Books by Russell Lynes

GOOD OLD MODERN

Russell Lynes

An Intimate Portrait of

New York 1973

GOOD OLD MODERN

The Museum of Modern Art

Atheneum

Copyright © 1973 by Russell Lynes
All rights reserved
Library of Congress catalog card number 72-94247
ISBN 0-689-10548-7
Published simultaneously in Canada by McClelland and Stewart Ltd.
Manufactured in the United States of America by
Kingsport Press, Inc., Kingsport, Tennessee
Designed by Harry Ford
First Edition

TO *John Kouwenhoven* AND *Eric Larrabee*

Dear Friends and Fellow Conspirators

Disclaimers and Acknowledgments

This account of the brief history of the Museum of Modern Art in New York is unofficial, unsubsidized, and unauthorized. The reader should know, however, that the author is not what might be called a "disinterested party," though I have never had any more official connection with the Museum than to be one of its many thousands of members. What I have written about the Museum in the past has occasionally ruffled the feathers of some of my friends there. I have not spared it or them when I thought they should be criticized or cautioned. I do not spare them in these pages, but neither do I go out of my way to feed the gossip mills.

A great many members of the curatorial, administrative, and archival staffs of the Museum, regardless of my unauthorized status, have gone to a great deal of trouble to answer my questions, make source materials available to me, and to help me in many friendly and generous ways. I will miss having no excuse to come and go as I please in parts of the Museum in which the public is not welcome, because I have made many new friends there and got to know some old friends better. No one whose cooperation I sought failed to help me—no one in the Museum, that is—and I am afraid that to some of them I made a nuisance of myself. To them I apologize. All of them I thank most warmly.

There are many individuals who have played roles of importance at the Museum who are not mentioned in these pages and who, but for the risk of making this book interminable, would have been and deserved to be mentioned. As a trustee of the Museum said to me, "You're lucky not to be writing an official history. You don't have to list everything." He was right. I have interviewed dozens of people—retired members of the staff, current ones and fired ones, trustees, friends and enemies of the Museum, critics, collectors, and artists. There are a number of quotations from interviews and letters in this book of which I have not given the sources, either because I was asked not to or because in a few cases I thought that doing so might cause needless embarrassment.

Some of the persons mentioned in this book as members of the Museum's staff are very old friends of mine. I was, one might say, present at the christening if not at the creation. When I was still an undergraduate at Yale, I was an occasional participant at the Sunday-afternoon parties at the Kirk Askews' where so many of the Museum's earliest staff were regulars. I have known Monroe Wheeler, John McAndrew, Allen Porter, and Agnes Rindge Claflin since before any of them worked for the Museum, and they were all there in its very early days. They are old and close friends. I have known, but less well, Alfred and Marga Barr, Philip Johnson, Henry-Russell Hitchcock, James Thrall Soby, and Beaumont Newhall since the early '30s. All of these friends, close and less close, have been generous with their help. They have searched their memories for me and in some cases their files as well. I am greatly in their debt.

I have never had the good fortune to meet Jere Abbott, who was so important to the Museum in its very first years, but I have benefited richly from his letters. In response to an inquiry of mine he wrote me a most informative and entertaining letter about the founding days of the Museum, and this initiated a correspondence that from my point of view was extremely rewarding, not just as material for this book but because Mr. Abbott is a letter writer of very great skill and charm.

It has been my good fortune to have three neighbors in the Berkshires, where much of this book was written, who are mines of information about the Museum. Dorothy Miller (Mrs. Holger Cahill) answered my hundreds of questions with both patience and brilliance, and led me to sources of great value and to speculations neither of us suspected. Her memory is extraordinary, so is her devotion to the Museum and to Alfred and Marga Barr. We talked for hours, many of them on the telephone. Elodie Courter Osborn, a very old and cherished friend, lives twenty minutes away in a different direction. She was at the Museum in its early, most dedicated, most inventive, and hardest-working days, and she remembers them with a combination of affection and humor which in no sense blurs her enthusiasm or her critical judgment. She read those pages of my manuscript which deal with the years she was at the Museum (from the early '30s until after World War II) and made many valuable suggestions and saved me from some egregious errors. My third neighbor, also twenty minutes away, is Andrew Carnduff Ritchie, who for eight years was the Director of Painting and Sculpture at the Museum and who left it to become director of the Yale University Art Gallery, from which he has now retired. His perspective on the Museum is more thoughtful, more penetrating, and more objective than that of anyone else with whom I have talked, in or out of the Museum. My gratitude to these three insiders, now outsiders, is profound.

It might be possible but it would be unreasonable to thank everyone who has contributed to this study. There are a few I cannot help but single out for special gratitude. Agnes Mongan, lately director of the Fogg Museum at Harvard, generously made the Paul Sachs archives available to me. They were invaluable. Eliza (Mrs. Bliss) Parkinson, whose association with the Museum started when as an enthusiastic youngster in the early '30s she was a member of the first Advisory Committee and by no means ended when she retired as President of the Museum, has talked both frankly and searchingly to me about the Museum's past and present. Henry Allen Moe, one of the wisest men alive, has shared with me his recollections of many years as an officer of the board. Edward M. M. Warburg, one of the original "Young Turks" and long a trustee, is a man of sharp insights and high humor, and he has been a frequent source of assistance. Glenway Wescott, a very old friend, who has watched the Museum's progress with the wit, precision, and penetration of the distinguished novelist and critic that he is, shared his views with me to my great benefit. So did Frances Lindley, James Johnson Sweeney, Virgil Thomson, R. Kirk Askew, Jr., Mrs. John D. Rockefeller 3rd, Marian Willard, Mary Sands Thompson, Edgar Kaufmann, Jr., Porter McCray, James Plaut, Nancy Newhall, Mrs. Donald Straus, William S. Paley, Louise Crane, Jimmy Ernst, and especially Eric Larrabee.

Of the present members of the staff on whom I have been an especial burden there are two I wish to thank most particularly: Elizabeth

Shaw, Director of Public Information, and Bernard Karpel, the Librarian. Mrs. Shaw is one of the busiest and at the same time seemingly most relaxed women with whom I have ever had the pleasure of working. No question that I asked her seemed to be too much trouble to find an answer to, and I asked and asked and asked. She dug out, or had her most amiable staff dig out, all sorts of entertaining or revealing pieces of old and new paper—clippings, speeches, releases, photographs, reports (entertaining is not the word for reports), letters, and memoranda. We laughed a great deal. What could I possibly have done without her? Mr. Karpel, for his part, gave me all the library privileges that normally are available only to the staff, and furthermore he let me poke into archives which, I'll wager, most of the staff do not know exist. He also let me borrow the key to the photocopying machine and let me take home items from his collections (when there were duplicates) that saved me hours and hours of tedious note-taking. Inga Forslund and Pearl Moeller, his two right hands, were greatly helpful to me and most pleasantly tolerant of my frequent presence. One former member of the staff, Elizabeth Chamberlain, was extremely helpful to me without knowing it. After she retired as Director of Public Information (she preceded Mrs. Shaw) she devoted herself to compiling a history of the Museum. It exists only in a typescript draft, but it was a constant and provocative guide to my researches. I am indebted to her for it.

I mention most of my printed sources as I go along, but there are a few I would like to mention here. The only book about the Museum's history is A. Conger Goodyear's *The Museum of Modern Art: The First Ten Years*. It was published by Mr. Goodyear in 1943. The best record of the Museum's activities from 1933 to 1963 is *The Bulletin of the Museum of Modern Art*. It was published somewhat irregularly for thirty years and then dropped for reasons of economy. This was, in my judgment, very poor economy indeed. Its thirty volumes have been "Published for the Museum by Arno Press, New York, 1967" in six volumes, with a seventh volume which is a useful index. There have been a great many articles written for magazines both here and abroad which have discussed the Museum's history and current activities, and there have been thousands upon thousands of news stories. The Museum's clipping files are excellent, and at this writing an effort is being made to see that these fragile, yellowing bits of paper are copied on microfilm and thus permanently preserved. They constitute an extraordinary ephemeral record of this extraordinary institution. The

best article on the Museum that I have encountered is "Action on West
Fifty-third Street," a two-part profile by Dwight Macdonald which
appeared in *The New Yorker*, December 12 and 19, 1953. More
recently *Art in America* devoted most of an issue to the Museum with
a lively text by Geoffrey T. Hellman. This was published in February
1964. Hellman had earlier written a profile of René d'Harnoncourt
for *The New Yorker* called "Imperturbable Noble" (May 7, 1960)
which d'Harnoncourt and many of his friends heartily disliked but
which nonetheless is filled with interesting information and insights
into its very complex subject. There is a wealth of material that deals
directly or tangentially with the Museum in the rich resources of the
Archives of American Art, an institution without which the social
history of the arts in America can scarcely be written. I found the
staff of the Archives in working on this book, as I have on earlier projects, to be unfailingly helpful, courteous, and resourceful.

There are a few members of the Museum's staff I have not mentioned
in these acknowledgments who took far more friendly trouble on my
behalf than duty dictated. I would like to thank them. They are
Margareta Akermark, Arthur Drexler, Linda Gordon, Earl Hatleberg,
Betsy Jones, Richard H. Koch, William S. Lieberman, Grace M.
Mayer, Waldo Rasmussen, William Rubin, Emily C. Stone, John
Szarkowski, and Willard Van Dyke.

A number of pairs of sharp eyes have looked at parts or all of my
manuscript. I would like to disclaim on their part any responsibility
for the final results. If I have slipped into errors of fact, the errors are
my responsibility, as are the judgments about events and persons. My
most especial thanks are to Allen Porter, whose long association with
the Museum made his an ideal pair of eyes; to Simon Michael Bessie,
my very old friend and publisher, who cooked up this project and
has generously tended the fire since he lit it several years ago; and to
Katherine Gauss Jackson, whose editorial judgment I trust above anyone else's, as I also cherish her friendship. My wife, who knows
museums from the inside (for a number of years she was on the staff
of the Metropolitan), has watched this book evolve with professional
as well as sympathetic eyes. Her criticisms have been precise and telling; her encouragement has been unfailing, and her constant company
during this excursion into her kind of world has been for me an im-
measurable delight.

NORTH EGREMONT, MASSACHUSETTS
OCTOBER 1972

Contents

Illustrations

Following page 238

Mrs. John D. Rockefeller, Jr. (*Rockefeller Archives*)

Miss Lizzie P. Bliss (*MOMA*) *

Mrs. Cornelius J. Sullivan (*photo George Platt Lynes*)

The Museum's first exhibition, 1929 (*photo Peter A. Juley & Son*)

Alfred H. Barr, Jr., 1939? (*MOMA*)

A. Conger Goodyear (*MOMA*)

Jere Abbott, 1933? (*photo George Platt Lynes*)

11 West 53rd St., the Museum's second home, 1936 (*courtesy Allen Porter*)

Elodie Courter preparing a Circulating Exhibition, 1940? (*photo Fritz Henle*)

The *Machine Art* show, 1934 (*photo Wurts Brothers*)

Abstract scultpure held up by U.S. Customs, 1936 (*photo Beaumont Newhall*)

Barr, Goodyear, and Cornelius Bliss, 1934 (*photo Paul Parker*)

Bauhaus Exhibition, 1938, in temporary quarters in Rockefeller Center (*photo Soichi Sunami*)

The "new" building at 11 West 53rd St., 1939 (*MOMA*)

Philip Goodwin and Edward Durell Stone, 1938? (*photo W. Sanders, Black Star*)

John McAndrew, 1939? (*courtesy Mr. McAndrew*)

* Photographs with credit given as "MOMA" are used courtesy of the Museum and bear no photographer's name on the prints. Dates are given in every case in which they are known. Dates followed by a question mark (?) are approximations.

xv

Following page 238

GOOD OLD MODERN

Chapter I *Mrs. Rockefeller's Wild Oat*

"The business of every modern museum," said Professor Frank
Jewett Mather of Princeton, "is to live as dangerously as possible."

Professor Mather was a little and twinkling man, a formidable
scholar in the arts and a traditionalist by inclination. He stood as he
said this before an audience of approximately 300 ladies in hats and
gloves and gentlemen in blue serge suits seated on little red chairs in
the drawing room of Mrs. Harold Irving Pratt's imposing house on the
corner of Park Avenue and 68th Street in New York. A group of
trustees, members, staff, and presumed or potential friends of the
Museum of Modern Art had gathered on April 19, 1934, to launch a
drive for funds and to take cognizance of the approaching fifth anniversary of the Museum's opening.

It was an occasion worth celebrating. The Museum, which was conceived by very wealthy parents in a time of great affluence, had been
born at a moment of national catastrophe, just ten days after the
stock-market crash of October 1929. The fact that it was not only
five years old but famous (though there were many who thought it
was merely infamous and was seeking further notoriety) was a matter
of great satisfaction to those daring ladies whose idea it had been, and
to the young men and women who had worked until all hours of the
night week after week to make it so. They all enjoyed living dangerously (at least so far as aesthetic matters were concerned), and they

3

took justifiable pride in what Professor Paul J. Sachs of Harvard called on that same afternoon "the daring originality of many of the twenty-nine exhibitions that the Museum of Modern Art has sponsored." When Professors Mather and Sachs finished their encomiums, the painter Walt Kuhn delivered a lecture using slides and paintings from the Lizzie P. Bliss Collection to demonstrate that modern art was not nearly as mysterious or outrageous as he presumed his audience to think it.

A great deal had to happen, however, before this afternoon of self-congratulation and instruction could take place. The seed of an idea had to be planted in soil that was rich and could be readily cultivated. Money had to fertilize it and intellectual energy had to work it. In retrospect it seems unlikely that any other cultural organization had as brief a germination as the Museum of Modern Art, but it was cultivated by people who were used to seeing their visions become realities, people whose wishes were indeed horses, and who, not stinting themselves, expected others to act as quickly and effectively as they did.

Mrs. John D. Rockefeller, Jr., Miss Lizzie P. Bliss, and Mrs. Cornelius J. Sullivan were the founding mothers of the Museum, and a formidable trio they were, women of spirit, vigor, adventurousness, and, not unimportantly, of commanding wealth.

In the winter of 1928–29 both Mrs. Rockefeller and Miss Bliss had gone to Egypt to escape the rigors of New York. They met there by chance, and they exchanged ideas about the desirability of starting a museum in New York devoted to what were then considered the rather outrageously advanced arts. When Mrs. Rockefeller was on her way home by ship, she encountered Mrs. Sullivan, with whom she discussed her conversations with Miss Bliss, and the fat, so to speak, was in the fire. Once back in New York "The Ladies," as they came to be referred to by the trustees and staff of the Museum, went to work in earnest.

None of them was a neophyte in matters of art—indeed, of the art that so many of their contemporaries thought not only distasteful but a calculated insult to the reason perpetrated by a group of dangerous Bolsheviks . . . or worse. Mrs. Rockefeller, who had been Abby Greene Aldrich, was the daughter of the powerful Senator Nelson W. Aldrich of Rhode Island, and her brother was Winthrop Aldrich of the Chase National Bank. She had acquired a taste for the arts, according to her biographer, Mary Ellen Chase, from her father, who had taken her to galleries in Europe and America when she was a young woman. Her concern was more than superficial. The year before the Museum of Modern Art came into being, she wrote to a friend: "To me art is one of the great resources of my life. I believe that it not only enriches the spiritual life, but that it makes one more sane and sympathetic, more observant and understanding, regardless of whatever age it springs from, whatever subjects it represents." Her concern with the arts of her own time, however, was a private and not a public matter. In the public eye she was a benefactor of such worthy organizations as the Young Women's Christian Association, the Girl Scouts, and the Red Cross, with gifts not merely of money but of her very considerable energies and organizing talents as well. The art in her house on West 54th Street, an eight-story brownstone mansion (indeed, the only eight-story private house in New York when it was built in 1912 for her father-in-law, John D. Sr., at a cost of $200,000), was, so far as visitors could observe, of a most conventional sort—precisely what one would expect in a very rich man's home. There were Old Masters in heavy frames; there was massive furniture covered in damask, and, to satisfy the taste of the master of the house, there were distinguished tapestries and many Chinese vases and other Oriental objects of art. The modern pictures were upstairs, out of sight in a "gallery" that Mrs. Rockefeller kept for her own pleasure and for the education of her five sons and her daughter. She bought paintings and prints by American artists, by George Bellows and "Pop" Hart, a particular favorite of hers, by Georgia O'Keeffe, Burchfield, Eilshemius, and Maurer.

"For many years," she wrote a few years after the Museum was a fact, "my husband and I collected things of the past." She had bought Japanese and Early American prints and, as she said, "went on to Buddhistic art and European china and all sorts of beautiful things that have been created in civilizations older than and different from ours." But she was evidently worried about whether these were the sorts of things that her children would "be interested in and want to live with." There were many groups of people and a number of dealers, she came to feel, who were helping to support and encourage modern painters and sculptors in America, but museums were doing almost nothing. She discussed her idea that there should be a museum of modern art such as those she had seen in Europe with her friend Martin A. Ryerson of Chicago, a distinguished collector of Impressionist paintings and the vice-president of the Chicago Art Institute; with Dr. Wilhelm Valentiner, the director of the Detroit Museum; with Lee Simonson, a designer for the stage and writer about the arts; and with others. So that when she encountered the other two ladies, she was already deeply concerned with how she might go about the establishment of such a museum.

Miss Bliss's education in the arts was of a quite different nature from Mrs. Rockefeller's, as was her collecting of it. She had fallen under the spell of the painter Arthur B. Davies, who was the guiding spirit (if not the moving force) of the International Exhibition of Modern Art in 1913. "The Armory Show," as the exhibition was then popularly known and has been called ever since, had picked up the art world in America by the heels and shaken it fiercely amid cries of delight from the adventurous artists and critics who had discovered the new art movements in Europe (the Post-Impressionists, the Cubists, the Expressionists, the Fauves, and other kinds of "wild beasts") and amid anguished moans from the old guard who were faithful to the academies. Under Davies' tutelage Miss Bliss, who was well known as a supporter of musical activities through her patronage of the Kneisel Quartet (but whose support of individual young musical students was done, as a friend of hers put it, "quietly—No mention"), became a very considerable collector of pictures. She bought five paintings from the Armory Show—two Redons, a pastel and an oil by Degas, and a landscape by Renoir—but this was only a beginning. She added Cézannes and Seurats, Matisses and Picassos and Toulouse-Lautrecs, more Renoirs and Degases and Redons—not just a few, but a formidable ten dozen paintings and drawings, most of them of exceedingly high quality. In her quiet way she commanded a great deal of influence in the New York art world, and in 1921 her pressure on the Metropolitan Museum was an important factor in its taking its first excursion into "modern" with an exhibition of Impressionist and Post-Impressionist works.

The wealth which permitted Lizzie Bliss (her friends called her Lillie) to indulge her taste and collector's acquisitiveness came from her father, an extremely successful textile merchant and manufacturer who was offered but declined the opportunity to be Vice-President by President McKinley and subsequently, though briefly, became his Secretary of the Interior. She never married, but devoted much of her life to the care of her mother, who was long an invalid. She was a shy woman with no airs and graces, complex within, yet natural without, and an accomplished pianist.

Miss Bliss was in her early sixties, about ten years older than Abby Rockefeller, when The Ladies foregathered. She lived in the penthouse at 1001 Park Avenue surrounded for the most part by rigorously conventional "good taste." The floor of her drawing room was covered

with a proper Persian carpet set about with Louis Quinze chairs and
sofas; over a marble mantel hung an elaborately carved gold mirror
on one side of which was Toulouse-Lautrec's little painting of "May
Belfort in Pink" and on the other a landscape by her friend and mentor,
Davies. The dining room was set with Chippendale and Sheraton and
console tables, like dozens of well-mannered dining rooms on Park
Avenue, but Miss Bliss, unlike any but a very few who looked down
into that fashionable canyon, had a gallery in which she hung the most
impressive part of her collection. It was a white room with a grand
piano in it, decorated in the most up-to-date 1920s manner which we
now call Art Deco but was then what was called "moderne" by some
and "modernistic" by others.

The third of The Ladies, Mary Quinn Sullivan, was of a very
different background and temperament from her colleagues. She was,
as a friend who knew her at the time of the founding of the Museum
describes her, "pure Irish mystic . . . a lovely person, with a fine eye
for art. I always felt that she went far deeper into the modern feeling
than the others did." But if she believed in elves and mystic experiences, she was also a woman of very considerable gaiety, charm, and
good looks ("She had a luminous face," another friend said of her,
"pink cheeks over a brown skin") and she had a practical appreciation
of detail. She was born on a farm near Indianapolis in 1877, the eldest
of seven children of second-generation immigrants from Ireland. She
evidenced a nice talent for drawing as a child, and when she was
twenty-two she arrived in New York determined to make her way as
a teacher of art, which she quite successfully did in the New York
public schools after studying at the Art Students League and the Pratt
Institute. In 1902 she went off to Europe on an excursion financed by
the New York schools to see how art was being taught there, and, of
course, this energetic and curious young woman came home with her
eyes filled with the new Impressionist and Post-Impressionist art that
was then considered so advanced. She taught at the DeWitt Clinton
High School until 1910, and then at Pratt as an instructor of design
and household arts and sciences. By 1912 she was back in Europe, this
time at the Slade School of Art in London, and there she listened to
the revolutionary lectures of Roger Fry, whose book of essays, *Vision
and Design* (along with Clive Bell's *Art*), was to be a bible for young
art-lovers of the '20s and '30s.

When she was forty, in 1917, she married a lawyer, Cornelius J.
Sullivan, who was seven years older than she. He had a large and
lucrative practice (his clients included John McGraw, manager of the

New York Giants, and the New York Board of Education), and they lived in an old and charming country house surrounded by lawns and trees and a picket fence, "nestling under the Astoria end of the Hell Gate Bridge," a country farm in a metropolis. Sullivan was a collector of rare books and paintings and a classmate at the Harvard Law School of John Quinn, one of the most adventurous collectors of his day, with whom he carried on a correspondence for years. The Sullivans gave dinner parties for thirty or more people at their pretty house filled with modern paintings, Georgian silver, and Early American furniture. It was considered a great treat by the young people who worked at the Museum to be invited. It was through Quinn, who had helped so greatly to make the Armory Show possible (he was no relation of Mary Quinn Sullivan), that she, like Miss Bliss, acquired a number of pictures from that exhibition to form the nucleus of a collection. Soon after they were married she and her husband started to assemble a somewhat more ambitious collection of Braque, Modigliani, Cézanne, Picasso, van Gogh, and others who are now considered masters but at that time were regarded by most art-lovers as being beyond the pale.

Lizzie Bliss and Mary Quinn had been friends since before the days of the Armory Show. They had spent afternoons together looking at gallery exhibitions, and it was through Miss Bliss that the future Mrs. Sullivan met Arthur B. Davies, whom they had helped to finance the Armory Show and who had preached to both of them the need for a museum for the new art. It was they who introduced Mrs. Rockefeller to Davies.

It might not be inaccurate to characterize the three Ladies thus: Abby Rockefeller was the most executive and the best organizer; Lizzie Bliss was the most thoughtful, and certainly the most retiring; and Mary Sullivan was, as her friend Peter Grimm, the New York real-estate tycoon, described her to Geoffrey T. Hellman, "a whizbang." It was a splendid combination of talents, tastes, and temperaments to launch an enterprise. It was also the source of a great deal of money, and the key to still more, though Mrs. Sullivan, compared with the other Ladies, was, as a friend of hers has put it, "a church mouse."

Late in May of 1929 Mr. A. Conger Goodyear's telephone rang at his New York address, and he was puzzled and surprised to hear the voice of a woman who identified herself as Mrs. Rockefeller's secretary. Would he, she asked, be willing to come to Mrs. Rockefeller's for luncheon at 10 West 54th Street on Wednesday of next week? Goodyear, whose permanent home was in Buffalo, New York, had not met Mrs. Rockefeller, and though the invitation seemed odd, he most assuredly had no intention of missing an opportunity to meet such a prominent figure and see her house and collection. "I accepted," he said in a speech at the Museum ten years later, "and since as usual I had nothing to wear, I went out and bought a very dignified gray suit which my Buffalo friends thereafter always called the Rockefeller suit."

Goodyear was a ramrod of a man with a close-cropped cannonball head and a military bearing. With good reason. He had been a colonel in the First World War and was to become a major general in the Second, in command of the Second Brigade of the New York Guard. He had graduated from Yale in the class of 1899, joined the family business, and subsequently become an officer in its several concerns, which included two lumber companies and the Buffalo and Susquehanna Railroad. It was not for any of these reasons that he was invited to Mrs. Rockefeller's for lunch. Indeed, he had not the slightest idea why he had been invited.

He arrived at the massive brownstone pile where the Museum's sculpture garden now is and discovered that two ladies were also guests at lunch and that he was the only man; this puzzled him even further. The ladies, of course, were Miss Bliss and Mrs. Sullivan, and they chatted amiably—it is not recorded about what they chatted, though it was presumably about art, as Goodyear had been a trustee of the Albright Gallery in Buffalo and briefly its president. Toward the middle of lunch Mrs. Rockefeller said to her friends, rather archly, it appears, "Shall we ask Mr. Goodyear the question we had in mind?" Miss Bliss and Mrs. Sullivan nodded their assent. "I had passed muster," the military Mr. Goodyear recalled, "and Mrs. Rockefeller proceeded to explain."

Would he, they wished to know, be willing to accept the chairmanship of a committee to organize "a new gallery or museum in New York that would exhibit works of art of the modern school"? He asked for a week to think it over, but he was obviously more than a little tempted and flattered, and sleeping on it seems to have been enough. He accepted the very next day.

The ladies had chosen their quarry with great care and acuity. First of all Goodyear was a collector, and though the Ladies may not have known it, his eye for a proper purchase had evidenced itself while he was still a Yale undergraduate. He had bought limited and fine and first editions of books, to which he later had the good sense to add a large batch of letters from William Makepeace Thackeray to Jane Octavia Brookfield. In 1927 he sold the bulk of his collection for $155,708 and was pleased to note that, as he calculated it, he had netted a profit of 18 percent a year during the period of his possession of the books and papers. But had the Ladies known of this, they would have been less interested than in the fact they well knew that he had a considerable collection of sculptures by Emile-Antoine Bourdelle and Aristide Maillol, in those days collected by few, and also paintings by van Gogh, Gauguin, Toulouse-Lautrec, Renoir, Seurat, and others—the very favorites of Miss Bliss and Mrs. Sullivan.

They also knew that he had had a falling out with the Albright Gallery in Buffalo over the purchase of a "pink-period" Picasso, "*La Toilette*." Goodyear's heart was on the side of modernism. In 1927, indeed, he had borrowed an international show from the Société Anonyme, Inc., a sort of floating collection of modern works assembled by Katherine S. Dreier and Marcel Duchamp, whose "Nude Descending a Staircase" had been the *cause célèbre* of the Armory Show. The trustees of the Albright were uneasy about Goodyear's taste, and when he purchased the Picasso for $5,000, they quite simply voted him out of a job and off the board. Mrs. Rockefeller had heard about this falling out, possibly from Mrs. Sullivan, who was closer to the gossip of the art market than she was. When seven years later Goodyear asked Mrs. Rockefeller how she had happened to turn to him, she wrote:

> I suggested [to Miss Bliss and Mrs. Sullivan] that we form ourselves into a committee of three and that we find a man to be president of the museum that was to be. We met again and after much thought decided that we would invite you to meet with us and discuss the possibility of your being president. We did this because we had been told of your efforts in the cause of modern art in Buffalo and that you had resigned the presidency of that museum because the trustees would not go along with you in your desire to show the best things in modern art.

They had picked the right man to get things moving, and he picked with their blessing three other members of the committee—a gentleman and a scholar and another lady of imposing wealth and cultural status, and possibly stature as well. The gentleman was Frank Crowninshield, the editor of *Vanity Fair*, a sophisticated monthly published

by Condé Nast, who also published *Vogue*. The scholar (also, to be
sure, very much of a gentleman) was Professor Paul J. Sachs of the
Fogg Museum of Harvard University. The lady was Mrs. W. Murray
Crane, whose fortune stemmed from the Crane Paper Company of
Dalton, Massachusetts.

Frank Crowninshield (whose full name was Francis Welch Crowninshield and was called by his friends "Crownie") was regarded by his
contemporaries as a man of commanding charm, urbanity, wit, and
tact. He inhabited the world of arts and letters, and his magazine was
at the same time glossy, chic, entertaining, and serious. He was a
collector of modern painting and sculpture with a sure, if not infallible, eye (he made some very bad guesses), a discoverer of writers
and photographers and pundits. He published, when they were first
heard from, such disparate writers as Noel Coward and e. e. cummings,
Robert Benchley and Clare Boothe, and in the May 1929 issue, which
was on the newsstands when Goodyear was lunching with the Ladies,
there was a piece by young Aldous Huxley on Thomas Mann, one by
Sherwood Anderson on small towns, an essay by D. H. Lawrence
called "Woman in Man's Image," and a full-page photograph of an
attractive young entertainer, Maurice Chevalier, by Edward Steichen,
who many years later became Director of the Photography Department
of the Museum of Modern Art. It was said that Crowninshield knew
everyone who mattered and could get any writer or artist, the most
famous and those just appearing above the horizon, to contribute to his
magazine. *Vanity Fair* was a window on the world of "the lively arts,"
as Crowninshield's friend Gilbert Seldes called them, to a whole generation of wide-eyed young aspirants to sophistication. Some of what it
published might today be called the serious side of "camp"; some of it
was simply serious; none of it was heavy-handed or solemn. Much of
it was to its knowing contemporaries outrageously funny; some of it
still is.

As in the case of Professor Sachs, what ultimately mattered most to
the Museum was Crowninshield's acquaintance among the young and
vigorous who were consumed with the new arts and with promoting
them, and his admiration for them and his belief in their beliefs.
Crowninshield was fifty-seven at the time the committee for the
Museum was organized; Sachs was fifty-one. Crowninshield was a
casually educated dilettante of the arts (he was principally educated
by tutors in France) whose dilettantism (to use the word in its original,
not its pejorative, sense) was precisely the right sort to guide a magazine of the arts in the 1920s. Sachs, by contrast, was a rigorously

trained scholar, a meticulous collector of drawings who refined his collection to the point where some of his friends thought it had become entirely impersonal. He kept replacing good examples with better ones, combing out what he considered the lesser ones, even those he loved, for he was a perfectionist. He had started out as a banker, working for the family firm of Goldman, Sachs, and he was thirty-six before he turned to teaching the fine arts at Harvard. He gave a course widely known in the profession as "the museum course," and in the 1930s and '40s there was scarcely an art museum of any stature whose director or chief curators had not been under Sachs's tutelage. His students were running, or otherwise engaged in, the Metropolitan Museum in New York, the Boston Museum of Fine Arts, the art museums in Worcester, Hartford, San Antonio, San Francisco, Buffalo, among others, and, as we shall see, the Museum of Modern Art. It was said that he was responsible for an entire generation of museum directors, and the observation was very nearly true. In his course he drilled them on administrative problems, on museum techniques, on connoisseurship, and when his ex-students would write him for advice he would often read their letters to his class—anonymously, of course —for their reactions.

Sachs was a tiny man physically, almost a dwarf. "Quite literally," one of the products of the museum course wrote to me, "everybody looked down on him." But no one looked down on him intellectually or as a man of very marked practical sense. "He was kind and generous and paternal, in the best sense of the word," his student of the 1920s wrote. "His great cross was a completely uncontrollable and furious temper. And you never knew what would trigger it, nor, I suspect, did he." He had a memory that was tantamount to total recall, and he used to say that instead of counting sheep to put himself to sleep, he would pick a museum, any museum that he had visited (and there can scarcely have been any in Europe or in America that he missed), and tour its galleries, seeing in his mind each picture and each object in its place. More important to the well-being of American museums, he not only had an extremely keen eye for the kind of scholar who should become a museum director or curator but he was fiercely loyal and always available to those he pinned his faith on.

So eager was Goodyear to be sure that Paul Sachs would join the new committee that he met Sachs at the pier on the North River in New York when he got off a ship returning from Europe. While Sachs was arguing with the customs men, Goodyear talked with Mrs. Sachs and a fellow passenger, Felix Warburg, the senior figure in the investment banking firm of Kuhn, Loeb & Company. (His son, Edward, later played an important role in the Museum's history.) Goodyear told Mrs. Sachs why he was there and asked if she thought her husband would accept; she replied, "Well . . . where art is concerned Paul is a Mormon." And Warburg, seeing how eager Goodyear was to make his invitation stick, said, "You are like me . . . when you really want a thing done you do it yourself."

When Sachs got back to Cambridge he wrote to Goodyear thanking him for his attentiveness in meeting him at the pier and saying that he was delighted to be a participant in this venture. He begged off, however, from raising money; the Fogg was problem enough in those ways. "I so frequently stand before the public as a mendicant," he wrote. What he liked best about the idea of the new museum was the vision of a kind of halfway house for art on its way from obscurity to immortality. "It is a dream I have long cherished," he wrote, "because it has seemed to me mandatory that in America we should have something comparable to the Tate Gallery in London and the Luxembourg in Paris from which works of art, when once they have established themselves in public judgment, may more or less automatically find their way into the great permanent collections of the community." Like many other dreams about the Museum, it never came to pass.

The fifth and final member of the original committee, Mrs. Winthrop Murray Crane, had been Josephine Boardman of Cleveland, born in 1873. She was the widow of a prominent Republican who had been Governor of Massachusetts and a Senator and had on several occasions declined cabinet posts offered him by President Theodore Roosevelt. He was the president of the Crane Paper Company, which had been founded by his grandfather, and he and Mrs. Crane had collected pictures, not by modern artists, many of which they had given or lent to the museum in Pittsfield, Massachusetts, which they did more than a little to support. It was Mrs. Crane's close friendship with Abby Rockefeller that got her involved with the committee. Mrs. Crane, who died in 1972 at the age of ninety-eight, lived for many years in a large apartment at 63rd Street and Fifth Avenue with seven servants and a view of Central Park, which, she confided to a friend in her very late years, she was glad she had bought because it assured her of protection from others wanting to build there and obstruct her view. On Thursday afternoons in Mrs. Crane's drawing room there gathered for years a group of ladies who were omnivorous seekers after culture to hear an "authority," or a novelist, or some other figure of the literary or art world talk about cultural matters. It was Mrs. Crane who provided the funds to found the Dalton School in New York, a private progressive institution for boys and girls that was for years considered to be far ahead of its time in educational practice. In some respects Mrs. Crane was a curious choice for the original committee, as her interest in modern art seems to have been moderate at the most. On the other hand, her concern with cultural affairs, though in a somewhat buck-shot manner, was intense, her good will toward the arts was surely genuine, and she was most certainly in a position to contribute hand-somely to the coffers of the Museum, which, indeed, she did over a great many years.

Here, then, was the committee. Goodyear was president and Lizzie Bliss was vice-president. Mrs. Rockefeller, who confessed that she knew almost nothing about business, was treasurer. The articulate Mr. Crowninshield was secretary. Paul Sachs was without title but was obviously the most experienced hand in museum matters and manage-ment. Mrs. Sullivan and Mrs. Crane were attendant but by no means idle figures.

The purpose of the museum which they envisioned seems to have been somewhat hazy even to the committee, though it was surely in the backs of the minds of the ladies and certainly not in the least obscure to Goodyear that one function of the "program," as they called it, was to put on public view (and record) works of art from the collections of the members of the committee themselves. There is no evidence to suggest that the committee was looking for any financial benefits in seeking public exposure of their treasures, though this has been a barb that some critics of the Museum have tried to make stick. It cannot be an injustice to suppose, however, that the ladies and Goodyear were pleased to acquire currency of another sort in the vindication of their taste and vision. If in doing so they increased the value of their collections, they certainly had no reason to object, and in any event, in their terms and from the eminence of their station, they were serving "the cause." Surely the number of paintings and sculptures, prints and drawings from the collections of its trustees in the Museum's exhibitions over the more than forty years of its ex-istence makes it obvious that it has been a showcase for trustee vanity —but in this it differs not at all from any other museum in America.

In the beginning, however, a program for release to the press and as a basis for soliciting financial support had to be concocted. The committee had decided that "to be on the safe side" it should set its goal for subscriptions at $100,000 a year for three years, and that it should start out, as Goodyear put it, with "a tentative program . . .

which included six exhibitions of one month each to open the following November."

This was not unreasonable daydreaming, though the committee had
none of the tools at hand to convert wishes into facts. And the committee had no gallery, no staff, no director, and no name for its brainchild. None of these problems seemed to worry it in the least, and it
attacked them simultaneously.

First of all there was the question of a name and a legal identity.
Goodyear tried "The Modern Gallery of Art" on Crowninshield, and,
like the editor he was, Crowninshield quibbled. "I have looked in the
telephone book," he wrote back, "and can find no trace of any similar
institution in New York. Would you think 'The Gallery of Modern
Art' a better name? . . . After all, 'The Modern Gallery of Art' might
mean a gallery recently constructed, planned and organized for old
art rather than a gallery devoted to modern art. But this is, of course,
quibbling."

Goodyear took the quibble seriously, and when he wrote to Mrs.
Crane just a few days later he had adopted Crowninshield's suggestion.
Within two weeks, however, the name had become The Museum of
Modern Art, which suggests that the committee already had in mind
not just a gallery for temporary exhibitions but a permanent collection
as its base. Some years later Goodyear explained: "Miss Katherine
Dreier, founder of the Société Anonyme in 1920, had used as a subtitle
for that institution 'Museum of Modern Art.' This was not known to
our founders at this time. When it was called to our attention it was
too late to do anything about it." Goodyear had proposed the name in
a letter to Mrs. Rockefeller in July at the same time that he had asked
her concurrence in going ahead to find quarters. She gave her blessing
to both.[1]

The next step was legalization. Goodyear appealed to Mrs. Sullivan's
husband to draw up incorporation papers, making sure "to so arrange
matters as to make subscriptions to the corporation deductible in calcu-
lating individual income tax reports." On July 31, 1929, an application
was made to the Regents of the University of the State of New York
for a charter. In the application the committee (and presumably it
was Sullivan's wording) had defined its intention as: "The establish-

---

[1] The problem of the name has never really been resolved. The Museum
is generally referred to in New York as "The Modern Museum" or just "The
Modern." Even officialdom does not always get it right. In 1957 the Mayor of
New York issued a "Certificate of Appreciation" and the name "Modern Museum of Art" was embossed on it.

ing and maintaining in the City of New York a museum of modern art, encouraging and developing the study of modern arts and the application of such arts to manufacture and practical life, and furnishing popular instruction." This somewhat quaint language, which sounds as though it might have been copied from the nineteenth-century application of the Cooper Union for a charter, obviously was calculated to make the museum sound not like a fanciful plaything of collectors but a serious educational undertaking.

The Regents granted a provisional charter on September 19 and said, in the equally quaint language of state universities: "if within five years the corporation shall acquire resources and equipment available for its use and support and sufficient and suitable for its chartered purposes in the judgment of the Regents of the University, and be maintaining an institution of educational usefulness and character satisfactory to them," then they would grant a permanent charter.

The committee decided, now that its institution was official, to expand and become a proper board of trustees. High on its list was Stephen C. Clark, whose inherited fortune was derived from the Singer Sewing Machine Company and Clark's O.N.T. Thread. Clark was a man with a very acute and personal eye as a collector. (He is not to be confused with his brother, Sterling Clark, whose very different taste was responsible for the Sterling and Francine Clark Art Institute in Williamstown, Massachusetts. The brothers were on somewhat less than friendly terms.) Stephen Clark's New York house, a gray stone Gothic country-house-in-the-city on 70th Street between Madison and Park avenues (it is now the Explorers Club), was filled with pictures from billiard room to attic. On the top floor was a large loft-like room which had been used by Clark's two sons and daughter and their friends as a gymnasium. Clark had bought a dozen or so paintings by Matisse and had engaged the services of Mrs. Eugene Speicher, whose husband was very well known in the '20s and '30s for his portraits painted somewhat in the Renoir manner, to decorate the gym. She did it with more gusto than tact. The red-checked table-cloths, the blue curtains, the polka-dot pillows, and the crockery were taken straight out of the Matisses, and the room had a sunniness and gaiety of considerable charm. It was dominated by Matisse's "Lady with the Plumes," and it is said that when Mr. Clark proudly showed the room to Matisse the painter was appalled. The idea of using his pictures as interior decoration infuriated him.

Matisse was by no means the only painter that Clark collected. Like Miss Bliss and Mrs. Sullivan, he helped to support Arthur B. Davies, who was a friend of his. But his taste, if discriminating, was catholic, and it ranged from El Greco to Peter Arno, the *New Yorker* cartoonist, whose drawings were hung on the walls of the staircase. He had a taste for the American landscapist Louis Eilshemius, for George Bellows, and he owned Thomas Eakins' magnificent portrait of his fiancée, Katherine, Corot's great "Port de la Rochelle," and a version of the same artist's "Castel Sant' Angelo," both of which he bought one day from a Corot exhibition at Knoedler's on 57th Street in New York. Seurat's "Side Show" (*"La Parade"*) hung in his library.

Clark was a man of great reserve who kept his own counsel and was called shy by some of his friends. His shyness was considered a carefully cultivated pose by those who did not like him, but, as one of those who worked with him at the Museum of Modern Art observed, "I think he really was shy and it sometimes made him do irrational things. But wouldn't you be shy if all through Yale you'd been known as 'Bathroom' Clark because your rich mother had had a tile bathroom installed in your college room?" But that he knew his own mind became quite apparent when he acted as both President and Chairman of the Board of the Museum about fifteen years after it opened. Indeed, when Goodyear first approached him to join the trustees of the as yet non-existent museum, he declined. "I am sorry to say," he wrote

> that, if I understood your plans correctly, I am in sympathy with only part of your program. The idea of holding exhibitions of modern art appeals to me strongly but I cannot get up any enthusiasm over the proposal to establish a permanent museum along the lines of the Tate or Luxembourg as I cannot see that either of those institutions does very much to encourage the best in modern art.

In view of what Goodyear had said to Sachs and Sachs had written to Goodyear about the Tate and the Luxembourg, the following from Goodyear to Clark, written a week later, seems merely opportunistic:

> I am very glad that after our discussion on the telephone last Friday, you have decided to accept the election as trustee of the Museum of Modern Art. . . . There is certainly no thought in my mind of ever establishing a museum that will be along the lines of the Luxembourg, which is at present moribund.

Goodyear also invited several other prominent collectors of modern art to join the trustees: Sam Lewisohn, whose New York house fairly burst with van Goghs and Gauguins, Cézannes and Renoirs, Matisses and Braques, and who seemed to sleep (but only seemed) through board meetings and had very positive ideas about what he liked and what he did not; Chester Dale, most of whose collection of nineteenth-century French paintings and a notorious "Crucifixion" by Salvador Dali are now in the National Gallery in Washington; Duncan Phillips, of Washington, who founded, maintained, and presided over one of the most delightful private museums open to the American public and whose taste ranged from the early Renaissance to canvases still wet from the brushes of his contemporaries and protégés. Edward Harkness declined Goodyear's invitation, so as an alternate he tried Martin A. Ryerson of Chicago, Mrs. Rockefeller's friend and advisor, but he too declined on grounds of age and distance.

For an institution that was still only a hope, not an actuality, its Board of Trustees was formidable indeed. Its roster must have given Robert W. De Forest, the president of the Metropolitan Museum, and the Egyptologist Herbert E. Winlock, its director, pause for thought.

It was, however, all very well to have an impressive Board of Trustees and some money both in the bank and promised. (Goodyear reported to Sachs early in August that subscriptions were already "a little over $50,000" against a proposed budget of $75,000 for the first year's operations.) But there had to be a place for the Museum to call home, and there had to be a housekeeper. In this case it seemed advisable to the committee to pick the housekeeper and have him help in selecting the premises and, indeed, what to put in them, though it had quite firm notions of its own about this. As the authority on museums and their keepers, the committee turned to Sachs with the expectation that he could produce a miracle, as he proceeded to do.

There has been great progress here in America during the year of your absence. The interest in museums and modern art in museums and in all that is connected with modern art and modernized art has greatly increased . . . it is a time for cooperation not irritation.

PAUL J. SACHS *in a letter to* ALFRED H. BARR, JR., March 1928

Chapter II The Man Who Came in out of the Fogg

Professor Sachs's miracle was a young scholar named Alfred Hamilton Barr, Jr. He was teaching the history of art at Wellesley College, an institution for young women in a fashionable and substantial Boston suburb. When Conger Goodyear asked Sachs to suggest a director for the new museum at an organization meeting in June of 1929, Sachs responded with characteristic alacrity that if they did not object to "a very young man," he had an immediate recommendation. On the other hand, if they had reservations, he would have to give the matter some further thought. The committee was evidently content to take Sachs's young man (one did not question his wisdom in such matters), and a few weeks later Barr was invited by Mrs. Rockefeller to visit her at her summer "cottage," called The Eyrie, in Seal Harbor, Maine. It cannot have looked much like a cottage to Barr as he approached it from its long driveway. Built of Maine granite and shingles, which had weathered for a good many winters, it seemed to wander down the hillside toward the water more like a resort hotel than like a casual family retreat from the formalities of New York. Here Barr was interviewed by Mrs. Rockefeller in a living room filled with Japanese pots in which the parlormaid fixed the flowers, carefully instructed by Mrs. Rockefeller to avoid Japanese "arrangements," which she considered too formal for the country. Mrs. Rockefeller, who, it has been said, "never ran out of questions," probed Barr's ideas of what a museum of modern art should be and listened attentively to his answers. She was evidently very favorably impressed with the young man's potentialities if less so by his person, and after his visit she wrote to Conger Goodyear: "I liked Mr. Barr and felt that his youth, enthusiasm and knowledge would make up for his not having a more impressive appearance."

Sachs had got to know Barr as one of his graduate students at the Fogg in 1924, and he had been so impressed by this rather fragile, thin-lipped and fine-featured, intense young man that he had written to his old friend Professor Charles Rufus Morey at Princeton to congratulate him "on the perfectly splendid student you have developed in Alfred Barr." He added, "I have no hesitation in saying that he acquitted himself better than any candidate during the time that I have been here. . . . One got the impression that he had thought deeply and ranged widely over the whole field [of the history of art]."

Barr was brought up in Presbyterian parsonages. He was born the son of a clergyman in Detroit, but after a brief stay in Chicago he moved with his family to Baltimore, where he spent most of his childhood and his youth and where, it is said, he played football on the Boys' Latin School team. He was twenty-two when he arrived in the autumn of 1924 at Harvard for graduate study as a Thayer Fellow and to take a job as assistant in the department of fine arts. In 1922 he had graduated from Princeton, where he had led a rather solitary existence with a very few friends, and he had taken his Master's degree there in 1923. He was then twenty-one and he had devised what he has since called a "five-year plan," though it is unlikely that he called it that at the time; it was not until 1928 that the Russians made the phrase a cliché. He intended to go from job to job, changing each year, traveling, doing graduate study. In the fall of 1923 he arrived at Vassar College in Poughkeepsie, New York, where he explored the mysteries of Renaissance art for young ladies in tweed skirts, sweaters, pearls, and saddle shoes and played occasional tennis with Henry Noble Mc-Cracken, Vassar's president. Barr puzzled the college community (and surely enraged a considerable number of faculty members and students) by hanging an exhibition of Kandinsky in Taylor Hall, which housed the art department's gallery. He entertained himself and the students by taking part in amateur theatricals (this was before the days of Vassar's and Hallie Flanagan's Experimental Theatre) and by wearing jackets that did not match his trousers. Such behavior was considered very eccentric and daring, and he was called "Mr. Mixed-Suits."

The Harvard appointment which followed the year at Vassar and a summer of intensive sightseeing in Europe (architecture ancient and modern, museums, galleries, movies) was for only a year, but he crammed into it everything he could lay an eye on, from the Middle Ages to modern sculpture, or turn an ear to. In September 1924 he wrote to Katherine Gauss, daughter of Christian Gauss, the Dean of Princeton who was the mentor of Edmund Wilson and Scott Fitzgerald: "Cambridge is a horble place to live in, loud and noisy and ugly. Harvard makes up for it though and more. Listen to the sweet tale of my courses: 1. Byzantine art, 2. Engraving and Etchings, 3. Theory and Practice of Representation and Design (Fun with watercolors and pencil and tempera), 4. Drawings—14th Italian, 14, 15th German, 18th French, 5. Modern Sculpture, 6. Florentine Painting, 7. Classical culture in the Middle Ages with *Rand*, 8. Prose and Poetry, Tudor and Stuart, 9. Russian Music . . . The last five I merely listen to and take notes—but aren't they swell? . . . I will be buried under work but will sing in my sepulchre—and Marcel Dupré is coming to play Bach's organ works *complete* and I will lunch with him. I am scarce contained!" Dupré, the most famous organist of his day, played all of Bach's organ music from memory.

At the conclusion of this year-long cram session Barr returned to Princeton as an instructor in the department of art and archeology. Before the year was out (this was 1925–26) Wellesley College offered Barr an associate professorship, a pleasant and uncommon leap over the rank of assistant professor and an attractive plum for a twenty-four-year-old scholar. Furthermore, this appointment brought him back to the neighborhood of Harvard, to Sachs's museum course and the lively atmosphere of the Fogg, which at that moment was training a group of young scholars who were to become extremely influential personages in the museum world, the art marketplace, and the profession of art historian.

Barr shared an apartment in Cambridge (Wellesley was only about half an hour away by train) with a slightly older young man from Dexter, Maine—Jere Abbott, whom he had met as a graduate student at Princeton and who later became his associate at the Museum of Modern Art for several years during its gestation, birth, and infancy.

Abbott, whose family had been the proprietors of a textile mill in Dexter since 1820,[1] went to Bowdoin College in Maine as an undergraduate and he planned to become a physicist. After a year of graduate study at Harvard he did indeed teach physics at Bowdoin for two years. He then "changed gears," to use his phrase, and went to Princeton with the intention of taking a graduate degree in history of art. I know of no other physicist who turned out to be the director of an art museum as well as a discriminating collector of modern art, but Abbott, whose talents included those of an accomplished amateur musician, has explained his shift from equations to the arts in this way:

> I "came" to modern art by way of modern music. A friend of mine at Bowdoin, who played the piano more expertly than did I, was exploratory and in that period, 1916–1920, in college, we played a lot of two-piano arrangements of Debussy, Stravinsky, Ravel and Satie. My friend was studying foreign languages and I physics! He went to Princeton for graduate work and it was my frequent visits to him there . . . which swung me into the history of art, for most of his friends were students in that field. Now do you believe in the theory of chance?

There were others in Sachs's course who were to cut a wide swath in the art world and leave a deep impression on American taste. James Rorimer was one of them; so were Henry-Russell Hitchcock, A. Everett Austin, and R. Kirk Askew, Jr. So were Agnes Rindge and, a little later, Agnes Mongan. Rorimer became the moving spirit who, with funds provided by John D. Rockefeller, Jr., brought into being The Cloisters, that remarkable museum of medieval art that looks down on the Hudson from a high bluff in Fort Tryon Park in New York. From there he moved to the directorship of the Metropolitan Museum. Hitchcock, who was for a time director of the museum at Smith College in Northampton, Massachusetts, played an important part in the development of the Museum of Modern Art's Architecture Department, and is today the undisputed dean of American architectural historians. Austin (called "Chick") had one of the most acutely perceptive and selective eyes of any museum man of his time—that plus panache and a sense of the theatrical that put the Wadsworth Atheneum in Hartford, Connecticut, among the liveliest museums of the 1930s, livelier than the Museum of Modern Art in many respects. It was there, for example, that in 1934 the chic segment of the *avant-*

1 In a letter dated February 23, 1971, Abbott wrote: "By the Grace of God we go into our 151st year this year."

garde in white ties and ballgowns gathered to see the first performance of Virgil Thomson's opera *Four Saints in Three Acts* with a libretto by Gertrude Stein and sets by Florine Stettheimer; the production was directed by John Houseman and the choreography by Frederick Ashton. Askew, as the head of Durlacher Brothers New York gallery (a long-established London firm of dealers in Old Masters) and later as its owner, became with his remarkable wife, Constance, the center of a coterie of artists, critics, composers, young collectors, editors, and writers. To the Askews' *salon* (or "saloon," as it was generally called by its regular Sunday-evening habitués) came quite literally all of those who were responsible for the direction of the Museum of Modern Art in its early days.

There were other and still younger men than Barr and Abbott and their contemporaries at the Fogg who were busy about the arts at Harvard and who later were movers and shakers in the Museum of Modern Art and elsewhere in the art world. They were undergraduate crusaders for enlightenment and advanced taste. They called themselves the Harvard Society for Contemporary Art, Inc., and they hired two rooms over the "Coop" (as the Harvard cooperative store is called) as a gallery in which to exhibit paintings and prints, sculpture and photographs. Lincoln Kirstein, an intense, humorless, beetle-browed nineteen-year-old of unlimited energy and very nearly unlimited intelligence and dramatically personal style and taste, was the moving spirit of the society. His two colleagues were Edward M. M. Warburg, later (but not much later) a trustee of the Museum of Modern Art and subsequently a Regent of the State of New York ("Lincoln brought me along with him," he says), and John Walker, whose primary interest turned from modern art to masterpieces of whatever time; he studied with Bernard Berenson, the doyen of connoisseurs, at his villa, I Tatti, in Florence and subsequently became the director of the National Gallery of Art in Washington. The young men decorated their rooms above the Coop in the most elegantly fashionable modern manner; they painted the ceilings silver, and set steel café chairs and tables with highly polished marble tops about the gallery.

According to Warburg, "Kirstein knew everybody—everybody, that is, who moved in literary and art circles," an exaggeration, of course, but in the circumstances a reasonable one. Kirstein was a poet; he published a novel (*Flesh Is Heir*) before he graduated from college in 1930; he founded and edited a literary magazine, *Hound and Horn*, to which a great many distinguished critics, poets, and writers of short stories were pleased to contribute. It published poems by Ezra Pound,

William Carlos Williams, and Allen Tate, short stories by Katherine Anne Porter, Sean O'Faolain, Kay Boyle, and Erskine Caldwell, critical essays by T. S. Eliot, Lewis Galantière, Matthew Josephson, and Herbert Read, photographs by Walker Evans, Ralph Steiner, and Charles Sheeler. These were just a few of the prominent names that graced the magazine's contents pages. In the age of "little magazines" *Hound and Horn* held its own with any of them. So far as the Harvard Society of Contemporary Art was concerned, Kirstein's most important gifts to it were an adventurousness of spirit, strong convictions about his own taste, and the ability to rally others to his cause. He persuaded collectors as important as Sam Lewisohn and Duncan Phillips to take pictures off their walls and send them to the Coop. Dealers like the Rehn Gallery and Valentine Dudensing and institutions as august as the Carnegie Institute in Pittsburgh lent pictures for the society's first exhibition, which opened on February 19, 1929. The first show was all Americans, and the young men had gathered works in oil by no less personages than Bellows and Davies, Prendergast, Sloan, Benton, Hopper, Robertson, K. H. Miller, Speicher, and Sterne, watercolors and drawings by Burchfield, Demuth, Kent, Marin, and Sterne, sculpture by Archipenko, Lachaise, and Laurent, prints by several of the painters, and a photograph by Stieglitz of Georgia O'Keeffe's hands, now a famous print. Such an exhibition was no mean undertaking for three undergraduates to collect, hang, catalogue, and supervise. "We did our homework there," Warburg recalls.

It has been said without any justification beyond a natural enthusiasm of the supporters of this youthful excursion that Mrs. Rockefeller and Mrs. Sullivan "got the idea for the Museum of Modern Art from the Harvard Society." It is nevertheless quite true that Kirstein, Warburg, and Walker anticipated by at least a year many ideas that were more grandly displayed by the Museum of Modern Art. The second exhibition of the society, for instance, was devised as a supplement to an exhibition at the Fogg of nineteenth- and twentieth-century French painters which, though it included Picasso, Derain, and Matisse, did not in the view of the young men give sufficient recognition to the new movements. Their show included Lurçat, Soutine, Vlaminck, Laurencin, Braque, Miró, Léger, Gris, and de Chirico among the painters, and also the sculptors Maillol, Despiau, Brancusi, and Orloff and a surprising miscellany of objects such as cigarette cases, wallets, book bindings, vases, bottles, and jewelry. On one occasion Alexander ("Sandy") Calder was invited to show his wire sculpture at the society's gallery, and legend (which Calder now denies) says that he arrived in Cambridge with nothing but a suitcase containing a few pieces of clothing, a coil of copper wire, and a pair of pliers. "He worked in his pajama bottoms," Warburg told me, "and used his big toe for a vice. He made his famous circus with moving figures, and we sold peanuts and stuff at the gallery. He also made a wire portrait of my father from a photograph and put a test tube in the lapel with a carnation in it." [2] On another occasion the society made headlines in newspapers as far from Cambridge as Denver and Paris with its exhibition of Buckminster Fuller's Dymaxion house.

The society, which was incorporated, had a small but distinguished board of trustees, a collection of eminent personages whom one would not expect to lend their prestige to an undergraduate venture: Edward W. Forbes, the director of the Fogg; John Nicholas Brown of Providence, a prominent collector of drawings who when he was born was known as "the richest baby in the world"; Philip Hofer, bibliophile and collector of drawings at Harvard; Professors Arthur Pope and Paul Sachs, also of Harvard; Sachs's brother, Arthur, a broker; and Felix M. Warburg, international banker and the father of "Eddie." Some of these men unquestionably applauded the enterprise of the young men who founded the society rather more than they applauded the works exhibited, for none of them was known as a man of experimental tastes. Between the time the society opened its first show in February 1929 and February two years later it had held twenty-one exhibitions. It had shown modern German printing, American cartoonists, Japanese and English handicrafts, an international photography exhibition, sculpture by Noguchi, and in December 1930 an exhibition of work of the Bauhaus nearly a decade before the Museum of Modern Art got around to it in 1938. Kirstein and Warburg and Walker all graduated in 1930, but the society went on until December 1931, when it was teetering on the edge of financial collapse. It rallied briefly with about $1,000 in donations, more than half of which came from students, and a gift of $700 from an anonymous donor.

Alfred Barr had, of course, watched the development and influence of the Harvard Society with interest and approval but, so far as I know, without participation in its activities. By the time its existence was threatened, he was already immersed in the second year of the Museum of Modern Art's emergence. He took time, however, to write to the Harvard *Crimson*, the university's daily paper, a letter encouraging support for the society's survival. "I have heard with astonishment and

2 "I took the circus along too, and showed it to the Harvard boys." *Calder, an Autobiography* (New York, 1966).

the utmost regret," he started his letter, "that the Harvard Society for Contemporary Art is about to close unless funds are provided for its continuation." After two paragraphs praising its accomplishments (including: "More than any other one factor the Society has persuaded the rest of America that Greater Boston is not as aloof from modern art as has been generally supposed") he concluded with a sentence of rebuke: "If the Harvard Society for Contemporary Art should die in the wealthiest academic community in the world, it would be little short of disgrace." It died, though one doubts that Harvard felt seriously disgraced, in 1933.

Several years before the society was founded, when Barr was teaching at Wellesley, Sachs had asked him for criticism of the Harvard course and for his suggestions. On New Year's Day of 1926 Barr responded with a letter which in some respects foreshadows what would happen at the Museum of Modern Art in the next fifteen years or so. He proposed a course on modern art that would deal not only with painting and sculpture but with music and poetry and draw on the talents not just of members of the academic community but of critics of various degrees of tolerance and distaste for modern art. He suggested that the young composer and critic Virgil Thomson (he was twenty-nine then) lecture on music and Professor John Livingston Lowes (the author of *Convention and Revolt in Poetry*, who became in 1927 the author of a work of scholarship that, as rarely happens, was a best-seller, *The Road to Xanadu*) and Bliss Perry, both of the Harvard faculty, lecture on poetry. "If Professors Edgell and Post [both art historians] could serve as antagonists, so much the better," Barr wrote. "Even Mr. Cortissoz [critic of the New York *Herald Tribune*] might be brought in to give his moribund opinions. . . . Mr. Ivins [curator of prints at the Metropolitan Museum and a brilliant essayist] I know could contribute gloriously as an antidote. Mr. Gilbert Seldes could present his seven lively arts [3] and Thomas Craven [author of *Men of Art*, a popular book bitterly attacked by many scholars primarily because it was so readable] could give his sober and very thoughtful opinions on modern painting." This was not to be just an intellectual circus, and Barr concluded: "Perhaps I am day dreaming, but I am really serious. No subject deserves a variety of attitudes so much as contemporary. . . ."

Nearly three years before Barr was appointed director of the new

3 *The Seven Lively Arts* by Gilbert Seldes (1924) dealt with the popular arts such as vaudeville, comic strips, movies, jazz, and other matters not then regarded as "serious."

museum Sachs had told his friend Sam Lewisohn about him in a letter. "In my deliberate opinion," he wrote, "Barr has thought more deeply on the subject of modern art . . . and has the ability to express his matured thoughts with more clarity than anyone else who is at present giving time and attention to this fascinating and difficult subject." Barr was twenty-five, and the occasion for Sachs's letter, which had been written at Barr's request, was an attempt to persuade Lewisohn to purchase a landscape by Corot that Barr very urgently wanted to acquire for the collection at Wellesley. Lewisohn did not rise to Sachs's bait. Indeed, there were many later times when Lewisohn as a trustee of the Museum of Modern Art did not succumb to Barr's eloquence.

Barr managed to continue his graduate studies by teaching for a year and then, with what he could save and abet by fellowships, studying for a year. He supplemented his income, but not by much, with an occasional book review for the *Saturday Review of Literature*, as it was then called. By 1927 he thought it essential to go to Europe again and see at first hand what was going on in London and Paris and, perhaps more important at that moment, in Germany. He wrote to Sachs: "Since graduating at Princeton I have been living hand to mouth— Now if I should go abroad I should have to go considerably in debt." He applied to Harvard for a fellowship "to enable me to spend a year in Europe. I wish to study *contemporary* European culture," he wrote, ". . . to gather material for a thesis, 'The Machine in Modern Art.' . . . Contemporary art is puzzling and chaotic but it is, to many of us, living and important in itself and as a manifestation of our amazing though none too lucid civilization. I confess I find the art of the present more interesting and moving than the art of Sung or even the Quattrocento." The fellowship did not materialize, but he went anyway. Sachs helped him with a "fellowship" of $400 which he took straight out of his own pocket and deposited in four installments to Barr's account in the Morgan Guaranty Bank in Paris.

Jere Abbott joined Barr in London in the autumn of 1927, "with the intent," he says, "of running about Europe, looking at anything which smacked of art." They met Wyndham Lewis there and found the novelist-essayist-painter (he was a leader of a group of artists who called themselves "Vorticists") a "colorful and brilliant" introduction to London's Bohemia. Through Lewis they met a woman named Nina Hamnett, "a painter of sorts, and a true Bohemian and trying, not too quietly, to wreck the Empire." She prodded the young men to go to Russia, a rare thing for American tourists or, indeed, Western Europeans to do in 1927, and she gave them a letter of introduction to an

Irish friend, a woman who was studying at the University of Moscow.

Barr and Abbott got to Russia on Christmas Day by a very circuitous route. First they went to Holland, where they were greatly impressed by the "modernity" of the Dutch architecture, posters, and book jackets and by the modern paintings that were to be seen in museums. "It is possible to discuss what is going on nationally," Barr wrote in a "Letter" to *The Arts* magazine, "and to a considerable extent internationally. Neither is at present possible in American museums." [4] Barr and Abbott also went to the Hook of Holland to look at the architecture of J. J. P. Oud, who had just completed a complex of workers' houses that was to establish Oud's international reputation as a master of modern architecture and, as he did nothing later to equal it, to climax it at the same time. They went to Paris looking for buildings by Le Corbusier, but found little. (His famous Savoye house at Poissy, a Paris suburb, was not completed until 1931.) They headed for Berlin and, according to Abbott, found the modern architecture disappointing and "heavy." The Bauhaus at Dessau, on the other hand, "opened a new world." Here Walter Gropius had built for his school a shimmering glass house just two years before. Here was a community of artists and students very much to Barr's taste—an interrelation of the several arts and many crafts, of architecture and industrial design and typography, an interplay that Barr had insisted upon in the course that he taught at Wellesley. "We had great entertainment there," Abbott has written. "We saw quite a bit of Klee and Feininger and others on the faculty. Feininger was extrovert and outgoing. Klee was quiet. Outside of art, his main interest was economics. His desk top— small shells, dried starfish, skeleton of a mouse, and some dried large spiders. But there was some humor there and great perception." In his preface to the catalogue of the Museum of Modern Art exhibition *Bauhaus 1919–1928*, which was published in 1938, Barr wrote:

> It is hard to recall when and how we in America first began to hear of the Bauhaus. . . . It may not have been until after the great Bauhaus exhibition of 1923 that reports reached America of a new kind of art school in Germany where famous expressionist painters such as Kandinsky were combining forces with craftsmen and industrial designers under the general direction of the architect, Gropius. . . . Some of the younger of us had just left college where courses in modern art began with Rubens and ended with a few superficial and often hostile remarks about van Gogh

4 *The Arts.* January 1928, pp. 48–49, "Dutch Letter" by A. H. B., Jr.

and Matisse; when the last word in imitation Gothic dormitories had windows with one carefully cracked pane to each picturesque casement. Others of us, in architectural schools, were beginning our courses with gigantic renderings of Doric capitals, or ending them with elaborate projects for Colonial gymnasiums and Romanesque skyscrapers. . . . It is no wonder then that young Americans began to turn their eyes toward the Bauhaus as the one school in the world where modern problems of design were approached realistically in a modern atmosphere.

From Dresden Barr wrote to Sachs on December 1, 1927, that he and Abbott were hoping to go to Russia "to study prewar 'primitivism' (my thesis) as well as post-Revolutionary painting, theatre and cinema." (He seems to have changed his mind about his thesis since he had written Sachs to apply for a fellowship a few months before to write a thesis about "The Machine in Modern Art.") He also, he told Sachs, hoped to see and study fifteenth-century painting. The young men got visas without difficulty in Berlin, and when they arrived in Moscow they were met at the railroad station in the early afternoon by Nina Hamnett's Irish friend, who took them to the Hotel Bristol. There they found the Mexican painter Diego Rivera (who later was a source of great embarrassment to the Rockefellers because of a mural in Radio City) and made friends with him. They found that there were very few foreigners in Moscow; they could move about just as they pleased, for, as Abbott recalls, "Intourist had been started but was so inefficient that nobody bothered with it." They were greatly impressed, however, by "the continuous marching of soldiers in the streets day and night. And they sang beautifully, often in four-part harmony and with solo voices."

The excitement of Moscow for Barr and Abbott was primarily in the film and the theater. On their first evening they saw Sergei Eisenstein's remarkable film *Potemkin,* and they met Eisenstein and made friends with him. He urged them to come to his laboratory and watch him edit the rushes of the film on which he was then at work. Meyerhold's production of *The Inspector General* they found "breathtaking." They were introduced to Meyerhold after the performance, as they had been to Eisenstein, and he invited them to drop into his morning rehearsals any time they wished.

"We almost at once began to sense the bind which the revolutionary government had gotten into in the arts," Abbott has written. "The few new apartments which had been built were bleak rather than modern

and miserably constructed. But in sculpture and painting and architecture the Russian powers were realizing that they could not be
'modern' and appeal to the masses at the same time. The masses laughed
at the stuff."

In a "Journal" that Barr wrote for *The Arts* he noted that there
might be some hope for modern architecture at the hands of two young
groups of designers, the Asnova and the OCA (Russian initials for
Society of Contemporary Architects), but, he said, "the private individual who might wish to attest to his membership in the *avant
garde* by patronizing the adventurous architect does not exist in Russia. There are men of wealth but they are careful to make no display
of it." So the only patrons were the bureaucratic ones, "alas, only a
little more advanced than . . . their American counterparts." For an
example he cited an apartment house for workers in government offices, the first of its kind, built in Moscow in 1926. Barr was not taken
in (he was rarely taken in) by its modern look. "It may be taken as
the epitome of modern Russian building," he wrote more in sadness
than in anger,

> for it demonstrates clearly a theoretical mastery of a problem
> which has been executed with remarkable technical incompetence.
> The interior techniques are pathetic: the piping crude, door fix-
> tures bad, garbage chutes impractical, doors even too wide; though
> these faults all must be blamed upon the lack of any fine tradition
> of craftsmanship rather than upon the architects.

Barr and Abbott were men with carpet-sweeper eyes; nothing
escaped them. They went to Leningrad and spent hours in the Hermit-
age collections. They went to Novgorod and visited the red brick
monasteries with their blue domes "hidden in white birch groves on
numerous islands." The twelfth- and thirteenth-century frescoes were
being cleaned while they were there, and they climbed the scaffold to
see them at arm's length. But in Moscow they found that the Museum
of Abstract Art had closed its doors and modern art was talked about
by docents in other museums as examples of "bourgeois decadence."
Barr recorded in his journal on January 6, 1928: "The exhibition to
which Diego Rivera was to take us was closed suddenly. Two reasons
were suggested by the Mexican: first, there were portraits of the opposition; second, in a composition representing Lenin's funeral some
figures were nude."

There was a constant flow of lengthy longhand letters from Barr in
Europe to Sachs in Cambridge describing in detail almost everything

he saw and frequently recommending color reproductions of modern works of art that he felt should be added to the Fogg's teaching collection. (In the 1920s, though today it seems hardly credible, color prints of modern pictures were very scarce in America. Even color reproductions of Cézanne and van Gogh and Renoir were hard to come by, and Picassos and Matisses scarcely existed at all; only the most adventurous college students had Cézanne reproductions on their walls. Most young people learned about modern art from a few magazines like the *Dial* and Frank Crowninshield's *Vanity Fair*.) Barr also sent manuscripts to Sachs for his comments, and in one such case Sachs, without revealing its source, tried the essay on his students and sent Barr their comments. In one letter Barr suggested that he was preparing a "critical bibliography" of modern art, a possible undertaking then as it would not be today except for a substantial team of scholars. Billions of words on modern art have piled up since 1928. He also wrote urging an exhibition of Russian icons on Sachs, who was enthusiastic, but the project was abandoned because of the problems of buying insurance on property owned by the Russian government.

Barr fussed at the reluctance of his contemporaries to accept the new art. He was a crusader and a missionary by nature and by inheritance, and he believed in the ultimate conversion and salvation of the Philistines . . . or so it appears. He was a zealot in the cause of art—all art and not just modern art—but it was the new and revolutionary, the expression of his contemporaries in every facet of the arts, to which he gave his enthusiasm most unreservedly and by whose lack of acceptance he was most saddened and sometimes irritated. Sachs took a somewhat more tolerant view, and in March 1928 when Barr was back in Paris he wrote to his protégé: "There has been great progress here in America during the year of your absence. The interest in museums and modern art in museums and in all that is connected with modern art and modernized art has greatly increased—witness the show at Lord & Taylor's, at Jordan Marsh and elsewhere . . . it is a time for co-operation not irritation."

By the fall of 1928 Barr was back at Wellesley giving his course in nineteenth- and twentieth-century art to a very small group of carefully selected students. There were just seven of them ("seven children," he called them), and he chose them on the basis of a questionnaire which tested their curiosity about the arts and their knowledge. "I went to Wellesley in the first place because I could do such a thing," he told me at the Museum in 1970 after his retirement. "I didn't give the children any marks or any examinations." (One of the children,

Ernestine Fantl, turned up on the staff of the Museum of Modern Art several years later as assistant curator of architecture.) It was a course, he said, that was based on the methods of Morey of Princeton, whose field was early Christian and medieval arts. "I was greatly impressed by his interest in various kinds of art—in architecture, in painting, sculpture, ivories, manuscripts. I liked that very much; it was not narrow. That had a good deal to do with it, and the Bauhaus, the whole business, the interrelation of the arts. I also," he continued, "got a great deal from Mather. This man really loved painting and painters. He never let you forget a slide was a slide and not a work of art, and he thought all color slides were bad and he wouldn't use them."

"Alfred got there without a chaperon," Mrs. Barr said to me on the same occasion. "He jumped into modern on his own."

The course at Wellesley was, in essence, the outline for Barr's later plans for the Museum, which developed very much in the same character as the course. It was the first course in modern art in any American college (if one discounts the courses in "modern art" that began with the Renaissance and ended with Winslow Homer), and it ranged over all of the arts, not just the visual arts of painting and sculpture, of photography and cinema, but concerning itself with the theater and with music and architecture and with machine-made objects. In his excellent profile of Barr in *The New Yorker* in 1953 Dwight Macdonald noted: "The girls rode the Boston and Albany from Wellesley to Boston to inspect the stations along the way that had been designed by the great nineteenth-century architect H. H. Richardson," and to study machine-made art "each student spent a dollar in the local five-and-ten on what seemed to her the best-designed objects, and these were then arranged on tables to form Constructivist designs."

Barr had finished his third year as an associate professor at Wellesley (one of them spent abroad) and had been offered a Carnegie fellowship to study at the Institute of Fine Arts at New York University when Sachs approached him in June 1929 about the Museum of Modern Art job. The Institute of Fine Arts was at that time rapidly gaining prestige as a center of art historical studies, and in the course of the next two decades, notably because of the influx of great German art historians in flight from Hitler and his bully boys, it surpassed Harvard as a graduate school in the arts. To be offered a fellowship there in 1929 was a considerable compliment, but the Museum—a new museum devoted entirely to what was new (or so it seemed then)—was irresistible. Barr reacted to Sachs's invitation in a letter of July 1 by proposing others who might fit the job. There was A. E. Gallatin, whose collection of modern paintings was hung on the first floor of a New York University building on Washington Square and was called The Gallery of Living Art. There was also Duncan Phillips, of Washington, who, Barr noted, "had much experience in collecting American painting." He also mentioned "Jacques Maurey of Paris (who has done most of Gallatin's buying) and a far better man, Dr. H. F. Hortlaub of the Mannheim Kunsthalle, which as you know is the most active modern collection in Europe." There was one other candidate whom he somewhat archly proposed. "The man who seems to me best fitted for the role has probably not occurred to you," Barr wrote. "He is a person of colossal energy, of great executive ability, of the most constructive imagination, and possessed by a passion for works of art. He has had great practical experience in all that pertains to great museums, he is able to guide men and control resources. I mean, of course, yourself. Why not?"

Having got that off his chest, Barr concluded with a cry from the heart: "The fact that you are even considering me as a possible participant in this great scheme has set my mind teeming with ideas and plans. This is something I could give my life to—unstintedly."

> *The Museum of Modern Art, which will open
> November 1, is very badly needed. There is a
> curious apathy toward current painting in this
> country. The average woman never buys any of it,
> decorating her home with prints that she obtains
> at the department stores, or with photographs of
> members of the family, or with elephant book-ends;
> the average man has never heard of it.*
> EDITORIAL, *New York Evening World*, September 7,
> 1929

Chapter III *Overture*

When Sachs wrote to Alfred Barr in Europe that "there has been great progress" in the interest in modern art in 1928, he essentially was reporting that a few grains of earth had been added to a mole hill, but that the mole hill was still far from becoming a mountain.

To say that there was little or no interest in the new movements in painting and sculpture and architecture would be far from the truth, though the interest was generally negative. There was indeed a very great deal of highly articulate (or at least noisy) professional as well as popular distaste for what was "modern" (as it was understood by its proponents) and what was generally called "modernistic" by those who could not abide any departure from academic traditions, the clichés of illustration, and the accepted forms and standards of Edwardian "good taste." Most people knew what was "beautiful" and they knew that the distortions, unconventional (read "unrealistic") colors, and abstractions of Picasso and Braque and Matisse, for example, were a conspiracy against all that was serious and decent. They

34

were not so much bothered by the subject matter (as they earlier had been by the garbage cans and clotheslines and whores and dirty urchins of the painters of the so-called "Ashcan School" which had erupted in New York in the first decade of the century); they were bothered because they could not see that there was any subject matter at all . . . certainly none that expressed a decent sentiment or provoked a noble emotion. What was art (i.e., ennobling) about a fragmented guitar, or an inaccurately outlined and flatly painted nude with her eyes in the wrong place in a spade-like head? How could anyone seriously call a tall piece of bronze that looked like a bifurcated clothes pin sculpture? Could you believe that a glass-and-concrete box that "they" talked about as "a machine for living" was architecture, much less a home?

It would be inaccurate to say that the general distaste for what was called modern started with the Armory Show of 1913, though it was then that the cork blew out of vintage American complacency with a pop that still echoes faintly in arguments about taste today. To define what is "modern" is a game that art historians rather solemnly play. Several years ago I asked Bates Lowry, who was then briefly the Director of the Museum of Modern Art, when modern art came into being, and with the assurance of a man who brooks no argument he said, "With Manet," which is to say about 1860. Others might agree with him if only because Manet was so violently attacked by the academicians and critics of his day (the same might be said for Caravaggio a couple of centuries before), but they would agree with reservations. It is comforting to think of Manet's gentlemen in business suits picnicking with nude ladies in the Bois or his mocking (and beautiful) parody of Giorgione's "Venus" called "Olympe" as the trumpets in an aesthetic charge, when they were actually more moral than aesthetic slaps in the academic face. Some would rather say that "modern" starts with the Impressionists, with Monet and Renoir, Pissarro and Degas and the American Mary Cassatt, or with the Post-Impressionists, Gauguin, Cézanne, Seurat, and van Gogh. To the young of the present it would seem that such men must be classified not with what is modern but with the Old Masters. Today modern painting seems to start for the middle-aged with the Fauves (Derain, Matisse, Braque) in the first decade of this century, with Picasso's and Juan Gris's Cubism, with Marcel Duchamp, the hero (or villain, as many regarded him) of the Armory Show because of his "Nude Descending a Staircase." To the young, I would assume, modern starts with the Abstract Expressionists, with Jackson Pollock and Rothko and "the School of New York," just as any movies made before the *Nouvelle Vague* of the 1950s are "classic," as are such old-fashioned sculptures as the pieces by Lipchitz and Henry Moore and Calder.

The founders of the Museum of Modern Art, however, seemed in no doubt about when modern art started. Conger Goodyear in the introductory chapter of his book on the early days of the Museum wrote in 1943:

> What is Modern Art? Most definitions use dates for their boundaries within which lies a territory of hazy character. For our purposes it has been agreed that Modern Art began fifty or sixty years ago with the Big Four of Post-Impressionism—Cézanne, Gauguin, Seurat and Van Gogh. The common characteristic of these men was originality.

(The common characteristic of all great painters, of course, has been originality, which can also be defined as a personal vision and an individual way of stating it.) After the Museum had been open for nearly seven years, Barr, in a statement justifying the need to build a new and bigger building, had a somewhat different definition. "Modern Art . . . ," he wrote, "is a relative, elastic term that serves continually to designate painting, sculpture, moving pictures, architecture, and the lesser visual arts, original and progressive in character, produced especially within the last three decades but including also 'pioneer ancestors' of the nineteenth century."

The men whom Goodyear cited as the fathers of modern art shared as a second common characteristic the disparagement of their academically minded contemporaries and the unrestrained ridicule of what might be called the informed if not the adventurous art public. To a considerable extent, it was their genuine experience that fostered the romantic myth that artists worth their salt are likely to be ignored by their contemporaries, a myth that the Museum of Modern Art by its dedication to the experimental has largely laid to rest in our time. As I have said elsewhere, it used to be that an artist hoped to be discovered before he died; now he can scarcely help being discovered. Today he hopes to be *revived* before he dies. There is, moreover, no place in which a contemporary (or should I say modern?) artist would rather be revived than in the galleries of the Museum of Modern Art with a "retrospective" of his work, a situation which has not in recent years been uncommon.

Such was not the case in the mid-'20s. The battle for the experimental arts was still in its early maneuverings, and the batteries drawn up to let loose their salvos against ignorance, indifference, and the hostility of active Philistinism, as it was so regarded by the embattled, were few and scattered compared with the offensive later to be mounted. No city of those which considered themselves cultural centers raised its guard higher to ward off modern art than Boston. When the Fogg Art Museum showed an exhibition of reproductions called *Living Art—Twenty Facsimiles* (they were given to the Fogg by Barr and Abbott), Barr baited the Boston critics into a reaction by calling Boston "a modern art pauper" in a piece in the Harvard *Crimson* of October 30, 1926, and by pronouncing that it was "surprising, and even shocking, to find so little interest in modern art in Boston." The critic of the Boston *Herald* announced that Cézanne was "a poor painter with bad eyesight," Gauguin a maker of "gross caricatures in the name of art," and van Gogh was dismissed as "a crazy galoot who painted for years in an insane asylum."

In New York the situation was somewhat more encouraging. If Royal Cortissoz of the *Herald Tribune* seemed to be a perpetual sorehead where anything non-conventional was concerned (he was the most amiable and gregarious of clubmen with his many friends), at least Henry McBride of the *Sun* looked upon what was new with a sympathetic and often uncommonly sensitive eye and became one of the staunchest critical supporters of the Museum of Modern Art. There were in New York, moreover, a number of commercial galleries that were (and had been for some time) devoted to painting and sculpture by the so-called "moderns." Even before the Armory Show of 1913 Alfred Stieglitz, the photographer, had shown works by Matisse and Picasso, Cézanne [1] and Toulouse-Lautrec, and American revolutionaries like Marin and Max Weber and Alfred Maurer in his 291 Gallery at 291 Fifth Avenue (also called the Photo-Secessionist Gallery). The Macbeth Gallery and the Modern Gallery were showing what *Art News* in February 1914 had dubbed "The Faddists" among the American artists, and also Europeans like Picasso, Braque, and Picabia. And in 1915 the Montross Gallery in New York gave Matisse a one-man show. In the mid-'20s, while Boston dragged its heels, the dealers on Fifth Avenue and those on 57th Street were showing modern paintings on their monk's-cloth or velvet or grass-cloth walls. The serious collector or the Saturday-afternoon gallery-goers could find "modern masters" at the Kraushaar Gallery, at Rehn's and Valentine Dudensing or at New Art Circle, as Barr's friend J. B. Neumann called his place. The "masters" were Derain and Bonnard, Segonzac, Dufy, Pascin, and

---

[1] Indeed, Stieglitz showed the first Cézanne exhibited in America, in 1911.

Laurencin, who seemed awfully up-to-date to the readers of Crownin-shield's *Vanity Fair,* where they were reproduced in color. Modern sculpture was less frequently seen in New York galleries, though the stately works of Maillol and Brancusi and Despiau graced the hushed elegance of Joseph Brummer's gallery at 27 East 57th Street along with ancient and medieval pieces of remarkable quality.

Obviously if there were successful dealers in "modern masters" there were also prosperous collectors willing—indeed, eager—to sit in arm-chairs before velvet-covered easels in the inner sanctums of the gal-leries and buy some of what was propped up in front of them, often, in those days, by a Negro minion in an alpaca jacket. Some of these collectors we have already met—Stephen C. Clark, Sam Lewisohn, and Conger Goodyear among others, well known to the trade if not yet to the art public. Some others, like Miss Bliss, bought under the guiding eye of an artist. Others relied on professional tastemakers, specialists in the arts whose business it was to know the art market and the tastes of their clients (or friends) and sufficiently eloquent to make their judgments acceptable. Scarcely any collection of importance in Amer-ica in the last seventy-five years has been made without the guidance of such a tastemaker, and the practice is, of course, still common today, and is likely to be common tomorrow. One advantage of being a mem-ber of the Board of Trustees of the Museum of Modern Art has always been that with the responsibility went the privilege of the advice of the director and the curators on personal collecting, though this privilege does not seem always to have been exercised. Members of the staff have acted as "scouts" for collectors on the board and watched out for "good buys" for their walls or their portfolios of prints and drawings. In a manner of speaking, they have acted in the art market in much the same manner as investment counselors do in the stock market, though the commodities may be bought for different reasons, and frequently are. Not all collectors of art are looking for capital growth in their investments in paint and canvas, in paper and ink, in stone and bronze; some are looking for aesthetic satisfaction and for personal (indeed, private) pleasure as well, and some are merely look-ing, as collectors have since the days of Aristotle and before, for the prestige that ownership of art affords to the socially ambitious. But in the 1920s modern art had not as yet become nearly as socially ac-ceptable as Old Masters, and there is a strong element of daring in the collections that were made in the days before the Museum of Modern Art made such collecting (and some of the collectors) chic.

A number of these pioneering (or prototypical) collections are

worth mentioning because they are part of the backdrop against which
the Museum of Modern Art first made its appearance on the stage. The
most famous and the least visible of these was in Merion, Pennsylvania,
a Philadelphia suburb. It was sequestered in the Barnes Foundation,
officially a public institution, but one from which the perpetually
petulant Dr. Albert C. Barnes, the inventor of Argyrol, managed to
exclude very nearly everyone who had a serious interest in what hung
on his walls. There were a hundred and more Renoirs, dozens of
Cézannes and Matisses and early Picassos (he balked at Picasso's cubism) and Soutines. His original mentor had been the painter William
Glackens, with whom he had played sandlot baseball as a boy in South
Philadelphia. Barnes could not abide what he considered the twaddle
of the art critics and the highbrows, and he refused to let them into his
Foundation to see his pictures, a policy which led some curators and
collectors and dealers and less official art-lovers to the most devious
subterfuges and masquerades to gain admission to his gallery. One
friend of mine passed himself off as a horticulturalist and asked access
to the gardens, hoping that Mrs. Barnes would say, "While you're here,
you know, we have some pictures you might like to look at." It
worked. On the other hand, when T. S. Eliot was lecturing at Bryn
Mawr College, just a few miles from Merion, his hostess sent her chauf-
feur to ask if the poet might see the collection, and the answer came
back, "Nuts!"

The only public gallery devoted entirely to new trends in painting
was A. E. Gallatin's Gallery of Living Art at New York University,
whose guiding spirits, as we have noted, were recommended by Barr
to Sachs as possible directors for the proposed Museum of Modern Art.
There was nothing like it in America when it was opened on December 12, 1927, and, as was remarked in 1943 in an official bulletin when
the collection became the property of the Philadelphia Museum of Art,
"it is a matter of surprise that no museum of this character had existed
in the United States, the most modern of all countries." Gallatin, the
scion of a distinguished family (his earliest American forebear was
Jefferson's Secretary of the Treasury and later Minister to France),
was trained as a lawyer but devoted himself to painting—to doing it,
to collecting it, and to writing about it. By the time Philadelphia
acquired the collection (Mr. Gallatin gave it to the museum) it numbered "nearly 170 works, carefully selected to illustrate the history of
creative art from 1906 to the present, with special emphasis on abstract
art." No more than half the works of art were ever shown at one time
in the New York University gallery. Milton Brown, in his *American*

Painting from the Armory Show to the Depression, says of Gallatin's holdings: "It was a minor collection which presented the tendency without the quality of modern art." It did, however, contain Miró's "Dog Barking at the Moon" and Picasso's "Three Musicians" along with examples of Mondrian, Arp, Lurçat, Maillol, Masson, Lipchitz, Klee, Chagall, de Chirico, Braque, and Brancusi and a number of Americans including Hartley, Louis Bouché, Knaths, and Preston Dickinson.

In 1941 the Museum of Modern Art asked Gallatin to present it with his collection and he declined. He later said, "I told them I wouldn't entertain the idea. It would have been like putting a good apple in a barrel of rotten ones." In 1972 the Museum borrowed ninety works of art from the Philadelphia Museum, including many from the Gallatin collection.

Two other major occurrences helped to endow modern art with respectability before the Museum of Modern Art was conceived. One was an exhibition and the other an auction. John Quinn played an important role in both.

In 1921 the Metropolitan Museum of Art in New York, prodded by Arthur B. Davies, Miss Bliss, Mrs. H. O. Havemeyer (whose magnificent collection of El Grecos, Goyas, Manets, Courbets, Renoirs, and dozens of other masterpieces and *objets d'art* later in the decade became the property of the museum by bequest), John Quinn, and several others, held its first, and for many years its only, exhibition of modern painting. "Modern" in this instance was Impressionists like Manet and Monet and Renoir and Post-Impressionists including Gauguin, Cézanne, Toulouse-Lautrec, Matisse, Derain, and pre-cubist Picasso. The museum trustees were grudgingly aware of the Post-Impressionists, and when Bryson Burroughs, the museum's curator of paintings and an associate of the National Academy of Design, was so bold as to buy Cézanne's *"La Colline des Pauvres"* in 1913 from the Armory Show, the museum's director, Dr. Edward Robinson, partly out of deference to the taste of the trustees, did his best to keep the news out of the papers. It was the first Cézanne bought by any American museum. Miss Bliss lent paintings from her collection to the Metropolitan show; so did Adolph Lewisohn (Sam's father), William Church Osborn, Mrs. Harry Payne Whitney (the sculptor better known as Gertrude Vanderbilt Whitney, founder in 1908 of the Whitney Studio Gallery on West Eighth Street and, ten years after the Metropolitan's modern show, of the Whitney Museum of American Art), and Walter C. Arensberg (who many years later gave his collection, which included the notorious "Nude Descending a Staircase" to the Philadelphia Museum). There were twenty-five lenders in all, seven of whom were anonymous. The exhibition was a long stride in making modern art socially acceptable, but even so it called down a torrent of vituperation such as had not been heard since the Armory Show, which Royal Cortissoz had called "not a movement and a principle" but "unadulterated cheek." No pictures provoked more venom than the twenty-eight paintings lent by John Quinn.

The role that Quinn played in the patronage and furthering of the modern movement in several of its aspects can scarcely be exaggerated. It has been told again and again, but briefly it is this:

John Quinn was a lawyer born in the town of Tiffin, Ohio, in 1870. His formal education consisted of a year at the University of Michigan and, after several years of reading law at night, a year at Harvard under John Henry Thayer, George Santayana, and William James. By 1906, when he was thirty-six, he opened his own law office in New York, and though his practice thrived (banking law was his specialty), he was quickly engaged with the arts and with artists and with the theater. As a lawyer he fought the battle of tariffs on works of art, and he defended the Irish Players when the New York police threatened to close down their production of Synge's *Playboy of the Western World*. Quinn was an exceedingly handsome man of classic features ("He was tall and aristocratic with a profile like a Roman coin's, only finer," one of his artist friends said of him). He was erect of carriage and possessed of driving energy, intelligence, and a distaste for the stuffiness of the Edwardian age. He cherished the idea that he was a gentleman, though he sometimes wondered if it were possible for an Irish boy from small-town Ohio to be a real gentleman. His memory, with which he confounded his opponents in court, was prodigious. It is recorded that one day, while he was shaving, a "lovely lady with a melodious voice" read aloud to him *The Waste Land*, which his friend T. S. Eliot had sent him. Thereafter he could recite the long and complex poem from memory without error.

Quinn is better known now as a champion and patron of the Abbey Players and the literary heroes of the Irish renaissance—his friends William Butler Yeats, J. M. Synge, James Stephens, Lady Gregory, James Joyce—than as an art collector, probably because his collection was disbursed. But it was nonetheless a formidable one and, unlike many collections, it was based to a very considerable degree on its owner's friendship with the men who made the art. For the purposes of our narrative Quinn's first head-on encounter with the battle for the new visual arts for recognition was his involvement with the Armory Show. The painter Walt Kuhn, who with Davies was the most active in every sense of the men on the committee that was organizing the exhibition, got Quinn to negotiate for the rental of the 69th Regiment Armory at 26th Street and Lexington Avenue. Quinn, according to Kuhn, "thought the whole scheme a crazy one," but Quinn was not the sort to be deterred by the outlandish when it was in a cause he thought worth fighting for alongside friends whom he trusted and admired. He became deeply involved and he obviously relished the hue and cry which the exhibition called forth from the press. "The Armory Show is pathological! It is hideous!" the *New York Times* declared, and it was called "vulgar, lawless, and profane." On the opening night of the show in the great hall hung with garlands of laurel Quinn made the welcoming speech: "It is the most complete art exhibition," he declaimed, "that has been held anywhere in the world during the last quarter of a century."

It was the pictures that Quinn lent to the Metropolitan eight years later that called forth the most vituperation, and some of them were works that in the flush of excitement and enthusiasm he had bought from the Armory Show. Indeed, he bought more from the show than any other collector—more items, that is. He spent $5,808.75 for several dozen paintings, bronzes, and prints, whereas the Metropolitan paid $6,700 for its single purchase, the Cézanne. In the interval between the Armory Show and the 1921 exhibition Quinn's taste, which was rather haphazard in 1913,[2] took a turn toward more solid fare, and Burroughs, when he went to see what he might borrow from Quinn for the exhibition, "sat for hours in amazement as a vivid parade of capital paintings was carried past his eyes." There were twenty-eight paintings that Burroughs wanted for the show, and Quinn lent them: "seven Redons, six Matisses, four Derains, three Picassos, two Gauguins, and one each by Van Gogh, Cézanne, Toulouse-Lautrec, Dufy, Rouault, and Vlaminck."

The exhibition opened on Tuesday, May 3, and the *American Art News* dated the following Saturday announced it as "the biggest piece of art news of the season." Two reasons justified their statement: "first, from the fact that it affords the best basis for an estimate of Post Impressionism that the country has yet had; second, from the recogni-

---

2 His purchases included Derain's "*La Fenêtre sur le Parc*" ($486); Kuhn's "Morning" ($600); an engraving, two watercolors, and three drawings by Pascin ($359); three oils by Jacques Villon ($540); three drawings (nudes) by Segonzac ($162); Redon's "*Initiation à l'Etude*" ($675); and so on.

tion of Modernism by a great institution like the Metropolitan. . . ."
The show included 126 pictures by twenty-two artists and illustrated,
according to *American Art News*, "Impressionism from its genesis
with Courbet [sic] and Manet, to its full development under Monet
and its wavering under Pissarro and Seurat . . . ; then it takes up the
Post-Impressionist revolt under Cézanne . . . and follows it to its extreme reach in Derain, Matisse and Picasso. It stops short of Cubism."
The magazine was completely accurate when it predicted: "It is sure
to arouse bitterness and enthusiasm," and, as is commonly the case, expressions of bitterness produced more newspaper lineage than did the
enthusiasm.

Four months after the show opened, a four-page flyer whose cover
bore the legend

A PROTEST

AGAINST THE PRESENT EXHIBITION

OF

DEGENERATE "MODERNISTIC" WORKS

IN THE

METROPOLITAN MUSEUM OF ART

was, according to the New York *Herald*, mailed "to many persons in
New York City." The flyer was signed by "A Committee of Citizens
and Supporters of the Museum" who intended to remain anonymous
and, at least so far as the press was concerned, succeeded. In the years
between 1921 and the present the language of the attacks, thanks to a
number of United States Congressmen and Senators, has become rather
familiar, but in 1921 it attracted attention. In its second sentence the
flyer threw down the gauntlet:

> We believe that these forms of so-called art are merely a symptom
> of a general movement throughout the world having for its object
> the breaking down of all law and order and the Revolutionary
> destruction of our entire social system.

And a few sentences later:

> This "Modernistic" degenerate cult is simply the Bolshevic phi-
> losophy applied to art.

Who was behind this opening of "the Temple of Art to the mentally
lame, halt and blind of the human race"? The answer was simply that
it was

organized by a coterie of European Traffickers in fraudulent art;
but the real cult of "Modernism" began with a small group of
neurotic Ego-Maniacs in Paris who styled themselves "Satanists"
—worshipers of Satan—the God of Ugliness.

It described "Modernistic" art as "a well-known form of insanity" and
referred to a speech made by an alienist, Dr. Charles W. Burr, at the
Philadelphia Museum, to prove it. It decried "these art crimes on the
walls of the splendid Museum." But it had special distaste for the
dealers:

> The sly dragging in of these ["Modernistic"] works is another
> proof of the crafty cunning of those who are trying to unload on
> the American dumping-ground more of the degenerate art-trash
> now in this exhibition and which is losing caste even now in
> Europe, where it originated.

In the final paragraph the "committee" (if it was a committee and
not an individual) lamely explained:

> We refrain from signing this protest only—because we wish to
> doubly emphasize our discontent, and also to escape the charge
> of merely seeking notoriety.

Not everyone, however, was equally reticent about coming forward
in defense of this conspiracy theory. A retired businessman named
Charles Vezin told a reporter from the *Herald* that he did not write
the circular but would be "proud to be the author." He had taken up
landscape painting since he gave up the dry-goods commission business and he had strong and verbose feelings about his avocation. A
more prominent artist, and surely a bonded one, Joseph Pennell,
blamed the show on John Quinn, "who," said Mr. Pennell, "had apparently been persuaded by dealers to make a hobby of the impressionist and post-impressionist schools." Mr. Pennell is further quoted
as saying to the *Herald* reporter that "post-impressionism . . . is pure
degeneracy, the same form of degeneracy that brought on the war";
he then added, with dubious accuracy, "and with peace it has been
abandoned even in Germany where it came from."

This was too much for Quinn. He issued a statement which the New
York papers and the art press broadcast for him, as they had broadcast
the flyer. "This is Ku Klux criticism," he said. "I was amazed that any
New York paper should publish such a screed. One does not argue
with degenerates who see nothing but degeneracy about them. . . .

I should no more think of replying in detail to that statement than I should of answering the ravings of a lot of lunatics. The whole thing reeks of ignorance. It is rancid with envy. It is filled with shrieks of impotent rage. Its vulgarity is equalled only by its cowardice. No one will be influenced by the attacks of self-admitted cowards. No one argues with anonymous libelers.

He did not stop at that, but that was the gist of it. With somewhat more humor, if less eloquence, the artist Robert Henri, by then very nearly an American patriarch of artists, said:

. . . The older men and the newer men [in the exhibition] are excellent, and we should be thankful to have an opportunity to see works of such distinctive character. The protest of the writers of the circular seems to be in keeping with the modern idea of prohibiting. Good heavens! we can't drink any more; surely we ought to be allowed to ruin ourselves looking at pictures.

The second event in which John Quinn played an essential role in helping to endow "modern" with social respectability in places few but important happened after his death. This was the sale of his collection on the orders of the executors of his estate. He died of cancer in 1924, and in his will he said that he thought that it was "better to take a loss than to carry them [the works of art] over for more than two years." Quinn had named two of his close friends who had scouted works of art for him, Arthur B. Davies and Henri Pierre Roché, to act as "advisers" on the disposition of the collection, which he did not want to "be consigned to the cold tomb of a museum and subjected to the stupid glance of the careless passer-by," a statement he borrowed from Edmond de Goncourt's instructions about the disposition of his collection. Obviously he would not have named advisers if he had not expected his executors to heed their advice. In spite of their warning, however, that it would be a catastrophe to the cause of modern art and to the finances of the estate to dump Quinn's considerable but generally thought to be outrageous collection on the market all at once, the executors were determined to stick to the letter of Quinn's will.

The dimensions and character of the Quinn collection are worth pausing to consider. One picture, and only one, Quinn had specified should be given to a museum; he left his finest Seurat, "The Circus," to the Louvre, which did not, as the Luxembourg also did not, own a

Seurat.[3] What was to be disposed of by sale included fifty Picassos. ("What agreeable and natural friendship one could have with him," Picasso said of Quinn after his death.) He had ten other Seurats besides the one he gave the Louvre and nineteen Matisses. He owned Rousseau's "Sleeping Gypsy," which Picasso had led him to; it was the last painting he bought before he died. (It brought $15,600 from the Paris dealer Bing at the Quinn sale in Paris and $30,000 when it was bought and given to the Museum of Modern Art by Mrs. Simon Guggenheim in 1939.) He owned an important El Greco, a "Christ Driving the Money Changers from the Temple," for which he paid $18,000, the most he ever paid for a painting. He had twenty-seven Brancusis, and paintings by Picabia and Redon and others and, of course, those we have already noted as being among his loans to the Metropolitan's 1921 exhibition. Not all of the objects got to the auction rooms. Marcel Duchamp and Roché bought all twenty-seven Brancusis, and the dealer Joseph Brummer sold a few items to private collectors. What did not go to Paris to be sold in 1926 (some 2,800 items in all; the market was thought to be better there than in New York) was sold in New York in February 1927. There were about 500 paintings and 300 sculptures in the New York sale, and the advisers were proven right; the prices were by no means what they might have been if the objects had been sold more sparingly and with greater fanfare.

Davies did not want to see the collection spread by the winds of chance to the four corners of the art world; he dearly hoped, as Quinn had wistfully hoped too, that he might get together $250,000 to buy the best of the French paintings and some of the others, and he appealed to the ladies who had helped to finance the Armory Show, Miss Bliss and Mrs. Sullivan. But the funds were not forthcoming. "Yet over their teacups," Aline Saarinen records in *The Proud Possessors*, "Miss Lillie Bliss and Mrs. Cornelius Sullivan deplored with him the loss of the Quinn collection and pondered whether, if New York had a permanent museum for modern art, Quinn's art might not have been saved. They began talking about doing something to correct the situation."

Whatever the leaves in the teacups may have foretold, the moment was soon at hand for their scheme to ripen. Once the Ladies put their minds to having a museum, events happened with what in retrospect

3 Quinn bought "The Circus" from the artist Paul Signac in 1922 and paid 150,000 francs, or about $15,000, for it.

seems like headlong speed. It was about five months between the day
Goodyear accepted Mrs. Rockefeller's invitation to lunch late in May
and the day the first visitors poured out of the elevators on the twelfth
floor of the Heckscher Building at the corner of Fifth Avenue and
57th Street to attend its opening. The months between Sachs's proposal to Barr that he be director of the Museum and its *vernissage*
were rather hectic, as one would expect. There was a staff to assemble,
small as it was; there was money to be extracted or pledged; there was
an exhibition to be decided upon, which turned out to be no easy matter, and the pictures to be borrowed, which, as it happened, took a
trip to Europe and a certain amount of diplomacy on Goodyear's part.

Barr made a second visit to Mrs. Rockefeller's cottage in Seal Harbor in August, and this time Jere Abbott had also been summoned
there. "I was about to set out on a trip around the Gaspé in a new
Stutz, to which I was over-attentive," he recalls, "when I was invited
by telephone. . . . Mrs. Rockefeller explained briefly the problem,
and when I arrived Alfred was also there. Attempting to conceal my
excitement, I agreed to help Alfred start the museum." It was not quite
as simple as Abbott recalls it to have been. He had been asked to establish an art department at Wesleyan University and he wired to Barr
that he was enthusiastic but uncertain about being able to give up such
an attractive prospect. "You know," he said in his telegram, "I would
rather work with you on this thing than anything I know." He suggested asking for Sachs's intervention with Wesleyan, and the following day he wired again: "Make no mistake as to my own feelings. . . .
Don't care what I'm called door clerk if necessary so long as I can
help. Salary you mention seems O.K. until they see whether I'm worth
anything or not." The proposed salary was $3,900 a year. The matter
was soon settled with the title of Associate Director.

Evidently Mrs. Rockefeller was more impressed by Barr on his second visit than on his first, for she wrote to Sachs: "Both my sisters and
I greatly enjoyed having Mr. Barr here for two days. We liked him
tremendously and I found him most sympathetic in every way. I like
his point of view and his ideas of what a modern museum of art should
be. I also feel that he not only has good taste, but good judgment."

She was less sure of his business ability and equally unsure of her
own. "We talked a little about the set up of the Museum from a purely
business point of view," she wrote. "Of course Mr. Barr has had very
little experience in this and I have had none at all." She was sure that
Sachs had the answer, and she added: "It would help me very much
indeed if you would be good enough to write me what business system

the Fogg Museum has worked out for Museums." As she was the treasurer of the committee, she also thought she ought to know what a treasurer did. She had opened an account at the Bankers Trust Company which could not be used until the incorporation papers were completed in September, but, she said, "I will pay any small bills that come along and then I will reimburse myself later."

There had been an exchange of communications about what Barr should be paid as the director of the new museum. The salary initially proposed by Sachs was $12,000 a year plus $3,000 for travel (Sachs expected Barr to go to Europe each year on scouting expeditions for the Museum and, as he put it in a letter to Goodyear, "do a certain amount of decent and legitimate entertaining"), but it was soon decided that this was a great deal more than any museum director in America was making. Crowninshield in a letter to Goodyear in August wrote that Mrs. Chester Dale and Mrs. Sullivan thought the salary "enormously high," pointed out that the director of the Minneapolis Museum was getting "only $5,000," and added that "$15,000 is a very high salary for a young man who has probably never, before this, earned $5,000." Barr had come nowhere near earning $5,000 at Wellesley; a new Associate Professor in those days got $3,000.[4] Crowninshield concluded:

> I like Barr and would personally like to give him everything in the world. It is merely a question of proceeding in a normal and prudent way. Might not our Directors—bankers, lawyers, etc.— think us a little wasteful if we start in on quite so lavish an arrangement with our Director. All this is in confidence.

The matter was settled, so Barr wrote to Sachs from New York early in August, at a salary of $10,000 with an additional $2,500 for travel. "There was absolutely no dickering," he said. "The matter is thus closed. I trust with satisfaction to all." Sachs's comment was, "I know of no scholar of any age who receives such compensation. On the other hand your responsibilities as a museum man are different."

During July and August Barr and Sachs were in constant communication. Sachs wrote to Barr that the money for the Museum seemed to be coming in in spite of the fact that it was "the worst season of the year for that sort of thing." Barr bombarded Sachs with memorandums about personnel, about a reference library ("I shall work for this and fight for it with enthusiasm"), and about the necessity of establishing

---

4 Today the starting salary for an associate professor at Wellesley is about $16,000, and with benefits about $19,000.

"a catalogue of modern works of art in Greater New York and ultimately throughout the country," something like the critical bibliography of modern art that he had suggested to Sachs in a letter from
Russia in 1928, that was conceivable then but would be next to impossible now because of the number of museums and galleries and private
collectors. He also wanted a photograph collection of modern works
and "a truly fine nineteenth-century collection." Nothing seemed impossible to Barr, but he wrote to Sachs, "May I ask you always in the
future never to hesitate to make even the least criticism of my conduct
or policies in relation to this business? It would reassure me to feel
that without assuming any troublesome responsibility you're yet ready
to give me your frank and immediate opinion *especially when ad-
versely critical.*" To Barr's ambitious plans for the Museum Sachs
wrote on August 1:

> . . . Now remember, Alfred, that we cannot get all the things
> that we want all at once. . . . We must not be worried by criti-
> cism; we must follow the line of least resistance in our Board of
> Trustees to start with, and as you gain their confidence, the rest
> will follow. The first thing to do is to plan in practical fashion for
> this winter. Attend to all business matters with meticulous care.

He concluded with his usual farsightedness: "After all, we are taking a
huge sum of money from the public which we propose to spend and
we must spend it wisely, so that we can get the support for a long permanent future."

Though the price of stocks was soaring and the hectic prosperity of
the '20s appeared to be irreversible, there was no shortage of space in
office buildings that might be adapted to the purposes of a new museum. "We have about ten locations under consideration," Barr wrote
to Sachs in mid-July. The committee had asked Crowninshield to find
suitable space for a gallery, and with the help of Mrs. Sullivan—who
turned to an ex-pupil of hers, Peter Grimm of the real-estate firm of
William A. White and Sons, which handled Rockefeller interests—
they hit upon space on the twelfth floor of the Heckscher Building on
the southwest corner of Fifth Avenue and 57th Street. The space occupied two thirds of the floor, with about 4,600 square feet of floor
space, and could be had for a rental of $12,000 a year. (Mrs. Rocke-
feller in a letter to Sachs, once the space had been decided on, thought
perhaps this amount might be reduced to nothing. "Would it be ad-

visable," she wrote, "to approach Mr. Heckscher to donate us a space in his building as his contribution to the work?" Whether Mr. Heckscher was approached or not, the rent was paid.) Barr figured that the open space, which had windows on just one side, could be divided into galleries that would provide about 3,800 square feet of wall space for hanging pictures, an office, a library, and a "porter's room for storage." The final plan was somewhat different, but Barr felt that his enthusiasm was justified on two counts; "it is perfectly located . . . in a well-known landmark, and secondly, the rent is very low—a little over $2.50 a foot in comparison with $3.50 and $4.00 in nearby buildings." Crowninshield got a friend, the architect H. T. Lindeberg, to lend him an experienced gallery designer who had worked for Duveen to "draw up estimates for floor covering, wall partitions, lighting, doors, etc." Mrs. Sullivan undertook to see to the remodeling and the furnishing, but one can be sure that whatever was done was under Barr's critical eye. He was not one to let the faintest trace of what he regarded as unsuitable creep in.

While the partitions were being put up and the walls covered with écru (or "natural") monk's cloth, which in the late '20s was *de rigueur* as a backdrop for what was modern, Barr was concerned with assembling a staff. The matter of Abbott's appointment was settled at a salary of $3,750, but there was still the question of secretarial help, and Barr appealed to Sachs to persuade Mary Sands, who was secretary to Edward Forbes, the director of the Fogg, to join him. She was by all accounts a model of good sense and efficiency and calm. "I had had a great deal of experience with museum directors," she recently said. She was, indeed, so familiar with the inner workings of the Fogg that on several occasions when Sachs had had to be away, he had asked her to take over his museum course; she believes that it was because Barr and Abbott had heard her lecture that they wanted her to help them with the almost infinite number of small details involved in borrowing and insuring works of art, in keeping records of shipping, of cataloguing, and labeling, which were essential to get the new museum running. She was then in her early thirties and the prospect of working in New York on a brand-new and experimental venture with eager and able young colleagues had irresistible charms for her. It was with great reluctance that Forbes let her go.

When the "loft space" which constituted the new museum was divided up, there were one large gallery about forty by fifteen feet, one medium-sized one, two small ones, and two offices. While the carpenters, plasterers, and electricians were bringing order out of a

void, Barr and Abbott were working in the Hotel Bristol and Mary
Sands was typing the catalogue Barr was writing. "Alfred was somebody we all stood in awe of," Mary Sands recalls. "He was not communicative at all. Even about the paintings he never seemed to be able
to express himself at all except in writing." When the trio finally
moved into the Heckscher Building, they were joined by an extremely attractive and socially agile young woman named Virginia
("Ginny") Carpenter from Chicago, who, Mary Sands was impressed
to note, "knew everybody." She was the daughter of the composer
John Alden Carpenter (he wrote the American ballets *Krazy Kat* and
Skyscrapers), and her mother, who was "socially prominent" (a phrase
more common in the '20s than now), was a decorator who happened
at that time to have come to New York to do over Elizabeth Arden's
hairdressing establishment. Mrs. Carpenter had been the moving spirit
in the founding of the Arts Club in Chicago in the '20s, an institution
which she and a number of her friends thought essential because at that
time the Art Institute showed no interest in modern art and no Chicago dealers were selling it. One of the early shows at the Arts Club
was of Picassos, and, as Miss Carpenter (now Mrs. Patrick C. Hill)
recalls, "It was there also that Stravinsky's *L'Histoire d'un Soldat* was
first performed in America." Young Ginny, in other words, was
brought up in an atmosphere congenial to the purposes of the new
museum.

The two other members of the staff were a young, blue-eyed Irish-
man named Patrick Codyre, who acted as messenger boy, office boy,
doorman, seller of catalogues, and general handyman, and a young
man named Cary Ross, who was ever present but not on the payroll.
Years later Mary Sands, who was not likely to miss anything, said, "I
always wondered where he came from and what he was doing." He
came, in fact, from Knoxville, Tennessee, and Abbott had met him
several years before when Ross, having graduated from Yale, was at
Johns Hopkins in Baltimore studying medicine. "He was rich," according to Abbott. "He'd spent a good deal of the '20s in Paris. He
was a friend of Hemingway and of Scott and Zelda Fitzgerald," and at
one time in the mid-'30s he arranged an exhibition at his studio-gallery
on 86th Street in New York of Zelda Fitzgerald's paintings and drawings, with an additional small show in the lobby of the Algonquin
Hotel. "He was as brilliant a conversationalist as I have ever known,"
Abbott recalls in a letter written in 1971. "He was a man to do odds
and ends in an intelligent way, to fill in, and he had ideas about presentation of exhibits." There is an interesting document about Ross

which, if it makes a simple statement, nevertheless leads to curious speculation. It is a photograph by Walker Evans of a portion of Ross's bedroom. Above twin beds of unsparingly Bauhaus design are two Picasso prints, rather large ones with wide mats. The prints, like the beds, are identical. Abbott remarks that Ross "found life rather trying." It has been suggested by a number of people that he was schizophrenic, and on several occasions, at least once while working for the Museum, he attempted to take his own life.

So, when the galleries were ready there were five on the payroll (which for the year came to less than $24,000, of which Barr got half) and one volunteer. Barr and Abbott shared an office which had two windows, Barr next to one and Abbott the other, with Mary Sands in a corner. Ross was "squashed into a funny closet," Mary Sands recalls, and Virginia Carpenter was stationed at the entrance with Pat Codyre. The Museum was a series of artificially lighted boxes. Beyond the entrance box was a gallery of medium size which looked into the main gallery, and from the entrance a visitor could see into the far room, where "an important picture" was selected to face the entrance. Nothing, of course, was ready for the opening until a few minutes before it happened.

There had been a dispute about what the initial exhibition should be. Goodyear proposed that a selection of pictures be borrowed for the occasion from the collection of Dr. Barnes of the Barnes Foundation. That, as anyone who knew the temperament of the Doctor could have guessed, was not feasible. Goodyear's alternative suggestion was: "paintings by Van Gogh and Gaugain [*sic*]. This should include paintings by Cézanne. The intention would be to show the founders of modern painting." Beyond this he had jotted down a list of possible exhibitions to succeed the opening show—paintings and sculptures by Americans, a show of Matisse ("There are enough first-class works by Matisse in this country . . . to make a first-class exhibition"), a show of Daumier and Toulouse-Lautrec, one of Derain followed by a Segonzac exhibition. But other ideas were suggested by other members of the committee. Mrs. Rockefeller and Miss Bliss at first wanted a combination of French and Americans, the standard French "founders of modern painting" and Ryder, Homer, Prendergast, Davies (of course), and Eakins. Sachs, on the other hand, thought that such a combination could not "be hung together with good effect," and he telegraphed Mrs. Rockefeller to that end. He also said in his wire:

IN MATTERS OF THIS SORT MY ADVICE IS THIS STOP LET ALL OF US ON THE BOARD SUBMIT OUR OPINIONS TO THE DIRECTOR AND LET HIM

ALSO TAKE INTO ACCOUNT THE EXPRESSION OF OUTSIDE OPINION AS IT
COMES TO HIM AND THEN LET HIM REACH A DECISION AFTER WEIGH-
ING ALL ARTISTIC ASPECTS AND INTERNAL AND EXTERNAL DIPLOMATIC
CONSIDERATIONS STOP IF OUR DIRECTOR IS WORTHY OF THE PLACE
HIS DECISIONS WILL BE CORRECT IN THE MAJORITY OF CASES STOP
AM FORWARDING COPY OF THIS TELEGRAM TO MR. CROWNIN-
SHIELD. . . .

Goodyear in the meanwhile, armed with letters of introduction from
Sachs, had gone to Europe to see what he might be able to borrow for
the French show which he hoped would follow an opening exhibition
of Americans. While he was abroad Crowninshield and Sachs and Barr
put their heads together, but to no avail. On September 4, 1929,
Crowninshield cabled Goodyear that they had caved in to the Ladies'
immutable position:

SACHS BARR AND I WANTED SMALL SHOW RYDER HOMER EAKINS LAST
TWO WEEKS OCTOBER FOLLOWED BY SEURAT VANGOGH CEZANNE IN
NOVEMBER STOP BUT FOUR LADIES ON COMMITTEE SOLIDLY AGAINST
US UNDER CIRCUMSTANCES FAVOR POSTPONING OPENING GALLERY
UNDER FRENCH SHOW STOP HAVING DIFFICULTIES CONTRACTOR AND
LANDLORD BUT SMOOTHING OUT NOW STOP HOW SOON CAN WE GET
THE FRENCH PICTURES TO NEW YORK FROM PARIS STOP BARR SACHS
AND I WILLING TO JOIN THE ADAMANTINE LADIES CHEERIO REGARDS
FROM US ALL

FRANK

The gentlemen of the committee were, after all, members of it at the
invitation of the adamantine Ladies, and they had little choice in the
matter when the Ladies put their foot down.

From the date on which this cable was dispatched there were still
two months before the scheduled opening of the Museum in early
November. Crowninshield found that he could insure the pictures borrowed from European dealers and collectors for thirty-five cents per
$100 of value, and he wired this information to Goodyear with an
expression of congratulations on "your wonderful energy and tact."
Goodyear was, in a manner of speaking, talking pictures off gallery
walls and out of storerooms in Paris, London, and Berlin. In the meanwhile Crowninshield was warming up the press, which, he hoped, in
turn would warm up the sentiments of the public.

In July Goodyear had drawn up "a statement to be sent to the public" setting forth the purposes of the Museum and had dispatched a
copy to Miss Bliss, who expressed "profound satisfaction and grati-

tude" that Goodyear was president of the committee but thought that "it might be wise to emphasize the fact that the exhibitions will be of American as well as foreign art." She was fearful that "Otherwise we might lose the interest of some pretty helpful people." When it was issued, the "Founders' Manifesto" asserted that it was the intention of the Museum ". . . to hold a series of exhibitions during the next two years which shall include as complete a representation as may be possible of the great modern masters—American and European—from Cézanne to the present day" and "to establish a permanent public museum which will acquire, from time to time, collections of the best modern works of art." On the other hand, there was a certain reticence about establishing ground rules for the future. "The possibilities of such an institution," it continued, "are so varied and so great that it seems unwise now to lay down too definite a program."

Barr had a program from the very beginning, but it was not to be made known to the public for more than two years, and then only gradually. Crowninshield, however, took on the function of informing the press that a new museum was about to come to pass, with the result that announcements and editorials appeared not only in the New York papers but in the hinterland (as New Yorkers think of everywhere else) as well.

On September 9, 1929, the *New York Times* in an editorial (probably written by Edward Alden Jewell, then the *Times* art critic) said, in part:

> Nothing has recently stirred more interest in art circles—and outside them for that matter—than the project to establish in this city a modern art museum. The plans are as yet tentative, but are promising. . . .
> Loan collections, it is stated, will be the basis of the activity of the new museum for a year or two. It must occasion a little surprise, not to say regret, that the first exhibition is to be French. American artists will feel that they might well have been given the earliest chance in an American museum of contemporary art to show what they can do. . . .

Sachs and Crowninshield and Barr must have wondered what the "adamantine Ladies" thought of that.

The New York *Herald Tribune* in an editorial published on the same day was concerned that a modern museum might be devoted, unlike the Luxembourg in Paris, to only the "left wing" segment of contemporary art and not do justice to the "salon." "On the other hand," it said,

> even if the exhibitions and acquisitions turn out to be chiefly representative of the left wing, an admirable purpose will be served. It will, after all, put that wing to the acid test.

The New York *Evening World*, the opening sentences of whose editorial appear at the head of this chapter, had a good deal more to say. This is the pertinent part of it:

> Art, in the imagination of the United States, is a collection of old masters brought over from Europe at fabulous expense, to be gaped at occasionally but never for a moment associated with ordinary living. With regard to pictures, we are in the position of the small Scandinavian cities with regard to the theatre. There save when an Ibsen comes along, there is almost nothing in the way of current dramatic composition and the productions consist chiefly of endless revivals of Shaw, Strindberg, Shakespeare and Wilde, with the result that many have got the idea that the classics are all that matter and that the modern theatre is to be thought of only with contempt. . . .
>
> So, certainly, with art. And a museum given over to modern pictures ought to do much to wake us up to our folly. In purchasing, mistakes will be made, of course. Men important now will be forgotten in twenty years, and men not important now may become immortal. Single judges can hardly hope to compete with the unerring judgment of posterity. But stocking masterpieces, we take it, is not the main idea. The object, apparently, is to acquaint Americans with what is going on, and that certainly the new museum can do.

Later in the month a good many cities scattered about the country heard of the impending birth of the Museum through a syndicated column by William B. McCormick, the art editor of Universal Service. After giving a rather straightforward account of the Museum's plans and noting that there was nothing like it in the nation, he concluded, "This department offers its congratulations and best wishes to the Museum of Modern Art."

Jewell followed the *Times* editorial several weeks later with a short piece accompanied by a number of pictures in the *New York Times Magazine,* and it evoked an indignant response from the painter and illustrator Albert Sterner which echoed in more moderate tones the extreme reaction to the Metropolitan's 1921 exhibition. The article was headed "Albert Sterner Questions/ Need for Modern Art Museum/ Sees Peculiar Modes and Mannerisms in Art as/ An Invention as Impermanent as the/ Queer Is Unenduring."

Jewell had illustrated his article with "Early Snow" by Vlaminck, Cézanne's "Olympia," a sculpture by Maillol called "Night," a Derain landscape, Ryder's "Pegasus," and a Diego Rivera called "Social Chaos." It is surprising that even so academic an illustrator as Sterner should have found this moderate selection to be examples, as he put it, of "unbridled self-expression." This, he wrote, is what Alfred Barr says "the people must want and support loyally in order that this venture shall finally take root and fulfill its mission and become permanent." "No one," he said,

> can gainsay the whim of a few wealthy and no doubt well-meaning people to gather together in a place specimens of any art or craft which amuse them and which like any other ephemeral fashions to which they subscribe, become their hobby, their exclusive toy with which they ride the crest of the wave on an exclusive beach where only the rich and idle may disport themselves—but the art of the world, the art we cherish and keep, art for the people, has never been explosive.

Sterner's discomfort at the thought of a museum devoted entirely to an art that, in his estimation, was not for the people had, of course, some justification. In the 1920s and for several decades after that the art which he regarded as "explosive" was primarily of concern to the somewhat adventurous rich, and to those who regarded themselves as having advanced or, as some would have said, highbrow taste. (It was at about that time when the English M.P. and humorist A. P. Herbert defined a highbrow as "the kind of person who looks at a sausage and thinks of Picasso.") It was also of vital interest to a limited number of scholars and curators, to some earnest and eager young people, and, of course, to artists seeking an escape from constraining conventions into new and personal discoveries of truth.

Perhaps inadvertently, but surely pertinently and to its financial advantage, one of the very first accomplishments of the Museum of Modern Art was to make modern art chic. Fashionable women dragged their reluctant husbands to openings, much as their grandmothers had dragged their grandfathers to the opera, less to see than to be seen. Such pretense has been and continues to be, one must admit, a primary fact of cultural life and support of the arts in America.

*Just as the Armory Show of 1913 was the opening
gun in the long bitter struggle for modern art in
this country, so the foundation of the new
museum marks the final apotheosis of modernism
and its acceptance by respectable society.*
LLOYD GOODRICH, *The Nation*, December 4, 1929

Chapter IV *Curtain Raiser on the
Twelfth Floor*

Many of the hundreds of ladies in cloche hats, which covered their
heads from their penciled eyebrows to the napes of their necks, who
came with their husbands or with friends to the Museum on the day it
opened to the public at nine on the morning of Friday, November 8,
1929, unquestionably had a sinking feeling in their stomachs. It came
not from what they saw at the Heckscher Building (though for some
it may have), but from what the morning paper had told them. On
that morning the headlines of the *New York Times* reported that
stocks on the New York Exchange had dropped from 5 to 66 points
and that U.S. Steel had hit a new low. It had been a miserable two
weeks. The bottom had dropped out of the stock market on October
24, and though the big banks had made a valiant and desperate try to
shore it up, five days later on the 29th panic had set in for fair. On that
day an unheard of sixteen million shares had changed hands as in-
vestors, many of whom had bought on precarious margins, struggled
to cut their losses. As if that were not tragedy enough for one day,
the *Times* also reported that a British airliner filled to capacity had
crashed into a hill on a flight to Berlin and all six occupants of the

plane had been killed. At Teterboro airfield in New Jersey a student pilot had fallen out of a plane, but his instructor had managed to right it and was saved. The account did not say what happened to the student.

Families as rich as the Rockefellers and as the Blisses then were, while they were unquestionably concerned for their fellow men, had holdings so secure and so broadly based that the fluctuations of the stock market, even ones of such violence as the present one which in so many instances had such tragic consequences, did not alter their way of life or their stance or, indeed, their sense of responsibility as a stabilizing influence. It was not so with the Sullivans and the Goodyears of the world of the 1920s, who, though exceedingly well heeled, were not above the effects of an erratic marketplace or an errant dollar. Not, to be sure, that they were suddenly poor—far from it—but the bloom was somewhat off their prosperity, and they could not have been unconcerned for the financing of their new museum in spite of the pledges that were already in hand.

The years of the subsequent Depression did not, in fact, do badly for the Museum. It had its beginnings in an era when the young, especially, were seeking forms of diversion and uplift, of new experience and discovery which cost them little or nothing. It was a time, for example, when young couples in New York spent Sunday afternoons riding from Washington Square to Fort Tryon Park at the top of Manhattan on the open upper decks of Fifth Avenue buses for a dime apiece. It took hours, and the longer the better. In those days before high-rise apartments bristled on the top of the Palisades it was a pleasure to look from Riverside Drive at the orange cliffs across the Hudson, which was still plied by blunt-nosed ferries. It was not, on the other hand, pleasant to find families living in shacks made of old crates and cartons in Central Park, or to see breadlines blocks long, or dozens of men and women gathered outside employment agencies looking for signs that offered $12 for a six-day week washing dishes in a restaurant. It was not a time when, as in the late 1960s and early 1970s, the young affected poverty and the ragged costumes of the indigent; they tried to look more prosperous and pulled together than they were, not less. Nor was it a time when the young had lost their sense of irony or humor or thought the world owed them a living because they were pure of heart and nobody else was. They were wide-eyed, of course, but they were not world-weary; they were looking for jobs and not kicks, and the Museum of Modern Art, then far from becoming an Establishment to be attacked as it now is, was the portal to a new world for many of them.

Few of them, however, were on hand when the Museum opened on Thursday afternoon to a select list of invited guests who were permitted to see it before the public came flocking in the following morning. A precedent was set that day which has become a Museum tradition. An "opening" at the Museum of Modern Art, while it has grown vastly in size and declined in elegance (except, perhaps, for those who are guests in the dreary Founders' Room on the Museum's sixth floor or at the houses of trustees for pre-opening dinners), is still looked upon by many New York Upper Bohemians as very nearly worth their while not to miss. But the days before the first opening were even more hectic than before the openings that occur so frequently at the Museum today. The initial opening involved the entire paid staff, all five of them, and not merely the staffs of a department or two whose members now may easily number in dozens, depending on which departments (Curatorial, Office of the Director, Publicity, etc.) may be called upon to get a show up and open. Barr and Abbott and Ross leaned the borrowed paintings against the monk's-cloth walls, looked at what they had done, and shifted them about until they finally arrived at the moment to hang them. Unsatisfied, they shifted them some more. Goodyear dropped by to see how things were going, and so did Mrs. Sullivan. Mrs. Rockefeller and Miss Bliss stayed away, not from any lack of interest but out of courtesy. Mary Sands, who had set up an essential system for keeping track of each precious item as it came in from a collector, a dealer, or a museum, was inundated by the paperwork she had devised. At the Hotel Bristol on West 46th Street, where Barr and Abbott lived, Barr, whose perfectionism has always been death on deadlines and on the printing budget, and who couldn't resist rewriting his copy after it had been set in galleys, was sweating out the text and layout (always a matter of acute aesthetic concern to him) for the catalogue. Crowninshield miraculously got it away from him and bulled it through the Condé Nast Press, which printed *Vanity Fair* and where he had important leverage, so that it was ready for the opening, not quite, but almost, a unique occurrence at the Museum in its early days.

It was a splendid production, 8½ by 11 inches, bound in yellow board, with a black spine and entitled

THE MUSEUM OF MODERN ART

FIRST LOAN EXHIBITION

NEW YORK

NOVEMBER

1 9 2 9

It included a list of those who had lent paintings and, as has been true of every such catalogue since, the names of the trustees of the Museum. Barr's foreword covered fifteen pages of amply leaded type, and following it was a list of other museums in America and Europe and one in Japan that owned works by the four artists, obviously an object lesson to Americans about their myopia. There were catalogue descriptions of thirty-five Cézannes (which included seven watercolors), twenty-six Gauguins (which included one drawing), seventeen Seurats (including four "oil studies" and six pencil drawings), and twenty-seven van Goghs, all of them oils. With the exception of one Cézanne watercolor and one Gauguin drawing which arrived too late to be engraved, all of the loans were reproduced as full pages, all in black and white. The first printing (and it was followed by several) was 3,000 copies.

On the morning of the private opening the *New York Times* ran a short item in column eight of the editorial page, not a spot likely to draw much attention, which announced that the new Museum of Modern Art would open its doors to invited friends that afternoon and to the public on the following day. It turned out to be a pleasant day, clear with the temperature hovering seasonably around fifty, and friends turned up in such numbers that the small galleries were jammed with what the papers the next day called "the socially elect." According to the New York *American*, "The large guest book soon acquired rows of distinguished names . . . and the occasion had about it an air of unique importance." The Boston *Transcript*, trying its best to be condescending, noted that "The art season in New York City, which lags a month or more behind Boston, has come to life with almost startling suddenness. . . . Thursday the newly created Museum of Modern Art opened the doors of its temporary galleries and held a house-warming. The invited guests, besides the usual group of socially elect, were Cézanne, Gauguin, Seurat and Van Gogh. . . ."

Many of the names that were socially prominent in the '20s have disappeared into obscurity in the last five decades—Mme. Alma Clayburgh, for example, the Julius Oppenheimers and the Paul Reinhardts, Leopoldine Damrosch and the John Alden Carpenters. They were there, and so was Lee Simonson, the theatrical designer, and the actress Dorothy Sands, who was Mary Sands's sister. More important to the trustees, however, was the most famous art dealer of his day and a contributor to the Museum's coffers, Sir Joseph Duveen, who was later to become Lord Duveen of Milbank as a reward for his generosity to the British Museum and the National Galleries of London.

It fell to Jere Abbott, for reasons he does not now recall, to escort Duveen around the exhibition. "There was something a bit like Hearst there," he has written, "the light, squeaky voice, the artificial exterior and the staccato gesture." Abbott met him at the elevator, and as Duveen walked into the dense crowd in the galleries, his first comment was, "You must do something about the ventilation at once." ("In the general minimum cost of planning and changing," Abbott says, "not much thought was given to ventilation." Some windows, to be sure, had been covered to afford more wall space for hanging pictures, and quite probably in their wildest dreams Barr and Mrs. Sullivan and Goodyear had anticipated no such crowds as turned up.) As Abbott guided Duveen around the rooms, the young associate director was astonished to discover that Duveen "was an extraordinary example of how partitioned the eyes can be. He undoubtedly knew Renaissance and Dutch and English art," he noted, "and yet otherwise he was blind."

"Ah yes. Who painted that?," pointing.
"Van Gogh."
"Oh! And that one over there?"
"Van Gogh."

From nine o'clock on the following morning until six that evening the elevators of the Heckscher Building coped with crowds such as they had never had to manage before. Several thousand persons streamed through the seven galleries, according to the *Herald Tribune,* and "among them were out-of-town connoisseurs who remained after the private opening to study further the exhibits which have been borrowed from public and private collections in all parts of Europe and America." The crush at the private opening, as at all private openings since, was obviously not conducive to seeing much except the backs of the heads of those who were jammed against the pictures, and the public opening cannot have been much better. The crowds, however, did not abate after the opening day. Indeed, the *Times* noted about two weeks after the opening that "attendance at the museum has increased steadily" and reported that on the second Saturday after the opening 2,868 persons had turned up. Henry McBride, who wrote a column for the magazine *Creative Art,* as well as being the critic for the New York *Sun,* suggested in the magazine's December issue that those who wanted to see the pictures at the new Museum should pick a rainy day. "In dry weather," he said, "try nine a.m. Otherwise you'll be jostled and perhaps not see some of the most important pictures at all." The situation was unprecedented. Lines formed out into Fifth Avenue, and for long periods the elevator operators had to refuse to take anybody more to the twelfth floor. "That's all for the Museum of Modern Art," they shouted, and then waited until they had thinned out the crowds aloft before taking others up. "Since then," McBride reported, "I have been informed by some art students that nine a.m. is an excellent hour at which to view the show; and I myself discovered that a heavy rainstorm thins out the enthusiasts."

If the crowds at the new museum were like the crowds that go to gallery openings today, and there is every reason to assume they were, they glanced at the pictures and talked about something else. There were, for example, other exhibitions in town, and as the game of gallery-going is somewhat competitive among its enthusiasts, comparisons were unquestionably made between the Museum's show and the one at the Newhouse Gallery, which had been selected by M. Edouard Raymond, the director of the National Museums of France. It had opened the week before the Museum's and was much more up-to-date. It had in it Utrillo, de Chirico, Gromaire, Soutine, and others including, of course, Picasso, Matisse, and Derain. Someone undoubtedly expressed regret that Arthur Davies who had died the year before could not see the new Museum of which he had dreamed, but it was appropriate and nice that there should be a show of his pictures currently at the Ferargil Gallery. At the Delphic Studios there were paintings and drawings by Orozco, the Mexican revolutionary.

Indeed, the Museum of Modern Art opened at a moment when there was plenty besides the catastrophe on Wall Street about which to make polite conversation. Noel Coward's *Bitter Sweet* had just opened and Gloria Swanson's "first all-talking" movie, called *The Trespassers,* was making crowds gape at the wonder of it all on Broadway. The Pulitzer Prize play of the year, to no one's surprise, was Elmer Rice's *Street Scene,* and the current best-sellers, which no intellectually self-respecting art-lover would have been caught dead with in his library, were Lloyd Douglas' *The Magnificent Obsession,* a pious and sentimental novel by a Lutheran clergyman, and Ripley's *Believe It or Not,* a reprint of his newspaper oddities about four-headed calves and Bantus with their feet on backward—or the equivalent. The very day the Museum opened Lucrezia Bori sang *Manon* at the Metropolitan Opera, and it was announced that Dorothy Parker had won the O. Henry Story Prize and $500 in gold for "Big Blonde." Earlier in the week Brooks Atkinson had given a pleasant review to *Berkeley Square,* which had opened at the Lyceum Theatre starring

Leslie Howard and Margalo Gillmore. Two days before the Museum became a reality had been election day, and the citizens of New York, neatly manipulated by the Tammany machine, had re-elected Jimmy Walker, the personality kid, for a second term as mayor by a resounding margin of 467,165 votes. The time was, in other words, still the Roaring Twenties when the Museum was born, though the moment was only a hair away from the doldrums of the Thirties.

It is more than likely that if Mrs. Rockefeller and her friends had not met for lunch with Goodyear in May of 1929 but had delayed another six months there would never have been a museum of modern art, or in any event The Museum of Modern Art, in New York at all. It was not the sort of scheme that would have been thought of in a moment of economic crisis, even probably by a Rockefeller. The family did, of course, launch Radio City in the teeth of the Depression as a spur to economic recovery, a venture of remarkable boldness as well as business acumen, but Abby's taste for modern art was scarcely encouraged by the other members of her family; it was merely tolerated as her idiosyncrasy. The moment, to be sure, was ripe for such an institution to emerge, though what form it might have taken and when is impossible to suppose.

There was no doubt, however, that the Museum was a fact, and a fact that elicited fulsome praise in some quarters, an uneasy skepticism in others, genuine distaste, as one knew it would, in others, and merriment in still others. The reaction from the press to the opening show was entirely favorable, and, as Goodyear said, "For this once, and this once only, not a finger of scorn was pointed." Some of it is worth recalling, if only because the Museum over the years has provided the art critics and reviewers with a most convenient and resilient whipping boy, always indignant but always ready to thumb its nose and come back for more.

Helen Appleton Read, the critic for the Brooklyn *Eagle*, greeted the opening exhibition as "a superlatively fine loan collection," and she set out to clarify a misty point about the Museum. "A comparison," she wrote,

> between the Modern Museum and the Luxembourg has frequently been made. . . . But in reality it has little in common with what people have so long believed, if erroneously, the Luxembourg stood for: namely, a representative collection of contemporary European art. . . . No, the Modern Museum is happily free from entangling red tape, progressive systems, and official alliances.

Art News declared: "The effect is tremendous, breathtaking, and if the exhibition has a flaw, it is that of too great power. Many a frail critical barque will be swamped. But sink or swim, it is a great experience and more than worth the real effort it demands." Such a response was echoed by Jewell in the *Times:*

> So superb is the initial offering that those of us who were prepared, perhaps, again to deplore the decision to start off with a French art show face palpable embarrassment. Quality disarms. And in view of the rewards so lavishly spread before a visitor's eye, it will be well to dissolve all carping in a more generous fluid of welcome.

Bryson Burroughs, the curator of paintings at the Metropolitan who had had the nerve to buy a Cézanne from the Armory Show, went out of his way to welcome the new Museum in the Metropolitan's own *Bulletin.* He called the opening a "noteworthy event" and praised the quality of the exhibition and the fact that "these men have [never] been more favorably shown, both as to the excellence of the examples chosen and the way in which they are displayed." A Boston critic, Jerome Klein, writing in the *Transcript,* used the occasion to take out after the Metropolitan under the headline "Metropolitan's Dilemma Is Solved":

> For a number of years the worthy trustees of America's greatest museum (the Metropolitan Museum of Art) have been subjected to considerable embarrassment; a great many people have had the bad taste to inquire in the public prints why the competent administrators of the museum have taken no cognizance of the emergence of art in the world of today.
>
> When at first such inquiries were made . . . the trustees, it was rumored, found the sight of a Cézanne or Van Gogh revolting to their delicate stomachs. . . .
>
> But the clamor grew and the trustees and their henchmen awoke one day to the horrible discovery that Cézanne and his upstarts had for years been taken up by the best society. . . . To make things worse, the academicians were beginning to imitate the moderns, and who was going to tell the sheep in wolf's clothing?

Several years later Walter Pach, a painter and a writer on art who had been one of the moving spirits in the organization of the Armory

Show, referred more succinctly to the Museum of Modern Art as "the Metropolitan's worst mistake."

Someone—it is not recorded who it was—said something about the exhibition that infuriated Alfred Barr, and a reporter (possibly the one who made the remark) quoted Barr in the New York *Sun:*

> "What's more, 99 per cent of the people looking at the pictures in this gallery are subnormal, and as for the artists, everybody knows all four of 'em were crazy!" His face reddened; his fist thumped; he turned and flung himself out the door.
>
> These words were actually spoken on the afternoon of November 12, 1929, in the vestibule of the Museum of Modern Art. . . .

This little item got on the press-service wires and turned up in papers far from New York. Barr has never let what he has considered inane criticism of what the Museum has exhibited go without comment, sometimes extremely sharp, sometimes laboriously judicial, but rarely, as in this case, petulant.

The exhibition closed on December 7, almost exactly a month after it had opened. In those four weeks some 47,000 people had crowded into the four galleries, an astonishingly large number, without, as the minutes of an early trustees' meeting revealed, a dollar having been spent on advertising. On the final day some 5,300 Johnny-come-latelies tried to get in to see what all the fuss was about.

Three days before the show closed, Lloyd Goodrich, who later became the director of the Whitney Museum, wrote in *The Nation:*

> Just as the Armory Show of 1913 was the opening gun in the long and bitter struggle for modern art in this country, so the foundation of the new museum marks the final apotheosis of modernism and its acceptance by respectable society.

He could scarcely have said anything which would have pleased the members of the committee or the young crew of intellectual laborers on the twelfth floor of the Heckscher Building more.

It is the most thoroughly alive museum in New York. Nobody goes out of a sense of duty. The crowd is an omnium gatherum. There you may see of a late afternoon such magnificos as the younger John D. Rockefeller. There you will also see Mrs. Schlitz from Washington Heights.
LOUIS SHERWIN, *New York Post*, December 26, 1929

Chapter V *Promise and Fulfillment*

It did not take long for the new Museum to get into the kind of trouble that for years was as much a part of its life's blood as red corpuscles are part of the blood of the healthy animal. Indeed, the second exhibition, which was called *Nineteen Living Americans*, set off not just the usual discordant "Why nineteen?" and "Why those particular nineteen?" but, "Ah, ha! The trustees are palming off on us what they have been collecting in order to increase the market value of their favorites."

In the meanwhile, during those first months in the Heckscher Building the staff, though half exhausted from coping with trustees, with paperwork, with collectors whom they hoped to woo and dealers from whom they might want to borrow, the press, the well-meaning, and the well-wishing, were in a state of something like euphoria. They sat up two thirds of the night at the Bristol Hotel in bull sessions that were partly practical, partly theoretical, partly dreaming about what the Museum might become. But, according to Jere Abbott, "One thing is certain. No one had any idea of the giant that had been created or at least, and unfortunately, its ultimate effect on the art market. It *had* to grow, and in growing, it somehow found an antibiotic for the original germ."

Mary Sands remembers those first months as "sheer fun," and unquestionably the difficulties under which they worked made for a kind of excitement, camaraderie, and dedication which appears in recent years to have vanished from the Museum. Tensions somehow resolved themselves because there was no time for them. At first, for example, Mary Sands, the only professionally trained museum person in the lot, thought that Ginny Carpenter was merely a "piece of social fluff," and Miss Carpenter seems to have regarded Miss Sands with a mixture of awe and resentment. This armed truce dissolved quickly into an affectionate mutual regard. "I came to realize," Mary Sands now recalls, "that Ginny was doing a very important thing. I was in the back room and I resented her being out front. She resented my being in the back where the decisions were made. On the night before the opening she drifted in after a party. There was something about the hanging that I didn't know, and she was dancing around and saying, 'At last we've found something Mary can't do!' "

Several years later when Barr wrote a money-raising pamphlet called *An Effort to Secure $3,250,000 for the Museum of Modern Art* he noted not only that the ventilation of the galleries was unsatisfactory "in spite of continual experiment with forced draught fans" (this was, to be sure, in the days before air-conditioning in offices) but that the staff was working under nearly impossible conditions, though it now seems that the Museum's staff never worked more harmoniously or more deftly than there. "In one office about fifteen feet square," Barr wrote, "the Director, the Associate Director, the Executive Secretary, and the Publicity Secretary are supposed to work with two typewriters, five telephones, and no space in which interviews may be held. A corner in a small storeroom at the opposite angle of the galleries has been converted into an office for the Assistant Secretary. In such quarters it is impossible to work efficiently or to receive conveniently visitors to the Museum."

They worked, however, with sufficient efficiency to put on six exhibitions between the time they opened in early November 1929 and the *Summer Exhibition: Painting and Sculpture* the next June. In those eight months 172,000 people came to see what the new Museum had to offer. This continuous stream of visitors infuriated the other occupants of the Heckscher Building because the elevators were constantly jammed and therefore uncomfortable and inconvenient for the tenants' customers and clients. The landlord threatened the Museum with dispossession; indeed, in the next year and a half he threatened the Museum three times. It was just one of many reasons why the Museum had to move.

But for the time being the staff and the trustees were stuck with their own modest prediction of what the appeal of the Museum might be. Goodyear dropped in frequently to see how things were going and to talk with Barr about exhibition plans and to hear his complaints about the physical shortcomings of the galleries. Mrs. Rockefeller came in rarely, but she sent her secretary with messages. Miss Bliss almost never showed up, though she used to drop in occasionally at the apartment that Barr and Abbott shared at the Bristol in order to listen to Abbott improvise on the piano, which he did with a skill that pleased her. Artists, not surprisingly, "drifted in and out," as Mary Sands remembers. "Max Weber came in one day and gave us all little block prints. Lachaise used to come in with his wife and so did Diego Rivera."

But the most constant visitor was a young woman named Margaret Scolari-Fitzmaurice, the daughter of a patrician Irish mother and an Italian father who was a prominent antiquarian in Rome. Miss Scolari, as she was called, first met Alfred Barr at the opening of the Museum's first exhibition. About twenty months later she became Mrs. Barr. She knew a great deal about Barr before they met, about his interests, his travels, and his friends. She had been teaching Italian at Vassar in 1928 while Barr was in Western Europe and Russia with Abbott, and Barr, who enjoyed writing letters, wrote at length to his friend from the Fogg, Henry-Russell Hitchcock, who was also teaching there. Hitchcock and "Daisy" (as she was called by her contemporaries then; today most of her friends call her "Marga") were friends, and Hitchcock, she says, used to read aloud to her the letters from this fascinating young friend of his. In the autumn of 1929 Daisy, who is also an art historian, had been granted a Carnegie fellowship to study at the Institute of Fine Arts of New York University, and there had been rumors of a "brilliant young scholar" from Harvard who was also coming on a Carnegie grant. "He did not, of course, come," she says. "He became the director of the Museum of Modern Art instead.

"Everyone there in those days was so young," she recalls. "The place vibrated. They all talked at the tops of their voices. Everything was going a mile a minute. Alfred was hanging shows and writing the catalogues at the same time. We ate crazy meals in terrible restaurants. In those days Alfred and Jere were out incessantly in the evening, in their white ties and toppers—two 'extra men,' a boon to New York." A boon most specifically, one assumes, to the trustees. Indeed, ever since the Museum was started, the bachelor members of the staff—and there have been many of them—have helped to round out the dinner parties of the trustees.

Work on the second exhibition had, obviously, started long before the opening of the first exhibition, and the pictures in it had been selected in a manner that taught the staff and the trustees a lesson. It was never repeated. The idea to show paintings by living Americans was Barr's. (The early suggestion of a show of dead Americans—Homer, Ryder, and Eakins—was put off until a few months later in the schedule. The change prompted one New York critic to complain that "The word museum connotes stability of purpose and execution of plans. Yet here we have the Museum of Modern Art changing exhibitions of great promise in the same casual way it appears to have arranged the second show in its programme.") The method of selecting the artists, however, seems to have been Goodyear's, not Barr's. It is most unlikely that Barr, as tactful as he was with his trustees and as careful of their education in the arts, would have suggested that the painters be picked by "a committee of trustees," as Goodyear has recorded. The choice was made in this fashion: a list of about 125 living American painters was submitted to each trustee with the request that he pick fifteen whose work he would like to see included in the show. These choices were then submitted to an executive committee, which made the final choice with, as Goodyear put it, "the fine Italian hand of Alfred Barr" to guide them. The intention was to make the show different from the usual Whitney Museum "annual" of American painting by having not just one picture by many artists but several by a few. There were 105 canvases selected for the exhibition.[1]

It was a suitable gesture to contemporary American artists, but it was a critical failure, and the attendance which it attracted said something about the American museum-goer's attitude toward native artists which is still substantially true today. Henry McBride of the *Sun* wrote: "Who are the best nineteen American living artists? Everyone consulted on the question knew definitely who they were, but unfortunately no two persons agreed." Where, he wanted to know, were Florine Stettheimer, Childe Hassam, Joseph Stella, George Luks, and Alexander Brook? Royal Cortissoz of the *Herald Tribune* found the show "drab," and Edward Alden Jewell of the *Times* commented that "eyebrows may well lift over certain participants." Other critics

1 The nineteen painters were Charles Burchfield, Charles Demuth, Preston Dickinson, Lyonel Feininger, George ("Pop") Hart, Edward Hopper, Bernard Karfiol, Rockwell Kent, Yasuo Kuniyoshi, Ernest Lawson, John Marin, Kenneth Hayes Miller, Georgia O'Keeffe, Jules Pascin, John Sloan, Eugene Speicher, Maurice Sterne, and Max Weber.

complained that not all of the artists were native-born Americans and that a couple of those who were no longer lived in America but were expatriates. Why the Japanese-born Kuniyoshi? And who was this unknown Lyonel Feininger, who was evidently born in America but lived in Germany? He, indeed, according to McBride, was "the surprise of the show" and was "doomed to be much talked about during the length of the exhibition." There were, of course, the usual wisecracks: a headline, for example, that read "Modern Art's Gentlemen Prefer Outsize Blonds," and the reference was to a voluptuous torso by Eugene Speicher and a "Susanna and the Elders" by Jules Pascin.

The number of visitors to the *Nineteen Americans* was just about half of those who came to the opening show. To be sure, the novelty of a hitherto unknown quantity had worn off somewhat, but the opportunity to see European paintings was a great deal more exciting to the art public than looking at the works of home-grown painters. Margaret Breuning, the critic of the New York *Evening Post,* said that the new Museum soon would "discover that if dead artists are not the only artists, they are decidedly the safer ones to handle." And she added: "The brilliant debut of the Museum of Modern Art is now historical. . . . Art has a strange way of making sudden converts." Another columnist in the *Post* noted: "But no little part of the attractiveness of the Museum of Modern Art is the fact that it does not draw merely the cognoscenti. It is the most thoroughly alive museum in New York. Nobody goes out of a sense of duty. The crowd is an omnium gatherum. There you may see of a late afternoon such magnificos as the younger John D. Rockefeller. There you will also see Mrs. Schlitz from Washington Heights."

But if the attendance was socially and intellectually a mixed bag (a state of affairs which unquestionably delighted Abby Rockefeller and Goodyear as much as it did Barr and Abbott), it was a far smaller bag for the American than the European shows. The comparison of attendance at the *Nineteen Americans* show and the opening show was not the only evidence of this. The worst-attended exhibition in the spring of 1930 was an attempt to give young artists a chance at the limelight. It was a show called *46 Painters and Sculptors Under 35 Years of Age,* and with it was a group of early watercolors by Charles Burchfield. The staff called the show *35/46* (forty-six under thirty-five), and only a third as many came to see it as came to *Nineteen Americans,* and even the American masters (Homer, Ryder, and Eakins), who are, to be sure, taken a great deal more seriously by a great many more people today than they were in 1930, attracted only a handful more than *35/46.*

The show of young Americans was up for only two weeks, or just half the length of time given to the American Old Masters. Not many of the names of those who were shown are especially familiar today. Of the fourteen sculptors the only one whose fame persists is Isamu Noguchi, though the reputation of John B. Flannagan is solid still, if quiet. Among the painters the best known now is Ben Shahn, but there were such valid if disparate talents as those of Peggy Bacon, Peter Blume, Arshile Gorky, Alexander Brook, Pavel Tchelitchew, Reginald Marsh, and Franklin Watkins. In his foreword to the catalogue Barr explained the cacophony of styles thus:

> If for the visitor the variety offered by these young painters and sculptors seems a confusion or even an anarchy of taste, let him remember that in our civilization it is almost impossible for the artist to avoid contact with scores of inherited traditions and exotic styles.

A substantial number of the paintings in *35/46* and *Nineteen Americans* came, not surprisingly, from the collections of the Museum's "founding fathers and mothers." It was, after all, their Museum (or so they regarded it) and they had been consulted about what was to be shown. The ballots are no longer available, but it would be interesting, in the light of the painters chosen, to know how many of those recommended were represented in trustee collections. In any event, Miss Bliss, Mrs. Rockefeller, Goodyear, Stephen Clark, Sam Lewisohn, and Crowninshield were among the lenders, and so was Jere Abbott. When Goodyear was discussing the forthcoming show with Alfred Stieglitz, the photographer-dealer asked him, "Do you want the best Marsden Hartleys?" and Goodyear is said to have replied, "We only want the works of men owned by the trustees. That's the only way we can run this Museum." Whether it was the somewhat tepid response to *Nineteen Americans* and *35/46* or because the trustees turned their eyes less frequently to American than to European art markets for their purchases, it was true that a decade later, in November 1940, the Museum found it politic to publish in its *Bulletin* an article entitled "American Art and the Museum," in effect a justification and apology for not having done more (though it professed to have done a great deal) about American artists. The artists, quite plainly distressed by what they regarded as being snubbed, had been snapping at the Museum's heels.

The exhibition that came between *Nineteen Americans* and *35/46* was called *Painting in Paris,* and it included ninety-nine works of art by twenty-six painters. As in the first two exhibitions, many of the pictures came from the drawing rooms, libraries, dining rooms, and galleries of eight out of the Museum's fourteen trustees. Henry Mc-Bride, generally one of the Museum's staunchest supporters in the press, fairly glowed with what he saw and what it meant. "It is even more important than the Armory Show," he wrote. "That was promise; this is fulfillment. . . . Time itself is the chooser and the results of the choosing [from the hundreds of artists in the Armory Show] are now in evidence in the rooms of the Heckscher Building." Cortissoz, as usual, grumbled his way through a few columns in the *Herald Tribune,* calling Picasso's "Seated Woman" "merely grotesque and repulsive" and protesting that "in the main the ancient sanctions of art are repudiated and 'beauty dead black comes again.' " By contrast, a piece in the *Post* was captioned "Modern Art Museum Glows with Life Even on Dull Days." The critic for *The New Yorker* magazine let out a cry of delight. The show, he said, was "one of the most thrilling experiences we have ever had. This is the latest five-star edition of breath-taking achievement."

The stars of the show were Picasso (Goodyear borrowed the very painting, *"La Toilette,"* over which he had quarreled with the Albright Gallery in Buffalo), Matisse (of whom, along with Picasso, the critic of the *American* said that it just went to "show to the full how thin is their art, how empty they are of ideas or anything like originality or charm"), Derain, Bonnard, Braque, Segonzac, and Rouault. The public flocked in in even greater numbers than they had for the opening exhibition. Indeed, 58,575 people stormed the Heckscher Building between January 10 and March 2, more than 10,000 more than had come to see Cézanne, Gauguin, Seurat, and van Gogh, and more, indeed, than came to look at any other exhibition the Museum held in its first three seasons.

Changes that were invisible to the public but of great importance to the future of the Museum were taking place during those first months when it was boldly stepping out into the unknown. Neither the trustees nor the staff members were temperamentally the sort to feel their way, though that is not to say that what Goodyear called Barr's "fine Italian hand" was not guiding the trustees toward his quite firmly defined but largely undisclosed concept of what the Museum should become. He scored his points deliberately in both senses of that word, both on purpose and by taking his time. It was of the greatest importance that he should bring his trustees along with him toward the goals he hoped to achieve—a museum as various as the arts of the time in which it happened, as experimental, as free of traditional tethers and prejudices, and as curious about the little, unnoticed, and unsuspected corners in which the arts lived where people lived—in everyday common artifacts, in the look of a poster, a label, a letterhead. Anything to which man applied his eyes and which might be given the dignity of an artist's or an artisan's or a designer's concern was, in Barr's concept, a proper study and province of the Museum. There was no object, he believed, from locomotive to saucepan, from aspirin bottle to street lamp to the lettering on the men's-room door, that should escape the critical eye and the studious concern of the Museum. The fine arts of painting and sculpture mattered most, perhaps, but the most minor of the arts and crafts that most people thought beneath the dignity of art mattered almost equally.

It has been said of Barr that he never suspended his critical judgment long enough to enjoy anything just for the fun of it. One of his very old friends and staunchest admirers said to me, "I never heard him say a really enthusiastic word about anything. He could not possibly say the gracious thing unless he meant it. Somebody would ask him to look at their collection and he'd say, 'You've got one picture that isn't bad.'" On the other hand, in a letter to his friend J. B. Neumann, the dealer, he wrote about a painting by Corot that he hoped to acquire for the museum at Wellesley when he was teaching there: "When I first saw it in your bedroom it hurt—it made my throat feel queer and my eyes smart—it is very beautiful. How you must hate to part with it."

The things that mattered to Barr mattered passionately, and one of the things that mattered most was the clarity of his critical judgment, its validity and freedom from cant. He tried to impress this on his trustees, not by telling them what they ought to like and why, but by deepening and expanding their critical faculties. Indeed, like the professor he was, he gave his trustees summer reading lists. He urged them especially to read Veblen's *Theory of the Leisure Class*, "one fundamental book," he said, "which I think every person interested in modern culture ought to read." He also gave them other books which, though they had little to do with painting, would, he believed, lead "to an independent and fresh attitude toward art" and of which he said, "Probably you will disagree with many of their conclusions, but the act of disagreement will, I think, prove valuable." Acts of disagreement about art ultimately contributed importantly to a clash between Barr and his trustees that sharply and painfully altered the course of his career (almost surely for the better) and the career of the Museum in a manner the benefits of which are still being argued.

But in the first months—indeed, in the first several years—there were no matters of essential disagreement to mar the progress of the Museum, though Barr and Goodyear argued furiously and amicably. Just a month after the first show opened, Mrs. Rockefeller as treasurer was able to report to her colleagues that subscriptions of $150,000 for two years were on the books. There was already talk of moving out of the Heckscher Building, not just because of the cramped quarters and the landlord's dismay over the elevators but because their surprise at their own success raised their sights to more ambitious exhibitions and more of them going on at one time. A Building Committee, which at that time had little intention of building, was looking at "various locations for a permanent home," which meant, for the most part, adaptable and available houses of the rich who were feeling poor, as many had begun to feel. Stephen Clark was the chairman of the committee, and he and Goodyear got the board's permission "to contract for the purchase of sixty feet frontage on 66th Street between Park and Madison avenues," but they thought better of it. It took a year and a half and, as was usual then and seems still to be, a gesture on the part of the Rockefellers before they made up their minds.

In the meanwhile an Advisory Committee had been organized in the spring of 1930, a sort of junior board of trustees or preparatory school for potential board members. The idea was first suggested by Crowninshield to Goodyear in a letter written in August of 1929 when their main concern was to get a good many collectors and socially prominent men and women somehow attached to the new Museum. "I think it is very important to have individuals like these in our background," Crowninshield wrote, "perhaps even on our stationery." In addition, he thought "it might be wise to have some sort of a committee of people definitely occupying positions in art museums, writers on art (not newspaper critics), perhaps a few painters with a definite leaning toward the modern French School—a man like George Biddle. . . ." He mentioned a few museum curators, among them Bryson Burroughs of the Metropolitan, and as an afterthought: "How about a lot of the young boys—Lincoln Kerstein [*sic*] of Harvard, young Walker of Harvard and young Abbott of Princeton?" Indeed, why not Abbott for Assistant Director to Barr: "He has been abroad a good deal, has money, has an attractive personality and is interested in modern art and writes well about it. Abbott and Barr would certainly make an excellent combination."

That part of Crowninshield's letter, as we have seen, was acted upon at once. The idea of a large Advisory Committee of "good" names was set aside in favor of a small Junior Advisory Committee of bright young people which took itself very seriously, worked very hard, and was patted on the head but otherwise pretty consistently ignored by the Board of Trustees.

The first Advisory Committee was organized in April 1930, with the brilliant youngish architect George Howe, of Philadelphia, as its chairman. (The building with which he and William Lescaze established their reputations, the Philadelphia Savings Fund Society, was not built until 1931–32). His chairmanship, however, lasted only a year. He was succeeded by Nelson Aldrich Rockefeller, Abby's second son, who had graduated from Dartmouth only two years before. He was twenty-three, and was working at Rockefeller Center, which was then a vast hole in the ground facing St. Patrick's Cathedral. Young Nelson, it has been recorded "proposed a more active and responsible role for his committee," and he made a report to the trustees in which he said:

We do not want to seem too pushy. We do not want to risk the reputation of the trustees, but we feel that we would have to take some chances. Will we be permitted to do some things which the trustees would not be willing to do in their position, providing we take full responsibility for these things? We feel that there is a real opportunity for a contribution on our part, and we do not want to be just the members of an important-sounding committee, . . . not to feel that our criticisms will just be dismissed as idle thoughts of a younger group. . . .

The Junior Advisory Committee introduced to the Museum's inner councils a number of men and women who forty years later are still of very considerable importance to the Museum. They have in the intervening years helped to build it (both literally and figuratively), to run it (both as trustees and as staff), and at least as importantly, on the part of some of them, helped to finance it. Almost at once on his appointment as chairman, young Nelson, who had as consuming a drive to run things then as he has ever had, appointed an Executive Committee of four men and two women. Two of the young men we have already met in these pages, two we have not, though they were equally important. Those we have met were Lincoln Kirstein and Edward M. M. Warburg, of the Harvard Society of Contemporary Art. Those we have not encountered were Philip Johnson, who was not then an architect, and James Johnson Sweeney, a poet and fledgling art critic and scholar from Chicago, author of a small book published in 1934 rather portentously entitled *Plastic Redirections in Twentieth Century Painting*. Johnson subsequently became director of the Museum's Department of Architecture and much later the Museum's official architect; Sweeney was for a time the Museum's Director of Painting and Sculpture, matters which will be delineated later in this portrait. The two women on the Executive Committee were Mrs. James B. Murphy and Mrs. D. Percy Morgan, but neither was nearly as important to the Museum as a very pretty young woman, as earnest as she was pretty, the niece of Lizzie Bliss. Nelson invited her to join the committee not long after it was established. Her name was Elizabeth Bliss (Mrs. John) Parkinson, and her mother, after her father's death, became Mrs. Conger Goodyear.

The Advisory Committee seems to have been as lively and as dedicated as it was ineffectual. Mrs. Rockefeller wrote to Goodyear: "I went to a very interesting and amusing meeting of the Junior Advisory Council [*sic*]. It amused me because, I told Nelson, they all acted as though they were super trustees." Mrs. Parkinson remembers the meetings with delight. "We used to meet all day," she told me, "screaming at each other, sitting on the floor and wanting to be heard. We had our bad moments. We criticized the trustees for emphasizing Europeans, particularly as we were having a depression and American artists needed help." The Advisory Committee had its innings and its come-uppance the year after Nelson took over its chairmanship. But several extremely important events in the Museum's history preceded that.

Miss Bliss died, the Museum held its first architecture exhibition (up to then everything shown had been painting or sculpture), and the Museum moved into a new home.

Lizzie P. Bliss died in March 1931, a month before her sixty-seventh birthday. Just ten years before, at the time when she and Quinn had been involved in the Impressionist and Post-Impressionist exhibition at the Metropolitan Museum, Quinn had mentioned her in a letter to his friend Léonce Rosenberg, an art dealer in Paris. Rosenberg had written to Quinn asking what he thought of holding a sale of Cubist pictures at the Anderson Gallery, then an important New York auction house. Quinn had replied by giving a list of American collectors of modern paintings with comments on the tastes of each. Of Miss Bliss he said: "She has bought very heavily of the work of an American artist, Arthur B. Davies, and others. She has been a rather heavy purchaser of works by Cézanne lately. She would not be interested in cubistic work at all. I know her well."

Her taste, in other words, was considered very advanced by those who clung to the Old Masters and to the academicians, to the landscapes of the Barbizon School, and even to such Impressionists as Pissarro, for example, and Americans like Childe Hassam and Mary Cassatt. On the other hand, she was not in Quinn's league of adventurousness or in Goodyear's or Crowninshield's or Clark's. "She seemed, quietly, to like Post-Impressionist painting," one of the "young Turks" has said of her, "and I came to believe that she truly did. I say that because, not unlike quite a few collectors, she had no taste outside of art and music. Those picture *frames!*" It might be unfair to her to say that she loved what her friend Arthur Davies told her to love, but if that were so, it does not mean that she loved them less than she might have had she discovered them for herself. He was her mentor, she his devoted pupil and, to put it politely, his patron—impolitely, but no less true, his best cash customer. "Impressed by his genius," wrote her friend Eleanor (Mrs. August) Belmont in the catalogue of the exhibition which the Museum of Modern Art held in her memory in the spring and summer of 1931, "she purchased first one painting, then several, then almost anything obtainable, from drawing to large canvas, as he finished it." In return, said Mrs. Belmont, herself a lavish patroness of music and particularly the Metropolitan Opera, "she broadened his horizon and revealed to him the rhythm of sound as he unfolded for her the rhythm of color and form." There never was a breath of scandal about their relationship, though at the time of the Armory Show there were those who wondered why Davies was so ostentatiously secretive about where he was getting money to put on the exhibition. Probably, as she was an extremely modest and reticent woman, she urged it on him. Davies, indeed, was a rather reticent man; it was not known until after his death that he had maintained two separate families, one in Yonkers, New York, and one in Italy.

In the catalogue of her collection (and also in Goodyear's history of the first ten years of the Museum) is a portion of a letter she wrote "To a Well-known Academician." It reveals a tolerant, clear, and articulate intelligence. Unfortunately, the original is either hidden or destroyed. What has been published reads:

> We are not so far apart as you seem to think in our ideas on art, for I yield to no one in my love, reverence and admiration for the beautiful things which have already been created in painting, sculpture and music. But you are an artist absorbed in your

own production with scant leisure and inclination to examine
patiently and judge fairly the work of the hosts of revolutionists,
innovators and modernists in this widespread movement through
the whole domain of art or to discriminate between what is false
and bad and what is sometimes crude, perhaps, but full of power
and promise for the enrichment of art which the majority of them
serve with a devotion as pure and honest as your own. There are
not yet many great men among them, but great men are scarce—
even among academicians.

The truth is you older men seem intolerant and supercilious, a
state of mind incomprehensible to a philosopher who looks on and
enjoys watching for *and finding* the new in music, painting and
literature who have something to say worth saying and claim for
themselves only the freedom to express it in their own way, a
claim which you have always maintained as your inalienable right.

The "academician" to whom this letter was addressed was surely no
innovator as a painter; indeed, as a painter he is all but forgotten. He
was, however, a very considerable innovator in another medium, and
he is presently enjoying an extremely fashionable revival. According
to Lizzie Bliss's niece Eliza Parkinson, the "well-known academician,"
was Louis Comfort Tiffany, the inventor of Favrile glass, the principal
proponent of Art Nouveau in America, the creator of many beautiful
and original objects, and the inspiration for a host of hideous imitations and some pleasant ones.[2]

On the day that Miss Bliss died the Museum opened its eleventh
show. It was not one which Miss Bliss would have liked particularly—
German Painting and Sculpture. She had no German works in her
collection. Her funeral was in the gallery of her apartment several days
later. On the center of the longest wall was Cézanne's great "Bather,"
flanked on one side by Daumier's "Laundress," and on the other by
Cézanne's portrait of his father, and stretching out beyond them more
Cézannes, Matisses, and a Gauguin. An adjoining wall was dominated
by Picasso's "Woman in White," and elsewhere in the room were his
"Green Still Life," several Davieses, Walt Kuhn's "Jeannette," and
Degas' "Race Course." Walter Hampden, as famous as any actor of
his day and most famous for his Cyrano de Bergerac, gave the eulogy.

Two months later these pictures and many others from Miss Bliss's
collection were hung on walls of the Museum's galleries as a memorial

---

2 Examples of Tiffany glass are included in the permanent design collection
of the Museum of Modern Art. They were much out of fashion in the 1930s.

exhibition to Miss Bliss. On this occasion, before the show was opened to the public a memorial meeting (one could not call it a service) was held for, as the *Times* put it, "only relatives and close friends of Miss Bliss, including those associated with her in the museum enterprise. . . ." There were three speeches; one by Mrs. Belmont ended with the quotation, "God gave us memory so that we might have roses in December." (Forty years later Mrs. Barr, in describing the meeting, remembered this and quoted it precisely, as did Miss Bliss's niece Eliza Parkinson.) Goodyear also made a speech and so did Mme. Olga Samaroff Stokowski, the wife of the conductor and a famous pianist. On the following day and for several weeks after, tributes appeared in the daily press.

The memorial meeting was quite suitably an occasion for music as well as speeches. Paul Nordoff, a pianist who was a beneficiary of Miss Bliss's patronage, as were so many young musicians, played a piece that he had written and dedicated to her. Mme. Stokowski in her speech called her friend "one of the really great music patrons in America with the rare ability to distinguish talent in immature musicians. Many famous musicians in this country are indebted to Miss Bliss for help when they were unknown." Three of these young musicians, a soprano, a violinist, and another pianist, also performed. In all of the comments about how much she had done for the arts the dominant impression is one of modesty. "She lived, most unassumingly, the life of a true patron of the arts," a painter wrote in the *Times*. "Apparently the gentlest, and certainly the most modest of women," Mrs. Belmont said, "she was absolutely independent in her taste. . . . Her outstanding characteristics were simplicity, tolerance, and understanding."

Miss Bliss had often discussed with Conger Goodyear her intention of leaving most of her collection and the best part of it to the Museum of Modern Art, which at that time most certainly had amassed no worldly goods and had, indeed, just drawn its first breath. When she died and the conditions of her will became known, it was evident that she was not disposed to take any chances on the stability of the new Museum. The pictures were to go to it on the condition that, in the view of her executors, the "Museum of Modern Art is sufficiently endowed and in the judgment of said Trustees on a firm financial basis and in the hands of a competent board of trustees." She also stipulated that three of her pictures could never be sold, but that if the Museum of Modern Art no longer wanted them—or, presumably, if it collapsed and disappeared—they should go to the Metropolitan

Museum of Art. Her choice is a measure of her taste. The three paintings were Cézanne's "Pines and Rocks" (also called "Blue Landscape"), his "Still Life with Apples," and the third, Daumier's "Laundress." The executors of the will decided that an endowment fund of $1,000,000 was sufficient to provide a "firm financial basis," and the Museum's trustees set out to raise the money.

It took a few years and a change of heart. On January 24, 1934, Alan Blackburn, Jr., a friend of Philip Johnson who had joined the staff with the title of Assistant Treasurer, wrote to Paul Sachs: "To date," he said, "we have raised $400,000: $100,000 from Carnegie, $200,000 from Mrs. Rockefeller, and $100,000 anonymously. We are expecting the trustees to give another $200,000. The Fund Committee which is headed by Mrs. Stanley Resor is responsible for $150,000 in smaller gifts." Three weeks later Barr wrote to Sachs saying that they hoped to get $100,000 "from the Warburgs" (Mr. and Mrs. Felix and their son, Edward) but that "Eddie has already complained of our pressing him." He also said that Mrs. Rockefeller "has decided to take 'no' for an answer from Mr. Clark." John Hay Whitney and his sister, Mrs. Charles S. Payson, had not yet been heard from.

When the trustees had put together $600,000, Cornelius N. Bliss, Lizzie's brother, who had replaced her on the Museum's board, and who was one of the executors of his sister's estate, persuaded the other executors to reduce their initial demand for an endowment of $1,000,000 to $600,000 (which had been raised), with the stipulation that they try to increase it to $750,000. Mr. Bliss, according to his daughter Eliza Bliss Parkinson, who later succeeded him as a member of the Museum's board, "wasn't very sympathetic to modern art or with the Museum, but he was devoted to Lillie." He has also been described by Monroe Wheeler, who several years after Miss Bliss's death became a member of the staff and still later a trustee, as "not a modern-art man. But he was very generous and very, very tolerant. He was a love of a man."

Miss Bliss surely would have approved. Those were, after all, hard times, and $600,000 was no mean sum. But not all of the collection, though surely the most important part of it, went to the Museum. "A number of ancient objects suitable to its collections," according to the press, went to the Metropolitan along with works by Davies and a Monet,[3] and as a result of this beneficence the secretary of the Metro-

---

3 The bequest to the Metropolitan included three oils, two watercolors, and two wax paintings by Davies, the Monet ("Etretat"), three Byzantine paintings, a beaten-silver camel and rider of Parthian workmanship, and a Chinese vase of the Yung Ching period.

politan's trustees wrote to Cornelius Bliss that his sister had been "declared a Benefactor of the Museum in grateful recognition of her generous gifts." It must have irked the staff of the Metropolitan and its director that the real plums had gone elsewhere, and to an upstart, at that. Miss Bliss spread the paintings by her friend Davies around— to the Brooklyn Museum, to the Utica Public Library, to the San Francisco Art Association, to the Portland Museum of Art in Oregon.

Two paintings by Davies which caused a considerable amount of acrimonious comment were left to the Tate Gallery (the National Gallery, Millbank) in London. They were called "Sleep" and "Line of Mountains," and the Tate Gallery turned them down. According to the New York *Herald Tribune*, "No reason for the rejection was contained in the formal notice from the Gallery received in New York this week." Mr. Hamilton, the attorney for the estate, said that "he did not know at what value the paintings were appraised. In art circles they were valued at $20,000 or more each." The piece went on to say that "Art dealers and painters were amazed at the action of the Tate Gallery. Many who criticized the action declared that American art was unappreciated in Europe. Others were pleased that the pictures were coming back to this country." *Art News* said, with questionable justification, that "it surely would have been more politic" if the Tate had just accepted the pictures and stowed them away, though the policy of the Museum of Modern Art over the years has been much like the Tate's. It declines what it does not want to include in its collection and it does not feel called upon to explain why. Nor should it.

On March 14, 1934, Goodyear wrote to Sachs that the matter of the Bliss collection was settled and explained about the concessions made by the executors. It was a considerable feather in the Museum's cap, he obviously thought, for he wrote:

> The establishment of the Museum as a permanent institution, and the definite inclusion of Miss Bliss' splendid bequest in our permanent collection, mark the conclusion of nearly five years since the founding of the Museum. Our success in raising so considerable a sum in the face of unfavorable financial conditions and the many demands from other sources is a striking evidence of interest and belief in the Museum.

The acquisition of the Bliss pictures was not the first step toward a permanent collection, but it most assuredly was the giant step. Even before the Museum had opened, Goodyear, Sachs, and Barr were "appointed" (or, probably more accurately, "self-appointed") as a

Committee on Gifts and Bequests, and as though to make the committee official, Goodyear had presented the brand-new Museum, on the very day it opened, with Aristide Maillol's bronze "Ile de France." Even this was not the first acquisition, for Sachs had already bought a drawing and eight prints for the Museum. Stephen C. Clark came next with the Museum's first gift of a painting, Edward Hopper's "House by the Railroad," and this was followed by three other trustee gifts of paintings from the *Nineteen Living Americans* show—a Burchfield, a Kenneth Hayes Miller, and a Karfiol. A gouache head by Picasso was the first foreign painting to belong to the collection, and it was given by a non-trustee who lived in Baltimore, Mrs. Saidie A. May. Later the same year Goodyear persuaded Maillol to give three large plaster reliefs, and Clark added Lehmbruck's "Standing Woman." There was talk of setting aside a room for this "permanent collection" of five pictures and eight sculptures, but it hardly seemed the moment to subtract from space in which to exhibit the scheduled shows.

The Bliss collection somehow made the Museum of Modern Art official as a museum and not just as a passing show. In an editorial in *The Arts* Forbes Watson wrote in just this vein. "The bequest is a nucleus round which to build," he said, "a magnet for other collections; a continuing living reply to the doubters; a passing on of the torch; a goodly heritage. It begins the transition of the Museum from a temporary place of exhibition to a permanent place of lasting activities and acquisitions."

The issue, however, was by no means as clear-cut or as impervious to interpretation as the words "permanent collection" would seem to imply. The nature of the collection (or more properly collections, as there are a number of them besides paintings and sculpture—prints, photographs, films, architecture, design, and so on), its needs, its uses, its validity—indeed, its permanence—have been argued since the beginning. They are still matters of dispute among the trustees, and between the trustees and the staff, which is constantly harassed by problems of exhibition space. In recent years the arguments have been extended to disputes between the Museum as an establishment and an increasingly dissident and articulate segment of the public. Acquisition of Miss Bliss's collection established not only the permanence of the collection but in a very real manner the permanence of the argument.

The Junior Advisory Committee, perhaps looking for a good solid issue with which to confront the trustees who they were afraid might ignore them, immediately raised the question of whether a museum devoted to what was "modern" should have a permanent collection at all. Goodyear, presumably speaking for his board, answered young Rockefeller and his "supertrustees" with a statement which was a metaphor, "The permanent collection will not be unchangeable," he wrote in *Creative Art* in December 1931. "It will have somewhat the same permanence a river has. With certain exceptions, no gift will be accepted under conditions that will not permit of its retirement by sale or otherwise as the trustees may think advisable. . . ." And he added: "The Museum of Modern Art should be a feeder, primarily to the Metropolitan Museum, but also to museums throughout the country. There would always be retained for its own collection a reasonable representation of the great men, but where yesterday we might have wanted twenty Cézannes, tomorrow five would suffice."

In a sense Goodyear was thinking of the Museum's collection in a manner that he had quite firmly told Stephen Clark in a letter about two years before was furthest from his mind—that is, as a sort of Luxembourg which would act as a feeder to the established cathedrals of art. He had not, however, mentioned the Metropolitan out of hand. A modest flirtation had been undertaken between Goodyear and William Sloane Coffin in early 1931 at just the time when Coffin was about to assume the presidency of the Metropolitan, commonly known at the Museum of Modern Art as "the museum uptown." Perhaps, Coffin had suggested, the Museum of Modern Art might take a hand in helping to spend the income from the Hearn Fund (about $15,000 a year), which had been left to the Metropolitan for the purchase of paintings by living American artists. Nothing concrete came of this proposal except the beginning of more friendly relations between the two museums which were to lead fifteen years later to a brief but abortive attempt at genuine cooperation between them.

But the real issue at that moment between the Advisory Committee and the trustees was the question about exhibiting more works by American artists. The Advisory Committee was, however, made to bide its time. Alfred Barr had something he thought far more important in mind, a first step and an extremely influential one toward making the Museum the kind of encompassing home for the advanced arts of the moment he wanted it to be.

Chapter VI *A Giant Step or Two*

When Alfred Barr and Jere Abbott came back from Europe in the fall of 1928, they brought with them a collection of posters which Barr, though few people would admit they were art, put up as an exhibition at Wellesley. They were precisely the kind of mass-produced examples of design that he wanted his students to pay attention to. "The posters cost us $125," he recalls, and the only other expense was thumbtacks. There was a student at Wellesley named Theodate Johnson, who, by her own account, was highly thought of "for some reason" by Barr as a budding actress. "He was a sort of fan of mine," she says. "I don't know why." Her older brother Philip Johnson, a dapper undergraduate from Cleveland with wavy brown hair and considerable wealth, was majoring in the classics at Harvard. According to Theodate, he came to her commencement in June 1929 and there she introduced him to Barr. According to Barr, he and Johnson met at the exhibition of posters on an occasion when Johnson came to see his sister perform. According to Johnson, he was introduced to Barr by his mother, who was president of the Wellesley Alumnae Association. It scarcely matters which version is the true one, though it demonstrates one of the problems of writing from other people's memories when no documentation exists. No matter. To say that the results of this casual meeting changed the course of American architecture would be an exaggeration, but to deny the importance of what Barr and

84

Johnson, who quickly became fast friends, did in the course of the next two decades to change the public taste in architecture and, as a consequence, the look of our cities and suburbs and campuses would be equally unjustified.

There was a third man involved. He was Henry-Russell Hitchcock, whose voice booms as loudly today as it did from his surprisingly red-bearded face forty years ago. He had graduated from Harvard in 1924 (having taken only three years to get his Bachelor's degree), spent a year in Europe as a Sheldon Fellow, and then two years as a tutor in the fine arts at Harvard. It was at this time he and Barr met and they have been ever since friends and admirers of each other's scholarship. "Alfred invited me to give a lecture in his Wellesley course," Hitchcock recalls, "and that was probably the first lecture I ever gave." He got his Master's degree in 1927, but declined to bother with a Ph.D.; he set out to be the premier architectural historian of America, and succeeded. His doctorates today are all honorary; his list of scholarly publications is almost endless. By 1930 Hitchcock was already, at the age of twenty-seven, an architectural historian to be reckoned with; he had published a book on Frank Lloyd Wright and one on modern architecture. Barr wrote of this pioneer volume in *Hound and Horn:*

> In *Modern Architecture* Henry-Russell Hitchcock, Jr., establishes himself as very possibly the foremost living historian of his subject. American books on modern architecture, with the exception of Lewis Mumford's, have been as provincial, as ill-informed, as complacent and as reactionary as are most American architects and American schools of architecture. This book is not.

Johnson, who was old for his class (he was twenty-four when he graduated in 1930), first became interested in architecture, by his own account, when he read an article by Hitchcock. He and Hitchcock met soon after this at Harvard, or so he says. (Mrs. Barr, on the other hand, says that she introduced Hitchcock to Johnson at Vassar when she and Hitchcock were both teaching there in 1928–29.) Under Hitchcock's tutelage Johnson's interest in architecture matured into considerable scholarship. He and Hitchcock traveled in Europe together in pursuit of modern buildings.

Hitchcock, Johnson, Barr, and Margaret Scolari-Fitzmaurice all turned up in Paris in the late spring of 1930. Barr and "Daisy" were there to get married and to gather pictures for the exhibition of Daumier and Corot which was scheduled for the fall at the Museum of Modern Art. They had gone to considerable trouble and expense to get the most elegant and proper wedding announcements engraved and printed, so that they might send them off from Paris not only to their friends but also to the trustees and friends of the Museum. They were married by a friend of Barr's in the Protestant church on the Quai d'Orsay, and the next day Mrs. Barr mailed the announcements she had addressed and stamped. Barr gave his, with money for postage, to the concierge of the Hôtel St. James et Albany, where they were staying. "The concierge pocketed the money," Mrs. Barr told me, "and none of the trustees got the announcements, and the feelings of some of them were hurt. So much for the French!" Barr had to pay a call on Miss Bliss when he got back to New York and explain what had happened. "There was no announcement for Mrs. Rockefeller," Mrs. Barr said, "and none for Jimsey Rorimer, who wasn't so pompous in those days. We had not a minute of honeymoon. We were always on the warpath [for paintings]. I was Alfred's interpreter in Europe."

For some time Barr had been planning in the back of his mind an exhibition of modern European architecture, and he had discussed it at length with Johnson. He was eager to break out of the pattern of shows of painting and sculpture. Johnson and Hitchcock were obviously the men to do the architecture show. No other Americans knew as much as they did about what was being built and had been built by the new revolutionary architects in Europe. In looking back at the summer of 1930 in Paris, Hitchcock now says, "Whether I had been approached before this I don't know—perhaps informally. At any rate, it was far enough along so it was decided that Philip and I were to do it, to pool our knowledge of European international-style architecture, and we were to go and collect the material, which we proceeded immediately to do. . . . Philip and I spent that summer and the next summer [collecting material], but there must have been a lot of work going on behind the scenes. We had to spend a great deal of time trying to persuade Mr. [Frank Lloyd] Wright to work with a bunch of wicked Europeans, but we did and he produced 'The House on the Mesa.' (It would be extremely interesting to know if there was ever a client for that.) Even at the time, the exhibition created a certain amount of stir."

The show, which was called *Modern Architecture: International Exhibition*, was the last one to be held in the Museum's galleries in the Heckscher Building, and its models and photographs were there, installed by Philip Johnson as "director" of the show, from February 9 until March 23, 1932. "Money was not easy in 1931," Barr recalls. "Our total budget was $68,000. Mrs. Rockefeller and Stephen Clark each said they would put up $10,000 if we got stuck for the architecture show." Johnson's father also helped to defray the costs, which, because of the elaborate models and their accumulation from abroad, were high. The work of more than fifty architects was included, and a catalogue called *Modern Architecture,* produced under the eyes of Barr, Hitchcock, and Johnson, included short essays on Wright, Gropius, Le Corbusier, Oud, Mies van der Rohe, Raymond Hood, Howe & Lescaze, Neutra, and Bowman Brothers. There was in addition a piece on housing by Lewis Mumford.

About 33,000 people (not a large number, as attendance went for other shows at the Museum that season) came to see the exhibition, which, because of its controversial character, had occupied a good deal of newspaper space, much of it devoted to asking the question, "Do you call this architecture? This utilitarian, unornamented, beautiless, so-called 'functional' building?" Barr's statement in the foreword of the catalogue did not by any means satisfy those critics who had been brought up in the Beaux Arts tradition of architecture. "The aesthetic principles of the International Style," he said, "are based primarily on the nature of modern materials and structure and upon modern requirements in planning." This sounds like an indisputable truism today, but then most people who thought about architecture at all thought that it was "Rubbish!" or "Balderdash!" It is not clear, even in the minds of Barr and Hitchcock and Johnson, which of them was responsible for the phrase "International Style," but it named a "school," or at least a period, of modern architecture, and it has stuck.[1]

"The question of the real historical potency must be to Philip and me an open question," Hitchcock said in 1971. "We have some reason to believe, if only because foreigners use the term 'International Style,' that, writing as we did at that period of maturation, just as things were beginning to change, our book became a kind of awkward bible, which it was not intended to be, of a closed style."

Twenty years after the show Johnson said to a reporter, speaking about it and about men such as Gropius and Mies and Le Corbusier, whose work was included in it, "Nobody considered these men seriously. Nobody thought of them as much of a threat. People were curious, that's all. Yet today the battle has been largely won. Twenty years ago I saw every modern building in Europe in one summer. Today our

---

1 Hitchcock has recently discovered that he used "international style" (lower case) in his 1930 book, *Modern Architecture.*

main job is simply taking adequate notice of all the fine contemporary work being done."

If this first architecture show was a giant step toward Barr's goals for broadening the Museum's areas of concern or, to put it less academically, its range, it also marked the first time that the Museum extended its physical horizons and literally cast its influence beyond the city of New York. This was the first "traveling exhibition." Scheduled for twelve museums and one department store,[2] it consisted of ten models, seventy-five photographs, and plans and explanatory placards. The director of the City Art Museum in St. Louis, Meyric R. Rogers, was so enthusiastic not just about this exhibition but about what it might portend, that he wrote: "From my experience here in St. Louis and in Baltimore I know how difficult it is for the museum at a distance from New York to obtain worthwhile exhibitions of modern work without the expenditure of an amount of time on the part of the museum executive out of all proportion to the calls of other sides of his work, to say nothing of the duplication of expenses incidental to exhibition. . . . I am sure that museums of high standards throughout the country would welcome opportunities of getting two or maybe three exhibitions every year the quality of which they could be assured would be up to the standards of the Modern Museum." A show similar to the one that went to the museums, but with photographs of the models instead of the models themselves, was prepared for smaller art galleries and universities. The Museum found itself with a whole new function and, in a very short time, a new and extremely active Department of Circulating Exhibitions.

Before that came into being, however, the trustees, egged on by Barr and encouraged by the success of the International Style show, established in the summer of 1932 a Department of Architecture. Philip Johnson, a member of the Junior Advisory Committee, was appointed as its obvious, though unpaid, chairman. He was also, in any formal sense, untrained, though his installation of the International Style exhibition, an exercise in three-dimensional design, had been called "brilliant" by the press and his historical foreword to the catalogue was regarded as "sound." It was not, in fact, until more than a decade later, in 1943, that Johnson got his architectural degree from Harvard.

2 Pennsylvania Art Museum, Philadelphia; Wadsworth Atheneum, Hartford; Buffalo Fine Arts Academy; Cleveland Museum of Art; Milwaukee Art Institute; Cincinnati Art Museum; Rochester (N.Y.) Memorial Art Gallery; Carnegie Institute, Pittsburgh; Toledo Museum of Art; Fogg Art Museum, Cambridge; Art Museum, Worcester, Mass.; Art Institute of Omaha; and the gallery of Bullock's Wilshire, Los Angeles.

Gropius, one of his heroes, and a refugee from Hitler's repression of the arts and more specifically from the formal disbandment of the Bauhaus at Dessau under government pressure in 1933, had by then been appointed dean of the Harvard School of Architecture. Johnson even before he received his formal degree was in informal practice. His first job, according to Edward Warburg, was the remaking and furnishing of Warburg's New York apartment, one floor of a three-story walk-up looking over the East River on Beekman Place. This was in 1934. "It was in strict International Style," Warburg has said, "with white linoleum floors, pigskin leather furniture, Mies van der Rohe chairs, ebony veneer on the walls, and a beautiful desk of the same material. The apartment was striking, much discussed and admired. It was so perfect. I can't explain my uneasiness. Why should I have felt that my entering it somehow spoiled the beautiful composition?"

Warburg's father did enter it and did spoil the composition rather violently if only temporarily. He was not in the best of health, but he managed to trudge up the three flights of steep steps, "tried his best to like the austerity" of the rooms, and then asked if he might make a telephone call. He sat on the edge of a chair and leaned forward to pick up the phone; the metal runners of the chair skidded on the white linoleum and "with a God-awful crash his jaw hit the desk." His son rushed to his aid, helped him up, and asked if he was all right. As Warburg recalls, "Still seeing stars, he pulled himself together and said, 'I guess so. But that's what I like about modern art—it's so functional!'"

When the establishment of a Department of Architecture at the Museum was announced in the press on July 2, 1932, the New York *American* accurately headlined its story: "Modern Museum Is Branching Out," and Johnson was called "the brilliant young authority on the history of architecture." Barr for his reasons and Johnson for his must have been pleased. Within two years and a half the Museum was already becoming "very different from what the noble gentry wanted," to use Barr's phrase, when they conceived of it as a way of correcting the lack of concern for the painters and sculptors they admired. "They wanted something related to the Tate and the Luxembourg." What they were beginning to get was a highly visible and somewhat sensational version of the course that Barr had given at Wellesley encompassing all the arts. Johnson, for his part, was getting not only the opportunity to teach the American public how to look at architecture (and not just what was being done at the moment but the antecedents of "modern" in the work of H. H. Richardson, Sullivan, Gill, "and other pioneers of modern architecture in America") but also the chance to exercise his remarkable talent for display and his caliper-like eye for measuring the quality of design.

Between the time the department became a fact and December 1934, when Johnson took off on an excursion that somewhat flabbergasted the trustees of the Museum and that appalled (if it did not surprise) many of his friends, the Museum had grown up to be in fact a museum and no longer just a gallery. It had moved into a new home, a house just west of Fifth Avenue on 53rd Street; it had acquired a Librarian and the beginnings of a distinguished Library, set up a Department of Circulating Exhibitions and a Film Library, initiated a Department of Publications with a professional in charge, launched a drive for several million dollars (and then backed down because of "the times," as the Depression was politely called), established a "branch" in Boston, expanded the Board of Trustees from the original nine to nineteen and the Advisory Committee from eight to twenty-one, and to top it off had a whirlwind affair with "Whistler's Mother." The wild oat which Mrs. Rockefeller had sown so modestly was producing a bumper (and many people thought bumptious) harvest.

During this time of burgeoning Johnson put on eight exhibitions of architecture and design. There was a show of *Early Modern Architecture: Chicago, 1870–1910*. There were several little shows having to do with the design of ordinary household objects and typography. One of these was called *Objects: 1900 and Today*, and it compared Art Nouveau lamps and furniture with its graceful flower forms with the strict chromium elegance of the Bauhaus. "It went over like a lead balloon," Johnson now recalls. "People then thought that Art Nouveau was best forgotten." There was an exhibition of the work of young architects of the Middle West and one called *America Can't Have Housing*. The purpose of the latter, which took up the entire fourth floor, was "three-fold," as the museum's *Bulletin* put it: "(1) To display the condition under which millions of people now live in New York. (2) To show the obstacles that stand in the way of changes in these conditions. (3) To show the advantages to the community of good housing and the results achieved in this field in foreign countries." To add reality to the models of "slum and super-slum" tenement rooms constructed for the display, live cockroaches were added. "The Architecture Room" in which the small shows were hung (they were largely photographs) was a small gallery scarcely fifteen feet square. Besides this busy schedule Johnson had arranged a selection of examples of modern American architecture for the triennial exposition of the decorative arts in Milan in 1933.

Of all of Johnson's early exhibitions, except his first, the one that caused the most comment and, in retrospect, was the most surprising, revealing, entertaining, and in some respects most influential was called *Machine Art,* and it took place in March 1934. Here in a museum, suddenly, were kitchen units (sinks and drainboards and cupboards), a nickel-plated cash register as clean-limbed as a racing sloop, a burglar-proof chest whose steel façade looked like the machine that probably made it, dinner plates, ball bearings, ceiling lamps. "The exhibition," said a Museum *Bulletin,* "will illustrate a victory in the long war between the Craft and the Machine." The show covered three floors of the new museum building, and there was nothing in it that was not manufactured in American factories and that could not be purchased by anyone who could afford it. "Another purpose of the exhibition," the *Bulletin* said, "is to serve as a practical guide to the buying public." The *Machine Art* show was the beginning of the Museum's career as a household tastemaker.

The reactions to the show were mixed, as the responses to such attempts to equate machine-made objects with art had been ever since Prince Albert tried to marry art and industry at the Crystal Palace Exposition in London in 1851. The victory of which the *Bulletin* spoke was more in the making of the objects than in their public acceptance as art, though over the years many of the designs first seriously shown there have become acceptable "good taste," and many others derived from them have turned into *kitsch* and supermarket "modren." Lest anyone think that there was not an eminently respectable authority for making the useful object into art, the catalogue (which had a picture of a ball bearing on its jacket) quoted from Plato a passage that was once an undisputed doctrine of modernism.

> By beauty of shapes I do not mean, as most people would suppose, the beauty of living figures or of pictures, but, to make my point clear, I mean straight lines and circles, and shapes, plane or solid, made from them by lathe, ruler and square. These are not, like other things, beautiful relatively, but always and absolutely.

The reliable Royal Cortissoz thought this a lot of pretentious nonsense, and in his column in the *Herald Tribune* he said, "It is calling the stuff 'art' that clouds the issue, that and dragging in Plato." Other critics got the point that Cortissoz missed, however, and one of them in the *Sun* said that he thought Johnson "our best showman and possibly the world's best. I'll say the world's best until proof to the contrary is submitted." Another in the *New York Times* said, "The

Machine Art show must certainly be said to constitute Philip Johnson's high-water mark to date as an exhibition maestro."

That December (1934) the Museum of Modern Art appeared in front-page headlines of a sort to which it was by no means accustomed and surely did not relish. Two members of the staff, Philip Johnson and Alan Blackburn, by then called Executive Director, had not only resigned but resigned for reasons that had nothing to do with the Museum. Blackburn, who had been hired in February 1932 in an effort to employ an experienced business hand in the management of the increasingly complicated ramifications of the Museum, was a school friend of Johnson from Cleveland. He was a man of rather small stature, "a very officious little gentleman, very nice-looking," as one of his colleagues at the Museum remembers him, "a good planner and organizer." Officially the trustees noted in their minutes that he "organized the business office, the workshop, the publicity department, the publications department and the department of circulating exhibitions," and that his "numerous and difficult duties were performed with tireless energy and devotion." Under the circumstances of his resignation, this wording must have called upon Goodyear's most tactful restraint.

"Two Quit Modern Art Museum/ For Sur-Realist Political Venture" was a two-column head on page one of the New York *Herald Tribune* for December 18. The New York *Post* took a still lighter tone: "Gray Shirts to See Huey/ To Put Hooey in Politics." The *New York Times*, characteristically, was more matter of fact: "TWO FORSAKE ART/ TO FOUND A PARTY/ Museum Modernists Prepare to Go to Louisiana at Once to Study Huey Long's Ways/ Gray Shirt Their Symbol/ Young Harvard Graduates Think Politics Needs More 'Emotion' and Less 'Intellectualism.'" It sounded like a college-boy gag. "Recently they became convinced," the *Herald Tribune* reported, "that, after all, abstract art left some major political and economic problems unsolved. Consequently both have turned in their resignations and will leave as soon as practicable for Louisiana to study the methods of Huey Long." Blackburn, from the newspaper accounts, appears to have done very nearly all the talking, and it was not funny nor was it evidently meant to be. They intended to call their party "The National Party," and though Blackburn insisted that they had no platform or program and "All we have is the strength of our convictions," their convictions evidently came from Lawrence Dennis' neo-fascist book *The Doom of Capitalism*. Dennis addressed their meetings, which took place in Johnson's elegantly modern apartment (like Warburg's) with a two-story living room. On one occasion, according to the press, a hundred "silver shirts" gathered there. The only statement made by Johnson quoted in the *Herald Tribune* was: "We're adventurers with an intellectual overlay, so we're almost articulate but not quite articulate." It is the only occasion to my knowledge when anybody ever called Johnson inarticulate. To paraphrase the critic for the *Sun* on Johnson's showmanship, he is possibly the world's most articulate architect.

Evidently the first that the trustees heard of Johnson's plan to quit the Museum for politics was when Nelson Rockefeller introduced Edward James Mathews, a young architect who was working on Rockefeller Center, to Johnson as the chairman of the Museum's Department of Architecture. According to Mathews, Johnson said, "Oh, I'm leaving in three weeks to be Huey Long's Minister of Fine Arts." Apparently Long gave Johnson and Blackburn very short shrift, and they were soon back in New York. Blackburn never returned to the Museum staff; Johnson, who many thought was Blackburn's dupe, not only returned to the Museum but eventually became a trustee and the Museum's official architect, a part of this portrait to be considered in its place. The trustees agreed with Abby Rockefeller that "every young man," as she said at the time, "is entitled to one bad mistake."

But before the small political tragi-comedy which involved the Museum rather obliquely was playing itself out, events far more important from the points of view of Barr and Goodyear and Abbott had happened and were happening. When the Barrs came back from Europe at the end of the summer that they were married, they moved into an apartment at 2 Beekman Place, a fashionable part of the city then and even more fashionable today. One of their friends, Frances Strunsky Collins, daughter of the *New York Times* correspondent Simeon Strunsky, was a fairly frequent caller. She had got to know Daisy Barr when Daisy was teaching Italian at Vassar. "None of their furniture had arrived from Germany," she remembers with amusement, "because it was a sort of commercial version of the hand-made Mies furniture that Philip had. There was a small bedroom with two narrow beds from Bloomingdale's side by side, two narrow chests of drawers painted dead black, and the beds had black headboards and footboards. As I remember, there was no furniture at all in the living room. Daisy and I would sit on the edge of the bed talking, and in the living room Alfred and Jere and Cary would be talking about the Museum."

In the spring of 1932 Abbott resigned his position as Associate Director of the Museum to accept the directorship of the Smith College Museum of Art in Northampton, Massachusetts. Quite apparently, a good deal of the charm and excitement had gone out of the job and out of his relationship with Barr after the Barrs's marriage and the bachelor quarters at the Hotel Bristol had been abandoned. Talks about the Smith position had been going on for at least six months before the announcement was made. Barr did not want to see Abbott go, but the trustees of the Museum saw a chance to save a little money, evidently, for Barr wrote to Sachs in February 1932: "The executive committee has decided to dispense with Jere by having him accept the Smith job. This may be the best thing for him to do, but it will be a long time, I fear, before we will find anyone to take his place. I do not feel that the trustees realize his value and tend to consider him merely as a lieutenant to me." To this Sachs replied in part: "Remember the times are very unusual; that everyone has very serious and unexpected problems."

Abbott appealed to Sachs for his advice even after this interchange between Barr and Sachs, and Sachs replied with a letter that had little bearing on Abbott's decision (which had evidently been made for him) but is nonetheless revealing. On March 2, 1932, Sachs wrote:

> And finally, you ought to weigh this in the balance:—that in my humble opinion the Modern Museum is destined to be one of the greatest institutions of its kind in the world, in spite of present conditions and possible discouragements, and in spite of the occasional pessimisms of Alfred. These difficulties and obstacles do not in the least discourage me. Such periods come periodically. In my opinion this epoch will pass, and for those persons and institutions who survive there will be again a bright and glowing future. I am, of course, a hopeless optimist. . . .

No one did replace Abbott, at least no one with his breadth of knowledge of the arts coupled with a sense of museumship and executive gifts, for a very long while. To take his place, there was a series of men, starting with Blackburn, who were regarded by the curators as "business types" and whom the trustees hoped would interject a businesslike atmosphere and efficiency into the conduct of the Museum's affairs. None of them succeeded, and not till a woman, Frances Hawkins, became Secretary of the Museum a decade later was there a firm, intelligent, and effective executive running (rather than direct-ing) the place.

Abbott missed the move into the new building and with it the at-tendant headaches. In December of 1931 Goodyear let the press know that the Museum was looking for a new home and said that it hoped to move into 11 West 53rd Street "if subscriptions can be secured sufficient in amount to satisfy the budget adopted by the trustees." He explained that "the experimental period of the Museum will come to an end with the present season," surely one of his most inaccurate public statements. If he had said "tentative period," he would have been close to the truth. "To justify its continued existence," he went on

> the Museum must have quarters more permanent and better suited to its uses than it has at present, Ultimately the endowment is equally essential, but with the large demands now made for emer-gency relief and the economic depression confronting us, it has been thought advisable to postpone any appeal for a considerable amount. . . .

Nearly three months before this announcement appeared in the papers Goodyear had written to Sachs telling him that at a trustees' meeting on October 6, with barely a quorum present, they had voted to "lease the house owned by Mr. Rockefeller on West 53rd Street for five years provided the money necessary for making alterations and annual subscriptions of not less than $80,000 for a period of three years can be secured. We have already practically been assured of the money for the alterations." Mr. Rockefeller reduced the rent his agent was asking from $10,000 to $8,000 and a lease was signed.

The house, as city houses went in those days, was a very large one, though by no means as large as the Rockefeller house on 54th Street on which it backed. It was built in 1900 of limestone and had a sixty-foot front on 53rd Street, and for some time a "To Let" sign had hung in one of its second-floor windows. It was five stories high, with Ionic columns on either side of its entrance on a slightly raised stoop. Wrought-iron balconies ornamented its third-floor windows, and above a heavy cornice there was still another story which was occupied by servants' rooms, and above that a penthouse. Its address, 11 West 53rd Street, has been the address of the Museum ever since.

Barr and Goodyear had all manner of plans for the new building. It was to have an "architecture room" for changing exhibitions of plans and models and photographs; it was to have a small auditorium, and a place in which to hang much of the Bliss collection and other pictures and objects in the permanent collection. It would have sufficient gallery space so that there could be several shows, besides the "permanent" one, going on at the same time, and there would be room "to carry on the museum's enlarged educational program," of which, I believe it is safe to say, no one had heard until then. Possibly the traveling architecture show, which was just about to start on its rounds, had assumed the distinction of a "program." It would also have space for executive offices, mostly on the top floor, where the servants' rooms had been and which could be reached by a tiny elevator just big enough, as one of the staff put it, "for one fat man and me."

The building had been refurbished by the first of May 1932, though some of its original fashionable qualities remained and made an uncommon contrast with the monk's-cloth walls on which pictures were hung by wire from picture moldings. The ceilings of what had once been the drawing room and living rooms and dining room were decorated with elaborate plaster ornament, with cartouches and dentils, and as partitions had been removed to make larger galleries, the ceilings of the rooms became, if anyone bothered to look at them, something of a sample book of Edwardian taste in architecturally applied ornament.

The opening of the new Museum on May 3, 1932, was greeted with congratulations on the one hand and catcalls on the other. William Sloane Coffin, the Metropolitan Museum's new president, and Alfred Barr shared a radio program on station WJZ a few days after the opening and said nice things about each other's institutions and made half-promises to each other. Mr. Coffin extended his "heartiest congratulations" to the staff and trustees of the Modern Museum and noted that "The frontier has no past, only a future. The frontier of art has no established tradition, no fixed judgment. For this reason the trustees of the older institution often hesitate and are timid in giving their stamp of approval to the experiments of the present. You are handicapped by no such inhibitions. The Museum of Modern Art 'believeth all things, hopeth all things, endureth all things,' and more than often your faith will be entirely justified by the judgment of posterity." Then he came to the nub of the matter:

When the so-called "wild creations" of today are regarded as the conservative standards of tomorrow is it too much to hope that you will permit some of them to come to the Metropolitan Museum of Art, leaving space on your walls for the new creations of the new day? If this museum will always remain modern, retaining faithfully the pioneer spirit of faith and adventure, you will have found what the ages have sought—the fountain of perpetual youth, whence shall well forever the spontaneous creative art of the future.

Barr responded in kind. "No other institution includes so wide a public as the Metropolitan," he said, "and to it should go ultimately the finest works of the foremost modern artists." But he was also being cautious, for he was not confident, as Goodyear seems to have been, that a reasonable deal with the Metropolitan could be negotiated. "We do not, however," Barr went on, "wish merely to become the feeder to other museums. To live we need the bone and sinew of a permanent collection which has strength and vigor, which looks toward the future but retains the support of the recent past."

It was noted on this occasion that relations between the two museums were closer since the election of two trustees of the Museum of Modern Art, Nelson A. Rockefeller and Cornelius N. Bliss (who, as we have seen, loved his sister but disliked modern art), to the board of the Metropolitan. Indeed, the art press had already commented on the fact that as a result of these elections the Metropolitan had started buying paintings from some of the livelier young painters, "definitely younger than any whose works have been admitted to the museum heretofore," men like John Steuart Curry, Reginald Marsh, Glenn O. Coleman, and Ogden Pleissner. And only seven months later Goodyear wrote to Sachs, who was then in Paris:

> You may be glad to know that we are at the point of making a definite arrangement with the Metropolitan. . . . On the face of it, it would seem that the Metropolitan gets everything and gives little. However, I am convinced that the happiest life for an institution or an individual is not to be troubled with too many possessions, and this scheme should result in keeping the Museum of Modern Art a living active institution abreast of the times.

Verbal bouquets were profuse on the occasion of the Museum's arrival in its new home. President Hoover, unquestionably prompted by Goodyear, wrote a letter which Barr read on the air at the time he and Coffin exchanged compliments. The President wrote: "The establishment of the Museum of Modern Art opens wide opportunities for appreciation by the public of the trends of the times in the fine arts and also for friendly emulation among contemporary artists of all countries." The press was generally complimentary, observing that

"In three seasons the Museum has won for itself a commanding position in the United States" and that "It is known everywhere in the world where the subject of art is discussed." It gave credit for this not to publicity-seeking but to "the reputation of the founders and to the intelligence and capacity for hard work of the directors and to the high standards that it set from the first. . . ." Another critic called it "young in years but rich in experience and accomplishment."

The same cannot be said of the press that greeted the opening exhibition at 11 West 53rd Street. Catcalls came not only from the conservative press but from the press that was usually friendly; they came from the Museum's own trustees and in various forms from a variety of artists as well.

The exhibition, which was called *Murals by American Painters and Photographers,* was the brainchild of the Advisory Committee and more specifically of Lincoln Kirstein. The Advisory Committee was for it because it gave American artists the kind of showing that the committee had been pestering the trustees for. Barr liked it because here was a chance to show photography as an independent art for the first time. It was, he said, "the wedge." Kirstein was in charge as director of the exhibition, and it was he who selected the painters to do the sketches for the murals and, according to the rules he set down, one completed panel to full scale. Julien Levy, whose upstairs gallery on Madison Avenue near 57th Street was, among other things, one of the very few galleries that took photography seriously, was in charge of selecting the photographers. Levy had been a friend of Kirstein at Harvard, and his father, a real-estate operator on a large scale in New York, had given him gallery space rent-free in a building he operated.

The Julien Levy Gallery, it should be noted, was one of the liveliest and most adventurous art-dealing establishments of the 1930s. It was here that Salvador Dali's little painting of limp watches (properly called "The Persistence of Memory") was first shown, and it could have been bought for $450. There too were the first shows in New York of the so-called "Neo-Romantics," Christian Bérard, Eugene Berman and his brother Leonid, and Tchelitchew, of the surrealists Joseph Cornell, Max Ernst, and Tanguy. It was there that the photographers Walker Evans and George Platt Lynes and Cartier-Bresson had their first New York shows, several years before there was such a thing as a Department of Photography at the Museum of Modern Art. Levy, a slender dark-haired man with sharp, aristocratic features, was married to Joella Loy, the beautiful daughter of a Surrealist poet and painter, Mina Loy, and they lived in an apartment on Seventh Avenue which had once been occupied by Polly Adler [3] and her girls, a fact which caused their doorbell to ring at the oddest hours. Their dark purple dining room was hung with panels painted for it by Berman, and the hall was decorated with photostats of front pages from a tabloid called the New York *Graphic* at the time of the Peaches and "Daddy" Browning scandal of 1927.

Sixty-five artists were invited to participate in the *Murals* show, and a few of them took occasion to adhere closely to the Communist party line, with results that threw some of the trustees into a state of near shock. One picture by Hugo Gellert which he called " 'Us Fellas Gotta Stick Together'—Al Capone," showed J. P. Morgan, John D. Rockefeller, Sr., President Hoover, and Henry Ford with Al Capone, "entrenched behind money bags," to use Goodyear's description of it, "operating a machine gun." Mrs. Parkinson in recalling the occasion said, "Somebody took pictures of the stuff to the Board of Trustees. They called it 'Commie stuff,' and Sam Lewisohn, who always woke up at the crucial moment, opened one eye, and said, 'As you are all aware . . .' We were *not* aware, and all hell broke loose!" The members of the Advisory Committee who were present at this session of the board went to Kirstein. He said flatly that if the Museum wouldn't show the paintings, he would have an independent show of them and make it quite clear that the Museum refused to show them. "Nelson paid a call on papa and on Mr. Morgan," Mrs. Parkinson recalls, "and they said they didn't mind. People jammed in. Some of the trustees wanted Lincoln fired. Nelson was marvelous; he backed Lincoln completely. A lot of the [Advisory] Committee resigned, and those who were loyal to Lincoln stayed. We had a much better committee afterwards."

The painters whose work had been challenged had a field day. The Museum had, evidently, risen to their bait (they would call it their "challenge"), and in the June 1932 issue of *New Masses* Hugo Gellert told his version of the story under the title "We Capture the Walls!" According to Gellert, when he delivered his mural to the Museum he was asked to do over the full-scale panel because he had done a horizontal one and not, as the specifications stated, a vertical one. Subsequently he received a letter, he does not say from whom, which read:

> I was thinking, when you are doing over your mural, if it would not be a good idea in a way to do the panel of Lenin instead of the one you did. . . . I think that the large figure of Lenin that you indicated would really be a definite and different aspect of

3 The author of *A House Is Not a Home* (New York, 1953).

the symbolism of the whole social struggle, and also as there is a single large figure, it might take you less time to do it over. Also, in a way—it is a more monumental design. . . . It was so terribly understanding of you to be willing to paint the panel over and the Museum and myself are really grateful.

Unfortunately, he does not say what the original subject of the panel had been. He quotes from a subsequent letter:

I must inform you that (unknown to me) any picture which can be interpreted as an offensive caricature or representation of a contemporary individual cannot be exhibited. This applies to part of your composition.

It is difficult to tell from Gellert's version of the story how much is what actually happened and how much is fact adjusted to conform to the party's line. It is equally hard to tell from Goodyear's version just what went on. Gellert's language is as patently in the *New Masses'* indignant tone of voice as Goodyear's is patently a glossing over, with the result that there is an aura of never-never land about both accounts. Gellert quotes conversations verbatim with unnamed persons in the Museum and telephone calls between unnamed artists and unnamed Museum staff members. He quotes statements made in meetings of the trustees which he could not possibly have heard and which, if they were made, surely none of the trustees would have relayed to him. (To wit: "How can Mr. Hoover come to the opening!" exclaimed Mr. Goodyear, "and how can I face J. P. Morgan if these pictures are hung in the museum of which I am a trustee!") "Throughout the entire procedure the museum was evasive," Gellert writes. "Even now it endeavors to place all the blame and responsibility upon the shoulders of Lincoln Kirstein, in spite of the fact that Nelson Rockefeller is chairman of the Advisory Committee." Goodyear says: "A committee of trustees at first was determined to throw out the foolish caricatures but finally they were wisely allowed to remain and attracted as little attention as they deserved." Gellert says: "The Museum crowded our paintings into a little room downstairs and later, finding that the attendance at that room was great, they moved them up to the fourth floor, where visitors were unaware of their existence." The published statistics of attendance at the Museum indicate that 15,336 persons saw the *Murals* show, somewhat fewer than half the number who attended any other exhibition that the Museum put on in 1932.

Gellert did not like the position taken by the New York press toward

the exhibition, especially Jewell of the *Times* and Murdock Pemberton of *The New Yorker*. "The critics," Gellert said, "are only too ready to be of service." He quotes Jewell:

> The exhibition is so bad as to give America something to think about for a long time. . . . The class struggle orgies may be dismissed as harmless trifles—not because of their theme, but because of the childish or generally uninspired way in which they are handled.

He also quotes Murdock Pemberton:

> The show easily divides itself into two classes: a few serious artists, who really hoped that they would snare a contract, or at least interest the American architect in their potentialities, and a great many young men who saw only an opportunity to stick out their tongues and have a little prankish fun with their hosts.

These comments which infuriated Gellert undoubtedly pleased Goodyear. In his book he adds a few more sour notes. Henry McBride said that it was "simply a disaster. It is the saddest event of a none too cheerful winter." Cortissoz, running true to form, wrote, "In sheer, dismal ineptitude the exhibition touches bottom." Jewell, in addition to what Gellert quoted, is quoted by Goodyear as observing that the show was "easel painting glorified into an ignominious failure."

To devote so much space in these pages to one of the Museum's early spectacular failures may seem, since the show was a minor one, unjustified, but it was the Museum's first head-on encounter with artists who were out to make a monkey of it and its stance and policies. But artists, who quite properly believe that they have more to gain or lose from the activities of the Museum than anyone else, have watched it with a degree of suspicion mixed with hope that the public cannot possibly summon up. No matter that the money has been put up by what Barr calls with polite irony "the noble gentry," and that the trustees consider it "our museum," as many of them still do. The artists' contribution to it is greater than theirs. They know that they can get along without the Museum but the Museum cannot get along without them. They also know that because the Museum exists it is easier for them to exist, and that the influence of the Museum on the market for their products is tremendous. For an artist to "make the Museum" is to "make the big time." It is Broadway, and, like Broadway, it is as much the artist's beloved enemy as it is his despised friend.

Everything had the frayed nerves of an opening night. The last pictures were still being hung while the cocktails were being served and somebody was fetching the catalogues from the printer in a private car. . . . What we've done is to turn into the bloody Establishment.

EDWARD M. M. WARBURG *in an interview*, 1970

Chapter VII *Innovation and Invention*

By the late spring of 1932 Alfred Barr had worked himself into a frenzy of fatigue. In the thirty months since the Museum had opened in the Heckscher Building it had held sixteen exhibitions and had organized and published sixteen illustrated catalogues with texts either written by Barr or prefaced by his comments. The staff by June of 1932 had grown from the original five to nine. (In 1970, when the Museum put on six times as many shows as it did in 1930, it had more than a hundred times as many employees. It reached its peak then with 531.) Even with the kind of volunteer help that Philip Johnson, Henry-Russell Hitchcock, Mrs. Barr, and Cary Ross provided, the struggle to gather the exhibitions, catalogue them, receive, insure, and hang them, and finally return the borrowed works of art was a Herculean task.

The relation of the Museum as it was then to the Museum it has become is somewhat like that of the handicraft shop to the belt-line factory. Barr had been at his workbench too long and the toil had told on him. He went to Goodyear asking that he be given three months' vacation to try to pull himself together. He could not sleep, his digestion troubled him, work which he usually enjoyed and for which he had a great capacity had become an anguish to him. Goodyear spoke to Mrs. Rockefeller, who asked Barr to let her physician give him a thorough going over. He could find nothing organically wrong and sent Barr to a "nerve specialist." Goodyear wrote about this to Paul Sachs. The nerve specialist, he reported, "tells him that it is necessary for him to take a year's rest." Sachs was not in the least surprised. "I have been disturbed by Alfred's appearance and by the clear indication (to my lay eyes) that he was on the verge of a nervous breakdown," he replied. "This view was further confirmed in the past week when I had lunch with him." There seems to have been no doubt in Goodyear's mind or Mrs. Rockefeller's or Sachs's what the trustees of the Museum should do, nor any hesitation in seeing that Barr, as Goodyear later put it, was given "every chance to work out his difficulties." The Museum granted Barr a year's leave of absence with half-salary, and he and his wife took off for Europe. After a few months of traveling and, as he never ceased to do, of studying and appraising works of art and architecture, music, films, theater, letters and birds—whose identification has long been his favorite relaxation and about which he is exceedingly knowledgeable—he was sleeping and eating well and beginning to feel like his customary energetic and dogged self.

In November a letter came from Goodyear which reached Barr in Rome asking him to handle the details of an exhibition of American art at the Musée du Jeu de Paume in Paris that was scheduled to open on the following March 15. Barr's rest had not been long enough nor was his recuperation nearly complete. He wrote to Sachs, who was staying at the Connaught Hotel in London: "He has asked me to be ready to go to Paris shortly to confer with M. Dezarrois regarding arrangements and again before the exhibition opens to take charge of hanging and 'details.'" All Barr's weariness and sleeplessness flooded back and he asked Sachs, as he so often did, what he should do. He was ready, he said, to resign from the Museum if necessary, or to give up his salary entirely, or to have the trustees hire someone in his place. He asked Sachs not to intervene on his behalf but merely to give him advice.

Sachs's reply, written three days later on November 27, was characteristically firm and kind, and exhorted Barr to stick to his guns. He spelled out the reasons:

> 1. *It is a fact*—that you are today the ablest man in the field of "Modern Art" in America. In addition you are highly competent both as scholar, teacher and Museum man, in other fields of art. . . .
>
> 2. *It is a fact*—you have been overworked by the trustees; that you have overworked yourself. . . .

3. *It is a fact*—that you are not well physically and nervously. . . .

4. *It is a fact* that your *first duty* is to regain your health completely—no matter about the consequences.

Therefore I say to you quite simply—do *not* agree *in any shape or form* to the President's request. . . .

About a week later Barr wrote to Sachs that he had followed this advice except to offer "to give up my half salary for two months to pay for a substitute."

Goodyear, having heard from Barr, wrote to Sachs about his concern: ". . . I am disturbed about Alfred, for if such a small thing as this would upset him so after six months absence, I hardly see how he will be able to go along with the Museum when his year's vacation is over." But the matter of the exhibition in Paris had been settled for other reasons. It was postponed, Goodyear said, "principally on account of the inter-allied debt feeling." There was, at the moment, no love lost between the French and the Americans over loans made during the First World War by the latter to the former. The exhibition had to wait for several years; it opened as *Trois Siècles d'Art aux Etats-Unis* at the Jeu de Paume in May 1938.

Barr had had a "very friendly letter" from Goodyear, he wrote to Sachs, "excusing me from participation in the American show." The letter had a postscript, later confirmed by cable, of the possible postponement of the exhibition.

The incident was closed. At the end of his year's absence Barr went back to work at the Museum as hard as he ever had, and he and Goodyear went back to arguing with each other. Twenty years later Barr wrote to Sachs: "You may remember that I had several very difficult arguments with him, but both he and I maintained a real affection for each other and both, I think, feel a certain pride in being able to go on working with each other in spite of occasional disagreements."

In retrospect the wonder is that there were as many meetings of the mind as there were. In temperament, in physical bearing, in standards of accomplishment, in background, and in what stood in the foreground of the ambitions of each they could scarcely have been more unalike. Goodyear, whom the staff at the Museum referred to as "Toughie," represented established money and the confident stance that so frequently goes with it. Barr represented the subtler inheritance of firm Protestantism and intellectual security with its different but equally confident stance. Barr, whose gaze during a conversation would become fixed on an indeterminate distance ("You'd know he wasn't there any more," one of his assistants said), had a concept for the Museum. He was quite willing to play by the rules his trustees set down, so long as he could bend them a little at a time to his own ends, which he justly identified with the Museum's best interests. Goodyear had an immediate concern for the Museum's success, and he worked at it. To him it meant money, crowds, the pleasure of his fellow trustees. It meant the exercise of his personal and by no means unadventurous or insensitive taste. It also meant not unwelcome personal kudos of a sort from which Mrs. Rockefeller and Miss Bliss, brought up in an age when it was considered indelicate for a lady's name to appear in the press except on the occasions of her birth, her marriage, and her death, would have shrunk. He was unquestionably pleased when his friend Crowninshield printed his picture in *Vanity Fair* as part of a monthly feature called "We Nominate for the Hall of Fame." With the photograph was the caption:

> Conger Goodyear because, a successful merchant, he made himself prominent also in the fine arts by his active interest and support; because he was the leading spirit in founding the Museum of Modern Art, of which he is the President; and because he owns one of the ten notable collections of modern French art.

He must have been less pleased—indeed, infuriated—when the magazine *Creative Art* in April 1932 reported a rumor that he meant to resign as president of the Museum. In a column called "News and Gossip," Walter Gutman wrote, in part:

> Various explanations are given. One is that his successful venture in backing Katharine Cornell has changed his interest from the *métier* of Toulouse-Lautrec to that of O'Neill. Others report that there have been several strained interludes between him and other backers of the Museum, especially the Rockefellers. A year ago in this column it was pointed out that Rockefeller City would be an ideal location for the Museum of Modern Art. Seemingly because of the jealousies of other potentates the Museum found permanent quarters merely on West 53rd Street. . . .

Goodyear was not the sort to brook that kind of nonsense, though he must have been quite aware that the Museum was then, as it has always been since, a breeder of art-world gossip and considered to be a jungle of personal jealousies, reckless ambitions, and character assassinations. The next issue of *Creative Art* backed down:

Unfortunately several statements about the Museum of Modern Art which were quite without foundation found their way into this column last month. Mr. Conger Goodyear did not resign from the Museum, and has no intention of doing so. . . .

Goodyear spent a great deal of time in the Museum in its first ten years. "He was very much around and immensely enjoyed the work," Monroe Wheeler recalls. Mrs. Barr says, "Goodyear fought Alfred tooth and nail. They were always fighting . . . terrible fights. But Goodyear was devoted to the Museum. Alfred was always fighting for ideas, not for himself." Their quarrels were essentially about matters of taste, about works of art on which they could not agree. "Goodyear always supported Alfred," Wheeler said, "except in the case of certain works of art he disapproved of. He wasn't altogether elastic." Goodyear quite clearly thought that Barr was altogether too damned elastic. Jere Abbott recalls Goodyear as "a huffy man and a complicated guy," but he also remembers that "Alfred and I had a wonderfully free hand in matters of exhibitions and Museum policy. I look back on it with amazement. Consider that board! No one on it was used to being said 'no' to. Yet there was no serious friction." Another staff member who was around in the early days, a young woman, remembers Goodyear as "a big ladies' man, but he was marvelous. . . . He was not an easy man. He was tough, very tough." He had a taste for the rambunctious young. "He liked us young Turks," Warburg said of him. "He was a very brusque guy. The last person you'd expect to have sensitivity. He was not a man of tact." And he added, "In those days when they were presidents of the board they acted as though they were directors of the Museum. Their taste mattered . . . not that they were custodians." Philip Johnson remembers him affectionately as "a bastard of the first order." "I admired him," Johnson says. "The more outrageous you were, the better he liked you. He was a curmudgeon . . . like old Harold Ickes." Another member of the staff, Allen Porter, who worked with Goodyear on the Jeu de Paume exhibition, has said, "We became very good friends, but he was a suspicious man and felt that people were always taking advantage of him, and he was grumpy. He soured when something went wrong. He went good and sour. . . ." By the end of his term as President, which lasted until 1939, he had good reason to sour, but in the meantime, in spite of the fact that he personally was having a difficult time financially, "he stayed with it and worked hard," and he and Barr fought if not exactly happily, at least productively.

* * *

"1933 was a lot of fun," Barr said in 1970, "a fine year! We picketed the Architectural League exhibition because it wasn't showing the work of the younger architects. We showed models in a shop across the street that Julien Levy's father allowed us to have there in one of his buildings. Howe and Lescaze refused to join the League show and joined our group." [1]

More important things went on at the Museum that year. The Department of Circulating Exhibitions was established, with a young Wellesley graduate, Elodie Courter, as its head, and it became in a few years the Museum's most influential instrument of tastemaking. In that year too was the Museum's first all-photographic exhibition, a show of prints by Walker Evans of American Victorian architecture; they were a gift to the Museum from Lincoln Kirstein. The first issue of the Museum's *Bulletin* appeared in June 1933. Warburg was appointed chairman of a committee "on the possibility of a department of film." In that same month C. E. Harbison of *Vanity Fair*'s "kennel department" presented the Museum with a German Shepherd dog named Don to patrol the building with the night watchman; his picture was in newspapers all over America. Holger Cahill, who advised Mrs. Rockefeller on her collection of American primitive art (most of which subsequently went to Colonial Williamsburg, a Rockefeller exercise in native archeology), took over as Acting Director during Barr's leave of absence. "Then began the flood of Americana under Cahill's direction," Goodyear recorded in his book. A large part of what was shown in the exhibition of *American Folk Art: The Art of the Common Man in America, 1750–1900* during the winter of 1932–33 came from Mrs. Rockefeller's hoard. Five months later this was followed by a show called *American Sources of Modern Art*, which displayed sculpture and pottery, textiles and gold and silver objects from Aztec, Mayan, Toltec, and Inca excavations. The title was a hard try, as Goodyear confessed, and it was, he recorded, "promptly qualified in the introduction to the catalogue: 'There is no intention here to insist that ancient American art is a major source of modern art.'" It was one of the Museum's earliest wanderings into pastures of culture in far distant times and places, but it was surely not the most curious. There had already been an exhibition in the fall of 1932 of Persian fresco painting, arranged by the American Institute for Persian Art and Archeology, for which there seems to have been no other excuse than that Mrs. Murray Crane and Sam Lewisohn and Miss Elizabeth Bliss and Sir Joseph Duveen were on the Institute's Board of Trustees or Advisory

---

1 George Howe and William Lescaze, the architects of the PSFS Building in Philadelphia, built in 1932, and famous as a "modern" skyscraper.

Council. It was simply a family affair. Having early in its career broken its nominal boundaries, carefully defined in its title as modern art, the Museum had no later compunction about considering that anything which struck its fancy was within its legitimate concern.

The event of 1933 that had the greatest impact on the Museum and its future, however, was none of these. It was the arrival on its staff of an extremely handsome Englishwoman in her late thirties with navy-blue eyes, fine features in a long oval face, and shining black hair. Her name was Iris Barry, and she was hired as Librarian, though the Museum had no library to speak of and the job was one for which she had no training whatsoever. She had been the film critic of the *Daily Mail* in London, and she had been summarily fired because she had written an uncomplimentary review of a film in which Marion Davies, the apple of the eye of the powerful publisher William Randolph Hearst, was starred. Iris Barry was scarcely gentle in her praise or blame; her eye was sharp and her pen witty, as the brief film notes which she wrote for the Museum's *Bulletin* attest. In addition to her job as reviewer in London, she had been co-founder in 1925 of an intellectually successful but financially impoverished film society, one of the first such societies anywhere.

In the fall of 1932 two close friends, the actor Charles Laughton and his wife, Elsa Lanchester, bought her a wardrobe and paid for her passage to New York. They sent her to their friends the Askews (Kirk and Constance), whose ménage in a brownstone on East 61st Street was a place to which artists and musicians, art historians and art dealers, writers, and collectors were attracted by the quality of the hospitality and of the conversation, the elegant and rather Victorian richness of the surroundings, and the intelligence and amiability and charm of the hosts. It was an elegant Upper Bohemian salon, a plush-lined kettle steaming with gossip of the art world. There on a Sunday evening one would encounter the composers Virgil Thomson and (less frequently) Aaron Copland, the painters Berman and Tchelitchew, who made many drawings of his hostess and painted a remarkable portrait of her holding a looking glass. There would be Lincoln Kirstein, A. Everett Austin, the young director of the Wadsworth Atheneum in Hartford, and occasionally his blonde wife, Helen; Julien Levy and Joella (who later became Mrs. Herbert Bayer, wife of the designer and painter from the Bauhaus); James Johnson Sweeney and Laura; Philip Johnson; Henry-Russell Hitchcock and John McAndrew, later Director of Architecture at the Museum; Joseph Brewer, at that time a young partner in the publishing firm Brewer, Warren and Putnam; Allen Porter, from upstate New York, who had given up working for the Buick Company to join Julien Levy in his gallery and later became Assistant Secretary of the Museum; Agnes Rindge, head of the Art Department at Vassar, who was briefly a Vice-Director of the Museum during the Second World War; and, since the circle of the Askews' acquaintance was wide, a great many others including, of course, the Alfred Barrs and Jere Abbott.

It was into this artistic compote that the Laughtons introduced Iris Barry, and either directly or only slightly indirectly it was through the Askews that she moved quite quickly into the orbit of the Museum. Philip Johnson, who was both supporting and directing the Architecture Department of the Museum at the time, was so impressed by the wit, agility, and knowledge of Iris Barry, whom he met at a cocktail party at Joseph Brewer's, that he told her she simply had to work for the Museum, that he would pay her salary and she would be the Librarian. ("I also gave her some money to buy a dress at Saks Fifth Avenue," Johnson says. "It was a terrible dress.") Some books, most of them given to the Museum by Goodyear, Johnson, and Henry-Russell Hitchcock, had accumulated helter-skelter in the penthouse of 11 West 53rd Street. In August 1933 Iris Barry climbed the stairs to the hot little room under the roof and went to work.

It is officially recorded that Miss Barry went to the Library School at Columbia University to learn her new profession; the present Librarian of the Museum, Bernard Karpel, who knew her well and worked with her for years, says, "I understand Iris went to library school for forty-eight hours," which is very likely to be only a small exaggeration if it is an exaggeration at all. The fact, however, that the Museum now had a Librarian inspired trustees to turn over books to it, most especially Mrs. Rockefeller. "The very fact that books accumulated in what might be called a disorderly way at the beginning," Karpel says, "was actually a great benefit. We have many things that a proper orderly accumulation never would have had."

Iris Barry, like the editors of *Vogue* and *Harper's Bazaar* in those days, always worked with a hat on, "always a very elegant hat," as a contemporary remembers. "What I liked about her," Karpel recalls, "was her mannish mind. I always talked to her as though there was a man across the table. She was logical, precise; she could be very short and direct, but there was no feeling of malice or deviousness about her . . . clean, sharp as a whistle." And he added, and it says something about the mores of the Depression, "So far as I knew, there was nothing that was not admirable about her . . . except for those people who constantly had to lend her money on Friday and hoped to get it back on Tuesday. Then they'd borrow from her on Wednesday. . . ."

Alfred Barr was in Europe when Miss Barry, as she was called, joined the Museum staff. She was in actuality Mrs. Alan Porter, the wife of an English poet and critic from whom she was divorced not long after she came to America.[2] There is no question that Barr shared Johnson's enthusiasm for her: she was extremely knowledgeable about films, and Barr's plans for a film library had been in the original prospectus for the Museum: "Not the least important collection," he had said in 1929, "might be a *filmotek*, a library of films. . . ." Three years later in a staff report to the corporation dated December 8, 1932, progress of a tentative sort (more hope than fact) was noted. It was quite probably Barr's polite way of calling to the trustees, "Ready or not, here we come!" The report said: "The establishment of a Motion Picture Department is almost an accomplished fact. . . . It is the plan that this department would show from time to time, films from all countries which are significant as art. . . . The collection in a film library of significant pictures is also contemplated." Miss Barry appeared to be (and indeed was) ideal for the creation of such a department. She had been the first film critic on any London newspaper, and her book *Let's Go to the Movies* was the first serious book of film criticism published in England.

Several years went by, however, before the Film Library became a fact. Soon after Iris Barry's arrival in New York she became involved with a scheme that Julien Levy promulgated to form an organization called the New York Film Society, the purpose of which was to show historic and foreign films which at that time were nowhere to be seen in New York. The committee of the society consisted of Levy, Iris Barry, Nelson Rockefeller, and Raoul de Roussy de Sales, and it sold subscriptions for five programs which were shown in a number of places (not theaters) in which a projector, a screen, and chairs might be set up. It rented the ballroom of the Essex House Hotel for the "grand opening." Iris Barry assembled the films, which at that time, was a matter of running down each to its source, to the company that had made it or, in some instances, imported it. There were no film libraries or depositories to which to turn. She put together a program called *The Motion Picture 1914-34* especially for the Wadsworth Atheneum in Hartford. It was not until the following year that the

2 He is not to be confused with Allen Porter, who was associated with the Museum for many years and was one of its mainstays.

Museum of Modern Art Film Library was organized, though a meeting had been held at Mrs. Rockefeller's in 1934 at the instigation of Alfred Barr and Miss Barry and Warburg. "I remember trying to persuade Miss Bliss that the movies were art, and convincing her by taking her to see *The Passion of Joan of Arc* [produced in 1928] at the Little Carnegie," Barr wrote. "I also recall sending her and Mrs. Rockefeller and Mr. Goodyear postcards from time to time recommending current films that seemed to me 'works of art.'"

Goodyear looked with very considerable skepticism upon the idea of the Museum's getting itself involved with motion pictures. He was in Europe when Warburg and John Hay Whitney, with the backing of Mrs. Rockefeller, made Barr's and Barry's scheme a part of the Museum's program. Once the decision was made, however, Goodyear gave it his support. In February of 1935 the Museum sent out a letter to several hundred college presidents and museum directors asking if they would be interested in a series such as the one prepared for Hartford to be shown in their institutions. About two hundred replies came back and eighty-four percent of them said that they would be interested.

At about this time there was a switch in the cast of characters. Iris Barry had divorced her poet husband and married a lean, blond, bespectacled, smooth-talking Wall Street customers' man named John E. Abbott, known to his friends as "Dick." He was five years younger than she. Things in Wall Street were, obviously, not very active in the mid-'30s, and Miss Barry persuaded the committee to make her husband Director of the proposed Film Library; she would act as Curator. "This sort of nepotism was not uncommon in the Museum," a colleague who admired Miss Barry but not Mr. Abbott commented many years later. In any case, Abbott was "engaged to prepare a report on the possibility of founding a Film Library," according to Goodyear, and the report evidently was largely written by his wife. John Hay Whitney, a thirty-one-year-old trustee of the Museum who at that time had some financial interest in the motion-picture business (years later he did handsomely with his investment in *Gone with the Wind*), took over the chairmanship of the committee on the Film Library, and he and the Rockefeller Foundation paid for Abbott's report. A few months later, in May 1935, with $100,000 from the Rockefeller Foundation and "private subscriptions totaling $60,000" (of which Whitney was the principal contributor), the Museum of Modern Art Film Library was set up as a separate corporation all of whose stock was held by the Museum. Whitney was president, Abbott vice-president, and Warburg was treasurer. As there was no room at II West 53rd Street, office space was rented at 485 Madison Avenue, and the Abbotts moved in with five employees to help them in what turned out to be a massive job of hunting, accumulation, sifting, cajoling, cataloguing, and distribution. In the Abbott-Barry report the purpose of the Film Library was set down as:

> to trace, catalog, assemble, exhibit and circulate to museums and colleges single films or programs of films in exactly the same manner in which the Museum traces, catalogs, exhibits and circulates paintings, sculpture, architectural photographs and models or reproductions of works of art, so that the film may be studied and enjoyed as any other one of the arts is studied and enjoyed.

The art of the film, however, was in a kind of jeopardy that the other arts with which the Museum was concerned were not. It was threatened with falling into dust. The storage vaults of the movie companies were jammed with reels of film, but the film was made of celluloid, and, as Miss Barry wrote in the Museum *Bulletin* in her first of many articles about the Film Library, "The chemical composition of celluloid is such that it is only a question of time before existing prints and negatives are dust and fragments. Unless something is done to restore and preserve outstanding films of the past, the motion picture from 1894 onwards will be as irrecoverably lost as the Commedia dell' Arte or the dancing of Nijinsky."

In general the movie-makers of Hollywood seemed rather flattered that the commercial product which had paid for their palatial homes and had built the movie palaces of the 1920s, the most ornate edifices since the golden churches of seventeenth-century Portugal and the baroque effulgences of Spain, was taken seriously as art. The Abbotts got on a train to Hollywood with letters of introduction from Jock Whitney and found themselves the center of "an alarmingly brilliant concourse of filmdom's great at Pickfair." Iris Barry described the evening in a Museum *Bulletin:*

> Certainly the gracious gesture of Mary Pickford in thus throwing open her famous house and herself acting as hostess could alone have afforded the infant Film Library so excellent an opportunity of putting its case before the aggregate film chiefs and, through the press which reported the somewhat unusual event, a wider circle of film employees and public. That evening, pioneers of the industry like Mack Sennett met newcomers like Walt Disney for

the first time, old acquaintances were renewed and new ones made, for Hollywood, contrary to report, is no more gregarious than any other community whose inhabitants work for a living and reside often twenty miles apart from one another. For once the exponents of this new art-industry who normally live for the immediate future and the work in hand, stopped the clock briefly to consider the past. They had been for the most part brilliantly successful, but had often, as a consequence, faced criticism proportionate to the enormous influence they exercised on the public imagination. Now an outside agency suddenly appeared, asking only permission to preserve a record of their endeavors, and seeking no financial contribution from them—at least, not for the moment.

After dinner the Abbotts showed a brief program of films and explained what the Film Library planned to do and why it was important to preserve the record of the art which many of them did not think of as an art at all but merely as a commercial product.

This glimpse of the birth and growth of an art which was peculiarly their own both surprised and moved this unique audience. The screen doubtless brought back memories of early struggles and half-forgotten triumphs, of former companions seldom remembered. There was a tiny, shocked gasp at the first appearance of Louis Wolheim in the program's brief excerpt from *All Quiet on the Western Front:* he had been dead so very short a time. Was fame so brief? Of course there ought to be a museum of the film!

Within a few months Harold Lloyd, who was at the party, had given eleven of his films to the Film Library, and Sam Goldwyn, who was also there, had given two. Another eleven came from Warner Brothers and seven from 20th Century-Fox. It was only a beginning.[3]

At the first showing of films in the Museum (the makeshift auditorium on the second floor could seat only 150 persons) Miss Barry wrote in her notes for the occasion: "We forget that it was only by a miracle, only just in time, that this retrospect of film-making was drawn out of limbo." Limbo, however, was exceedingly generous. It produced two million feet of film from the Edison Company and an

---

3 John Hay Whitney recalls that a bill for the evening's entertainment came from Mary Pickford that "included everything—even the wood burned in the fireplace."

equal amount from the American Biograph and Muscotope Company, for which D. W. Griffith had made his early and revolutionary films. "The films poured in by the hundreds, and during the first years the major efforts of the Film Department were devoted just to seeing what many of the unlabeled cans contained." There was no great difficulty in finding prints, Miss Barry wrote, of the early films from 1895 to 1912: "by token purchase, gift or loan . . . from film pioneers or their heirs most of the outstanding early films were obtained." And she noted, "In one instance Mr. William Jamison of the Film Library's staff found a print of the *Execution of Mary Queen of Scots* (much spotted with tobacco juice) in an open garbage can in the Bronx. Another day a total stranger telephoned to offer a film which she had had in her hat-closet for many years." (Unfortunately, Miss Barry did not explain how it happened that a member of her staff was looking in garbage cans in the Bronx.) By 1941, six years after the Film Library was founded, she wrote: "the Film Library has accumulated sixteen million feet of film; it would take three thousand hours, or 365 eight-hour days, to see it all."

While the Film Library was going about its business of looking in trash cans and hat closets and the warehouses of movie companies from its headquarters on Madison Avenue, the fifth floor of 11 West 53rd Street was humming like a beehive. In some respects those who worked there look back on it with amusement and pleasure as a time of experiment, late hours, excitement, lively gossip, cramped quarters. They were something like a small Salvation Army band blowing their horns and banging their tambourines, collecting converts and money, and passing out literature that would save the souls of the doubters and scoffers. Not everything was bathed in the warm light of brotherly love on the fifth floor, however, and not everyone was more interested in "the word" than in himself.

Barr, Johnson, Blackburn, and Warburg (who worked as a volunteer) had offices on the floor that had once been reserved for the Rockefeller cooks and parlormaids, butlers and houseboys, laundress and seamstress. So also did Ernestine M. Fantl, Elodie Courter, Dorothy Miller, and Frances Strunsky Collins. It would be difficult to put together on a single floor in a single New York house so high a concentration of artistic intelligence, temperament, and, probably not by accident, good looks.

Blackburn was not welcomed back to the Museum after his excursion to Louisiana with Johnson. "I guess the trustees thought he was politically unreliable, or something," Johnson says. But he was still there when Ernestine Fantl was hired and when Elodie Courter came fresh out of Wellesley to work at first as a volunteer. Miss Fantl had been a student in Barr's course at Wellesley, one of "the seven children" who had been accepted for the course after being given a test of fifty questions designed to discover their knowledge of and sophistication in the arts of the day. It was a list of names of artists and composers and writers, the titles of books and movies and schools of artists, headed by the question: "What is the significance of each of the following in relation to modern artistic expression?" Some of the names not obvious to the young of the '20s now seem over-obvious, such as George Gershwin, Henri Matisse, Frank Lloyd Wright, James Joyce; others seem remote: Frans Masereel, Harriet Monroe, Boleslavsky. But there is *Saks Fifth Avenue* (answer: "Through its advertisements and show windows this department store has done more to popularize modern mannerisms in pictorial and decorative arts than any two proselytizing critics"), and there is *The Zoning Law* (answer: "Ordinance in New York and other large cities governing the height of tall buildings in proportion to the width of the street, thus safeguarding light. Resulting in the 'stepback' design of the newer skyscrapers, this law is of infinitely greater importance to American architecture than all the still-born and sentimental archaisms of the so-called revolutionary architects.") Today the questionnaire, which Frank Crowninshield was pleased to publish in *Vanity Fair* in August 1927, is still entertaining and a challenge or, to some, a chance both to show off and to show their age. Frankl? Antheil? Suprematism? Meyerhold? All these names were bandied about by the bright young people of the 1920s and '30s including, there can be no doubt, Ernestine Fantl, who, if she was not familiar with them before she took Barr's course, certainly was when she finished.

Barr was impressed by Miss Fantl's intelligence and articulateness, and when she graduated from Wellesley he wrote a letter of introduction for her to his good friend J. B. Neumann, the New York art dealer. "This is Miss Ernestine Fantl," he said, "who you will remember as among my students possibly the most mature in the understanding of modern art. She wants a job in a gallery and spoke of yours as the one that most interested her. I think you will find her both charming and able." She got the job.

In the spring of 1933 while Barr was still in Europe she was hired by Philip Johnson as his secretary, and he paid her salary. She was assigned by him to help with the arrangements for a summer exhibition, a show of French and German paintings that was selected by Stephen Clark. It was hung by Miss Fantl, who also had a good deal to say about what was in it, and it was, according to Goodyear, "the most successful showing in the warm-weather period that the Museum had put on." Indeed, it was so successful that much of it was held over and included in an exhibition called *Modern European Painting* that opened in October.

By that time Miss Fantl (these were the days when "everybody did everything" at the Museum) had been put in charge of the Publications Department, which seems not to have existed at all until she was given it to nurse. Heretofore everybody belonged in a manner of speaking to the Publications Department. Catalogues, which were the Museum's only publications except for money-raising brochures, had come under Barr's eye, or Jere Abbott's so long as he was there, but in June 1933 (while Miss Fantl was working on the summer show) the Museum issued its first number of *The Bulletin of the Museum of Modern Art*. It was a four-page illustrated news sheet on glossy paper, 7½ by 10 inches, saying what was going on in the Museum, giving its schedule for future shows, and some comment including one- or two-sentence critiques of current films by Iris Barry. (To wit: "CAVALCADE . . . Theatrical where it should be cinematic, dense with false sentiment and inverted patriotism, this nostalgic pseudo-newsreel which has proved to be very popular is admirably mounted and capably cast, but is emphatically not a piece that calls for praise or imitation." And, by contrast: "SHE DONE HIM WRONG . . . The Hollywood product at its vital best—perfect pace, brilliant execution, robust approach to and attack on a simple subject, and a perfect vehicle for that original screen personality, Mae West.") In the first issue there was also a letter from Henri Matisse "after visiting the Exhibition of *American Sources of Modern Art*." It was, of course, stylishly printed in French, but even so reads rather like a commercial for the Museum and for the dead civilizations of ancient Mexico and Central America. The *Bulletin's* masthead listed all nineteen of the trustees and all twenty-one members of the Advisory Committee and, below the other lists, just two members of the staff, Barr and Blackburn. Barr was still in Europe when the first issue of the *Bulletin* was published, but on its first page it printed a cablegram sent by him from Stuttgart on May 28 which started with the sentence: "Invitation to write for the first number Museum Bulletin comes in midst of year's leave generously granted by trustees." (Obviously, he was not going to be inveigled into writing an

article any more than he had been willing to get involved with the
Jeu de Paume exhibition.) The rest of his telegram had to do with how
many more museums there were in Stuttgart than in New York, which
was twenty times its size.

It had evidently been more of a job to get out this first issue of the
Bulletin than Blackburn had expected, and Miss Fantl, as a consequence
(and probably because she needed a title to retain her on the payroll),
was given the responsibility for the Publications Department. She occupied this position until November 1935, when she was appointed
Curator of Architecture and Industrial Design, a position she held until
February 1937. She is remembered by her colleagues as not only extremely effective and ambitious and intelligent, with a very discerning
eye, but also as "very much on the make." On a trip to London
she met John Carter, a distinguished English bibliophile and author
and a very handsome young man of aristocratic bearing in his
late twenties or early thirties, and they were married, not long after,
in America. They returned to London and, as Ernestine Carter, Miss
Fantl did indeed "make it." She became an extremely well-known
journalist and fashion writer and a few years ago was among those
honored (Order of the British Empire) on the Queen's birthday.

When Elodie Courter joined the group on the fifth floor in 1933
there was no place for her to work except in a back room with "Billy,"
the mail clerk. She was given a little desk by a window. "I don't think
dear Billy had had a bath since he left Ireland seven years before," she
says. "I thought I'd die in that room! Billy had been out of a job for a
long while, and he'd promised the Virgin to thank her every day if he
got one. So every day he went in his lunch hour to St. Patrick's."
(The Cathedral is just two blocks from the Museum.) Miss Courter
was fresh out of Wellesley, where she had taken all the art and architecture courses she could find, but she did not have Barr's famous
course; he had left by the time she got there. She had, she recalls, been
to all of the Museum's exhibitions in the Heckscher Building, and she
was determined to get a job working for the Museum in spite of the
advice of the Placement Bureau at Wellesley that there simply were
no jobs there. She turned up at the door, and Mr. Tremp, who was a
sort of receptionist-custodian-friend-and-counsellor-to-all-comers (his
official title was "Assistant at Information Desk"), recognized her as a
regular visitor. Tremp in the course of time became one of the Museum's most cherished employees. He was "a sort of hunchback, with
a long thin face, a long nose, and awkward movement," Miss Courter
recalls, "a terribly sweet man." She asked him about a job, and he

said, "There's nothing that I know of, but if you could stop in to see Mr. Blackburn, he could talk to you about it." Miss Courter was an extremely attractive young woman with brown hair and a somewhat heart-shaped face, a spontaneous smile, and a mind that was clear and sharp, exact and humorous. Blackburn was impressed. "Mr. Blackburn said that if I could type there was a job identifying about two thousand slides that Eddie Warburg and Philip Johnson had brought back from Europe. 'You have to do it on a typewriter,' he said. 'We've had three volunteers now and we can't read their handwritings.' All I knew about typewriters was where the letters were. As soon as graduation was over I got a typing book and tried to learn in two weeks." She had allowed herself the time between graduation and the Fourth of July weekend to master the typewriter, and then she turned up at the Museum and was closeted with Billy O'Leary, a typewriter, and a pile of slides. On one occasion she was told to take over the switchboard. She got the operator to show her what to do, but, she says, "That was very embarrassing. I got two calls crossed. Eddie Warburg was talking to Mrs. Rockefeller and Blackburn was talking to somebody about Warburg and they could all hear everything, and I just yanked all the cords."

This young volunteer was soon on the payroll and in November 1935 took over the mechanics of the circulating exhibitions. She organized what in effect was the only department of its sort in any museum. She ran it with such skill, such attention to detail, and such understanding of the facilities available in other museums and in schools and colleges that some years later (and some years after Miss Courter had become Mrs. Robert Osborn and had left the Museum), when UNESCO needed to provide a manual for the international exchange of exhibitions, it was to her that they turned. The book, called *Manual of Travelling Exhibitions*, was published in France in 1953, twenty years after the efficient Miss Courter fouled up the switchboard.

The Museum of Modern Art most assuredly did not invent the touring art exhibition, nor does it claim to have. The first exhibition circulated by the Museum was, as we have seen, the International Style architecture show, which was financed partly by the Museum and partly by eleven other museums that subscribed to it. The idea of circulating shows, however, goes back to a suggestion which was made before the Museum opened by W. R. Valentiner, the director of the Detroit Institute of Arts. When the new museum was first announced in September 1929, he wrote: "I am wondering whether there might be a possibility of arranging that some of your exhibitions, or at least a part of them, be sent on for exhibition here at our museum. . . . If our museum could have the opportunity of showing the sort of exhibitions I know yours will be, it would be an excellent way of stimulating an interest in this branch of art."

The next was a traveling one-man-one-picture show—Whistler's "Mother," borrowed from the Louvre for an exhibition of American painting in 1932 and whose peregrinations are, as we shall see, part of another story. Planning the details of its travels, however, had been an important lesson to the Museum in the problems of circulating exhibitions. "Blackburn had set up the mechanics," Miss Courter recalls, "so that it would be one month in each museum, and the letters were all formulated before the painting arrived from Europe—how they were to open it, how they were to handle the publicity . . . special letters to the Railway Express. It was in this way that the real mechanics of doing this sort of thing were established." The first traveling exhibition that Miss Courter herself organized was an *International Exhibition of Theatre Arts* which had been directed by the prominent theatrical designer Lee Simonson in January 1934. It initially consisted of some 750 items from five centuries (the earliest being Primaticcio drawings from the Stockholm Museum and Inigo Jones's designs for a Ben Jonson masque) and from eleven countries. It was a show of great variety and style, and to reduce it to manageable size for circulation was no mean problem. It was also the first, but by no means the only, excursion of the Museum into the arts of the theater.

Six years later, in an account of the activities of the department over which Miss Courter presided, the *Bulletin* recorded that the Museum "has sent out nearly one hundred exhibitions which have been shown over a thousand times in 222 cities in the United States, Canada, and Hawaii. These exhibitions have been in such demand that it has been impossible to keep pace with requests for them. . . ." It was the curators of the several departments and Miss Courter who picked the objects to travel, or, as she says, "We would design the exhibition or choose the paintings to be included. The curators of each department helped to decide and then Alfred would say, 'Don't use that painting. Use this one.'" It was also Barr who had the final word about what was to be said about each object that went out on circulation. In one instance Miss Courter had asked a friend outside the Museum to select from a large number of photographs of American sculpture an educational exhibition and write the captions; the friend suggested that the show include an example or two of nineteenth-century graveyard sculpture as having been an important manifestation of American stone-cutting and taste. Dorothy Miller was horrified: "Alfred would never put up with that. The Museum can't give that sort of thing its approval." The Museum had a "line" to which it adhered. It was certainly not a straight line, but it just as certainly was determined by Barr's taste. That is not to say that Barr thought that in the long run his taste about individual works of art was infallible; he knew that his guesses (it would be politer to say judgments, for they were never haphazard) could not always be right; indeed, that they could more often than not be wrong. He once said: "When it acquires a dozen recent paintings, it [the Museum] will be lucky if in ten years three will still seem worth looking at, if in twenty only one will survive. For the future the important thing is acquiring this one; the other nine will be forgiven and forgotten. . . . Sooner or later time will eliminate them. In any case, it is already clear that errors of omission are by far the most serious, for they are usually irrevocable." Nonetheless the statements that went out with the circulating exhibitions were the current version of the gospel according to the Director, and no nonsense!

Barr's most faithful disciple and one of the Barrs's closest friends was another of the young ladies who came to inhabit the servants' rooms on the fifth floor. She was Dorothy Miller, who became in 1938 Mrs. Holger Cahill, the wife of "Eddie" (as he was called) Cahill, who stood in for Barr during the year of his absence and was later the director of the WPA Art Project—the open-handed program for the support of artists in the Depression. Without it much good art and many good artists would have sunk without a trace along with a lot of bad art and bad artists who, though financially aided by the program, blessedly did.

Dorothy Miller, because she played a very substantial role in selecting what American artists would be exhibited at the Museum over many years, is looked upon by artists either as a benign goddess or as a disdainful one, depending on whether or not she smiled on their work and included them in her shows, which over many years attempted to show relatively unknown American artists and most particularly those who did not live and exhibit in New York. But if there were skirmishes they were minor ones—border incidents, one might call them—in the perpetual war between artists and museums which are punctuated by periods of peace and by love feasts.

Miss Miller first heard about the Museum of Modern Art when she was working in an apprentice class at the Newark (New Jersey) Museum. (It anticipated the museum course at the Fogg by a year.) She had graduated from Smith College in 1925, and she read an article about the new museum by Barr in a magazine called *Charm*, then published by Bamberger's department store in Newark. Barr's friend Katherine Gauss, also a Smith graduate, was a fledgling editor at *Charm*[4] and had asked him to write the article. (Many years later he said to a journalist who was reporting on the art world that as a young man "I didn't know any girl at Vassar and only one girl at Smith who would go to a gallery. And it's possible that she went only because I wanted to go." This Smith girl was Katherine Gauss.) Miss Miller determined to get a job at the Museum. Unlike Miss Courter, she did not go herself to apply, but sent a friend to investigate. There were no full-time jobs, but she was hired at a dollar an hour to work part-time for Holger Cahill on the catalogue he was preparing for the exhibition of *American Painting and Sculpture, 1862–1932.* "Eddie sold the trustees on a series of primitive shows," she says, "and in the spring of 1933 put on the Aztec, Mayan, etc., show *American Sources of Modern Art.* The trustees insisted on the title, though it didn't make much sense. I worked on this show for nothing. I had a marvelous time. It was great material."

This was during the time of Barr's absence in Europe, but when he came back he asked Miss Miller to work on the catalogue of the Lee Simonson theater exhibition, and she also helped Simonson install the show. Barr asked if she would like to go on working with the Museum, but she said that she had agreed to work with Cahill on a vast exhibition that he was gathering. It was called *The First Municipal Art Exhibition*, and it was held in 1934 at the RCA Building, which faced the plaza in Rockefeller Center, in space remodeled to the tune of $50,000 contributed by the Rockefellers.

It ran, however, headlong into a controversy that had the artists of New York in an uproar. The Rockefellers had commissioned Diego Rivera to paint a mural in Rockefeller Center, and Rivera had submitted sketches (now in the Museum's collection) for the 1,071 square feet which he was allotted. They had a theme—the emancipation of mankind through technology, which seemed right for the time and the place. The result, however, did not conform to the sketches, and, as Aline Saarinen reported, "Rivera apparently decided to bite the capitalist hand that was feeding him $21,500." The head of Lenin appeared

4 She later, as Katherine Gauss Jackson, became Book Review Editor of *Harper's Magazine*, a post she held from 1939 to 1969.

prominently in the fresco, and Nelson Rockefeller, as tactfully as he could, tried to suggest that perhaps this wasn't the most suitable figure for the site and the circumstances; Rivera, though he was a friend of Nelson's mother, who had been a patron of his for some time, stuck to his guns. The management of Rockefeller Center responded with weapons of its own. They hung canvas curtains in front of the mural and then proceeded to hack it off the wall. The artists of New York were shocked (and so, evidently, was young Rockefeller, who has often erroneously been blamed for what happened); so were the newspapers, even some of those that thought Rivera was in the wrong. The story broke in the papers on the very day that trucks were going out to collect pictures for the Municipal Art Exhibition. Half of the artists said they most certainly wouldn't show in Mr. Rockefeller's galleries, and it took a great deal of persuasion to convince some of them to return to the fold. Not all of them did.

The economic pressures of the Depression had driven a great many artists who heartily disliked each other's work and ideas more or less into each other's arms. "Suddenly there seems to be lots of art in America," Henry McBride wrote in the New York *Sun* on March 13, 1934. "One of the journalistic experts of the town describing the First Municipal Art Exhibition . . . called it 'a mile of art.' This is a careful bit of understatement. . . . I liked every bit of it, but I thought it about six miles long." It was New York's attempt to help its local painters and sculptors before the WPA project was organized, and it was held under the auspices of Mayor Fiorello La Guardia. All of the works were for sale. Here was a painting by Henry W. Watrous, the president of the National Academy, hanging between two "revolutionaries," John Marin and Arthur Dove. "It had always been thought," said McBride, "that blood would have to be shed before such a thing could happen." Nearby was Florine Stettheimer's big canvas "In Memory of P. T. Barnum." Miss Stettheimer was very much in the art news at the time as the designer of the sets and costumes for the Virgil Thomson–Gertrude Stein opera *Four Saints in Three Acts*, which had recently had its première at "Chick Austin's Museum" or just "at Chick's," as the Wadsworth Atheneum in Hartford was generally called by those who were (or wished to pass themselves off as being) sophisticated in such matters.

"One of the most puzzling items on display," McBride noted, "is a 'Mobile' by young Alexander Calder of Paris and New York. In it some globes are suspended on wires and there are other contraptions that suggest a wireless apparatus, or possibly a recording instrument for Professor Einstein. Many people will pass it right by, mistaking it for a heating device, or something of that sort; yet it was one of the first things sold, going to the Museum of Modern Art; and the purchase does great credit to the new museum, for the 'Mobile' is precisely the kind of exploring art that a modern museum should feature."

The exhibition was installed in thirty-one galleries with approximately 5,000 running feet of wall space (hence "the mile of art"), and works by about 500 artists added up to 1,500 items. The selection for the exhibition was made by the directors of the Whitney, the Metropolitan, the Brooklyn Museum, and the Modern, as well as the presidents of the National Academy, the American Society of Painters, Sculptors and Gravers, and Cahill. It was by all odds the biggest show of American contemporary art, let alone local art, that New York had ever seen. It did not retain this distinction for long.

When the work on this show was completed, Barr again asked Miss Miller to work for him on a catalogue, this time on the Bliss collection. Again she declined, as she had started working on the municipal art exhibition's successor, the Independents' show. It contained some 5,000 pictures and objects by anyone who wanted to pay the registration fee of $2.00. "What a mess!" Miss Miller says. There was no selection committee and no jury. "But John Sloan was still president [of the Society of Independent Artists], and Kuniyoshi and all the boys were there. We called this one *Five Miles of Art*." It was when this was over that Miss Miller formally applied to Barr for a job. He seemed rather distracted and faraway, as he sometimes did, but when his mind came back to Miss Miller's question he said that he would ask the trustees if he could have an assistant. After a few weeks Dorothy Miller found herself sharing the penthouse at 11 West 53rd Street with Iris Barry and several stacks of books.

The autumn of 1934, when Dorothy Miller joined the staff, was one of those not infrequent moments in the Museum's history when it was pleased "to point with pride" at itself and its accomplishments. It was now ready to celebrate its fifth birthday, which it did with a show called *Fifth Anniversary Exhibition—Modern Works of Art*. It included some 218 works (153 paintings from Cézanne to Grant Wood; 34 sculptures and constructions, and 31 examples of architecture and industrial arts), and an impressive catalogue was produced for the occasion. The Museum had come a remarkably long way since the day in May 1929 when "the Ladies" invited Mr. Goodyear to lunch and asked him to form a committee to start a modern museum. It had opened its doors in the teeth of a financial gale and had sped boldly ahead while others were trimming their sails. It had been both buffeted and supported by criticism and had enjoyed the clamor. By the end of 1934 the Museum was sending its *Bulletin* and other publications to 1,100 members (in 1970 it had more than thirty-five times that many). It had put on thirty-five exhibitions and it had raised $600,000 to "qualify for" the bequest of the Bliss collection and so to establish itself firmly as a museum and not just a gallery of passing shows. "On the whole," Goodyear wrote in the *Bulletin* for December 1934, "We may point with pride. . . ."

The Depression had not, in fact, done badly by the arts, though it had not by the end of 1934 done well by the artists. In October 1932, one of the worst of the bad years, the *Literary Digest* in a piece captioned "Art Blooms in Summer" remarked that "The effect of the Depression on art is paradoxical" and, quoting *Art News*, said, "New York and its environs have witnessed more exhibition activity during the past summer than in many years." The Whitney Museum, which frequently closed in the summer, stayed open. The Metropolitan put on a special show called *Taste of Today*, and "As statistical confirmation of this increased art interest during the dog days, the Museum of Modern Art informs us that its daily average attendance was more than double that of the two previous summers." The very fact that exhibitions were as cheap a form of entertainment as anyone could find (there were no admission charges in 1932) unquestionably contributed to the crowds; so, as *Art News* pointed out, did the fact that many people who would have gone to Europe could not afford to; they stayed home for their culture. These were the days, too, of the inexpensive concerts in the Lewisohn Stadium at the City College and free concerts in many city parks. It would never have occurred to anyone to call New York or any other American city "Fun City" in those dark days, but the days and evenings were not without their compensations. It was even safe to stroll in the parks.

In November of 1934 the Museum of Modern Art added a slight extra fillip to the cultural scene (and a good deal of rather rude gaiety to the daily press) by inviting Gertrude Stein to lecture on Picasso to its members at the Colony Club. The papers referred to her as "the most talked-about but least read of American authors" (probably with not a little justification) and captioned their stories with such headlines as "Gertrude Stein Avers an Oil Painting Is an Oil Painting" and "Stein, Stein, Stein Talks, Talks, Talks." It was inevitable, too, that in the days of Rudy Vallee's fame as a crooner some paper would use the headline "The Stein Song." It was the Sarasota (Florida) *Tribune* that did.

The problem of what was modern and what was "modern" had not, however, been resolved, and the Museum's *Bulletin* published a short essay by Barr in its May 1934 issue which undertook to throw some light on this mystifying question. None of the definitions which had been valid when Cubism, for example, was new seemed to apply in the age of Surrealism, he noted, as none of the definitions of modern by Ruskin when he defended Turner and Holman Hunt in the 1850s as "modern painters" could apply to the Cubists.

Barr concluded his essay or, perhaps more accurately, brought it to an end thus:

> Since the war, art has become an affair of immense and confusing variety, of obscurities and contradictions, of the emergence of new principles and the renascence of old ones. . . . The truth is that modern art cannot be defined with any degree of finality either in time or in character and any attempt to do so implies a blind faith, insufficient knowledge, or an academic lack of realism.

A few months later Barr was a member of the prize jury for the 1934 Carnegie International Exhibition in Pittsburgh, which in those days annually attracted a great deal of attention, especially if the prize happened to go to an American artist. A reporter for the Associated Press asked the three jurors—Elizabeth Luther Cary, for many years a New York art critic, Gifford Beal, a painter and member of the National Academy, and Barr—"what they expected to find in the prize picture."

"Merit," said Miss Cary.

"Workmanship and intelligence," said Mr. Beal.

"I have no beliefs," said Mr. Barr.

One of the reporters who were present at the interview pressed him further and asked, "But how are you going to judge these pictures?"

"By looking at them," Barr replied.

*The Museum of Modern Art receives more
publicity than any museum in the world.*
A MUSEUM STAFF REPORT, 1933

Chapter **VIII** *The Bittersweet Taste
of Fame*

Modesty may have been a characteristic of a number of the persons
important to the Museum of Modern Art in its early days—Abby
Rockefeller and Lizzie Bliss, for example—but the same cannot be said
of the institution itself then or, indeed, now. Part of its determined
function has been since the start to shake the public out of its lethargy
toward the arts of its own day, and the Museum's "product," as you
might call it, has consistently had built-in shock value. "You call that
art!" the public says (not asks), and the Museum replies in ringing
tones, "Yes, we call that art!" Every time the Museum has hung an
abstract picture upside down by mistake, which it inevitably has now
and then, the newspapers have had a field day with the notion shared
by the public that neither the Museum nor the artist "knows which
end is up." At least once the Museum contributed to this belief in its
own publication, *The Museum of Modern Art Bulletin,* by printing a
photograph of "Abstract Portrait of Marcel Duchamp" by Katherine S. Dreier upside down, and took occasion to correct the error
by printing it right side up in the next issue. This unintentional frivol-
ity, however, has been entirely inconsequential compared with the
publicity that the Museum has sought with concerted efforts from
the day when Crowninshield gave a lunch party for the press before
the Museum opened for the first time.

In many respects the Museum is a public-relations organization just as surely as is any commercial "PR" firm: it is concerned with making the public aware of a product and leading the public to accept its judgment and follow its taste. When its policies, its judgments, its taste have been attacked in the press, it has very frequently sought means of rejoinder, ways of answering back. It has always been touchy (though it used to be touchier in its earlier days than it is now) [1] and had a way of making it seem as though it were being picked on by oafs and Philistines. Its spirit was a missionary spirit; it believed that it had "the word"; and that, since the word came to it by something close to (if not identical with) divine revelation, there was something immoral about disputing it. It would be a mistake to underestimate the value to the Museum (and in many respects to the public) of this solemn belief in its own rightness, even when the belief slipped over into self-righteousness as it not infrequently did. It was the missionary zeal, its conviction that it was right and that right must prevail, that made the Museum not only infuriating to many but surely one of the most remarkable cultural institutions, one of the most influential, and, though there are those who would call it a sacred cow, one of the most durable idols of our iconoclastic age.

It is well to remember that the Museum grew up in a time of "causes." The crash which happened a few days before the Museum opened was spectacular if horrifying, but the doldrums which followed it were debilitating and angering, and the ache of poverty and unemployment or just of scrimping did not seem to yield to the medicines that Roosevelt and his New Deal concocted and tried to administer. Adult readers attempted to escape by the hundreds of thousands into the romantic pages of *Anthony Adverse*, a swashbuckling novel of the Napoleonic era by Hervey Allen. The young frantically danced the Lindy Hop and the Big Apple and swarmed to "battles of swing" fought out, among juvenile screams of delight, by Benny Goodman and "Satchmo" Armstrong, by Gene Krupa and by the big bands of Tommy Dorsey, "Duke" Ellington, and Artie Shaw. Many of the intellectual young turned sharp left politically and some became card-carrying Communists, and a great many more proudly called themselves liberals and supported the Spanish Republicans against Franco, raised money to buy them ambulances and to hire pilots. To conservatives they were known as "parlor pinks." A relative few turned sharp right, as Johnson and Blackburn did. In the comfortable but pinched middle, ladies read *The Green Light* by Lloyd C. Douglas and thought

[1] It had more reason to be. It was part of a genuine *avant-garde* in those days.

solemn thoughts about cozy religion, and the men read Dale Carnegie's *How to Win Friends and Influence People*, hoping to raise their salaries if, indeed, they were lucky enough to have any. A great many people believed that there was something radically wrong with a society in which there were such inequities of wealth, such great resources and yet such great unemployment, and they sought ways out of this dilemma, usually not by radical means but by organizations—by labor unions, by an array of government bureaus or government-administered schemes—WPA, NRA, AAA, FSA, etc., etc., called by the cynical "alphabet soup." Some flirted, but not for long, with a scheme called Technocracy, which was going to cure the world's evils with a new price system based on energy. "Erg" (now found only in crossword puzzles) was a word on the lips of bankers and taxi drivers, parlor economists and editorial writers. It was a straw, and straws were something to grasp at.

It was in this atmosphere that the Museum of Modern Art was passing its infancy and childhood. If the new in art was a blow for freedom from outworn ideas, if turning the old aesthetic values upside down would reveal the soggy bottom of the conventions which had made such a mess of art as well as of society, so much the better. Some of the American artists of the '30s took the aesthetic path to salvation, basing their revolt on the lessons taught some years before by Picasso and Matisse and Braque; some took the road of social protest and followed men like Diego Rivera and Orozco, political as well as artistic revolutionaries of Mexico; some sought a new kind of reality in fantasy, in Freud, and in satire. The Museum, in an orderly, methodical, and thoroughly scholarly manner (the manner of Alfred Barr, that is), exposed all of these revolts one after another to the public, and the public that was interested, that tiny but often articulate segment, made the Museum one of its causes.

The Museum had tasted printer's ink early and found it delicious. In May 1930 the weekly humor magazine *Life* (whose title was bought a few years later by Henry Luce for Time Inc.) published an issue called "The Modern Art Number." On its cover was a parody of a Picasso portrait of a woman, and inside were cartoon travesties of modern painting and sculpture. "Not yet a year old," Goodyear gleefully wrote in his book, "and the leading comic weekly thought our field worthy of a special number." He called it "a perfect tribute."

In 1931 the Museum took on a public-relations firm (in those days they were generally called, less elegantly but more accurately, "press agents"). It was the Phoenix News Publicity Bureau, and it reported "at the end of its year's work that 1,694 clippings had been assembled from 626 newspapers and 68 magazines." "Special emphasis," Alan Blackburn wrote in a report to the trustees, "was placed on developing a national distribution of news." But it was decided to fire the press agent and take on a new member of the staff to do the job. In the fall of 1933 Blackburn reported that "The Museum of Modern Art receives more publicity than any other Museum in the world," and he explained why:

> Because of its many departments, the Museum's news appears in practically every section of the newspaper from real estate to editorial. Museum releases have appeared in magazines like *Skyscraper Management* and *Railroad Weekly*. In addition to a large volume of local New York publicity, the Museum has tripled its national distribution and doubled its foreign distribution.

That spring the Museum had tried a publicity stunt that was not only a failure but an embarrassment. In Barr's absence in Europe, Samuel A. Lewisohn, at that time Secretary of the Board of Trustees, arranged an exhibition of paintings that Maurice Sterne had made in Bali and other islands in the South Pacific. Someone (no one cares to remember who) thought it would be a splendid idea to have Sterne's wife dance in front of the paintings in native costume for the benefit of newsreel cameras. The movie-makers thought this a bonanza, but when the cameramen arrived at 11 West 53rd Street some of the more conservative members of the staff thought it a dreadful and shaming thing to have happen in the Museum, and an argument broke out. It was "an undignified argument," as a journalist described it in the *Saturday Evening Post,* and "the cameramen departed in a nasty mood without any pictures that they could use."

It may well have been the sobering effect of this unpleasant scene that prompted Goodyear and Blackburn, before Barr got back from Europe, to employ Sarah Newmeyer to organize a Publicity Department for the Museum. She arrived, redheaded and exploding with ideas, in August 1933. She was no neophyte. She had worked in Cleveland as the secretary of an eccentric manufacturer who assigned numbers to his friends and associates and even to his wife and children and referred to them by number, not by name. She had written sentimental fiction for popular magazines and struggled with plays for Broadway. She was on the West Coast writing for a living when the Museum offered her a job, and the prospect of steady work in a lively young institution attracted her. On her way to New York she stopped for a few days in Chicago (there was no through train from coast to coast) and went to look at the World's Fair, an exposition which gave a great many Americans their first glimpse of what was new in architecture. There she saw Whistler's "Mother," which the Museum of Modern Art had persuaded the Louvre to lend for an exhibition in New York and for a subsequent tour of the country. It was with schemes for capitalizing on "Mother" that Miss Newmeyer arrived at the Museum.

The visit of "Mother" to America was the result of delicate negotiations between Goodyear and the officials of Les Musées de France, the official bureaucracy which has all the museums of France under its aegis. The occasion for the request was an exhibition of *American Painting and Sculpture, 1862–1932* that the Museum of Modern Art planned for the fall of 1932. The painting, originally called by Whistler "Arrangement in Gray and Black, No. 1," was not only the best-known painting by any American artist, but in the eyes of the Museum it was a moral and aesthetic object lesson to all Americans. Was it not shocking that when it had been offered for sale in America fifty years earlier this masterpiece, this symbol of motherhood, could not find a buyer with the $1,000 that was asked for it by the artist, and that the French government had picked it up for a mere $400 in 1889? At first it was stipulated that the picture would be lent on the agreement that the Museum of Modern Art insure it for $1,000,000, which certainly did its publicity value no disfavor, but the Louvre came down in its price and agreed, as Goodyear has recorded, "that half that amount would be sufficient." A certain inevitable official pomp attended the gesture: "As was rather solemnly announced at the time, the loan was regarded 'as an act of international good will on the part of the French government and a reaffirmation of the artistic solidarity of France and the United States.' "

Suddenly attendance at the Museum leaped to a figure that nearly doubled the number who had come to any exhibition it had held thus far. More than 102,000 people pressed into the newly opened galleries, three times as many as had come to the International Style show, more than six times as many as saw the murals that caused such consternation. But when Sarah Newmeyer saw the painting at the Chicago fair, she was appalled to discover no mention of the Museum's having brought it to America, a situation which caused the press-agent blood in her veins to boil. "By the time I hit New York," she is reported to have said, "I was hopping mad. The first thing I did was to get 'Mother' back in the fold."

She did this by sending press releases to newspapers everywhere in the country saying that "Mother's" next stop would be the Cleveland Museum and that she would not have been about to arrive there if the Museum of Modern Art had not engaged in delicate negotiations with the Louvre. She explained that the Louvre valued the painting at a million dollars; she did not say that it had relented on the insurance and came down to half of that. She arranged to have the picture photographed in each city in which it was shown, along with a front page of the paper on which there was a story telling of its arrival; these she sent to the Louvre as proof that the painting was in good condition. This evidently appealed to the local editors, and they were glad to cooperate with front-page stories. Governors and mayors were on hand to greet the painting and get their pictures taken with it in city after city. The picture was "guarded by armored cars, motorcycle police, or a troop of cavalry." In Boston the Museum of Fine Arts put on extra guards, two police dogs, to make sure that thieves did not steal "Mother" in the night. (It is not quite clear what a thief would have done to dispose profitably of such a large and totally familiar painting, but the dogs made a good story. Famous paintings were rarely if ever held for ransom in those days, as they occasionally have been in recent years.)

In all it was estimated that two million persons went to museums to see Whistler's "Mother," though a press agent's figures are, like his claims of quality, never to be taken literally. It is undeniable, however, that the U.S. Post Office issued a three-cent stamp (then sufficient for a first-class letter) with Whistler's "Mother" on it. Whistler's composition, it appeared, was not good enough for them, and they were persuaded by the florists' lobby to place a bunch of flowers in a vase at the lady's feet. Alfred Barr was infuriated by this outrage to an artist's integrity and sent off a characteristically burning letter to the Postmaster General.

On its way back to Paris the painting appeared again at the Museum of Modern Art for just four days in May 1934. Miss Newmeyer was determined to get a final splurge of publicity for the Museum, and she managed with considerable difficulty to get Mrs. James Roosevelt, the President's mother, to pose at the Museum with the painting. Mrs. Roosevelt, who was reluctant to come to the Museum at all, was finally persuaded to "unveil" the painting which had been unveiled a dozen or more times by then, but she would not pose with it alone. She said it would be "too pretentious," and insisted that two men pose with her. "It was too bad," Miss Newmeyer told a reporter. "The Number One Mother of the United States with the Number One Mother of the world of art. What a natural that would have been!"

Allen Porter, who worked with Sarah Newmeyer for many years as editor of the *Bulletin* and as Assistant Secretary of the Museum (he turned down the job of Secretary), and who became known as "Mr. Museum," has said of her: "She was a real zany, but she was a good press woman because she would never take 'no.' The secretary of the *Trib*'s editor would say he was busy and when she looked up Sarah was in his office. They were all scared of her. Like a lot of those girls, she got too big for her buttons."

But it was not until she had been there for fifteen years that the Museum decided that it could get along better without her than with her. The triumphant moment of her career, or so she thought it to be, came in 1935, about eighteen months after the Whistler went back to the Louvre. The story, however, is certainly not Sarah Newmeyer's but Alfred Barr's.

Fifteen years before the Museum put on its one-man exhibition of van Gogh, which it did in November 1935, the Montross Gallery, a New York dealer, had shown thirty-two van Gogh oils and thirty-five drawings, watercolors, and lithographs. The exhibition lasted for three weeks, and, as Frank Crowninshield wrote many years later, "not one single item among them found a purchaser, notwithstanding the fact that the fame of the painter had been greatly enhanced during the thirty years following his death." [2] The Museum had, of course, included twenty-five paintings by him and a watercolor, a drawing, and a gouache in its first exhibition, and his work was by no means unknown to anyone who had even a casual interest in art in New York. It was in March 1935 that the trustees of the Museum gave Barr a green light to arrange a van Gogh exhibition.

The Advisory Committee, always, it seemed, more eager to look ahead than look back, took prompt and energetic exception to the plan, and it sent a formal and strongly worded resolution to the trustees:

Resolved: That the van Gogh exhibition be abandoned because:
1. van Gogh was well represented at the first Museum show in 1929.
2. van Gogh died 45 years ago and his influence on contemporary painting has waned.
3. There is such a similarity of impulse behind van Gogh's

2 From a preface to a catalogue of a Parke-Bernet sale of paintings from the collections of James W. Barney and Frank Crowninshield, October 26, 1944.

painting that a one man show would prove less interesting than can now be imagined.

4. The Museum is much criticized for not being up to date, and a van Gogh show would increase this criticism.

5. A van Gogh show would be excessively expensive.

The trustees, as usual, ignored the Advisory Committee, and late in May Barr sailed for Europe with his wife to see what paintings and drawings could be borrowed from the Kröller-Müller Foundation, which was then situated near The Hague, and from the engineer V. W. van Gogh, who was the painter's nephew. There were some 300 paintings by van Gogh in the Kröller-Müller collection, and Barr spent weeks sifting from them what he wanted to borrow. In July Goodyear turned up in The Hague, and with the help of Grenville T. Emmet, the United States Minister to Holland, an agreement was concluded. Initially the exhibition had been expected to cost $7,146.67 for shipping, insurance in transport, packing, collecting, and five months of insurance in America. This was based on borrowing forty oils and fifty watercolors and drawings with a value of $40,000 on each of the paintings and $2,000 on each drawing and watercolor.[3] The agreement which was finally made came to a higher figure. It was based on a cost to the Museum, including everything, of $13,750. The Museum, however, was not in this deal by itself; three other museums had agreed to put up a total of $5,250, and Goodyear expected to take in about $5,000 from the admissions which would be charged during the eight weeks when the pictures would be on show at 11 West 53rd Street before going on the road to Boston, Cleveland, and San Francisco.

The response was, quite literally, overwhelming, and for this Sarah Newmeyer is due a share of the credit. The exhibition had the Museum almost entirely to itself. There were thirty oils and thirty-five drawings from the Kröller-Müller, thirteen oils and six drawings from V. W. van Gogh, and twenty-three oils and nineteen drawings from other collectors, including five of the trustees—Clark, Goodyear, Mrs. Rockefeller, Mrs. Sullivan, and Sachs. There was an excellent catalogue (the first printing of 4,000 copies was soon exhausted), the text of which consisted almost entirely of excerpts from van Gogh's letters, supplemented by a chronology of the artist's life, a list of the books he had read and from which he quoted in his letters, and, as a dig at New

3 This estimate, undated, is in the P. J. Sachs file for 1936 in the Fogg Museum archives.

York, a list of American museums in whose collections his work was included. There were six of them; none was in New York.[4]

According to Roger Butterfield, who wrote an article called "The Museum and the Redhead" for the *Saturday Evening Post* in 1947, Miss Newmeyer said to him, "We played the van Gogh show like a polo game—dribbled the ball down the field first, and then, bang, right between the goal posts! It was a honey, if I do say so myself."

As soon as Barr departed for The Hague, she put out a release to the newspapers saying that he was to find van Goghs that had never been seen in America, and she embellished it with a sentimental account of van Gogh's life. She played down the incident of his cutting off his ear and sending it to a prostitute, but the newspapers did not. "I wanted to emphasize his art," she told Butterfield. "You can go all through my releases and you won't find a word about van Gogh's ear. That's one they can't pin on me." By the time the exhibition opened in November the press coverage had already made it famous and nearly every suburban housewife knew about van Gogh's ear.

The crowds that turned up at the Museum were so great that it was necessary to call the police to keep the lines in order. They stretched down 53rd Street past the side of St. Thomas' Church, up Fifth Avenue to 54th Street, and around that corner. The Fifth Avenue Association, a group of merchants that attempts to keep Fifth Avenue from the tarnishes of honky-tonk and forbids signs that project over the sidewalk, was furious that the Museum hung a banner from its façade announcing the exhibition. The banner was not, however, within 100 feet of the Avenue, and was therefore outside the Association's jurisdiction. In the last week of the show the building got so dense with art-lovers and curiosity-seekers that as three people emerged from the door of the Museum just three more were allowed by the police to take their places. The exhibition was open in New York for sixty-two days and the attendance exceeded even that which came to see Whistler's "Mother" and her attendant American paintings; 123,339 visitors were clicked in on the counters in the hands of the guards at the door, and more than $20,000 was collected in admission fees at twenty-five cents a head. The show was even more successful in San Francisco than in New York. According to Goodyear, "227,540 persons crowded the galleries of the Palace of the Legion of Honor, and over $30,000 in admission fees were paid in the first week." People came

4 Barr later corrected this statement. There was, he found, a watercolor in the Metropolitan. The six museums were the Albright Gallery in Buffalo, the Phillips Gallery in Washington, the Chicago Art Institute, the Toledo Museum, the Detroit Art Institute, and the Kansas City Museum.

from as far away as 900 miles in trains marked "Van Gogh Special."
By the time the exhibition had gone to other museums (fifteen other
cities wanted the exhibition, but, Goodyear said "time did not permit") the total attendance was 878,709. Then in late January of 1937
the pictures came back to New York and were shown at the Museum
for just two weeks, and 19,002 more persons came to see them.

It is unlikely—indeed, inconceivable—that any other art exhibition
has ever had such an immediate impact on the public taste as the van
Gogh show. The Armory Show of 1913 may have produced more lines
of newspaper and magazine coverage, but whereas most of the comment on the Armory Show was vituperative or caustic or wisecrack-
ing, the reception of the van Gogh show was open-armed. Here were
vibrant color and vigorous drawing which nearly everyone, except
Royal Cortissoz of the *Herald Tribune*, could understand, and even
someone who could not understand it could enjoy it. Store windows
on Fifth Avenue were filled with ladies' dresses in van Gogh colors,
displayed in front of color reproductions of his paintings. His sun-
flowers bloomed on shower curtains, on scarves, on tablecloths and
bathmats and ashtrays. It was as though in the depths of the Depression, as those days were called, a bright and cheerful light had been let
in. No matter that it came from a dark soul and an often deranged
mind. Wasn't everybody's soul feeling somewhat dark and his mind
somewhat off its track then? Or so people said, or felt like saying.
Empathy certainly had something to do with the success in 1935 of the
artist who had died in 1890 having sold in his lifetime $109 worth of
his art.

The critical success of the exhibition matched its popular success.
Superlatives blossomed in newspapers and magazines as splendid as the
adjectives on movie-palace marquees. "Superb," said the *New York
Times*. "Fraught with wonder," said *Art News*. "The most thorough,
the most exemplary, and the most stimulating exhibition of modern
art it has yet put on," said *The New Yorker*. "Magnificent," said the
Boston *Transcript*. In the *Herald Tribune* Cortissoz muttered, "It is
enough to keep him in honorable memory. To hail him as a great
artist is sheer absurdity."

Sarah Newmeyer gave Roger Butterfield a "poem" by one of the
night watchmen at the Museum. His name was James Ryan and he
wrote:

> *Poor Vincent van Gogh*
> *Was certainly slow,*
> *To sell his work so cheap.*

Were he alive today
He'd make it pay;
A fortune in dollars he'd reap.

But he had nothing in Life
But sorrow and strife;
His days were often sad.
He got no credit
And little merit.
It was enough to drive him mad.

Now, when he is dead,
His fame, it has spread
To different parts of the world.
At the Museum of Art
It got a good start;
His name on a flag is unfurled.

After the closing of the van Gogh exhibition, things at the Museum quieted down for a few months, but only for a few months. There was another explosive exhibition simmering on the Museum's back burner. In the intervening quiet months Ernestine Fantl, by then Curator of the Department of Architecture and Design, put on a show of advertising posters by the remarkable French designer Cassandre, whose witty and stylish and thoroughly modern Dubonnet advertisements will be remembered by anyone who was in France in the 1930s or, indeed, several decades later.[5] They had staying power, for the little man in his bowler holding his glass of red apéritif had, as Miss Fantl said in the catalogue of the show, "the universal appeal of Mickey Mouse." The exhibition unquestionably had a salutary though, from the Museum's point of view, all too minor effect on American poster design, but very few persons bothered to come to see it.

The same was true of two other exhibitions in the early months of 1936. They were on view at the same time as the Cassandre show and they were *New Acquisitions: The Collection of Mrs. John D. Rockefeller, Jr.* and *The Architecture of Henry Hobson Richardson.* Mrs. Rockefeller in 1935 had given the Museum 36 oils and 105 watercolors and pastels, nearly all by American artists and mostly by artists who were still living. The Richardson show was the work of Philip John-

5 In the autumn of 1971 there was a small retrospective exhibition of some of the posters that were in the original show and are owned by the Museum.

son, once again in the Museum's fold after his escapade in politics, and Henry-Russell Hitchcock. According to Johnson, this exhibition, like the one in which he had compared Art Nouveau objects with what was brand new, went over "like a lead balloon." Philip Goodwin, a distinguished architect and a member of the Board of Trustees of the Museum, said to Johnson, "What do you want to show Richardson for? This is the kind of stuff I was turning my back on forty years ago." Goodwin was of exactly the right generation to have wanted to break away from the influence of Richardson, but the time had come by the 1930s when the bright young men would inevitably rediscover the work of this physically tremendous and tremendously gifted and influential man who had dominated American architecture in the 1880s. If the show at the Museum did little for the popular reputation of the architect who designed Trinity Church in Boston and the City Hall in Albany and dozens of "Richardsonian" houses, libraries, and railroad stations, the publication by the Museum of Hitchcock's monumental book on Richardson [6] revived and established his reputation as an American genius once and for all. It also established Hitchcock's reputation as an architectural historian beyond any question of doubt.

Fewer than 10,000 people came to look at these three exhibitions, very nearly an all-time low for attendance in the Museum's first ten years.

One would have thought that by 1936, twenty-three years after the Armory Show, even if the public did not like Cubism and abstract art, it at least would not have been infuriated by them. The fact of the matter, however, seems to be that nearly sixty years after the Armory Show most people are no more convinced, or perhaps one should say no more acquiescent, than they were then. They will not even notice its influence on advertising and packaging, so used are they to it, but they most certainly would not hang it on their walls at home or put non-representational little sculptures on their living-room tables or mantelpieces.

On March 3, 1936, the *New York Times*, under Edward Alden Jewell's byline, ran a full-column story with the lead: "The most elaborate, complex, and in a sense at least, the most bewildering exhibition arranged thus far in the career of the Museum of Modern Art was opened privately with a reception last evening." The show was called *Cubism and Abstract Art* and it occupied all four floors of the Mu-

6 Henry-Russell Hitchcock, *The Architecture of H. H. Richardson and His Times* (Museum of Modern Art, New York, 1936). Reprinted in paperback by MIT Press (Cambridge, Mass., 1966).

seum's gallery space. On the façade of the building a Calder "mobile" fluttered from a flagpole over the entrance. It was a show after Barr's own heart. It included not just paintings and sculpture but "drawings, prints, constructions, architecture, furniture, rugs, theatre design, the movies, typography and photography." Jewell found it a "maze" and a "journey through strange worlds," but he was obviously fascinated and he was grateful to discover that there was a historically planned sequence for him to follow, starting with known quantities like Gauguin and van Gogh before slipping into Matisse and Picasso, Franz Marc, Feininger, and Kandinsky. "Whether the exhibition as a whole," he wrote, "may be said to pursue a sequence as sharply defined and as taut as this is open to question." In any event the show, he believed with justification, was a monumental undertaking and the juxtapositions of kinds of art (he called them "consanguineous expressions") were "brilliant." It would not surprise him in the least if "This effort . . . may send Barr and his associates to beds of complete exhaustion for a month or more," and he added, "but while they lie unconscious we may enjoy the fruits of such protensive toil."

According to Dorothy Miller, looking back thirty-five years, the show was put together "in no time flat." "Alfred had it all in his head," she says. "I don't actually know how long it took to borrow the stuff, but I do remember Alfred's laying out the catalogue on the living-room floor of their apartment. He would never let that catalogue be reprinted when it sold out; he thought it was a hasty job, though, of course, it was the only thing of its kind then." [7]

The exhibition was held up for a week while Goodyear wrangled with the United States Customs officials over what he estimated to be $100,000 worth of abstract sculpture from Europe. According to Paragraph 1807 of the Tariff Act and a definition made in 1930, sculpture in order to be eligible for importation as art rather than as raw material or as utilitarian objects (on which there was a 40 percent duty based on the consigner's valuation), had to be "imitations of natural objects, chiefly of the human form . . . in their true proportion of length, breadth and thickness." There were nineteen pieces which Barr had borrowed that the men in the customs house could not measure properly or put heads or tails to—three each by Giacometti, Laurens, Vantongerloo, and Duchamp-Villon, two by Boccioni, and one each by Arp, Moore, Gonzales, Nicholson, and Miró. This was not the Museum's first run-in with the Customs. In May of the preceding

---

7 Like the Museum *Bulletins* this catalogue has been reproduced for the Museum by Arno, New York, and is again available.

year the Museum had put up a show of *African Negro Art* and, as the
Bulletin explained,

> Many objects . . . had been refused free entrance because it was
> impossible to prove that certain sculptures were not more than
> second replicas, or because the artist's signature could not be pro-
> duced, or because no date of manufacture could be found, or be-
> cause ancient bells, drums, spoons, necklaces, fans, stools and
> headrests were considered by the examiners to be objects of utility
> and not works of art. As a result the Museum was forced to give
> bond, the premium on which amounted to $700.[8]

The press had a delightful time with the sculpture that the Customs
said was not sculpture at all, and Sarah Newmeyer must have been
delighted as the clippings came pouring in from cities and towns all
over America showing the Boccioni "Unique Forms of Continuity in
Space" and an abstract head in wood and plaster with the caption
"Would You Call These Things Art?" What might be called the more
sophisticated daily press took the exhibition in stride if not always
with complete approval. Some of the diehards, like Thomas Craven,
muttered about "the toys" that the Museum was calling sculpture
and an arm of the government was not. The Associated Press put
a story on the wire on what it called "the Museum of Modern Art's
latest successful bid for crowded galleries," but devoted a good portion
of the piece to quotations from Barr explaining why "abstract art
today needs no defense." "It has become one of the many ways to
paint or carve or model," he said, though he cautioned, "It is not yet a
kind of art which people like without study and some sacrifice of
prejudice."

Quite probably the most significant reaction to the exhibition was
what happened in the commercial art galleries in New York. The van
Gogh show had had an immediate and highly visible effect on commercial tastemaking, on drygoods and fashions and crockery. It had
"over-popularized" in a manner that any committed highbrow would
find disgusting the work of a serious man who deserved better of posterity. The commercial reaction to the *Cubism and Abstract Art* exhibition was of a very different nature—of a nature, indeed, which the
Museum had not evoked before but which was in years to come the
reason for its being called "the Bourse of the modern art market." For
the first time the galleries rode on its coattails and held exhibitions

8 *The Bulletin of the Museum of Modern Art*, Vol. 3, No. 5 (April 1936),
discusses the Museum's encounters with the Customs at some length.

that were intended to capitalize on the taste and reputation of the Museum. One could go straight from the Museum to the Reinhardt Gallery a few blocks away and look at a group of works by American artists who called themselves "Concretionists," although "Abstractionists," the *Times* said, would have suited them as well. They were George L. K. Morris, John Ferren, Charles G. Shaw, Charles Biderman, and Alexander Calder. At the René Gimpel Gallery there was a show of work by Emmanuel Gondouin ("cubistic and abstract paintings") while the Squibb Building Galleries were showing Hilaire Hiler and Carl Holty. Only the Julien Levy Gallery and Pierre Matisse seemed to be anticipating the Museum at that moment. Levy was showing the American Surrealist Walter Quirt (he had already exhibited Dali several years before); the Matisse Gallery was where de Chirico, Miró, and the young Mr. Calder could be seen. Surrealism was standing in line to make its debut at the Museum just a few months later.

Ten days after the Museum's *Cubism and Abstract Art* show opened, Henry McBride looked about him at what else was going on and in his column in the *Sun* said: "Do you begin to see glimmerings of a rapport between the mental states of these artists and the mental state of society in general?

> You know what they all say about modern life, don't you? And about modern civilization, too? It has a familiar echo, has it not, to just what the enemies of these new artists say about them? As though the poor artists could help being like the times they live in! Why blame the artists for that! What had they to do with making the world the way it is at present? I ask you!

There were not many people who thought that it was the function of the artist to represent the current chaos by being himself chaotic. The visual arts were, in the opinion of most Americans, meant to be a relief from what bothered them, an escape into pleasant sentiments or sensualities, into sunlit meadows or the floors of forests mottled with sunshine, or into tufted boudoirs. Art was meant to dignify toil and idealize virtue, to record the features of man or, better, to improve on them; or it was meant to amuse, to titillate, to evoke nostalgia. It could be legitimately awe-inspiring, but religious art had come on hard times and had turned mawkish, for the most part. What could these people find for themselves in distortions, in what looked like arbitrary ugliness, in base caricature? The fact that very few people giggled at it had some significance. It was not really a laughing matter (though they made jokes about it and still do); it was infuriating. It was an

insult, and its perpetrators were called crazy and their work was compared to the rantings of diseased minds. It cannot be accurately recorded that hoards of scoffers or enthusiasts or curiosity-seekers came
to look at the exhibition. About 125,000 had come to see the van Gogh;
fewer than a quarter of that number, about 30,000, came to contem-
plate (or cast an eye over) the work of the Cubists and the Abstractionists. Henry McBride's comment on the state of the world probably
escaped the notice of all but a few conscientious readers of art news.
It recalls, however, a remark made twenty-three years earlier by a
banker, James A. Stillman, who had been shown around the Armory
Show by the sculptor Rudolf Evans. "Something is wrong with the
world," he said. "These men know."

There was a still ruder shock to come, and this time it evoked a considerable amount of merriment, much of it not only good-humored
but somewhat in the spirit of the matter at hand. Figuratively speaking,
Barr was conducting a public course in the history of the modern
movement, and his blackboard (or, possibly more accurately, projection screen) was the Museum. One might even go so far as to say that
what he was using is what has come to be called in recent years "multi-
media" techniques: he had as many projectors as there were galleries
and as many media as there were ways of making an object. Having
brought his "class" (anybody could qualify; this was not Wellesley
but New York City and beyond) from Corot and Daumier in the mid-
nineteenth century, through the Post-Impressionists, to the Fauves and
the Cubists and Abstractionists, he had prepared them for the Dadaists,
the Surrealists, and other Fantasists.

He gave the public very little time to digest abstraction or to collect
its wits before, in a manner of speaking, he dropped a poached egg in
its lap. The *Abstract* show closed in late April and *Fantastic Art, Dada,
and Surrealism* opened in early December. In the meanwhile there had
been a number of small exhibitions. Monroe Wheeler, not at that time
a member of the staff, had been a "guest director" and put on a handsome, influential show called *Modern Painters and Sculptors as Illustrators*. It had, Wheeler says, "considerable reverberations. It was
scheduled for six weeks in the spring, and it was so successful that they
continued it all through the summer." Serious book illustration was
considered *infra dig* by most American artists in the 1930s; the same
was demonstrated to be not true in Europe, where Picasso, Matisse,
Rouault, Gris, Braque, Maillol, and many others did drawings for

elegant small and expensive editions. During one week of the summer while the *Illustrators* were on view, so also were Edward Steichen's hybrid delphiniums for reasons which only the trustees of the Museum of Modern Art could possibly conceive of, even if they could not explain them. Steichen was a friend, an influence in the art world, a master photographer, and, presumably, he wanted more people to admire his hobby than he could entertain at his place in Connecticut. His friends at the Museum obliged him. (This was not Barr's doing; he was in Europe at the time.) To the best of my knowledge, this is the only occasion on which the Museum acted as though it were a branch of the Garden Clubs of America. Also during the summer there was an exhibition of *A Private Collection on Loan.* The printed record merely records the lender as "anonymous," but this sort of show was for a number of years a standard procedure, for practical reasons. Collectors were delighted to get their treasures out of their town houses while they were away in Europe or Bar Harbor or Newport or Cooperstown for the summer and have the Museum insure them and provide guardianship. The Museum found this a way not only to get an exhibition inexpensively, and to give the public a chance to see works that were not otherwise available as a group, but also to flatter the ego of the collector and, hopefully, influence his determination of what he might ultimately do with his collection. It was one of the many traps the Museum baited which occasionally caught something for the permanent collection.

In its November 1936 number, which appeared about six weeks before the Surrealist exhibition at the Museum, *Harper's Bazaar* accurately forecast: "One sure thing, you aren't going to find a solitary place to hide from surrealism this winter." Surrealism was in the atmosphere. There had been an important Surrealist exhibition the season before in London, and Chick Austin with Julien Levy's help, had long since staged "the first exclusively Surrealist exhibition in America" at the Wadsworth Atheneum in Hartford. That was in 1931, five years before the Museum's show, and it had contained the work of Dali, de Chirico, Max Ernst, Picasso, Pierre Roy, Sauvage, and Masson. Julien Levy had held shows of Surrealists each year from 1932 to 1936, and the Pierre Matisse Gallery had shown Miró in 1932 and again in 1935. The names of the men shown at Hartford, plus those of Man Ray (photographer and painter), Arp, Tanguy, and Magritte, were familiar to those who conscientiously kept up with what went on in New York galleries. Dali's extraordinarily frenetic capacity for self-promotion had done more to put Surrealism into the common tongue than all of the gallery exhibitions. He was, as one journalist put it, "every city editor's idea of what an artist should be: sleek, witty, photogenic and willing to do anything—and that means anything—for publicity." The line between promoting himself and demeaning himself seemed not to exist in his mind. "Anything" included throwing himself through the plate-glass window of a Fifth Avenue store front, posing on a grand piano in the middle of a pond, or leading a Hereford bull solemnly into a drawing room. *Harper's Bazaar* continued its prediction of "no place to hide" from Surrealism by adding:

> Department stores have gone demented on the subject for their windows. Dress designers, advertising artists and photographers, short stories in the *Saturday Evening Post,* everywhere, surrealism. Only—sometimes, and most times, it has no more to do with surrealism than the man in the moon (who maybe has, though). Mr. Levy, who is naturally taut and intense, never has looked more t. and i. than he did when he assured us that Schiaparelli is the *only* designer who understands surrealism. . . .

Alfred and Marga Barr were in Paris during the summer of 1936 gathering material for the Surrealist exhibition, and discovered to their dismay that all was not peace in the house of art and that, not unusually, factions of aestheticians were not speaking to each other. "Paul Eluard and André Breton were the established high priests of Surrealism," Mrs. Barr recalls, "but they had fought and were at odds. They had once collected together, but now they weren't speaking to each other. Breton tried to keep a hold on his flock. There was a terrible split-up, and it was an uphill job to get the show. Eluard was very friendly. It was Breton who was hostile, and we had endless sessions with Georges Hugnet." Part of the problem was that Breton and Hugnet (who later wrote two essays for the catalogue of the show) [9] wanted the exhibition to be exclusively Surrealist; Barr wanted it to include Dada manifestations and the work of the what he called "Fantasists." It did not help matters that Picasso was a friend of Paul Eluard. "Picasso enjoys being bitchy," Mrs. Barr says. "Alfred wanted to borrow some small figurines from him, and Picasso denied that Surrealism had affected him in any way. Finally he said, '*Eh, bien. Je*

9 These essays arrived too late to be included in the first printing of the catalogue, but were published in the *Bulletin* of the Museum, Vol. 4, Nos. 2–3 (November, December 1936) and are called "Dada" and "In the Light of Surrealism." They were translated from the French by Mrs. Barr.

dis "oui," ' and told me to go to Kahnweiler's [gallery] at eleven the next morning and that he'd phone Kahnweiler and tell him the details. I waited until one thirty and Picasso never phoned."

The exhibition nonetheless was ready to open on December 2, and the opening was, as Allen Porter recalls, "the first really grand, chic opening we'd ever had. Everybody was there, but everybody you ever heard of, and the clothes were marvelous!" There were some 700 objects in the show, which was divided into a section with fantastic art from the fifteenth and sixteenth centuries, another of seventeenth- and eighteenth-century fantasies, and a third section from the French Revolution to the World War (as it was called in 1936, not World War I). There was a section of the precursors in the twentieth century of Dada, of art independent of the "movements," "collateral material" by children, by folk artists, and by the insane. There was work by Dürer, Holbein, da Vinci, and by Tristan Tzara, Tanguy, Dali, Breton, and many dozens of others. To describe the exhibition is impossible, so varied and so broad was its scope. Even the critics who thought that the Museum and all its personnel had taken leave of their senses were impressed by the vast amount of research and labor of accumulation that the exhibition represented. The result was "bewildering" because of the variety, the richness, the unexpected, and the shocking, to say nothing of what a great many who came to look thought to be the irrelevant.

One entered the conventional façade of the Museum through the glass doors which had taken the place of wrought-iron ones and came face to face with an enormous pair of lips painted against a bright blue sky and above a landscape by Man Ray. It was called "Observatory Time—the Lovers." Above this was "Rotating Apparatus," a painting by Marcel Duchamp, whose "Nude Descending a Staircase" had been the *enfant terrible* of the Armory Show (and which had been nick-named "Explosion in a Shingle Factory"). A reporter from *The New Yorker* recorded that at the foot of the stairs stood an enormous mask "ornamented with a strange miscellany of household utensils, including a mousetrap, bits of wire, hairbrushes, etc., and as I was going up I met an intensely respectable couple coming down. The man had a solid substantial air, most probably a banker, a man with an instinctive feeling for values, and after gazing in awe-struck astonishment at the mask for a moment, he turned to his wife and said unsmilingly: 'Never throw anything away.' " Upstairs there were nearly fifty paintings by Max Ernst. (One bore the title "The Gramineous Bicycle Garnished with Bells the Pilfered Greybeards and the Echinoderms Bending the

Spine to Look for Caresses." It was a printed botanical chart that Ernst
had worked on with gouache.) There were about two dozen pieces by
the sculptor Hans Arp, and a small wire-and-wood cage which was
filled with lumps of sugar and a thermometer and was called by its
creator, Duchamp, "Why Not Sneeze?" The most widely publicized
piece in the show, and one which the Museum has never been allowed
to forget either by its friends or by its critics (the former amused, the
latter incensed) was Meret Oppenheim's "The Fur-lined Teacup,"
which was, unlike many objects in the show, precisely what its title
said it was. It was, moreover, sitting on a fur-lined saucer and accompanied by a fur-lined teaspoon.

"There is much about Surrealism and its predecessor, Dada," Barr
wrote in his introduction to Hugnet's essays,

> that may seem wantonly outrageous and iconoclastic; in fact,
> these movements in advocating anti-rational values seem almost
> to have declared war on the conventions and standards of estab-
> lished Society. But it may be remembered that the Dadaists and
> Surrealists hold Society responsible for the Great War, the Treaty
> of Versailles, post-war inflation, rearmament, and a variety of
> social, political and economic follies which have made the realities
> of Christendom in their eyes a spectacle of madness just as shock-
> ing as their most outrageous super-realities may be to the outside
> world.

Barr, obviously, was saying much the same thing that McBride had
said of the attitude of the artists in the *Cubism and Abstract Art* show
and that the banker who had visited the Armory Show had said many
years earlier. But the critics—that is, those most widely read by the
public—either did not read Barr or did not heed him. Thomas Craven
referred to the show as "one of the foulest doses of art ever com-
pounded by the international apothecaries," and said that "freaks of
art belong in the tent show along with the two-headed calf and the
tattooed idiot." The *Literary Digest* called the artists "the Marx
brothers of the art world," which was an unintentional compliment
that the artists must have enjoyed if they noticed it, and referred to the
contributors to the show as "zanies." Whoever wrote the piece was
happy to find three ingenious cartoon devices by Rube Goldberg and
Walt Disney's "Wolf Pacifier." Not all of the critics were infuriated
or thought the show a bad joke. It was taken seriously by much of the
art press, by *The New Yorker*, by Elizabeth McCausland, and by
Henry McBride and Royal Cortissoz, who, though he couldn't stand

it, gave it his full attention and what he considered its due. Setting Cortissoz' column next to McBride's today and comparing what they have to say about Dali says much about them:

Cortissoz: "So in the case of Salvador Dali . . . we have to deal with an unmistakable talent. He is an executant in the polished, meticulous tradition of that otherwise very different type, Meissonier, capable of extraordinarily skillful miniaturistic effects. He is also capable of a certain breadth, and his 'Puzzle of Autumn,' with its fine landscape and luminous sky, is undoubtedly the best thing in the show."

McBride: "If Mr. Dali were to drop psychiatry for a moment his career would end instantly for he is no more a painter than the old ladies who copy pictures in the Louvre."

Just as *Harper's Bazaar* predicted, Surrealism, or rather what passed for it or teased it or tried to copy it, was everywhere. Dali did a series of windows for Bonwit Teller in New York (he was furious when he sent someone to get a live lobster and it turned out not to be, as he expected, bright red). Filene's in Boston and Blum's in Philadelphia had "surrealist windows" done by Copeland Displays Inc., and the Associated Press put a story on the wire about the fact that in New York "One may dress like a surrealist painting or like a Southern belle of the '60s nowadays, and be in the height of fashion either way." A photograph that appeared in newspapers, dozens of them, everywhere in America showed two models in ornate hats. "Even Millinery Goes Dada," the caption read. There were endless newspaper and magazine cartoons with a deadening sameness about their presumed fantasies.

In the spring of 1968, nearly thirty-two years after the Dada-Surrealist show closed in the house at 11 West 53rd Street (50,000 people had come to see it), the Museum opened a show in its vastly larger and more flexible complex of buildings at the same address. It was called *Dada, Surrealism, and Their Heritage*. It seemed to those who had witnessed the excitement of the 1936 show rather cozy and nostalgic. There in a glass case was "The Fur-lined Teacup." Out in the garden (but close enough to be seen through the glass wall at the back of the first floor) was Dali's "Rainy Taxi," a contrivance he had made for the World's Fair of 1939—a beat-up cab with a female mannequin sitting in the front seat being doused with a continual spray of water. (Dali got some live snails from a nearby restaurant to live with the mannequin in the taxi, but, alas, they perished of the experiment.)

But something had been added to this opening that had occurred to no one in 1936. Outside on 53rd Street behind police barricades there was a peaceful demonstration of about 300 young artists and their friends. Some of them carried placards: "Bourgeoisie Zoo" and "This is a Money Circus. Down with Art, Up with the Revolution," and some of the demonstrators shouted at the arriving guests (among them the aged Marcel Duchamp in a dinner jacket): "All you rich old ladies go back to Schrafft's," and "Surrealism means Revolution, not spectator sports." A young instructor from Princeton carrying a banner announcing a group called The Transformation said, "Dada and Surrealism are art that is really happening in life, not in museums." Upstairs on the Museum's sixth floor, drinks and chicken à la Ritz were being served to 250 special guests. Duchamp was asked by a reporter what he thought. "Certainly I approve of the demonstrators," he said, "as long as they are not violent." Dali's comment was: "I'm very proud of the hippies. I approve of any kind of manifesto. But, unfortunately, many of the young people today have no information. Dada was a protest against the bourgeoisie, yes—but by the aristocracy, not by the man in the street."

The members of the cast at the Museum had changed considerably in thirty-six years, of course, and those who were still on hand (and there were not a few of them) were gray and sedate, not, as they had been, bright-eyed and dashing. The Museum, which has always had a composite but recognizable personality, was nonetheless still up to its old tricks with its old *noblesse oblige.* In its customary aristocratic manner it was still baiting the smug tastes of the bourgeoisie. It seems entirely unlikely that among "the rich old ladies" at whom the picketers shouted there was one who would have been caught dead in a restaurant so patently bourgeois as Schrafft's.

The Museum of Modern Art is in a more strategic position than any other institution to lead the attack on the fundamental cultural question in our time: "How can Art be restored to a more healthy relationship to life of the community?"
ARTEMAS PACKARD *in A Report on the Development of the Museum of Modern Art*, February 1938

Chapter IX *Eruptive Interlude*

If the face that the Museum turned toward the world in the early and mid-'30s was at once serious and impudent, what was going on on the fourth and fifth floors of 11 West 53rd Street was not quite so confident in its posture. The Museum, in a sense, was a palace in which the revolution was permanent, and there was an air of intrigue which caused the Museum to be overlaid with an aura of scandal. It is not easy—indeed, it is not possible—to say just what was scandalous in any real sense. I was warned long ago that to tell the Museum's true story would be to invite libel suits, but in my opinion, and from my observations and researches, the Museum seems to have run about true to form in its institutional nepotisms, its jockeyings for power, its undercuttings and overthrowings, its who-was-having-an-affair-with-whom, and, as is not uncommon in institutions concerned with the arts, overtones and undercurrents of homosexual as well as heterosexual intrigues, jealousies, infightings, and back-bitings. It was a magnet for gossip and accusations of favoritism; it still is. Business as usual at the Museum of Modern Art was a combination of euphoria, intellectual brilliance, scholarship, hard work (more in the early years on everybody's part than now), and confrontations of temperaments that were sometimes in balance and often at swords' points.

By 1936 the nature of the Museum's Board of Trustees had changed radically from the original intimate group that called itself "the Committee." Mrs. Sullivan resigned from the board in October 1933; her husband had died the year before, leaving her far from destitute but not very rich. His will had provided specific bequests to his sisters, a will written before "the crash," and what was left for his widow was not all that he had intended it to be. Mrs. Sullivan opened a gallery in a brownstone on East 56th Street in New York. It later moved to 460 Park Avenue where she shared a gallery with Lois Shaw, and Jere Abbott recalls buying there for the Smith College Art Gallery, of which by then he was the director, a sketch of a lady with a monkey for Seurat's *"La Grande Jatte"* and two Seurat drawings. In April 1937 a very large portion of the Sullivans' collection was sold at auction at the Anderson Galleries. It took three sessions to complete the sale: the first evening there were 95 watercolors, drawings, and paintings, the second evening a group of 165 prints, 48 more paintings, and a dozen Degas bronzes. The final session, on a Saturday afternoon, was devoted to the decorative arts, mostly English and Early American, listed as 210 items in the sale catalogue. The prices by today's standards seem ridiculously low for the paintings, prints, drawings, and bronzes, but the difference is not merely a matter of inflation; it is the shift in taste that accounts for the differences. A Modigliani drawing, for example, went for $30, a Redon watercolor for $35, a Degas bronze of a dancer for $125. The highest price brought by any work of art in the sale was fetched by a Seurat drawing, "Woman Reading." It was 11½ by 8½ inches and had been lent by Mrs. Sullivan to the first exhibition the Museum had held. It went for $5,700.[1]

Two years later, on December 5, 1939, Mrs. Sullivan died of pleurisy and diabetes at the age of sixty, the evening before what of her collection she had kept for herself was to be sold at auction at the Parke-Bernet Galleries. Abby Rockefeller bought from this sale "Window at Vers" by Derain, which Mrs. Sullivan had acquired at the notorious sale of the John Quinn collection, and a limestone "Head" by Modigliani, and she presented them to the Museum in memory of her friend and co-conspirator in the cause of modern art.

In May 1935 the board lost another member of the original Committee. Frank Crowninshield resigned, and the reason for his resignation, contained in a letter to the President, Conger Goodyear, is not known, as, for some reason, it was "struck from the minutes of the

[1] These prices are taken from a marked copy of the sale catalogue in the possession of Mr. and Mrs. Alfred Barr.

meeting at which it was presented." It is logical to assume that part of the reason was that his magazine, *Vanity Fair,* was in financial trouble, for in that same year it ceased publication and was "incorporated" into another of the Condé Nast publications, *Vogue.* (In publishing circles the combined magazine was wryly referred to for a while as *Vague.*) This was not the first time that Crowninshield had found it expedient to reduce his commitment to the Museum. He resigned as Secretary of the Board in March 1930, just a few months after the Museum had opened, "on account of the pressure of other duties." He may have been disconcerted by the rejection of some works of art that he had offered to the Museum for the permanent collection, as anyone might be. Many potential donors, indeed, subsequently have been disconcerted. The Museum's Acquisition Committee, of which Barr was the mentor if not the chairman (the chairman was always a trustee), was not sentimental about what it would and would not accept as gifts either from collectors or from artists.

In the early days of the Museum, Jere Abbott recalls, Crowninshield was, "quietly in the background, missing nothing." He was a collector who, by his own account, "never collected an object or figure, from Africa or Oceania, because of anything curious about it, or because of its utility or historic interest. Everything has been chosen entirely because of its aesthetic significance; its form, feeling, structure and plastic values." He was a teetotaler and a *bon vivant* with, as he said, "a perhaps preposterous liking for the new, as against the old, in painting, music, architecture, night clubs, dances, food and women." Before he died, thinking that "it would make a frightful mess" if he left his collection for others to take care of, he sold it at auction at Parke-Bernet for $181,747. It was made up of a great variety of paintings and drawings, of prints and bronzes and primitive sculptures. Nearly all of the paintings, drawings, and prints were by his contemporaries (he was three years younger than Matisse and nine years older than Picasso), though there were very few Americans among them. The sale catalogue, looked at today, reveals a man of catholic if fashionably *avant-garde* tastes and personal delights, adventurous and with an eye for quality. His collection has the feel of one made by a man for himself, not one, as so many of the Museum trustees' collections have been and are, made by hired "experts" and "scouts."

The average age of the board dropped sharply with the introduction to it of two young men, each of whom subsequently became President of the Museum: John Hay ("Jock") Whitney and Nelson A. Rockefeller, Abby's second son. It would have been difficult to find anywhere two young men so preposterously rich and at the same time so determined to justify themselves by the intelligent use of their money and their energies. Neither was a "do-gooder," in the pejorative sense of that overworked epithet, but each had been brought up to a sense of public responsibility.

Whitney was twenty-six years old when he was invited to join the board and was elected to it in September 1930. He had been properly instructed in the ways of a God-fearing young gentleman at the Groton School, he had been a student both at Yale and at Oxford, and even as an undergraduate he had demonstrated his concern with the promotion of cultural matters by giving the Yale University Press a fund of $100,000 for the purpose of distributing its scholarly publications to small college libraries that couldn't afford to buy them. He was generally thought of by the public (for he was in the public eye) as a rich young playboy and a theatrical plunger. They knew about his vast fortune, the principal origins of which, like that of the Rockefellers, were in the Standard Oil Company. They knew about his racing stables and polo ponies, and some knew about his affiliation with David O. Selznick and Hollywood. His first significant contributions to the Museum were in the founding of the Film Library, for which, as we have seen, he was able to open doors to the film industry's illustrious patricians (if that is the proper word). He was an early collector of modern paintings, and he is still a very considerable collector, with John Rewald, the foremost authority on the Impressionists, as his advisor.

Nelson Rockefeller's elevation to the Board in 1932 was a different matter. He had been picked out of her five sons by Mrs. Rockefeller as the one who was going to be involved in art, and though I have encountered some disagreement among his friends about how genuine is his concern for the arts (most of them believe he is deeply involved), there is no question in anyone's mind about the extent of his efforts on behalf of the Museum or of his support, both financial and thoughtful, of its growth and influence. He has, in the vernacular, put his money where his mouth is. He has also been quoted by members of the Museum's staff as having said, "I learned about politics in the Museum of Modern Art," which is not difficult to believe. The statement fits the characters of both Rockefeller and the Museum. Nelson graduated from Dartmouth College in 1930, and while he was in college and a member of the outing club he had, according to one of the Museum's curators whom he caused to be dropped some years later, "taken wonderful photographs, really very good, very distinguished." He had also played on the soccer team and edited a magazine called *Fine Arts*. When he became chairman of the Junior Advisory Committee of the Museum almost immediately on graduation from college, he was more interested in architecture than in painting, for the very good reason that he had got involved in the building of Rockefeller Center, of which he was made a director in 1931. In February 1932 he was elected to the board of the Museum, by which time he was twenty-three. His mother was eager to push him along or, more precisely—for he had all the self-generated push toward power that he needed—to help him into a position of influence in the Museum. Two years after he was elected to the board Mrs. Rockefeller wrote to Paul Sachs: "When I talked with Nelson I found he was not very anxious to be secretary of the Museum, but preferred being chairman of a committee. At the present moment I do not know how this will work out." The following week she wrote to Sachs: "Mr. Goodyear appointed several committees. He made me chairman of the Exhibitions Committee, which I have accepted because I feel that I can be very helpful to Alfred in that position. Nelson was made chairman of the Finance Committee."

Mrs. Rockefeller was not by any means merely ambitious for her son; she was ambitious for the Museum and was confident that he could serve its ends. "Mother loved a good fight," Nelson said some years later, after his mother had died, but she fought with humor and dignity and generosity, never with bitterness, never claiming more knowledge than she had, like the New England patrician (there is no question of the word here) that she was. She was rather square-jawed, with a long, slender nose and dark eyes, and to the somber Rockefeller ménage she brought a presence at once aristocratic and easy. She abided by the blue-nosed Bible Belt morality of the Rockefellers, which permitted not a drop of spirits in the house, but she entertained her intimate friends and the artists whose work she bought with a glass of sherry in her upstairs gallery out of sight of her husband, who could not understand, even if he could tolerate, her taste for modern paintings and prints.

She had the gift that few persons of great wealth possess of being extremely generous to those who worked in the vineyards that she supervised, like the Museum, without condescension or ostentation or in any sense being patronizing. As a result those whom she helped felt grateful to her but not beholden, a nice distinction that can result only from modesty combined with spontaneous generosity. Instances of her generosity pop up everywhere. When Mary Sands, the first secretary to work for the Museum, left to be married, Mrs. Rocke-

feller sent her a check for $250, a munificent sum indeed in the De-
pression. When Elodie Courter in 1935 was awarded a Carnegie
Fellowship to spend a summer at the Sorbonne in Paris, she was given
a leave of absence without pay, and, as she was supporting her parents,
was pinched for funds; Mrs. Rockefeller volunteered to pay her salary,
a matter of $500. (Out of his own pocket Barr paid her expenses from
Paris to Holland so that she could see the Kröller-Müller collection,
from which he was then making his selection for the van Gogh
exhibition.)

Mrs. Rockefeller felt identified not only with the Museum but with
its staff in a manner that is not common between trustees and the
employees of their institutions. When young Edward M. M. Warburg
became a trustee of the Museum in November 1932 (he was then
twenty-four), he and Mrs. Rockefeller disagreed about the relationship between trustees and staff. It was his contention that the Director
should have a completely free hand to arrange exhibitions as he
pleased without interference from the trustees, and that if the trustees
decided that they did not approve what the Director did, then they
should fire him and get another Director. Mrs. Rockefeller did not like
this distinction, as she put it, "between 'we' and 'they'" and insisted
that "they," in the persons of the Director and other principal members
of the staff, should be elected to the board and sit on it as voting
members. "The fact of the matter," Warburg has said, "was that most
of the trustees, Mrs. Rockefeller, Goodyear, Sam Lewisohn, and some
of the others, were frustrated museum directors."

Mrs. Rockefeller had her own way in this matter, as in many other
matters having to do with Museum policy, though she managed never
to ruffle anyone's feathers—not, in any case, so far as I have been able
to discover. I have talked with no one who worked with or for her,
and I have talked with a great many, who does not speak of her with
delight and does not reveal affection and respect.

At about the same time that "the young Turks," as Warburg calls
them, were elected to the board, a number of other young men joined
the staff of the Museum who in varying degrees and for varying
lengths of time contributed to its reputation and its operations. The
first of these was Thomas Dabney Mabry, Jr., who succeeded to the
job, if not at once to the title, that was abandoned by Alan Blackburn
when he took off for Louisiana and Huey Long. Mabry was hired as
Assistant Treasurer in June 1935 and became Secretary of the Museum
in the following January. What experience, if any, he had for either
of these positions seems today to be a matter only of conjecture

among those who knew him. He was an intimate friend of Lincoln Kirstein, whom he had known at Harvard and with whom he had traveled abroad, and it was Kirstein who introduced him to the Museum, or, to use a euphemism common to fraternities and to the Museum, "brought him in." Kirstein's influence in the 1930s on the composition of the staff was more important than his influence on the aesthetics of the Museum; he and Barr rarely saw eye to eye on aesthetic matters, but they had many friends in common. Mabry had an office next to Barr's with a window between them so that they could pass correspondence back and forth, and it was Mabry's job to relieve Barr of administrative duties—when he could be got to relinquish them, which, it seems, was never easy for him to do. Mabry was generally very well liked by the staff, an amiable and charming presence among them, but his contemporaries remember him as not having been "in the center of things," nor having exercised the authority to which his position (he became Executive Director) entitled him. Mabry's tenure was not long, though it came at a very active time in the Museum's history, and he was the victim eventually of Nelson Rockefeller's attempts to inject business methods throughout the Museum, an ambition many of his successors have endeavored without notable success to achieve.

More important to the development of the Museum's reputation and to its stature was the hiring in 1935 of a young art historian named Beaumont Newhall, who had been the victim of a number of cutbacks in the budgets of other museums. Newhall, who established the Photography Department a few years later, was still another product of Paul Sachs's museum course at the Fogg ("a model of instruction in museum work," he has called it, "a seminar in the days before seminars were popular"). He worked as a lecturer at the Philadelphia Museum, "to tell everybody everything about all the art in the place." He was then twenty-two. When he left there he was hired by the Metropolitan Museum as "curator in residence" of the Cloisters, but was let go after eighteen months because of a change, as he recalls, in administration. The Cloisters had been taken under the wing of John D. Rockefeller, Jr. (the Rockefellers seemed to be into everything), and from a rather miscellaneous collection of structural stones and sculptures assembled in Spain by the sculptor George Gray Barnard it emerged as the most distinguished "branch" museum in America. Newhall was a tall young man with dark hair, a beetling brow, and a deep voice. It was Henry-Russell Hitchcock, whom he had known at Harvard and for whom he had taken photographs of architecture, who brought him into the Museum. He came as Librarian to replace Iris Barry, who had become totally occupied with the development of the film collection. His experience as a librarian consisted of cataloguing his tutor's library at Harvard. He had known Barr in his Wellesley days and, Newhall says, "He was prejudiced in my favor." Barr offered him a starting salary of $1,500, but was persuaded to raise it to $1,800, and on the day he arrived for work Barr was putting up the van Gogh exhibition. "Take off your coat," Barr said, "and help me hang these pictures."

Newhall was Librarian from the time he joined the staff until he left for the Army in World War II. In the early years of his job he pieced out his very modest income by acting as the Museum's photographer, and it was he who took the picture of the abstract sculptures that the Customs officials had called hardware and which appeared in newspapers all across the country. He set up a darkroom in part of the men's room on the office floor, and a shelf he had erected made the route from the door to the toilet an obstacle course. "Such," he said, "were the primitive conditions in the Museum in those days." His concern with photography went far beyond the odd jobs he had done in the medium for the Museum and for Hitchcock; his interest was scholarly as well. "In 1932," he says, "I began to see the possibilities of combining my photographic and art-historical interests." He contributed reviews and articles on photography to scholarly journals and popular art magazines (popular, that is, as opposed to scholarly; they had small circulations). He contributed a preface to the catalogue of the Second International Salon of Photography at the Pennsylvania Museum of Art, and he delivered a paper on "Photography and the Artist" before the august assembly of the College Art Association. It was a considerable output for a young man who was busy earning a living as a curator and lecturer. It was his concern with photography that led to his most useful and lasting contribution to the Museum and to one of the Museum's liveliest departments.

"Alfred could see I was really keen on photography," he has told me, "and one fine day he stopped me in the corridor and asked me, 'Would you like to do a photographic show?' I said I most certainly would."

Barr had long wanted an exhibition of photographs on a scale with the biggest of the painting exhibitions and given the same importance as had been given them. Photographs had been shown in the West 53rd Street building before, as we have seen—the photomurals which received such a bad press in 1932 and the Walker Evans pictures of nineteenth-century houses, donated by Lincoln Kirstein, in the following year. Barr had a far more ambitious plan. He asked Newhall what sort of show he thought should be done. "I think the first thing to do is probably to have a look at the medium," Newhall said, "and see what's happened since it began." Such a program fitted precisely with Barr's scheme of using the Museum as a means of educating the public not merely in what was new in the arts but in how they had evolved and where they seemed to be heading. This was the approach he had used in the *Fantastic Art, Dada and Surrealism* show with such success. Barr told Newhall he had budgeted $5,000 for the exhibition. "Very good in those days . . . still pretty good," according to Newhall. "Just as I was about to crow about this, Barr added a little footnote: 'You'll probably have to travel to Europe,' he said, and I quickly added, 'Why, certainly.'" This was in 1936, and Newhall, on the strength of it, called up Nancy Wynne and said, "Now we can get married." They promptly did and went off to Europe to look at and collect not just photographs but examples of the photograph's mechanical predecessors. They were back in a few months with several thousand items which included engravings copied by heliographic plates, a portrait done by a gadget called a physionotrace which employed a sort of pantograph to transfer a tracing of a sitter's features from the glass plate behind which he sat to a copper plate, the "earliest daguerreotype in existence," which was a still-life made by Daguerre in 1837, and so on. They also had a few early cameras and some primitive darkroom equipment.

"In those days," Newhall says, "each member of the staff had his own exhibition and it was his responsibility. There were no committees, and everyone pitched in and helped whoever was making the exhibition."

For advice Newhall turned to the most knowledgeable and at the same time least constricted connoisseur of photography he could find. He immediately asked Alfred Stieglitz to serve as his chief advisor. "Stieglitz refused," Nancy Newhall later reported. "It was years before Newhall realized that Stieglitz expressly had founded An American Place [in 1930] to counteract, so far as he could, the intellectual exhibitionism of the Museum of Modern Art." In his own words Stieglitz had written to a friend: "I have nothing against the Museum of Modern Art except one thing and that is that the politics and the social set-up come before all else. It may have to be that way in order to run an institution. But I refuse to believe it. In short, the Museum has really no standard whatever. No integrity of any kind. Of course

there is always a well-meaning 'the best we could do under the circumstances,' etc. etc." In commenting on Newhall's request that he be an
advisor he said: "I feared I could be of no use, as I felt that in spite of
its good intentions the Museum was doing more harm than good. . . .
The reason [for not supporting him] was that I realized that the spirit
of what he was doing was absolutely contrary to all I have given my
life to. In short, that he was doing exactly what I felt was a falsification
of values—primarily because of ignorance." One cannot help but find
in these words the rancor of an old innovator toward the new ones.

Newhall had a warm reception elsewhere, and those who sponsored
his exhibition and helped him assemble it were a distinguished group
of men. Charles Peignot, the director of the remarkably handsome and
graphically sophisticated magazine (now defunct) *Arts et Métiers
Graphiques,* published in Paris, was one. Edward J. Steichen was
another, and others were Alexey Brodovitch, the art director of
Harper's Bazaar and not only a typographer of great skill and invention but a photographer and teacher of photographers, and Moholy-
Nagy, a refugee from the Bauhaus then running an art school in
Chicago, a pioneer in abstract photography, a theorist of photography,
and a remarkable teacher. About Stieglitz Newhall merely says, "He
would have nothing to do with me. He said, 'This young man doesn't
know what he's talking about.' "

The exhibition was a pivotal one. For the first time in America
photography was given the same full dignity in an art museum that
had heretofore been reserved for painting, sculpture, and prints. The
catalogue which Newhall wrote to accompany the exhibition (only
3,000 copies were initially printed and it was reissued the next year [2])
was a readable and extensively illustrated piece of scholarly research
that commanded respect (indeed, it still does), and the defenders of
photography in the perennial argument "Is photography an art?" got
a leg up on at least some of their dogmatic opponents. The show
was called by what Newhall now considers "a terrible name." It was
Photography: 1839–1937, and included in it were 841 prints old and
modern, scientific and spur-of-the-moment (there was a section of
newspaper photographs); there were stills from films, early aerial
shots, and color in the days when color was far less reliable than it is
today. There were pictures from Europe and America; none from
the Orient or Africa.

Newhall had nothing to do with the Museum's next photographic

2 It was reissued under the title *Photography: A Short Critical History* with
the Museum's imprint.

show, which was a collection of pictures by Walker Evans, the Museum's first attempt to give the full range of a single photographer's work. It was put together by Lincoln Kirstein and Thomas Mabry in 1938, and Kirstein, who wrote the text for the catalogue, took the "responsibility for the selection of the pictures" and, for reasons which are now obscure, went to the trouble of saying that they were "presented without sponsorship or connection with the policies, aesthetic or political, of the institutions, publications or government agencies for which some of the work has been done." Some of the pictures had been taken for the Farm Security Agency, for which Evans worked during the Depression; most, however, were not, though Kirstein may have wished to divest himself of any obligation to that agency, with whose director Evans was not sympathetic. The catalogue contained nearly ninety plates, and was a model of photographic publishing by letter-press; it was reprinted for popular sale thirty years after its original issue. "The exhibition and the book were widely and seriously—and for the most part sympathetically—reviewed," John Szarkowski recalls in a 1971 catalogue of an exhibition of work by Evans held at the Museum thirty-three years after the first show.

There was one influential photographer who became extremely important to the Museum's photographic ambitions who, however, took sharp exception to the Evans book. It was Ansel Adams and he wrote to Edward Weston. "Walker Evans' book gave me a hernia. I am so *goddam* mad over what people think America is from the left tier. Stinks, social and otherwise, are a poor excuse and imitation of the real beauty and power of the land and of the people inhabiting it. Evans has some beautiful things but they are lost in the shuffle of social significance." And he wrote to Georgia O'Keeffe: "I think the book is atrocious. But not Evans' work in the true sense . . . it's the putting of it all in a book of that kind—mixed social meanings, documentation, esthetics, sophistication (social slumming) etc. Just why the Museum would undertake to present that book is a mystery to me. . . ." And to another friend, David McAlpin, he wrote in part: "I certainly do not like Kirstein's article in the book in question. So glib and so limited! O well. But I still think Evans has made some beautiful pictures."

Szarkowski found a piece by Thomas Mabry in *Harper's Bazaar* "the most perceptive" of any of the reviews of Evans' work. Mabry wrote that it had "a power which reveals a potential order and morality at the very moment that it pictures the ordinary, the vulgar, and the casually corrupt." In retrospect Mabry and Kirstein seem more

right than Adams. It is the quality of the pictorial vision that survives
and not the social comment, an observation that can be made about
any "social" art that outlives its "message."

The Evans show was a giant step in the direction of the establishment of a Photography Department, but it was followed by two other
demonstrations of Barr's concern with the seriousness of the medium.
The first was the inclusion of sixty photographs by American photographers in an exhibition of American art sent to the Jeu de Paume
in Paris in 1938, and the other was a section in the Museum's tenth-
anniversary show in 1939, both of which exhibitions are important in
the Museum's history and which we will look at in another context.
The establishment of the department, however, belongs to this chapter
—if not chronologically, at least reasonably.

The decision to form a department was announced in the Museum
Bulletin in December 1940. By then it was clear that there was considerable public interest in photographs on exhibition. (By then, for
example, there were some 8,000 camera clubs in America and everyman
had become a self-styled "artist with the lens.") Newhall, as Librarian,
had been collecting the documents of photography—books, prints,
slides, technical manuals—and so the Museum had accumulated the
basic reference tools of a research center for study of the medium's
history. The photographic shows were comparatively easy for the
Department of Circulating Exhibitions to put on the road, and the
Photography: 1839–1937 exhibition had traveled not just to museums
but to department-store galleries. "We worked with something we
wouldn't tolerate today," Newhall says, "cardboard panels three by
four feet with holes cut in them and covered with plastic material."
Barr said, "One of the most vigorous and popular arts of our time,
photography has long been recognized by the Museum. . . . It is
hoped that the Department will serve as a center for those artists who
have chosen photography as their medium."

Early in 1940 Newhall was visiting his friend Ansel Adams, who had
so emphatically criticized the Walker Evans book two years before.
The distinguished West Coast photographer had been a protégé of
Alfred Stieglitz and exhibited in his gallery, An American Place.
Newhall explained to him his hopes for a Department of Photography
at the Museum. In the introduction to a book which Adams had published in 1935, *Making a Photograph*, he had, Newhall says, "visualized a department almost exactly like that which I'd visualized for the

Museum. I told him about our hopes. We were sitting in Yosemite National Park having a drink, and he threw his drink into the bushes and said, 'We'll call Dave McAlpin right now.' "

David H. McAlpin, a grandnephew of John D. Rockefeller, Sr. (and hence a cousin of Nelson Rockefeller), lived in Princeton and worked in New York as a broker. He was a collector of "fine and rare" photographs, an enthusiastic amateur photographer, and an habitué of Stieglitz' gallery. "He said he'd put up $1,000 to buy photographs," Newhall says, "and he gave an equal amount to the Metropolitan for the same purpose, and sat back to see who'd spend the money best. We bought the most fastest. I bought the entire Moholy-Nagy one-man show. . . . We got a lot of things, and Dave backed us."

When the department was established, McAlpin was appointed chairman of the Committee on Photography (he was also elected a trustee of the Museum) and he paid Adams' way to New York to work with Newhall in the capacity of vice-chairman of the committee. "We opened the department with a small exhibition," Newhall says, "in retrospect not nearly so good as the 1937 one, called *Sixty Photographs*. Then came the war clouds and I got into uniform and my wife took over the department." His wife, Nancy, recalls that when Alfred Barr came to look at this first exhibition of the new department while it was being installed, he peered at the close-ups by Stieglitz, Strand, Atget, Weston, and Adams, and asked, "Why do all the photographers have to photograph bushes?"

It is to the credit of the early trustees of the Museum that they continually questioned whether their museum was doing everything it should be doing. It was not that they distrusted Barr's vision of a museum that dealt with all the contemporary arts, but they liked to be reassured, and there was in their behavior a constant hint that they were concerned about his ability to convert into practical action his theoretical objectives. Besides, the trustees felt that they should be *doing* something, have their fingers in the pie and on the pulse at the same time, or, as a trustee-pecked administrator might put it, "messing in operations." To this end, at the suggestion of Nelson Rockefeller, they employed in 1935 the services of Professor Artemas Packard, the chairman of the art department at Dartmouth College, "to conduct an investigation to determine in what way the Museum could most effectively aid in the development of esthetic values in American life."

Professor Packard worked at the Museum for a year, and the "only place we could find for him," Barr wrote Mrs. Rockefeller at the time, "would be in one of the maids' rooms on the rear of the fifth floor, moving Miss Newmeyer to the penthouse bathroom." Since she was the Publicity Secretary, she could not, he noted, "work outside the building." At the end of a year Packard went off to ponder and write his findings and recommendations. In January 1936, while he was still at the Museum, he made some preliminary suggestions to the trustees. They started some soul-searching that was taken most seriously by the Junior Advisory Committee, which put its collective mind on problems of education and industrial design. In 1938 Packard produced a final 138-page document that spelled out in considerable detail and in plain words what the position of the Museum should be in relation to other museums and to schools and colleges, and how it should respond "to the characteristic interests and needs of contemporary society." In his introduction Packard says:

> It is only too apparent that its [the Museum's] present enviable reputation has been largely built on the care with which it has avoided catering to the "popular" interest. Yet "popular instruction" is one of the major objects for which the institution exists. . . . What we are really confronted with is the need for two quite consciously and deliberately different kinds of enterprise; on the one hand, the search for what is best in Art according to the highest standards of critical discrimination, and, on the other, the provision of facilities for popular instruction *in accordance with the public need.*

He looked at the exhibition program ("the Museum should strive to keep both the specialized and the popular interest equally in mind," and "a proper balance between 'advanced' and retrospective shows and between the exhibition of works by American and foreign artists. The Museum's program has apparently received some unfavorable criticism on this score"). He looked at what he called "the importance of interesting men," by which he meant getting men involved ("one of the greatest barriers to the healthy development of art interest in America is unquestionably the fact that it has been so largely cultivated hitherto as of interest primarily to women"). He looked at "the museum and the scholar"; he suggested (indeed, urged) the possibility of the Museum's publishing a "popular monthly magazine covering the whole range of the visual arts of the present day"; he proposed that the Museum produce educational films, have a gallery for beginners, and so on and on. He left no bypath unexplored, and he even went so far as to suggest abandoning the phrase "Modern Art," which must have profoundly shocked not only some of the trustees but most especially Alfred Barr. He thought the phrase constituted "a serious stumbling block" and said, "I cannot emphasize too strongly the desirability of using such terms as 'present-day' or 'contemporary' rather than 'modern' and of seeking to correct, wherever it appears, any tendency to look upon the Museum of Modern Art as primarily an agency for the dissemination of propaganda in favor of any particular modern school of expression." The Museum of Modern Art did not heed his advice in this regard; indeed, it later got into a rather furious internecine squabble with the Boston Institute over the distinction between "modern" and "contemporary."

In general, however, the *Packard Report*, as it is still called (and it is still regarded as one of the Museum's basic documents), was given close attention. In his book on the first ten years of the Museum, Conger Goodyear wrote: "Mr. Packard's report is full of meat and might well be made required annual reading for the Trustees." Barr and Dorothy Miller and others who were involved with the Museum's early days speak of Packard with both affection and respect. He and his wife died in an automobile accident in 1961.

At about the time Mabry and Newhall went to work for the Museum and Packard was working on his report, another youngish man in his mid-thirties edged his way (or was edged) into the Museum, where he became one of the most important members of the executive staff and, in terms of service, one of the longest-lived and most influential. This was Monroe Wheeler, a small, wiry man with a tanned face somewhat monkey-like and dark, amused, and eager eyes. He was (and still is) an excellent raconteur with a clever wit which was frank and sparingly acid, extraordinary social poise and conversational timing which endeared him alike to artists and to dowagers, an intelligence that was entirely self-disciplined, and an eye that was self-taught. "He came from nowhere," one of the trustees, who was in no doubt where she came from, said of him, "and he was marvelous. He was a diplomatist." It was as a diplomat, an organizer, and a publisher, not as a scholar, that he made his career in the Museum. He was liaison man not only between the staff and the trustees (he became a member of the board after a few years) but between the Museum and foreign collectors, governments, artists, and other museums.

Wheeler had in fact come from the Chicago suburb of Evanston, where he was born in 1900. His father was a food broker, a book collector who had his own private printing press, and an amateur painter. Wheeler did not go to college, but he says that as a boy in his teens he "haunted the Chicago Art Institute," a wonderfully rich introduction for any young man to the visual arts. He also made friends with Harriet Monroe, the poet who had made a national reputation by writing the "Columbian Ode" which was read to many thousands of visitors on the opening day of the Columbian Exposition, the very great World's Fair in Chicago in 1893. She had founded the influential and innovative *Poetry: A Magazine of Verse* in 1912 and was its editor. Through her Wheeler met Mrs. William Vaughn Moody, the widow of the Indiana playwright and poet, whom he remembers as "a great literary hostess." At her house he talked with Tagore and Masefield and Edward Arlington Robinson, and his very nearly endless collection of famous literary, artistic, and musical acquaintances and friends got its start. It should be noted that Wheeler, while he has spent a lifetime collecting famous people (and delights in talking about them), has most assuredly been collected in turn by them, for he is a man of charm, perception, and a very contagious enthusiasm. He realized as a young man, he says, that he "had no basic talent in the arts," but it was artists and literary people whose company he most enjoyed, and he began, in his words, "seeking contacts and circumstances that would bring me close to creative persons and their interests and needs."

Before he was twenty he met Glenway Wescott, an eighteen-year-old student at the University of Chicago, and Yvor Winters, who was almost exactly Wheeler's age. Both were promising poets, and a year or so later Wheeler, in his first excursion into publishing, printed small books of their verse, *The Bitterns* by Wescott (1920) and *The Immobile Wind* by Winters (1921). Under the same imprint (Mannequin Press) he also issued a slim volume, *Go Go*, by William Carlos Williams. "In 1921," he says, "I made friends with Marianne Moore, Robert Frost, and Padraic Colum." In this same year Wheeler and Wescott went to Europe together (they have shared a ménage ever since), and it was in Paris that Wheeler added the novelist Ford Madox Ford to his collection and first got involved with the world of painters and sculptors. He came back to America in 1923 and supported himself and Wescott (who was writing *The Apple of the Eye*, his first novel) by working at public relations for a New York bank. The novel was published in 1924, and three years later Wescott's *The*

Grandmothers won the Harper Prize Novel contest and went through seventeen printings in three months. Wheeler and Wescott went back to Europe, this time to live there until 1934. By this time Wheeler's roster included Raymond Mortimer and Cyril Connolly, the British critics, Katherine Anne Porter, who was then living in Paris, Dame Edith and Sir Osbert Sitwell, Somerset Maugham, Jean Cocteau, Aaron Copland, and the painters Soutine, Tchelitchew, Kristians Tonny, Bérard, Berman, and a palette of others. (His friendship with Miró and Matisse and acquaintance with Picasso came later.) They were, and those who are alive still are, his very good friends, for he has a considerable talent, as a profile in *Apollo* magazine said of him in 1964, "for keeping the age-old friendships on the boil."

Wheeler and Wescott came back to America in 1934, the delightful years of living as expatriates, so fashionable (and inexpensive) for literary figures in the 1920s and early '30s, having lost their charms. Wheeler's first association with the Museum of Modern Art came about almost at once through his friendship with Lincoln Kirstein (to whom he was introduced by the photographer, George Platt Lynes) and Philip Hofer, at that time assistant director of the Morgan Library. Hofer, who later joined the Harvard faculty, was a well-known and greatly respected bibliophile even then and a collector of books and drawings of great discrimination. Kirstein and Hofer persuaded Wheeler to join the Museum's Library Committee, of which Walter P. Chrysler, Jr., was then chairman. Wheeler soon succeeded to that position and became a member of the Advisory Committee. More important to Wheeler's career, however, was Barr's invitation to him (urged on by the Advisory Committee) to direct an exhibition of book bindings by Ignaz Wiemeler, a German whom Wheeler still regards as "one of the greatest binders that ever lived." While Wheeler had been living in France he had established himself as a typographer and publisher of de-luxe limited editions. He and a friend, Barbara Harrison, started a company called Harrison of Paris with offices on the sixth floor of the Palais Royal. Miss Harrison's father had been governor general of the Philippines and she was an heiress to a Gold Rush fortune, a collector of paintings, and a patroness of the arts who was not content to be on the periphery but got to the root of the matter (she helped to support Soutine, for example, when he was penniless and unknown). She and Wheeler performed a kind of publishing that was popular with collectors in the '20s and '30s. The books were issued in very small editions and on several grades and kinds of handmade paper, each copy numbered. Wheeler designed them and had them printed by the best craftsmen he could find in Europe, with the result that Harrison of Paris books were models of a sort of publishing one rarely encounters today in America. It was Wheeler's interest and expertise in contemporary "fine printing" and "fine binding," as bibliophiles call them, that first involved him in the affairs of the Museum.

In Paris in 1931, three years before he brought the offices of Harrison of Paris to New York, he had been director of the American section of what he describes as "a large international exhibition of the arts of the book" at the Petit Palais, and he had seen Wiemeler's work there. He met Wiemeler, ordered a binding for himself, and got photographs of many others. Kirstein interested the Advisory Committee in the possibilities of a show. "It was a small exhibition," Wheeler says, "but it made a tremendous impression on people who know quality in bookbinding. I can remember Paul Mellon coming in and ordering a binding for his wife for one of her favorite texts." This exhibition was in the autumn of 1935, and Wheeler's next show for the Museum was *Modern Painters and Sculptors as Illustrators*, which he did with Philip Hofer and which we have already noted as one of the first of the influential small exhibitions to be held in the 53rd Street house.

A good many seeds were sown by the Museum in the mid-'30s which were not to bear fruit for a number of years but which, when they did, had a good deal to do directly or indirectly with shaping the taste of a great many people. In 1936–37 the Advisory Committee, which had been brooding on what it should do about the design of household objects since Johnson's *Machine Art* exhibition in 1934, asked Wheeler to investigate how the Museum might venture to "improve," to use Wheeler's word, "the quality of the things that people use every day." More specifically, he was asked "to prepare a report on the possibilities of a department of Industrial Design." He spent, he recalls, "a lot of time on it." "I wrote to people all over the country," he says, "asking what they thought the need was, and the response was overwhelming." One of the people to whom he wrote was Paul Sachs. His letter was three pages of single-spaced typing and was, in effect, a précis of the 113-page report that he made to the Advisory Committee in June 1938. On the top of the first page of the letter Sachs wrote in pencil, "Museum class." It would be interesting to know what the eager young art historians and future museum directors had to say about putting kitchen utensils and bathroom hardware into museums. Sachs's reply to Wheeler was brief, noncommittal, and, of course, polite. The gist of Wheeler's letter was in this paragraph, which occurred near the end:

> In other words, we believe that the same serious consideration should be given to household articles that was given to beautiful and useful objects in the past, and which is still currently given to painting and sculpture. In this way we hope to provide many people with a source of aesthetic gratification of which they are not now aware, as well as a sense of the continuity of art in the history of mankind.

These rather lordly words, which seem to get re-invented, or in any case re-stated, by the tastemakers of each generation who wish (or, indeed, feel morally impelled) to correct the sagging taste of the preceding generation, have been common in America at least since the 1840s. They echo the preachments of Andrew Jackson Downing, who tried to make gentlemen and farmers look with a more sensitive eye at the contents of their parlors. The "refinement of the public taste" has always been considered a function of American museums, and museum directors have always hoped to hit as close to home as possible. When a few years later the Museum of Modern Art established a Department of Industrial Design, it managed to hit its target more frequently than most museums had in the past, and Wheeler's report had a good deal to do with paving the way—or, to put it more bluntly, with prying money out of trustees and foundations for the establishment of the department.

Wheeler's name appeared on the Museum's payroll for the first time in September 1938 when he became Director of the Membership Department. There had been a Membership Committee from the very earliest days of the Museum, and Mrs. Murray Crane had been its first chairman. In the first year there were 405 members; by the end of 1934 there were 1,200, and successful efforts were under way to get more than just New Yorkers involved. In those days a basic $10 membership afforded (and continued for some time to afford) not just free access to the exhibitions (indeed, there was usually no charge for admission) and invitations to openings and (as it now is) to the members' dining room; it also assured members of free copies of the Museum's publications.

A branch of the Museum was established in Boston in 1935 and was called The Boston Museum of Modern Art. It held exhibitions (sent to it by the "home office") and in two years it had acquired 700 members, a small portion of whose dues was paid to the mother institution. Early in 1938 James S. Plaut was named Director of the Boston branch, and by the time the year was out the Boston Museum of Modern Art had become the Institute of Modern Art and had disaffiliated itself from the New York museum. In his report to the Membership Committee early the following year Wheeler referred to this act of infidelity, as it was regarded in the drawing rooms in New York where the committee met, as "the secession of Boston." It was not the only setback. There was briefly a Washington (D.C.) Museum of Modern Art— very briefly. In 1937, with Mrs. Dwight F. Davis, the wife of the ex-Secretary of War, as chairman, it leased space in the Metropolitan Club for a gallery. It held five shows, to which, it was claimed, 20,000 persons came. It gave up after two years for lack of support by the citizens, many of whom are transients, of the nation's capital. Thirty years after the collapse of Washington and the secession of Boston the Museum's annual report declared that it then in 1969 had more than 40,000 members who contributed $456,055 a year to its support.

Wheeler's tenure as Director of Membership was brief; indeed, it lasted only ten months, at which time he was appointed by Nelson Rockefeller, who by then was President of the Museum, as Director of Publications, a title which inaccurately described the many functions of management and diplomacy that ultimately fell under his aegis. It was as the Museum's publisher, however, that he, to quote from the English art magazine *Apollo*, "literally transformed the image of the modern art book." "Under his directorship," the article (unsigned) says, "a Museum of Modern Art publication has come to mean the highest standard of book production." It should be added that none of these several hundred books was published as a "coffee table" object to flatter the cultural egos of the Museum's members. They were scholarly catalogues, for the most part, and a few distinguished monographs such as the Matisse and Picasso volumes written by Alfred Barr. This was publishing seriously conceived and aesthetically executed, and it set new standards for museum publication in America.

The Museum of Modern Art was, you will recall, chartered as an educational institution, a fact of which some of its trustees (including Mr. Rockefeller) kept reminding themselves. In the public eye its educational purpose seemed often to get lost behind the glamour and excitement of its flying in the face of acceptable taste, in the crowds of curiosity-seekers who came to giggle at its extravagances (as they were thought of) and its lunacies. Even the young who thought of themselves as the *avant-garde* felt a kind of private, proprietary interest in the Museum, as though it were their club to which it was really awfully generous of the Museum to permit the Philistines access. It was one of the prices that had to be paid by the sensitive to the thick-skinned, by the forward-looking to the reactionaries.

This was not, however, the attitude of the young members of the Advisory Committee or of the Director, who believed that to make converts it was necessary to open young eyes to the new truth, or at least not shut them off from discovering delights for themselves by interposing between them and the arts old, academic prejudices and conventional methods of teaching. In the 1930s "progressive education" was still looked upon by most parents as dangerous license and by a good many schoolteachers as a caving-in of the old standards of learning. It was regarded as "faddist," as something that John Dewey and Teachers College at Columbia University perpetrated for their own questionable if not quite immoral ends. Worst of all, it was "progressive."

But Barr, at heart not a schoolmaster but a scholar, recognized that the Museum should be involved in the whole educational process, not just adult education. And so, not long after the Museum opened its doors, he and Mrs. Sullivan, an art educator by profession, invited a number of chairmen of New York City high-school art departments to sit down with them and see what the Museum might do that would be helpful. In the characteristic style of one of the educators reporting some years later, "Discussion centered on the need of guiding adolescents toward a full understanding of the arts of their time, and plans were made to utilize the contents and services of the Museum toward this end." The report also put into Barr's voice a note of desperation which it is unlikely was actually there. It said: "Mr. Barr observed that to create public opinion favorable to art the only hope lay in educating the young people who can still be influenced by bringing them and their teachers in constant contact with the best art of our time in museums and in the community." The upshot of this conference was to give art students and teachers membership in the Museum for one dollar each, and in October 1932 Barr put together a collection called *A Brief Summary of Modern Painting in Color Reproduction* for showing in schools. It was in such demand, not only in New York but in colleges and schools elsewhere, that a duplicate of it was assembled and sent traveling.

It was, however, the inclination of the Museum, as it is of most growing institutions, to officialize the spontaneous and to departmentalize the general, which is to say change natural language into jargon. In the same issue of the Museum's *Bulletin* that announced Monroe Wheeler's "Report Covering a Proposed Industrial Art Project," as he called it (it was called "Report on Multiple Exhibitions of Objects of Daily Household Use" in the *Bulletin*), there was the announcement that the Museum "has secured the services of Mr. Victor d'Amico, head of the department of fine arts at the Fieldston School, to work out an educational project through which the Museum's material would become more useful to and more used by secondary schools in New York."

Victor d'Amico, a small man with the gait of a boxer and a pleasantly rugged face, black hair, and a not surprising, considering his name, Latin look, was a born and bred New Yorker (one of eleven children) who had made a reputation as a teacher and by a study that he had done for the Rockefeller Foundation on art in the secondary schools. When the Advisory Committee, taking its cue from the *Packard Report*, decided that it should be "looking towards a better integration of art with other subjects in the curriculum," Eliza Parkinson had been designated chairman of a committee to do something about it. She turned to Barr, and Barr turned to the General Education Board. The board recommended d'Amico.

"Barr hired me part-time in 1937," d'Amico says. "He'd arranged an exhibition of color reproductions of modern art and he said to me, 'Take it from here.' I was otherwise head of the department at Fieldston. I came to the Museum from five to ten evenings and on Saturdays and some Sundays to organize the program. I believe in mixing in the manual because we learn through our hands as much as through the visual. In those days Kandinsky was not only an unexplained wonder, he was considered a hoax, but if you could get the kids making their own abstractions and begin to wonder why it was better if they did it this way rather than that way, and then you showed them the Kandinsky, they got the idea."

D'Amico started two programs more or less at the same time, and both prospered. The first was the high-school program. ("There seemed to be less happening in the high schools in modern art than at any other level," he recalls. "At that time there was an antagonism to modern art, and it mostly came from the parents. There's one basic difference, I found out, between the adult and the kid. The young person argues to find out; the adult argues in order not to be disturbed. They'd rather be against.") The second program was the Young People's Gallery, which opened in 1939.

"I don't think Barr was much interested," d'Amico says. "Eliza Parkinson took me under her wing." Barr, in fact, resented having any gallery space taken away from the Museum's collections.

During the first year of the program it was Mrs. Parkinson who found the money to get it started. "I think the initial money must have come from the Advisory Committee," she says now, and the record shows that she is right. The initial money, however, was not enough to continue the program after the first trial year, and the William C. Whitney Foundation put up a necessary $2,000 in April 1938 and repeated the grant the next year. The public schools that were invited to participate responded with a great deal more alacrity than the private schools, most of which, it appears, thought they were already sufficiently engaged in art education and in those days were rather uppity about programs that involved the public schools. The program consisted not only of shows that traveled to the schools, but also visits to the galleries of the Museum, student membership tickets, a teacher-training program, and slide talks that could be used in the classroom. (There were some objections that this took the initiative away from the teachers.) Closer to d'Amico's heart than what went out of the Museum to the schools was the Young People's Gallery, to which boys and girls came on Saturdays. "It was both an exposure and a participation," d'Amico says, "and it was all for young people. They helped to arrange the exhibitions, and then I had a kind of wainscoting around the room that opened out into desks—tables to work on, and when they'd done their pictures or constructions or whatever, they'd fold them back up and the exhibition would be in place. One of the students in the first class was Bill Rubin." William S. Rubin became Chief Curator of the Collection of Painting and Sculpture of the Museum in 1969, after Barr's retirement.

The General Education Board of New York (not to be confused with the city's Board of Education) was impressed by the response of the schools, the evident excitement of the children, and no doubt the interest of the Rockefellers in the project. As a result, the board put up $20,100 to support the project for three years. From ten participating schools in 1937 the number had grown to more than forty by 1944 and there were seven Saturday classes to which 200 city-school children came. In that year the program ran into a financial crisis and, according to d'Amico, "The schools said, 'We can't give this up.' So they contributed to the fund, and up to a few years ago they gave $13,000 a year toward the program and [in 1970] still are."

This is not the place to trace the history of the Museum's educa-

tional projects to their waning in the late '60s, but one of the most
far-reaching of its projects with more impact than the programs in
New York's schools was started in 1942 and died just about twenty
years later in 1963. It was called the National Committee on Art Education, and it grew out of a meeting of fewer than a dozen art teachers
who did not feel that they had been given a hearing at a meeting of
"the annual conference of a large art association." They did not intend
to form a committee and they did not want to be one of those organizations beholden to "business interests on whose support most art
organizations depend." D'Amico had invited them to meet at the
Museum to discuss their mutual problems, and of course they did find
that they were a committee and the Museum was their sponsor. Within
a few years the committee had a thousand members and held annual
conferences at the Museum. "It was one of the finest things that happened to the Museum," Monroe Wheeler has said, "because when it
came to exploring the potentialities, Victor discovered that the greatest
obstacle was that there weren't any teachers. So the big task was to
educate the teachers first." The committee became in essence the
Museum's shock troops or, perhaps more accurately, its educational
underground. In any case, its members carried the word into primary
and secondary schools and into colleges in all parts of the country, and
did it with the zeal of converts and the devotion of missionary priests.

By 1938 the Museum had launched every significant program for the
propagation of the faith that it was ever going to launch. Its exhibitions
were famous; its Film Library was gathering momentum at a gratifying rate; its Library was fast becoming the best library on modern art
anywhere; its circulating exhibitions peppered the map of America;
its permanent collection was soundly based in the bequest of Lizzie
Bliss; Photography, though not yet dignified by being a separate department, was an accepted part of the program. Architecture, though
it had its ups and downs and frequently changing curatorial leadership,
was deeply rooted. Industrial design, which had first found a toehold
with Philip Johnson's exhibitions of *Objects: 1900 and Today* and
Machine Art, had now been formalized by the acceptance of Wheeler's
report. The Museum's publications, which were to become increasingly
distinguished, were already among the most sought-after books on the
modern movement and had established a reputation for quality of
reproduction, readability, and scholarship. It is true that the Museum
in its role as an arm of international diplomacy had not yet flexed its

muscles, but its first efforts in that direction were only a few months away.

There was, however, some major destruction and building to be undertaken—indeed, there was a new cathedral of taste to be erected—before the normal business of the Museum could be resumed.

Art is almost the only luxury the Rockefellers can afford. Not in terms of dollars and cents, of course.

ALINE B. SAARINEN, *The Proud Possessors*, 1958

Chapter X *Burning and Building Bridges*

Fiorello La Guardia, the round little "fusion" Mayor of New York, who is remembered by those who were children in the 1930s for his reading of the comic strips on the radio during a newspaper strike and as an honest political fireball by most of their parents, had a vision of a cultural center for New York. La Guardia did nothing by halves. "The proposed art center . . . is no fantastic dream," he said, "although it is startling in its magnitude." On September 21, 1936, at the time when Barr and his crew were putting together the *Fantastic Art, Dada and Surrealism* show, La Guardia announced that he had $14,000,000 in pledges from private donors for his project, which was to house an opera house, a symphony hall, and a museum. (He hoped that "the opera house and the symphony hall can be so arranged that they can be thrown together to provide one enormous hall for conventions.") One of the suggestions made by the Municipal Art Committee that had taken the Mayor's project in hand was to incorporate the Museum of Modern Art into the "center."

One thing of which its trustees and Director were sure was that the Museum was not going to bury its independence or its identity in somebody else's grand schemes. It had a rather splendid scheme of its own, though it was not a vast and, as it turned out, unrealizable one like the Mayor's. A simple $1,500,000 would serve the trustees' purposes, though they did not say so at the outset.

Ten days after the Mayor announced his $14,000,000 project, the front page of the *New York Times* carried a story that was headlined "MODERN ART GROUP TO HAVE A NEW HOME." The article that followed explained that the Museum would "erect a new building on the site now occupied by Nos. 9, 11, 13, 15, 17, and 19 West 53rd Street" and would stay in its present quarters until the following June. The new land would give it 135-foot frontage and 100 feet in depth, and "in the rear it abuts on the residence of John D. Rockefeller, Jr., at 10 West 54th Street."

Four days later, on October 5, the New York *Sun* reported that Mr. Rockefeller's house, which had been built for his father in 1895, was "probably scheduled for the wrecker's ball." Eleven days after that it was formally announced that the building would indeed come down, and that the Rockefellers were taking what seemed like a step down in the world; they were renting an apartment on Park Avenue. It was, moreover, only sixteen rooms. The paper said that Mr. and Mrs. Rockefeller "issued no statement explaining their motives for the move" but that one of the rumors was that they "simply had become tired of living alone in an eight-story private residence and sought the comparative ease and simplicity of housekeeping in an apartment." There was speculation that the site of the house might be used for an apartment building; there was no suggestion that it might become a garden for the Museum.

By the following May La Guardia's plan for his civic center had been officially postponed by the Mayor "until after the elections." The Mayor was re-elected, but the plan passed into oblivion; the excitement had gone out of the project and it was not until many years later that something resembling La Guardia's scheme came to life in Lincoln Center.

In order to demonstrate the need for a new and much larger home for the Museum's treasures, its temporary exhibitions, and its encounters with the public through its library, films, and circulating exhibitions, Alfred Barr drew up a document in 1936 which, in a sense, started all over again at the beginning. He explained in one section "Why the Museum of Modern Art was Founded," and defined "modern art" as "a relative, elastic term" that concerned itself with the art of the "last three decades" and its ancestors going back as far as Delacroix. For the money-minded he pointed out that the sales values of "modern" had increased tremendously in a relatively few years, and he specifically cited Seurat's *"La Grande Jatte,"* which was sold at the artist's death in 1891 for $200. In 1925 it was bought by the Chicago Art Institute

for about $25,000 and "in 1930 an offer of over $400,000 was refused."
He added, "This represents an increase in 'bid' value of about 200,000
percent in forty years." This was the sort of talk to which collectors
who were potential donors liked to listen. He also explained that there
were many foreign museums devoted exclusively to modern art, that
"Modern art is a difficult problem for a large museum of historic art
such as the Metropolitan Museum," and he emphasized "the advantages
of a separate Museum of Modern Art." He concluded with the national
and international importance of the Museum, noting that "The rest of
the United States looks more or less consciously to New York for
leadership in art," and that "the Museum . . . was planned not merely
as a local institution but so that it might be of service to the whole nation." Furthermore, he added a statement from Dr. Gustav Pauli, the
director of the Hamburg (Germany) Museum, who had recently been
lecturing at Harvard: "You have to fulfill a very important mission as
an international means of the highest cultural relationships. Art seems
to us the best and finest bridge leading toward an understanding among
civilized nations."

This preamble of eight pages was supported by charts and figures
showing the increased activities of the Museum in the last seven years,
the number of visitors who asked Mr. Tremp, the guardian of the door,
to see the permanent collection and had to be told there was no place
to show it (there were 200 inquiries in six weeks), why an auditorium
was essential for showing films and for lectures, how the Film Library
had to rent office space outside the Museum, and how crowded the
staff offices were. A pathetic statement announced that "There is no
packing room, no locker space, no rest room."

Barr explained that the land which had been acquired on 53rd Street
cost $465,000. Of this, $215,000 had come from the Endowment Fund
(which, you will recall, had been raised to guarantee the Museum's
stability so that it could inherit the Bliss collection) and $250,000 had
been contributed by Abby Rockefeller.

"What may be of even greater importance," the report continues,
"is the possibility of the continuation of the new street (now extend-
ing from 49th to 51st Streets between 5th and 6th Avenues in Rockefeller Center) through 52nd Street to 53rd Street." This had been a
plan promoted by Nelson Rockefeller, a splendid mall that would join
the Museum to Rockefeller Center with the Museum facing it from
the north. There also seemed a chance that La Guardia's dream center
might face on this mall from the west and that thus "the new Museum
will be situated in a location unequaled in America for public useful-

ness." This mall seemed such a likely possibility that Nelson Rockefeller wanted the façade of the Museum designed so that it would center on the mall, and for a while plans were held up on this account. The Rockefellers, however, were thwarted in their hopes to buy the properties between 51st and 53rd Streets which would have made the mall possible. The former famous speakeasy, and by the mid-'30s an even more famous restaurant, "21," would not sell its building, and without that land the scheme fell through. Philip Goodwin, a trustee of the Museum and the architect of the proposed building, was quoted in the New York *Herald Tribune* on May 12, 1937, as saying: "We couldn't wait any longer. We went ahead and designed a building which we thought was equally adapted to face either a comparatively narrow street or an open plaza."

Before the wrecker's ball got to the house at 11 West 53rd Street in which the Museum had been living in cramped quarters since it moved out of the Heckscher Building in 1932, plans had been made for temporary galleries and offices and storage rooms in Rockefeller Center. The galleries and storage rooms were underground or, as it was more politely called, on "the concourse" of what was then the Time-Life Building at 14 West 49th Street. The offices were in the same building on the fifteenth floor. The building at 11 West 53rd Street closed in April; the new galleries opened on June 23 with three modest shows: a summer exhibition called *Painting and Sculpture from the Museum Collection and on Loan*, a *Project for a Community Center by Architects, Painters and Sculptors Collaborative*, and stills of movies called *A Brief Survey of the American Film*. Between the time it moved into temporary quarters and the opening of the brand-new building on 53rd Street, thirty-one exhibitions were held below ground, in "air-cooled" galleries, as they were then called, and several of them were shows of considerable importance in the Museum's career: the Walker Evans *American Photographs* was there; so was the first public exposure (in photographs) of Frank Lloyd Wright's remarkable house built for Edgar Kaufmann over a waterfall at Bear Run, Pennsylvania, and called "Fallingwater"; so was the work of the source of many of Barr's ideas, an exposition of the *Bauhaus: 1918–1928*.

It is a temptation to say that it was "business as usual" at the Museum during its underground residence, but business was never either usual or "as usual" in that eruptive, contrary, intense, embattled institution. The trustees sat heavily and sometimes despairingly on the fluttering lid of a pot that continuously bubbled with young energy, rivalries, dreaminess, and, from their point of view, inefficiencies. There was a moment in 1937 when a committee of the trustees (Goodyear, Stephen Clark, and Nelson Rockefeller) put their heads together and produced a report the obvious intention of which was to limit what must have seemed to them the chaos of the Museum's administrative procedures. The report recommended that there should be an Executive Vice-President, "or some similar title," the duties of that office to be "the correlation of the activities of the different departments of the Museum and the executive management of the Museum's affairs." It is obvious that some departments weren't speaking to other departments. The report also suggested that "at some future time" the Museum should hire a "salaried member of the Museum's staff" to serve as a full-time paid president, and that the heads of the board be called chairman and vice-chairman. The board accepted these proposals of the committee with evident relief, but the man whom the committee had in mind as a paid president, Joseph Hudnut, dean of the Harvard Architectural School, thought their invitation over for a few months and then declined. "And that," said Goodyear, "was the end of the attempt to secure a salaried president." [1]

Just two months after the Museum moved into the Time-Life Building an architect who had turned teacher moved into the job which Ernestine Fantl gave up when she married and went to live in London. John McAndrew became the Museum's Curator of Architecture, and in doing so he kept the Sachs-Barr-Abbott-Hitchcock-Johnson line (with its offshoots in Wellesley) unbroken. From the time he was an undergraduate he was a member of the "family" (one is tempted to say the Modern Art Mafia) which was to be in charge of taste in a great many museums throughout the country for the next four decades. McAndrew had majored in the fine arts at Harvard and graduated, by a curricular quirk, with a Bachelor of Science degree. (In those days a Bachelor of Arts at Harvard was awarded only to students who qualified in Latin or Greek. McAndrew's father, who had been Superintendent of Schools in Chicago, did not believe in the teaching of Latin in his school system or in having his children study it.) After he graduated McAndrew went to architectural school at Harvard (he did not get his degree then, but did some years later), and from there to work for the New York architect Aymar Embury, a fashionable, talented, and altogether traditional designer mostly of domestic architecture and schools. McAndrew was a victim of the Depression, which

[1] This concept of a paid president was again explored and again discarded by William S. Paley in his regime as President of the Board in the late 1960s and early 1970s.

hit the architects' offices early and hard, and in 1932 he was hired by Vassar College as an assistant professor to teach the history of architecture, courses in art history, and a practical course in architectural drafting. Agnes Rindge was the chairman of the Vassar department, and she, too, was a "Fogg product" and an important member of the family; for a brief period during World War II she acted, as we have noted, as a Vice-Director of the Museum of Modern Art. She was a member of the coterie that gossiped about the arts and drank bootlegged liquor (or homemade gin) at the Askews' on Sunday evenings, and who kept running into each other in European museums during the summer.

McAndrew got to know Barr after Barr's and Abbott's trip to Europe in 1927–28. McAndrew went to a lecture on modern painting that Barr gave at the Fogg. "He gave quotations in Latin and never translated them, and he handed around big color reproductions of radical modern paintings—you know, Cézanne etc. I was introduced to him at a party afterwards. But," he says, "I got to know the Barrs better in the summer of 1935 in Rome because Daisy was there." He had met Daisy at the Askews' when she was teaching at Vassar and Henry-Russell Hitchcock had brought her there. "The Askews," he recalls, "decided that she was the ideal bride for Russell." Hitchcock and McAndrew were classmates at Harvard. McAndrew met Philip Johnson "by accident" in a gallery in Europe in the summer of 1929. "We traveled together and the Bauhaus was the climax of our trip. Philip was there to perfect his German," McAndrew says, "and Alfred had told him where to go and what to look at."

So it is not surprising that when there was a vacancy in the Architecture Department, McAndrew should be offered the job. He had been invited to give a few lectures at the Institute of Fine Arts of New York University and discovered that he was "being looked over." On another occasion he was called in by Goodyear "to give an opinion on something," he does not remember what. In April of 1937 he was offered the job at the Museum. "It was late in the academic year to find someone to replace me. But I went to McCracken [2] and he said, 'Don't be crazy. Go now. We'll find someone.' I picked Richard Krautheimer, who was then recently from Germany and teaching at the University of Louisville, to do the history part. John Coolidge, then at Columbia, did the 'modern,' and I got a draftsman from Ed Stone's office to do the practical course. Vassar will never be able to repay me

2 Henry Noble McCracken, president of Vassar College.

the debt they owe me for leaving and making room for Richard Krautheimer." [3]

McAndrew was thirty-three when he established himself in a Museum office on the fifteenth floor of the Time-Life Building with a salary of $3,500 a year. He was then a bachelor, with black hair, a very agile wit, and a reputation among his students as an extraordinary teacher and lively lecturer. He was a scholar who seemed to remember in detail every building he had ever seen, what the weather had been like on the day he saw it, and what he had had for lunch and dinner. His memory, indeed, rivaled Barr's, and he had the capacity for making what he liked sound remarkable and what he disapproved of seem dreadful. What came in between seemed to him of less than no interest. It was, to use words he frequently employed then and does today, "tiresome" or "dreary." Buildings were "tiresome," so were people and books and meals, or they could be "ravishing" or "a catastrophe." He had the un-academic attribute of being able to write simply, clearly, and without jargon, though he was a perfectionist and, like many perfectionists, a procrastinator. He put off committing himself to paper . . . sometimes for years. He had, moreover, a very considerable gift for indignation, a sort of stiff-necked intolerance toward compromise, especially in aesthetic matters and particularly where his convictions of what was right and proper collided with what someone else thought was expedient. Especially as a young man he was likely to take as a personal affront any opposition to his ideas of how things should be done, and in the eyes of some colleagues and employers this made him difficult to work with and led him, indeed, into rifts with good friends (nearly always very temporary) and battles with administrators and trustees, sometimes much to his disadvantage. He had, on the other hand, a tremendous capacity for enjoyment. He was a gourmet of food and painting and architecture, design and music, and he had a way of using the words commonly used to describe one of these to describe the others: stone was the color of melon; you could eat a baroque façade with a spoon; a fresco could be as rich in color as raspberries or as thin as skimmed milk. A building, on the other hand, could be vintage Le Corbu, or creampuff modern, a monument could be a layer cake or a layer cake

3 Richard Krautheimer became a professor at the Institute of Fine Arts and is recognized as one of the great art historians of his time. John Coolidge became a professor of fine arts at Harvard and the director of the Fogg Museum. McAndrew, some years after he left the Museum of Modern Art, became chairman of the art department at Wellesley College and director of its museum.

monumental. Taste to him was a matter of all the senses, all of them fastidious.

"When I first got to the Museum," he says, "I worked on a few minor shows and much on the Bauhaus show." It was at that time that he first heard that Frank Lloyd Wright had built a new house for Edgar Kaufmann, the Pittsburgh department-store owner. He wrote to Mr. Kaufmann to ask if he could see the house and was told that it was not in Pittsburgh, but in Bear Run some miles away, and he was invited for the weekend. "I think," he says, "I was the first person from the outside world to see it. Edgar and I became great chums from then on, and I arranged to have a one-house show." The Edgar referred to was the son of the owner; he had worked at Wright's eyrie at Taliesen in Wisconsin and had persuaded his father to commission Wright, and Wright to accept the job. The site was left to Wright, and he chose to put the house over a waterfall, with results that became famous.

McAndrew has called the exhibition a "one-man one-house show." It was small; it consisted only of photographs and plans (*Architectural Forum* collaborated in the arrangements and published an article), but a few years later it led to a large, expensive (too expensive, the trustees thought) Wright exhibition with many models and a battle with the Master's temperament which made the arrangements for and the installation of the show a cliffhanger until the last minute. More importantly, the one-house show led to the involvement of Edgar Kaufmann, Jr., in the Museum's affairs, a fruitful if occasionally stormy one for a number of years.

At the same time that the Evans photographs and a group of Rouault prints (an exhibition put together by Monroe Wheeler) were on show in late September and October of 1938, McAndrew had installed the first of an annual series of exhibitions of inexpensive "useful objects" as a way of trying to encourage the manufacture and sale of "good design." The first exhibition was limited to things—tableware, glass, pottery, cooking utensils, and a variety of other objects for personal or household use—that could be bought for less than $5.00. The show was called *Useful Household Objects Under $5.00*, and Goodyear refers to it in his book as "a delight to shoppers" which "undoubtedly improved the quality of many Christmas gifts." McAndrew enlisted the help and advice of a small committee to search out and select the objects. Kaufmann, who had been working in his father's store in Pittsburgh, "knew the trade well," McAndrew says, "and he produced all sorts of things, some highly suitable and hard to find, and urged us to have handicrafts as well as industrial design." Elodie Courter, who was in charge of circulating exhibitions, was also on the Selection Committee, and she saw to it that the show went on the road. There was, she reported, "enthusiastic comment whenever it was shown," and those who showed it asked for another show next year. "Visitors purchased many of the objects . . . from lenders and local distributors in their cities . . . ; several wholesalers and manufacturers received gratifying requests from all over the country, and several . . . found enough attendant business in the provinces to establish new retail outlets. . . ." There is little wonder that the chosen manufacturers were delighted. Here was the Museum's stamp of "good design" (or, if you prefer, "good taste") on their products, every bit as good as the Good Housekeeping Seal of Approval and, from their point of view even better. "Many manufacturers whose merchandise had not been included in the exhibition," Miss Courter reported, "wrote the Museum asking that their product be considered another year."

Here was grass-roots tastemaking with a vengeance, and those who thought the Museum's posture in matters of taste to be somewhat too lordly and too smug (and there were many then as there are today) were either amused or infuriated. The posture, however, was in the spirit of Wheeler's report on industrial design as a proper concern of the Museum and it put into practice an admonition that he had quoted from another report [3] on what museums should be doing, to wit:

> Metropolitan museums situated in New York have an exceptional opportunity to guide popular taste in the appreciation of artistic values in objects of common use. New York is one of the greatest shopping centers in the country and the influence of its taste radiates to every part of the land.

The first such show was followed by seven others. In the second year the objects cost up to $10; by 1946 they were up to $25, and in 1948 the exhibition was called *100 Useful Objects of Fine Design, Available Under $100*. After that the *Useful Objects* shows were abandoned, but in 1951 they were succeeded by the *Good Design* exhibitions.

In the history of the arts of our time the Bauhaus exhibition on which McAndrew worked with Herbert Bayer and Mr. and Mrs. Walter Gropius and, of course, Alfred Barr was a great deal more important than the *Useful Objects* shows, but it had a great deal less

3 *The Civic Value of Museums* by Professor T. R. Adams (New York, 1937).

impact on the public or, indeed, on the taste of critics. It was, to use a phrase of the art historian Erwin Panofsky, a *"flop d'estime."* The show opened on December 6, 1938, and, as Goodyear says, "brought forth a good deal of severe criticism." Henry H. Saylor, who for years was the editor of the *Journal* of the American Institute of Architects, wrote in a "Journal" that he published in *Architectural Forum* in January 1939 apropos of the Bauhaus show:

> . . . talking with Frederick Ackerman in an earnest effort to re-orient my mind, I asked him what the present agglomeration of abstracts . . . and distorted forms meant. "I spent about ten years of my life trying to find out," he said, "and now my complacency with regard to the whole thing is summed up in 'What the hell does it matter?' "

Bayer installed the exhibition and Mr. and Mrs. Gropius edited the catalogue, a document of prime importance perhaps most particularly in the relation of art and politics. The tensions of the time in which it was produced are vividly suggested by the omission of the names of artists whose work was included in the show but who are not identified because they might be subject to political reprisals. The Nazis had abolished the Bauhaus; many of its faculty—artists, designers, architects, craftsmen—had fled from Germany; others were still there, and it would have been a danger to them to be identified with an art and an institution that Hitler found "depraved." It was almost exactly nine months after the Bauhaus show opened at the Museum that Hitler's troops invaded Poland.

The attacks in the press on the Bauhaus show ("confusing, and still worse . . . gadgety"; "clumsily installed"; "little short of a fiasco"; "chaotic"; "something essentially heavy, forced and repellent in most of the Bauhaus work"; and so on) were so disturbing to the trustees of the Museum that Barr and McAndrew prepared "notes on the reception of the Bauhaus Exhibition" in which they analyzed the criticisms. Goodyear says, with what seems not much conviction, that they "perhaps tempered the breeze somewhat." It was the last exhibition in the temporary quarters in Rockefeller Center.

There had been during the "temporary quarters" period, however, an exhibition which had concerned Goodyear, Barr, and McAndrew a great deal more than the Bauhaus show, and had taken a great deal more of their thought and energies. It was a dream of Goodyear's come true, but was a dream with more than a few nightmarish aspects. It was a considerably grander version of the Jeu de Paume American exhibition for which he had tried to get Barr to give up his sabbatical (when he was ill) in 1932. It was an accomplishment of which Goodyear was extremely (probably excessively) proud, and he devotes a full chapter of his book on the Museum's first ten years to it. It does not, in retrospect, seem to justify the same amount of space here.

Goodyear's original plan for an American exhibition in Paris was, you will recall, abandoned not only because of Barr's inability to take it on but because, as Goodyear later put it, "There was the little matter of the inter-allied debt which had not produced any noticeable amount of the good will desirable for such an occasion." Goodyear, however, was very nearly cussed in his determination that sooner or later he was going to see a splendid display of the American arts in Paris, and considering the run-around that he got from French officials, it is something of a miracle that his determination did not go limp and vanish. Goodyear made advances to French officials in 1933 who, he said, "lacked something of cordiality." By 1935 he had decided that the next move had to come from the French and only an official invitation would be acceptable. Backstairs exchanges of pleasantries between museum officials (the director of the Louvre and Barr) were all very well, but the Museum must stand on its dignity. Between December 1935 and February 1937 cables and letters were exchanged with long pauses between them. One sticking point was that the French insisted that the Museum of Modern Art pay all of the expenses of the show and that the receipts from admissions and from the sale of the catalogue should be divided equally between them. Goodyear found the proposal preposterous, and for a while the matter bogged down on that issue. Finally in March 1937 a letter came from the French Embassy in Washington saying that it had received a cable from the Ministry of Foreign Affairs in Paris "accepting fully the conditions set forth" in the letter that Goodyear had written the ministry in September 1936.

In one sense this was a victory, but in another it was a complete defeat. The acquiescence came too late. It would have been impossible to mount an ambitious exhibition by the summer of 1937, and Goodyear took it upon himself to tell the French Ambassador by letter that the Museum "must, with regret, abandon the expedition." He did this without consulting his fellow trustees, and his letter must have been rather characteristically curt, for, as he says, "a committee of trustees . . . prepared and forwarded resolutions expressing our regret and our appreciation of the kind offices of the Ambassador."

Barr and Goodyear, however, had one friend in Paris, Eustache de Lorey, who seemed as determined as they were that the show should come off. It was he who had acted as go-between with the directors of the Louvre and the Jeu de Paume, and he would not let the matter drop. In June 1937 he told Barr and Goodyear that "the French authorities would accede to everything [the Museum] wished," and Goodyear added, "there was received from the Minister a form of contract conforming exactly to our original proposals, which for nine months had been the subject of wearisome correspondence."

Two floors of the Musée du Jeu de Paume, which looks across the Tuileries gardens to its counterpart, the Orangerie, were put at the disposal of the Museum of Modern Art for a period of three months, June, July, and August 1938. Work to pin down the plans for the show and assemble it started at once. It was to encompass three centuries of American art. Goodyear, at the trustees' behest, was in command, and he undertook with Dorothy Miller's help to assemble the painting, sculpture, and prints; McAndrew with Elizabeth Mock as his assistant worked on architecture; Newhall, then still Librarian, was assigned the photographic show, and Iris Barry and Dick Abbott, with the help of Allen Porter, who had recently joined the Film Library staff, put together a history of the American movies. According to Goodyear, Barr was "frequently consulted"; according to McAndrew, he was "passionately interested" and worked furiously at it, and one can be sure he would not have let it be otherwise. In the issue of the Museum *Bulletin* published in May 1938 to tell the Museum's members about the forthcoming exhibition, Barr gives all the credit for the painting, sculpture, and print section of the show to Goodyear and Dorothy Miller; furthermore, he not only says that the American share of the funds to pay for the exhibition were contributed by Mrs. Rockefeller and Goodyear, but adds: "Mr. Goodyear (who will not be given an opportunity to censor these lines) has also borne not only the difficult responsibility of choosing the painting and sculpture but, in addition, has given most generously of his time and enthusiasm during six years of negotiation."

Goodyear obviously had been having the time of his life; he was acting (and had been acting for several years since he first started negotiating) just like a museum director. "At various times during the preceding years," he wrote, "I had been going up and down the land, looking over all the principal art museums and many of the private collections of painting and sculpture from Boston to San Francisco and in the far south." He put together what was in part a very distinguished exhibition. Eighteenth-century American painting had some stature with collectors then, but the nineteenth century was generally shrugged off by those who considered themselves sophisticated in such matters. Goodyear's selection of nineteenth-century paintings was not only extremely perceptive, it was innovative as well. Unfortunately, he was frustrated by being unable to borrow a number of paintings he very much wanted the French to see. He could not, for example, persuade the Jefferson Medical College in Philadelphia to lend Eakins' "The Gross Clinic" or the National Gallery in Washington to part with Ryder's "Jonah and the Whale" and "The Flying Dutchman," but what he did manage was a rich banquet that included fourteen Homers, nine Whistlers, six Eakinses, three Sargents, and single examples of Bingham, Cassatt, Inness, Morse (the splendid portrait of Lafayette), and so on. There was fortunately one Audubon (the "Snowy Owls"); possibly because he was born a Frenchman (indeed, he thought himself to be the lost Dauphin) it was the picture the French seemed to like best.

The matter of twentieth-century American paintings posed a quite different problem. Goodyear made the mistake, as he recognized later, of inviting forty artists to select canvases from their works and send them to the Museum. "Thirty-six of the forty accepted and the result was lamentable," he wrote. Only "six or seven" of those submitted were sent to Paris; the rest of the contemporary paintings were chosen by Goodyear with Dorothy Miller and Barr looking over his shoulder. ("He insisted," John McAndrew recalls, "that we send Speicher's portrait of Katharine Cornell. He had backed her plays and they were very good friends.") The list of painters whose work was sent reflects more or less what one would expect of the Museum's taste in the 1930s. It ranged from the Ashcan School to abstractionists, from social realists to the rather sentimental figure painters and to the regionalists.[4]

As for sculpture, the nineteenth century then scarcely mattered and from the Museum's point of view the less attention paid to it, the better. It was entirely out of fashion, but Goodyear included one bronze ("Bronco Buster") by Remington, two reliefs by Saint-Gaudens, and "five examples in the folk art collection." There were, however, pieces by five contemporaries: Epstein, Zorach, Lachaise, Carl Walters, and Mina Harkavy. Lest any aspect of the "fine arts" be neglected, there were prints by Audubon, Currier & Ives, Cassatt, Bellows, and Whistler.

4 The list included Henri, Luks, Bellows, Marin, Demuth, Stella, Dove, O'Keeffe, Sheeler, Weber, Sterne, Kuhn, Karfiol, Kane, Kuniyoshi, Speicher, Burchfield, Hopper, Benton, Pop Hart, Grant Wood, Gropper, Shahn, Prestopino, Gorky, and Peter Blume.

McAndrew's and Elizabeth Mock's problem was, obviously, a very different one. The paintings and sculpture were to be installed on the second floor of the Jeu de Paume and the architecture, photographs, and films were to occupy the first floor. "We got plans from the Jeu de Paume which turned out not to be accurate," McAndrew says. "We had quite a large section for architecture downstairs. There wasn't much problem upstairs because there were galleries and it was just a question of hanging." McAndrew used big photographic blow-ups, elaborate models, and extensive explanatory labels. "On entering the architecture section," he wrote in the *Bulletin*, "the visitor will see, high above his head, two giant fir-wood maps. From Spain, England, and Holland on the map of Europe streamers stretch to those places on the map of the United States where colonists from the three European nations settled." When the visitor got his bearings (if he did) he could then follow the development of "monumental architecture through the Colonial and Early Federal Periods," down through the fantasies of the Victorian era which America shared with much of Europe, to the fathers of modern American building—H. H. Richardson, Louis Sullivan, and Frank Lloyd Wright. But on the way there was an eye-opener which was the hit of the show.

It was what McAndrew calls "the domestic vernacular" that the French found fascinating: adobe pueblos of the Southwest, the stone barns of Pennsylvania, and, more than any others, the wooden houses of New England. "We thought they'd like the Santa Fé things," McAndrew says. "No, it's just like Algeria. We had quite a big section of wood houses with a piece of balloon frame and all sorts of photos. 'Tiens! *toute de bois,* and it's still standing there from the seventeenth century!' they said. It was just about the time when vernacular architecture was beginning to cross-fertilize with modern, and Le Corbusier was using stone, etc. Lewis Mumford was very enthusiastic about it, and said that the history of American architecture had never been told this way before."

Evidently many fewer visitors to the exhibition looked at the paintings and sculpture than at the architecture and the film showings (five a day) on the first floor. Indeed, when the show opened on Thursday, May 24, at three in the afternoon, crowds clutching tricolored invitations from the American Ambassador or the French Ministry of Education poured in. "It was undoubtedly a gala," Goodyear wrote. "No one could see much of the pictures or the sculpture, but those who came could see each other and be seen, which is, after all, the purpose of a *vernissage*." There was, however, a line waiting to see the films, and he was greatly encouraged. His nose was somewhat out of joint, to be sure, because His Excellency the American Ambassador, Mr. Bullitt, was unable to be there; he simply had to go to London to keep a date with his tailor. Gertrude Stein wasn't at the opening because, as Allen Porter recalls, "She thought it all too dreadful." The Ambassador turned up several days later on May 27, when, "following a quaint French custom," as Goodyear put it, "the exhibition was formally opened by the Minister of Education." The Ambassador, he noted, was "now fully clothed."

With the exception of the architecture, films, and photographs, the critical reception of the exhibition in the Paris press was, according to McAndrew, "absolutely vicious." "They missed the point about all sorts of things," he recalls. "They thought the nineteenth century was dull and academic and the modern part was bad imitation French. The French were then just beginning to yip that they did not have very good modern painting because it had all been taken away from them by those American millionaires, when they'd turned it down for ages themselves."

McAndrew's memory is accurate, and the press clippings bear him out. One Paris paper said, "Quantities of second-rate [nineteenth-century] artists encumber the walls." Eakins and Ryder were paired by one writer, who said, "Eakins, who was a mere analyst, freezes the atmosphere, Ryder befogs it." Copley and Stuart were regarded as "far behind the English portraitists." Goodyear quotes another writer as saying that he would "give all the paintings in the United States for a few meters of American film." But the best diatribe of all came from the critic of *Gringoire*, André Villeboeuf: "Here is painting justly called 'international'; without origin, without taste; marked only by an originality that accents the indecency of its arrogance, the puerility of its vanity," a statement which Goodyear thought could be "envied by our favorite American castigator." He meant, of course, Royal Cortissoz of the New York *Herald Tribune*.

Not all of the comment was so disparaging, to be sure, and some of it came close to being, if not complimentary, at least friendly. Not nearly as many people came to see the exhibition as Goodyear had hoped. There was a show of British art in the Louvre, and the city was plastered with posters announcing it. There were almost no posters for the American show. The American community in Paris paid it little heed and gave it little support, and the American Embassy all but ignored it.

On balance Goodyear thought it was good that the show had been held. It was not his fault if the French were blind to the qualities of American painting. They turned up with great regularity for the playing of the films (Allen Porter ran the projector and went through his program five times each day), and the architecture section of the show had been a considerable critical and popular success. "I got a telegram from Nelson and his mother saying 'You saved the Paris show,'" McAndrew told me, and he added, "It's a pity in a way that the show couldn't have been later. It would have been a big success."

There is no question that European attitudes toward American art have changed greatly since the Second World War. It is true that the Museum of Modern Art has been a prime factor in shifting the world's center of art, the place where artists want to come and where they want to exhibit and be recognized, from Paris to New York. It is also true that the building in which the Museum was about to take up a new and more ambitious life (a model of it was in the Paris show) played no small part in expanding the Museum's influence abroad and in enforcing the impact of its tastes at home.

*The youth, when nature and art attract him,
thinks that with a vigorous effort he can soon
penetrate into the innermost sanctuary; the man,
after long wanderings, finds himself still in the
outer court.*
From GOETHE'S *introduction to the periodical*
PROPYLAEN, *quoted by* PAUL SACHS *in his address to
the trustees of the Museum of Modern Art on its
tenth anniversary*

Chapter XI *Home Is Where You
Hang Your Collection*

Who should be the architect of the new building? Choosing was a
pleasant prospect but a troublesome question. Here was an institution
that stood at once for the adventurous, the serious, and the refined,
the forward-looking (not just the up-to-date), whose mission it was
to instruct and improve taste and which was devoted to the morality
of "honest" architecture. Here, moreover, was the institution that in
1932 had introduced the International Style to America—indeed, given
it its name in an exhibition that Edward Durell Stone many years later
said "did for architecture what the famous Armory Show had done
for painting. . . . I know of no single event which so profoundly influenced the architecture of the twentieth century." Whoever the
architect should be, he (or, as it turned out, they) should further the
lessons already begun on the Museum's walls.

Alfred Barr thought that just five living architects were of sufficient
stature to undertake the design of the Museum, and four of them were
Europeans. It was not that he wanted a foreign architect, as some of

his trustees thought at the time. "No," he says, "not foreign, distinguished. There was only one distinguished American, Frank Lloyd Wright, and I knew we couldn't work with him, and that Swiss, Corbu,[1] we'd already found he was impossible to work with. So I suggested Oud and Gropius and Mies."[2] He got permission from the Building Committee (Goodyear, Nelson Rockefeller, and Stephen Clark, as chairman) to consult these men when he was in Europe in the summer of 1936. Oud eliminated himself; he did not want to leave Holland, and, besides, Barr said, "He'd done all his best work in the '20s and was tired." Gropius was not interested; he had recently set up practice near London. Mies *was* interested. The reasons for setting aside the names of Wright and Le Corbusier dated back to the 1932 International Style show. Wright had behaved like such a prima donna over his part of the exhibition that the thought of sweating out the problems of building a museum with him seemed appalling. Le Corbusier had, quite simply, accused the Museum of having stolen his models, called the Museum the Rockefellers' institute and the Rockefellers pigs (*"les cochons Rockefeller"*), and, until a photostat of a check was made public to prove that he had been amply paid, threatened to sue. Even if Barr had had the temerity to work with Wright or Le Corbusier, the trustees most certainly would not have. And, as matters resolved themselves, they did not want to work with Mies van der Rohe either.

The only architect on the board of the Museum in 1936 was Philip Lippincott Goodwin, who had been elected in April 1934. It was to him that the Building Committee turned for advice, and in the end, it was he whom the committee appointed as architect for the new building. He is described by those who knew him (and there are many still at the Museum who did) as a man of "exquisite taste," "so much loved," "a very generous and thoughtful man who was always doing things for people," "one of the most loved of the Museum's close friends." Indeed, he contributed his architect's fee to the building fund. He was wise as well as gentle and friendly. Professionally he was an architect with the eclectic tastes of the Edwardian era and his roots were in the neo-classicism of the Paris Ecole des Beaux Arts. He was "an old-time New Yorker" who built gentlemanly houses for ladies and gentlemen of wealth, "for people with the money and taste," as an obituary put it, "to be free from the limitations of functional econ-

---

1   Charles-Edouard Jeanneret, called "Le Corbusier" and, by the professionals, "Le Corbu" or "Corbu" or even just "Corb."
2   J. J. Oud, Walter Gropius, and Mies van der Rohe.

omy." He was a confirmed bachelor, a product of Groton and Yale (class of 1907), and as a young man he had been a draftsman for the New York firm of Delano and Aldrich, celebrated for its impeccable tastefulness. His own work was described as "felicitous," and it was said that "he stubbornly resisted being hurried into second-rate design or inferior execution." He was the author of a book on the smaller chateaux of Touraine, and, indeed, he lived part of the time in an imitation chateau on a hilltop in Cornwall, Connecticut.

None of this, however, explains his association with the Museum of Modern Art. The explanation lies in his activities as a collector with, as Barr put it, "fastidious taste." Furthermore, as Arthur Drexler said, "His own eye was very personal." He had started collecting under the guidance of Stieglitz, but he was soon very much on his own. Those who saw his collection in the duplex penthouse in which he lived on Fifth Avenue say that the most important pictures and sculptures were on the first floor and the more personal ones on the floor above. Downstairs were a famous Marin watercolor ("Lower Manhattan," 1920), Brancusi's "Blonde Negress," a Léger, a de Chirico, a small Picasso tempera ("The Rape," 1920), Nadelman's charming polychromed wooden sculpture of a woman at a piano, and so on. Upstairs were, among others, pictures by Paul Cadmus and Jared French, protégés and friends of Lincoln Kirstein.[3]

It was evident to the Building Committee that Goodwin alone was not the man to design a modern structure that would be a lesson and an example and a declaration of faith in the new forms all in one, and Goodwin was unquestionably as aware of this as they. It was Nelson Rockefeller who proposed that young Edward Durell Stone, then thirty-four, be associated with him and who, according to John McAndrew, "arranged this shotgun marriage." Stone, who was born in the university town of Fayetteville, Arkansas (and says he has never graduated from anywhere since junior high school), had worked as the principal designer under Raymond Hood and Wallace K. Harrison on the vast Radio City Music Hall and the smaller Center Theatre. He had got his training at Harvard when Edgell was its dean of architecture, at the Massachusetts Institute of Technology, and during two years in Europe on a traveling fellowship. He had looked hard and enthusiastically at the new architecture in Sweden and France and

---

3 When Goodwin died in 1958, he left the major part of his collection to the Museum of Modern Art, and a special exhibition of it was held. The collection is described and much of it illustrated in the Museum's *Bulletin*, Vol. 26, No. 1 (Fall 1958).

studied Le Corbusier's published designs and doctrines. One of the men who had worked with him at Radio City was Donald Deskey, who had done the interior furnishings, and it was he who got Stone the job of designing a house in Mount Kisco, New York, for Richard H. Mandel, an associate of Deskey's. The house was, Stone says, the first in the new International Style "in the East"; it called forth a good deal of comment and, from those who were enthusiastic about the new style, a good deal of praise. This was in 1933. In the following year he did another house in the same vicinity and in somewhat the same manner which so "shocked the vicinity's sensibilities," he recalls in his book, *The Evolution of an Architect,* that "zoning ordinances were modified to prevent further desecration of a synthetic colonial community."

Times were hard and jobs were scarce for architects then, and Stone worked for $40 a week on the two houses. When he had finished them he did odd jobs, one of which was to work on the displays for the Museum of Science and Industry which Nelson Rockefeller was organizing in the RCA Building in Rockefeller Center. "One day," Stone recalls, "I overheard Wally [Harrison] say to Nelson, 'What about Ed?' I didn't know what the hell was going on." It was soon after this that Stone was asked if he wanted to work with Goodwin on the design of the new Museum.

The decision to engage Goodwin with Stone as his associate was made while Barr was in Europe collecting material for the Surrealist exhibition, and he received a very long cable from Goodwin telling him that the Museum was to be designed by an American. It appears that Barr still hoped that the façade of the Museum might be designed by Mies and he encouraged him to come to America. "Mies arrived and we had no money for him," Barr says, but Philip Johnson engaged the enthusiasm of the Stanley Resors (he was the head of the J. Walter Thompson advertising agency) for commissioning Mies to design a country house for them in Jackson Hole, Wyoming, and his long and distinguished career in America as teacher and builder was thus launched.

There exist in the files of the Study Center of the Museum half a dozen sketches for the façade and first-floor interior of the early stages of the designs that Goodwin and Stone worked on. The first façades were copybook modern, or so they now seem, but the sketches for the first floor show a curved ramp to the second floor which, by a slight stretch of the imagination, can be said to anticipate Wright's ramp in the Guggenheim Museum. There is also a drawing that shows how the Museum might have looked if it had been joined to Rockefeller Center by the street which Nelson Rockefeller so much wanted to open.

But the atmosphere in which the plans for the building emerged was lightened with flashes of temperament and clouded with beetling brows. Barr declined to partake of the consultations of the Building Committee, and seems to have been sorry later that he absented himself. As Director of the Museum, he had not been consulted in the final decision about the architect of his Museum, and he was offended. It was, however, characteristic of Goodyear and Rockefeller to take such matters into their own hands (as Goodyear had taken the Paris show into his own hands) and to brush aside as impractical the very kind of judgment by which Barr had made the Museum's quality and its reputation. But neither Goodyear nor Rockefeller nor, it seems, Stephen Clark was notable for tact. "Toughie" Goodyear made up for it by bluster, Nelson by back-slapping and "Hiya, Fella," and Clark by relative silence which may or may not have masked a genuine shyness. That is not to say that Barr's ideas were not communicated to the committee, for, as Stone put it, "Alfred was calling the shots from behind the scenes." He had appointed John McAndrew, whom he hired after the deliberations of the committee were under way, as his emissary and the interpreter of his strongly held opinions about the needs of the Museum.

McAndrew had known Stone when they were both in the architectural school at Harvard (Stone was a few years older than McAndrew) and they spoke a common language. "Goodwin felt deeply about certain things," McAndrew recalls, "about a certain elegance and clarity in design and plan, and Ed Stone would always say 'yes' to anybody, whatever they proposed, and Phil Goodwin would suffer." The meetings were, McAndrew says, "stormy." "Clark didn't say much. Nelson and Goodyear were awfully rough on Goodwin. They were just not very nice to him." There was a good deal of discussion about "how to make the frame of a building that could have concrete-slab floors with no beams so that partitions could be moved around; they argued about did it have to be air-conditioned or didn't it? There was endless talk about the little auditorium down below. Acoustical experts were brought in, but they forgot the fact that the subway was right there and they spent a great deal of money raising it from 92 percent perfect to 96 percent; that was all fine except that every four minutes a train went by and the whole thing shuddered. There was the question of furnishing it [the auditorium] and Alfred had the idea that Klee should design it, but it cost too much and anyway Klee died about then. There was a suggestion that Calder should design the lights on the landings, but the committee didn't do that."

But however stormy the sessions, however acquiescent Stone appeared to be (he obviously took the suggestions he wanted and ignored many of the others, as any architect must), the plans of the building were far enough along by March 1937 so that the Building Committee could present them to the trustees as a whole. The Museum was to be a six-story building of 1,390,000 cubic feet, with an auditorium and lounge and shipping rooms below street level and a members' lounge on the top. It was estimated that it would cost one dollar a cubic foot to construct, and in those times that meant a fairly luxurious building. The trustees approved, and in the Museum *Bulletin* for July 1937 the new building was announced to members and a photograph of the model, as it then was, was printed on the cover. "Through the generosity of its trustees, friends and patrons," the *Bulletin* said, "the Museum of Modern Art has already raised more than three-fourths of the million dollars necessary for the erection of its new building." The *Bulletin* promised that the façade would be white marble and that there would be a tower at the west end which would rise twenty-six feet "above the penthouse level." The first three floors were designed for exhibitions, the fourth for offices, a projection room, and a shipping department for the Film Library, which would finally come home to roost, and the Museum's Library and print room. On the fifth floor the Director and the curators would have their offices, and the penthouse would include "several rest rooms and a large conference room, surrounded by a wide terrace."

The model was widely reproduced in papers in New York and elsewhere, and it seemed preposterous to a good many editorial writers that anybody had the nerve to call it architecture. "The new 'functional' architecture, so called," said the Lexington (Kentucky) *Leader*, "has no excuse for being." And it also moved him to say, "There is no concern felt to make the exterior beautiful, pleasing to the eye and conformable to architectural principles as these have been developed through the ages." In further saying that he preferred the Mellon Institute, which had just been completed in Pittsburgh at a cost of $10,000,000 and was a "replica of a Greek temple of the Periclean age, thoroughly modern in its equipment . . . as completely functional as the most practical engineer could wish," he was speaking for millions upon millions of his fellow citizens who thought that "functionalism" was an insult to their sensibilities, a somehow treasonable flouting of all that was good and noble and beautiful in the heritage of architecture. Ten years later, of course, the Museum looked, if not quaint, at least comfortably old-fashioned. The "curtain wall" of unmitigated and unadorned glass was beginning to become a cliché, and gas stations and diners and supermarkets were Internationally un-Stylish. What Frank Lloyd Wright called "the flat-chested style" of architecture had in many debased and misconstrued forms taken over almost everywhere except in the old suburbs, where Tudor and French Provincial and Colonial tastes still persisted, and in the new mass-produced Levittowns, where Cape Cod cottages and the emerging ranch house were the accepted middle-class dream.

The building as it was built resembled but did not duplicate the model whose photograph was distributed. The tower at the west end was eliminated, and the other changes were largely in the façade and principally in the material of which it was made. Instead of white marble there was a vast area of a new translucent material called Thermolux on which Alfred Barr insisted because he wanted the interior lit by diffused daylight. The Building Committee and the architects had opposed him, and so he turned to Sachs. Sachs, as he customarily did, came to Barr's support. Barr wrote to thank him, and said, "You made a phone call—you said *fiat lux* in a loud voice [to the Building Committee] and like magic *there was light*." (In practice, the light that came through the Thermolux sandwich of spun glass between two sheets of clear glass turned out to be far too intense; a false wall had to be built behind it and artificial light substituted for sunlight.) Four months after the photograph of the model was published, plans for the building were filed with the Building Department of New York City and a loan of $800,000 was negotiated with the Chase National Bank at 2½ percent interest for three years. Nelson Rockefeller, who was in charge of raising the money to build the new Museum, had a million dollars in subscriptions in hand by the time the new building was opened in May 1939, about six months later than had been announced in the *Bulletin*.

One-thing-at-a-time has never marked the Museum's character. Indeed, it was a circus with more than the usual metaphoric three rings, though usually its activities were within its own walls or, as in the case of the circulating exhibitions, initiated by it. But while the new building was being planned, haggled over, and financed, Goodyear had got involved with the World's Fair that was scheduled by New Yorkers to rise in 1939 on the Flushing meadows with the Trylon and Perisphere designed by Wallace K. Harrison as its symbol. In June 1936 there had been the notion in the Fair Committee that it would be nice to "confer with representatives of the Museum of Modern Art for the erection of

a 'Town of Modern Art' to portray at the fair the town of the future."
Nothing came of this, but in the same spirit the Museum held at just
about the same time a show of *Modern Exposition Architecture*. With
enlarged photographs, models, sketches, and plans of what had been
done in Stockholm in 1930, in Cologne in 1928, in Milan in 1933, in
Brussels in 1935, and in Chicago in 1933, it hoped to have some influence on the architecture of the New York fair. About two years later
Grover Whalen, who was the City Commissioner for the fair, asked
Goodyear to organize and chair a committee for a vast exhibition of
American painting, and the committee he collected represented every
shade and shadow of artistic opinion from the most staid to the most
advanced, the most politically conservative to the most radical. There
were the directors of the Metropolitan, the Whitney, and the Brooklyn museums, the presidents of the American Federation of Art, the
National Academy of Design, the Artists' Congress, and the New York
Society of Women Painters, plus William Zorach, Paul Manship,
Eugene Speicher, Stuart Davis, and Hugo Gellert, who, you will recall,
was the man who had violently attacked the Museum over the refusal
of political paintings for the exhibition of *Murals by American Painters
and Sculptors* in 1932.

Holger Cahill, who had been Acting Director of the Museum while
Barr was in Europe in 1932, was named director of the exhibition, and
the New York *Herald Tribune* reported on August 15, 1938, that
"Cahill expects more than 15,000 works to be submitted and 800
shown." There were to be six regional committees to do the initial
weeding, and Cahill said that "the keynote" would be Democracy in
Art. "Care," he said, "will be taken to see that every school of artistic
thought, from the most extreme modern, through middle of the road,
to conservative is represented." American artists living in Paris sent a
cable protesting that their work would have to be shipped to New
York to be judged and they resented the expense.

The exhibition was called *American Art Today* and it was as various
as the tastes of the juries that selected the sculpture, painting, and
prints. More than a thousand objects were displayed, and Alfred Barr's
first broom, Dorothy Miller, was there frantically helping her husband,
Cahill, to get the show "hung." "It was all so terribly last-minute," she
says. "The macadam of the floors was still soft; the rigs we used to
move the sculpture and our feet sank into it." [4] Grover Whalen had

---

4 The Museum bought nine paintings out of the exhibition, four of them by
the Chicago artists Mitchell Siporin, Gustaf Dalstrom, Raymond Breinin, and
Rainey Bennett. The other five were by Edward Chavez, Everett Spruce, Adolf
Dehn, Joseph Hirsch, and Byron Thomas.

warned Cahill that he would need someone to work with him who was familiar with the complexities of the fair, and he lent him his own secretary, Elizabeth Litchfield (known as "Giggles"). She became, as she said to Dorothy Miller, "tainted with art," and subsequently joined the Museum's staff as Barr's secretary, at a considerable reduction in salary, and remained as a mainstay of the Museum.

If things were hectic on Flushing meadows in the weeks before the fair opened on April 20, they were frantic on 53rd Street. If, as Edward Warburg had said of ordinary life in the Museum in the early days, "Everything had the frayed nerves of an opening night," this was *Walpurgisnacht!*

There was the exhibition to be gathered and its catalogue to be written, and this was to be an exhibition on which the Museum could stake its reputation and demonstrate the breadth of its concerns. Even its title, *Art in Our Time,* seemed lordly. It was not only intended to celebrate the opening of the Museum's first "permanent home," it also celebrated the Museum's tenth birthday, and was therefore a declaration of its accomplishments and a pledge to its future. It was, moreover, the Museum's bait and offering to the hundreds of thousands of people who were expected to flock to New York to see the fair. But the show was just one of dozens of problems—planning problems, labor problems, problems with city red tape, social problems, publicity problems, and problems of protocol.

In December 1938, six months before the scheduled date for the opening, Mrs. Cornelius N. Bliss, Monroe Wheeler, and Tom Mabry had put their heads together and thought up a plan for a Modern Art Ball to be held at the Ritz or the Waldorf-Astoria "one week prior to the opening." The idea, of course, was to make publicity, not to raise money. "It was suggested," the minutes of the meeting record, "that all the costumes be designed by modern artists and that numerous prizes, consisting of modern works of art, be awarded to those wearing the best costumes." After a good deal of discussion with the larger Committee on the Opening, the plan was abandoned for fear that such a splurge might have "an adverse effect on Foundations and friends of the Museum" at a time when money was still acutely needed for the building fund.

It seemed advisable to Nelson Rockefeller, who was the imminent heir apparent to Goodyear as President of the Museum, to hire an expert in public relations who could accomplish more than Sarah Newmeyer. She was a spectacularly good press agent, as we have seen, but she did not seem to him quite up to the dignity and dimensions of the occasion. At his own expense he hired Julian Street, Jr., and appointed

him Secretary of the Museum at $7,500 a year, with his duties defined
(in part) as: "Preparation and placing, if possible of news and pictures . . . ; conducting important people [in New York for the
World's Fair] through the building and making news of the occasion;
making contacts with agencies, etc., in regard to distribution of information about the Museum; representing the Museum on such occasions
as are not covered by the Director or the Executive Director. . . ."
The program that he concocted for the opening of the Museum was
an impressive one. Evidently without difficulty he engaged the cooperation of the Columbia Broadcasting System to make its facilities
available for a radio broadcast the evening of the formal opening on
May 10, and he was instrumental in putting together an imposing radio
show.

There were, however, a good many things to be put in order before
that evening arrived. Indeed, one of the things that seemed to take forever to materialize was the absolutely essential Certificate of Occu-
pancy from the New York City Department of Buildings. If the building should be opened to the public and there were any sort of accident
or catastrophe, the trustees of the Museum would be financially responsible. Happily, the certificate arrived on April 21, nearly three
weeks before the deadline.

Then there was the matter of the garden on the north side of the
building to be resolved. In 1937, two years before the new building
was completed, John D. Rockefeller, Jr., had given the Museum a
piece of land where his and Abby's house had stood, but it was a small
strip that ran only seventy-five feet along 54th Street. "About a week
before we opened," John McAndrew says, "we found we could have
some extra land [lent by Mr. Rockefeller], not just the little piece we
had, for a garden." It meant that the areas of plate glass on the north
side would look out, as they do today, on a pleasant space set about
with trees and sculpture. The expanded garden was 400 feet long by
100 feet deep. "Alfred and I sat up all one night, and I made a model
of the whole garden with steel-wool trees while Alfred placed sculptures where they could be seen best—that is, so that you wouldn't
come in and see everything at once but had to turn corners." They
had to work with a very tight budget; nothing had been set aside for
this unexpected purpose. Inexpensive plywood pavilions were built and
cheap woven wood fencing was used to break up the space. To provide variety in the surface McAndrew used pebbles of two different
colors in free-form patterns, and women complained that the pebbles
were death on their high heels. "It wasn't really dry by the time the

Museum opened," McAndrew explained. "We wanted to mix a little cement powder and sand with the pebbles so that they would be solid, but it didn't get done." Nelson Rockefeller had the gardener from Radio City come to do the planting (trees and shrubs were donated by trustees), but he and McAndrew did not see eye to eye. "I had an awful fight to get in birch trees," McAndrew said. "He said they wouldn't grow in the city, and I remembered the beautiful birches behind my cousin Stephen Brown's house on Madison Avenue and 39th Street, and we put them in and they did very well." [5]

The last few weeks before the opening were a strain on everyone involved. When I asked McAndrew, who had been responsible for selecting all of the furniture for the building, about the opening, he said, "I remember the weeks *before* the opening. People were working almost all night, and I think the last couple of days quite a few people actually did work all night." Allen Porter said, "Everybody did everything. You painted, you hung. Did you know that after all the wiring and lighting fixtures were in, the electrical union very cleverly discovered the day before the opening that all that stuff was non-union made? Of course they knew it all along, and so they wouldn't touch anything. It had to be all taken down, taken out, rewired, rehung at such a vast cost in overtime that you wouldn't believe it." On the afternoon of the day of the opening Dorothy Miller and Alfred Barr found that there was nothing in three small sculpture galleries. "Nothing had been placed, and at about five o'clock we started pushing pedestals around," Dorothy Miller said. "We had a system of pushing them with one foot and holding on above. At six thirty Alfred said, 'I've got to go put on a dinner jacket,' and he left, and I took a piece of silk and went about flicking the dust off the pictures that hadn't been dusted. I was there until about eight thirty, and then I went home [to the Village] to dress. I was so exhausted I fell asleep and never did get to the opening."

Two days before the official opening the trustees put the building to its first formal use. On the evening of May 8 they had a dinner (it might almost be called a banquet) in the Trustees' Room on the penthouse floor. It was followed by speeches and a formal meeting. The occasion was a momentous one in the history of the Museum, and everyone there was well aware of it. It marked the end of an era and of a regime, and the beginning of a new manner of life for the Museum and its staff. The moment was encrusted with suitable ceremony.

5　Thirty-three years later birch trees (though not the same ones, as the garden has been redesigned several times) thrive in the Museum's garden.

"Sandy" Calder had designed silver candelabra which looped their way among greens and lilies down a long table set with glasses for three wines. The husbands and wives of trustees were there, and, as Mrs. Barr recalls, "Abby Rockefeller had on a most glorious deep red long dress by Lanvin; you know, he cut everything on the bias. She looked magnificent." The speeches were limited to two, the first by Paul Sachs, a serious consideration in two parts of "the Problem which faces American museums" and "the specific problems of the Museum of Modern Art," and the second by Goodyear, which was chatty and informal.

Sachs, the scholar, spoke like a scholar. He berated American museums for their "comparatively mediocre" scholarship, and deplored the laxness of the training of most young men for the museum professions, and the inadequate quality and standards of publication. "The problem, as I see it," he said, "for American museums in the future is how to develop within their walls a more severe discipline; how to avoid the sentimental." When he spoke to his second topic, the problems of the Museum of Modern Art, he said with prescience that "in the coming decade energy and funds must be allocated with enthusiasm on a larger scale to *films*, to *architecture*, to *photographs*, and to the *library;* for it is through these that the greatest number of young people can be reached—a fact, I fear, which too few of our generation appreciate." He praised the Museum's catalogues, but stressed the "need of more leisurely scholarly work" and for fellowships for scholars in twentieth-century art. He urged a slower tempo lest the Museum "burn out our able personnel"; he exhorted the trustees to consider the importance of a "choice permanent collection of moderate size—a collection which may serve as a sort of stabilizer or measuring rod—a sort of *background of quality.* . . ."

Sachs was an élitist, as, indeed, were most if not all of his fellow trustees, a position which is heartily challenged today by those who would reform the Museum's posture and heartily (if not in so many words) still supported by the Museum's older trustees. Sachs put his belief in these words on that evening: "The Museum of Modern Art has a duty to the great public. But in serving an élite it will reach, better than in any other way, the great general public by means of work done to meet the most exacting standards of an élite."

Before he sat down to accept the applause of his social if not in most cases his intellectual peers, he had a final caution to pronounce. He warned them against *"the danger of timidity"* and he underlined the words in his manuscript. "The Museum must continue to take risks," he said. "It has taken risks, with its eyes open, from the very start. It must not stop taking risks:—for the reputation of the Museum of Modern Art will rest upon its successes more than upon its mistakes. In the field of modern art chances must be taken. The Museum should continue to be a pioneer:—bold and uncompromising."

Goodyear was at his most affable; the grouch and curmudgeon was wreathed in smiles as he reviewed the brief history of the Museum, praising his fellow trustees and most especially Mrs. Rockefeller, and letting his momentary eloquence fall benignly on a few members of the staff. He spoke tenderly of Lizzie Bliss; he recalled the day on which he had waited on the pier for Sachs's boat to dock so that he might ask him to become one of the committee to organize the Museum, and he noted that "At this particular time our Eddie [Warburg] was still happily roaming in his rompers at Harvard." But his greatest compliments went to his principal antagonist, who was also in many respects his friend—Alfred Barr. "The pituitary gland, you know, has a very profound influence in the growth of the body," he said. "The skeleton cannot prosper without it, and when its activity is diminished, this leads to obesity and mental defects. Our pituitary gland is Alfred Barr. . . . It is useless for me to attempt to tell you what Alfred has done for us. I need only say, look about you." He added a compliment for Tom Mabry to the laurels he was bestowing and he mentioned Iris Barry and Dick Abbott pleasantly in connection with the Film Library, but gave the principal credit for its success to Jock Whitney. He praised nearly all of the other trustees, but no other members of the staff. Not surprisingly, he singled out the husband of one trustee, John D. Rockefeller, Jr. ("Without his cooperation and generosity certainly this building could not be"), and told a story about him which, he said, "I think is characteristic.

He was in London with Mrs. Rockefeller and looking for a quiet place in which to spend a weekend. A friend recommended a little inn at Chagford in Devon, saying: "If you go, you will drive in from the north and you will see first the front of the lovely buildings and an ugly gasoline station. I have urged the landlady to move it away, but she will not, as she says it is her backlog," and Mr. Rockefeller said, "Have you ever thought—that is my backlog too?"

It was on the occasion of this dinner and meeting that Conger Goodyear stepped down from the presidency of the Museum and turned it over to Nelson Rockefeller, who was then thirty years old.

"His finger," Goodyear said, "has been usefully employed in practically every one of our pies." He had been chairman of the Advisory Committee (but not its first chairman, as Goodyear said; the architect George Howe was forgotten that evening), Treasurer of the Museum and chairman of the Finance Committee, a member of the Executive Committee and of the Building Committee. "Sometimes his mother has stressed Nelson's youth as a detriment," Goodyear said, "but I can't agree that youth is any handicap." [6]

On that same evening Stephen C. Clark was elected the Museum's first Chairman of the Board, a gesture of thanks for his "time and money in the creation of this building" but also with the unmentioned (but surely not unknown to anyone in the room) hope that his remarkable collection might in time be given or bequeathed to the Museum. If Clark had known what he was letting himself in for during the next five years, he might have thought better of accepting the honorific post that was bestowed on him.

Clark that evening was home with a minor illness, and Nelson read a telegram from him which praised Goodyear and congratulated Nelson. Then Nelson, who remarked that his mother "feels that there should be no other speakers tonight," said, "Since I am not permitted to express my feelings in words, I should like to present to Mr. Goodyear this painting by Mr. Harnett, as a token of my personal admiration and esteem for what he has done for the Museum." Moreover, he said that to him the picture seemed to symbolize the Museum in various of its aspects and "to typify the Museum's interest in American art." The painting, called "Playbill and Dollar Bill," was a rather far-fetched joke, a *trompe l'oeil* presumably by William M. Harnett, who worked his charming magic in the last decades of the nineteenth century.[7] With the presentation of the picture the meeting was adjourned and the trustees and their spouses swept into the shining new elevators and descended to the lower floors to see what delicious confection Barr and his colleagues had wrought under the ambitious name *Art in Our Time* for the Museum's tenth birthday.

Since they had the building all to themselves (certainly not the case for those who came to the official opening two nights later), they were able to see the exhibition in its pristine, if not entirely

6 He was also by this time the president of what *Time* Magazine called "the huge landlording enterprise of Rockefeller Center" and a director of Creole Petroleum Corp., a subsidiary of Standard Oil of New Jersey, with properties in Venezuela.

7   The attribution of this picture has been called dubious by Alfred Frankenstein, the principal authority on Harnett, in his book *After the Hunt*.

final, condition. It was the kind of show that would take a conscientious connoisseur or amateur several weeks to look at. There were 205 oil paintings, 20 watercolors, 21 large prints, 76 pieces of sculpture and construction, 63 photographs by seven American photographers, plus an architecture exhibition of *Houses and Housing*, and *A Cycle of Seventy Films*. As Goodyear noted in his preface to the catalogue of the show, "The exhibition galleries provide three times the space available heretofore."

Barr, never for a moment forgetting that the Museum was by its charter an educational institution (or that he was by conviction and habit an educator), conceived of *Art in Our Time* as an outline of the Museum's curriculum. It presented, he said, "achievements of living artists together with the work of certain important masters of yesterday," and he made clear that it was quite different from the "special exhibition of modern art in other New York museums at the time of the Fair" not only because it did not confine itself to American work but because it included matters with which most museums did not concern themselves, such as chairs by Le Corbusier and Mies van der Rohe and a "one-piece" bathroom made of sheet metal and designed by Buckminster Fuller. Oliver Larkin observed (in his book *Art and Life in America*) about the show of American painting that Cahill had done for the World's Fair, "If any common denominator emerged, it was a fresh consciousness of the American environment and a greater emphasis on factual content than on form." Almost the exact opposite was true of Barr's show, which had virtually nothing to do with the American (or any other) environment as such and placed a great deal more emphasis on form than on factual content. In American painting it went back as far as the 1860s—"Landscape with Figures" by Winslow Homer (owned then by the new Chairman of the Board and now at Yale); the earliest European painting was a Renoir of 1876, "*Le Moulin de la Galette*," lent by Jock Whitney, who was the new First Vice-President. In each of its aspects the show displayed the very latest objects that were being made. As the trustees came down the stairs from the second floor, hanging above their heads at the landing was a brand-new mobile by Calder, commissioned for the occasion. It was called "Lobster Trap and Fishtail."

Two days later the floodgates opened.

Forty dinner parties on the evening of May 10, arranged by trustees and committee members, gave assurance that the most fashionable and influential members not just of the New York community but from afar were on hand to ornament the official opening of the new building. Mr. and Mrs. Robert Woods Bliss of Washington (she was a trustee) borrowed a house on Gramercy Park from their friends the Samuel Little Barlows, as, according to the press, "they maintain a house in New York but found it too small for their guest list." The list included the Swedish, Danish, and Norwegian Ministers and their wives, Sir Kenneth and Lady Clark [8] of London, Mrs. Vincent Astor, and President and Mrs. Dodds of Princeton, among others. Conger Goodyear, having no dining room of his own big enough (and presumably every friend of his who had one was already giving a party for the Museum), held his dinner at Hampshire House, a hotel on Central Park South. His most newsworthy guest was Anne Morrow (Mrs. Charles A.) Lindbergh, whose accounts of her flights with her husband, *North to the Orient* and *Listen! the Wind* (published that same year), had made her famous in her own right. A reporter noted that she looked "thinner and more wistful than ever . . . in a simple soft blue gown." On Goodyear's right was the formidable Ruth Vanderbilt Twombly in black lace. Frank Crowninshield was, of course, at his friend Conger's party, as were Salvador Dali and his wife, Gala (in a burgundy dress that "glittered with paillettes and gold embroidery"), the Alfred Barrs, the celebrated actress Lillian Gish, and the sculptor Jo Davidson, heavily bearded in the days when beards were thought suitable only for artists.

Not all the parties were as brilliant as the Blisses' and Goodyear's, but Monroe Wheeler and his committee to plan the opening had enticed advocates of the Museum to entertain and had parceled out the celebrities and near-celebrities with some respect for fairness. Sarah Newmeyer had the mimeograph machine grinding out press releases which found every hamlet in the nation, or so it seemed, and local papers happily reported what homefolks had been there, in their "Social Notes from All Over" columns. A Richmond, Indiana, paper, for example, reported that Mrs. M. F. Johnson, the director of the Richmond Art Association, had written to "a friend": "The much advertised new Modern Art building was opened on the evening of May 10, with a grand reception to members and guests. . . . I saw New York's four hundred en masse in an awful crush. Evidently modern art has captured the attention of this group. . . ."

In the vernacular of the '30s, "she said a mouthful!"

Seven thousand women—carefully, and many elaborately, dressed—and men—in white ties and opera hats or at the very least in dinner

8 Sir Kenneth was then the director of the National Gallery in London. He later became Lord Clark and because of his book and television series is now jokingly known as Lord Clark of Civilization.

jackets—pressed through the wide-open glass doors on 53rd Street into the first floor of the Museum. Mrs. Nicholas Murray Butler, the wife of the president of Columbia University, who had been at Goodyear's dinner, took one look and said, "You couldn't drag me in there," and went home. Mrs. Cornelius Vanderbilt, a tall, imposing figure in rose lace with a bandeau of matching lamé around her gray hair, struggled in with Katherine Anne Porter and George Platt Lynes (there is a photograph to prove it), and so did Mrs. Vincent Astor in black net and pearls. Nobody, of course, could see anything, but, as Goodyear had said of the Jeu de Paume show, that was not the purpose of a *vernissage:* it wasn't even to see other people that most of them came, it was to be seen. People struck out for the garden when the press on the first floor got too great, and many of them took the elevators to the members' penthouse. One couple found that the best way not to get pushed about was to ride the elevators. "We're just riding up and down for the fun of it," they said.[9]

Jimmy Ernst, the painter, who was then in his late teens and worked for the Museum as an office boy, said, "I remember seeing La Guardia walking around making snide remarks at the Seurats and the Sheelers. I don't know whether he didn't like them or just wanted to be clever. And then the Roosevelt speech, which I thought was rather impressive. . . ."

The radio program that Julian Street, Jr., had arranged for the evening was in anyone's terms "impressive." Lowell Thomas was the announcer who introduced Edward Bruce, then the chief of the Treasury Department of Fine Arts, Edsel Ford, who talked about "the industrial aspects of modern art" (and said, "I think the time is not far away when it will be possible for us all to live in homes furnished with objects of 'museum quality' even though their cost be trifling"), and John Hay Whitney, who talked about the Film Library. Then Hollywood was switched in and Walt Disney talked about the significance of historically important films to the future. From there the pick-up went to Chicago where Robert M. Hutchins, the young and educationally adventurous president of the University of Chicago, said, among other things, "People have eyes and perceive. Perception can be taught. Perception is understanding." From him the program went precisely at 10:45 to the White House.

"My friends," said Franklin Delano Roosevelt, "when men dedicate

9 Most of this information is taken from the observations of society reporters; some is from my own memory. My best source has been a column by Patricia Coffin, a journalist with humor and a sharp eye, who was then a reporter for the New York *World-Telegram.*

a new edifice for a common enterprise they are at once celebrating an achievement and announcing a purpose. They cannot refrain nor could they properly be excused from making clear what that purpose is."

The President talked for fifteen minutes, speaking slowly in his flat New York accent words that had been written for him by a number of people at the Museum but which were principally the composition of the distinguished philosopher Irwin Edman, who professed at Columbia and was a graceful stylist. The talk covered the various activities of the Museum and emphasized most emphatically the traveling exhibitions which were likely to have been seen and would be seen in the future by many more people than had ever got (or were likely to get) to 53rd Street. "And most important of all," he said, "the standards of American taste will inevitably be raised by this bringing into far-flung communities results of the latest and finest achievements in all the arts." Surely no more official statement was ever made about the tastemaking role of the Museum than this.

The opening statements were more memorable than the concluding ones in Roosevelt's speech. "We are dedicating this building to the cause of peace and to the pursuits of peace," he said after his first few sentences.

> The arts that ennoble and refine life flourish only in the atmosphere of peace. And in this hour of dedication we are glad again to bear witness before all the world to our faith in the sanctity of free institutions. For we know that only where men are free can the arts flourish and the civilization of national culture reach full flower.
>
> The arts cannot thrive except where men are free to be themselves and to be in charge of the discipline of their own energies and ardors. The conditions for democracy and for art are one and the same.

It is well to remember that the World's Fair which opened just a few weeks before these words were said by Roosevelt was also dedicated to the pursuits of peace, and that less than four months later the Nazi *Luftwaffe* bombed the cities of Poland and Hitler's tanks and infantry crossed its borders to lay the country waste and to detonate the world's most devastating war.

Two things roiled the surface brilliance of the evening, one a prank and the other an oversight which became known as "Nelson's goof."

Those who had come to the party had received elaborate engraved invitations on which appeared the names of all the trustees. The intention was not merely to make the party socially impressive to members but to make sure that invitations were put in the hands of relatively prosperous people who might be induced by an aura of elegance to join the Museum—a routine kind of promotion for a museum, any museum, to undertake. But it ruffled the feathers of Frances Collins, the young woman in charge of publications, and made her, as she recalls, "extremely indignant." Not only was the invitation pretentious, she thought, but it was an outrage that some of the staff—the telephone operator and Jimmy Ernst, the office boy, for example—were not invited to the party. "You've got to remember," she said, "that I was extremely young and terribly snooty. Nelson's people had put a team of efficiency experts in the Museum because he thought that the Museum ought to be put on a paying basis, and there were a lot of tensions and the staff was in a passion of moral indignation." [10] She called her friend Joseph Blumenthal of the Spiral Press (which printed the Museum's catalogues and was for many years one of the finest presses in the country) and asked him if he would print on toilet paper a mock invitation which she would write. "He said he had some beautiful handmade Italian paper and would use that. He designed and I wrote this abominably impudent 'invitation.' It was kid stuff," she said, "let's face it."

The "invitation" was a four-page "French fold" on the front sheet of which was printed a simple crown in outline and under it the words in small sansserif capitals, to wit:

OIL THAT GLITTERS
IS NOT GOLD

Inside was the flying horse of Socony-Vacuum as a crest at the top of the third page and below it the invitation printed in a script that imitated engraving. It looked like this, which is reproduced from the original:

10 Beaumont Newhall was photographing the new Library at just about this time when one of Nelson's efficiency experts came in. Newhall didn't know who he was and said, "Here, hold this, and press the button when I tell you." He gave him flash equipment to work.

The Empress of Blandings
and
Mister Charles Boyer
request the honor of

Mrs. Collins *presence*

at the semi-public opening of the new

Museum of Standard Oil

11 West 53rd Street, New York, N. Y.

Wednesday evening, May the 10th

from nine until one o'clock

Better dresses - 5th floor

R. S. V. P.
this card will admit two persons
or one person and two dogs or . . .

"The night of the opening," Mrs. Collins said, "I had on a severe and I thought terribly sophisticated black dress, and I encountered Lincoln Kirstein resplendent in white tie and tails. He kissed me and said, 'This is the kiss of death.' Apparently Lincoln had got hold of one of these invitations and shown it to Nelson. Lincoln was playing Caligula. Not very long after that Mr. Rockefeller suggested to Mr. Mabry that my services should be dispensed with; that I was dangerous. Tom did fire me, but he didn't want to. Evidently Nelson had said, 'Better get her out of here fast or she might burn the place down.' "

"Nelson's goof" was a quite different matter which, unlike Frances Collins' prank, had rather far-reaching consequences. The staff, if not the trustees, were greatly amused by what their young colleague had done. Nobody was amused by Nelson's oversight.

There were some trustees who thought that the radio program "was unsuited to the importance of the occasion," but more important than that was the fact that during the broadcast "no mention was made of various founders and trustees whose efforts were largely responsible for the success of the Museum today. It was also regretted that no mention was made of the architects of the new building."

The crux of the matter does not emerge from these quotations from the minutes of a meeting of the Membership Committee which was held just a week after the opening. The simple truth was that Conger Goodyear's feelings were hurt. "If you give ten years of your life to the presidency of an institution and not be acknowledged by the new president," Monroe Wheeler said, "well, it attracted attention." Rockefeller came to the meeting of the Membership Committee to explain, and the minutes record the gist of what he said:

> Mr. Rockefeller expressed profound regret concerning the omissions referred to, and assumed entire responsibility for them. . . . He explained in detail the problems of interesting a radio audience of millions of people, and the severity of the radio companies in deleting any references to people or events which would not interest the average radio listener.
>
> Mr. Rockefeller further explained that these matters of acknowledgement had been thoroughly dealt with at the dinner meeting of the Trustees. . . .

It is quite probable, of course, that if Rockefeller had explained these exigencies to Goodyear before the fact, hurt feelings would have been avoided. Though this may, on the other hand, have been inevitable. There was no great love lost between Goodyear and young Nelson. It is interesting, though the significance of it cannot be measured, that after Goodyear had given to the Library of the Museum his scrapbooks of correspondence and memorabilia, he withdrew the volume that deals with the end of his presidency and the beginning of Rockefeller's. According to Bernard Karpel, the Museum's Librarian, Goodyear felt it more discreet to remove that volume, and his family evidently does not know what has become of it. Goodyear's interest in the Museum dwindled rapidly after this incident, and his collection of paintings and sculpture for the most part found a permanent home not on 53rd Street, as Barr had hoped it would, but in the Albright-Knox Art Gallery in his hometown of Buffalo, New York.

Whatever the momentary internal difficulties may have been, the critical reception of the new building and its first exhibition was generally enthusiastic. Royal Cortissoz in the *Herald Tribune* took his usual swipe at the Museum. "The Museum of Modern Art," he wrote the following Sunday, "makes its new building rather difficult to approach in the right mood. It has committed itself to one of the most forbidding façades in the annals of the city, a bold essay in that style which may be in harmony with the Mesopotamian word 'functionalism' but which, in its ugliness, looks just like so much vacuity. Once inside the building, however, it is apparent that the architect has well acquitted himself." No one in the Museum much cared what Cortissoz said, but they did pay attention to Lewis Mumford, who was then writing a regular column of architectural criticism for *The New Yorker*. He most certainly did not go overboard in his enthusiasm, which was, indeed, restrained, but there were things about the building that pleased him. He liked the entrance, "a very happy introduction to the building" which "calls attention to . . . the generally intelligent and gracious use of curved forms throughout the building." He liked the fact that one could see through the building to the garden as one came in, and he liked the main stairs "as they mount upward against a stunning frieze of statuesque green plants." He especially liked the way the flexible interior space for the galleries had been used. "This innovation," he said, "is bound to affect every future program for museum building."

The exhibition in general fared even better than the building. Henry McBride, a friend but never a fatuous one, said in the *Sun*, "New York has the opportunity to study the finest and most complete exposition of the 'modern idea' that has yet been put together anywhere in the world." *The New Yorker* said that "The show itself is generally superb. . . . All in all, the most sumptuously arranged and consistently interesting exhibition we've had in New York for some time." Jewell of the *Times* was equally stirred, as were the critics for *Art News* and the *Magazine of Art*. Cortissoz was polite.

It was a triumphant climax to the Museum's first decade. It was the 112th show that the Museum had put on, and more than a million and a half people (many of them, of course, repeaters) had come to see what was on the Museum's walls and pedestals and what hung from its ceilings. "Not all of those shows commanded a general acclaim," Goodyear wrote in his preface to the catalogue for *Art in Our Time;* "many were frowned upon by the ultra-conservative; a few were scorned by the advanced liberals.

"In the tenth year of its existence," Goodyear said, "the Museum of Modern Art comes of age, a precocious accomplishment."

It was indeed precocious; there was no arguing with that—a ten-

year-old in a million-dollar home on a million-dollar lot with a past
that was already scandalous and distinguished and a character that was
praised and excoriated and a future that was championed and attacked.
It seemed almost too good to be true. Indeed, in some respects it was
too good to be true.

But the staff was not worrying about that at the moment. Everyone
was exhausted from the weeks of getting ready for the balloon ascen-
sion. Mrs. Rockefeller was quite aware of that and sensitive, as always,
to the feelings of those who worked for and with her. She must, however, have been thoroughly pleased with the way things had worked
out. It was her wild oat that had produced such a delightful and aston-
ishing crop, and now her second son was about to take over the farm.

Before they had had a chance to catch their breath each member of
the staff received what Allen Porter says was "a wonderful letter from
Mrs. Rockefeller. It was like a shot in the arm. You couldn't believe
it." It read:

> The opening of the new building of the Museum of Modern
> Art marks the climax of its work during the past ten years. The
> Trustees were tremendously enthusiastic when they visited the
> building and the new exhibition on Monday night. They were
> greatly impressed with the arrangement of the galleries, the deco-
> rations and furnishings, the lighting and the perfection of work-
> manship throughout. An unbelievable job has been done, and the
> Museum has taken another important step forward.
>
> This has all been made possible by the work which you and the
> other members of the staff have done. . . . We hope that you will
> accept the enclosed token of our personal gratitude.
>
> With many thanks and best wishes.

The letter was signed by Abby Rockefeller, Stephen Clark, and Nelson
Rockefeller. Goodyear's name was curiously missing.

The enclosure was a month's salary.

Musical chairs. *A game in which the players walk to music around a row of chairs containing one chair fewer than the number of players. When the music stops, the players rush to sit down, and the one left without a chair is eliminated.*
THE AMERICAN HERITAGE DICTIONARY OF THE ENGLISH LANGUAGE, 1969

Chapter XII *Musical Chairs and Other War Games*

The new building was by no means the glass-and-marble bower of bliss that the staff had envisioned, and life in it was different in tempo, in atmosphere, and above all in spirit from life in the Museum's make-shift earlier homes. In a manner of speaking, what had been a mission-ary church in a Philistine jungle with a small band of passionately devoted young proselytizers dedicated to making converts began to look curiously like, and take on the airs and graces of, a cathedral of the new culture. The Museum had floated from place to place; it had proudly called itself an experimental laboratory (Barr's phrase); it de-lighted in shoving a challenging fist in the public face, and just when it looked as though its program had settled down, it would sprout an-other new department and make a new and unconventional assault on the public sensibilities. It had lived on purposeful improvisation; it had done the best it could with inadequate space, half-remodeled interiors, false walls, and cans of paint in colors no one had seen in a museum before. It had flouted the dignity of the Fifth Avenue Association, which had objected to its banners, challenged the Metropolitan Mu-seum, and refused to be swallowed up in the Mayor's grandiose scheme for a cultural center. Whatever anybody might say about how its new home looked like a factory because it had no fluted columns or carved cornices, nobody denied that it was an establishment and was likely to stay put for some time. Nobody thought of it as part of "the Establishment," as the phrase had not yet got into the common American argot, but in today's language it was incontestably the Establishment's baby grown up.

The immediate impact on the staff, which was as full of bounce as ever, as full of schemes (and schemings), was "Wild! All of a sudden," as Dorothy Miller said, "we had a lot more space and no staff."

As new presidents are wont to do in educational and philanthropic as well as in business organizations, one of Nelson Rockefeller's first official acts as President of the Museum was to try "to put the house in order." In such transfers of power, the new incumbent often looks about him to see how he can shuffle the staff and dispense with some of it, either as "an unfortunate but necessary measure of economy" or as "getting rid of dead wood." Rockefeller had already introduced a team of "efficiency experts" into the Museum to comb the staff and its procedures in the hope of bringing expenses somewhat into line with income.

Unlike those museums in New York that occupy city property—the Metropolitan, the Natural History, the Brooklyn, for instance—the Museum of Modern Art had no financial help from the city in the maintenance of its plant or in paying for guardianship, and could expect none. It lived entirely on the beneficence of its trustees and friends, with some minor foundation support, the dues paid by its members, and the quarters collected at the door from visitors. The annual budget in 1939 was about $500,000, and though Rockefeller had no illusions about putting the Museum on a paying basis, he did hope to keep the annual deficit from getting out of hand. His approach was more realistic than that of one of his fellow trustees, Mrs. Murray Crane, whose long suit was "culture." She naïvely suggested that "Since we always seem to have a deficit, shouldn't we set something aside each year to meet it?" David McAlpin, when he was elected to the board and became chairman of the Photography Committee, wrote to Ansel Adams, "The total costs for [the] 1940 fiscal year are over $500,000. Income from sources outside the Board are about $200,000. So you can figure out what it costs to be a trustee!" One of the ways that Rockefeller hoped to reduce the burden on the trustees, or at least not let it increase inordinately, was a more efficient use of personnel in the Museum. The staff was by no means large in 1939, and to reduce it at a time when it might have been expected to expand (which, indeed, it did in the following year) is remembered now by some who were there as a rather gratuitous gesture, surely not calculated to maintain morale.

Very soon after the opening of the new building Alfred and Margaret Barr sailed to Europe to finish the work of collecting the Museum's first important exhibition of Picasso, a show which opened on November 15, 1939, with the title *Picasso: Forty Years of His Art.* Barr had started work on the show as long ago as 1931, and it had been several times postponed. Finally it had been rescued by an agreement that Barr made with Daniel Catton Rich, then director of fine arts of the Art Institute of Chicago, for the two museums to finance the exhibition and the catalogue jointly and to show it first in New York and then in Chicago. It was while Barr was putting the final touches on the show that something close to panic crept in among some of the younger but important members of the staff. First Frances Collins was fired for her prank, which cannot have surprised anyone, though it offended her colleagues' sense of loyalty. Far more important, however, were the dismissal a few days later of Tom Mabry, the Executive Director, and the resignation of John Ekstrom, the superintendent who had been in charge of the carpenters, frame-makers, maintenance men, and guards, and who had designed the movable walls which made the exhibition space so flexible. Both Mabry and Ekstrom, a man on whose friendliness, manual skills, and imagination the curators heavily depended, were very popular with their colleagues. There are conflicting stories of how these departures came about, but it was generally thought among the staff that the firing of Mabry and Frances Collins and of a number of men on the maintenance staff had taken place entirely without Barr's knowledge or consent, though he was, after all, the Museum's Director. Several of the staff, according to Beaumont Newhall, decided to cable to Barr in Paris, but they thought it unwise to do so from the Museum. "We were so terrified of the establishment (I guess you'd call it that now)," he says, "that we went over to my apartment to send a cable for fear the wires might be tapped or somebody might be reading the carbon copies, and we told Alfred that we'd stand by him and create a museum wherever he wanted." A few days later, Newhall says, a cable came from Barr saying, "Sit tight until I return." When Barr got back he said, according to Newhall, "Well, it just had to happen and I couldn't do it." It was plain to the staff that "he didn't have any power any more. And for a long time we just floated."

The decline in Barr's administrative authority worked gratifyingly to the advantage of two other men in the Museum. Monroe Wheeler was "asked by Nelson," as he explains it, "to take over publications." It was a job for which his previous experience qualified him. Not only had he been a publisher and a publicist, but he moved with an easy and self-assured gait among the arts, had high standards of book production, acquaintance with the printing industry, and, as we have noted, though he was no scholar himself, he respected scholarship in others. Above all, he was extremely well liked by the trustees and by most of the staff and was a useful bridge between them. The other member of the organization who found himself elevated to a more responsible position by Barr's decline in influence over the mechanics (not over the standards) of the Museum was John ("Dick") Abbott. He had been the titular director of the Film Library since it was founded, though his wife, Iris Barry, with the title of Curator, had been its fountain of ideas; it had been her taste, judgment, and knowledge that in just a few years had made the Film Library a unique scholarly resource and one of the juicier—to use a '30s word—public attractions of the Museum. In the new building with its auditorium, its projection room, its storage space for film, its offices and shipping facilities, the Film Library had been able to rejoin the family. There were, therefore, no physical complications in the way of Abbott's wearing two administrative hats at the same time. From the point of view of the staff, he wore neither of them gracefully. From the point of view of the trustees, he was, at least for a time, their man.

Before Wheeler took over the publications of the Museum they had already established a reputation for excellence. From the Museum's first catalogue for the opening show, care had been lavished on the typographical design, the quality of the plates, and the presswork. Under Barr's critical eye Jere Abbott had laid out the catalogue, and as typography was one of the arts that everyone encountered every day, it was therefore of as much concern to Barr as the design of household objects or architecture or any of the other arts considered not "fine" but "applied." This meant, of course, that every piece of printed paper, every letterhead, envelope, exhibition label, and door sign was scrutinized and critically weighed for the quality of its design. Allen Porter encountered Barr standing in the hall on the office floor of the new building one day shortly after it had been built and he appeared to be staring at the wall in deep concentration. Porter, who wanted to consult him, finally spoke up, and Barr said, "I'm not sure I like the way 'MEN' is printed on that door." When Monroe Wheeler was put in charge of preparations for the opening of the new building, one thing that fell to him quite properly was the design of the new letterheads, always to a typographer a finicky and challenging job. He took great care, and after considerable discussion a design was approved and thousands of letterheads and envelopes were printed. Instead of giving the address of the Museum as 11 *West* 53rd Street it was 11 *East*. Those who felt that Wheeler was a little over-conscious of what was chic explained that east of Fifth Avenue was fashionable and west was less so, and this was consequently a natural error for Wheeler to make. "We were using it for scratch paper for years," a member of the staff said.

There was always a struggle to get the catalogues of exhibitions out on time—in time, that is, for the opening of the exhibitions many of them recorded. The struggle was partly a contest between scholarship and practical publishing, between two kinds of perfectionism, one scholarly, the other a firm belief in the sanctity of deadlines. It was in some degree a contest between Barr's "integrity" and Wheeler's "efficiency," though the words greatly oversimplify what was a complicated relationship between these two men, a relationship that was never an easy one, though neither of them would openly admit it. Where contention surfaced, it was never on personal grounds but on "what is best for the Museum." They have generally conceded each other's virtues, but not always with enthusiasm. In their different ways they were both artists: Barr a writer of great clarity, often of elegance, and, especially in his private correspondence, of considerable humor; Wheeler a designer with originality, style, and wit, whose principal gifts were social. Barr's turn of mind was philosophic and speculative; Wheeler's was practical and pragmatic. In many respects they supplemented and complemented one another, and, so far as the publications of the Museum were concerned, they made each other's work excellent.

In the earliest days of the Museum, members received all of the Museum's catalogues, the cost of which exceeded the basic membership dues of $10. Those that were sold were priced just slightly above the cost of manufacturing them, as it was accurately believed that the catalogues were an important instrument in spreading the "word." Nelson Rockefeller's efficiency men thought this unbusinesslike and recommended that the prices be raised to a point where the catalogues might bring a reasonable profit to the institution. Frances Collins, when confronted with this in a meeting, was, as she says, "in a passion of moral indignation, and I blew my mind. I decided I was Joan of

Arc, and I was probably very insolent." It unquestionably contributed to her being fired later because of the "phony invitation," and to Wheeler's being stepped up from head of the Membership Department to Director of Publications. With his appointment the Museum's publishing became much more like that of a commercial house, not in style or content but in distribution. Soon members were receiving only some and not all of the catalogues as a benefit of their membership, and the firm of Simon and Schuster was handling the distribution of the books to the usual publishing outlets.

To trace the Museum's publishing career through its more than 300 books would serve no useful purpose here. The extent of its influence, however, on the acceptance of the arts it concerned itself with, on the practice of other museums and their publishing, and most especially on the students who used the books in their college libraries, if not measurable, can at least be suggested. The principal publications were, of course, catalogues of the Museum's exhibitions, and since many of these were sent to all Museum members, the Museum was in a sense running a book club. But in addition to the catalogues there were little manuals such as Alfred Barr's *What Is Modern Painting?* which went into many editions and many languages. There were similar short pamphlets on *What Is Modern Architecture?* by Arthur Drexler, which followed a *Guide to Modern Architecture: Northeast States* by John McAndrew, and two short books on modern design by Edgar Kaufmann, Jr.[1] There were long monographs such as Alfred Barr's *Matisse: His Art and His Public* (1951) and his *Picasso: Fifty Years of His Art*, which grew out of the catalogue for *Picasso: Forty Years of His Art*, published in 1939. There were books which became standard texts in their fields like Andrew Carnduff Ritchie's *Sculpture of the Twentieth Century* (1952), John Rewald's *The History of Impressionism* (revised edition 1961) and *Post-Impressionism from Van Gogh to Gauguin* (revised edition 1963), and Beaumont Newhall's *The History of Photography* (1949). The Museum's all-time best-seller was the catalogue of the photographic exhibition which Edward Steichen devised in 1955, called *The Family of Man.* To this writing it has sold more than 3,500,000 copies and it is still selling, mainly in a paperback edition.

Five years after Wheeler took over the direction of the Museum's publications he reported to the trustees that in the previous year (1945) the Museum had sold "50,000 books, 22,000 color reproductions, and

---

1 *What Is Modern Design?* (1950) and *What Is Modern Interior Design?* (1953).

70,000 post cards" and "during the past three years our book sales have increased 300 percent." By 1967, when he retired from the Museum's staff and became an "advisor," 300 books had been published by the Museum under his supervision. Many of them had been chosen for their typography to be included in "The Fifty Best Books of the Year," an accolade bestowed by the American Institute of Graphic Arts and much prized by designers of books. Many of them had been translated into foreign languages. "Soon after the war," Wheeler said, "Nelson sent me around the world to explore the possibilities of foreign-language editions of the Museum's publications and to look into foreign distribution. I arranged exhibitions of the books, sometimes in museums and sometimes in bookshops, and this was what really launched the international sale and distribution."

Andrew Ritchie, who became a central figure in the life of the Museum in 1949 as Director of the Department of Painting and Sculpture, said of the Museum's catalogues, "They were always done under the pressure of time. We were criticized for not being scholarly enough, but I'm not sure a catalogue somebody has spent thirteen years on isn't worse—a lot of insignificant detail. Shows were planned two or three years ahead, but even so . . . Art historians are interested in interpreting the gospel, not in preaching it. We were preaching it. Our attempts to improve scholarship [about modern art] were subject to taking risks and to the need for speed. What we did never would have been done by the academics. We were trying to be both preacher and scholar, and Museum publications were attempts to write for a broad public."

Wheeler had been Director of Publications for only a little over a year before he was given, to use his phrase, "another hat to wear." In 1940 Rockefeller decided that Wheeler should be Director of Exhibitions as well as the Museum's publisher. "They were always changing people's titles in those days," Wheeler said. When the appointment was announced in the Museum's *Bulletin*, John Hay Whitney, at that time briefly the President of the Board, as Rockefeller had gone to Washington to run the Office of the Coordinator of Inter-American Affairs, said "The position . . . has been created largely to relieve some of the burden of responsibility so long carried by Alfred H. Barr, Jr., who has been Director of the Museum since it was founded in 1929. . . . This newly created position . . . will enable Mr. Barr to devote more time to research and to develop the Museum's collections."

Barr's job was little by little being shaved away by the sharp knives of the trustees; they were fully aware of the Museum's debt to him; they looked upon him with a combination of awe (for his intellect and the intensity of his dedication), affection (for his devotion and style and humor), and dependence (for his advice on their own collecting and his perpetually bubbling fountain of ideas for the Museum). As this whittling increased, Wheeler found himself in a position to hope that he might succeed Barr as Director of the Museum, or so, in any case, it appeared to his colleagues.

Wheeler was ambitious, which was plain to those who worked with him and for him. He was wily and sure of his opinions about persons without in any sense being vicious. He enjoyed organizational intrigues, the jockeyings for favor and position, and he liked to hold the reins and to keep them taut. Though he said that "titles didn't mean anything in the Museum, we all did everything," he enjoyed the prestige which titles gave him, as, to be sure, nearly every man in an organization does. His new job and his new title put him in a position of very considerable power in the Museum's affairs, and he enjoyed it. He used it, however, with a sense of his own shortcomings—his amateur status, one might say, among experts—but also with a sense of confidence in his abilities as an organizer and manager and as a clever hand at dealing with temperament in others. A somewhat boastful man himself, he understood the uses of flattery. Modesty was not a virtue he practiced or regarded as especially virtuous in others. He had an eye for getting the right people to design the exhibitions over which he was the titular presence. "He was accurate about deadlines and he was enormously competent, and he allowed people a great deal of freedom when it came to designing a particular show," George Amberg, who at one time worked under him, said. "He had a sensitivity to know intuitively whether or not something would be good." He was also a martinet about budgets for exhibitions, which no one else in the Museum, as nearly as I have been able to discover, was. Wheeler insisted, and it did not improve his popularity with curators, on firm figures for the expense of a show before he would submit them for the consideration of the trustees. He would never compromise on quality and he found the vagueness, the unbusinesslike attitude of the "experts" aggravating; he would not have said, as his good friend Lincoln Kirstein, who had built a great ballet company on brilliance, conviction, and intuition, once did, "If I were businesslike, we wouldn't be in business." And though this statement might well serve as a motto for every artistic organization, Wheeler knew that it could not work for him as a channel between the curators and the trustees. "Monroe did not heed Alfred's advice as he should have," Amberg said. "I think on Monroe's side there was a feeling of competition, not on Alfred's side. But Alfred had enormous authority because he was a great expert. I think Monroe's contribution to the Museum was enormous, but he had his problems. He is a very complex person."

In 1940 Wheeler's chances of becoming Director of the Museum must have looked fairly good to him. He had already made many friends on the board who liked him not only for his charm and social adeptness but for his efficiency as an organizer and as an unofficial pipeline to what was going on when they were not on hand to see for themselves. As Eliza Parkinson said, "Most of the staff was intellectual and not socially knowing. He became the link between the staff and the trustees."

The Museum had not occupied its new home for more than a few months before relations between the trustees and the staff had deteriorated to such an uncomfortable degree that they sorely needed shoring up, and shoring up was not what they got. The firing of Collins and Mabry and a number of members of the custodial staff and Barr's evident helplessness in the face of trustee pressures and of trustees' taking matters into their own hands so dampened the spirits of the staff that there was among them a feeling of frustration that bordered on helplessness. Stephen Clark, the new Chairman of the Board, was beginning to take his responsibilities seriously in the early '40s, and Barr seemed to him a hurdle and a hindrance, not an executive with whom he could possibly, much less happily, work. Relations between them declined rapidly and, it almost seemed, catastrophically. Rockefeller, young and idealistic and genuinely fond of Barr (they frequently spent hours together rehanging and rearranging Rockefeller's collection and they enjoyed each other's company, though it is difficult to think of two temperaments less alike), believed that the age of great fortunes and great endowments for museums was at an end. As John McAndrew recalls it, "He was less involved in personal vendettas [than Goodyear and Clark] and he called in the professional efficiency sharks to reorganize MOMA into something self-supporting. We had been running—rather well—on morale: the efficiency boys tried to substitute system, and it failed to work, and morale was broken."

Allen Porter puts the collapse of morale in somewhat different terms: "Everybody was so busy you couldn't find them," he says. "They all took three- and four-hour lunches. Originally the hours were nine to five, but since no one came in they were changed to nine-thirty to five-thirty, and then they didn't come in until ten and then ordered up their breakfast. Then in the afternoon they had tea at four. I didn't go. I should have, but I didn't play politics."

Porter himself stuck to a strict schedule; someone had to, though that is not to say that many in positions of authority were less conscientious than he or that they did not often work long into the evening.

In the first months of Rockefeller's presidency of the Museum, internal politics were predominant and there was a great deal of jockeying for position on the staff. Besides the heads that got cracked, at least one department got the supports cut out from under it. This was McAndrew's Department of Architecture and Design. His staff was reduced. ("Architecture shows did not make money," he says, and, as someone else suggested, McAndrew had trouble staying within his budgets.) Clark and Goodyear had not liked the role he had played on the Building Committee and neither had Rockefeller. McAndrew was not one to be over-impressed by trustees; indeed, he was not unlikely to be rather high-handed with them, and, as one of his colleagues said, "He was very elegant and just got their dander up. Every now and then various trustees would ask him about something and he would more or less say, 'I'm too busy to tell you." McAndrew resigned late in 1940. "Alfred told me the depressing news," he recalls, "that the Architecture Department would be getting precious little money henceforth, and that things looked very bad. I asked if it wouldn't be a good idea to resign before the ax fell." In fact Nelson Rockefeller found him "incompatible" and wanted him off the staff, a position in which Stephen Clark concurred. Some of McAndrew's friends thought that Barr did not put up a fight on his behalf, and were dismayed; others believed that Barr put his own job on the line, but his threat was to no avail. A couple of months after McAndrew had left the Museum, Barr wrote about his worries to Paul Sachs. He was deeply concerned, he said, about the disintegration of the Museum, and the fact that it was relaxing its standards of excellence and distinction in favor of mediocrity just because mediocre people were easier to get along with than really gifted ones, "as if organization were an end in itself." He wrote enthusiastically of McAndrew, who, he said, had done "a superb job at the Museum," who was "extraordinarily learned in the history of architecture, a brilliant designer, a lucid and exciting lecturer with wide knowledge and deep cultivation." He spoke of him "as a person of courage, integrity and conscience . . . charming and excellent company." And he added, "He was, I say with conviction, the most brilliant person on our staff, at once sensitive and energetic." Barr was very evidently, as he said, "profoundly angry . . . and alarmed about its [McAndrew's departure] effect on the morale of the staff." But by that time it was too late to repair the damage. McAndrew had left the Museum.

So had Nelson Rockefeller. He had gone to Washington to assume the post of Coordinator of the Office of Inter-American Affairs, a brand-new bureau created in the summer of 1940 when the war in Europe was about nine months old. Most Americans believed by then that it would be only a matter of time before their country would be a great deal more than peripherally involved. Belgium and the Netherlands had fallen like skittles before the German *blitzkrieg,* and the "saturation bombing" of Rotterdam was a horror never before witnessed by man and a foretaste of a new, all-involving brand of warfare. In May the British, the French, and the Americans held their breath while more than 850 boats of every size and description evacuated 338,-000 British and French troops from the harbor of Dunkirk, and their hearts sank when the French Army collapsed in June and Maréchal Pétain presently became the head of a puppet government in Vichy.

Rockefeller's appointment by President Roosevelt as a "dollar-a-year man" was, according to an Associated Press wire story of August 17, "to counter the Fascist influence in Latin America." Rockefeller's qualifications for the job were described as his experience as a director of the Creole Petroleum Corporation, which had its headquarters in Venezuela, the fact that he had "set the Creole company into co-operation with the Government of Venezuela in improving education, health and general social conditions," and that he had built a hotel in Caracas as "a test tube to show the value of Latin America as a land of profitable North American investment." For the moment, in any case, he had no intention of giving up the presidency of the Museum, and the AP story pointed out that "he has sponsored shows of Latin American art in New York. . . . A Mexican exhibition is there now."

Up to that time the Museum had held just one important Latin American show—works by Diego Rivera—though paintings by Rivera, Siqueiros, Orozco (of Mexico), and Portinari (of Brazil) had been included in the show with which the new building was opened, and works by some of them had been shown earlier at the Museum. The Mexican exhibition, whose full name was *Twenty Centuries of Mexican Art,* was in the Museum partly as the result of McAndrew's doing. During the summer of 1940 before he left the Museum, he had gone to Mexico for a vacation. An exhibition of pre-Columbian Mexican art had been prepared for the Jeu de Paume in Paris, but the war had started before it was shipped and the show, of course, was canceled. Certainly no one was sending valuable works of art to Europe at that time. Neither were valuable works of art being committed to ships which might be picked off by the torpedoes of German submarines, and so an exhibition of Brancusi sculpture which had been scheduled for the Museum of Modern Art had also been canceled. McAndrew got wind of the Mexican show from Diego Rivera, at whose house in a suburb of Mexico City he had seen photographs of what had been assembled. When he got back to New York he suggested to Barr that what had been assembled for the Jeu de Paume would make an interesting show for the Museum. Barr in turn told Nelson Rockefeller, who found it much to his taste and certainly in keeping with his official efforts on behalf of "hemisphere solidarity." As a result Rockefeller went to Mexico City, taking Dick Abbott with him, and, as McAndrew says, "saw not as much of Rivera and Dr. Medioní [who had helped to assemble the material] as of President Cardenas." The show "grew and grew with Cardenas' blessing (he and Nelson hit it off notably), and soon a huge show, many times bigger than the original, was promised by the Mexican government."

At Barr's insistence, McAndrew went back to Mexico City. McAndrew says, "There was really nothing for me to do, though the real reason was that Alfred feared Abbott would make enemies, and furthermore I knew Spanish." Barr's fears had not been baseless, for, as McAndrew later learned, "Miguel Covarrubias had wired the Museum that Dick must be recalled at once; Miguel said he could not be responsible for his life."

The exhibition when it arrived filled the entire Museum. More than 5,000 pieces were shipped to the Museum from Mexico, and in addition more than 100 objects were borrowed for the show from the New York Museum of Natural History. The Mexican treasures were packed in three freight cars and guarded by Mexican soldiers to the Texas border. From there two Texas cowboys rode the roof of the train all the way to New York, a gesture which suggests the publicity shenanigans of Sarah Newmeyer. McAndrew was in charge of installing the exhibition, which consisted not only of pre-Columbian sculpture but of colonial paintings and sculpture, folk art, and work by current artists. The catalogue was printed in both English and Spanish (partly paid for by the Mexican government and partly by the Museum); Monroe Wheeler went to Mexico to supervise its production.

"It was the last time the entire Museum was devoted to a single show," McAndrew says. "We even used the garden as a Mexican market and put a lot of the folk art there." Installing it was, moreover, one of the last examples of the carnival kind of morale that made the early days of the Museum so gratifying to those who worked there.

"The Museum was still running on morale rather than on system," McAndrew says. "The morale was terrific. George Valliant of the Museum of Natural History helped us and he would work all night, and there wasn't a girl in the place who wouldn't have cut off her left arm for him. He'd zip them off to the St. Regis [Hotel] for a drink and a sandwich and zip them back. In those days the young people would say, 'We'll sweep the floors for nothing because we want to work in this wonderful, wonderful place,' and we'd have to turn them down right and left. Most of my department came in as volunteers. We were the social center because we were right where you got off the elevator, and when things got too bad for Alfred he used to come in and warm himself."

Five months after he had left for Washington, Rockefeller came to the conclusion that he could not be both Coordinator of Inter-American Affairs and President of the Museum, so he resigned the latter job. At about the same time he established "The Inter-American Fund" for the purchase of works of art in Latin American countries. Barr and Edgar Kaufmann went off together to Cuba and Mexico, and Lincoln Kirstein roamed the capitals of South America. In all, they bought fifty-eight paintings and sculptures for the Museum's collections. John Hay Whitney was elected by the board to replace Rockefeller. Whitney, who was then thirty-six, had been a trustee for a decade and his principal interest, as we have seen, was the Film Library. "I shall not diminish my interest in the Film Library," his published statement said, "but hope to participate increasingly in all the Museum's other activities." He was not President for long. In May 1942 he was commissioned a colonel in the Air Force (he wound up in the Office of Strategic Services, General Donovan's intelligence agency) and Stephen Clark assumed the job of President of the Museum as well as that of Chairman of the Board.

Clark's right-hand man was John ("Dick") Abbott, who had been elevated to the position of Executive Director when Mabry was dismissed, and his career was a futile one and not long-lived in (or out of) the Museum. Goodyear, it is said, "took an instant dislike to him," and so it was not until after Goodyear had turned the presidency of the Museum over to Nelson Rockefeller and Mabry had been dismissed that Abbott came into his own. Because of his experience as a broker in Wall Street he was regarded as a "money man" and a practical operator, and so he was named the Executive Director, whose function was to keep the Museum's daily operations running smoothly and its purse plump. It was he who was also supposed to be the calm center in a storm of temperaments, and as Clark liked him and trusted him and looked upon him, it is repeatedly said, "as a sort of son," his influence in the Museum was exceedingly important for a time—a time, indeed, of troubles. Henry Allen Moe, the director of the Guggenheim Foundation, who became a trustee of the Museum at the behest of his good friend Clark (and has been an important figure in the Museum's councils for many years), remembers Abbott as "a most useful fellow," and says, "He was a good enough administrator, and he was so sensitive to the winds of change that he was a good listening device for all the board members."

It is likely that it was because he was known to the staff as a "listening device" that he was so heartily disliked and distrusted by so many of them. "He treated the staff terribly," one says, and another: "I used to lie awake nights worrying about him. He was the menace of the Museum. Am I the only one who thought of him as a Hitler? He was the very opposite of Monroe [Wheeler]. You always felt this very scheming thing going on. You never knew what he was up to, and he had a habit of insisting that you write a memorandum to him, and he would never answer a single memorandum except by telephone, and then if you would quote him, he'd say he never said that. It suited his purposes, and he never put anything in writing, so you couldn't prove it. It was a very slippery period indeed." These statements were made by two of the Museum's most devoted and efficient staff members, an associate curator and the director of a department, Dorothy Miller and Elodie Courter. Eliza Parkinson recalls Abbott as not so much devious as dull. "Abbott just wasn't very bright," she says, "and you had to be bright in that company." Jimmy Ernst, who saw him with the eye of a perceptive office boy, says, "I thought he was very slick, and there was something aggressive about him born out of a measure of ignorance. Iris was the intellect in that thing."

Iris Barry (Mrs. Abbott) was not only the intellect of the family, she was also the one their colleagues enjoyed and respected. "Everyone liked Iris and didn't like Dick," Allen Porter said, and George Amberg, who was willing to give Abbott his due as an administrator, said, "He was no match for Iris, I dare say. Nobody was."

Abbott's importance in the history of the Museum is slight except as a cat's-paw for wiser and better-intentioned persons than himself.

Whitney, as chairman of the Film Library, had seen him in operation more closely than other trustees and evidently thought well enough of him to see him given authority in the Museum next only to Barr's. In any event, someone was needed to take Mabry's place and to keep those wheels turning which Barr was too preoccupied to tend. It was not that Barr wanted any authority to slip from his fingers; he did not, and though his whole heart belonged to the Museum, his intellect and his instincts belonged to what went into it and issued from it—as additions to the collections, as works for temporary exhibition, as words to be put on labels and in catalogues, as traveling shows. While the storm around him grew and threatened his stronghold, he withdrew further and further into the basic intellectual concerns of the Museum as he envisioned them, and in a manner of speaking he barred his door to the problems of the men and women who had their own battles for recognition, for budgets, and for trustee approval and sympathy. It became more and more difficult for his colleagues to get him to make decisions, to answer their urgent questions (at least the questions that seemed urgent to them), and to put his mind on their problems. They liked and admired and, many of them, cherished him no less, but they felt cut loose from his concern. It was in this atmosphere that Abbott collected more and more administrative power to himself. It was also in this atmosphere that the "war programs" of the Museum evolved.

The first war involvements were not programs at all. The summer before the war started, Barr had brought from Europe a number of Picassos borrowed mostly from private collectors, a few dealers, and from Picasso himself. Gertrude Stein had allowed the portrait of herself to be taken down from her wall and shipped to New York. Elsa Schiaparelli, the couturière, had lent "Bird Cage and Playing Cards," and so had half a dozen other collectors in France let the Museum borrow from their collections. Most important of all, Picasso had sent pictures and pieces of sculpture from all of the periods of his work; he even sent the vast "Guernica" and a great many of the studies for it. Furthermore, there were still in the Museum's possession paintings, including Rousseau's "Sleeping Gypsy," that had been borrowed for the *Art in Our Time* exhibition with which the new building had opened. Obviously they could not be committed to the hazards of travel back to their homes, and many of the collectors were happy to have them in so remote a place as America. Barr sent letters to all of the collectors saying that the Museum would hold onto the pictures, would insure them, and treat them as it would its own collection or he would send them elsewhere in America if that was what the owners wanted. The Museum could not be responsible if New York was bombed, though precautions to get the pictures to safe places along with the rest of the Museum's holdings would, of course, be taken. Most of the owners signed releases on these grounds, and the Museum found itself custodian of what a member of the staff called "riches for us because our collection wasn't very large at the time, and so we had things to exhibit."

From the end of January into April of 1940, however, the Museum had such things to exhibit as it had never been the privilege of New Yorkers to see in their city. One of the most unlikely exhibitions the Museum ever held was called simply *Italian Masters,* and it came to 53rd Street more or less by accident. A great many people, including good friends of the Museum and a very vocal segment of the New York community of artists, thought it outrageous that a collection of first-quality Italian paintings and sculptures from the Renaissance and the Age of the Baroque should come to rest for a little over two months on the third floor of the Museum of Modern Art . . . of all places! No one, however, was sorry that they came to rest somewhere in New York, and the Metropolitan had refused them house room. They were a magnificent lot of paintings and bronzes and marbles and terracottas of inestimable value; they were insured for $26,000,000; today it would be . . . $126,000,000? Easily! They ranged chronologically from Masaccio's "Crucifixion" (1426) from the Naples Museum to a Pietro Longhi portrait of 1765. But this is only a hint. There was Giovanni Bellini's "Madonna with St. Catherine and John the Baptist" from the Academy in Venice, Fra Angelico's "Naming of John the Baptist" from Florence, Titian's "Portrait of Pope Paul III" (Naples) and Mantegna's "St. George," also from the Academy in Venice. There was Michelangelo's bas-relief of the "Madonna and Child," Verrocchio's elegant "David," and Donatello's "Bust of a Young Man," all three from the Bargello in Florence, and an "Annunciation" in terracotta by Andrea della Robbia, lent by an anonymous private collector. Better known than any of these to the public and to every child who looked at picture books that contained even the smallest sample of art were Botticelli's "Birth of Venus" from the Uffizi and Raphael's "Madonna of the Chair" from the Pitti in Florence. In all there were twenty-eight pieces, and the press, with characteristic delight in irrelevant statistics, noted that when crated they weighed ten tons. They were accompanied by two packers sent by the Italian government to supervise their crating, and they were attended by special guards with visible revolvers twenty-four hours a day when they were on exhibition. When they were sent from Chicago to New York they came in a special air-conditioned freight car that was attached to the Commodore Vanderbilt express, one of what were then known as the "crack trains" of the New York Central, and they were accompanied from the station to the Museum by mounted police. The agile hand of Sarah Newmeyer was evident in the managing of the publicity. The parade of the pictures was photographed by news photographers standing on the tops of cars along the path cleared by police sirens, and floodlights were installed at the Museum's entrance so that newsreel cameras could record the arrival of the crates. One piece of unplanned and unexpected publicity was inadvertently provided by the reticent Greta Garbo. She wanted to see the paintings and arrived to look at them a day before they were to be open to the public. Allen Porter was told of her presence in the Museum and, saying to himself (according to a press report), "I mustn't faint, I mustn't faint," escorted the great lady of the films through the half-hung exhibition. Garbo and Porter have been friends ever since.

The great collection of Italian masterpieces was in America to be shown at the San Francisco World's Fair of 1939. Daniel Catton Rich had arranged to have it stop in Chicago to be exhibited at the Art Institute over the Christmas holidays, and since it had to get to the port of New York and the Italian ocean liner *Rex* for the voyage home it could logically be shown there. Even before the pictures had left San Francisco the Italian government had decreed that never again would such national treasures be allowed to leave their country. The opportunity to show them was offered to the Metropolitan Museum and was turned down by William M. Ivins, a lawyer turned curator and a brilliant albeit crusty man who was then the acting director. He thought it preposterous to pay $5,000 a week for the privilege of showing the pictures, and he'd be damned if he'd let the Italian packers in his Museum. According to Monroe Wheeler, he got wind of this and told Barr and Rockefeller; they not only decided that the Museum should get the pictures for exhibition but they believed, with justification, that by charging special admission to see them they could more than cover the costs incurred in meeting the Italian government's stipulations about their guardianship. "There was a rumor," Wheeler says, "that if the Met wouldn't take them the Brooklyn Museum would. And we certainly couldn't let them be shown in New York and not in Manhattan."

The works of art were on view from January 26 to April 7 and very nearly 300,000 people (or twice as many admissions as were needed to meet the costs) came to see them, and a great many seized the opportunity to vote for their favorites. Titian's "Pope Paul III" placed first by a handy margin, followed by Raphael's "Madonna of the Chair" and, as a rather poor third, Botticelli's "Birth of Venus." The least-popular pictures in the show were—not surprisingly, considering the taste of the time—two Baroque paintings, the Longhi portrait and a Guercino of "The Bath of Diana."

"The show would have looked much better at the Met," Rich, the director of the Chicago Art Institute, recalls. "They put too much light on the pictures, and when I was looking at the sculpture I felt I was in a shower." By and large, however, the press was friendly to the manner in which Barr mounted the show, though there was a certain amount of criticism of its being in the Museum at all. Stephen Clark issued a statement intended to forestall such criticism. "Our acceptance of this exhibition of Italian masterpieces," he said, "does not indicate a change in the established policy of the Museum or any shifting of its emphasis on the contemporary arts. Great masterpieces are not, however, bound by any period, and the influence of the Italian Renaissance and Baroque upon the modern artist is fundamental and continuous." He also took pains to point out that "The Museum will show simultaneously . . . an exhibition of work of some of the greatest modern artists of both the European and American schools."

About a week after the exhibition closed in early April a group of New York painters who called themselves American Abstract Artists let fly with a broadside captioned "How Modern Is the Museum of Modern Art?" It was signed with fifty-two names, and it had a field day at the Museum's expense. It criticized everything the Museum had done that was not what they considered "modern," and did it with gusto. It lambasted the *Art in Our Time* show with which the new building had opened. "Whose time? Sargent, Homer, LaFarge, Hartnett [*sic*]? Or Picasso, Braque, Léger and Mondrian? Which time? . . . And MODERN MASTERS (to counterbalance the Italian Masters, as this feeble demonstration from a great period was advertised) Eakins, Homer, Ryder, Whistler—died 1916, 1910, 1917, 1903. Those are the only Americans included. . . ." It asked, "Is the Museum a business?" and after flaying about at a contest the Museum was conducting with the cooperation of the newspaper *PM* for "the artist as reporter," it said: "Why not build pyramids? Why not tear down the Museum and build a pyramid! As big as Radio City! With 100,000 slaves! Think of the publicity!" And so on. The broadside reproduced an item from Leonard Lyons' column in the New York *Post* for March 21, 1940:

Art Dept.: Nelson Rockefeller, head of the Museum of Modern Art, told a group that the Museum is spending more money than it is receiving—that this was the first time he ever was engaging in show-business, but that the off-balance wasn't worrying him. . . . "It's all right," Rockefeller assured. "The Greatest Showman of our times—a man in Washington—works on the same principle."

The artists' comment on this was: "What is this—a three ring CIRCUS? How about Billy (Aquacade) Rose as the next trustee?"

This was one of the earliest public outcries made by artists against the Museum. The one at the time of the mural show in 1932 was, you will recall, an attack on political grounds. This one was aesthetic, and there were many to come, several of them during the war. The Museum never took these attacks casually, and when the Federation of Modern Painters and Sculptors Inc. broadcast a mimeographed attack on the Museum in January 1942 and others in 1943, and 1944, James Thrall Soby, who by then was Director of Paintings and Sculpture, went to very considerable pains to answer the attacks point by point, not for public consumption but for the staff and trustees and the Advisory Committee. These attacks were essentially against what was presumed to be the Museum's casual attitude toward American artists, and the first was provoked by a show called *Americans 1942—18 Artists from 9 States*. The Museum was accused of "reducing American art to a demonstration of geography." In the following year the Federation attacked another show of Americans called *Realists and Magic Realists* on the grounds that, as Soby paraphrased the complaint, "realism as the show defined it didn't amount to much" and that "it wasn't the Museum's business to define tendencies in modern art" but only to "search for true art." The exhibition which Soby and Dorothy Miller did in the following year, called *Romantic Painting in America*, impelled the Federation to call for "the abandonment of shows which emphasize works rightly considered out-moded even in the Victorian era," which showed more enthusiasm in the Federation for self-promotion than for art-historical accuracy. The Museum was also attacked for its ethnological shows (American Indians and Mexicans) and scientific shows (industrial design, architecture, etc.), but at the root of the attacks was what the Federation believed to be the Museum's lack of basic concern for the contemporary American artist, and an over-emphasis on what was then new in Europe. Soby pointed out that what was going on in Europe in the arts was a great deal more interesting than what was going on in America. "You cannot possibly present twentieth-century American painting," he said, "as we have presented School of Paris painting. The revolutionary impact is not there. . . ." He might also have pointed out (as a list in the *Bulletin* of the Museum did in November 1940) that there were works by 127 Americans in the Museum's "permanent" collections, and that work by more than 700 American painters, sculptors, and graphic artists had been shown in the first eleven years of the Museum's existence.

Some of the attacks by artists on the Museum were considered "irresponsible" by members of the staff and by trustees, and, strictly speaking, they may have been more impassioned than accurate, more touchy than justified in some cases. The very fact that they made the Museum defend itself, made it examine and justify itself, cannot but have been in the long run salutary.

But there was a bigger war on, bigger pressures on the Museum and bigger pressures on European artists, than those which American artists were subjected to in 1940.

Keeping pictures that were already in New York from danger was one thing; getting artists out of Europe was quite another, and, of course, a great deal more complex. An organization called the International Rescue Committee was at work in Marseille soon after the fall of France—and during an interval in which there was still a "zone" that the Germans by agreement with the Vichy government did not "occupy." Both the Barrs worked with the rescue committee, but Mrs. Barr, fluent in many European languages, used the Barrs's apartment as an office, and most of the correspondence (and there was a great deal of red tape to be cut) went out from there. "The first difficulty," she says, "was clearing the names with the State Department. They seemed to be concerned only if the artists were communists. They didn't care if they were fascists." The committee had to find sponsors for anyone whom they hoped to bring in before a visa could be obtained. "A guarantee of $3,000 per person had to be put up—per person, that is, not per couple," Mrs. Barr says, "and then passage by boat cost $400. The people who were most helpful with money were Philip Goodwin, Curt Valentin [the dealer], and Jo Davidson, who said that if we could sell his bust of '*La Pasionaria*' [2] for $10,000, he'd give the money to the fund. Alfred worked on the

2 Dolores Ibarruri, heroine of the Spanish Republicans in the revolution of 1936.

trustees, and some of them and their friends raised the money and the fund got the $10,000."

One of the artists whom the Barrs were instrumental in getting to America was the Surrealist painter Max Ernst, whose son was Jimmy. "In my case," he says, "I got a postcard at the Museum from my father, who was in a French concentration camp, where he was held because he was technically still a German even though he'd lived in France since 1920 or '21. It was in pencil, the way you were allowed to write —I have the card somewhere still—asking me to help get him out. I shot into Barr's office with the postcard, and things began to happen immediately. He and Frances Perkins [Roosevelt's Secretary of Labor], through David Hare, the sculptor, who was then married to Perkins' daughter, Suzy—the Department of Immigration was then in the Department of Labor . . . A lot of these people like Chagall and Masson were brought over, and Barr had a great deal to do with all that."

"It is hard to believe now," Mrs. Barr says, "that the artists had no contacts in America except the Museum of Modern Art."

The sculptor Lipchitz, the painters Yves Tanguy and André Masson Mrs. Barr remembers as among those brought to America by the Museum's efforts, but unfortunately the correspondence has been misplaced (not lost, Mrs. Barr thinks, because she is quite sure it did not get thrown out) and so the record is vague. An account of the work of the International Rescue Committee was written by Varian Fry, its moving spirit, a friend and fellow editor with Lincoln Kirstein on *Hound and Horn*. The book is called *Surrender on Demand* [3] and tells the stories of many men and women, mostly intellectuals, whom the committee rescued at great personal risk. By no means all of the artists who made their precarious ways to New York (some via Martinique and Haiti) are mentioned. Possibly the most peculiar story was that of Max Ernst, who met and became involved with Peggy Guggenheim, already a very adventurous collector of paintings (and painters). She managed to get herself and him seats on a plane, an almost unheard-of stroke of expensive good fortune, and they flew to America from Lisbon. On their arrival Ernst was grabbed by the immigration officials and spent several days on Ellis Island, which he found very entertaining but during which Peggy Guggenheim was frantic. He was finally released when his son Jimmy showed up with a letter from the Museum of Modern Art. "Soon after Pearl Harbor," Miss Guggen-

3 Published in 1945 by Random House, New York.

heim wrote in her entertaining autobiography,[4] "we were married, as I did not want to live in sin with an enemy alien."

The Museum's official war programs were of a very different nature from its unofficial but heartily supported rescue efforts. In 1940 and 1941 a great many institutions of a great many different kinds were looking for ways in which they might help "the war effort," though the involvement of the United States was, at least ostensibly, a matter more of sympathy and anticipation than of action. On June 20, 1941, the Central Press service issued a wire story which appeared in many newspapers with a lead paragraph that read: "The latest and strangest recruit in Uncle Sam's defense line-up is—the museum!" A photograph of John Hay Whitney accompanied the piece, and he was quoted as saying: "Does it seem strange to you to think of a museum as a weapon in national defense?" A museum could, he said, "educate, inspire, and strengthen the hearts and wills of free men in the defense of their own freedom." It was a familiar kind of rhetoric in the days when there was a sense of doom which hung over the Western world and much of the Eastern world as well. It was a time of large statements and inspirational oratory, when skepticism was hushed and a great deal of "made work" was devised to give everyone a sense of participation in the national effort. Not everyone, to be sure, was convinced; there was bitterness between the interventionists and the isolationists, and, when the war began in Europe and for two years after that, those who were for "America First" were in the majority. At one extreme were the followers of Father Coughlin, the Silver Shirts of America, and the German American Bund, at the other extreme were the Communists and their "fellow travelers," with William Z. Foster and Earl Browder at their head. Both extremes were dedicated to keeping America out of the war until the *Wehrmacht* invaded Russia in June 1941 and the American Communists suddenly became interventionists, encouraging labor to work for the war effort rather than to sabotage it. It was not until Pearl Harbor was bombed in December 1941 that men like Philip Johnson of the far right and Ben Shahn of the left found themselves engaged in a common cause. Conservative artists and radical artists and artists of the middle joined in an organization called Artists for Victory, whose "constituent groups," Oliver Larkin recalled in *Art and Life in America*, "acted as citizens

4 *Confessions of an Art Addict* by Peggy Guggenheim (New York, 1960).

to whom the preservation of a civilized world was more important than the differences between the National Academy and the Artists' Congress."

But the Museum of Modern Art was in the fray before that, or, perhaps more accurately, the preliminaries of the fray. In April 1941 the Museum announced a poster competition, *Posters for National Defense*, with $2,000 in prizes divided between two categories, the U.S. Air Corps and National Defense Savings Bonds and Stamps. The jury was composed of "the directors and curators of the Museum," and the *Bulletin* said: "The Museum feels that in a time of national emergency the artists of a country are as important an asset as men skilled in other fields, and that the nation's first-rate talent should be utilized by the government for its official design work. . . . Discussions have been held with officials of the Army and the Treasury who have expressed remarkable enthusiasm. . . ." John C. Atherton and Joseph Binder took the honors in both categories, Atherton winning first place in the Defense Bonds and second place in Air Force recruitment, and Binder doing just the opposite. In July through September the competitive posters were shown at the Museum, and Atherton's bond poster was reproduced on a massive scale on a building at the corner of Fifth Avenue and 42nd Street in New York.

Before the poster show went up, a large exhibition called *Britain at War* had opened at the Museum in late May. Barr had got the approval of the trustees for the show many months before. It was, he told them, to be selected by Sir Kenneth Clark, the director of the National Gallery in London, who had "excellent taste and a wide knowledge in the field of modern art." Delays in shipping caused by the hazards of a submarine-infested Atlantic delayed the show beyond its intended date, but when it opened it was accompanied by a catalogue which included a short poem by T. S. Eliot called "Defense of the Islands," an essay by Herbert Read on "The War as Seen by British Artists," and several other pieces. One by Monroe Wheeler on "The Artist and National Defense" concluded with the sentence, "Those whose work is shown here have fought well without guns." Not nearly as many people came to look at the show as had been expected; it was cut back from two floors of the Museum to one floor to make way for the *Prize-Winning Defense Posters* and a group of Picassos which had been held in custody by the Museum from the show of the year before because, it was said, "of hundreds of requests from teachers and students, especially outside New York City, who had been unable to see the earlier show." It was a perfect example of the Museum's talent for making capital out of expediency.

After the bombing of Pearl Harbor the Museum's war program took a very different shape. In his as yet unpublished memoirs James Thrall Soby tells of getting a phone call from Dick Abbott saying that "the Museum was deluged with requests for help in art matters by the Armed Services" and was there anything Soby could do to help? The upshot of this was Soby's assuming the position of Director of "something called the Armed Services Program" by mid-January, and, he writes, "I was at work in the Museum in what certainly was the smallest office ever inhabited by a grown human male."

Soby was by no means new to the Museum or to the cause for which it stood. It was a cause to which he had nearly a dozen years before pledged his allegiance, his intelligence, his bank account, and his perceptive and adventurous critical eye. The scion of a Hartford family which had made its fortune in the manufacture of pay telephones, he had spent a couple of years at Williams College (which many years later gave him an honorary degree). He bought his first picture when he was a college sophomore in 1925, a print of a Maxfield Parrish, the meticulous romantic illustrator who was widely known for his Mazda electric-bulb advertisements. It was, Soby says, "a nude but sensibly misty young girl perched on a swing over an Arcadian terrace." Five years later in January 1930 he bought a Matisse and a Derain from the Valentine Gallery in New York and his career as a serious collector had begun. He was, he recalls, rather frightened by what he had done, and turned to Chick Austin, the director of the Wadsworth Atheneum in Hartford, for support. He had not known Austin until then, but Austin was, of course, enchanted to find a young collector in his constituency, and they became fast friends. "Chick took hold of him," Virgil Thomson says. "His taste was formed under Chick's guidance." It was, moreover, through Austin that he met Alfred Barr and Julien Levy. Five years after he had bought his first paintings he published his first critical book, *After Picasso*, a study of what he called the Neo-Romantics, a group of painters that included Eugene and Leonid Berman, Tchelitchew, Bérard, and Kristians Tonny, a group of "official" Surrealists (Ernst, Arp, Masson, and Man Ray), "non-official" Surrealists (Picasso, Miró, and Roy), and some painters he called artists of "the newer objectivity" (Tanguy, Giacometti, and Dali). Barr reviewed the book for the *Saturday Review of Literature* and praised it for the soundness of its scholarly method and its "examination of philosophical, social as well as artistic values" which added up to "a lucid, interesting and much needed book." At about the same time Soby acquired a part (49 percent) interest in Julien Levy's gallery, but stayed in the background. Levy was the only dealer in New York handling the Surrealists then; indeed, as Soby says, "he was as close to being an official surrealist himself as one could come without signing one of André Breton's guidelines to the surrealist faith." His association with Levy was Soby's only commercial participation in the art world, and he sold his interest back to Levy when he became a member of the Advisory Committee of the Museum in the late 1930s.

Soby was a good choice to take on the Armed Services Program; he was energetic and well organized. He and Barr had become good friends and greatly admired each other's qualities and opinions. Soby, moreover, had a talent for working with people younger than himself; his manner was easy and friendly, he put on no airs and graces, and he had the gift of humor. He was, he says, glad to find something "an aging art critic" could do for the war effort.

The program that evolved was partly therapy, partly exhibitions, partly morale-sustaining, and partly making the Museum's facilities and talents available to Nelson Rockefeller and his Office of Inter-American Affairs. Soby worked with Army Special Services to get art materials into camps for the use of men in uniform. He arranged for the use of the Museum's garden for parties for soldiers and sailors. (At one of them, he writes, "I remember that in the middle of one of her most famous songs Miss [Gracie] Fields stopped abruptly, cast a baleful look at the life-size nude bronze of St. John the Baptist, and shouted out, 'Such a brash young man.' She then went on with her song.") He managed to get together an exhibition on the uses of *The Arts in Therapy* which was praised by the Surgeons General of the Army and the Navy, and to set up a national competition for new designs and objects to be used in occupational therapy.

The Museum held a long series of exhibitions that related to the war effort in a considerable variety of ways. There were shows of *Wartime Housing*, of *U.S. Army Illustrators*, of *Anti-hoarding Pictures by New York School Children*. A very ambitious photographic exhibition called *Road to Victory* was selected by Edward Steichen, then a lieutenant commander in the Navy, and mounted by the ex-Bauhaus designer Herbert Bayer, with a text by Steichen's brother-in-law, the poet Carl Sandburg. Everyone, it appears, was impressed. Jewell in the *New York Times* called it "the season's most moving experience." Carlyle Burrows in the New York *Herald Tribune* said it was "a show of inspiring purposes . . . a declaration of power and an affirmation of our will to win the war. . . . At every stage in a spectacular tour of the second floor galleries there is a dramatic spot with a compelling message." And even the *Daily Worker* was impressed and reported, "It is the most sensational exhibit of photographs that ever was shown in these parts. What a country to fight for!"

Besides the exhibitions having to do with the war, there was also business as usual at the Museum, and the public seemed to appreciate it. Briefly after Pearl Harbor, attendance at the Museum dropped off, but within a month it had climbed beyond the levels it had sustained before the war. Men in uniform were admitted to the galleries and to the film showings without charge, and many found refuge there. In August 1944 Soby and Victor d'Amico, who was in charge of the Museum's Education Department, organized an art center for veterans, a project in which Abby Rockefeller had a particular interest. "Men who have served in the Army, Navy, Marines and Merchant Marine," the announcement said, "are invited to sketch, paint, or model under the guidance of skilled artists and craftsmen." D'Amico says: "I asked one fellow why he had taken up art and he said, 'Well, I just came back from destroying everything. I made up my mind that if I ever got out of the army and out of the war I was never going to destroy another thing in my life, and I decided that art was the thing that I would do." Another man said to d'Amico, "Art is like a good night's sleep. You come away refreshed and at peace." The program was such a success that it lasted for four years.

In the garden of the Museum at the end toward Fifth Avenue a Garden Canteen was installed, with "garden chairs and tables under umbrellas," with a cement dance floor and ping-pong tables. There, under the aegis of the Salvation Army, young ladies from the Junior League sold sandwiches, doughnuts, and coffee "at cost" to servicemen and their friends (the "public" was not admitted).

In a sense the Museum was a minor war industry, and, like other such enterprises, entered into contracts with the procurement bureaus of the federal government. Its product was cultural, to be sure. It executed thirty-eight contracts with the Office of the Coordinator of Inter-American Affairs, the Library of Congress, the Office of War Information, "and other agencies" before the war was over, and the contracts added up to $1,590,234. It put together nineteen exhibitions of contemporary American painting which Nelson Rockefeller's office shipped around Latin America; it conducted an industrial-design competition; it adapted documentary films to be shown in Spanish- and Portuguese-speaking countries. It ran a hemisphere poster competition, analyzed enemy propaganda films, and put together architecture and photography exhibitions for London, Cairo, Stockholm, Rio de Janeiro, Mexico City, and so on and on. Obviously, Rockefeller was its biggest customer, and Monroe Wheeler from the Museum worked in Washington as a part-time consultant to the Coordinator's office during much of the war.

The six years between the opening of the Museum's new home on 53rd Street and the collapse of the German Army in 1945 were in a great many respects the most turbulent of the Museum's history. If there was a single stabilizing element in these years of unrest, it was the war itself. It was the one thing that the staff and the trustees seemed to agree on. There was no question that the Museum had a role to play in its own special corner of the war effort. There was also no question that a good many of the staff had to play roles closer to where the action took place. Jock Whitney, as we have seen, left for the Air Force. Beaumont Newhall had joined the Navy, and Allen Porter was in the Army; they were both members of the dedicated central corps of the Museum's staff. Elliot Noyes, who had come in as Director of the Department of Industrial Design after McAndrew left, was in the Pentagon designing gliders. Paul Magriel, who briefly was the Curator of the Dance Archives, a department set up at the behest and by the generosity of Lincoln Kirstein, had joined the Army.

There had been a great many more exhibitions in the Museum related in one way or another to the war than I have mentioned here. There was, moreover, a program of musical events which started in 1940 with a *Festival of Brazilian Music* held in the basement auditorium at the same time that the paintings of the Brazilian artist Portinari were hanging on the walls upstairs. By April 1941 a Music Committee had been organized and Carleton Sprague Smith was its chairman. With Louise Crane, the daughter of Mrs. Murray Crane of the trustees, as its sponsor, the committee presented a series of "coffee concerts"— jazz, *Four Saints in Three Acts* performed by the original cast as an oratorio, several evenings of Latin American music, and "concert swing"—and, as Miss Crane says, "They were as successful as the capacity of the auditorium allowed." In February 1943 the committee presented "one of the earliest public performances by John Cage of his prepared piano," and the following month Virgil Thomson, then the music critic of the New York *Herald Tribune*, started a series of five *Serenade Concerts*, the proceeds from which went to the Mu-

"*The Adamantine Ladies*" (left to right), *Mrs. John D. (Abby) Rockefeller, Jr., Miss Lizzie P. Bliss, and Mrs. Cornelius J. (Mary) Sullivan, conspired in May 1929 to found a museum for their "outrageous" modern art.*

The Modern's first exhibition was paintings by van Gogh, Gauguin, Cézanne, and Seurat in galleries on the twelfth floor of the Hecksher Building.

When it opened, Alfred H. Barr, Jr., aged twenty-nine, was the Museum's Director, A. Conger Goodyear its President, and Jere Abbott its Vice-Director.

In 1933 the Museum moved to a Rockefeller house at 11 West 53rd Street on the site of its present building.

Elodie Courter ran the Department of Circulating Exhibitions from 1936 to 1947 and probably introduced modern art to more people than anyone in the Museum.

In 1934 the Machine Art *show provoked one critic to say, "It is calling the stuff art that clouds the issue," and another to say that Philip Johnson who directed it was "our best showman and possibly the world's best."*

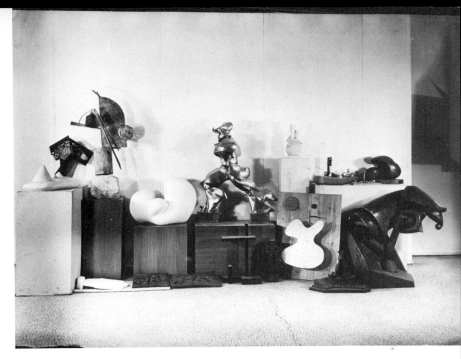

These sixteen pieces borrowed from Europe for the Cubism and Abstract *show were held up by customs as not being "imitations of natural objects" and hence not duty-free art.*

In 1934 Cornelius Bliss (right) handed Goodyear in Barr's presence a document transferring his late sister Lizzie's collection to the Museum—its first substantial acquisition. Behind Bliss hung Picasso's "Woman in White," later transferred to the Metropolitan Museum. The Modern wishes it had it back.

The Museum went underground in 1937–39 and set up shop in the concourse of Rockefeller Center while its new building was under construction. The Bauhaus exhibition, more influential than popular, was shown there.

The new building, designed by Philip Goodwin and Edward Durell Stone (upper right), and its interiors furnished by John McAndrew (lower right) opened in November 1939. The press attacked it as showing "no concern . . . to make the exterior beautiful."

When Goodyear resigned in 1939 as the Museum's first President, Nelson A. Rockefeller (aged thirty) replaced him, and Stephen C. Clark became Chairman of the Board.

John Hay ("Jock") Whitney, at various times President and Board Chairman of the Museum, was a moving spirit in founding the Film Library. At left are Iris Barry (black hat), the Film Library's creator, curator, and guiding genius, with the actress Gloria Swanson.

The members' penthouse when it was opened in 1939 was a showcase of modern furniture, much of it now in the Design Collection.

RIGHT: *James Thrall Soby, collector, critic, and trustee, served the Museum for many years in many capacities. During World War II he directed the Museum's War Services Program.*

LEFT: *The museum exhibited in 194(a remarkable collection of Italian mas terpieces lent by the Italian Governmen because the Metropolitan Museum re fused to show them.*

In 1942 photographer Lt. Com. Edward Steichen (later Director of the Museum's photography department) mounted an extraordinary exhibition called Road to Victory. *His brother-in-law, Carl Sandburg* (left), *wrote the captions.*

During World War II, the Museum's sculpture garden became an entertainment center for troops of all the Allied nations.

René d'Harnoncourt (left) joined the Museum staff in 1944 and became Director four years later, a position he occupied until 1968. Here he sits in the library with Victor d'Amico.

Edgar Kaufman, Jr. (right) directed the Good Design *shows of the 1950's, which had such an impact on manufacturers, retailers, and householders. With him is Alexander Girard.*

Philip Johnson, MOMA's official architect, trustee, and one-time director of the Architecture Department, in his private sculpture gallery in New Canaan, Connecticut, 1970.

This photograph of Monroe Wheeler was taken in 1943, two years after he was appointed Director of Exhibitions in addition to his job as Director of Publications.

RIGHT: James Johnson Sweeney's tenure as Director of the Department of Painting and Sculpture was a brief (January 1945 to November 1947) and stormy one.

After eight years as Director of the Department of Painting and Sculpture, Andrew Carnduff Ritchie left in 1957 to become Director of the Yale University Art Gallery.

Alfred Barr in 1967 with Alexander Calder's "Gibraltar."

Dorothy Miller (Mrs. Holger Cahill) was a curator for more than thirty years, and the influence of her judgment on American artists' careers was profound.

Chief Curator of Drawings, William S. Lieberman, has held a variety of important curatorial positions since he joined the staff in 1943.

ABOVE: *Arthur Drexler, head of the Architecture and Design Department, discusses an installation with René d'Harnoncourt.*

LEFT: *John Szarkowski succeeded Steichen as Director of the Department of Photography in 1962. In 1967 he put on a show called* Once Invisible, *for which he is measuring a strip of Muybridge photographs.*

William A. M. Burden, President of the Museum from 1953 to 1959, was succeeded by Blanchette Rockefeller (Mrs. John D., 3rd) who served for five years and was later reelected in 1972.

A fire in the Museum in 1958 did extensive smoke and water damage and cost the life of one man. The destruction of paintings, though serious, was largely averted by the action of the staff who, like Bernard Karpel the librarian (right), carried out millions of dollars worth of pictures.

Porter McCray, in 1961, when he was Director of the International Council of the Museum with Mlle Dubreuil of the Louvre at the opening of a show of masterpieces of French drawings in American collections.

The "Jazz in the Garden" concerts were initiated in the summer of 1960. Social "jazz" in the garden has been perennial since 1939. Champagne glasses adorned Rodin's "John the Baptist" at the reopening of the Museum in 1964.

William Rubin, who became Chief Curator of the Painting and Sculpture Collection after Barr's retirement, first came to the Museum as a child to paint on Saturday mornings.

Allen Porter ("Mr. Museum") retired in 1965 to live in a remodeled Victorian church and installed a gazebo in his garden in 1972.

Mrs. Lyndon B. Johnson rededicated the Museum after its expansion in 1964. Left to right, *Adlai Stevenson, d'Harnoncourt, Mrs. Johnson, Mrs. David Rockefeller and Mr. Rockefeller, Barr, Richard Koch, and Mrs. d'Harnoncourt.*

Willard Van Dyke, head of the Film Department, and Eliza Parkinson gaze up, as most people had to, at d'Harnoncourt, "the gentle giant," at a party in the Founders' Room.

Bates Lowry was briefly Director of the Museum from July 1968 to May 1969.

William S. Paley (left) was President of the Museum when he hired John Hightower as Director in May 1970. Hightower's incumbency lasted twenty months.

Richard E. Oldenburg was appointed the fifth Director of the Museum and Mrs. John D. Rockefeller, 3rd, was elected its President for the second time, both in 1972.

When Alfred Barr retired in 1967 after thirty-seven years, he said that one of his greatest pleasures in the Museum was "the most beautiful garden in New York," designed by his old friend Philip Johnson. The photograph below was taken of Barr in Stockbridge, Massachusetts, two years later.

seum's Armed Services Program and the Stage Door Canteen.

While the Museum was buzzing with all these activities, the cross-currents on the executive floor of the building were growing more and more turbulent. The relationship between Stephen Clark in his dual capacity of President and Chairman of the Board and Alfred Barr in his capacity as Director was deteriorating at a rapidly accelerating speed. When finally it collapsed, in October 1943, the Museum suffered a wound from which many of Barr's friends believe it has never fully recovered.

*Art historians sometimes seem moved as much by
intellectual vanity as by love of truth, critics and
museum people by partisanship or love of
power, collectors by concern for prestige or the
values of the art market or simple pride of
possession.*
ALFRED H. BARR, JR., *in the catalogue of the James
Thrall Soby Collection, 1961*

Chapter XIII *Fired!*

Bernard Karpel, who had taken Beaumont Newhall's place as the
Librarian of the Museum of Modern Art when Newhall joined the
Navy, walked into the library one morning early in 1944 and found a
carpenter sawing one of the library tables in two. "I was a little bit
astonished," he says, and so he went to see Frances Hawkins, who
had been Secretary of the Museum for a year or more. "She was as
astonished as I was. But I left it at that. I had other fish to fry." Not
for several days did he discover that a cubicle was being erected in a
corner of the library reading room to provide a placc for Alfred Barr
to work. The Director had been fired, he learned, but was being given
minimal house room to work on his books.

Barr was following a piece of advice he had given to others with
whom the higher powers in the Museum had wished to dispense. "Just
don't go away," he would say, believing that if they didn't, the storm
might blow over. He could not be bodily ejected, and, as his wife said
some years later, "Of course Alfred would not leave. It was his Museum. The Museum was his mistress."

Stephen Clark and Barr had been on a collision course for longer than just the two years that Clark had been both President of the Museum and the Chairman of its Board. They evidently liked and respected each other in their somewhat reticent fashions, but just as Barr found Clark's taste in pictures limited and inelastic and stuck in a single generation, so Clark found Barr's taste unaccountable, erratic, and, he was free to say in some instances, frivolous. When Barr exhibited in 1942 a highly decorated shoeshine stand by a New York "primitive" named Joe Milone (it had been discovered by the then relatively unknown but now famous sculptor Louise Nevelson), Clark thought that Barr had taken leave of his senses. Barr, to whom a beautiful object was a beautiful object (and therefore worthy of showing in the Museum, whether it was officially "art" or not), wrote:

> Joe Milone's shoeshine furniture is as festive as a Christmas tree, jubilant as a circus wagon. It is like a lavish wedding cake, a baroque shrine or a super-juke box. . . . Yet it is purer, more personal and simple hearted than any of these. We must respect the enthusiasm and devotion of the man who made it. . . .

To compound what Clark considered Barr's felonious assault on taste and on the dignity of the Museum, Barr supported an exhibition of paintings by a retired Brooklyn manufacturer of slippers and dresses named Morris Hirshfield. Hirshfield, who had taken to art at the age of sixty-seven, had been unearthed by the art dealer Hudson Walker, who introduced his work to Sidney Janis. Hirshfield devoted himself to subjects such as tigers and flowers and women, sometimes nude. His manner was somewhat that of the Douanier Rousseau, though he thought himself superior in talent, for when Janis showed him Rousseau's "The Dream," which Janis had bought, he said, "Shrubs. Good shrubs. But the lady—she's too swollen. I can fix her up for you." The critics, however, shared neither Hirshfield's nor Janis' nor Barr's enthusiasm for his talent. "It was, in fact," John Brooks wrote years later in *The New Yorker*,[1] "one of the most hated shows the Museum of Modern Art ever put on." Janis in his book on Hirshfield had noted that in his days as a slipper manufacturer the salesmen's samples were made only in left feet, and this explained why in very nearly all the painter's nudes the women had two left feet. *Art Digest*, which had no love for the Museum, referred to Hirshfield as "The Master of the Two Left Feet," and Emily Genauer, the critic then for the New York *World-Telegram*, declared that the show was "a frivolous and

1 "Why Fight It?", a profile of Sidney Janis by John Brooks, *The New Yorker*, November 12, 1960.

ill-considered gesture with Mr. Hirshfield the goat." Clark was no happier than the critics, and he, after all, as President of the Museum, had to take some responsibility for what he considered Barr's distasteful lapse of judgment in permitting Sidney Janis to direct and hang such a show in the Museum.

But matters of taste were by no means the only factors setting Clark and Barr at loggerheads. Barr was, without question, the lightning rod of the Museum. He not only attracted the thunderbolts which attacked it, but he also attracted the wreaths of laurel which were tossed to it. In most people's minds who knew about the Museum he *was* the Museum. So he was also to the curators and directors of departments who worked with him. He did not, however, have the place in hand; indeed, to Clark he seemed to be frittering away his time with details of scholarship and not even getting his own writing done. He was wasting time tinkering with other curators' manuscripts. He was not accepting invitations to give even such prestigious lectures as a series he had been asked to give at Bryn Mawr College. He most assuredly was not minding the store. Indeed, Clark believed that Barr's only use to the Museum had come down to what he wrote, and that otherwise he was a burden on the institution. For a time in 1943 James Thrall Soby was appointed Assistant Director to take over some of Barr's functions, not in the management of the Museum (which was under Dick Abbott's fluttering wing) but in matters having to do with its artistic activities.

Admittedly this was a very difficult moment for Clark to try to hold the reins, and, happily for him, he had the support of Mrs. Rockefeller. "In undertaking the management of the Museum during the war years," he wrote some years later to Abby Rockefeller's biographer,[2] "we were faced with an unusually difficult situation. Our chief concern was to try to keep the organization intact and to make the members of the staff work together in harmony." This was obviously a Herculean task, too big for Clark; harmony, as we have seen, was not achieved. "For Mrs. Rockefeller and me," he continued, "this was a novel experience. Neither of us had ever seen at such close range the group of individuals who composed the staff of the Museum." He found most of them "likable, extremely intelligent, and filled with a boundless enthusiasm for the Museum and all that it stood for." However, he also discovered that "some were very temperamental in character, and there was occasionally bickering, jealousy, and dissension

2 *Abby Aldrich Rockefeller*, by Mary Ellen Chase (New York, 1950).

among them." The situation, he said, called for "someone . . . to quiet their emotions, soothe their wounded feelings, and disengage them from violent controversies." He conceded that, "In this field Mrs. Rockefeller had no equal. Everybody liked and admired her, and so great was her tact and understanding that, even when she had a disagreeable duty to perform, she left no scars behind."

Clark did leave scars behind, and at least one wound that took a long time to heal, though apparently it did heal after many years. The clash between Clark and Barr might have been fatal—fatal for Barr's career, quite possibly, and crippling for the Museum, whose central nervous system and much of its muscle he had been and for the next nearly thirty years continued to be.

But let us look at these two men, each strong in a different way and each sensitive, both dedicated, both with a sense of public responsibility and of private indulgence in the pleasures of the arts, both with intuitive taste, though their tastes were not equally educated or equally daring.

Clark was a tall and rangy man, generally considered to be handsome, and he liked to walk. He was up early in the morning and headed on foot downtown from his vast house on 70th Street on his way to his office. His good friend Henry Allen Moe was always in his office at the Guggenheim Foundation at Fifth Avenue and 45th Street by eight o'clock. "So," Moe recalls, "he used to stop in there, and we'd talk for half an hour or an hour about the Museum—and I do say this, that's where the decisions got made." He would then walk up Fifth Avenue past St. Patrick's Cathedral and Rockefeller Center to the Museum. "Mr. Clark used to drop in early," Allen Porter recalls. "Fortunately, I was an early riser. He loved a piece of gossip. I was scared to death of him: he seemed so simple on the surface, and then he'd come out with something terrific. He also could be furious. I'll never forget one day in the office. We used to try out modern furniture. He sat on a chair and it tipped and he fell on his face and he said, 'Get that thing out of here!' It was one of those things that looked wonderful in a drawing, but it bit people."

On Wednesdays Clark would take Monroe Wheeler to lunch at the University Club, the splendid Renaissance palace designed by McKim, Mead and White, just a block north of the Museum and a short stone's throw from the Museum's garden. "He would come back to the Museum," Wheeler says, "and all the details of the Museum's various programs were discussed in great detail, and then he would go down the hall and see Alfred. It's hard to imagine how immense an additional burden it was to Alfred to move from the small place into the new building. As Director he was responsible for the entire institution —it was a colossal burden. He couldn't make all those decisions."

The decisions that Clark made were discussed in detail with Mrs. Rockefeller, and any incident that took place was gone over and weighed by them. The staff found him very laconic. "You almost had to read what he was thinking," Andrew Ritchie recalls. He said little at meetings and his was "a powerful silence," according to Jere Abbott. "I felt he was the one member of the board who could pounce." He kept a sharp eye on the Museum's finances, and Victor d'Amico remembers that twice a year he had to submit to Clark and Mrs. Rockefeller his budget for the operation of the educational program. "He would say to me," d'Amico recalls, " 'Victor, is there anything here where you're wasting any money?' I said, 'I don't know,' and he said, 'I just want to tell you something about wealthy people. Money is not just money; it's a symbol. You waste a penny or a thousand dollars and it's the same thing.' " And d'Amico added, "I liked him very much."

So did many other members of the staff, though he seemed greatly removed from them, a distant figure and a lonely man. Several of the women on the Board of Trustees speak of him as "difficult," but do not define him further. His daughter, Betsy, to whom he was devoted, died during the war, and his three sons, it is said, were a disappointment to him. His wife was, as Moe put it, "one of the completest ladies I have ever known." She was almost invariably to be seen in a simple navy-blue dress with white at the throat and at the cuffs. One evening at the opening of an exhibition of the Clark collection at Knoedler's, a charity benefit, an eager young man said to Mrs. Clark, "Don't you think the new Greco your husband has bought is marvelous?" And Mrs. Clark replied with faint mockery, "Oh, I don't know anything about the pictures. Stephen buys the pictures, I buy the wine and the cigars."

As a collector Clark prided himself on the fact that he never had a dealer as an advisor or a curator for his collection, and that his eye was entirely his own. "When I was a boy in my teens," he told Henry Moe, "I'd sell one and buy another when a picture hadn't lived up to my first expectations. It was all my own judgment, nobody else's." Andrew Ritchie, who sat with him on the Acquisitions Committee of the Museum, said, "He had very definite ideas about what was good. 'Matisse is out,' he said, and sold all he had." His taste, which was subject to change, was basically for the Impressionists and Post-Impressionists, though that was by no means the limit of it. Some years after the war, in the early 1950s, he resigned from the Acquisitions Committee. "I think his split with the Museum came, like Conger Goodyear's," Ritchie recalls, "over Pollock. He couldn't take Pollock." According to Eliza Parkinson, it was a Rothko that floored Goodyear, and Dorothy Miller recalls that it was Giacometti whom Clark found reprehensible. "He couldn't stand the Giacometti chariot and left the committee," she said. "Imagine! He just couldn't stand Giacometti." Moe had a somewhat different perspective on Clark's taste and on the Museum. "He had the respect of everybody by reason of his force of character and his connoisseurship," Moe said, "so that if there was an exhibition going up and there was a picture on the wall that he didn't approve of for that particular exhibition, he'd walk up and take it off the wall."

It seems unlikely that any trustee in any museum in New York would take it upon himself today to snatch a picture off the wall of an exhibition because it displeased him or he thought it unsuitable, and it cannot have pleased Clark's curators then. It is well to remember, though, that the belief of the trustees that the Museum was their possession, bailiwick, and private indulgence was a great deal stronger in the early 1940s than it is in the 1970s, although some of that attitude persists. Clark had, after all, given the Museum the first painting it had ever owned, Edward Hopper's "House by the Railroad." He gave it early in 1930, just a few months after the Museum opened its doors. Glenway Wescott, who watched the back-and-forth between his friend Monroe Wheeler and Clark, said to me, "Of course Alfred doesn't like pretty pictures, and Monroe does, and Monroe not only felt that he wanted Mr. Clark's pictures for the Museum, but he also felt that the taste of the great collector was an essential part of the story of the taste of the Museum." This observation about the difference between Barr's taste and Clark's is borne out by Allen Porter, who remembered that "Clark wanted to give the lady with the white plumes [by Matisse] [3] to the Museum, and Alfred said it was cheesecake and didn't want it in the collection."

"It was Alfred's directness and honesty and passionate, passionate feeling about things that put Stephen Clark off and made him feel that he couldn't work with this man," one of Barr's associates has said. "Without knowing it, Alfred made Stephen Clark feel like a fool because Alfred was always right."

Presumably, no one is "always right." Barr would have been the

3 Its proper title is "White Plumes" and it was painted by Matisse in 1919. It ultimately found a permanent home in the Minneapolis Institute of Art.

first to say so, and he often expressed his doubts about his own judgments on works of art. In the long run, he expected to be proven wrong more often than right, though this reasonable acknowledgment of historical perspective on taste did not dampen his enthusiasm or convictions of the moment.

The lightning struck in October 1943. Clark wrote Barr a letter that left him momentarily stunned. It scolded. It berated. It accused. It was gauche and harsh and carping, and copies of it were sent to Philip Goodwin, Conger Goodyear, Mrs. Rockefeller, and James Thrall Soby. Only Soby rallied to Barr's defense and offered to resign. He did not like the way the Museum was developing, he said, and he did not want to carry on with Barr on the shelf. At first Clark suggested that Barr's salary be cut to $6,000 a year and that he could supplement this with royalties from books he wrote for the Museum. In November Clark lowered the boom still further: he would not even let Barr have an office in the Museum, much less one near the Library. Then he thought better of this and reversed his field somewhat. He offered Barr the job of Curator of the Museum Collections, which he hoped might be stored and shown in a new and separate building after the war.

Paul Sachs was no longer an active trustee of the Museum when Barr got fired—and "fired" is the word he used and his wife still uses to describe what someone else might call more politely but less accurately "a shift in responsibilities." The fact is that he was dismissed from the job of Director as surely as Mrs. Clark might have dismissed an unsatisfactory butler. Barr wrote to Sachs, as he was accustomed to do when he wanted advice or, occasionally, just to blow off steam. "Really, Paul," he wrote, "I am still pretty damn sore, and I feel that there are many undersurface forces at work which I can't put in writing. . . . I'm afraid the Museum is in real danger—and I'm no longer strong enough to fight a losing battle."

About four months later, early in April 1944, Barr wrote to Sachs again, saying that the plan to make him the Curator of the Collections had collapsed, and that the Executive Committee of the board wanted Barr to spend his time just writing. Clark, he said, had threatened to resign from the board if anyone questioned the reversal of his decision and added that he'd "take his fifty thousand a year with him." Barr was named Advisory Director that spring.

As one would expect in such a situation, there was a distinct choosing up of sides within the Museum, and accusations of duplicity and double dealing flew through the air like knives. The curatorial staff

stood by Barr. Dick Abbott and Frances Hawkins, the Secretary of the
Museum who had been recommended for the job by Lincoln Kirstein,
were thought by most of the staff to have worked on Clark and to be
responsible for Barr's being fired. Frances Hawkins was a small, thin,
and lively woman who had worked as an executive for Martha Graham
and her dance troupe, and Allen Porter, who worked closely with her,
remembers her as "wonderful, a good woman executive without being
overpowering . . . bright and quick." Though Barr was told at the
time that Abbott was out to get him, he has since said that he does not
believe this to have been the case. Others, who are unwilling to exon-
erate Abbott, thought that Wheeler was also at Clark's elbow in this
matter, but, whatever the truth may have been (and everyone who
played a major role in the Museum's politics at the time is now reluctant to lay blame on anyone with the exception of Abbott, who
has long been safely dead), it was Clark who made the decision. As
Barr said to Sachs, Clark was at heart a collector who distrusted the
intellectual and educational approach to gathering a museum collection, and he thought that Barr's only use to the Museum was as a
scholar and writer. "Damn it, Paul," Barr wrote, "is this true? Were all
the planning and all those exhibitions, and the paintings I have bought,
and the standards I have fought for—was it someone else?"

We have seen a good deal of Barr in the pages of this book, but
there is a great deal more about Barr that should be understood if the
Museum is to be understood. This moment in his career, while he was,
in his words, "on the shelf," is a reasonable time to look at the man
from some perspectives which this narrative has not before made convenient.

"I think," James Soby wrote in a letter in 1971, "the prevalent view
of Alfred as a cold and remote scholar is totally wrong. He was and is
an extremely warm human being, especially with his close friends."
Surely there is nothing of the pedant about him in his personal correspondence with friends, or, in any event, in those letters I have had
the pleasure of reading . . . and a few of which are quoted in these
pages. They are casual, vivid, and slangy. When he was studying at
Harvard and Katherine Gauss was a student at Smith, he sent her a
"bluff sheet" with all the likeliest fashionable clichés in it for impressing
the sophisticated with one's knowledge of music.

In the section on the Russians, for example, he said of Tchaikovski
("often written -kowsky"): "It is fashionable now to look down on

him as lacking both the profundity and the true spirit of Slavic music."
Of Moussorgski he said, "Wrote the greatest Russian opera, *Boris
Godunov* (just say *Boris*—it sounds more familiar)." Of Rimski-
Korsakoff he said in part, "Orchestrated Moussorgski's *Boris*. (It is
fashionable to regret this because M's harmonic system is akin to very
modern music. R-K's more pleasant.") The "bluff sheet" deals with
each composer in somewhat more impressive detail than indicated here,
and if young Miss Gauss actually memorized it, she must have sounded
very knowledgeable indeed, and very up-to-date in her opinions.

He was an eager sports fan or, more accurately, an eager spectator
of sports, and, as with anything he puts his mind to, his critical faculties
of performance were always analytical. His mother once said to him,
"Can't you just enjoy yourself without having to be critical?" and his
reply was, "But don't you understand that being critical is a large part
of the enjoyment?" By "critical" he obviously meant not "disparaging"
but "analytical." About a Princeton-Harvard football game which
Princeton won handily, he wrote a friend: "It was marvelous, one of
the great days of one's life—first hopeful, then encouraged, then surprised, then confident, then amazed, then dumfounded, then utterly
incredulous, then religious (or equivalent) and finally dionysiac. I lost
my much beloved hat—the four year old one and got a horrible black
Latin Quarter one in exchange—but what nobler fate could befall an
old and faithful hat than to be sacrificed on the altar (or should one
say the goal posts) of Victory . . . and the odds 2 to 1 agin us. . . ."

He played tennis and golf in Greensboro, Vermont, far up in the
state near the Canadian border, where he had gone for summer vacations with his parents, and where for years he has had a house on the
lake to which he goes still to write, to watch birds, to cut brush. The
community is, or, rather, was fifty years and more ago a resort to
which many academics went for their long summer vacations. It was
unpretentious (and largely still is) and set in rolling wooded hills under a wide sky. Those who enjoy it are fiercely loyal to it, and when
Mrs. Barr went there first as a bride, she was asked if she didn't think
it was the "most beautiful place" she'd ever seen. "Certainly not," she
said. "Does it compare with the Italian lakes?" She has not changed
her mind.

There is, whatever Soby may say (and he surely would agree),
something of the remote scholar about Barr, the preoccupied scholar
whose mind often drifted away from the consideration of practical
problems in the presence of members of his staff. As one of them said,
"Suddenly you'd know he just wasn't there." Where he was it was

difficult to tell, but it was assumed that he was back in the book or the exhibition on which he was then working. He could, as Soby has said, "be impatient with people who took up his time needlessly." He was "one of the few people in the world who could answer the question, 'Have you got a moment?' by saying flatly, 'No, I haven't.'" In staff meetings he could be extremely critical of his colleagues, "taking little details," as one said, "and making causes out of them." Some members of the staff resented this; on the other hand, McAndrew, like Barr a man with a critical and precise mind, said to me, "You see, Alfred is a very distinguished teacher, as well as all these other things." George Amberg, who was the Curator of the Dance Archives at the Museum in the 1940s, said not long before he died in 1971, "Alfred was a difficult person, but, my God, who cares? When somebody has his extraordinary talents . . . And he was always very fair. He was uncomfortable in a meeting. He stuck to the point. He wanted it precise. Most of the time he said nothing. If and when he spoke, it was always precise and courteous." Andrew Ritchie, who is a Scotch Presbyterian by birth, observed that Barr's background was North Irish Presbyterian, which was even more rigorously Calvinist than his own, and that therefore Barr was even fiercer than he in standing on principle. On another occasion Ritchie changed the theological figure of speech but not the sentiment. "You can't undercut the Pope," he said. "Alfred *was* the Pope."

As Pope he was sometimes moody in his papal palace, and his entourage sometimes thought him vindictive. He was, it appeared to them, suspicious that those who served his church were angling for his papal crown or, if not that, trying to undermine his spiritual, if not necessarily his temporal, authority, which after 1944 was exerted by influence rather than by office. He picked away at Wheeler and at Ritchie and even, it is said, at his successor to the directorship, René d'Harnoncourt. "He was mean to them," one of the trustees told me, "but I think he was also devoted to them."

Barr liked to work with young people; he liked to help them, to teach them, and to use them as backboards off which to bounce his ideas. The role of Cary Ross—who was, you will recall, very much around with Barr and Jere Abbott in the earliest days of the Museum—seems to have been that of backboard. "Alfred liked a sort of younger faithful person," McAndrew says, "who would go around with him that he could talk to, not that he wanted to hear his answers, but Alfred's thinking often took place best when he was talking, and there was a series of a sort of satellites. . . . He would often ask their advice and opinions, which I don't think meant anything. It was his way of thinking and working." Dorothy Miller, who worked more closely with Barr than any other member of the staff for many years, speaks of his wanting to push younger people into doing things on their own. " 'You do it,' he'd say, 'and put your name on it.' " When Elodie Courter went to the Sorbonne on a Carnegie Fellowship in 1935, she was twenty-three and new on the Museum's staff. "I had about fifty or sixty dollars," she says, "and some money that Alfred gave me, and I did a little traveling. Alfred was very cute about it. He said, 'You can pay me back for the rest of your life—twenty-five cents a week—but I think it's important while you're here that you get around and see a few things.' "

To a whole generation of young curators (and some not so young— his near contemporaries) Barr was, as James Plaut has said, "the most powerful man in the field." Plaut was for many years the director of the Boston Institute of Contemporary Art (which had a furious row with the Museum of Modern Art in 1948, as we shall see), and he said, "I felt I was a protégé of Alfred, and he treated me that way. He's the only greatness of the Museum of Modern Art. He put together a cult, a Barr cult concerned with the whole lot of creative forces of our time. No one else compares with him. He used to be a sort of seven-teenth-century man in the political in-fighting with the passion of a revivalist."

No one questioned Barr's power, but some looked on it with the deepest suspicion. Francis Henry Taylor, the director of the Metro-politan Museum from 1940 to 1954, referred to the Museum of Modern Art as "that whorehouse on 53rd Street." Barr was called a "Svengali" for the skill with which he manipulated his Board of Trustees, though if this were true, he would not have let himself be manipulated out of the directorship. He has been said to have controlled the art press and the market for modern painting and sculpture, and while he unques-tionably had a very considerable influence on the press and the market through what he chose to show at the Museum and buy for its collec-tions, control was not only beyond his powers but beyond his wishes. The fact was that the press listened to him usually with respect and the dealers watched what the Museum did with an eagle eye. "Don't forget the Museum was the Bourse," Andrew Ritchie said. "Everything we did the dealers knew about before we did it, and prices were af-fected accordingly. It was inevitable." Many of those who followed Barr's judgments regarded him with the awe generally accorded only to gurus; some of those who thought his judgments mistaken regarded him not just as in error but as a vicious enemy of what was good, true, and beautiful, and somehow in cahoots with an underground movement that was trying to destroy not only art but the body politic as well.

In his excellent "profile" of Barr and the Museum of Modern Art which Dwight Macdonald wrote for *The New Yorker* in 1953, he says:

If Wyndham Lewis's "America I Presume" is to be trusted, Barr is the sinister personification of "modernism" to the members of the University Club, which, from the northwest corner of Fifty-fourth Street and Fifth Avenue, commands an excellent view of the back of the Museum of Modern Art. "Club members are accustomed to watch the Museum's Mr. Alfred Barr, Jr., whom they can see in his office," Lewis writes in his book. "They point at him with trembling fingers, indignation painted upon their massive countenances, for they are decent fellows, most of them. 'There he is,' I have heard them mutter to each other darkly, 'thinking up some new outrage.' And I'll swear the fellow knows he's being looked at and enjoys it. I have seen him surrounded by millionaires, examining some leering monstrosity upon the walls of his so-called Museum. He looks like a defrocked Spanish Jesuit. And for all I know, he is."

Some resentments and mistrusts of Barr were long-lived, and let us leap ahead for a moment to see how. In the mid-'60s Glenway Wescott, Marianne Moore, and Virgil Thomson believed that Barr should be elected a member of the National Institute of Arts and Letters, but, as Wescott recalls, "There was no possibility of our getting him into the membership. He was put up. Marianne put him up for the department of literature, and Virgil and I talked most eloquently, and the painters [who were members] were just outraged, and they said that it was almost treason that he had done, that he had taken all their market away." The artist members about whom Wescott was talking were, he said, "great people who were in the museums at one point or another, like Leon Kroll and Watrous and Gardner Cox" but their vogue had passed and they were not benefiting from the boom in the art market of the 1960s. The older architects in the institute were no happier about Barr than the painters. They were men raised in the Beaux Arts tradition, and what the Museum had put over on them in the early '30s with the International Style exhibition had not been forgiven. Wescott a few years later tried a different tack. "I had the idea of putting him up for the medal." The medal's proper name is the institute's "Award for Distinguished Service to the Arts." By this time the mood had changed greatly and "The people who formerly had been against him said, 'Look, it doesn't matter what kind of man he was, he made a market for art in this country. When we were young, people didn't feel that they had to have pictures on their walls. They had flowered wallpaper or at the most a print, but he suddenly made it all right.' This was in 1968."

When Wescott prepared his remarks for the presentation of the medal, Barr asked if he might see them so that he would know in what vein to reply. "I gave him my text," Wescott said, "and he corrected something in it because he didn't want to be given credit individually for what he regarded as belonging to the Museum as a whole." When Barr telephoned Wescott to make this small correction, he said, "I want to tell you, before we start talking about me, something that will interest you and sadden you, and I would forget it if I were to talk about what we have to talk about, and that is that the pilgrim hawk that used to nest on the top of the Queensborough Bridge has departed." Wescott, as those who are familiar with this extraordinary writer's work well know, is the author of a short novel called *The Pilgrim Hawk*, published in 1940.

In his brief presentation speech (fewer than 500 words) Wescott said

Today for the first time in history, this country is exporting its paintings and sculpture. It is a better world for artists than that into which my generation and our elders were born. This, for the most part, the Museum of Modern Art, with Alfred Barr's ardent, persistent spirit decisive in every respect, brought about. . . .

He has newly defined, clarified, coordinated the language having to do with art, so that the intention and accomplishment of a given artist can be characterized and praised without in any sense defying or insulting opposite artists. Post-Barr, we seem not to have had any merely verbal, unintentional quarrelsomeness in aesthetics. He has enabled hundreds of thousands of art-lovers to converse happily about what they love, and thus to teach one another in the best way.

There were many young painters to whom Barr was a somewhat distant but at the same time highly visible landmark. They thought of him as remote and cool; they were somewhat frightened of him, not just because he controlled their destinies (which he would ardently deny) but because of his unflappable critical and analytical attitude toward their work. "The first time he got fired," Jimmy Ernst says, "I remember meeting him and saying that the artists wanted to do something about this. They're very upset. . . . He was the Museum. After that, instead of being concerned with culture, they became cultivators. Anyway, Barr got very upset and he said, 'No, absolutely no. I want nothing at all.' He became very firm. Whether there were reasons for it or only whether he kind of wanted to separate himself from it—from the artists—I don't know. I loved this man."

Some years later, Ernst remembers, when Barr first saw the "glowing panels" of Mark Rothko, he said to him, "Do you know what you've done?"

"Mark wasn't usually at a loss for words," Ernst says, "but this time he said, 'What do you mean?' and Barr said, 'You've performed a miracle,' and then he said again, 'Do you know what you've done?' and Mark understood. That was the beginning of Mark. I suspect things like this happened very frequently."

The painter Ralston Crawford, an abstractionist just a few years younger than Barr, said, "Barr was not inclined to be educated by the painters. He had other sources." On the other hand, in the days of The Club, a group of New York artists who met in the Village one evening a week, Barr would frequently turn up, as one of them said, "and make things very uncomfortable for us—in a real sense, not a nasty sense, in an intellectual sense." One evening "all kinds of people were sitting around a table, talking about the School of New York (when it became the School of New York, that was the end of the Club—the moment we allowed it to be called that name), and Barr got up and said, 'What are you going to do now?' and everybody got terribly angry, and somebody said, 'What's the matter? You got nothing to sell to your trustees? You gotta have something new?'" On another occasion the group held a three-day symposium "in a loft that New York University was paying the rent for" and Barr sat there as an observer. Out of this came a publication and a protest. The publication was a record of the discussion as part of *Documents of Modern Art;* the protest was by a group that called themselves The Eighteen against the policies of the Metropolitan Museum toward contemporary American painting. The Hearn Fund, which had been given to the Metropolitan for the purpose of purchasing modern Americans, had sat unused in that museum's coffers. When the Metropolitan was under pressure from artists to use it, Francis Taylor decided to have a big "catch-all" exhibition for which artists would submit their work to regional juries that would then pass along their choices to a master jury at the Metropolitan. The Club thought that the museum should be confident enough of its own taste to make its own selections, and they decided to boycott the exhibition. The boycott was Adolph Gottlieb's idea, and Barnett Newman delivered the ultimatum to the *New York Times* and the *Herald Tribune* on a Sunday evening when things were slow, and "The Irascible Eighteen," as they were called, made the front pages the following morning.

It would have been out of character for Barr to make any public comment on such a declaration by artists against another museum, but he was quick to answer attacks on his own museum. In 1946 *Harper's Magazine* published an article by Lincoln Kirstein called "The State of Modern Painting." In it Kirstein, whom no one could call a Philistine, defined a new kind of opposition to what he called "the general acceptance and canonization of abstract painting—a modern Abstract Academy that, like its other academic predecessors, now wins prizes in eminently respectable national salons." He made it quite clear that he was in no way opposed to "the use of unhampered imagination, experiment in new method or material, or what is loosely called distortion." He was opposed to "improvisation as method, deformation as a formula and painting (which is a serious matter) as an amusement manipulated by interior decorators and high-pressure salesmen." "The Museum of Modern Art in promulgating its useful catalogues . . . has done its job almost too well," he wrote. "Today most young painters, thanks to the Museum's publications, feel that the past fifty years or more are more instructive and worthy of imitation than the past five hundred years." Of the Museum of Modern Art's permanent collections (which "just as the written words in the museum's catalogues, remains in the mind") he said, "They represent, after all, just one kind of picture selected as a demonstration of the development of what seems to the men who collect them to be a significant body of tendencies. But they are infrequently good models, too often charts of dead ends, unselective and feeble imitations of renowned paintings by famous signatures."

Barr could not have been expected to be unmoved by this kind of summation of his Museum's collection, which he had helped to build with such care. Furthermore, *Harper's Magazine* just a little over four years before had published an attack on the Museum and more specifically on Barr himself. It was by Emily Genauer, who had been for twelve years the art critic of the New York *World-Telegram*, and it was called "The Fur-lined Museum." In it Miss Genauer said of Barr,

"Whisper-voiced, he rarely smiles, and when he does the effect—in the apt phrase of one of his friends—suggests soil erosion. His appearance gives the impression of no great strength or of will." Of his taste she wrote, "Yet some defect of judgment or of initiative seems to have dogged his steps. Chiefly it may have been an uncertainty such as was suggested in *The New Yorker* cartoon of a man in an art gallery saying, 'I know all about art but I don't know what I like.' " About his buying for the Museum's permanent collection she said, "How does it [the Museum] justify the purchase of Van Gogh's 'Starry Night' and Rousseau's 'Sleeping Gypsy' (with money given by Mrs. Simon Guggenheim) for over $25,000 each?" Of his relations with artists she wrote: "But the heart of Barr's difficulty seems to have been a failure to keep in touch with—or to appreciate—the important things which have been going on in the contemporary art world unless these happened to have attracted the attention and admiration within the closed circle in Fifty-third Street." Of his relations with the trustees who fired him, she said, "During his tenure as director he handled his trustees with the diplomacy of a Talleyrand." On the exhibitions in the Museum, Miss Genauer wrote: "The emphasis has been largely upon two elements: (1) Those Sure Things which it has inherited, and which as time has gone on have been accepted as classics by wider and wider audiences; and (2) Those Shockers (the fantastic, the precious, the bizarre, and the decadent) which excite the crowd that might be called the Café Society of the Arts." On what American painters the Museum had not included in its permanent collection she cites specifically Bluemner, Boardman Robinson, Waldo Pierce, David Burliuk, and Henry Varnum Poor. With the exception of Burliuk, all of them had been shown at the Museum, one of them (Poor) four times. She lists among the artists the Museum did own "the proficient but uninspired realist, Edward Hopper" and "a large fifth-rate canvas by the contemporary neo-romanticist, Tchelitchew," a picture called "Hide and Seek," which, whatever its merits, is today the most popular picture in the Museum's collection. "And," she said, "there are eight of Alexander Calder's 'mobiles' and 'stabiles'—arrangements of wood and metal segments that are suspended from lengths of cord and wire, to be moved by a motor or a passing breeze."

It has little significance in this narrative, but there is some amusement in seeing what Miss Genauer wrote twenty-two years later when she was doing a column on art for the New York *Herald Tribune;* she said, "MOMA, they're whispering sadly in studios, galleries, art-lovers' living rooms, has grown middle-aged. . . . There's no question but she has lost the pliancy, the bounce, the rapturous enthusiasm of her youth. She has grown a little cautious."

There is, however, some significance in the way the trustees rallied to Barr's support in 1944. Paul Sachs wrote to Frederick Lewis Allen, the editor-in-chief of *Harper's*, in part:

> Now that I have read the "cheap," superficial and unfair article with care—an article utterly unworthy of the best traditions of a serious journal—I think that you, as an able and imaginative editor who enjoys public confidence, would be very sorry indeed that you ever gave your editorial sanction to the article. It may be good spicy reading for the uninformed (and they are legion in all fields of honest human effort), but those who know and understand are not only incensed but bitter about an article that they consider completely unfair.

Editors are not likely to be moved by such letters as this one from Sachs, and Allen's reply was courteous but noncommittal. Letters like Sachs's are part of an editor's daily diet and he gets used to them, but the fact was that Allen, as I know from personal conversation with him at the time, was uneasy about having published the article. He would not have denied what Sachs said when he wrote about Barr, "He, more than any other one person, has 'made' the Museum. Starting at scratch, he has given the Museum a national and an international reputation. Generous and powerful trustees can never manage without a gifted director. . . . About all this and much besides Miss Genauer seems to me quite unaware."

An editorial in the August 1–31, 1944, issue of *Art News* said of Miss Genauer's article:

> What value the Harper's article had in part as an objective appraisal, however, was unfortunately destroyed by a constant undercurrent of *a priori* animosity, and even more, by an all too obvious intent to smear the Museum's director. Indeed, this violent personal attack on Alfred Barr, filled with unpleasant irrelevancies, was so pointed and in such poor taste that it takes the entire article from the category of the answerable into that of the questionable —to the extent that one must suspect its motives. . . .

To accompany the editorial, which filled a full two-column page, *Art News* published an article by Agnes Mongan, a curator at the Fogg Museum (and some years later its director), called "What Makes a Museum Modern?" It was not a reply to the Genauer article; Miss

Mongan would have thought this beneath her dignity. It was, rather, a brief review of the Museum's accomplishment on the occasion of its fifteenth-anniversary exhibition, which was called *Art in Progress*. Miss Mongan said:

> The record of the Museum of Modern Art is an astonishing and enviable one for any institution which has existed a brief decade and a half. In that time it has achieved both national leadership and international fame. Neither is easily won. Both are well-deserved awards of a wisely flexible policy, generous private support, and the unremitting intellectual and physical labor of a brilliantly endowed staff.

The Genauer article caused sufficient disturbance within the walls of the Museum so that James Soby produced a lengthy (sixteen legal-size pages) memorandum "for internal consumption only, that is, for circulation among the Trustees and staff members." It takes "The Fur-Lined Museum" apart almost sentence by sentence, premise by premise, accusation by accusation, and answers it . . . or at least comments on it. He concludes, for those who actually read the memorandum to the last page, with

> But the refutation of Miss Genauer's second charge [that the museum's past record had been bad] is the overwhelming fact that the Museum during its first fifteen years has won world-wide esteem as the greatest institution anywhere for the advancement, enjoyment, and understanding of the 20th century visual arts. We shall have our hands full living up to the first fifteen years.

The first charge, that the Museum was torn by internal dissension, Soby discards. "Any growing institution," he writes, "is expected to have points of disagreement among its Trustees and staff; indeed . . . these disagreements are a healthy complement to the process of growing up."

Neither the scholar in Barr, nor the collector, nor the individual was impressed by Miss Genauer's article, though no one likes to have devious motives imputed to him and no one likes to be called names. Barr was not in the least worried about the effect on himself; he had already been dropped from his job, and being kicked while down by a journalist was of no great matter to a man who had just been kicked out by the Chairman of his Board. Barr, however, did not like to have his "mistress" insulted either by a "working stiff" of the press or by his friend Lincoln Kirstein. I discovered this at first hand.

One morning at *Harper's Magazine,* of which I was an editor (though I had not been when Miss Genauer's piece was published), I had a phone call from James Soby asking me to lunch with him and Barr, an invitation I was puzzled by but glad to accept. It was soon after the publication of Kirstein's article. We met in a restaurant behind the Museum a few days later, and Barr said to me, "What is this conspiracy against modern art that *Harper's* and the *Atlantic Monthly* and the Hearst press are engaged in?"

I suggested that if there were a conspiracy the conspirators must have sat down and conspired together on plans. "Can you imagine the editors of the *Atlantic* and the Hearst press and *Harper's* sitting down to discuss their editorial policies, much less agree on them?" I asked. "You can't have a conspiracy without conspirators."

Barr and Soby conceded that this was true.

But let us get back to our narrative. "When Alfred was fired," one of his colleagues said recently, "the staff just fell apart. It was so shocking. And then there was this long period when we went along until this awful person finally lost power and was out."

"The awful person" referred to was Dick Abbott. Abbott and Clark worked more and more closely, and they were so much together and seemingly so close that in the gossip mill that was the Museum there were raised eyebrows. Daniel Catton Rich recalls with amusement a conversation he had at the time with Juliana Force, the director of the Whitney Museum in the days when it was still on West Eighth Street in the Village.

"What is this between Clark and Abbott?" he asked.

"Innocence," she replied.

Abbott divorced Iris Barry (or Iris Barry divorced him, depending on whose version one believes), and when he remarried in the mid-'40s Clark was his witness at a civil ceremony which took place at Abbott's apartment because Abbott was suffering from a pulmonary ailment. Abbott's tenure at the Museum did not last long after that. He was divorced from his new wife, he had "trouble with the bottle," as one of his colleagues put his problem, and he was eased off the Museum's staff early in 1948. This did not happen, however, until Clark had found another job for him as manager of a restaurant; in fact, the job was arranged for before he was told that he was no longer welcome on the Museum staff. The new job was not a success either. "He was on the Museum's board for a couple of years even after he got fired,"

Allen Porter recalls, "and he took great delight in coming to meetings and bitching things up." Abbott died in the early 1950s, the victim of a domestic accident. He fell and killed himself.

There were other casualties of a less dramatic but more important character. When Beaumont Newhall returned to the Museum after the war to resume his job as Curator of Photography, a position which had been held down for him by his wife, Nancy, while he was in the Navy, he discovered that the situation was not at all what he expected it to be. In December of 1945 Mrs. Newhall was told by Stieglitz to "watch out for Steichen" because, he said, Steichen (who had been in charge of combat photography for the Navy in the Pacific and was by then Captain Steichen) "wants to take over the department." The warnings were justified. According to Tom Maloney, who then edited the annual *U.S. Camera*, he was approached by Henry Allen Moe, who asked him if he thought Steichen would be interested in taking over the directorship of the Photography Department. Several days later at a lunch in Washington, Maloney asked Steichen what he thought. "I'd love it," Steichen said. Moe reported these conversations to the trustees, who agreed to make such an arrangement so long as it did not increase the Museum's budget. According to Nancy Newhall it was Steichen's and Maloney's plan to get $100,000 from ten manufacturers of photographic equipment to give initial support to the new program, and they envisioned the erection of a structure eighty feet square in the Museum's garden in which to hold shows. None of the members of the Photography Committee of the Museum was consulted about this scheme. David McAlpin, the committee's chairman, told the Newhalls that he first heard about it at a trustees' meeting.

Steichen intended to have Newhall continue as curator of the department, of which Steichen was to be boss, a proposal which Newhall, who had built the department from scratch and whose interest in photography was scholarly and aesthetic and not spectacular, found entirely unacceptable. So did his friend and supporter McAlpin; so did the photographers whose work he had introduced into the Museum and who had helped him found the department, most particularly Ansel Adams (who wrote of Steichen as "the anti-Christ of photography: clever, sharp, self-promoting and materialistic"); so did the Advisory Committee of the Museum; so did James Soby and Alfred Barr.

Marian Willard was the chairman of the Advisory Committee at the time Newhall was "fired," for that was what the situation was considered by his colleagues to be. She recalls that "this was the first time that commercial money, I believe, came into the Museum in such a way." The way was to pay Steichen's salary. The Advisory Committee felt that the trustees were being "disloyal to the staff to treat Newhall as they did." It was "one of the things that got us concerned about the direction the Museum was taking"; it was one of the things, indeed, that led the Advisory Committee to resign in a body, which it did in the spring of 1946 in protest against the fact that all its investigations and recommendations to the trustees were ignored. ("It is the reluctant conclusion of the Advisory Committee," the letter of resignation said, "that the services of such a Committee are not welcome. . . .") The committee which disapproved of the way Newhall was being shunted about and the publicity-seeking implied by Steichen's appointment was made up of a very considerable list of influential individuals. As a committee it had been in existence for seventeen years, first with George Howe as its chairman and then headed by Nelson Rockefeller as his first official connection with the Museum. It became clear to Miss Willard; to Dorothy Shaver, the president of Lord and Taylor; to William W. Wurster, the dean of architecture at MIT; to Davidson Taylor, a vice-president of CBS; to C. H. Gray, the president of Bard College; to the editor of *Town and Country*, Harry Bull; to the theatrical designer Jo Mielziner; and the others on the committee that they were merely ornamental, and they wanted no further part of it.

Newhall wanted no part of being Steichen's lieutenant. "Steichen counted on Beaumont and needed a top-flight man next to him," Bernard Karpel says, "but Beaumont did not want to be second fiddle. . . . You couldn't be second fiddle to Steichen. You had to be a slave to Steichen. Beaumont knew that he couldn't survive in the shadow of Steichen's kind of volcanic domination, and he left. Steichen didn't want him to go."

It is generally believed that Steichen was instrumental in getting Newhall the job which he held for many years as director of George Eastman House, the photographic museum of the Eastman Kodak Company in Rochester. Steichen was Director of the Museum's Photography Department until he retired at the age of eighty-three in 1962.

Still another post-war departure from the Museum and a serious curtailment of its programs came with the resignation in 1947 of Elodie Courter (by then Mrs. Robert Osborn) as Director of the Department of Circulating Exhibitions. ("Elodie was the kind," Barr said, "who when she left the Museum it took four people to replace her.") She had asked for a leave of absence to have a child and she had been encouraged to return to her job whenever she felt she wanted to. Her pediatrician, Dr. Benjamin Spock, when she told him that the time had come for her to make up her mind whether to go back to the Museum, asked her, "What do you do at the Museum?" She explained what her department did, and he said, "I think I'd let somebody else pack the pictures." "That seemed such a blow to me," she said recently, "I wasn't sure what I was going to do. So for that reason I took on doing the teaching portfolios, which was something I didn't have to be at the Museum regularly to do."

The circulating exhibitions, under Miss Courter's surveillance, had grown tremendously in scope, in geographical spread, and in influence, but by 1945 the Policy Committee of the trustees "in the interests of efficiency and economy" recommended that the "circulating exhibitions should be radically reduced in number and the charge . . . considerably increased." The department showed a deficit of more than $19,000 in the year ending July 1945, and during that year the number of shows on the road had been cut back from 136 to 75.

"The circulating exhibitions," Monroe Wheeler said, "were always a problem because they were so expensive to develop year after year. We couldn't get enough from the recipients of the exhibitions because they didn't have enough money."

Dorothy Miller said of them in 1971, "I can't tell you how many artists through the years from all over the country have said, 'Oh, my, you don't know what your circulating exhibitions were like out in Portland, Oregon,' or wherever. It was important to do it then. It isn't now."

Sarah Newmeyer, who had headed the Publicity Department of the Museum since she had first put "Whistler's Mother" on front pages across the country in 1933, resigned from the Museum in the spring of 1948, not without encouragement. She resigned, according to an announcement in the Museum *Bulletin*, "to devote full time to the completion of a book on which she had done much research and preliminary work during the past several years." The book, *Enjoying Modern Art*, was published in 1955, not long before her death. She moved to Sturbridge Village to do the publicity for that "Early American" Massachusetts town and, it is said, "put it on the map." Her house in Sturbridge was flooded at the time of a hurricane which struck New England so violently that summer and, as Allen Porter reports the incident, "When the storm was over she went to her house with an electrician. They waded into the water and turned on the electricity and they were both electrocuted."

Frances Hawkins, who was briefly the very effective Secretary of the Museum, left under quite different circumstances and for different reasons. In January of 1945 Barr wrote to Sachs that Frances Hawkins had resigned, "officially no reason given, but obviously the same reason" for which Soby had also resigned as Assistant Director: Barr's dismissal. Miss Hawkins, it is evident, found working with Stephen Clark not to her taste, and Agnes Mongan wrote a memo to Sachs in which she said:

> For your own information, John McAndrew told me last night that Frances Hawkins when she resigned recently, wrote six or eight pages giving the reasons for her resignation. Clark replied that she was neurotic and should see a psychiatrist. The following week she presented Clark with statements from three of New York's eminent psychiatrists, each of whom said that she was one of the sanest women he had ever seen.

There were many other comings and goings at the Museum in the last half of the 1940s. One promising arrival and subsequent stepchild was the Dance Archives. Late in 1939 Lincoln Kirstein, who was a member of the Advisory Committee and with George Balanchine a founder of the American School of the Ballet, the American Ballet Company, and the Ballet Caravan, persuaded the Museum to set up a library of the dance, and to it he contributed his own burgeoning collection and the collections of Gordon Craig and Fred King. At his behest Paul Magriel, who had written extensively on the history of the dance, was appointed librarian of the collections. Within a year of their official establishment in April 1940 the Dance Archives had held seven small exhibitions in the Museum (all of which had traveled under Elodie Courter's circulating-exhibitions program) and prepared two exhibitions only for traveling. ("We were young then," Magriel now says, "and we got a lot done in a hurry.") By 1942 both Kirstein and Magriel were in the Army and George Amberg (who was many years later to establish at NYU the first doctoral program anywhere in cinema) took over as Archivist. By 1943 the program had withered on the vine. The Museum's trustees had found it a financial burden which they were no longer inclined to support; Alfred Barr, who never had been convinced that the materials belonged in the Museum and was by then Director of the Collections, paid it no heed, and Kirstein was fairly thoroughly disenchanted with Barr and the Museum. He gave the most valuable of the early books on the dance to the Harvard Library on extended loan, and the rest of the collections went to the New York Public Library's Theatre Collection and are now in the library at Lincoln Center, where, Magriel says, "they belong and get much more use than they ever would at the Museum."

There were a number of far more important arrivals in the 1940s than those I have mentioned, but they belong to what might justifiably be called a different era in the Museum's history. It would be inaccurate to call the era "post-Barr" but not entirely inaccurate, for though his voice persisted as that of the Museum's aesthetic conscience until 1967 when he retired, authority over the Museum's business and its staff and programs became somebody else's responsibility. The era can accurately be called post-war—post World War II, that is. The Museum's internal wars continued much as before, though the issues were different and so were many of the contestants.

What followed was an interregnum when the Museum was administered by a staff committee. "However," Dorothy Miller recalls, "there was a sort of path worn in the floor toward the little alcove that Alfred was working in within the library—he was writing his Picasso book then—because everybody had to ask his advice about everything."

*This place is a madhouse, because of the pressures,
the number of people who want to get into the act,
and a temperamental board of trustees and
staff. He holds it together. He moves from one crisis
to another.*
ALFRED H. BARR, JR., *in an interview with*
GEOFFREY T. HELLMAN, 1960

Chapter XIV *A Gentle Giant*

In the mid-'30s, nearly ten years before Alfred Barr was ejected from the Director's office of the Museum, he and Mrs. Barr invited the Nelson Rockefellers to dinner at their sparely furnished apartment in 2 Beekman Place. The occasion was to introduce Nelson to René d'Harnoncourt, a towering man of noble lineage and an authority on primitive arts. Barr thought that d'Harnoncourt might at some time be useful to the Museum. D'Harnoncourt at that time was teaching the history of art at Sarah Lawrence College in Bronxville, a New York suburb, and he had met Barr earlier when he was conducting a radio program called *Art in America* which was heard on thirty-six stations and was a sort of Cook's Tour from the art of the Colonies to the present.

Mrs. Barr, a not easily flustered woman, was in something of a fluster about having Nelson and Tod Rockefeller for dinner for the first time, and she asked Philip Johnson (he then lived in the same building as the Barrs) what she should cook for them. Johnson suggested *osso buco*, a veal knuckle, which she served in an especially dark gravy and which looked mountainous on a plate. It was a dish which as an Italian she cooked particularly well. It was not, however, a success. The Rocke-

264

fellers evidently had never seen such a concoction before and left it only politely nibbled at. The meeting of the d'Harnoncourts and the Rockefellers, however, initiated what later became a long and close friendship which did indeed turn out, as Barr could not have foreseen, to have a profound influence on the Museum of Modern Art, on d'Harnoncourt's career, and on his own.

D'Harnoncourt is most often referred to by those who knew him as "an enormous man." He stood six feet seven and weighed 230 pounds. His voice was deep, his laugh was frequent, and contagious. Like many tall men, he was inclined to stoop a little and his very broad and heavy shoulders were slightly rounded. He characteristically sat with his right elbow on the arm of a chair, with his forefinger in the corner of his right eye, and though he was slightly deaf (a condition which increased as he grew older and may have contributed to his death) he would not abide a hearing aid. His wife, Sarah, a handsome, striking figure, was nearly as tall as he. ("I was on my way to the Art Institute in Chicago," he is said to have said, "and there on Michigan Boulevard I found myself face to face with a woman who could look into my eyes.") They were, and were frequently called, "an impressive couple."

D'Harnoncourt was a count, though he dropped the title when he was a young man. He was the scion of a noble Austrian family, and "a descendant," as Geoffrey Hellman wrote in *The New Yorker* in 1960, "direct and collateral, of a cloud of Middle European noblemen who flourished as chamberlains and provosts to a cloud of Dukes of Lorraine, Counts of Luxembourg, and Hapsburg emperors." In 1924, after the Austro-Hungarian Empire fell apart, his family estates were expropriated by Czechoslovakia. He was twenty-three at the time. The equivalent of $60,000 which his father had left to young René in 1922 was, he said, "worth one necktie and a pair of suspenders" by the time the legacy got to him.

Like the early education of the sons of most such families, René's was largely at the hands of governesses and tutors. In his teens he lived in Graz, where he went first to school and then to the university. Already multi-lingual, he had a gift for learning, an interest in art and poetry, and a talent for drawing. He devoted his working hours at the university primarily to chemistry and his leisure to the arts—to making pictures, to collecting engravings by early German masters, and, with a few friends with whom he formed a club, to putting on exhibitions of modern art. For the first time in that rigid academic community they introduced prints by Picasso and Matisse, and, no doubt, were looked upon as radicals. From Graz he had gone in 1922 to the Technische Hochschule in Vienna, where he worked on a dissertation on *The Creosote Contents of Certain Coals of Southern Yugoslavia* which he thought might ultimately lead to his making a living in creosote technology. (Many years later he came on his dissertation, which had been published in a technical journal, and tried to reread it. He was amused to find that he "couldn't understand a word of it.") In 1925 he decided on North America as a likely place to make his fortune, but he could not get on the quota for entry to the United States and so settled for Mexico.

When he arrived at Veracruz, d'Harnoncourt had the equivalent of $19 in his pocket and discovered that this was $31 less than the Mexican immigration authorities considered the minimum for entry into their country. He borrowed $31 from a fellow passenger to demonstrate to the officials that he was solvent and repaid it as soon as he had passed the barrier. He found no charms in Veracruz and headed straight for Mexico City, and as no one there seemed sufficiently impressed with his knowledge of Yugoslovian creosote to hire him, and as foreign companies engaged with chemicals were staffed by their own nationals, he turned his skill as a facile draftsman into a means of supporting himself. He first got a job through a man who had befriended him on the ship from Europe, doing, as he has said, somewhat sexy posters for a cigarette called Buen Tono. He then fell into retouching photographs, painting dials on pocket watches, making sketches of bullfights which he sold to tourists, and putting up window displays for department stores and druggist shops. There was one stretch of a few weeks when his total worth was a peso a week, which, he noted, "was marvelous for my figure."

This skillful-hand-to-hungry-mouth existence lasted for just about a year, and then d'Harnoncourt had the good fortune to encounter an antique dealer named Bauer whom he had known in Austria and got a job with him selling furniture. "When he was away, which was a good deal," d'Harnoncourt said, "I was sales manager. When he was around I was the delivery boy." Through this job he met an American collector whom he greatly impressed with his extensive, albeit youthful, knowledge of antiquities—the kind of knowledge that an accurate, discerning, and intensely interested eye acquires almost automatically. The collector was William Green, the executive vice-president of a subsidiary of Standard Oil of New Jersey with headquarters in Mexico. (In one way or another Standard Oil kept popping up in d'Harnoncourt's career.) Green put d'Harnoncourt on a retainer of twenty-five pesos a day, a sum he regarded as magnificent, for the peso was then worth fifty cents and had, he said, the purchasing value of a dollar. D'Harnoncourt acted as an antiques scout, and this led to still other clients but most importantly to Frederick Davis, an American who owned the Sonora News Company, which handled, along with its staple printed commodities, Mexican curios. Davis invited d'Harnoncourt to take over this aspect of the business, and he quickly expanded it to include contemporary Indian artifacts of unusual quality, and he went so far as to arrange in the store the first commercial exhibition of work by the powerful revolutionaries Rivera and Orozco and by Tamayo and Covarrubias. For many years after d'Harnoncourt had moved to New York, Davis was his closest friend in Mexico; indeed, Davis kept an apartment in his house so long as he lived for the use of the d'Harnoncourts, and they used it frequently.

D'Harnoncourt also met the Dwight W. Morrows in Mexico City. Morrow, who had been a partner in J. P. Morgan and Company, was appointed United States Ambassador to Mexico by President Coolidge in 1927 (he became greatly popular in that role) and d'Harnoncourt helped him and Mrs. Morrow to fill their house in Mexico City with native handicrafts and works of art. Mrs. Morrow, a tiny dynamo of a woman with humor and great charm, wrote a children's book about Mexico called *The Painted Pig* and d'Harnoncourt illustrated it. Far more important, however, was his involvement with the craftsmen among Mexican Indians. He showed them examples of ancient works by their distant forebears, and, as his friend the author Stuart Chase wrote, "suddenly, mysteriously, something long dead came back to life."

In 1929 the Mexican Ministry of Education asked d'Harnoncourt to put together forty-eight collections of Mexican folk art, "one for each of the United States—which would be sent around to various American schools to show the children what was being done in Mexico." In the following years the Carnegie Corporation financed a much larger single exhibition of Mexican arts at the behest of Ambassador Morrow, who, d'Harnoncourt said, "felt that public opinion about Mexico was so bad in this country, what with the talk of bandits, revolutions, and so on, that it might help if we could show that Mexico produced some nice art." The exhibition opened at the Metropolitan Museum in October of 1930, and d'Harnoncourt was on hand to help to install it. He spent the better part of the next year traveling with the exhibition around the country, and gave more than two hundred talks about Mexican art in museums, clubs, and schools. As a side issue he autographed copies of two children's books of his own about Mexico, *The Hole in the Wall* and *Mexicana: A Book of Pictures*. By the time he finished his trip he had seen more of the United States than most Americans, had been courted by many eager mothers who thought it would be nice to marry a daughter to an Austrian count, and had been introduced to the seductive extravagance of Hollywood in its palmy days.

It was in 1934 that he took the part-time teaching job at Sarah Lawrence College and at the same time the supervision of the *Art in America* radio program. By then he was to all intents and purposes, if not yet officially, a citizen of the United States, and in 1937 he became a half-time employee of the Commissioner of Indian Affairs in the Department of Justice. He had met the Commissioner, John Collier, in Mexico. Collier had been impressed by his knowledge of the Indian arts and with his skill in encouraging them without interfering in their native qualities, and d'Harnoncourt was appointed assistant general manager of a newly organized Indian Arts and Crafts Board. Three years later he was the manager. "One of our objects," he told Geoffrey Hellman, "was to help North American Indians obtain some economic independence through their native crafts. They now earn a great deal that way."

D'Harnoncourt became legally a citizen in 1939, and that same year he put together a large American Indian exhibition at the San Francisco World's Fair. Out of it grew an even more impressive show for the Museum of Modern Art. It was partly paid for by government agencies, and it was d'Harnoncourt's first official act for the Museum. Two months before the show was to be installed he presented to the trustees scale models of three floors of the Museum with each object to be shown in its place. D'Harnoncourt liked to work in this way, and as long as he did installations for the Museum, which was for many years, he always organized them completely in scale drawings, with everything where it would be, its lighting precisely conceived, the backgrounds painted in their final colors. First he drew each object which he had selected individually, then he drew them together in groups, so that he could be certain of their relationships in scale and in context. When he had these juxtapositions determined to his satisfaction, he worked on a floor plan, "providing open vistas between one section and another," as he told Hellman, "wherever there was a close relationship between their contents, and introducing closed units only where unique local styles had developed." He chose the colors against which sculptures or handicrafts or other objects were to be shown "as symbolic aids," to approximate the light and backgrounds where they were made—the green of the jungle, the white light of the full sun, the red of rocks and tan of desert.

The *Indian Arts of the United States* exhibition made an immediate reputation for d'Harnoncourt in New York as a master of installation. He had displayed more than 1,000 objects with a kind of dramatic lighting that is now not uncommon but was then a revelation not just of his technique but primarily of the quality of the objects. He put up a canvas mural twelve by sixty feet and hung it in a curve from wall to wall; it was a full-scale replica of ancient animal and figure drawings from the canyon walls of Utah. On the sidewalk in front of the Museum he installed a totem pole which could be easily seen from Fifth Avenue, and which must have annoyed the Fifth Avenue Association as much as the Calder mobile had nearly a decade before. There were objects of pottery, of weaving, of basketry, dolls, ceremonial figures, costumes, masks, implements of the household and of the chase. There were Indians in the Museum making sand paintings on the floor, and they would quit when anyone tried to photograph them because, they insisted, their art was of itself a mysterious force "capable of harm when not controlled."

It was not the dramatic effect that d'Harnoncourt was interested in; it was in focusing the visitor's eye on the objects in such a manner that they could be made new and newly visible and be comprehended. "Installation is a very complicated and exciting subject, and it requires humility," he said. "Who comes first, the installer or the guy who's being installed? I never over-emphasize dramatic settings. A museum director shouldn't *add* to a work of art; he must *not* prostitute the whole thing and finally make a peepshow of it." The effect of d'Harnoncourt's installations has been far-reaching. It has also been abused. Some years after he put on the Indian show he was at a conference of art educators at the Museum's People's Art Center, and he took out after "museum directors who attempt to improve on the beauty of a work of art by an over-ambitious exhibition of it." According to the *New York Times*, "As an example he told of an exhibit of primitive ivory figures. The figures were set in a glass case and were played upon by shifting blue and green lights, causing a grotesque effect. 'If some museum directors like to do that sort of thing,' Mr. d'Harnoncourt said, 'let them use eggs, not works of art.' "

It had taken d'Harnoncourt two years to assemble the exhibition of Indian arts for the Museum and to prepare with Frederic H. Douglas a comprehensive catalogue with many illustrations which is at once a guide to the show and a textbook of its subject. "A representative picture of Indian art in the United States," he called it. Nelson Rockefeller was impressed by the success of the show as he had been earlier impressed by the character of the man, and in 1943 he invited d'Harnoncourt to join the staff of the Inter-American Affairs office as head of his art section. D'Harnoncourt went there on loan from the Department of the Interior, and from then on his career was closely tied to a series of Rockefellers and to what they regarded as "Mother's Museum."

D'Harnoncourt became officially attached to the Museum staff in 1944 with the curious title of Vice-President in Charge of Foreign Activities and Director of the Department of Manual Industries. He arrived at the fifth-floor offices in 53rd Street at a moment when Barr was in limbo and the staff was in the doldrums. He knew Monroe Wheeler well by then; they had worked together on projects for the Coordinator's office, which, as we have noted, had many contracts with the Museum for exhibitions and films and publications. He also knew Barr well, and had a profound admiration for him which was coupled with a genuine affection. There seems little doubt that Rockefeller, without much difficulty, persuaded Stephen Clark to take d'Harnoncourt onto the Museum's staff with every intention of seeing to it that after a period of apprenticeship he would become the Museum's Director. "Nelson decided very early in his friendship with René," Wheeler said, "that he wanted to make him Director of the Museum, but René was not a modern-art man." One of the trustees said, "It was very cleverly done. Nelson got him in just to be around and get a sense of the place and so that the staff would get to know him."

There was most certainly nothing naïve about d'Harnoncourt, and he must have been fully aware of Rockefeller's plans for him, though a member of the curatorial staff has said, "I remember when René first came I had lunch with him and he said, 'You know, I don't want anyone to think that I'm trying to be Director of the Museum. I'm not an administrator in any sense. It's just not my sort of work.' And I'm sure he meant it."

For several years after Barr was fired the Museum was ostensibly managed by a committee of trustees, with the various heads of departments reporting each to a designated member of the board. It was neither an orderly nor a successful manner of keeping the ambitions and temperaments of the staff in balance, and in 1946 the management of the Museum was centered in what was called the Coordination Committee, of which d'Harnoncourt was named chairman by Rockefeller, who resumed the presidency of the board that year. The committee was made up of d'Harnoncourt, Wheeler, Barr, Abbott, and Ione Ulrich, who had succeeded Frances Hawkins as Secretary of the Museum. "We met every Wednesday morning," Wheeler recalled, "and all policy was discussed there. René was chairman (I think I must have been vice-chairman; I remember presiding at some meetings), and after a few years of this he was in control anyway, and he'd proved himself sympathetic to every side—everything we wanted to do—and it was that committee at my instigation that recommended to the trustees that he become Director. Of course it was long in Nelson's mind."

The year after the Coordination Committee was organized James Johnson Sweeney became the head of the Department of Painting and Sculpture. He took over from Soby who, when his friend Barr was fired, had volunteered to hold the reins in that department until someone else could be found. Sweeney recalls hearing the director of a European museum ask Marian Willard, chairman of the Advisory Committee, who was showing him around, who was the director of her Museum. "There are seven directors," she replied.

She scarcely exaggerated. During the committee-managed interregnum which lasted from the time Barr was fired until 1950 when d'Harnoncourt was appointed Director of the Museum, no individual was officially in charge, and though many of the staff looked to d'Harnoncourt as the guiding hand, the heads of departments were, not surprisingly, autonomous or, in any case, thought that they should be. The case of James Johnson Sweeney throws some light as well on the trustees' attitude toward "their" staff.

In the *Bulletin* published in January 1945 the Museum officially announced the appointment of Sweeney, "well-known writer and lecturer on modern art," as "Director of the Museum's Department of Painting and Sculpture." It noted that Sweeney had "long been associated with the Museum as a member of its Advisory Committee, and has directed and written the catalog for several exhibitions, *African Negro Sculpture* [1935], *Joan Miró* [1941], and *Alexander Calder Sculpture and Constructions* [1943]." Obviously to reassure Sweeney that he was to be his own boss and make the final decisions about what he exhibited and what the Museum purchased at his behest, the announcement specifically stated that "As director of the Department of Painting and Sculpture he will be responsible for the Museum's acquisitions in those fields as well as in the graphic arts. In a reorganization of the Department . . . there has been a considerable revision of duties, making the department head in the future fully responsible for the activities of the Department during his tenure of office."

Sweeney was very much his own man, an individualist with a some-what gravelly voice and a big, robust laugh, an independent income, and a sharply critical eye and pen. He was a poet who looked like an athlete, and indeed was one, and he became an art critic somewhat by accident. Born in 1900, he lived mostly in Cincinnati and Chicago, where his father was in the importing business. He graduated from Georgetown University in 1922 and went from there to Cambridge, England, to take his "tripos." "I used to send poetry to A.E. in Dub-lin," he says, "and he wrote back, 'If you chance to be in Dublin, come and see me.' " Sweeney made a point of going to Dublin and one eve-ning "found A.E. and another man looking at a catalogue of the Quinn collection, and they couldn't understand these things—Modigliani and Rouault and the others. 'This crazy stuff, what do you think of it?' I was frightened to death, but I said, 'I think they're mighty fine,' and I told them why I liked it." The man who was visiting George William Russell (A.E.) that evening was Edward Alden Jewell, who was then the art critic for the *Christian Science Monitor* in Boston. "Three years later I went to see him when he had become the critic for the *New York Times,* and he asked me to do two one-thousand-word pieces at two cents a word on Rouault and Modigliani, and I went on doing that for three or four years. I also answered an attack by Sean O'Flaherty that Russell printed in his magazine, the *Irish Statesman,* and he wrote that he didn't agree with a word of it but would print it in full over two issues of the magazine."

In 1934 Sweeney published a small volume called *Plastic Redirec-tions in Twentieth Century Painting* which established him as a critics' critic and an interpreter to be reckoned with. It was the year after this that he directed his first exhibition for the Museum. By the time he was invited to join the staff of the Museum, he was widely known in the art world not only as a critic and scholar but as a fiercely meticu-lous arranger of paintings and sculpture for exhibition.

"They asked me what I should be paid," he recalls, "and I said I'd take whatever René was being paid—not Alfred, because I thought he was getting more and should be paid more than anyone. I found that René was not being paid by the Museum but by Nelson—$10,000, which was what Monroe was being paid. It was what I got paid, too."

He did not get paid it for long.

"When I took on the job as director of the department," Sweeney said, "I took it on the condition that I could not only arrange exhibi-tions but supervise their publicity, and that I could not only make recommendations for purchases to the Acquisitions Committee, but that I could say 'no' to things I didn't think should be acquired."

It was apparent that he did not want Barr, who was an old friend but obviously a man of strong opinions with which he permitted no trifling, or the trustees to tell him what he could and could not do.

"Henry Moe," he said, "tried to talk me out of the veto, but I wouldn't agree."

Later when Rockefeller came back to the presidency of the Museum in 1946, he put his foot down. "No," he said, "it won't be done that way." He made it quite clear that he was not going to give anyone "veto power," an expression then much in the press, as it was being furiously argued about in the initial meetings of the United Nations and was a sore subject. Sweeney said, "On the Board only Paul Sachs backed me up." It was, you will recall, Sachs's belief that you gave a director his head; you did not tell him what to do. If you did not like what he did, then you fired him.

On November 15, 1946, twenty-two months after Sweeney's appointment was announced by the Museum, the *Art Digest* ran a piece headed "Sweeney Resigns." "From behind the iron curtain," the lead of the piece said,

> that the Museum of Modern Art has always maintained between the public and its administrative activities, the art world learned the other day, largely by hearsay, that James Johnson Sweeney, brilliant head of the painting and sculpture department, had resigned. At first the information was semi-denied, then it was semi-confirmed through a letter from Nelson Rockefeller, Modern's President. Thousands of words were typed or printed, and still 57th Street didn't know if it was coming or going or delayed in transit. What had happened to cost the museum one of its few competent leaders? Was Sweeney fired or disgusted?

What had happened was that the trustees had decided (or, more properly, Nelson and his mother and Henry Moe had decided) on several ways of by-passing Sweeney and the agreement under which he was hired. In the first place it voted that "election to the Board will be determined by ability and should not be ex-officio." (Wheeler, Barr, and Abbott were then members of the board, and Sweeney quite naturally expected to be elected to it as the Museum's most important departmental director.) It further decided that "in as much as the function of the Board . . . is to shape and guide policy on a broad basis, with the program itself carried out by the staff in view of the fact that the staff had contributed much [*sic!*] to the development of policy and program, it was important to continue such a relationship." It was also decided that no members of the staff might serve on the Executive Committee but they might attend meetings if they were invited; they had, however, no right to a vote. This was decided because, it was said, "Nelson wanted one place to discuss matters without staff present."

Sweeney might have put up with being excluded from the board (though there are those who say he resigned because of it), but when the Coordination Committee was quite obviously organized to exclude him, he gave his resignation to Rockefeller. His decision in all probability made life easier for the trustees of the Museum; he was an "inconvenient" Director—a man, in other words, whose principles took precedence over his trustees' convenience. It was not in his nature to play the game of diplomacy at which d'Harnoncourt and Wheeler were so adept and effective, and if his resignation served the Museum's trustees, it was taken in ill part by much of the art community and especially by a distinguished group of artists who protested politely but firmly in a letter to the *New York Times*.[1] The letter said, in part:

> The role of the Museum of Modern Art, as leader in public education in modern art, has had in Mr. Sweeney one who is foremost in its interpretation. In the activities of the museum which have specific reference to contemporary painting and sculpture, we feel that Mr. Sweeney's abilities to give meaningful direction are rare. The absence of his knowledge and vision would be a source of great regret to us, and to many others, artists and laymen alike.

Sweeney wrote a measured reply to the *Times* explaining the reasons for his resignation in some detail, and pointed out that when the Coordination Committee was organized, one member of it (d'Harnoncourt) was designated Director of Curatorial Departments, which, he said, "abolished, all save in name and salary," the position he occupied.

The Catholic magazine *America*, whose art column was written by Barry Byrne, praised Sweeney for his stand and for his not being, as it said, one of "the courtier type of persons, adept at the shades of deference to be paid to people of varying importance, financial and

---

1 The letter was signed by Stuart Davis, Romare Beardon, Peter Blume, Byron Browne, Paul Burlin, Alexander Calder, Russell Cowles, Ralston Crawford, Arthur Dove, Lyonel Feininger, Louis Guglielmi, William Hayter, Karl Knaths, Yasuo Kuniyoshi, Jacob Lawrence, Le Corbusier, Julian Levi, Jack Levine, Loren MacIver, John Marin, Robert Motherwell, Georgia O'Keeffe, Amédée Ozenfant, Jackson Pollock, I. Rice Pereira, Abe Rattner, Kurt Seligmann, and Niles Spencer.

social, as these might have weight in the control of a particular museum." Sweeney, however, was by no means lost to the New York art world, nor was his influence diminished, though it was interrupted. In 1952 he became the director of the Guggenheim Museum, a position in many respects better suited to his tastes, at least until he found himself embattled against the temper and temperament of Frank Lloyd Wright, who accepted the job of designing the Guggenheim's new building in spite of his frank distaste for painting and sculpture and, indeed, for any art but his own.

The departure of James Johnson Sweeney may have reduced some tensions at the Museum, but life under the Coordination Committee cannot be said to have been peaceful. The calm with which d'Harnoncourt seemed to endow the surface of the troubled waters was real enough in many respects, but there was roiling beneath which had a way of exploding through at intervals. James Thrall Soby, by then a trustee, took over the chairmanship of the Painting and Sculpture Committee, though not as the department's Staff Director, a job for the time being left vacant. He and Barr got along famously, enjoyed each other's humor (and they both had it), respected each other's taste, and saw eye to eye far more often than not. Soby and d'Harnoncourt liked and admired each other, and the problem of status which had irked Sweeney was resolved by Soby's service on the board. A new member joined the staff of the Museum when Elodie Courter decided not to come back after producing a son. Porter McCray, who had worked with d'Harnoncourt and Rockefeller in the Coordinator's Office and later as director of the Inter-American Office of the National Gallery in Washington, took over as Director of Circulating Exhibitions. McCray had been trained as an architect at Yale (where he had been instrumental in starting a modern-art society), and he came into the Rockefeller orbit through Rockefeller's architect, Wallace Harrison, who had known McCray at Yale and asked him to join the Coordinator's office.

The Architecture Department was in a state, as usual, of transition. After McAndrew left and Philip Johnson was in the Army, the department was run during the war by Elizabeth Mock who had been an assistant to McAndrew. She had been a Frank Lloyd Wright disciple at Taliesen and was then the wife of a Swiss architect, Rudolf Mock. She edited a small book in 1944 called *Built in U.S.A.* which was, according to a Museum *Bulletin,* "the most successful book on architecture ever published by the Museum" up to that time. In 1946 she and the illustrator Robert Osborn produced another popular Museum publication which twenty-five and more years later is not only sound in its advice but still looks very much in the current style. It was called *If You Want to Build a House*. Mrs. Mock resigned in 1946, leaving the Architecture Department in a sort of administrative limbo. In 1949 Philip Johnson became Director of the Architecture and Design Department (by now combined) as well as its angel, though he was neither an employee nor as yet a trustee. He was, however, a presence in the Museum, with an office there from which he conducted Museum business and the practice of architecture as well. He hired two young people who have since become distinguished as journalists and critics of architecture, Ada Louise Huxtable, the architectural critic for the *New York Times,* and Peter Blake, the editor of *Architectural Forum.* Mrs. Huxtable was a student at the New York University Institute of Fine Arts specializing in architectural history. Johnson hired her on the basis of some papers she had written on Early American domestic architecture. She worked for three years at the Museum as an assistant in the department, and then went to Italy in 1950 on a Fulbright Fellowship. Blake was at the Museum even more briefly. After he got out of the Army in 1947 he spent a year at Pratt Institute studying architecture and came to the Museum in 1948 as Curator of Architecture. He left shortly after Mrs. Huxtable did, to go to work for the *Architectural Forum.* "It was a peculiar situation," he has said.

It was during the interregnum that John Abbott was eased out, and Allen Porter was made Acting Secretary. Porter insists that he never wanted to have a position in the Museum any more important than "acting," though he was several times offered the job of Secretary. He managed, as few did who worked in the Museum over a long period of time, to keep out of the political in-fighting. He enjoyed his job, but he also enjoyed his freedom. He was quite willing to work long hours when it was useful to do so; there was no job in the Museum that was beneath him if it needed doing or if he thought that by doing it he could help build morale. He was quite as likely to be found selling postcards in the Museum's bookshop, or at the information desk, or greeting visitors at an evening "opening," as signing the payroll. He seemed to know everyone, and all of the "regulars," who could be counted on to appear at openings, knew him. He had an apartment less than a block from the Museum, the ballroom floor of what was once the Chauncey M. Depew mansion, and in Barrytown, New York, he owned a small wooden church which he had converted into a house and to which he retired in 1964. He decorated the apartment and the house mostly in red, for Porter is color-blind, and the only color that he can recognize is red. He lives in a world, he says, that "is like the old black-and-white movies." There seems to have been no one intimately involved in the history of the Museum who was more universally liked and respected by all levels of the staff. I have encountered no one whose face does not brighten at the mention of his name. He is a gossip, but a kindly gossip, and no one has had occasion to fear him.

Soby's tenure as the head of the Painting and Sculpture Department was not very long-lived. He knew it was an interim matter and he wanted it to be. From his point of view, as also from René d'Harnoncourt's, the primary concern was Barr's position in the Museum. At the time when d'Harnoncourt was taken on as a curiously titled vice-president, Barr's status was at its nadir, and d'Harnoncourt agreed to join the staff of the Museum only on the condition that Barr would be kept on in a dignified and responsible position. "René felt that Alfred had created the Museum," Mrs. Parkinson has said, "and he said, 'I can't understand how everybody wants to get rid of the man who *is* the Museum.'" "Everybody," of course, was a small group of trustees who felt that they had come to the end of their rope. "Alfred had all the ideas for what a modern museum should be, but he couldn't run it, couldn't handle the people, and it got bigger and bigger with more and more people, and he simply couldn't manage," one trustee said. "When Alfred was demoted, he so resented it and felt so badly. Furthermore, he had around him many people who tried to interfere with everything that anyone else [i.e., d'Harnoncourt] did. They felt that Alfred should be the only one to run the Museum."

There was, to be sure, a good deal of choosing up of sides among the staff when it became obvious that d'Harnoncourt was going to take over. A Barr camp and a d'Harnoncourt camp, not entirely based on personal loyalties, emerged; there were those who were for Barr as the intellectual symbol of the Museum, its cultural integrity, its uncompromising concern with quality (though some looked upon this with raised eyebrows and muttered about expedience and favoritism especially when it came to pampering the tastes of the trustees). On the other hand, there were those who were perfectly willing to concede Barr's personal and intellectual and scholarly virtues but who could not abide the manner in which he did things, found him impatient with their problems and inattentive to their departmental needs. They lined themselves up with d'Harnoncourt with sighs of relief that there was somebody to talk to who seemed to have infinite patience, kindliness, concern, and a gift for making people get along if not always happily together, at least in an aura of suspended warfare.

It was d'Harnoncourt who insisted that Barr be part of the Coordination Committee and that he be made Director of the Museum's Collections. "René didn't want to get along without Alfred and Alfred couldn't function without René," Mrs. Parkinson told me many years after this partnership was formed. "In order to run the Museum, in order to make a Museum as great as this one was, René needed exactly what Alfred had, the vision, the ideas, the knowledge, the taste, and the passion for the place. So their careers became utterly interdependent. I wonder what it would have been like if they had been together at the top—co-directors, on an equal footing, and so without Alfred's resentment and hurt feelings."

Other museums in recent years have, indeed, tried such an arrangement—a general director and an aesthetic director—and it has not been notably successful, though it might have been in this case. Barr's control over the Departments of Painting and Sculpture and Prints through the Acquisitions Committee (he never took charge of the collections of the Film Library or the Department of Photography) was essentially unofficial. His voice was firm, and so were his opinions about matters of current exhibitions, but the very fact that his position did not give him administrative powers over those matters led, on occasion (as in the case of Sweeney and later with other heads of departments), to outbursts of vituperation and squabbling. D'Harnoncourt could, as a trustee said, "handle the prima donnas," and in saying so he meant not only the staff but the trustees as well, for there were always trustees who stood on their prerogatives (and their bank accounts) and liked to throw their weight around—to meddle in departmental affairs that were outside their aegis. I suggested to Henry Allen Moe that a good deal of d'Harnoncourt's ability to handle the trustees came from the undisputed fact that he was the social equal or superior of all of them. "If that's only a hunch," Dr. Moe said, "it's a very good hunch."

Several years before Dr. Moe made this comment, Edward Warburg, who has known the Museum's inner workings longer than any member of its board except Barr himself, said to me, "You should know that René was the luckiest thing that ever happened to the Museum. He made the setting for what Alfred had to do. He was a courtly Old World gentleman; he loved to waltz and to hack around."

It was not only the setting for what Barr "had to do" that d'Harnon-court made possible, it was also the setting for what others had to do. If occasionally individuals got out of hand, as was inevitable in an organization that capitalized on the temperament of its staff rather than suppressing it, the presence of d'Harnoncourt kept "the situation" from ever getting out of hand. Most problems had a way of dissolving before his quiet, deliberate, and wholly sympathetic manner of dealing with them. He was an "open door" administrator. Any member of the staff who wanted to talk with him would find himself welcomed and listened to. He would sit behind his enormous Art Nouveau desk with his finger in his eye and hear what his colleague had to say, and then he would very frequently answer with a long story which seemed to have nothing to do with the problem at hand. His fund of stories which were essentially parables seemed to suggest an answer to any problem put to him, and if not everyone went away satisfied that his problem had been solved, he was likely to go away reassured. D'Harnoncourt much preferred to have people make their own decisions. Indeed, I have been told again and again that it was very difficult to get a precise answer out of him, but I have never been told this with anything but a sort of surprised admiration for d'Harnoncourt's ability to administer without seeming to manage.

It was surely not d'Harnoncourt's social status that impressed his colleagues who were his intellectual peers, nor the other members of the staff from those who guarded the doors or tended the out-of-sight mechanisms of the building to the ablest and the crankiest secretaries and the most ambitious or pretentious junior curators. Their regard for him was not based merely on the fact that he was, as Victor d'Amico said, "a very lovable man . . . a child all his life with great imagination who loved teaching and loved people." He was, I have frequently been told, "an image," a "father figure," "a guy who had everything—who spoke all the European languages and could speak to painters and scholars and collectors on terms of equality. He knew his stuff." From the point of view of many of the staff, he was their voice with the trustees. He gave the impression of being on everybody's side and nobody's side; he was on the Museum's side, and to this end the staff and the trustees were equally important, equally his responsibility, and equally worth his most diplomatic schemes and efforts.

"He had an astounding quality that so few people have," one of the curators who knew him longest said, "and that was an infinite patience and a sort of Viennese ability to make a plan, an invisible plan, and then slowly to work toward its accomplishment. He was that way with people always. He was infinitely tactful, and often quite devious, so devious that you didn't know what he was getting at."

He was, it appears, both unflappable and generous. There were times when Barr nagged at him, tried to cut him down in meetings, "tried to thwart him, was rude and disagreeable," according to a trustee who liked both men keenly. "René would never resent it," she said. "He felt that this is the way Alfred felt because of what had happened. He was concerned about what was best for the Museum, and he had such enormous respect for Alfred's mind and ideas. He said to me, 'Alfred behaves perfectly terribly to me, but I know perfectly well that Alfred is very fond of me.' It was extraordinary that it worked. He just didn't expect to be disliked. He was full of love for people and never expected that they were not full of love for him."

Such a statement might be taken as fatuous if variations on it had not been made to me by so many men and women who worked with d'Harnoncourt. George Amberg, a man not given to superlatives without weighing them, said to me not long before he died, "I have no words to describe René. He was absolutely extraordinary and with all this very human, very warm, very understanding, one of the few important people who have no personal vanity whatsoever, none at all. . . . Everybody who worked with René loved to work with him. He was very generous in helping people, in understanding people and advising people, and at the same time he was very diplomatic."

The adjective "diplomatic" is applied to him more frequently than any other, and with good reason. To maintain even a semblance of peace in the affairs of the Museum required not just tact and tolerance, it demanded all the arts of flattery, patience, and persuasion, of manipulation, cajolery, and polite connivance that are masked by the outward calm of diplomacy. D'Harnoncourt was not only extremely adept at these arts, but enjoyed them and seems not to have used them for his own ends. His satisfaction was in seeing his plans work out, however long they might take to come to fruition. He could bide his time, sometimes to some persons infuriatingly so. "He was extremely difficult to get a decision out of," one curator commented. "He was too vain to wear a hearing aid and he heard little of what was said to him. He would sit with his finger hooked into his right eye and his navel showing—he couldn't remember to button his shirt. He was a master of back-door diplomacy, and he loved his machinations with Nelson." On the other hand, part of this indecision revealed itself in what I have repeatedly been told was his "inability to fire anyone," considered admirable by some and by some a weakness. The result was that incompetents were either kept on or were shifted into jobs where their incompetence made no difference, into made work, cooked-up projects to keep them busy—in any case, on the payroll. One of the Museum's most active trustees, Eliza Parkinson, was head of the International Council of the Museum and had an assistant she found impossibly inefficient and asked d'Harnoncourt to fire her. She told me that when he demurred, she said, " 'I'll fire her and you comfort her,' and that's what we did." On another occasion a head of a department was causing more than usual internal strife. "It took two years to get him fired," I was told. "René felt terribly about hurting anyone's career. He felt strongly about a man's job being his job, and he didn't want to take it away from him."

When d'Harnoncourt became the Director of the Museum it had "the most terrible reputation because so many people had been fired," Mrs. Parkinson said, and added with justification, "It has the same reputation now." It was partly a wish to correct this unfortunate view of the Museum and partly just native concern for people that stayed d'Harnoncourt's hand. "He would sit up half the night with somebody's problems—personal problems—with perfectly amazing kindness," one member of the staff said to me, and I heard many variations on this same theme. If some staff member did something he found distasteful or thought was not in the interests of the Museum, he did not send for him to bawl him out; he would "come and call very politely" at his office and make his presence felt.

With the trustees his technique was somewhat different, but it was no less personal. With a large board—and the board of the Museum by the time d'Harnoncourt became Director had thirty-four members —there are always some workers, some whose names are ornamental, and some whose only use is in their checkbooks, but all of them like to feel as though they are privy to the institution's secrets and plans. They also like to believe that their opinions are important to the Director. D'Harnoncourt made a practice of telephoning them. "He knew what they were interested in," a trustee said, "and if something came up that interested one trustee or another particularly, he'd call him up and get him involved." He also used the telephone to "defuse" a trustee who, he thought, might torpedo a plan when it was presented to the board if he had not had it explained to him in advance. "In this way he always had the support he needed."

His success with his trustees and most notably with the various members of the Rockefeller family with whom he had to do—Abby, as the founding mother, Nelson as President, Mrs. John D. (Blanchette) 3rd, as President, and David as Chairman of the Board—led to his being referred to as a "courtier," an epithet which he despised. There is no question that the Rockefellers were the reigning family of the Museum and that the dynasty persisted from the inception of the Museum without surcease to the time when d'Harnoncourt retired, and still continues and is likely to continue for some time. The accusation that d'Harnoncourt paid court to the Rockefellers is frequently made by those who were (and are) critical of him, and by some who obviously liked him. The fact of his noble forebears gave rise to the epithet. In some cases personal jealousy unquestionably gave it bite; in other cases loyalty to Barr (who was also accused, especially in the early days of the Museum, of paying court to the Rockefellers) prompted Barr's friends to point the finger at d'Harnoncourt; in other cases it was used as a way of explaining his success by those who believed, as one of them said to me, that "René was a whiz in his own field, but it didn't stretch into other fields and he didn't know it." (There are others who contradict this and say that he was far too modest about claiming any expertise in modern art, that he did, indeed, know a great deal.) The fact that he helped Nelson Rockefeller form his extraordinary collection of primitive art and that he was at Nelson's beck and call as a personal advisor in such matters also was used to give substance to the accusation of "courtier."

In his *New Yorker* profile of d'Harnoncourt, Geoffrey Hellman put a good deal of emphasis on d'Harnoncourt's noble lineage and drew a parallel between his ancestors' roles as courtiers and the relationship in which d'Harnoncourt found himself to Rockefeller, whose "unspoken rank is at least ducal." It unquestionably stamped the word "courtier" on d'Harnoncourt in a good many minds, including many of those who worked for him. "Of course when you know a person, you never think that a profile is quite right," one of them said. "But actually it gave us some clue to René." His own reaction to the profile was one of great distaste. He said of it, "I felt as though I were standing naked on a street corner in somebody else's body."

A story about d'Harnoncourt and a remark he once made reveal much about his quality. One time when he was away from the Museum attending a meeting in New Orleans, John Szarkowski, the Director of the Department of Photography at the Museum, was about to put up an exhibition that included photographs of transvestites. At the last minute he had second thoughts about whether it might not be considered offensive—not that there was anything obscene about the pictures, but this was at a time when public exposure of sexual deviations was not taken for granted as it now is. He consulted the President of the Museum and the lawyer on the staff, and together they decided that it might be a good idea to telephone d'Harnoncourt and see what he thought.

When the question was put to him, he replied, as he often did, with a question. It settled the matter.

"Do the photographs make fun of anybody?" he asked.

The answer was that they most certainly did not, and the show was hung.

D'Harnoncourt consistently backed his curators so long as he felt that in no sense were they compromising with quality. He frequently spent long evenings at the Museum helping to hang shows—as another pair of hands and eyes, not as an interfering superior. They counted on him; indeed, one of his trustees went so far as to say, "You couldn't get anything done while he was away." On one occasion when he was away on an extended trip to Europe there was a rumor seeping through the Museum that he was going to resign and not come back. Barr reassured the staff. "René would never leave us in the lurch that way," he said.

In his memoir, *File on Spratling*, William Spratling, who lived much of his life in Mexico and contributed greatly to the revival and dissemination of Mexican crafts, wrote: "I remember years ago that René d'Harnoncourt . . . remarked to me that he had arrived at the conclusion that the definition of a superior *maestro* was one who could recognize a superior instrument, or tool, and utilize it.' "

To d'Harnoncourt the Museum was a superior tool, and he utilized it with all the skill he could muster for nearly twenty-five years.

*We do not consider it our job to force
contemporary art in one direction or another
through propaganda or patronage, much as
enthusiasts for a particular dogma would like to
have us do so. For in the final analysis it is not
our job to lead artists, but to follow them—at a
close yet respectful distance.*
JAMES THRALL SOBY *in* MUSEUM NEWS, June 15, 1944

Chapter XV *The Harvest*

When the notorious *Fantastic Art, Dada, and Surrealism* exhibition
closed in early 1937, Alfred Barr recommended to the Museum's
Acquisitions Committee that it approve the purchase for the permanent
collection of "The Fur-lined Teacup," which had caused such merriment and shock. The committee in 1937 was chaired by Sam Lewisohn,
whose heart belonged to the Impressionists and Post-Impressionists,
and Conger Goodyear and Philip Goodwin, both of somewhat more
advanced tastes, were its other members. The committee could not
have thought that Barr was joking; he did not take such matters
lightly. They did, however, turn down the "Teacup," so Barr bought
it for $50 and nine years later put it in the "study collection" of the
Museum. In 1968 it turned up again as part of a large reminiscent
Surrealism exhibition at the Museum, and Barr again recommended
that it be included in the permanent collection. This time the committee agreed with alacrity.[1]

Except for the interlude between the time when Clark fired Barr

[1]   Officially in the interval it was on "extended loan" from the artist, an interesting and meaningless euphemism.

284

and the time he was named Director of the Collections in 1947 at the insistence of René d'Harnoncourt, Barr had the collection under his eye and influence from before the Museum opened in 1929 until his retirement in 1967. (Since that time he has compiled its history, not as yet published.) In the statement of purpose that was printed as a folder in the summer of 1929 with the title *A New Art Museum* Barr included the following statement: "The ultimate purpose will be to acquire, from time to time, either by gift or by purchase, the best modern works of art. . . ." You will recall that in their early deliberations the founders of the Museum thought of it as a sort of Luxembourg, an idea which they sometimes seemed to take seriously and sometimes denied was in their minds. In the folder, the following appeared:

> For the last dozen years New York's great museum—the Metropolitan—has often been criticized because it did not add the works of the leading "modernists" to its collections. Nevertheless the Metropolitan's policy . . . is reasonable. As a great museum, it may justly take the stand that it wishes to acquire only those works of art which seem certainly and permanently valuable. It can well afford to wait until the present shall become the past. . . . But the public interested in modern art does not wish to wait. . . .

The intention, however, was clearly spelled out that the new Museum "would attempt to establish a very fine collection of the immediate ancestors, American and European, of the modern movement. . . ." Barr stated, furthermore, that in due course the new Museum "would probably expand beyond the narrow limits of painting and sculpture" and embrace drawings and prints, photographs and examples of typography, objects of industrial design, architecture, stage design, furniture, and the decorative arts. He also mentioned, as we have noted, "the *filmotek*, a library of films."

Barr, of course, had a way of making his prognostications become facts, and while the opinions and policies of the Museum's trustees often vacillated, they usually fell in line behind Barr. There have been a good many shifts in policy regarding the Museum's collection in the last forty-odd years. There have been a number of gestures toward the Metropolitan and a number of hurried retreats from unprepared positions, or positions that, if prepared, were found to be temperamentally untenable. Today, however, the collection appears to be what Barr wanted it to be all along—an assemblage of important "masterpieces" of modern art of all varieties regarded as "the permanent collection," and a group of objects considered interesting but unessential and therefore available for trading or sale to improve the quality of the permanent collection. This in turn is backed up by the "study collections," objects of interest primarily to scholars, less for their intrinsic quality than for what they represent in the development of their particular arts. No one, for instance, is likely to insist that a blue glass Art Deco radio from the 1920s should be in the permanent collection, though it is an entertaining and useful document of the taste of its era.

"Alfred," said one of his staunch supporters who worked with him for years on the Museum's holdings, "is one of the great collectors of all time."

Be this as it may, the Museum's collection, which is in a constant state of refinement, if that is the word, is generally regarded by those who administer the citadels of taste in our time as the greatest collection of modern art anywhere in the world. How it came to be that is the subject of this chapter, and to tell its story necessitates looking again at the earliest days of the Museum and also at some of its most recent ones.

There was an acquisitions committee which called itself the Committee on Gifts and Bequests, as we noted in Chapter V, even before the Museum opened, and its members were Goodyear, Sachs, and Barr. As though to justify its existence, Goodyear gave a Maillol bronze and Sachs bought for it a drawing and some prints. Clark followed with the Museum's first owned painting, a Hopper, and soon were added to these a Burchfield, a Kenneth Hayes Miller, a Karfiol, and a gouache by Picasso, the Museum's first painting by a foreign artist. This much we have already said, but these gifts were more friendly gestures than pledges of faith in the future of the Museum as an important collector.

In 1931 Barr thought it was time to take firmer steps and he wrote to Mrs. Rockefeller: ". . . we must have or we must budget sufficient funds . . . to pay for space for a beginning of the permanent collection or at least a collection borrowed from our friends which might be of a rotating nature. I do not believe that we could continue the quality of our past exhibitions even at four a year and that we ought to have a supplementary exhibition of more or less permanence."

Mrs. Rockefeller raised a pertinent question and one which, indeed, was a troublesome one for many years: ". . . probably no one will give us collections," she replied, "while we are still in the uncertain stage. . . . The part that distresses me most is how we are going to remain modern and at the same time satisfy donors that the pictures they give us will not be disposed of in a manner that would be objectionable to them."

Gertrude Stein is said to have written about the Museum of Modern Art, though no one seems able to track it down, "A museum can either be a museum or it can be modern, but it cannot be both." "When is modern?" is a question that has never been resolved and is likely never to be, any more, it seems, than the problem of "What is a museum?" seems likely to be settled, though both of these questions seemed more readily answerable in 1930 than they do now. In any case, there was no question in the minds of the founders of the Museum of Modern Art that there was any contradiction in terms in the name or the function they blessed it with. To be a museum meant having a collection. To be modern meant . . . well, what did it mean? It certainly meant one thing to Mrs. Rockefeller, another thing to Goodyear, and something quite else to Clark, and to none of them did it mean what it meant to Barr.

Goodyear in 1931, in defining the future of a collection for the Museum, came close to the mark. "The permanent collection will not be unchangeable," he said. "It will have somewhat the same permanence that a river has. With certain exceptions, no gift will be accepted under conditions that will not permit of its retirement by sale or otherwise as the trustees may think advisable. . . ."

The Museum's first major windfall was, of course, Lizzie Bliss's magnificent collection of Impressionists and Post-Impressionists, which became the property of the Museum in 1934 when the trustees of Miss Bliss's estate were satisfied by the raising of $600,000 that the Museum was indeed a serious and presumably permanent institution. Even before this, however, the Museum had held an exhibition of part of its modest collection soon after it moved into the house on 53rd Street. There were in all ten paintings and nine sculptures. Twelve of them were already in the collection in 1930; the next three years produced only nine more, but among them was what has been called "the first important European painting in the Museum's permanent collection," the portrait of Dr. Mayer-Hermann by the German painter Otto Dix. It was Philip Johnson's first of many important gifts to the Museum. These were lean years for acquisitions, however. "Lack of space, emphasis on temporary shows, and the Depression were discouraging," Barr has written in his summary of the collections.

If they were lean, they were not inactive. It was in 1931 that the first of several flirtations between the Museum of Modern Art and the Metropolitan Museum of Art began. Goodyear and William Sloane Coffin, the president of the Metropolitan's board, discussed the possibility that the Modern Museum might lend a hand with advice about how the Metropolitan should spend the $15,000 that its Hearn Fund provided each year for the purchase of contemporary American paintings. But the flirtation never got even so far as holding hands. It was not long after Mr. Coffin had made his flowery speech at the opening of the Museum's new home in 1932 that negotiations between the two institutions resulted in informal talks between trustee committees of both institutions. Goodyear suggested that his Museum might limit its concerns to what had gone on in the last fifty years in American and European art, and that the Metropolitan might buy works from it that were older than fifty years and had stood the test of twenty years in the Modern's collection. The discussions petered out and nothing transpired between the two institutions until Francis Henry Taylor, the long-nosed, portly, and genial, if sharp-tongued, director of the Metropolitan tried to revive some interest in collaboration. In 1941 he wrote a letter to John Hay Whitney, who was briefly at that time the President of the Modern, suggesting that it might be a good idea to discuss ways in which "these two institutions may in the near future draw closer and closer to each other." Whitney turned the matter over to Barr, who responded at once that he sincerely hoped that they could "work out a sensible, intelligent, and friendly cooperation."

Taylor's and Barr's temperaments were as far apart as their tastes. Taylor's humor was bawdy, his manner expansive, his opinions outspoken, his appetites Lucullan. He was born a Philadelphia patrician, and had, like Barr, done graduate work in the fine arts (his field was medieval) at Princeton. He was a believer in the museum as a democratic institution that belonged not to a handful of scholars but to the public, which he said, "have had their bellyful of prestige and pink Tennessee marble." He was the same age as Barr when he first assumed the directorship of a museum: he was twenty-seven when he was hired by the Worcester Museum, one of the most distinguished small museums in the country, and it was more distinguished when he left in 1940 to take over the director's office at the Metropolitan. He endeared himself not at all to the academic community with a small book called *Babel's Tower* on the bind in which scholarship held museums. He was not anti-scholarship, but he was anti-pedant, and the scholars who were also pedants despised him.

"Taylor's attitude toward modern art," Calvin Tomkins wrote in *Merchants and Masterpieces*, "like everything else about Taylor was highly complicated. He did not dismiss or condemn it out of hand, as some people accused him of doing. Taylor took modern art very seriously, seeing in it a frightening reflection of the moral crisis that threatened all humanity." But if he was serious, he could also be extremely mordant in his comments on what he thought phony or pretentious or second-rate. In an article in the *Atlantic Monthly* in 1948 he wrote that "the contemporary artist has been reduced to the status of a flat-chested pelican, strutting upon the intellectual wastelands and beaches, content to take whatever nourishment he can from his own too meager breast." He was also quite frank to express his distaste for "those pansies" at the Museum of Modern Art.

One of the things that Taylor and Barr had in common was the respect of Paul Sachs. When the trustees of the Metropolitan asked Sachs for his recommendation for a director, it was Taylor who headed his list, just as it had been Barr who headed his list for the Modern. But they were unable to come to any agreement about how the Met and the Modern should or could work together. The talks went on for a number of years—indeed, even after Barr had been fired and James Johnson Sweeney was briefly head of the Painting and Sculpture Department at 53rd Street. Sweeney and Taylor got along famously. They liked each other, they laughed together, and they respected each other. "We cooked up a deal," Sweeney told me, "whereby the Hearn Fund at the Met could be spent by the Modern, and the Met would eventually get the pictures. But Mrs. Rockefeller said to me, 'Jim, I've been talking to Nelson and he'd prefer to wait until he returns after the war.' And I guess that was the end of that. One reason we thought it would work was because Nelson was a trustee of both places."

Neither Taylor nor Barr was willing to let it go at that, and by September 1947 not only the Met and the Modern had arrived at an agreement but the Whitney Museum of American Art, with which the Met had been collaborating on purchases since 1943, joined in a "Three Museum Agreement." Barr issued a statement to the staff of his museum on September 25 which was subsequently published in part in the Museum's *Bulletin* for the edification of Museum members. Essentially the agreement divided the pie in three large if unequal slices. The Metropolitan was to concern itself with "older art which, for convenience, is referred to as 'classic art' "; the Whitney was to stick to American art of whatever era; and the Modern was to devote itself to "both American and foreign modern art." There was nothing very surprising about that, to be sure, but the agreement also provided for some transfers of works of art which, as reasonable as they looked at the time, led to recriminations and to uneasiness in the minds of collectors who had been considering giving or bequeathing paintings and sculptures to the Modern.

The Museum of Modern Art agreed to sell to the Metropolitan "paintings and sculptures which the two museums agree have passed from the category of modern to that of 'classic.'" In all, the Modern sold twenty-six works to the Metropolitan (though the agreement initially called for a total of forty, for which the Metropolitan was to pay $191,000 in four annual installments). Those that changed hands included Daumier's "Laundress" from the Bliss collection, Cézanne's "Man in a Blue Cap," a Maillol torso called "Ile de France" (Goodyear's gift), and Picasso's "Woman in White," which Barr wishes he had not let go, though at the time he is said to have thought it "too pretty." In all, the list to be sold included twenty-six paintings, bronzes, and drawings—two Cézannes, four Despiaus, three Kolbes, five Maillols, three Matisses, two Picassos (including "*La Coiffure*," which Barr regrets more than the "Woman in White"), a Redon, two Rouaults, three Seurat drawings, and a Signac—and fourteen examples of American folk art.[2]

On its part, the Metropolitan let the Modern Museum have on extended loan Maillol's "Chained Action" and Picasso's portrait of "Gertrude Stein," which it "did not consider inappropriate for lending," although Miss Stein thought quite the opposite. It was the one picture from her collection that she specifically bequeathed to anyone or any institution because she felt confident of its (and her) immortality in the halls of the Metropolitan. She had said of it that it was "the only reproduction of me which is always I for me," and Picasso, when he was told that it did not look like Miss Stein, is said to have replied, "It will."

In his staff memorandum Barr explained that the funds which the Museum received from transfers to the Metropolitan would be used for purchasing other works of art by "distinguished American and foreign artists and younger artists whose reputations are not yet established." The Metropolitan had agreed that "whenever a work bought from the Museum of Modern Art is exhibited, catalogued or repro-

2 These were subsequently reclaimed by John D. Rockefeller, Jr., and added to the Abby Aldrich Rockefeller Collection of Folk Art at Williamsburg, Virginia.

duced it will refer to the name of the Museum of Modern Art and the name of the original donor who gave the work to that Museum."

The agreement between the Metropolitan and the Modern lasted somewhat uneasily for five years. Barr was never sanguine about letting works which the Museum had acquired as gifts or by purchase slip away from him, especially if they were of such a quality and importance as to be considered suitable for the "mausoleum uptown," as the Metropolitan was sometimes referred to by the staff at 53rd Street. Barr's position as collector and caretaker and scholar is entirely understandable. His intention—indeed, his most dearly held prerogative—was to use his influence, his knowledge, and his diplomatic skills to improve the quality of his museum's collections by whatever legitimate means were at hand. He was uneasy, and so were the Museum's trustees, lest collectors who owned works that the Museum coveted might be reluctant to give or bequeath them to what not only seemed but was publicly announced to be an impermanent collection. The Whitney Museum had already broken off its agreement with the Metropolitan for reasons that were partly matters of temperament, partly policy, and partly financial, but which need not concern us here. And on February 15, 1953, the Museum of Modern Art with some fanfare announced "An Important Change of Policy." Barr later referred to it as "a crucial decision."

The announcement was made by John Hay Whitney, then the Chairman of the Museum's Board. "The Museum has come to believe," the statement released to the press and later published in the *Bulletin*, said,

> that its former policy, by which all the works of art in its possession would eventually be transferred to other institutions, did not work out to the benefit of its public. It now believes it essential for the understanding and enjoyment of its entire collection to have permanently on public view masterpieces of the modern movement, beginning with the latter half of the nineteenth century. The Museum plans to set aside special galleries for this purpose and to transfer to them, from its collections, outstanding paintings and sculptures which it considers have passed the test of time, and to acquire additional works of art of equal excellence for permanent retention.

Essentially this is the Museum's policy today, though I doubt if it would make so sharp a distinction now between what is "its public" and the public that invades "other institutions." The time seems to have passed when it was easy to divide the shockables from the un-shockables on the grounds that they liked "traditional" or "modern." But when Whitney made his statement the Museum was somewhat more on the defensive (and therefore more aggressive) than it is today; the "modern movement" needed to have a ring drawn around it for purposes of self-identification. So the release continued with a state-ment that the Museum "believes now, as always, that the major portion of its collection cannot remain static," that "it must attempt to include all significant and promising aspects of today's artistic production," and that this in turn would lead to such an overwhelming lot of paint-ings and sculptures and objects that, with the exception of a "perma-nent nucleus . . . composed only of great masterworks," everything else was subject to being sent to the bench or even to the bush leagues, or becoming part of a trade.

The Metropolitan Museum was not the only institution with which the Modern had been having trouble. Another institution which had been one of its farm teams, to stretch the metaphor, was the Boston Institute of Modern Art. You will recall that it had initially been the Boston Museum of Modern Art until it decided to break its umbilical cord from MOMA in 1938 and set up on its own, an infidelity, as we have noted, which was referred to on 53rd Street as the "secession of Boston." James Plaut, the director, had written to Conger Goodyear, "Although we were organized as a chapter of the Museum of Modern Art in New York, we have in three years developed an educational philosophy which is independent of the purposes and aims of the par-ent institution." Ten years later Plaut and the president of the insti-tute, Nelson W. Aldrich, took a further and, it was felt at the home of the ex-parent, treasonable step. It changed its name to the Institute of Contemporary Art and in a manifesto it said right out in public where everyone could read it that the "cult" of modern art was "A Cult of Bewilderment," and that "this cult rested on the hazardous foundations of obscurity and negation, and utilized a private, often secret, language which required the aid of an interpreter." These were harsh words indeed. The institute had slapped Mother's face, and it went on slapping it sentence after sentence. "Valid artistic ex-pression was often exploited for purposes of propaganda or sensa-tionalism; and once the gap between artist and public was widened sufficiently, it became an attractive playground for double-talk, op-portunism and chicanery at the public expense." "Modern art," it said, "denoting simply the art of our times, came to signify for millions something unintelligible, even meaningless. Today, however, 'modern art' describes a style which is taken for granted; it has had time to run its course and, in the pattern of all historic styles, has become both dated and academic."

The reaction at 53rd Street was initially one of shocked and lofty silence. *Newsweek* reported (the manifesto was very widely publicized and in many quarters heartily cheered): ". . . from the glass-blocked citadel that is the Museum of Modern Art in New York came this classic answer: 'No statement,' it said. 'And no comment.' "

A great many others, however, were charmed to comment, and they licked their chops, over what was almost universally assumed to be an attack aimed specifically at the Museum of Modern Art and not, as the institute hoped its manifesto would be, a way of clearing the air and setting its own course. Emily Genauer "hailed the stand as the first victory in the fight against irresponsibility in art," according to *Life*, which let itself go with a six-page piece called "Revolt in Boston: Shootin' Resumes in the Art World." The article was illustrated with paintings by Paul Burlin, William Baziotes, and George L. K. Morris as examples of what the institute was attacking (though it was not) and followed it by a series of color reproductions of paintings "of this century which they believe are chiefly rooted in native traditions that are romantic or realistic." [3] These pictures were chosen from an exhibition then at the institute which was called *Milestones of American Painting in Our Century*, and the directors of five major museums [4] which had lent pictures to this show wrote an infuriated letter to the editors of *Life* which said, in part:

> In the selection of the pictures [for the exhibition] and in the catalogue . . . there is no attempt to "slant" the exhibition in order to promote or discredit any particular schools; on the contrary, the aim is to represent impartially the chief tendencies of the period including abstract, surrealist and other trends.
>
> Yet your article, in both text and captions, represents the exhibition as an attempt to discredit "modern" tendencies, to decry "foreign influences" and to gratify "native traditions." . . . Your article is a deliberate misrepresentation of the aim and character of the exhibition. . . .

3 The pictures reproduced were by Sloan, Bellows, Kuniyoshi, Watkins, Levine, Burchfield, Feininger, and Kuhn.
4 Addison Gallery, Chicago Art Institute, St. Louis Museum, Corcoran Gallery, and Cleveland Museum.

The Museum of Modern Art finally issued a reply to the manifesto, and *Life* quoted a few sentences from it in an article which appeared just about a year after the institute's manifesto. "We detest the policy of the totalitarian state," the Modern Museum's statement said. "We would be seriously remiss in our duty . . . were we not willing to stand against the intimidation of progressive artists through pressure of invective and ridicule. . . . The word 'modern' is valuable."

The word "totalitarian" was common in the art world in those days as a piece of counter-invective. It seems rather quaint today in the context in which the Museum used it then, as though the institute in Boston by using the word "contemporary" instead of "modern" were marching out the storm troops and clapping artists in jail. Many years after the fracas had passed into limbo, James Plaut said, "We couldn't conceivably have envisaged the flurry caused by the change in name. We were a young institution feeling its oats and wanting its own identity. We felt badly about the ruckus. Lincoln Kirstein said he was ashamed of Boston and called me a Philistine in print, which I considered high praise from Kirstein. He attacked us vigorously." Plaut says that he coined the term "contemporary art." "We wanted to broaden our spectrum," he said. "We felt that MOMA had pre-empted modern art with its own definition, and we felt more things were involved, a broader definition of involving oneself with the meaningful arts of our time. It was a semantical game. The *avant-garde* had become an academy, an academy of the left. I do not mean that politically."

In a sense this ruckus is a diversion from the subject of this chapter, the museum as a collector of works of art. On the other hand, it is a revelation of the Museum's opinion of itself and its function as arbiter of what is and what is not "modern," be it contemporary or not, and its collecting has been based (as any important collecting has to be based) as much on exclusivity as on inclusiveness—on the exercise, in other words, of its taste. The result (or one result) of the ruckus was the publication in March 1950 of still another manifesto, this one called "A Statement on Modern Art," and it bore the names of the Institute of Contemporary Art, the Museum of Modern Art, and the Whitney Museum of American Art. It was a burying of the hatchets with which the "Contemporary" and the "Modern" had been cracking each other's skulls. They buried them in a three-page discourse on the evils of chauvinism, intolerance, and bigotry, and the virtues of freedom, objectivity, tolerance, and humanism. In reading these platitudes today one is constrained to remember that this was the era of Mc-

Carthyism and of Congressman Dondero, when every artist who
wasn't of what Paul Burlin called the "Kiss-mummy" school of painting was regarded in some circles as a subversive or a "pervert." It was
the time when an exhibition of American painting traveling in Europe
under the auspices of the State Department had recently been recalled
because Congressman Fred E. Busbey of Illinois declared that there
were works in it that were by Communists. It took some courage in
that era to stand up for what was looked upon by the American
Legion, the Daughters of the American Revolution, and the Knights
of Columbus and a great many others as un-American. Congressman
Busby had said, "The movement of modern art is a revolution against
the conventional and natural things of life as expressed in art." Many
citizens nodded in agreement when he further observed:

> Without exception the paintings in the State Department's group
> that portray a person make him or her unnatural. The skin is not
> reproduced as it would be naturally, but as sullen, ashen gray.
> Features of the face are always depressed and melancholy. That
> is what the Communists and other extremists want to portray.
> They want to tell the foreigners that the people are despondent,
> broken down or of hideous shape—thoroughly dissatisfied with
> their lot and eager for change.

Put in such a context, the manifesto of the three museums seems to
have a good deal more bite than it does today. But, in any case, it is
evident that the Modern Museum had brought the Contemporary
Institute to heel and to a confession of its heresy in public.

The Museum of Modern Art's concept of a fluid collection made a
rather spectacular public appearance in 1944, just a decade after it had
acquired the Bliss collection. Barr, whatever were his differences with
Stephen Clark at that moment, was still the dominant intellect of the
Museum and the shepherd of its taste, and he and the trustees took a
step the nature of which, in Barr's restrained words, "caused some
doubt as to policy." A public auction was held at the Parke-Bernet
Galleries (then at 30 East 57th Street) on the evening of May 11 of
"Notable Modern Paintings and Sculptures" which belonged to the
Museum, "With Additions from Members of the Board of Trustees
and Advisory Committee." In the foreword to the sale catalogue was
a one-page explanation of the Museum's reasons for taking such a step.
Its first paragraph read:

The Museum of Modern Art is selling certain of its nineteenth century works of art to provide funds for the purchase of twentieth century works, chiefly by living artists. A number of these nineteenth century paintings and sculptures came to the Museum as gifts or bequests from our friends, and the proceeds from the sale of these particular works will be spent with the utmost care, for modern art of exceptional quality. It is our intention to perpetuate the generosity of donors to the Museum Collection by making sure that their names are applied only to works comparable in importance to those originally given us.

The foreword also explained that there were some twentieth-century works included in the sale because with the proceeds the Museum hoped, by selling lesser works (or near duplicates), to "improve our coverage of an artist's development." It also took care to point out that "No work by any living North or Latin American artist has been included in the sale."

The most surprising items listed in the catalogue (it included 108 items in all) were four oils and four watercolors by Cézanne, two Seurat drawings (which there seems to have been some reason to look askance at; their provenance, if not shady, was at least vague), all from the Bliss collection. One of the Cézannes, a portrait of the artist's wife, appeared as a considerable surprise; two others were still-lifes of high quality ("The Water Can" and "Pears and Knife"), and the watercolors included a view of "Mont Ste. Victoire." There were also a Matisse from the Bliss collection and a Matisse and two large Picassos contributed by Clark from his own collection. Some other items were contributed by Frank Crowninshield—two watercolors, one by Segonzac and the other by Dufy, and a bronze of a dancer by Despiau. "Financially," Barr records in his outline of the collections, "the sale was fairly satisfactory. . . ." (It netted the Museum $64,070.)

It was the fact that the works of art were disposed of by a well-publicized auction that "caused some doubt as to policy." If they had been sold to dealers or traded for other works and this had been done without fanfare, it is likely that no stir would have been caused, though the brouhaha aroused by the Metropolitan Museum's deals in 1972 would suggest the contrary. Public disposal of works of art which have been given to a museum is very likely to turn away potential donors who, in giving their treasures to a museum collection, believe that they are assuring their gifts and themselves a certain immortality. An older and more firmly established institution than the Museum was in

1944 (it was just in its middle teens) is in a position to take a somewhat loftier stance than an upstart, and an upstart with something of a chip on its shoulder. The Museum never held an auction like this one again, though in 1960 when it was in the midst of a drive to raise $25,000,000 to add two new wings and a new sculpture garden there was an auction of "Modern Paintings, Drawings, Sculptures," also at Parke-Bernet (by then moved to 980 Madison Avenue), for the "Benefit of the Thirtieth Anniversary Fund." In this case the works sold were "donated by private collectors, artists and American and European dealers." Of all the works offered, Barr selected fifty, and his choice was "based upon the monetary as well as the artistic value of the works." The auction was carried by closed-circuit television to Chicago, Dallas, and Los Angeles, and the results were rewarding. This time the take was $504,000.

Only part of the reason for the 1944 auction was financial. The Museum collection had grown to an unmanageable (or at least far from exposable) size even by 1940. There were then some 217 paintings in the collection, 383 prints and drawings, and 103 pieces of sculpture, with an insurance value of just over $700,000.[5] Even the tripled gallery space in the new building, which had, Barr said, "brightened hope for showing continuously a modicum of the collection," was entirely inadequate. Part of the reason for this was exhibitions like *Art in Our Time*, the Mexican show, and d'Harnoncourt's American Indian exhibition, which spread virtually all over the building. "The Museum," Barr wrote in a memorandum to the Advisory Committee in March 1941, "now has a large and valuable collection but at the moment, with the woods full of Indians, the casual visitor would not be aware of it." Even if half of the Museum's exhibition space were given over to showing the collection, this was inadequate, and furthermore, Barr said, there was no "accessible study storage" space which could be used for making the Museum's riches available to scholars. Later, in the summer of 1945 (at which time Barr was not yet officially the Director of Collections), he put up a show with Dorothy Miller's help that covered two whole floors of the Museum with 355 works— "the first comprehensive show of the collection since 1933 when 12 paintings and 9 sculptures comprised all the Museum owned."

There had been nothing Topsy-like in the way the collection had grown and was to continue to grow. Its upbringing was most carefully supervised and disciplined, and Barr meant it when he said that no gift

5 There were 75 American paintings and 36 sculptures as compared with 81 paintings and 43 sculptures from the School of Paris.

would be accepted as permanent, though in the course of time this policy changed and the nucleus came to be regarded as inviolable. What the Museum bought or accepted as gifts was from 1934 to 1944 the province of the Acquisitions Committee, and its chairmanship was at different times held by Stephen Clark and Sam Lewisohn, whose very considerable collections Barr hoped the Museum would someday inherit. Edward M. M. Warburg, still a "young Turk" in 1936, was chairman that year and again from 1939 to 1942. In 1944 the committee changed its name to the somewhat more lordly sounding Committee on the Museum Collections, and James Thrall Soby took over its chairmanship. The committee was indeed concerned with more than just acquisitions; it also determined how the collection should be shown, what works of art might be lent to other institutions, and made other such decisions of administration.

The new name has stuck, but there have been many chairmen since then. The single lines of continuity until 1967, when Barr retired, were Barr and Soby, though the chairmanship frequently fell to one or another especially interested if not always especially qualified trustee. According to the Museum's published policy, anyone "inside or outside the Museum might recommend a work of art which he believes should be added to the collection." In practice, so far as painting and sculpture, drawing and prints were concerned, very little got to the committee for decision that had not first passed through Barr's fine sieve and did not have his support. It was over this situation, you will recall, that James Johnson Sweeney quit the Museum as Director of the Department of Painting and Sculpture. It was for similar reasons that a number of Sweeney's successors left to take jobs in other museums where they would have a freer hand to recommend what they wanted to their trustees, and therefore feel they had a hand in shaping the collections under their aegis. The most distinguished of these was Andrew Carnduff Ritchie, who left the directorship of the Albright-Knox Gallery in Buffalo to take on the Painting and Sculpture Department at the Modern in 1950 and resigned after eight years to become the director of the Art Gallery at Yale.

The discussions at the meetings of the committee were free-wheeling and often lengthy. Barr could be eloquent about what he wanted the committee to approve, and its members sometimes felt overwhelmed by his willingness to fight for pieces that individuals on the committee did not like. Sometimes they balked completely, as when Goodyear resigned over the acquisition of a Rothko and Clark over the Giacometti "Chariot." As Barr has put it in his historical outline of the collections: "In 1947, encouraged by newspaper criticism, some older members of the committee on Museum Collections vigorously questioned the validity of certain acquisitions including paintings called 'abstract expressionism.' Purchase was difficult. . . ." A lady member of the committee for many years told me, "If Alfred didn't like it, it didn't get into the collections . . . all the collections . . . . everything except film. On a few occasions it is true that the committee just couldn't stomach certain pictures, and on those occasions Philip Johnson [a member of the committee continuously since 1957], who was always there (they were a tremendous trio—Philip, Jim Soby, and Alfred), would simply buy it and then a few years later he would offer it as a gift to the Museum and the trustees would always accept it."

There was a parallel example of this in 1958 when the painter Jasper Johns first appeared on the horizon of the New York art world. Barr had seen the show of his work at the Leo Castelli Gallery and had reserved four of the paintings for the Museum's consideration. Soby liked them; they were, he thought, a very refreshing change from abstract expressionism and evidence of a new spirit. One of the four pictures, painted in encaustic on newspaper, was of the American flag. To buy four paintings by one artist at the same time seemed a little extravagant to some members of the committee, but Barr pointed out to them that when Morris Graves first turned up they had bought a dozen and had never regretted it. What the decision came down to was to buy all but "Flag" because, though the committee liked it, it was fearful lest the Museum might be exposed to attack from the American Legion or some other group of chauvinists. The full board of trustees agreed with this. So Philip Johnson bought the picture for himself and has it in his collection, ready to give it to the Museum whenever they may want it. (Johnson also used Jasper Johns's work to ornament the New York State Theatre, which he designed for New York's Lincoln Center.)

When d'Harnoncourt was Director of the Museum, it was not his custom to sit regularly with the Collections Committee; he had a life of meetings, and he did not pose as an expert on the modern arts, as we have noted. He was, however, at a meeting at which the question of whether to buy the Picasso sculpture called "She-goat" was presented to the committee by Barr. Word had just come from Picasso's Paris dealer, Kahnweiler, that the cast of the goat which had been at the Brussels World Fair was for sale. He had been trying to get it for some time, he said, and it was one of just two casts; the other was in

Picasso's garden. He was asking 30,000,000 francs for it (about $72,000), and Barr said that in his opinion it was "possibly Picasso's greatest sculpture." When the committee had agreed to buy the piece, d'Harnoncourt said, "I've never been so partial to any goat in my life."

William S. Rubin, who became the Chief Curator of Painting and Sculpture Collections after Barr's retirement, says, "The committee is now extremely forward-looking and open to new ideas. I gather that was not always the case and Alfred ran into terrific opposition." He cited the example of "the black Stella," which Barr had bullied through the committee. "If you look back at the minutes of that meeting, you see that Alfred had to virtually force it down their throats . . . for a price of about $600 or $900 for this very large picture. This period is very recherché now and these pictures are worth $45,000 and $50,000 if you can find them of that quality. The committee changed markedly after that, and by the time I came it was really quite a liberal committee, and they thought that nobody who replaced Alfred could fight quite the same battle and they were right. Our problems have tended to be mutual problems—where to get the money for something we all want."

That, of course, has been a very large part of the problem of forming a collection with a shape, not just a hodge-podge, from the very beginning. It was that which led to the first of the auctions; but it had led before that to the conditions under which the Museum would receive gifts of works of art.

Abby Rockefeller made her first substantial gift of paintings and sculpture to the Museum in 1936. It was quite clear to her, as it was to her fellow trustees and to Barr, that it was accepted with the condition that any piece of it might be sold if that seemed advisable as a means of improving the collection. The gift included 36 oil paintings, predominantly by Americans, and 105 watercolors, gouaches, and pastels. (That was the year that the Rockefellers' tremendous house on 54th Street was torn down and they moved into an apartment. Mrs. Rockefeller's private gallery was no more, and her husband surely was relieved to have her modern pictures off his premises.) There was one restriction on disposing of pieces in the gift, a restriction imposed as a matter of policy early in the Museum's history. No work of art by a living American could be sold for any other reason than to purchase another, and presumably superior, work by the same artist. Goodyear had insisted on this because of an incident that had happened when he was on the board of the Albright Gallery in Buffalo. The gallery had sold at auction the work of a number of American artists once famous but by then out of fashion, and they were hurt not only in their pride but in their purses as well. The pictures had brought very low prices, and the artists, not surprisingly, complained with vigor. In subsequent years many of the pictures by Americans in Mrs. Rockefeller's gift were exchanged "to improve the quality." The same condition did not and does not apply to works by European artists (it does apply to Latin American artists), and, according to Dorothy Miller, "a good many other museums follow this same policy."

The year before she gave her pictures, Mrs. Rockefeller gave Barr $1,000 to spend in Europe. It was the first purchase money the Museum had ever received, and Barr came back with "three Dada collages, an oil by Max Ernst, a Schwitters collage, a large Masson pastel, a Tanguy gouache and two suprematist oils by Malevich." In 1936, moved by the plight of artists in the Depression, Mrs. Rockefeller gave $2,500 to buy American art and another $2,000 for "purchase abroad." (It was a frustrating year for Barr. Chagall's "I and the Village" was on the market for $1,500 and he could only raise $1,000; van Gogh's "Starry Night" could be had for $30,000, La Fresnaye's "Conquest of the Air" for $6,000, and, worst—or best—of all, Picasso's "Three Musicians" of 1921 could be had for $10,000, but Barr could get promises of only $4,800, and the picture went to the A. E. Gallatin Collection. These frustrations, however, ultimately had a happy ending, as we shall see.)

It was two years later, in 1938, that as the world grew sourer the Museum's purchasing funds were substantially sweetened. 1938 was the year that Neville Chamberlain went off with his furled umbrella to visit Hitler at Berchtesgaden in hopes of resolving the German-Czech crisis, and a few weeks later, on September 29, the notorious Munich Conference which was to assure "peace in our time" sold out the Czechs and made Hitler's war of conquest an inevitability. The year had begun happily for the Museum. In January Mrs. Rockefeller gave $20,000 to establish a "purchase fund" and her son Nelson added another $11,500 in his mother's name. Even more auspicious for the future of the Museum's collections, Mrs. Simon Guggenheim appeared on the Museum's horizon and with her the dawn of a quite different sort of day.

Until Mrs. Rockefeller and Mrs. Guggenheim opened their purses for the purpose of expanding and raising the level of the Museum's collections, the total purchase funds during the years 1935 through 1937, as an example, had been $8,560, with additional gifts from the Advisory Committee of $4,500. Late in 1937 Mrs. Guggenheim, who was an inveterate walker and an explorer of New York, dropped into the Museum on one of her occasional visits and said that she would like to speak to the Director. No one on the staff knew her, but she was quite apparently somebody, and she was taken to see Barr. With very little if any beating about the bush (Mrs. Guggenheim was a woman who knew her own mind, respected the opinions of experts, and also knew what she did not know) she said that she would like to give the Museum a painting, "an important modern painting," indeed. It did not necessarily have to be a picture she liked, but it had to be one which the Acquisitions Committee wanted with unanimous enthusiasm and which they were convinced would "become a masterpiece." She had one other stipulation: the picture must be bought from the Valentine Gallery, which was run by her friend Valentine Dudensing.

It did not take Barr long to get to the Valentine Gallery, where he found Picasso's "Mirror," painted in 1932. It was to be had for $10,000. Mrs. Guggenheim approved of the purchase, though she did not like the picture (it is said that she came to like it deeply in later years), and gave the funds to buy it. Her next gift was an even more magnanimous one. The Museum had borrowed Rousseau's "Sleeping Gypsy" from a Swiss collector for its tenth-anniversary exhibition, *Art in Our Time*, with which it opened the new building in 1939. When it was borrowed the picture was not for sale, but before it was to return to Europe it became available for $30,000. Barr went to Mrs. Guggenheim and explained to her what a remarkable opportunity had arisen to acquire this "masterpiece," and once again Mrs. Guggenheim acquiesced.

This was the beginning of a long association between the Museum and Mrs. Guggenheim, one which evidently gave her a good deal of pleasure and satisfaction and enriched the Museum tremendously. Mrs. Guggenheim was the widow of a Senator from Colorado. She and her husband, who died in 1925, had collected Italian primitives under the eye of Bernard Berenson, but owned no modern works. She lived in an apartment at the corner of Fifth Avenue and 86th Street, and she knew who lived in each mansion along the avenue and who had lived there before, and delighted in collecting and retailing to her friends small pieces of gossip about them. Her particular friend at the Museum became Dorothy Miller, whom she would telephone frequently and say, "Dorothy, would you like to have lunch and go for a little drive?" She would then pick Miss Miller up at the Museum and they would go exploring. "Her knowledge of New York real estate was prodigious," Miss Miller says. "She was a very interesting woman with very good brains. When she was in Washington with her husband, she was deeply interested in politics and would be in the gallery of the Senate every day it was in session."

Mrs. Guggenheim, small of stature and with a rather long, distinguished face, a long nose, and inquisitive eyes, was independent in her judgment about most things but extremely modest about paintings. After her first two gifts to the Museum she was encouraged to establish a fund for the acquisition of paintings and sculpture, which she proceeded to do. Nothing, however, was bought with her fund that she did not approve, and nothing was bought except "masterworks." "There were very few times when she refused anything that Alfred and the committee wanted," Dorothy Miller said. "She would buy only three of five Picasso bronzes of the '50s. They were reasonable, and with them we could fill in a big gap in the collection with her fund, but she didn't care about two of them. Fortunately, another trustee did. Another time there was a late Picasso painting we wanted and she said, 'I think I've bought enough Picassos.' But usually she said, 'If the committee likes it, that's all I want to know. I don't have to like it.' "

Several of the pictures that Barr thought had been lost to the Museum in 1936 were bought with Mrs. Guggenheim's fund. In all, she gave the Museum more than a million dollars. She paid for the Chagall "I and the Village," and with her fund the Museum eventually got La Fresnaye's "Conquest of the Air" and a different version of Picasso's "Three Musicians," larger than the one the Museum lost to Philadelphia. In all, the Museum acquired sixty-nine paintings and sculptures with Mrs. Guggenheim's money, including Picasso's "She-goat." By the 1960s the fund amounted to about $150,000 a year, but by that time, as William Rubin noted, "Even Mrs. Guggenheim's money could not be said to pay for one or even half of a masterpiece a year." And Miss Miller said, "Mrs. Guggenheim couldn't understand the inflation in the art market. The fund was $50,000 at first—we paid that much for 'The Three Musicians.' She could never quite see why the fund should be $500,000 if we were to continue to buy such things in the '60s."

Mrs. Guggenheim was elected to the Museum's board in 1940, by which time she was sixty-two, and later became an Honorary Trustee for Life. So long as she was able she came regularly to the Museum to see what was new and to look again and again at the collection she did so much to enhance. She liked to eavesdrop on others in the galleries, and she enjoyed the details of how the Museum went about its daily business. In her later years her hearing deserted her and her eyes grew dim, so that she could neither listen to music nor read or watch television. "I'm bored to death," she would tell Miss Miller. She was furious at her doctors for saving her life when she went into a coma from a bleeding ulcer. "They should have let me go," she said. "They had no right to save me." When she finally did go in 1970, she was ninety-three. Barr's book on the Museum collections is dedicated to her by the Museum's trustees, ". . . in profound gratitude for the unequaled generosity, concern for excellence, and modesty of spirit with which, over three decades, she yearly enriched the Museum's Collection of Painting and Sculpture." [6]

There have, of course, been a great many others who have enriched the collections—hundreds of others, indeed, all of whom possibly deserve being mentioned but only a few of whom can be cited here. By no means all gifts to the Museum have been inspired by high cultural motives or the purest unselfish generosity. Contributions to cultural institutions are to some donors a civic responsibility which they are happy to accept, though their duty is sweetened by applause. Indeed, it is sometimes sweetened by having their names carved in marble within the portals of the institutions on which they have bestowed their beneficence. Or if not carved in marble, then printed in annual reports, in either case a long-established American tradition. In other cases, of course, works of art are bought with the intention of having them reappraised at a higher price than was paid for them and then given to an institution in order to take advantage of the tax benefits that thus accrue to the donor along with the prestige. Many American museums have benefited greatly from this not entirely admirable practice, and the Museum of Modern Art has been one of them. Let it not be said that all or even many reappraisals have been dishonestly arrived at. The art market has been so inflationary in the last two decades that it is scarcely possible to buy with a good eye or good advice and not see one's investment gratifyingly soar. This tax advantage to the donor, however, has been very nearly the only way in which the Museum has received any help from government until very recently. The Museum, to be sure, is on tax-exempt property, but until 1971, when it had a grant from the New York State Council on

6 Barr's book on the collections was still in manuscript when I was permitted to consult it, and as of the publication of this book, it is not yet in print. R. L.

the Arts for $320,000, it had received no direct government subsidy of any sort. In other words, its government assistance has come primarily from the advantages given to persons who have made donations to its funds or its collections. In this way the Museum has enjoyed private support condoned by government tax policy to an extent that no European museum enjoys—indeed, to an extent no European museum enjoys even with direct government handouts. The Museum's collections, then, have been substantially government-made or, more accurately, made possible.

Aside from Mrs. Guggenheim and Miss Bliss, other especially magnanimous donors to the Museum's painting and sculpture collections have been Mrs. Rockefeller (who in 1939 added to her gift of paintings and drawings thirty-six pieces of sculpture and fifty-four works from her American folk art collection [7]), Philip Johnson, James Thrall Soby, Nelson and David Rockefeller, Mrs. John D. Rockefeller 3rd, G. David Thompson, Mr. and Mrs. Samuel Marx of Chicago who gave the Museum several very distinguished Matisses, including "The Moroccans," and Sidney Janis, all of whom, with the exception of Thompson, and the Marxes have previously appeared in these pages. In 1954 the trustees decided to make a special category of archangels called Patrons of the Museum's Collections "to honor the donors of the principal purchase funds and works of art" and specified that their names should not only be "inscribed in publications" but also appear "on a plaque at the entrance to the collection's galleries." This list is now about sixty names long and includes artists (Maillol, for instance, and Picasso) and a few generous dealers.[8]

Philip Johnson, as we have noted, gave the Museum its first "important European painting" by Otto Dix, but he also gave about the same time a painting of the "Bauhaus Stairway" by Oscar Schlemmer (which hung for years on the staircase to the second floor at 11 West 53rd Street). It was in an exhibition in Stuttgart which was closed down by Hitler's orders in 1933 and, Dorothy Miller says, "Philip bought it then and there for the Museum." He has been generous to the Museum's collections ("fantastically generous," Miss Miller says) ever since, and in 1967 he sent Barr the card file of his own collection and said, "Choose whatever you want as promised gifts." Barr made

7 Among these were the pieces transferred to the Metropolitan Museum and later added to Mrs. Rockefeller's collection at Williamsburg along with the remaining forty pieces, with the exception of Pickett's "Manchester Valley," which MOMA still has.

8 There were fifty-seven names so listed in the 1970–71 Annual Report of the Museum.

up a list of about forty works. Among them were things the Acquisitions Committee had failed to buy and of which Johnson had said, "I'll buy it and give it to you later." Johnson has at his place in New Canaan, Connecticut, near his "glass house," a painting gallery (underground) and a sculpture gallery, both of which he designed.

James Thrall Soby, who, like Philip Johnson, has been close to the Museum since its earliest days as an unpaid staff member, member of the Acquisitions Committee and the Committee on Collections, and a trustee, lent his collection of painting and sculpture for a benefit exhibition at the Knoedler Galleries on 57th Street in New York for the month of February 1961. The money from tickets sold for the opening (it was a fashionable jam of people in evening dresses and black ties from top to bottom of the splendid building that venerable firm then occupied) and for daily admission was to benefit the Museum's Library, now unquestionably the foremost library on modern art anywhere. It included forty-eight paintings and ten sculptures, all of which had been "pledged or given" to the Museum by Soby. "Of exceptional interest," Barr noted, "were Bacon's 'Study of a Baboon,' Balthus's 'The Street,' eight paintings by de Chirico (unmatched in any other collection), Miró's unique 'Still Life with an Old Shoe' and 'Self-Portrait,' Shahn's 'Liberation' and Picasso's 'Seated Woman' of 1927."

"Promised gifts" have played and will play in the future a major role in the enrichment of the Museum's collections. As an example of this, there was an early Picasso that had been owned by Roland Penrose, who felt impelled to sell it, but the price was far beyond Barr's budget. It was "Girl with a Mandolin," and Barr went to Nelson Rockefeller with his problem. He explained that, though it seemed expensive, it was less than "a miserable little Gauguin still-life" which had recently gone for more at a London auction. Rockefeller bought it and promised that he would eventually give it or leave it to the Museum. There are, according to Dorothy Miller, "twenty-five or twenty-eight things in Nelson's collection in that category." Recently when Nelson was selling some of his paintings ("There are times, you know, when even Rockefellers feel poor, and, besides, he says he wants to return to his first love, which was Chinese porcelains"), he wanted it made clear to Barr and to Rubin that none of the pictures he had promised to the Museum were among those he intended to sell.

Nelson's younger brother David, who is chairman of the Chase Manhattan Bank and became chairman of the Museum's board in 1962 [9] ("He is the only one of the Rockefellers who is really making

9 He stepped down in 1972.

money; all the other brothers are just spending it"), has also bought paintings suggested by Barr and Rubin and Dorothy Miller. They have in some cases been pictures that "the Museum very much needs," and David has bought them and promised that they will eventually become part of the Museum's collection. "For all our great Matisses," Rubin said, "we haven't a single Fauve-period Matisse. One of the great Fauve pieces came up for sale in London last year and we alerted David. He gave us the go-ahead and we won it, at quite a good price. We were willing to go higher. The Museum may not get it for many years, but when a museum builds a collection, that's the way it builds."

One of the most curious stories of "promised" works of art that someday will join the Museum's collection has to do with the Stein Collection—some of which was Gertrude's and some of which belonged to her brothers Leo and Michael. While Bates Lowry was briefly Director of the Museum he and his curators heard that the Stein Collection could be had for $6 million, and William Lieberman was dispatched to London to have a look at it. The price seemed right to him, but the Museum had no such funds at its disposal. On twenty-four hours' notice four trustees and a friend who could well afford to join them agreed to buy the collection. Whitney, Nelson Rockefeller, Paley, and André Meyer, not an insider at the Museum but very much an insider as a collector, each put up $1 million, and David Rockefeller put up $2 million. Each of them assured the Museum that he would give at least one picture to the Museum's collection, and it was further hoped but not declared that eventually more of the Stein collection would become the Museum's property. Richard Koch, the Museum's Administrator, met with the five men in the Museum's storage rooms where the collection was displayed. He held a hat from which they drew lots to determine the order in which they could make their choices. Each of the men, with the exception of Whitney, came with an expert advisor to help him choose. It has been said, and disputed, that Whitney did less well than the others, but there is no question that the Museum did very well indeed. This was amply demonstrated when the Stein collection was shown at the Museum in 1970.

The Museum also builds by the unprompted enthusiasm of collectors with minds of their own and tastes that are personal. Such a one was G. David Thompson, who lived in Pittsburgh and said he was in "steel," though the bigwigs in steel did not seem to recognize him as one of themselves. He was, however, a man of considerable wealth, and is described unerringly by those who have told me about him as "a rough diamond" and a "self-made man." When he first started to collect he patronized Edith Halpert's Downtown Gallery and bought Americans such as Stuart Davis, Charles Sheeler, and the Pittsburgh primitive John Kane. Then he got involved with the dealer Curt Valentin, and his tastes changed, becoming more adventurous and a great deal more confident. He served on the Museum's Committee on Collections, where he seems to have been in some degree "the life of the party." He liked to bring up a work by an artist he had discovered for himself and none of the others had heard of ("He spent all of his time after he retired in galleries and studios here and abroad"), and he would say, "I was in his studio in Milan (or Paris) and I think this is the best he's done . . . better than the one I bought." Before meetings of the committee he frequently spent several hours looking at the Museum's collection. "I like to walk through and see what we have," he would say, "before we decide what we're going to get." He was a man of excellent good humor and something of a practical joker. When the Museum was deep in a drive to raise a very large sum of money to expand its buildings (and hence facilities for showing the collections) he told Barr that he had a check for him that he had promised for the drive and handed him a check for $1,000. "He watched Alfred be polite . . . and pale," one who was there recalled, "and then he gave him another check for $100,000." Once his gallery (he had built a gallery onto his house in Pittsburgh) was broken into and some paintings were stolen. He called Elizabeth Shaw, the Director of Public Information, who was in the country for the weekend, hoping that she could help to publicize the theft and thereby increase the chances of recovering the paintings. He said, "Tell Alfred that none of the things I've promised the Museum were taken."

Collecting became a passion with him. "If he saw something in somebody's house he wanted," Miss Miller says, "he just wouldn't rest till he had pried it off the wall." He not only gave the Museum money to buy pictures that the committee wanted and he was enthusiastic about, but he also gave pictures and sculptures to the Museum, the two most notable being Picasso's "Two Nudes" (1906) and Henry Moore's sculpture in two parts, "Reclining Figure II" (1960). He offered his collection, which was put together by a restless process of buying and selling and trading, to the city of Pittsburgh; it was said to be worth $5,000,000, but the city fathers, unwilling to put up a building to house it, declined. The collection was most notable for a large group of Paul Klees and a large number of Giacomettis, which with part of the collection were subsequently sold in Europe. Thompson died at sixty-eight, the victim of a physician's misjudgment. He had a house near David Rockefeller's in Seal Harbor, Maine, and was taken ill with what the local doctor thought was a heart attack. Rockefeller offered to have him flown to Pittsburgh in his private plane, but the doctor cautioned against it. When he finally was flown to Pittsburgh ten days later, it was discovered that he had an intestinal obstruction. It was too late to save him.

Sidney Janis gave his collection of ninety-eight paintings and sculptures to the Museum in the late spring of 1967. "That the Janis collection should find a home at a great museum," he said, "has long been my hope, and happily the museum of my first love, the Museum of Modern Art, has graciously accepted it." The Museum was delighted to be gracious; moreover, it was somewhat surprised that it was given the opportunity so to be. William Rubin told Dorothy Miller that he thought Janis might smile upon the idea of making the Museum the recipient of his beneficence. "I was surprised," Miss Miller said. "I would have thought he would give his things to a college or a small museum where it would be the most notable part of a collection and immortalize their name."

Janis was certainly no stranger to the Museum. His first association with it went back to 1933, when he was a member of the Advisory Committee with Eliza Parkinson, Philip Johnson, Lincoln Kirstein, Monroe Wheeler, and other young men and women, and, as we have noted, it was he who in 1942 had at Barr's invitation (but his own instigation) put on the Morris Hirshfield exhibition that Stephen Clark so detested. He was already a collector in the early '30s. He and his wife had been a dance team on the vaudeville circuit, and then he had gone into the shirt business, producing a single model of white shirt with two breast pockets which he called "M'Lord." As John Brooks in his *New Yorker* profile of Janis wrote, "M'Lord's charmed life continued through the stock-market crash and into the Depression, when people seemed to be more eager than ever for two-pocket shirts, however empty the pockets might be." Janis started collecting in a modest way in 1925 with the purchase of a Whistler etching, which he soon turned in (with some cash) for a small Matisse oil, which in turn he got rid of in 1929 to buy his first expensive painting (now in the Museum), Picasso's famous "Painter and His Model" of 1928. In 1934 he was invited to show his collection at the Walker Art Center in Minneapolis, and by that time it was already an imposing assemblage of six Picassos, three Klees, two Légers, pictures by de Chirico, Matisse, Gris, Dali, Gorky, and other examples of what at that time was very advanced and adventurous taste. It also included Rousseau's big canvas of "The Dream" which Hirshfield had wanted to touch up for Janis, and which Janis sold to Nelson Rockefeller for "more than $100,000." Rockefeller promptly gave it to the Museum. In the summer of 1935 Janis lent his pictures anonymously to the Museum, where they were on display in the 53rd Street house from early June to late September along with the Museum's own collection.

It was thirteen years later that Janis went into the art-dealing business and opened a gallery on East 57th Street with an exhibition of nineteen Légers. The prices were moderate, some of them lower than $1,000, but Janis managed to sell only two of them. He began to assemble a "stable" of artists, not well known but not unknown when he took them on, who have become the most famous members of the so-called New York School—Baziotes, Gorky, Guston, Jackson Pollock, Rothko, Gottlieb, Kline, de Kooning, Motherwell, all of them "abstract expressionists," all of them now afforded by only the most affluent collectors. He was, Barr said, "the most brilliant new dealer, in terms of business acumen, to have appeared in New York since the war."

It would be inaccurate to say that Janis kept his private collecting distinct from his business in the art world, because objects went in and out of his collection to his gallery. He sequestered, however, those things that he most wanted for his collection and, it is said of him, "He bought very carefully only those things that he truly liked." When he made his gift to the Museum, it was with the stipulation that he would give one tenth of the collection each year for the next ten years, but the whole of the gift was shown at the Museum in 1968. By then there were eight Picassos, four Légers, eight Mondrians, three Giacomettis, six Dubuffets, an "important" Paul Klee, and important recent (and living) Americans—Gorky, Tobey, de Kooning, Kline, Pollock, and so on. The collection ranged from early Cubist and Futurist pictures through "Pop." It took up the entire first floor of the east wing of the Museum and the main entrance hall, and it subsequently traveled to several American museums and was shown abroad under the auspices of the Museum's International Council.

No strings were attached to the Janis collection. If the Museum's Director of Painting and Sculpture Collections and his committee want to sell items in it or use them for trading purposes, this is permissible under the terms of the gift. However, what is acquired as a result of sales or trades must bear the name of the Sidney and Harriet Janis Collection on its label. Indeed, several of the Janis Mondrians were sold (as the Museum is rich in works of that artist) and the proceeds were used to buy a very large Jackson Pollock, as being "in the spirit" of Janis' collection.

Late in 1972, four years after the collection was shown at the Museum, a catalogue of it was published with the title *Three Generations of Twentieth Century Art: The Sidney and Harriet Janis Collection of the Museum of Modern Art*. Richard E. Oldenburg, by then the Museum's newest Director, described the catalogue as "the most detailed that the Museum of Modern Art has ever published on any part of its collection." It was 231 pages long (not including the "Acknowledgments," "Foreword" by Alfred Barr, and "Preface" by William Rubin) with all the regular academic accouterments including "Notes," a "Chronology" (liberally adorned with photographs of the Janises and the Janis Gallery), and a "Catalogue Raisonné."

The contributions of Blanchette Rockefeller (Mrs. John D., 3rd) and Mrs. Parkinson to the Museum's collections belong more properly to a different part of the Museum's story and will be told there. Let it merely be noted at this point that their concern with the collections was early, long, and essential to their growth.

The Museum, like nearly all "charitable institutions," has had occasional windfalls that it had no reason to anticipate. When Kay Sage, the widow of the Surrealist painter Yves Tanguy, died in 1963, she left the Museum the largest bequest it had received up to that time for the purchase of paintings and sculpture. It was $100,000. Some years before that, in 1947, the Museum received word from a lawyer who was settling the estate of Anna Erickson Levene that she had bequeathed to the Museum three early paintings by Juan Gris and a Derain of 1900. She was the widow of Dr. Phoebus A. T. Levene, and no one at the Museum had ever heard of him or her. "Our best Gris is one of those," a curator said, "the 'Guitar with Flowers.' " Much more recently, in the mid-'50s, Larry Aldrich, a prominent dress designer and a friend of William Lieberman, the Museum's Curator of Prints and Drawings, asked Barr to have lunch with him. He proposed that he give a fund of $10,000 a year with a stipulation which became difficult to meet as prices of art went up. He wanted his fund to be used for the purchase of the work of artists not yet represented in the Museum's collection and "nothing could cost over $1,000." He had been a collector of late nineteenth- and early twentieth-century art, but he decided to sell his collection at auction. In the preface to the catalogue he explained that he had enjoyed what he had, but that he wanted to collect his contemporaries. He explained to Barr that he hoped to learn from what the Museum bought with his fund. That is not, however, how the story turned out. "He soon outstripped us," I was told, "He had much more time to cover the waterfront in the galleries and studios than we had as we got more and more hectically busy. He soon knew a great deal more than we did." The fund was given for two five-year periods, with the result that the collection was enriched and the hearts of many young artists gladdened. In the meantime Aldrich has built his own private museum in Connecticut to house his collection of aspiring—and by now many recognized—Americans.

To offset the surprises there have been a number of bitter disappointments. There were three major collections that the Museum hoped to inherit from three of its oldest friends, men who had been with it since its birth and all of whom had served on the Acquisitions and Collection committees . . . Conger Goodyear, Sam Lewisohn, and Stephen Clark.

Goodyear, you will recall, had been a trustee and the president of the Albright Gallery in Buffalo before he was tapped by Mrs. Rockefeller to be president of "the committee" which founded the Museum. He had, moreover, left Buffalo in a huff and, it seemed apparent, had transferred his allegiance and his affections to the new Museum. To be sure, his feelings were hurt more than a little at the time when he surrendered the presidency of the Museum to Nelson Rockefeller, and, moreover, Goodyear had resigned from the Collections Committee because he couldn't stomach a painting by Mark Rothko which Barr and the committee wanted to acquire. Nonetheless Barr and his colleagues and trustees expected that Goodyear's collection would come to the Museum on his death. Goodyear, however, had quite different plans for it, inspired, it seems, by a certain degree of vindictiveness which was coupled with an old loyalty to Buffalo.

Goodyear was furious when the name of Seymour Knox, a banker who had been extremely generous to the Albright, got his name attached to it and it became the Albright-Knox Gallery. "He used to sit in his study and stew over ways to get back at Knox," I was told, and his stewing resulted in a very odd scheme. He left the pictures from his collection to Buffalo with the condition that they had to be sold and the proceeds used to buy the works of young artists. So the Albright-Knox Gallery got the collection and couldn't keep it, with the result that they sold the pictures and sculptures to comply with the will and then with other funds bought the most important ones back. The prize of the collection, which is in Buffalo and which Barr still regrets slipped through his fingers, is a magnificent Gauguin nude from his Tahiti period.

The Lewisohn story is of a very different nature. His taste in American painters ran to the work of Jack Levine, Georgia O'Keeffe, and Burchfield, and he progressed into abstraction only as far as Stuart Davis. His house was filled with paintings of excellent quality, with Cézannes and van Goghs, with Renoirs and Gauguins and Utrillos. He wanted his collection to have "the best" example of an artist's work, and he kept improving the quality of his collection right up to his death. The sculptor Sidney Simon, who was his son-in-law, recalls that Lewisohn went to a gallery in New York to see an exhibition of landscapes by the wife of his friend, the great Washington collector, Duncan Phillips. Phillips buttonholed him and said, "Which one do you like?" Lewisohn in a slight fluster pointed to one, and Phillips said to the dealer, "Mr. Lewisohn wants to buy this one." "When he got home," Simon says, "he was depressed and he told Margaret, his wife, who said, 'Don't worry, Sam. So-and-so is getting married next week and we'll give it to her as a wedding present.' Sam didn't sell pictures he decided weren't up to snuff. He gave them away."

In 1949 he was elected to the board of trustees of the Metropolitan Museum, and he was assigned to the committee which was shepherded by Robert Beverly Hale to spend the income from the Hearn Fund on contemporary American works. Lewisohn was delighted. Whereas at the Modern Museum he was feeling rather old-hat in his tastes, at the Metropolitan he felt "young and wild," and he went about with Hale to studios and galleries enjoying himself enormously. He died in 1951. The most important pieces of the Lewisohn collection went to the Metropolitan. The Museum of Modern Art got three pictures, —Picasso's "Pierrot," Rouault's "Three Judges," Shahn's "Violin Player," and a bronze "Torso of a Woman" by Maillol. Later Mrs. Lewisohn bequeathed Cézanne's "*L'Estaque*," a Soutine of "Maria Lani," and Maurice Sterne's "After the Rain."

Stephen Clark left the Museum precisely nothing. The cause of his disaffection was only partly aesthetic, only somewhat a matter of the convictions of his taste, which were strong and very personally evolved over years of looking at and buying works of art and disposing of what no longer pleased him. He had sold all of his Matisses, of which, you'll recall, he had had a roomful in his house on 70th Street. He bought Corot and Eakins and Bellows and Winslow Homer, remarkably fine examples of each, and if these were not what the Museum of Modern Art wanted (possibly they were), they were chosen by a sharp eye and a sensitive one. Clark's split with the Collections Committee came, you will remember, over Giacometti's "Chariot," which, if looked at with the same eye that bought Corot's remarkable "Port de la Rochelle" (perhaps his greatest landscape), looks rather unsatisfying —indeed, rather silly—and so it must have looked to Clark, however it looks to us. But the *coup de grâce* of Clark's relationship to the Museum had nothing to do with personal taste in the arts. At the time of the thirtieth anniversary of the Museum, when it was conducting a drive for $25,000,000, someone, I do not know who, told Clark that "We've put you down for a million dollars." This was not the sort of thing one said to Clark; this was not the kind of arrogant bite that he would tolerate, nor the kind of pressure that it would ever have occurred to him to put on anyone else. This was not within his definition of how a gentleman behaved to another gentleman. He left his pictures to the Yale Art Gallery and the Metropolitan Museum. A friend of Clark's in Cooperstown, where Clark had a summer place and was the chairman of the board of the New York State Historical Museum, in explaining Clark's disenchantment with the Modern Museum said, "All those homosexuals bothered him, and he really didn't like the pictures." His disaffection, then, seems to have been a matter of taste, manners, and distaste, three powerful social considerations, subject to scrutiny but never to be taken lightly.

The present state of the Museum's permanent collection is one of vast riches and perennial poverty. To all intents and purposes there are no funds that can be relied on to expand the collection; on the other hand, there are a great many works of art owned by the Museum that can be traded or sold to buy works that its trustees, at the urging of its curators, feel are necessary to its well-being. Within the last few years one of its most lucrative sources of works of art was cut off when the Internal Revenue Service ruled that artists could not take tax deductions at market value of works that they gave to museums or other educational institutions. (The same ruling applies to authors' manuscripts given to libraries. In both cases only the literal cost of materials is tax deductible.) Museums, of course, were under no obligation to accept works they did not want, but works by artists they very much wanted for their collections were acquired through gifts from artists, especially those whose work commanded high prices and who found themselves in high tax brackets. It worked to the advantage of both the museum and the artist and was, indeed, an important indirect government subsidy of the arts.[10]

Gifts, however, continue to come in and will come in for years, even if only those that have been promised arrive as expected, and so long as it is to a donor's advantage to make tax-deductible gifts. Some of these will be accepted, as they have been in the past, only with the condition that they may be used for sale or trading to improve the collection. "We often take bad things by great artists who are well represented in the collection," Rubin explained, "and sell them. For example, we have sold a couple of very minor Picassos, a couple of very minor Mirós, an average Redon out of a great group of Redons, some minor Rouaults—third-rate little gouaches—two Léger décors that we never showed and one Léger which was something of a duplicate, a nice picture, not a great one, and there was a Cézanne, a smallish one of Mont Ste. Victoire. That was the picture we offered Picasso in exchange for the great metal sculptures that he'd never been willing to release, and Picasso really didn't like the Cézanne that much. We then turned around and used that Cézanne as a major element in an exchange to acquire Picasso's great 'Charnel House,' the picture inspired by the scenes in the concentration camps, that was being offered at a little under a million dollars and which we could never have touched otherwise and one we terribly wanted because someday the 'Guernica' will go back to Spain. . . . Picasso was pleased by this and has given the Museum a model of a rod sculpture he did some years ago as a monument to Apollinaire (and was turned down), and the Museum is now going to have it made in cor-ten steel."

And so it goes, and so it will continue to go, in all probability. Barr had acquired Picasso's "*Les Demoiselles d'Avignon*" by trading a "mediocre" Degas of race horses out of the Bliss collection to the dealer Jacques Seligman, and he got the van Gogh "Starry Night," which had been far beyond his reach in 1936, by trading for it a minor Degas pastel and a "minor sketchy" Toulouse-Lautrec and a few other minor items. It was the Museum's first van Gogh and is quite possibly its greatest.

But the collection of painting and sculpture is only a part, if the most highly visible and valuable part, of the Museum's collections. How the other collections were formed and how they grew is a very different story.

10 The ruling has been challenged and at this writing stands a chance of being modified, if not reversed.

*It is old enough now so that a generation it educated
to revere Barr instead of Berenson, Cézanne
instead of Fra Angelico, visits the permanent
collection to show old favorites to its children
and grandchildren.*

JOHN CANADAY, *The New York Times*, June 18, 1967

Chapter XVI *The Gleanings*

At a conference in May 1972 of those minor Maecenases who administer state and federal funds for the support of the arts, Eric Larrabee, the director of the New York State arts council, said in a speech to his peers, "Can you imagine industrial design in this country over the past quarter of a century without the design collection of the Museum of Modern Art?"

Larrabee could have said "over the past thirty-eight years." The Museum's design collection had its genesis in the *Machine Art* exhibition of 1934, which, as you will recall, caused many more raised eyebrows than exclamations of approval, more "What is this stuff doing in a museum?" than "It's high time that machine-made objects of good design should be recognized as art." Some of the objects from that exhibition—a self-aligning ball bearing, a chair by Marcel Breuer, a brass boat propeller, a chemical flask, and some tumblers by Walter Dorwin Teague, for example—were squirreled away and became the nucleus of what has become a unique collection. No other museum has anything to touch it as a revelation of what might be called "high taste" (or highbrow taste) in design in this century. Indeed, it reaches back into the later years of the nineteenth century, as other collections of the Museum do, and for much the same reasons. It has its equivalents

316

of van Goghs, Cézannes, and Lautrecs. It includes, for example, a number of bentwood chairs, now enjoying a revival, designed by Thonet as early as 1860. To them can be traced concepts which turned up much later in the bent plywood furniture of Alvar Aalto and bent metal tubing of Breuer and Mies van der Rohe. The collection, in other words, is concerned with origins of modern design as well as with what the machine has produced in our time. It is also concerned with what can be called the overthrow of the Victorian academic traditions of design, and so the collection has an example of Louis Sullivan's intricate architectural ornament, and examples of objects generally classified as "decorative arts," such as furniture, lamps, vases, jewel boxes, and other idiosyncratic manifestations of Art Nouveau from the turn of the century. The bulk of the collection, of course, consists of objects produced more or less within the span of the Museum's existence, dating, that is to say, from the 1920s.

It is, of course, impossible to demonstrate the direct relationship between the Museum's design collection and the effect it has had on designers. In that regard the fact that the Museum has made such a collection is more important than any individual object in it. Unlike paintings, mechanically made objects are not unique. Theoretically, anyone could with patience and a healthy budget duplicate the Museum's design collection, with the exception of some objects, like the Tiffany glass, which are the unique products of craftsmen's hands and not of machine tools. Many other museums are rich, of course, in the products of craftsmen; many museums have extensive collections of "decorative arts." The Museum of Modern Art is concerned "primarily with mass-produced useful objects made to serve a specific purpose." It is for this reason that "decorative arts" would seem an anomaly if applied to most of what the Museum's collection contains, "and so," says Arthur Drexler, Director of the Architecture and Design Department, "the term 'design,' or 'industrial design,' has been used instead." The importance of the design collection is essentially that it takes seriously (indeed, often solemnly) what manufacturers turn out for a mass (and sometimes for a class) market, and that its curators and directors have been able to convince manufacturers—at least a few manufacturers—that "good design" is good business.

The *Useful Objects* exhibitions, which started under the regime of John McAndrew in the late 1930s and were continued by Edgar Kaufmann, Jr., in the 1940s, were, as we have already seen, so attractive to a segment of the public that manufacturers competed to have their products selected for them. Some objects from these exhibitions found their way into the design collection, which, like the painting-and-sculpture collection, is divided now into a "permanent" and a "study" collection. But this sort of acquisition was at best haphazard. Usually the objects were donated by the manufacturer if the Museum wanted them, but there was no established pattern for acquiring the necessary materials to add up to an orderly, scholarly, and historically useful record of modern design.

The Design Department and the Architecture Department were separate after McAndrew "jumped or fell" from his position of director of a department that encompassed both. Eliot Noyes, who came to the Museum from Harvard, where he was studying with Gropius and Marcel Breuer, both late of the Bauhaus, and with the recommendation of Dean Hudnut, became Director of a Department of Industrial Design in 1940. A competition that he organized in that year and called *Organic Design in Home Furnishings* ("That title still makes my skin crawl," Arthur Drexler says) produced the prototype of the now famous Eames chair, which, along with a chair by Eero Saarinen, Eames's collaborator, is now in the design collection. During World War II Noyes, who is a sailplane pilot for recreation and a licensed airplane pilot for his own business transportation and to tote his family around on holidays, worked in the Pentagon designing gliders that were used for troop and equipment transport. He returned to the Museum only briefly when he got out of uniform, and after he left, the principal figure for a number of years in the Design Department was once more Edgar Kaufmann.

Life in the department under Kaufmann's executive direction was stormy. Evidently Kaufmann shared with a number of other heads of departments at the Museum before and after him a shortage of executive skill and tact that produced more than a little anguish among those who worked for and with him. Feelings were hurt and tears were shed, but no one questioned the skill of his eye, the integrity of his judgment, or the remarkable determination with which he tackled both manufacturers and merchandisers for the production and distribution of what he firmly believed in as excellence. Furthermore, though he was a self-made scholar (he did not go to college, much less graduate school, though he had worked with Wright at Taliesen), nobody questioned his scholarship; his knowledge of design was by no means confined to the present any more than it was confined to America and Western Europe. His formal education in the arts, in other words, was in kind not unlike that of Monroe Wheeler or James Soby, Lincoln Kirstein or Philip Johnson, or of Arthur Drexler, who succeeded him. Not one of them was a bonded art historian; none was a trained curator, a normal situation at the Museum of Modern Art which has frequently provoked the scorn (and surely the envy) of scholars and trained museum professionals. The line between dedicated and informed amateurism and professionalism is often fine indeed in the administration and promulgation of the arts, as it is not in the making or performing of them.

In 1950 Edgar Kaufmann initiated a series of *Good Design* exhibitions. To accomplish this he sought and achieved the cooperation of the Merchandise Mart in Chicago, which he encouraged to hold two such shows a year, with the selection of what was exhibited determined by the Museum—which meant largely by himself. From these two shows a single one was derived for exhibition at the Museum. "He did a superb job," Wheeler said many years after the shows were abandoned. "A little tag was devised identifying the Museum as approving the objects, and this eventually had a great influence on the manufacturers who wanted to have the Museum of Modern Art's acceptance." The exhibitions were discontinued after 1955 because, according to Drexler, "the material was running pretty thin, and they were big shows that took a lot of time and got on everybody's nerves here, and, besides, it had become a sort of shoppers' service." Furthermore, the tag which said that an object had been selected for the *Good Design* exhibition was "misunderstood" and promoted by the manufacturers as a Museum of Modern Art "award." But the exhibitions had served their purpose. Kaufmann, with the weight of the Museum behind him, had convinced several manufacturers to put "good design" into production, in spite of the often difficult technical problems of working in new materials (plastic and metal and plywood) for which they did not have the machinery. Furthermore, he had convinced furniture buyers in department stores to display the end products. "To get an audience for modern design," Drexler said, "you first have to get the stuff in the stores, and the people who were stopping this were the buyers." In those days Bloomingdale's in New York was the leader in acceptance and promotion of modern furniture, and it was Kaufmann who convinced them to take it on.

In January 1948 the Museum announced an "international competition for low-cost furniture design" with Kaufmann as the director of the competition and a jury (of which he was not one) that included d'Harnoncourt, Mies van der Rohe, Catherine Bauer (who had won a prize given by Kaufmann's father through *Fortune* magazine for an article on the relationship between industry and the arts),[1] and several

---

1 Catherine Bauer, a housing specialist, later married William Wurster, dean of the MIT Architectural School.

others. The competition was "open to designers in all countries" and there were prizes for the "best design for a seating unit" and for "best design for a storage unit." The first prize was $5,000, the second $2,500, the third $1,250, and the competition was jointly sponsored by the Museum and by Museum Design Project, Inc., "a non-profit organization set up by representatives of the trade." In the annual report for 1948 it was stated that "entrants from foreign countries alone number more than seven hundred," and the upshot was a publication in 1950 illustrating the prize winners "as presented to the jury and as finally manufactured where the pieces are in production."

While he was working on an exhibition of *Textiles and Ornamental Arts of India* in 1955 Kaufmann suddenly resigned from the unpaid position he occupied at the Museum. It was not the first time he had offered his resignation. On several occasions he had put it in writing on d'Harnoncourt's Art Nouveau desk and d'Harnoncourt had pushed it aside and pretended not to see it, believing that the storm would pass, which, indeed, it did. This time, however, the resignation was accepted, considerably, it is said, to Kaufmann's surprise. The issue was a press release having to do with his department which he had not seen and approved, and it included statements to which he took exception. Monroe Wheeler recalls, "I remember so clearly how Edgar walked into my office and said, 'You can understand how in view of what has happened I cannot continue the directorship of the *Textiles and Arts of India.*' He felt so strongly that he left immediately, and I had to take over." The upshot was unfortunate for Kaufmann and for the Museum. Kaufmann felt that his resignation had been handled in such a way that it looked as though he had been fired, and he was resentful of the fact that Alfred Barr had not rallied to his support. Indeed, it seemed to him that Barr had been instrumental in letting him go. What had been a friendship of long standing and mutual respect and warmth became, at least on Kaufmann's part, an arm's-length acquaintance. "I thought the world of Alfred," Kaufmann said many years later. "I'm not sure I still do." He also believed that Wheeler wanted to get rid of him. "Monroe got Alfred bounced," he said. "I was one of the dividends. . . . Alfred knew this was going on. He had no reason not to spill the beans. I didn't accept this. Monroe was fighting Alfred for power. He was playing for big stakes, and he did not get what he hoped for." At the time Kaufmann left, the Museum was about to send an exhibition of *Fifty Years of American Art* to Europe. "All the Feiningers in it belonged to Kaufmann," a trustee said, "and he withdrew them."

Distortions occur as memories dim, sores fester or are healed over, real and unintended, or even unsuspected, slights are forgotten or rankle, and they are worth recalling only as they seem to indicate the temper of a time and place. Such abrasive incidents and relationships, such doubts of loyalty and suspicions of connivance and undercutting and favoritism, such star-crossed friendships and affairs of the heart were in character, not out of it, behind the Museum's glass but not transparent walls. If the Museum had worked like a well-greased precision machine instead of like a cranky, temperamental, thrown-together Rube-Goldbergian fantasy, which it often seemed to be, it would have produced a product as dull as it was efficient. The Museum was inspired by passions and plagued by pettinesses. If it was sometimes outrageous, it was surely not dull. No one can deny its impact.

The residue of Kaufmann's incumbency in the Design Department was a greatly increased and enriched collection of objects, not just those that he searched out and got manufacturers to give to the collection but things that he bought and gave himself—chairs by Wright and van der Rohe, and glass by Tiffany, for example. But the methodical development of the collection started when Arthur Drexler became head of the Department of Architecture and Design; the two functions were put together by Philip Johnson before Drexler took over.

Drexler was twenty-six years old when he came to the Museum. For the preceding two years he had been the architectural editor of *Interiors,* a magazine of serious intent not to be confused with magazines for the general run of chintzy interior decorators. Before that he worked for George Nelson, the industrial designer and architect who had left the editorship of *Architectural Forum* to set up his own office. "George hired me," Drexler says, "because he wanted somebody to talk to." Nelson at that time had been commissioned by *Holiday* magazine to do a series of articles on "holiday houses" in various parts of the country. Drexler did the traveling and the selecting and the reporting, and got the photographs taken, and did first drafts of the articles, which Nelson, an able and witty writer, then rewrote. "I couldn't have afforded that much travel," Drexler said. "I saw a lot of the country I never would have seen otherwise. I got to see an awful lot of stuff and a lot of people, and it was immensely useful, though it was often boring and lonely." Before that he had worked at being what he calls an "artistic hack" for an architectural firm in New York. "I was supposed to take what everybody else did and take the curse off it by making it 'artistic.'" (The quotation marks were in his voice.) His only formal architectural training was a year before World

War II at Cooper Union, where he learned to do renderings. It was Philip Johnson who persuaded him, with not much difficulty, to leave his editorial job at *Interiors* and come to the Museum as Curator of Architecture. Johnson was the Director of the department, which also included industrial design. Kaufmann's *Good Design* project was a quite separate operation, and, it is said, Kaufmann was not at all sanguine about what was going on in the way of decisions about design under Johnson. At best theirs was a chilly friendship.

The chief squirrel (who was also in large part a ferret) of the design collection was Greta Daniel. She was a refugee from Germany, where most of her friends were destroyed during the war. She had been an apprentice curator in the museum in Essen ("from which we got not only Greta," Drexler says, "but Matisse's 'Blue Window' via Switzerland"), and when she first came to the Modern Museum she worked for Kaufmann and then, Drexler says, "came into the department and started to build the collection." She was methodical, determined, sensitive, and modest. "At that time life here was much more leisurely," Drexler says. "The whole thing, the whole office for the department was no bigger than this small office, and it was all done out of everybody's pocket. It was very nice. Greta would go shopping and she'd be allowed, I don't know, $22.75 a year, and she'd come back with all these goodies, most of which she'd squeezed out of manufacturers and designers." Johnson would go over the "goodies" and then there would be "the most strenuous, soul-searching review as each ash tray was examined for its proportions and workmanship and material and truth —the honestness, the seriousness, the moral righteousness of the whole thing was not to be believed! Philip, thank God, is an unreconstructed aesthete." Thus the collection grew with Greta Daniel as its conscience and its buyer, tracking down "the best knife, fork, and spoon and the best teacup. She was a walking encyclopedia of everything produced both here and abroad, and worked like a dog for the wages of a porter. She died in the early '60s—a terrible loss to the Museum and to me. She carried a card file in her head, and after her death we had pandemonium." Kaufmann remembers her as "nosy, fussy, smarmy, and self-seeking."

She had, however, systematized the design collection and revealed its shortcomings as well as plugged many of the holes in it. The department has some purchase funds, but Drexler does not feel that "we have to have everything." The funds have come largely from members of the advisory committee of the department, "a handful of people who have been very interested and very generous." "When I have

$10,000 or $12,000 in the bank, I feel I'm in superb shape," Drexler says. "I have to work hard to spend it." Some of the items in the design collection, if not priceless, almost seem so. The Art Nouveau desk which d'Harnoncourt had in his office (until Drexler rescued it from him) was designed by Hector Guimard, whose wife came to New York after World War II, when the Museum "bought some stuff, including his own desk and two chairs and side chairs and jewelry, more or less as charity." Recently a small bronze twelve inches high by Guimard brought $17,000 at auction. "What would his own desk bring?" Drexler asks. In the Museum's sculpture garden is one of Guimard's elegant Art Nouveau entrance gates in cast iron for the Paris Métro. It was bought in 1958 for about $1,500. In 1958, when Drexler and Greta Daniel produced an exhibition of *Twentieth Century Design from the Collection of the Museum of Modern Art* and a very handsome catalogue (now out of print) to go with it, the design collection comprised "some 850 examples, representing all the arts of manufacture." In 1972 the collection contained approximately 2,000 such objects.

But this is only one aspect of the design collection. You may recall that when Alfred Barr and Jere Abbott went to France and Russia and Germany in 1927–28 they brought back with them a collection of posters with which Barr made an exhibition for his students at Wellesley. Four years after the Museum opened and before there was a department of design the Museum held a poster competition. In that same year there was an exhibition of Toulouse-Lautrec posters, and in 1936 Ernestine Fantl, then the Curator of Architecture, put on an exhibition of posters by Cassandre. The nucleus of the poster collection was what Barr and Abbott and also Philip Johnson had picked up in Europe and given to the Museum. During the war there were two more poster competitions (National Defense in 1941 and United Hemisphere in 1942), and by the time the war was over, the Museum had held, in all, nineteen poster exhibitions. Posters, in other words, were a continual, if not a major, part of the Museum's exhibition program. "Competitions were very popular in those days," Drexler said. "Architects and designers had time on their hands and it seemed like a democratic way of finding talent. There were competitions for home furnishings, for lamps, playground equipment, and especially for posters. We also had a polio poster competition."

The poster collection is under the wing of the Architecture and Design Department because "it's an applied art—a utility." And Drexler explained that "It's been put together in a much more cavalier manner with much less discrimination in keeping stuff out. There's been much more readiness to absorb the material because it's easier to cope with." The result is a collection built up by Mildred Constantine, who came to the Museum after the war, "very handsomely." Drexler calls it "an astonishingly comprehensive collection," and believes there is none to equal it anywhere. The collection also includes graphic ephemera of various kinds—Christmas cards, packages, throw-aways, and so on.

Architecture, obviously, is harder to collect than graphic design or useful objects. The Museum has a collection of architectural models, which are extremely expensive to make, to store, and to maintain. It also, of course, has an extensive collection of architectural photographs, dating back to the International Style exhibition of 1932, and some architectural studies and drawings. "Since we are the only museum with a department and a full-time curatorial staff in architecture and design," Drexler said, "it has always seemed to me very important to have a collection of architectural material, and gradually we've been building this up. The problem, of course, is space." What he would like is "a continuing exhibition of key buildings and key ideas in modern architecture. During the next ten years I want to get this really launched." At present the most important single collection of models is a large group given to the Museum by Mies van der Rohe's office.

Some of the architecture and design collection—chairs and vases, lamps and jewel boxes, models, and so on—is continually on view in the Philip Goodwin Gallery on the third floor of the Museum's east wing. As for the study collection, it is not greatly used by designers and students, but, Drexler says, "In fifty years it will be a fascinating thing. It's the also-rans, the minor variants, whatever for some reason has caught our attention but just not quite made it. From time to time we have taken material from the study collection and put it in the permanent collection." In other words his department has its "Fur-lined Teacups" too.

On the fourth floor of the Museum one steps out of the elevator (if he has a pass to get that far) into a hall hung with big blow-ups of stills from movies that are by any definition of time or quality historic. If he goes straight ahead a few steps and turns left, he finds himself at the beginning of a long, narrow corridor whose walls are also hung with blow-ups. If he walks to the end, he passes the offices of the Film Library's executive staff and a projection room, and at the very end he faces a closed door with the words *Department of Photography* painted on it. Beyond this door is a room filled with filing cabinets, bookshelves, black flat boxes, and a couple of large tables at which there are usually a few young people looking at photographs. Behind glass walls at the right are two offices, and at the far side is a door on which in brown wooden letters ten inches high is the name of the great French nineteenth-century photographer Atget. Behind this door is John Szarkowski's office; he is the Director of the Department of Photography. Customarily he is smoking a pipe and looking worried, or possibly just concentrated, for he is a man who smiles readily and laughs easily. He succeeded Edward Steichen, who, you will recall, caused considerable consternation in the bosom of the Museum family when he was put in over Beaumont Newhall, the department's first Director, who left rather than play second fiddle to "the great man" of photography.

Steichen was a showman as well as a remarkable photographer whose pictures for many years graced the pages of Crowninshield's *Vanity Fair* and of its sister magazine *Vogue*. He had done two very successful exhibitions for the Museum during the Second World War, *Road to Victory* in 1942 and *Power in the Pacific* in 1945, at which times he was chief of the U.S. Navy's photographic department. His first exhibition after he became Director of the Museum's department in 1947 was photographs by Alfred Stieglitz, whose protégé he had been when he first came to New York as a very young man in 1900. Steichen was sixty-seven when he took on the job at the Museum, or two years older than what was generally considered the retirement age, another factor that did not especially endear him to some of his new colleagues. He was, moreover, used to "command," in the Navy sense, and he was a "personality" in the public-relations sense. He liked to be called "Captain Steichen." He was an "ornament" to the Museum, and he knew it, and he stayed on as Director of the Photography Department until 1961, when he retired at the age of eighty-two with great fanfare.

During his incumbency the Museum held forty-three photographic exhibitions, the most noteworthy of which from a publicity point of view was *The Family of Man*. It was a smash hit; it was even a financial success. As with *Road to Victory*, its installation was as spectacular, if not more spectacular, than the photographs in it. It was a vast photo-essay, a literary formula basically, with much of the emotional and visual quality provided by sheer bigness of the blow-ups and its rather sententious message sharpened by juxtapositions of opposites—wheat-fields and landscapes of boulders, peasants and patricians, a sort of "look at all these nice folks in all these strange places who belong to this family." It was produced in 1955 at a moment when the world was briefly tired of warring (the conflict in Korea had ceased in 1953), and some of it was superficially and hopefully, if not actually, a "family." The show was considered magnificent and noble, and the book which was made from it, with an introduction by Steichen and a prologue by his brother-in-law, the poet Carl Sandburg, sold, as we have noted, millions of copies and is still selling.

One of the exhibitions that Steichen had put on was called *Seventy Photographers Look at New York*. There was no one who knew more about New York's image on film than Grace Mayer, curator of prints at the Museum of the City of New York, and Steichen turned to her for her expert help. She was the author of a book called *Once upon a City*, which was about the firm of photographers known as Byron and its extraordinary record of New York from before the turn of the century until well into this century. Two years after the New York photographers' exhibition at the Museum Steichen invited her to join his staff. He needed her. She was not only extremely knowledgeable about photographic history, but she was a trained and meticulous archivist and a collector. Steichen was none of these things; indeed, Barr thought that the photographic collection, of which Newhall and his wife had been such careful custodians, was being allowed to drift into something of a shambles. Miss Mayer became Assistant to the Director and a worshipful acolyte of her boss. She tidied up the collection, added to it, got proper cabinets and boxes for it, and, according to Szarkowski, "did a great deal to avoid deterioration and loss."

Szarkowski took over the direction of the Photography Department in 1962 after Steichen's retirement. He is not sure who recommended him for the job, but he did know that Steichen and Henry Allen Moe (whose voice on the Board of Trustees, though always extremely quiet, was listened to with a respect that very nearly approximated awe) were acquainted with a book he had done on the architecture of Louis Sullivan (*The Idea of Louis Sullivan*) and were impressed by it. "My basic perspective, though I knew something about museums, was that of a photographer," he says. After he graduated from the University of Wisconsin in 1948, he went to work for the Walker Art Center in Minneapolis (H. Harvard Arnason was then its director) as a photographer, but, as he explained, it was a small museum and he soon found himself "involved in various things." From there he went to teach photography at the Albright Art School in Buffalo, and it was there that he was fascinated by Sullivan's Guaranty Building and spent his spare time for two years (1951–53) taking pictures of it under all sorts of conditions. In the following year with the aid of a Guggenheim

Fellowship his photographic examination of Sullivan continued, and when the Chicago Art Institute decided to hold a centenary exhibition of Sullivan's work with Edgar Kaufmann as its guest director, Szarkowski went to work on the show. His book came out in 1956, the centennial of Sullivan's birth. Before he joined the Museum of Modern Art he had known Beaumont Newhall and had had an exhibition of his photographs at George Eastman House in Rochester, of which Newhall was the director.

"Before I came to the Museum," he said, "I never had the chance to work in a distinguished and sizable collection of photographs. Practically nobody had. Most museum photo collections are small and trivial or specialized in certain periods and without historical range, nothing in which one could immerse oneself and come out with a sense of what photography is about."

In 1958, under Steichen's aegis, the Museum had held a large exhibition of 500 photographs taken between 1838 and 1958 by 300 photographers in eighteen countries. All of them were selected from the Museum's collection, which in that year contained some 5,800 prints, 3,000 of which were in the "collection" and 2,800 in the "study collection." Szarkowski, in other words, had something to immerse himself in when he arrived four years later. Considering the billions of photographs that are taken each year and the millions that are published, 5,000 is a drop—less than a drop, a minim—in the bucket, even if the bucket were full of interesting photographs.

The collection was started in 1933, seven years before there was a Department of Photography, with a gift from Lincoln Kirstein of eighty photographs by Walker Evans of Victorian houses, a project, you will recall, that was initiated by Kirstein and financed by him. It took a firm step forward when Beaumont Newhall, at Barr's suggestion, put together his historical survey which was called *Photography, 1839–1937*. A great many prints collected for possible use in that show (and for the book that was published under the same title) were not included in the exhibition. "The collection started, I am sure," Szarkowski says, "before anybody had a philosophical framework or even an idea of what precisely was the purpose or function or goal or outline or rationale."

In some respects the very fact that the collection grew in a casual way rather than following an orderly and preconceived plan has given it a kind of variety and depth that it surely would not have otherwise had. Steichen, remembering that as a young man he had found that Stieglitz would not infrequently buy a couple of prints from a young photographer who he thought had some promise for $5.00 a piece, did the same thing (at the same price) many years later at the Museum. According to Szarkowski, there has been "a double standard in the photography collection, a double standard of formality in terms of acquiring work. So, much has been inexpensive, ephemeral, and gifts from photographers." It was in this manner that much of the study collection was assembled; very little of it went through the complex machinery of the Acquisitions Committee. "The thing is that you get the material first, and five or ten years later, if it looks good," Szarkowski says, "then it becomes part of the Museum's official collection.

"Steichen didn't add to the collection in any logical, coherent, systematic way," Szarkowski says, "but he added a lot of very wonderful stuff. He never cared where it ended up or if it was properly registered, and half the time it wasn't paid for or had been permanently 'borrowed' from the photographer, and the record-keeping and housekeeping of it was certainly not entirely methodical. His basic training was as an artist, not as a collector, and artists don't tend to treat art with the same respect as curators. In some respects Steichen treated the exhibitions with a good deal more casualness than we do now. To a considerable degree, the collection was a by-product of the exhibition program—but not entirely."

When Szarkowski first became the Director of his department, purchases for his collection had to follow the same procedure as the expensive purchases of paintings and sculptures, drawings and prints. One day a long meeting of the committee lasted on toward six thirty in the evening, and it came Szarkowski's turn to present the photographs he wanted to purchase for the committee's approval. "I happened to glance out of the window of the committee room," he said, "and there down in 53rd Street was a line of Rolls Royces and Cadillacs waiting to take the members of the committee home. I don't suppose their engines had been running all this time, but if they had, they would have been spending money on just gasoline a lot faster than I was on photographs. It was impressive that the committee really did listen to my spiel and really seemed to be interested. They didn't argue; they were even less sure of their expertise in photography than in painting and sculpture." This procedure no longer obtains; like other departments, Photography has its own committee with a trustee chairman and several other trustees and "interested persons" who approve or disapprove of the purchases that Szarkowski and his curators want to make. "He is very persuasive," a member of the committee told me. "We nearly always approve."

By 1964 the collection had grown to "about 7,000 prints," and they were housed in what is called the Edward Steichen Photography Center in the east wing of the Museum, which was opened that year. The department now had its own gallery, in which important photographs from the collection are shown on a more or less permanent basis, and a small gallery for temporary shows, often of the work of individual photographers, some very much alive, some long dead.

"In photography," Szarkowski says of the collection, "it is not the individual masterpiece but the accumulation of a photographer's work that matters most. It is not the individual statement, because the masterpiece does not have the same relevance in the non-traditional arts as it does in painting and sculpture, and one of the limitations of most photographic collections made by serious and competent people arises from the fact that they've tried to collect masterpieces only—great prints. That's the 'fine-art prejudice.' "

The most important, and surely the most expensive, single acquisition the Photography Department has ever made came in 1969, when it bought the negatives and prints of the modest French genius Eugene Atget from Berenice Abbott, herself a distinguished photographer many of whose prints are to be found in the Museum's permanent collection. It was not until the sale was very nearly consummated that Szarkowski discovered that the collection was half owned by Julien Levy. Levy, you will remember, was the first dealer to import the Surrealists to America in the early 1930s; he was also at that time the only dealer who held regular exhibitions by photographers. It was he who, with Kirstein, had put on the exhibition at the Museum of murals by painters and photographers in 1932 that caused a slight political flurry and evoked vigorous and non-political denunciation from very nearly all the critics. The story of how Levy and Abbott came to own the Atgets is worth telling briefly, as I do not believe it has been recorded elsewhere.

In 1927 Levy was in Paris working on a film with Marcel Duchamp in the studio of Man Ray, the photographer and Surrealist painter. His ambitions to be a film maker were never realized in any very great degree, but his fascination with the movies and with still photography led him not only to organizing a film society in New York with Iris Barry but to collecting and exhibiting photographs. When he was in Paris, he said, "I lived around the corner from Atget's studio and I used to go every day and buy a few prints. He wouldn't sell in quantity. He was a very old man and very charming. The prints cost five or ten francs apiece, and he would never sell more in a day than he was willing to reprint to put back in his scrapbooks. If he sold five in a day, he'd shut up shop." Berenice Abbott was in Paris when Atget died at the age of seventy-one. "She knew that I was interested," Levy says, "and she went over to the studio and the concierge was putting the collection into the garbage. He was closing the studio out. So Berenice screamed and said, 'What do I do? Who's in charge here?' Nobody seemed to be interested. The furniture was sold and the photographs were considered valueless. Berenice promised that within a week she'd get $1,000 for them, and she wired me. She didn't have a penny—could I find someone, etc., etc." Levy had inherited "a small nest egg" from his mother, and, he said, "that was the first time I drew anything on my mother's account." Levy and Abbott "went into partnership" on the agreement that Abbott would arrange to get the prints and the glass negatives to the United States. "I agreed to be anonymous," Levy said. For years Abbott used the pictures for lectures, and from many of the negatives she made prints which were sold in small portfolios, beautiful prints and now of considerable value as having been made by her, for she is a craftsman of great skill and perception. The Museum is said to have paid $80,000 for the collection "with the aid of a gift from Shirley C. Burden," a photographer and a member of the Museum's Photography Committee.

This is not the place for a critical evaluation of Atget. He spent years quietly going about Paris and its suburbs with his bulky camera, taking pictures of shop fronts, of scenes in parks, of trees, of unimportant cobbled streets and of boulevards, of occasional palaces and their gardens, of prostitutes and pushcarts and babies in prams. He was a documentary photographer to whom many later photographers owe a great debt. Berenice Abbott is one of them; Walker Evans and Brassaï and André Kertész are others. It is also said that the painters Utrillo and Braque used his prints as sources for their work, and in his sometimes eccentric and always personal vision the Surrealists found much to wonder at.

The basic reason for the photography collection's existence, according to Szarkowski, is "to exhibit it, to study it, to reproduce it, and above all to preserve it." From his personal point of view, an essential importance of the collection is "the accidental insights that come from accidental juxtapositions of prints that you'd never be smart enough to put together on purpose." Photography to him is "the only great nineteenth-century invention that has any muscle tone left. We've just begun to understand it," he said. "Maybe the automobile begins to be comparable. Photography is much more important than the steam engine or any of those things." He was a good deal more than half serious when he said this. The collection is used by photographers "who want to learn what their tradition is about," and on any given day there are usually as many as 1,000 photographs outside the Museum at loan exhibitions and another 2,500 in the Museum's own traveling shows. Furthermore, the collection is used as a research source by authors and publishers of textbooks, so that the department is also in "the cultural-history business," and it is in this sense a useful showcase for photographers and a means of steering business their way. As of 1972 the collection included about 7,000 prints, exclusive of the Atget collection, which numbers about 3,500 prints and 1,000 negatives, and approximately 4,000 prints in the study collection, and it grows, if not every day, at least every week.

In 1966, when Willard Van Dyke became Director of the Museum's Film Library, he promptly changed its name to the Department of Film. "Library" was a misnomer for a complex of activities which went far beyond the collection of film "footage" and its preservation and lending and rental services. "The name 'Library,' " said Margareta Akermark, Van Dyke's associate, "was originally used to persuade the film companies that we were a serious study center and not in competition with them. It sounded nice and stuffy." It was Iris Barry (Mrs. John "Dick" Abbott), whom we first encountered many chapters ago, who had been the clever, saucy, knowledgeable, and energetic guiding hand in the establishment of the Library. Miss Barry continued to run it, to write her astute and witty film notes, and to charm gifts out of film companies and movie stars. In addition to what she had got out of the Biograph Company's warehouses (those rare, in several senses, very early D. W. Griffith films), out of the Edison Company and Samuel Goldwyn and Harold Lloyd, gifts flooded in from the heroes and heroines of early filmdom—Douglas Fairbanks, Sr., and the dour William S. Hart, both of whom gave nearly every picture they had made, and Gloria Swanson, Colleen Moore, Douglas Fairbanks, Jr., Richard Barthelmess, and Irene Castle added their films by the mile.

"Iris knew a great deal about films," her friend Virgil Thomson, the composer and critic, said. "She had a sacred flame about them. She could look at films for days on end and actually remember everything she had seen. She got herself a kind of steady situation doing book reviews for Irita Van Doren at the *Herald Tribune* [where Thomson was music critic]. Iris said that the book reviews gave her far more prestige with the Museum's trustees than anything she knew about films. The Museum was always terribly aware of newspaper prestige."

Another, but far less close, friend, George Amberg, who had been the Curator of the Dance Archives at the Museum in the '40s and became a professor of cinema at New York University, said of Miss Barry not long before he died in 1971, "She was an extraordinary woman. To a certain extent, it is owing to Iris that I'm doing what I'm doing. She had a vision about what the cinema amounted to that was absolutely unequaled at the time, an insight into films that I don't think anyone has equaled. Her major program notes are still one of the great documents, a slender little book that unfortunately she didn't continue."

Film Notes was published as a sixty-eight-page *Bulletin* by the Museum in 1949. In a sense it is a brief history of the early cinema, with comments on many individual films. In the introduction Miss Barry wrote:

> When films of the past were first made available for study and re-enjoyment by the Museum of Modern Art in 1935, only then could a critique of the motion picture as a whole have been undertaken. Until that time, the art of the motion picture could never have possessed an art historian since films invariably vanished some months after their release and only recollections and opinions remained.
>
> First to be able to re-examine those actual works which, step by step, had created this new form of expression, the staff of the Museum's Film Library became necessarily its first commentators. . . .

Something less than a year after the *Film Notes* were published, Miss Barry left for Europe before Christmas 1950 and asked Margareta Akermark to look after the things in her apartment. Miss Akermark found them all carefully tagged with instructions as to what to do with them—"give this to so-and-so," "return this chair to so-and-so." Some mystery surrounds Miss Barry's departure, but Miss Akermark believes, as do other of her friends, that she had had a cancer scare and did not expect to return to the Museum. She did not, however, make her intentions known to d'Harnoncourt or to anyone in the Museum's administration. Allen Porter, who had worked for her when he first went to the Museum and before that when she and Julien Levy organized their short-lived film society, said, "She wrote the Museum that summer and said the Film Library could take its old film and stuff it.

The reason why was not clear." There appear to be almost as many stories about why she did not return as there are people who profess to know the answer. The one thing that most of them agree on is that she met a man in Marseille referred to as "Pierre Somebody," fell in love with him, and settled down in Fayence. For several years her name disappeared entirely from the publications of the Museum, but in 1956 she was referred to in the *Bulletin* as "the Library's European representative," as she was presumably chasing down rare documentary films for the collection. "She did go to the Cannes film festival the year after she left, to represent the Museum," Miss Akermark says. "It was really an excuse for the Museum to pay her a pittance."

During her tenure as Curator and then Director, the Library had grown far beyond the 16,000,000 feet of film of which she had boasted in 1941, only six years after she started collecting. Richard Griffith, her successor as Curator (no new Director was appointed until Van Dyke was hired by d'Harnoncourt), wrote in 1956: "During World War II the staff of the Library spent most of its time and energies supplying a host of government agencies with films for strategic, informational, and morale purposes." A very considerable part of this activity was, of course, helping Nelson Rockefeller with his friendship crusade in Latin America. After the war, collecting had picked up again and the problem of preservation of the Library's holdings had become crucial. "By the time of Miss Barry's retirement," Griffith wrote, "the Film Library was having to run very fast to stay in the same place." Indeed, he said, "The very success of the Film Library had saddled it with burdens it was unable to bear."

Bear both financially and emotionally, that is. It was a heart-breaking sight to watch reels of old film begin to ooze with a glutinous matter as the celluloid disintegrated into what eventually became a yellow dust. Transferring it was exceedingly expensive, and at that time even the new stock had no promise of longevity. Griffith estimated that it would cost $100,000 just to save the Biograph collection for a limited time. "In earlier years . . . duplicating at the first sign of trouble was regarded as a rare emergency measure," he wrote. "With the advancing age of the collection, the stage of emergency became chronic."

Such was the state of affairs when Iris Barry, for whatever reason, jumped ship. If she left trouble behind, she also left a most extraordinary legacy of influence. "No one else could have done what Iris did," Amberg said. "She had a sense of history. She made the young realize that this was a legitimate field of study, and she trained several very able young people herself. Jay Leyda, now at Yale, was one of them."

When the Film Library came into being in 1935 there was only one accredited academic course in motion pictures anywhere in the country. It was at the University of Southern California, Hollywood's close academic neighbor. By 1952 there were 575 film courses being given in more that fifty colleges and universities, and a decade later there were more than 800 such courses. As of this writing, there are well over 2,000. In 1970 New York University announced the first "Ph.D. program in cinema" and said, "At other universities, students interested in film scholarship on the doctoral level are required to take their degree under the supervision of other departments, such as English, drama or communications." They quoted Amberg, whose program it was and who had fought for and got approval for it from the New York State Board of Regents. He said: "This is the first time cinema studies has been fully recognized as a legitimate, autonomous academic subject." Two years later Willard Van Dyke remarked to me, "I have heard a horror story that there are some 300 or 400 candidates for Ph.D.'s in film at NYU!" (Actually there were about thirty.) When Iris Barry and Julien Levy started their short-lived film society, it was virtually unique in America. Now there are more than 4,000 active film societies; most of them are on college campuses, but many are under the aegis of museums or are quite independent community activities run by and for the delectation of dedicated film enthusiasts. Once the Museum's Film Library was the sole source of historic films; now there are dozens of commercial and non-profit sources for the rental of many of the same films.

In 1939 a meeting was held at the Museum of Modern Art at which "all the existing institutions organized the International Federation of Film Archives." The British Film Institute and the Cinémathèque Française in Paris had been founded after the Museum's Film Library and were, quite frankly, the offspring of its inspiration. In the federation are now represented most European countries (except France, whose director pulled out because, as Van Dyke says, "He couldn't run it the way he wanted to") and Iron Curtain countries and those in the Far East—about thirty in all. Until her death Miss Barry was the "lifetime founding president" of the federation.

Almost precisely thirty years after she had helped to found the Federation, word came in 1969 from Miss Barry to Margareta Akermark at the Museum that she was extremely ill and broke. She was in a hospital in Marseille suffering from the terminal phase of the cancer which had threatened her for nearly twenty years. The hospital, she said, was like a scene out of the once shattering film on the dehumanizing of

modern life, *Metropolis*. Miss Akermark, who had worked in the Film
Library when Miss Barry was still its head, turned to James Soby.
Soby and Warburg, Whitney and Philip Johnson and Nelson Rockefeller put together a fund to pay Miss Barry's hospital bills and to give
her such comfort as money could provide. They had all known her
from the beginning of her American career; they were all genuinely
fond of her, and they were all sensitive to the remarkable and far-
reaching circles of influence which had emanated from her sudden and
fortuitous descent upon New York in 1932. She died on December 22,
1969. "The brassy little girl from Birmingham," as Alistair Cooke
called her in a tribute in the *New York Times*, was seventy-four. "For
all the hundreds of thousands who now accept the Museum Film Department as an inevitable amenity of New York City," he wrote, "she
was their pioneer public servant. She would have laughed herself sick
at the thought."

Shortly after Miss Barry's "retirement," as her departure was officially called, a new invention changed the character of the film-preser-
vation problem. In 1952 a film stock called triacetate was invented that
chemists insisted would last "as long as the finest paper, or approximately four hundred years." According to Richard Griffith, the Film
Library was "aflame with this discovery" and set out to find the funds
to put all of its important films on this new material. $25,000 was
forthcoming from the Rockefeller Foundation if the Museum could
raise a similar amount. There followed the work of the usual committees, which put on benefit performances of films, raised $18,000
among themselves and friends, and even, it appears, a little money from
the film industry, not generally known for its support to cultural institutions, even when that would appear to be in its own long-range
interest. By 1956 the Committee for the Film Library Collection had
$52,361.50 in hand and donations were still coming in. Twelve years
later, though much film had been transferred to triacetate, Willard
Van Dyke wrote in *Arts in Society*, "Money must be forthcoming to
solve this problem or the problem will solve itself—through total disintegration."

Richard Griffith, Miss Barry's successor, was more housekeeper (in
many respects that is what a curator is supposed to be) than innovator.
"When Griffith came in," Amberg said, "Iris was such a powerful personality that all he could do was continue what she had started. He was
in a miserable position, but he kept things going." Miss Barry would
not recommend to d'Harnoncourt that Griffith be made Director of
the department, though her advice was sought. "He was a man of great

fairness," Amberg said. "He had good judgment but many blind spots, which Iris did not. There were thousands of films he simply rejected because he couldn't see them, and he finally was interested just in documentary." Van Dyke said of him, "During the War he worked in Capra's unit on the *Why We Fight* series, which was made by the Signal Corps. He had an encyclopedic memory for stock material. Officially, he resigned because of ill health. He stayed until November 1965. He had a little trouble with the sauce."

When Van Dyke became Director of the department in 1966, Margareta Akermark provided the essential continuity. Like many another mainstay of the Museum (including Iris Barry), she was encouraged to join the staff by one of the Museum's inner circle whom she met at a cocktail party. In her case it was Edward Warburg, and the year was 1941. She had just arrived by freighter from Sweden, where she was born ("Eddie said I was the last of the immigrants"). She had traveled extensively ("to learn languages"), but she had no knowledge of films. Her first job was at the information desk in the Museum's front hall (she found herself back in the hall many years later in 1972 for a few weeks when the Museum's security guards went on strike; this time she was selling tickets for the film showings), but not long after her arrival Miss Barry needed help in the Film Library. When Allen Porter was drafted into the Army, where he spent all of his time after basic training at Fort Dix working as a sergeant in the Signal Corps film center on Long Island, she took over his job as Circulation Director of the Film Library. Not only did she greatly extend the services of the Film Library to educational institutions and film societies, but she also became a dogged expert at unearthing rare films to fill gaps in the collection. For a time under Griffith she was the Library's Executive Secretary (providing the administrative skills which Griffith lacked), and on Van Dyke's appointment she became his Associate Director.

When Willard Van Dyke was appointed by d'Harnoncourt, who had spent a good deal of time scanning the field of possible candidates for the job, there were many raised eyebrows. They were raised not because Van Dyke was not liked and respected by those in the field but because, as one film educator said, "Some positions at the Museum are wide open to criticism, like the appointment of Van Dyke. It's impossible to do it right. You do it right for some and you do it wrong for others." It was considered "a peculiar choice" by some, primarily because of his reputation as "a documentary person." His first excursion into films (he had been a still photographer) was as a cameraman on *The River*, which was made in 1937 by Pare Lorentz with government funds and a score by Virgil Thomson. He had produced *The City* with Ralph Steiner two years later, which, according to the Museum's press department, "established him as a leader in the field of the documentary." His list of documentary "credits" is long and impressive, as are the film-festival prizes that they won for him. He had been producer-director of television films, films for industry, and films for foundations. He had given Hollywood a wide berth, though he is well versed in what it has produced. He had taught courses in the production of films at City College in New York and had been a visiting lecturer at NYU, Yale, Dartmouth, and Bradford College. There was no doubt, however, that he was a "documentary person." He was, moreover, considered to be rather conservative in his tastes, and though he had been much involved in films that were considered *avant-garde* in his younger days, there were those (as there are always those) who were afraid that he was no longer interested in the *avant-garde* and in what the young experimental film-makers were up to. They could have spared their misgivings.

In 1972 he said: "Last year we had a very small budget of $2,500 for purchasing films. Now we have no funds except a memorial fund established by the friends of the late Sidney Meyers, the director of *The Quiet One*, for the purchase of works by young film makers, and a number of years ago Joseph Strick gave us a thousand or two a year for several years for the same purpose." There was, he said, "an explosion of young film-makers about ten years ago," and there are now many young men and women who send their "stuff" to the Museum. "The way we respond to that," he explained, "is by a program we call 'Cinéprobe.' It's one of our most adventurous things, I guess. Not everything we show has to be a masterpiece, but it should be on an informational basis. With that in mind we offer the film-makers the opportunity to bring their films here, no matter how difficult or how unused the audience is to it. At five thirty on alternate Tuesdays they show films and we insist that they remain and face the audience and answer whatever questions are put to them. The audience is very rough on some of them, really rough. Last year Humble Oil put up some money so that we could pay the film-makers a small honorarium, which made us feel that we were not exploiting them and it added dignity to their position." Less experimental but sometimes just as controversial is a series called *What's Happening?* that is part of the Museum's film program. "They are films of a political nature or that deal with major problems," Van Dyke said, "black problems, student unrest, and that sort of thing. We're going to have to find some financing somewhere to keep that going." He seemed in no doubt that he would find it. Margareta Akermark has a favorite series of her own that runs in the midday on Wednesdays. "When the movie houses stopped running shorts," she said, "people never got to see that sort of thing, so we started a series of shorts, documentaries and art films, and they are very popular."

The audience for the film showings (the auditorium, several stories underground, holds 480) runs at a fairly constant rate. "Year in and year out," Miss Akermark said, "we can figure on about seventy-five percent capacity." They are all ages, but a number of older ones can be counted on to "come from across the street," from the branch public library, just as a way to kill time. "If we hold a series by one director, for example," she said, "the attendance goes right up. At the same time a new film by Jean-Luc Godard was showing to about four people in a New York commercial theater, we were showing Godard to standing room only. Not that we let people stand; when the auditorium is full, that's it. A guard had to threaten to remove Susan Sontag physically. She sat down in the aisle and said, 'I haven't seen this Godard, and I'm not going to leave.'" ("I'd bet she won," Van Dyke interjected.) "We were filled to capacity for every single Godard," Miss Akermark continued, "yet he's death at the box office. We showed every film he's ever made, including early shorts. It was young people who felt they had to see everything as part of their education." "We had a complaint from the teacher of a film class at Rutgers which met at two thirty," Van Dyke said. "Nobody'd shown up for the whole week! They were all here."

What this suggests about the impact of the Museum's film involvement on the young is self-evident and needs no exploring here, but the exhibition function and the collecting function of the Film Department are in many respects perfectly parallel with the same functions in the Painting and Sculpture Department. They are separate strands that are interwoven into a program without losing their individual identities.

The film collection, unlike the other collections, has been built almost entirely on gifts—gifts not of money but of films. It took persistence and patience rather than cash, for example, to find and identify prints of such early classics as Lumière's *Teasing the Gardener*, which was one of the very first films to be shown for an audience (it was projected in the 1890s in the basement of a Paris café); *A Trip to the Moon* by the ex-magician Georges Méliès, made in 1902; and Edwin S. Porter's *Great Train Robbery* of the following year, and his *Dream of a Rarebit Fiend*, made in nine days in 1906 at a cost of $350. What Miss Barry turned up in the first years of the Film Library was, Van Dyke says, "practically the whole history of the early days of the film," which included, "of course, the first masterpieces, Griffith's *Birth of a Nation* and *Intolerance*." Once it was in possession of a great deal of footage, the Film Library was then in a position to fill the gaps in its collection by swapping with other film archives. In this way, as more and more countries established their own libraries of film, more and more avenues of trading opened up. At first all the archives needed the Museum's Film Library, as it alone had materials they all wanted; they were delighted to swap their national product for what the Museum could supply. In general, this back-and-forth continues to be a most amicable sort of international exchange. "The Russian archives have given us ninety titles in exchange for our things," Van Dyke said. "One thing we have that they didn't have and very much wanted was the Eisenstein footage for *Thunder over Mexico*. Our first exchange with the Russians a few years ago was Griffith's *Orphans of the Storm*, and they had some Griffith films we didn't have. Then they sent us a print of *Earth* which had footage in it which had never been shown over there. It's an official agency called Gosfilmofund; it was one of the founding members of the International Federation of Film Archives. Our relations with them are excellent."

Van Dyke noted wryly that Gosfilmofund has more than 400 employees and the British Film Institute about 170, whereas his department has twenty, "including three projectionists who serve the staff and run the seventeen weekly auditorium screenings."

The collection has had its setbacks. In the early '50s the Film Library began to feel the hot breath of television, that hungriest of all media, on the back of its neck. At first the new industry came more or less hat in hand, seeking help in finding documentary films, a project in which the Library was pleased to cooperate. Soon after this, however, a member of a new trustee Committee on Films and Television was quoted in a Museum *Bulletin* as saying: "It would seem that the Film Library's very success in building a cultural interest in films of the past has brought in rivals whose interest in the field is purely commercial." Film companies that had given prints of their products to the Museum started to put restrictions on them; what they had considered dead or at least outdated suddenly became the apple of the bleary eye of the late-night TV audience. Broadcasters started to buy the rights to old "fiction" films, and Harold Lloyd, for example, who had been so open-handed in giving his films in the early days, discovered that they were worth a great deal more than just catnip to an in-group's nostalgia. "He released *The Best of Lloyd*," Van Dyke said, "and we lost *Safety Last* and some others, and his distributors wouldn't let him give them back to us. They belong to his estate now, and they have all sorts of plans for them."

In 1955 Richard Griffith had written in the Museum's *Bulletin*, "It is becoming increasingly plain to the industry at large that it is the Film Library's very use of once-famous, long-unseen films which has restored their value." It seemed then a high price for success, a bite to the feeding hand, but the effect of the Library's foresight has been a more important kind of harvest, the kind in which museums ostensibly are more interested, a harvest of cultural concern, enlightenment, and intellectual effectiveness.

The Film Department, for those who are interested in figures, now claims the possession of 22,000,000 feet of movie film which represents "between 5,000 and 6,000 items.". In 1971 its budget was close to $300,000, about $125,000 of which was recovered from rental of films. "One thing we don't get any financial credit for," Van Dyke explained, "is the number of people who come to the Museum only to go to the auditorium. If that were taken into account, the cost of running the department would be very small." The department has no budget for the purchase of films, but now and then someone gives a small general fund of a few thousand dollars, usually a trustee, for the Director to use at his discretion. Gifts of films, however, do continue, and the Museum had an uncommon windfall in 1967 when Janus Films, an importer of European movies, gave the Museum twenty-seven "major film classics," as they were called—and with reason. "That the directorial credits for these films should read like a who's who of contemporary cinema," Van Dyke wrote in the foreword to a pamphlet announcing the gift, "will come as no surprise to those aware of the Janus standard." Nine directors were represented, including Antonioni and Olmi and Truffaut, but by all odds the most impressive part of the gift was eighteen films directed by Ingmar Bergman and another for which he had written the script. "It might have taken the Department of Film years to collect such an impressive body of films," Van Dyke said, "and make it available for research and study."

Like the Photography Department, the Film Department has its study center available for qualified researchers, with "moviolas" (a gadget which makes it possible for an individual to look at a film or a section of a film as often as he may want; it sits on a table, is hand-operated, and is most commonly used by film-makers for editing).

The department also has a vast collection of movie reviews and clippings that date back to 1911. The collection of books on films is in the Museum Library, a situation Van Dyke would like to remedy. "It would be more convenient if the books were in the study center," he says. Some of the important books on the films have been written by members of the staff and published by the Museum itself. "We are not publishing as much as I'd like to see us," Van Dyke said. "But what can you do? One of the reasons is that everybody is overworked, and there's just no time for writing."

It is not possible in a brief space to give an accurate impression of the scope of the Film Department's riches, though the extent of its influence has, I hope, been suggested. The collection is deep historically and broad in the range of its concerns. Much of what it owns is of more historical than aesthetic interest, of more value as experimentation than as accomplishment. But it is all there in some degree—reportage, documentary, early serials (hard to come by, as at one time nobody, but nobody, thought they were worth anything), early and late animations, "epics" and "westerns," "masterpieces" and musicals and thrillers and casual comment, "art" films and films on the arts, abstractions, and scientific investigations, many kinds of "shorts," teaching films and propaganda films and films made for television—enough film to keep a single projector running eight hours a day for a year and a half.

And the search goes on. Masterpieces of the past are still missing (many Chaplin films, for example) and recent films are unavailable or too expensive to acquire. It might be said that the Museum's Film Department is not, and cannot afford to be, any more static than the product in which it deals.

Not long before Professor Sachs was first asked to be a member of the committee to found the Museum, he quite frankly did not in the least like modern paintings and drawings. Indeed, he detested them. "When I took French Painting at Harvard with Mr. Sachs," John McAndrew said many years later, "his last lecture stopped after about half an hour. He'd shown some Cézannes, saying that they had a feeling of great weight. Then he showed some van Goghs and a Gauguin and said, 'Gentlemen, we are being asked to admire the works of madmen and children. Class is over,' and stamped out of the room." Sachs had an eye for quality, albeit in some instances a reluctant one. "His conversion was absolutely genuine," McAndrew said. "He had already bought his neo-classic Picasso drawing of 'The Bathers,' which he hated when he first got it, but he knew it was a good drawing."

It was Sachs who in a modest sense founded the Museum's collection of prints and drawings. The month that the Museum opened in 1929 he presented it with four German prints, which he had purchased at the Weyhe Gallery in New York, and a few days later he bought for the Museum the first drawing that it owned, George Grosz's uncharacteristically sympathetic portrait of a woman, his mother-in-law, Anna Peters. Sachs's gesture was not forgotten. Thirty-two years later, in 1961, Blanchette (Mrs. John D., 3rd) Rockefeller, then President of the Museum, announced the formation of "The Paul J. Sachs Committee on Drawings and Prints," the function of which was to act, in a manner of speaking, as foster parents of the drawing-and-print collection. Sachs was no longer an active trustee; he was, as a number of good and faithful servants became, an "Honorary Trustee for Life." He was, however, named the chairman of the committee that bore his name, and he chose its members. For the occasion Mrs. Rockefeller recalled a statement that Sachs had made at the trustees' party at the time of the Museum's tenth anniversary when the "new" building was opened for the first time. "The Museum of the future," he had said, "should embrace in addition to traditional and well-understood museum functions those of study, teaching, reference, and research."

The first substantial leg up for the print-and-drawing collection was the Lizzie Bliss bequest, which had also been the first substantial gift of paintings. It was, Barr said, "the most valuable addition to the print collection during the Museum's first dozen years." There were fifty prints in all, "among them major works" by Cézanne, Renoir, Gauguin, and Redon. There were also a number of drawings, including the Seurat of his mother, subsequently sold at auction along with a number of other pieces from the Bliss bequest which, as we have noted, Barr felt were expendable. (William S. Lieberman, Chief Curator of Drawings, referred to it as "Seurat's greatest drawing. . . . It never would have been sold by me.") Other friends of the Museum enriched the print collection in the 1930s. J. B. Neumann, the dealer for whom Barr had such great respect and admiration, gave a series of Beckmann etchings in 1932 and later added portfolios of lithographs by Arp and Schwitters. Mrs. Saidie A. May gave "a dozen good French prints," and Ambroise Vollard, the Paris publisher and dealer, was so impressed by the exhibition of *Modern Painters and Sculptors as Illustrators* which Monroe Wheeler put on at the Museum in 1936 (Barr calls it "the Museum's first important print exhibition") that he and

Rouault gave the Museum a series of Rouault's prints, "31 very rare inscribed proofs for the great '*Miserere et Guerre*.'"

But as important as these gifts were, they were minor compared with the largesse with which Abby Rockefeller bestowed the collection in 1940. She had started collecting prints before she had any notion that she might be the founding mother of a modern museum, though the idea was surely in the back of her mind that there should be such a place. She started buying in 1927 under the eye of one of the family architects, Duncan Candler, whose advice she frequently followed. Once the Museum was opened and it seemed assured that it would persist, she began to buy prints on a rather grand scale with the Museum's collection in mind. In 1931 she gave Barr a "small fund" (it was $500) to enable him to buy prints in Paris which, she said, would eventually belong to the Museum. Her own primary interest was in prints by American artists, and she bought the graphic work of her friend Arthur B. Davies, Walt Kuhn, Stuart Davis, Kuniyoshi, and "scores of others." Lieberman, who knows the print collection better than anyone else and who knew Mrs. Rockefeller and how she bought for her collection, says: "She was quite of her own opinion, really quite frankly and truthfully a collector of great taste and foresight." Her biographer, Mary Ellen Chase, said much the same thing of her: "Her tastes in art were definite, even unyielding. She knew precisely what she liked and did not like; and she was not easily persuaded to alter her judgments. The pictures and prints which she bought, first of all for herself, reflect her own inclinations and enjoyments." The collection she presented to the Museum in 1940 consisted of 1,600 etchings, lithographs, dry-points, and woodcuts.

Before she gave the collection she made quite sure that it was going to be adequately cared for. When the new building was being planned in the late 1930s she urged on the Building Committee (and probably most directly on her son Nelson) the desirability of including a print room. Prints, she suggested, were within the range of small incomes, and in a "museum concerned with encouraging the widespread collecting of original works of art by living artists," as Barr paraphrased her wishes, there should be a place where prints could be studied and treated with the same curatorial respect as paintings. The Building Committee acceded to her wishes (as who in the Museum didn't?). Space was provided, but the collection went into storage for the next nine years because of World War II. "The space intended for it," Barr wrote, "was used instead for the study of films in connection with various defense and war offices."

Mrs. Rockefeller, however, was not deterred in her enthusiasm for buying prints for the Museum, or in the care and feeding of the collection. In 1945 she paid to have Carl O. Schniewind, of the Chicago Art Institute, catalogue the collection, and she took to buying prints again. She indulged her special delight in Frenchmen who were at work around 1900—men like Bonnard and Signac. "Her tastes were definite," Barr said, "but occasionally she would be persuaded to purchase works which she herself did not admire." It was obviously Barr who did the persuading, and one of these prints was Picasso's "Minotauromachy." It was this formidable monster that provoked her to say that it should be listed as purchased with a "Fund for Prints Which Mrs. Rockefeller Doesn't Like." In the following year, 1946, she gave a group of prints which, on the other hand, she very much liked—a collection of lithographs by Toulouse-Lautrec which Lieberman regards as one of the three greatest collections within the collection. The other two are very rare van Gogh prints ("Certainly no other museum in New York has them, and probably no museum in the country") and a collection of Edvard Munch, which Lieberman himself assembled.

Early on the morning of April 5, 1948, Mrs. Rockefeller died of a heart attack at her apartment at 740 Park Avenue. She and her husband had returned a few days before from a "winter vacation," as the *New York Times* called it, in Tucson, Arizona. They had been there about five weeks. Mrs. Rockefeller's self-imposed duties as an especially dedicated and operative chairman of and server on boards and committees (she might have been called an executive philanthropist) had taken some toll of her strength, and the winter vacation was intended to be a restorative—not, apparently, that she was worried about herself, nor was anyone worried about her. Almost the minute they got home she and her husband went to their place at Pocantico Hills, and two days later on Sunday the Rockefeller clans gathered for a family reunion—five Rockefeller sons, a daughter (Mrs. Abby Rockefeller Milton Pardee), and eighteen grandchildren. Mrs. Rockefeller and her husband drove back to New York that evening, and early the next morning Mrs. Rockefeller was seized. The family physician was called and he and Mr. Rockefeller were with her when she died at eight o'clock. She was seventy-three.

Mrs. Rockefeller never saw the completed print room for which she had successfully lobbied with her friends, her son, and her curatorial conspirators, but when it came into being in 1949 it bore her name—The Abby Aldrich Rockefeller Print Room. She had bestowed on the Museum a great deal more than works of art. She had firmly established it as a family responsibility, which has been assumed most notably by two of her sons and one of her daughters-in-law: Nelson and Blanchette as Presidents and the youngest of her sons, David, as Chairman of the Board. She had also left the Museum a residue of humor and modesty, which it needed and could use more of, and a wealth of stories of her generosity to artists as well as to members of the Museum staff. Early in the Depression she had given a number of artists jobs to keep them busy and the wolves from their doors, even if in retrospect they seem rather odd and inappropriate assignments. She paid Ben Shahn $250 apiece to paint portraits of the Rockefeller horses; Marguerite Zorach, the wife of the sculptor, she commissioned to do an embroidered portrait of the Rockefeller family out of doors at The Eyrie in Maine. She had Charles Sheeler painting pictures of Williamsburg. "She deplored the long period between creation and appreciation," Aline Saarinen wrote of her in *The Proud Possessors*, "and later, when she got interested in founding the Museum of Modern Art, her major hope was that the Museum would close that tragic gap."

One gap she was never able to close was that between her husband's view of art and her own. "We never lack material for lively arguments," her husband said. "Modern art and the King James Version can forever keep us young." One day during the war she invited a couple of friends to lunch in the Museum garden and see the *Airways to Peace* exhibition. "She was always trying to get John to take an interest in the Museum," a friend of hers recalls, "and after lunch she said, 'Now we must go up and have a look at the war show with the maps and all that. John, I think you'd like to have a look at that.' And suddenly he panicked, and was rather rude and hurried away. Apparently he realized that he had been rude to his wife, and the next morning he gave her—that is, he gave the Museum—the other end of the garden." This was the piece of land that Mr. Rockefeller had lent to the Museum just a week or so before the new building opened and which Barr and McAndrew had stayed up nights to make into a garden. Mrs. Rockefeller had, it is said, always been very sure that the money she spent on her own collection of modern paintings and prints was "Aldrich money" and not "Rockefeller money," and Aline Saarinen notes that "her total purchasing was probably less than the $1,200,000 which her husband allegedly spent on the Unicorn Tapestries" which he gave to the Metropolitan Museum for his (and its) medieval collection at The Cloisters.

When the new print room opened in 1949 William S. ("Bill")

Lieberman, who was twenty-five, was appointed its Curator. He had gone to Swarthmore College, and after his graduation in 1943 and before going to Harvard to take Sachs's museum course, he applied for a summer job as a volunteer at the Museum. He was put to work for Monroe Wheeler in the Exhibitions and Publications Department doing odd jobs. He came back to the Museum two years later, and this time he was hired as an assistant by Barr, who had emerged from his doghouse in the corner of the library early in 1947 with the title of Director of the Museum Collections. With the exception of Barr and Dorothy Miller, there is no one who knows the Museum's painting and sculpture collections better or who has worked with them longer than Lieberman, and there is surely no one who knows the collection of prints, illustrated books, and drawings as he does. There is, indeed, scarcely any aspect of the Museum's programs in which he has not had a role to play. He was worked on a great many big and important shows, such as the Modigliani exhibition as long ago as 1951, more recently the Jackson Pollock and Dubuffet shows in 1967 and 1968, and still more recently the intensely nostalgic, impressive, and entertaining exhibition of the *Collections of Gertrude Stein and Her Family* in 1970. He has also put on dozens and dozens of smaller exhibitions, of which eighty-odd have been prints and drawings, and he has written books for the Museum, some slim and some substantial, in connection with exhibitions he has directed. A bibliography of Lieberman's output would include as well a long list of *Bulletin* articles and catalogue notes, magazine and newspaper articles, and several fat volumes: *Picasso: Blue and Rose Periods* (1954), *Matisse: Fifty Years of His Graphic Art* (1956), and *Edvard Munch* (1969).

Bill Lieberman is a slender, rather elegant man who speaks with what might be characterized as a New York private-school drawl. He is careful not to single out those who have been especially generous to the Museum's print collection lest, it would appear, someone else might be offended by not being mentioned. ("You will find their names listed in the *Bulletins*," he says.) In his long tenure at the Museum he has watched a good many curators and three Directors of the Museum come and go, and has seen his own position of importance wax on some occasions and wane on others. He has, by his own account, raised a good deal of money with which to buy objects for the painting and sculpture collections and also for the print and drawing collections, and it is apparent that he enjoys the game. His biography as released by the Museum's Publicity Department says: "Mr. Lieberman collects 18th-century silver boxes, Japanese prints of the Meiji era, and first editions of one British and two American authors." It is characteristic that he does not say who they are. He engages actively, and evidently with wit, in intra-museum politics, and he is a disappointed man who is said to play his cards close to his chest.

Nine years after Lieberman took over the Print Room the collection had more than doubled, and a Museum *Bulletin* in 1958 declared that "although the Print Room measures only 500 square feet, it houses the world's most important collection of modern graphic art." In 1972 Lieberman said, "The collection now is the greatest collection of twentieth-century prints in the world." If the collection has a weakness, which Lieberman says it has, it is in late-nineteenth-century prints. He has no endowed funds with which to purchase prints and drawings, but he has a gift for finding what he needs among Museum friends and trustees and most especially from the Rockefellers (Nelson, Blanchette, and David), who feel it incumbent on them to carry on Abby Rockefeller's project.

Mrs. Rockefeller's enthusiasm for prints was more than matched by Professor Sachs's enthusiasm for drawings, and the drawing gallery in the Museum is named for him. No one at the Museum, to my knowledge, has claimed that the Museum has "the greatest collection of modern drawings in the world," the claim it makes for its painting and sculpture and print collections, though it might be difficult to dispute the claim were it made. The print and drawing collections of most art museums must of necessity take a far wider historical view with, quite probably, a less doctrinaire definition of what is "modern." A great collection (or a terrible one) cannot be made except by eyes that are not only expert but opinionated, and no one will contest the assertion that the eyes which have made the Museum's collection are both. "I believe in a study collection that *is* a study collection," Lieberman says. "For instance, we have a large collection of Rodin forgeries. I cannot believe in a study collection that is a grabbag of crap. In the drawing collection there is a lot of stuff that no one will ever study. But there are some drawings of no great quality as drawings that are of interest as studies for paintings and sculptures in the collection. The print collection, on the other hand, is like a library. I consider the whole print collection to be a study collection."

Bernard Karpel, the Librarian of the Museum, appeared a long time ago in these pages. It was he who took over the Library from Beaumont Newhall when the Department of Photography became official in 1940. It was he who said, "The very fact that books accumulated in what might be called a disorderly way at the beginning was actually a great benefit. We have many things that a proper and orderly accumulation never would have had."

Karpel is a professionals' professional, a stocky, round-faced, and extremely—almost overly—articulate man with iron-gray hair. He talks not just in whole, punctuated sentences but in organized paragraphs, and makes eminently good sense. He remembers everything and, if the two can be divided, is more bibliographer than librarian at heart. He has made dozens of bibliographies of artists for Museum catalogues, and has undertaken to do a bibliography of all American art for the Archives of American Art, a bureau of the Smithsonian Institution. He first came to the Museum on loan for ninety days from the Art Division of the New York Public Library in 1939 at the invitation of Iris Barry, who, he says, "wasn't talking to Newhall." His stay lasted a good deal more than ninety days. With a hiatus to go to war from 1942 to 1945 he was a constant, dogged fixture. In his first year, he recalls, Newhall had worked out "a budget for everything of $1,500—books, periodicals, binding, supplies." This was for 1940–41. "But when I came," Karpel says, "the eminent gentlemen on the fifth floor cut it in half to $750 for the year." He recommended that he be allowed to sell what he called "non-modern art books, like *Egyptian Wall Paintings*," and, he says, "The trustees reluctantly agreed, and that's how I made up my other $750."

During his tenure he assembled "the greatest library on modern art in the world." It was not he, however, who so described it to me, not he nor another member of the staff. It was a distinguished English critic who comes from London a couple of times a year to work where he knows he will find the books and periodicals he needs for his researches in modern art. Moreover, Janet Flanner, who for many years has been *The New Yorker*'s Paris correspondent, writing under the name Genêt, said of the Museum Library when she was working on "profiles" of Matisse and Braque, "I suppose the material is somewhere in Paris, but you can't find it. Everything I needed was in the Modern. Besides, it's the only library in the world where they let me smoke."

By no means all of the superlatives about the Museum's collections come from within.

*I am sure that in the long run we will obtain that
stability which possibly precedes ossification.*
A. CONGER GOODYEAR *in a letter to* PAUL J. SACHS,
December 28, 1932

Chapter XVII *Happy Birthday*

It took the Museum of Modern Art a year to celebrate its twenty-fifth birthday ("a fine youthful age," the *Herald Tribune* said), and it started with a party. It was a very wordy party such as only institutions on anniversaries ever think is a pleasure. It took place on the afternoon of October 19, 1954, in the newly redesigned garden behind the Museum on the land that Mr. Rockefeller had given to make up for his gaucheness to his wife. Philip Johnson, the chairman of the Museum's Architecture Committee but not yet a trustee, had completely redone the place with reflecting pools and fountains, birch trees and weeping beeches, and it not only looked elegant and civilized, but the sound of water struggling against the noise of traffic was friendly and almost suburban. A platform was built against the high wall of glazed grayish brick at the back of the garden, and from there issued forth a river of invited congratulations and self-congratulations presided over by William A. M. Burden. A trustee of the Museum since 1944, Burden had succeeded Nelson Rockefeller as President in 1953. The audience he faced was carefully chosen—trustees, benefactors, directors of other museums, foundation executives, "important friends," critics, and a sprinkling of scholars and artists. "No matter whom you invite," Allen Porter, who spent most of the afternoon shaking hands with arriving guests as the "official greeter" of the Museum, said, "there are always some gripes and hurt feelings."

349

As is customary on such occasions in such well-connected institutions, there was a statement from the President of the United States. It was Eisenhower at that time. "We all worked on his statement," Porter recalls, "and we sent him several to choose from." (The Museum's board fairly groaned with good Republicans who reinforced their loyalties with their checkbooks; two of them were rewarded with ambassadorships—Whitney to England and Burden to Belgium.) The statement the President chose was about 300 words long and its theme was "Freedom of the Arts": ". . . freedom of the arts is a basic freedom," he said, "one of the pillars of liberty in our land. . . . As long as artists are at liberty to feel with high personal intensity, as long as artists are free to create with sincerity and conviction, there will be healthy controversy and progress in art." The dense political haze which had made Senator Joe McCarthy a prime enemy of most of the intellectual community had begun to dissipate (the famous "McCarthy hearings" were over and the Senate was then debating the question of censoring him), but though Eisenhower had taken a stand against "the book burners" and had attacked "thought control" with the arrows he shot in the air but intended for McCarthy, the memory of "suppression" and of "blacklisting" was still fresh in the minds of the artistic and academic worlds. Words about intellectual freedom from high places were welcome.

In addition to the President's statement there were six speeches. August Heckscher, then chief editorial writer for the *Herald Tribune* (he many years later became Mayor Lindsay's official keeper of the city's culture and Commissioner of Parks), talked philosophically about "Modern Art and Mid-Century Development," and remembers the occasion as one of the "most successful speeches I ever made." He was followed by Dag Hammarskjöld, the Secretary-General of the United Nations, a most articulate and perceptive man, who spoke of art with the same modest assurance with which he spoke of politics. "Modern art teaches us," he said, "to see by forcing us to use our senses, our intellect and our sensibility to follow on its road of exploration." Then he quoted Ezra Pound, something a good many presumed liberals still cannot bring themselves to do, confusing art with politics: "It makes us seers—seers like Ezra Pound when, in the first of his Pisan Cantos, he senses 'the enormous tragedy of the dream in the peasant's bent shoulders.' Seers—and explorers—these we must be if we are to prevail."

When it became René d'Harnoncourt's turn to speak on "The Museum 1929–1954," he managed in about ten minutes to touch all the bases. He scurried from the purpose of the Museum's founders to the collections, from there to the Film Library, and then to Publications (". . . initiated by exhibition catalogues, [the publications program] has grown to include works on individual artists and movements until it has become a representative documentation of the art of our day"). Next was a sentence which bowed in the direction of the circulating exhibitions, which had been seen in "over 800 communities in the United States and thirty-nine foreign countries." Then came "good design" (though he did not call it that), the educational programs in and out of the Museum "for a more fruitful and deeper enjoyment of the arts." (He conscientiously avoided the shibboleth "art appreciation.") Before he had finished he had also nodded to the exhibitions of housing and city planning, to the war programs and the Veterans' Art Center, and "the establishment of an extensive international program of exhibitions," by which he meant the labors of the International Council. He thanked without naming names all sorts of benefactors, committees, foundations, and members for their financial support, and concluded by saying that the Museum "had grown . . . into an institution of broad scope and varied activities. It now looks forward to a future in which it hopes to continue and increase its public services in a spirit of dedication to its original purposes, carried forward with awareness of the needs of a changing world."

If d'Harnoncourt touched all the bases, Burden and Paul Sachs placed flowers in the buttonholes of all the trustees (or most of them) and the heads of all departments, past and present. They were obviously taking no chances on repeating "Nelson's goof," as Rockefeller's failure to mention Conger Goodyear on the occasion of the tenth anniversary was called. Goodyear got mentioned this time (". . . who captained the ship with vigor, humor, and common sense for the first ten crucial years"). Stephen Clark was "wise and sensitive," Jock Whitney was "quiet and modest," and Nelson was praised for his "energy, imagination, and drive." Barr got more than a single flower; his was a horseshoe of blossoms. His was "single-minded devotion," and he, moreover, was "that dedicated and courageous scholar who is generally recognized as one of the world's greatest authorities on modern art." D'Harnoncourt, on the other hand, was a "genial giant" with "creative imagination, tact, humor and all-around ability."

When Burden sat down, Sachs talked about "The Early Years," called himself "an old retired museum man," and spoke of what had been "the crying need for its creation." "Twenty-five years ago," he said, "we were all, as a matter of course, reading modern literature;

we were listening to modern music; *but* in spite of the excitement engendered by the Armory Show of 1913, our country was, on the whole, antagonistic to modern art." He then passed out his posies with special attention to the founding mothers (Rockefeller, Bliss, and Sullivan), to Goodyear, and to Clark, who "more than any other single trustee, gave his time and thought to keeping this Museum going during the war years when the younger men were away." He reached back and mentioned some of the young men and women who had helped to shape the place and who had quit or died or been fired—Jere Abbott, Sweeney, Newhall, Dick Abbott, Iris Barry, McAndrew, Elizabeth Mock, and Cahill—and some who had stuck—Dorothy Miller, Philip Johnson, and Barr and d'Harnoncourt, of course. He did not mention Monroe Wheeler, but then Wheeler was not a scholar and Sachs had little use for museum men who were not scholars. He should have, because he mentioned the "steady stream" of "sound publications" over which Wheeler had presided.

It was what the Museum had done to change the climate, however, about which he was most concerned and was most eloquent. "They have continued to take chances," he said. "They have avoided the dangers that dog the footsteps of the complacent. They have made the Museum a telling instrument in the field of general education." He spoke more accurately than many museum trustees and directors would have conceded when he said, "Their influence and example have liberalized the policies of every one of our leading museums—even the most complacent." In his final burst of—well, complacency he said:

> Through courageous, audacious and crusading leadership, the Museum has changed the climate of public opinion from one of hostility to one that is today open-minded and receptive to all aspects of modern art. No longer is the new dismissed with contempt and ridicule. Instead, there is in the art world of America an attitude of curiosity, reflected in books and periodicals, in the daily press—yes, even in the universities.

The final speaker, Mayor Robert Wagner of New York, who had been given both a topic and a prepared speech by the Museum—"The Museum and the City"—failed to turn up on time to give it. Somebody read it for him, but there would have been small loss if it had been skipped entirely. It had to do with how the Museum was "a typical New York institution," which must have been the slip of somebody's pen. The Museum never liked to be thought of as typical of anything. Unique, of course; typical—well, hardly.

In his speech Burden, with a tact not always characteristic of museum presidents, had spoken warmly not just of art but of artists, a number of whom, as we have noted, had actually been invited. "In our community," Burden said, "the artist is, by necessity, the leader whose genius we follow. The vigor and excellence of his work is the life blood of all our endeavors. If we take pride in our achievements, it is pride in transmitting his message."

The transmission of the artists' message filled three floors of the Museum on that afternoon and for several months. Barr and Dorothy Miller had put together an exhibition of what they regarded as the cream of the Museum's collection of paintings, and Lieberman had put up a show of American prints. Sculpture was in the garden, which, like the Print Room, was named in memory of Abby Aldrich Rockefeller, as was inevitable. A passing show, or even a series of passing shows, was not to be the monument to this august moment in the Museum's history, this moment which, though it did not seem so at the time, was a watershed in its career. The monument was a book called *Masters of Modern Art*, and monumental it was.

The book, which was printed in Holland, contained seventy-two tipped-in color plates and twice as many black-and-whites. Barr was its editor, and the text of the main part (the section on paintings, sculpture, drawings, and prints) was written by him with occasional paragraphs by William Lieberman. It is lively, anecdotal, precise, and without a trace of pomposity or obscurantism. It is, moreover, filled with quotations from the artists whose work is illustrated, and in most cases their words attempt to explain the pictures and sculptures that are reproduced. They are frequently less revealing than their authors meant them to be and far less telling than Barr's comments. Each curatorial department of the Museum has a section of the book devoted to the "modern" development of the art with which it is concerned (architecture, industrial design, film, photography, graphic design and typography) and each is illustrated with examples from the Museum's collections. The book is a model of art-book making; the text is carefully adjusted so that each object discussed in it is always next to its illustration. It is, in other words, what one would expect of an expensive birthday cake—delicious, filled with prizes and almost, but not quite, too pretty to consume. The nub of the matter is in the Foreword over the name of John Hay Whitney, Chairman of the Board. After noting that the book "deals with many branches of contemporary visual art produced in forty countries over

the past seventy-five years," Whitney says: "That it is possible to select the illustrations for this book entirely from the Museum's own
collection is a matter of considerable pride to us." In other words, the
Museum was in possession of much of the best of all that mattered in
the arts of the last seventy-five years, and if it did not have all of the
best, it had by inference more of the best than anybody else.

According to d'Harnoncourt, by the time of its twenty-fifth anniversary the Museum had "organized some 820 exhibitions in all
branches of the modern visual arts and their relevant backgrounds."
Only 567 of these had been shown at the Museum; the other 253
had been traveling exhibitions prepared by the Museum. So far as the
fame of the Museum was concerned and the spread of its influence, the
traveling shows were as important as the others.[1] In its first year the
Museum installed nine exhibitions; in its twenty-fifth year it had
nineteen. In the first year it had fewer than a dozen employees; in its
twenty-fifth its payroll was over 200. In its first year the Museum was
one cohesive, overworked department; twenty-five years later it had
burgeoned into eleven "curatorial and program departments" that included Education, Circulating Exhibitions, the Library, and Television
as well as those mentioned above, and there was a host of men and
women (121 to be precise) working at business, publicity, security,
conservation, and housekeeping jobs. It was far from the cozy madhouse it had once been. In its first year, exhibitions had cost just under
$20,000 to gather and mount, and it had cost about $15,000 to produce
the catalogues to go with them. Twenty-five years later the "curatorial and educational" expenses (which included publications) were
$814,868 and the total expenses for operating the whole place had
risen from $100,000 to just short of $1,500,000. In both the first and
the twenty-fifth years there was an excess of income over expenses
(much of the income was, of course, the donations of trustees), a situation which must make the administrators and trustees of the Museum
today wistful indeed.[2]

The Museum was riding the crest of its popularity and influence.
Barr and d'Harnoncourt, Wheeler and Johnson, Soby and Dorothy
Miller and Andrew Ritchie were at the peak of their prowess and their

1 Early in 1972 the number of in-museum exhibitions had reached 1,000.
2 In 1929–30 about 85 percent of income was "contributions" from trustees
and "friends"; in 1953–54 only about 21 percent came from similar sources. The
rest came from admission fees, memberships, publication and sales, circulating
exhibitions, "special grants" rental of films, and endowment income. The surplus
in 1930 was $23,167.58. In 1954 it was $3,818. These balance sheets appear in the
Museum's *Bulletin*, Vol. 22, No. 1–2 (Fall-Winter 1954).

influence on opinion. They were, moreover, supported by some comparative youngsters of promise, such as Arthur Drexler and William Lieberman, Margareta Akermark and Mildred Constantine, and the idea of retirement was as remote as the idea that the Museum might one day seem out of date. In the late 1930s some of the young staff had talked about how they might retire when they got to be fifty, thinking that by then they would no longer be young enough to keep their fresh point of view; they even went so far as to consult an insurance expert on retirement funds. "The insurance people thought we were nuts," one of them recalls. As they grew older, they evidently thought they had been nuts, too. In their fifties they had never been more confident.

With good reason. The Museum's influence was felt—indeed, it was seen—in every corner of the art world. Through Victor d'Amico's National Committee on Art Education, the teaching of art in a great many schools had already been radically changed. Barr's method of hanging pictures by their relationship to each other rather than their comparative square footage had changed many museum galleries from dead symmetrical arrangements to inviting, intellectual challenges. D'Harnoncourt's imaginative and masterly techniques for showing objects in relation to their origins and cultures and his remarkable sense of drama-without-corn had taken objects out of glass cases and given them light and breathing space and had taught a permanent lesson, better learned in some places than in others, to museums everywhere. The circulating exhibitions had made once-shocking modern architecture and the distortions and abstractions of modern sculpture and painting nearly as familiar in Kansas City as in New York, if not necessarily as acceptable or as fashionable. The Museum, and most particularly Barr, with its catalogues had set a new standard for museum publishing. "I believe," the director of a university art department said, "that Barr should go down in history if for no other reason than for the revolution he brought about in making the catalogue of an exhibition a basic part of the exhibition itself and a permanent record for posterity with all the bibliographic apparati, etc." It was Karpel's dogged and imaginative development of the Museum's Library and his skill as a bibliographer that made this kind of innovation possible.

The Museum had made the films a legitimate subject for study and, moreover, taught a large and unacademic public the pleasures of early and foreign films and revived the satisfactions, grave and hilarious, which had been hidden away in cans in movie-company warehouses. It did much the same for photography, not just by revealing prints of the nostalgic past and promoting what it considered best of the present, but by giving photography the dignity of an art which, like the best of journalism and belles-lettres, has more than passing impact and validity. The Museum had, indeed, taken on "the environment" long before the word became a cliché and a political bandwagon. It had dealt seriously and attractively (and sometimes dogmatically) with architecture and city planning, with the quality of posters for highways, and with the design of the automobiles that traveled them.[3] It had concerned itself with the intimate environment—with domestic architecture on a small scale, with textiles and furniture, with the mechanical and hand tools that make servantless life workable and pleasing. "You can make art out of anything," a character in *Cadwallader*, a satirical novel, said, "out of marble or thread or gold or earth or wood or anything but meat and cooked vegetables." The Museum had tried them all except meat and cooked vegetables and had made them socially acceptable. It had made modern art chic as well as fashionable. It even provided meat and cooked vegetables for its members in the restaurant on its sixth floor, and some of the members preferred the food to the art. In 1953 *The New Yorker* reported overhearing a lady who was going down in the elevator from the members' penthouse say, "Someday we *must* get off and look at the pictures." In 1954 the Museum had members on every continent and in extremely remote cities. There were 21,474 of them in all, quite possibly the largest membership of any art museum anywhere at the time.

A Yale professor who participated in the Seminars in American Studies in Salzburg in the mid-'50s discovered, to his surprise, as he wrote to me, "that all the students [who were Europeans] regarded the Museum of Modern Art as the real beacon of American culture and the major force in establishing a receptive audience for contemporary forms of expression throughout the civilized world." So did a great many American students who first encountered not only the works of Picasso and Braque and Matisse in the Museum's traveling shows, but those of Cézanne and van Gogh and Gauguin. It was a time in which the Museum seemed more interested in interpreting history than in trying to make history. ("When they stopped recording history and began making it," an artist said to me, "they entered the world of fashion.") It was a time when young artists everywhere in America looked, if not for inspiration, at least for information about what was officially considered new and significant in their profession

3 Before 1954 the Museum had held two exhibitions of automobiles. "All were selected . . . primarily for their excellence as works of art."

—largely as it was practiced in Europe. That is not to say that the Museum ignored the arts of America, but that was not where its heart seemed to be. In the early missionary days of the Museum, when it was struggling to become the established voice of authority, even though it may not have admitted to itself that it was, many of the young rallied to help it become so. They crowded into its shows (of course they still do) because they knew they would find there revelations that they would find nowhere else—which cannot be said of the Museum today. The Museum was a cause and a mission, and so it was a center for passionate loyalty, an emotion far different from the compassionate loyalty with which many of its very old friends regard it today. In the early days, like wheat germ, it was "good for you"; like an intellectual and aesthetic roughage, it kept the bowels of the mind open. It was the place to go. As Monroe Wheeler said, "When I was a young man in New York, people used to meet their dates under the clock at the Biltmore Hotel. Now they say, 'I'll meet you at the Museum,' and *the* museum they mean is this one." It was also a place to be seen, especially at the evening openings, where the costumes of the well-to-do young were often eccentric (but never sloppy) and tiaras and white ties were not uncommon. There was an air on such occasions of the bishop and his canons welcoming their patrons and the faithful congregation into the cathedral close.

The fact that the Museum was a moving force in the creation of private collections quite obviously had an effect on the market for art, on the careers of artists, and on the profits and preferences of dealers. Barr and Dorothy Miller went shopping for the Rockefellers and the Whitneys and for other trustees, sometimes demanding, as Julien Levy recalls from his days as a dealer, a "museum discount" for their patrons, presumably on the assumption that perhaps the Museum would become the ultimate home of what they bought. (In many cases, of course, it has.) Curators, indeed, used to go "Christmas shopping" for trustees. What they bought mattered, and not just to those they bought it for. "If Alfred Barr got off a plane in Rome or New Delhi and, having a few hours, went into town," a retired museum director once said to me, "and visiting a local gallery, spoke well of an artist's work, the little artist became a great one instantly. The dealer quickly added three zeros to his prices; museums and collectors rushed to buy." He added what many artists have felt achingly in their bones to be true and have said so. "The Museum's approval was obligatory if an artist was to have a career." Aline Saarinen wrote in *The Proud Possessors* at just about the time of the Museum's twenty-fifth birthday: "Yet the Museum of Modern Art has been and continues to be the most ardent champion of modern art and the most important tastemaking institution in the world. No single advisor, including Berenson, has ever played so influential—or often so dictatorial—a role for so many collectors."

Such, briefly, was the status of the Museum at the time of its birthday party—exceedingly influential, gratified by its international reputation, proud of its collections and its constituency, with a new garden and a new wing (the annex called the "21 Building" at 21 West 53rd Street) [4] to its building, a comparatively peaceable (if badly underpaid) staff, no noticeable competition from any other institution, and a miraculously balanced budget. It felt called upon to brook no questions of its intentions or of its authority. It was a moment for rejoicing, or so everyone there seemed to think, for making more ambitious plans than ever, for confidence in the future. No one at the birthday party in the garden could have foreseen how different would be the mood and manners, the morality and crusades of the urgent and assertive '60s from those of the optimistic '50s, or the trial by fire which the Museum was about to face.

4 It was built in 1951 with funds from the estate of Grace Rainey Rogers.

*As I emerged from Elizabeth Arden's at noon
yesterday my heart fell into my boots. . . . The
Museum is lucky to have saved so much. After all,
there might have been civil war with Chicago!*
MRS. JOHN WISE *in a letter to the Museum,*
April 16, 1958

Chapter XVIII *Fire!*

On April 15, 1958, shortly after noon, a trustee of the Museum of Modern Art who had heard a news flash on the radio that the Museum was in trouble telephoned to find out what was going on.

"We're having a fire today, sir," the unflappable switchboard operator said. "Please call back tomorrow."

Daniel Catton Rich, the director of the Art Institute of Chicago, and one of the most highly regarded museum men of his day, was sitting in his office with his curators at just about this same time. He was holding a staff meeting. The door burst open without warning and Rich looked up to see the institute's public-relations head. She looked thunderstruck.

"Alfred Barr just called to say the Modern Museum's on fire," she said. "I thought you'd like to know."

Rich had lent Seurat's *"La Grande Jatte"* to the Museum of Modern Art, Seurat's masterpiece, the apple of the Art Institute's eye, the example Barr had used in a money-raising pamphlet in 1936, as we noted, to demonstrate how the market value of modern paintings could miraculously skyrocket. Frederick Clay Bartlett, who gave it to the Art Institute, had paid $24,000 for it and a few years later had turned down an offer of $450,000 from a French syndicate.[1] The picture was given to the Art Institute with the stipulation that it could be lent only once to another institution, and it was insured on this occasion for $1,000,000. Rich called the Museum of Modern Art at once and got no answer.

"So I called the Dorset Hotel, where I usually stayed in New York," he recalls. "It is just down the street from the Museum garden on 54th Street. The manager said, 'Yes, there are fire engines in the street. I'll go look.' He came back in a minute and said, 'Yes, the Museum does seem to be on fire.' "

Rich and the institute's conservator, Louis Pomerantz, were on a plane to New York within the hour and in 54th Street by mid-afternoon.

" 'We won't discuss this on the plane,' I said to Pomerantz," Rich recalls. "We got there after the fire was out. We could see through the windows of the Whitney where the pictures had been moved, and there was a large canvas about the size of the Seurat very badly damaged, but Pomerantz said, 'That's not it. That's the wrong kind of stretcher.' You can imagine how we felt."

John McAndrew called that afternoon from Wellesley to talk to Emily Woodruff Stone, the head of the Museum's Membership Department and an old friend of McAndrew's wife, Betty. The Museum operator said, "I'm sorry, I can't take your call. There's a fire in the building."

"Betty's stepmother had lent a little Seurat to the Seurat show," McAndrew said. "We didn't know whether we believed what the operator said or not, and then just by accident we called our travel agent, who was just down the block, about something else, and she said, 'By the way, there's a fire in the Museum of Modern Art, lots of fire engines.' This was early afternoon. Before we had drinks before dinner, we had a telegram from René saying that Betty's stepmother's picture was O.K. Was that good staff work!"

The fire started on the second floor of the Museum just before noon. The building was undergoing considerable renovation; according to the National Fire Protection Association, which issued a detailed report on the fire, it was making "required improvements to smooth out traffic and building problems" because of "the increasing interest in modern art." Moreover, "a $630,000 modernization of the

[1] These figures are from Aline Saarinen's *The Proud Possessors* (1958). She does not give their source, and they may or may not be more accurate than those Barr used twenty-two years earlier.

air-conditioning system was in progress."

The work on the second floor was nearly completed. All of the paintings on that floor had been taken from the walls and movable partitions when the work started—with the exception of a tremendous Monet of "Water Lilies," seven feet high and nineteen long.[2] It had been left where it had been permanently installed on a hardboard partition, and to protect it during the work an enclosure, also of hardboard, had been built around it. The smaller, easily transportable canvases from the collection had been removed to temporary storage in the annex building which had been added to the main building in 1951. There were, however, seven large paintings which, because of their size and the difficulty of moving them to the annex, had been removed from the walls but stored between partitions to protect them from flying plaster dust and possible flying paint. The renovations on the second floor were completed except for the painting of the walls and ceilings, which was about half done. There were wooden scaffolds still in place and painters' drop-cloths were strewn about. There were also thirty-five gallons of paint in open cans on the floor when the painters went out to lunch.

There are two theories of how the fire started. One, which many of the staff seem to remember best, is that the villain was a spark from the electrical equipment, a new alarm system, which was being installed. The other theory seems more likely. The workmen, some of whom smoked on the job, had started cleaning up the mess that the renovations had caused, and there was an accumulation of rubbish on the floor. Somebody, so this theory goes, dropped a lighted cigarette onto one of the painters' drop-cloths. In any event, one of the plasterers came back from his lunch and found a small fire in one of the drop-cloths near the open paint cans. "He yelled for help," the NFPA report says, "and a guard responded. They tried to put out the fire with an extinguisher, but it was advancing rapidly. The paint in the open cans caught quickly and then fire flashed over the newly painted panels. The wooden scaffolding and rubbish collections nearby added fuel to the flames. The paint and paneling gave off thick black smoke."

Smoke was as wicked as flame—indeed, in the final assessment, a good deal more wicked. It filled the main staircase and poured into the new air-conditioning ducts and the openings that had been made for new pipes and conduits. It filled the fire stairs and the area between the glass wall of the south façade and the false wall that had early been

2   "The Water Lilies" (*"Les Nymphéas"*) was purchased in 1955 with funds provided by Mrs. Simon Guggenheim.

built behind it when it was discovered that glass let in too much light and heat. Smoke, in other words, spread all through the building from the second floor to the members' penthouse on the sixth.

But it was slow to get into the Library. Bernard Karpel left his Library office and was on his way out to lunch just after twelve o'clock. "The first thing I knew about the fire," he said, "was when I came out of the annex door and a large piece of plate glass missed taking off my left arm by about twelve inches." On the sixth floor in what is now the members' art-lending service one of the curators, Sam Hunter, had found himself and one of the Museum's good friends, Mrs. Gertrud Mellon, enveloped in acrid smoke. He had, according to Karpel, picked up "a rubber plant or something heavy" and smashed the window with it. No general fire alarm had been sounded in the building "for fear of panic," but an alarm had been sounded on the office floors in the main building and in the basement. It had not been sounded in the annex.

Elizabeth Shaw, the Museum's remarkably cool-headed, imaginative, and sensible Director of Public Information, was well accustomed to coping with the Museum's public crises. Many years later she said, "I was in my office on the fourth floor, and I think I saw a *Life* photographer before I saw a fireman." Since she stuck to her business, this was probably quite true. However, when Karpel emerged fortunately in one piece, 53rd Street was filled with firemen, with pumpers and hook-and-ladders, with police prowl cars, ambulances, and hundreds of people standing in front of the Donnell Library directly across the street from the Museum. It was a docile day ("the pleasantest of the spring so far," *The New Yorker* noted) and, according to Karpel, "The crowd stood there looking up—warm, quiet, concerned as though they thought this is my house, my family, my kids." As they watched, the firemen started at the west end of the building methodically breaking through the heavy Thermolux glass that Barr had been so insistent be installed nineteen years before. They used their ladders as rams, and as each glass panel was shattered, dark greasy smoke billowed out and the false wall supported by two-by-fours slowly became visible from the street. No one in the crowd, except perhaps a few Museum employees, knew if paintings still hung on those walls. The firemen were looking for flame, not smoke, and it was not until they got to the east end of the building that flame leaped out.

Looking down on this scene from the Museum's penthouse terrace were about 200 people, some of whom had been there when the fire started. The others had climbed there by the fire stairs, as the rising smoke had turned them back from their attempt to head down to the street exit. One woman got as far as the fifth floor of the annex, and rushed into the Architecture Department; finding herself enveloped in smoke, she smashed the window with a telephone, threw her purse and shoes and straw hat out, and screamed for help. The firemen in the street saw her and, as *The New Yorker* reported (one of the editors had been lunching in the Museum garden when the fire broke out), "Perhaps fearing that she would try to follow them [her belongings], the firemen ran an extension ladder up to the window, bringing it to rest at a perilous angle to the sill. A fireman climbed the ladder and slowly, slowly helped the lady out of the window, over that quadrant of thin air, onto the topmost rungs. We felt sick, watching. . . ." She made it, though there was a moment when the crowd gasped as she squirmed in the fireman's arms to adjust her dress. She was followed by another woman with somewhat more aplomb in the arms of another fireman.

Alfred Barr and about fifteen of his colleagues were in the executive offices on the fifth floor of the main building when the smoke got dangerously dense as it poured out of the open ducts. There were a number of typists, Helen Franc of Circulating Exhibitions, Sarah Rubenstein, the Comptroller, and a young man, David Vance, a clerk in the Registrar's office. On the extreme southeast corner of the fifth floor there was a high window of heavy plate glass that was not intended to open, but by climbing on a desk and using the heavy legs of a swivel chair, Barr and Vance managed to smash the window and clear the jagged edges at the sill. Then by means of a chair on the desk they climbed out onto the roof of the house next door. It was a house (or, more precisely, two brownstones put together) owned by the Rockefellers and lived in by one of them, Mrs. E. Parmelee Prentice, sister of John D., Jr. McAndrew, to whom Barr related what had happened, recalls, "In no time at all the butler appeared and said to Alfred, 'You cannot come onto the roof of this house,' or something like that. And Alfred thought quickly, 'What do you do with servants? You treat them like servants,' and he said, 'There will be many more coming. Have the stairs clear so that they can get down out of the fire.' And the butler said, 'Yes, sir,' and led the way."

At noon, five minutes before the fire started, Allen Porter, Acting Secretary of the Museum, had gone to lunch in a nearby Italian restaurant. He came sauntering back and found that 54th Street was blocked. "I asked a cop what was up, and he said the Museum was on fire." He made his way through the Whitney to 53rd Street and found

Stephen Clark arguing with a policeman who would not let him in. Then while they were arguing Nelson Rockefeller came along. He had been walking down Fifth Avenue when he saw the fire equipment and ran down the block. He identified Clark and Porter, whom he told to stay and identify other Museum staff for the police as they came back from lunch, got a fireman's helmet, rubber coat, and boots, and dove into the building. It was he who kept the firemen from breaking through the false wall on the third floor with their axes. On the other side of that wall was the *"Grande Jatte"* and the greatest Seurat exhibition that had ever been held anywhere.

Not a single Seurat suffered any damage except, at the worst, a slight film of smoke which offered the Conservation Department no real problems. D'Harnoncourt had not been in the Museum when the fire started, and when he got there he went straight to the sixth floor of the annex with some electricians, thinking the telephone operator was stranded there, which she turned out not to be. From there he went down to the third floor and found Rockefeller in his helmet and, no doubt, his element. With the help of a sort of bucket line of thirty of the Museum's staff—guards, secretaries, carpenters, curators, librarians, the maintenance crew—the paintings were carried down the stairs and into the Whitney Museum next door. The *"Grande Jatte"* was a special problem. Because of its size (with its frame it weighed 500 pounds) and its importance, it had been very carefully fixed to the wall, a protecting glass had been put in front of it, it rested on a raised platform, and lest anyone get too close to it, there was a barricade. Karpel, who was there "carrying millions of dollars' worth of art," said: "The removal of the barricade, the removal of the protecting glass . . . all this had to be done in the face of all the excitement, all the heat, all the smoke, with great quiet and precision. That's the time when the crew really came through. René was there supervising it. It was remarkable to see how they worked, slowly undoing things in exactly the reverse order in which they'd been done, very carefully, very deliberately. They could have been doing it on a moonlit night in their own backyard. It was carefully handled like a tender babe, wrapped and sealed in paper, covered with a tarpaulin, and wheeled into the Whitney."

The exhibition of paintings by Juan Gris offered less of a problem. They were hung on the first floor, where the smoke was minimal, and they were more easily removed. They were taken to Rockefeller Center. One of the heart-stopping aspects of these two shows, the Seurat and the Gris, was that both artists had died as young men

(Seurat at thirty-two, Gris at forty) and that these exhibitions represented a very substantial portion of their entire work. The Seurat
show had been assembled by Rich for Chicago and Barr for the Museum of Modern Art ("Alfred and I had talked about a Seurat show
for years," Rich said); it had been in Chicago before it came to New
York. To have lost the two would have been a catastrophe of unthinkable proportions.

The fire was officially "under control," which meant that it was out,
by one five, exactly an hour after it had started, and the minute the
last of the borrowed paintings was safely out of the building, d'Harnoncourt's secretary, Ellen Seipp, started sending telegrams to everyone who had lent a picture to the exhibitions. "By three fifteen,"
d'Harnoncourt said, "143 telegrams had gone out, informing every
lender what had happened." Three weeks later the Museum reopened
the two exhibitions, and no one who had lent to the shows refused
to let his picture be shown again. One woman who had lent a painting and been furious when she heard of the fire but had got a wire that
afternoon saying her picture was safe wrote, "Any museum that can
have a fire and a wire on the same day must be all right."

Not everything was all right at the Museum. Far from it.

Much of the building was a smoke-scarred, waterlogged, glass-
strewn shambles. An electrician was dead, face down in six inches of
water on the second floor; he had led the firemen there early in the
fire, and the NFPA report said: "The clawed finger marks on the
smoke-smudged wall were mute testimony that he had lost his way
in the dense smoke." His name was Rubin Geller; he was a contract
electrician in his fifties, and he left a widow and three grown children.
He died of smoke poisoning.

Water dripped from the blistered ceilings and lay in deep puddles
on the floor. There had been a misunderstanding. A plumber mis-
takenly reported to the firemen that a standpipe that was out of commission had been repaired, and when they attached their hoses to the
Siamese connection and started their pump, "water pouring from a
four-inch opening on the fifth floor began cascading down the rear
stairwell and collecting on lower floors." "It came down those stairs
like Niagara," Allen Porter said. One result was that a great deal of
correspondence that had been stored in the basement got soaked.
"Some people helped themselves to some of it," Porter said, "to get
autographs of Picasso and people."

Thirty firemen were injured, including those overcome by smoke,
but there were no fatalities among them. Fire Commissioner Cava-

naugh was on hand to supervise the work, and it was he who gave Nelson Rockefeller his outfit and let him into the building. It was fortunate that he had. "It is a three-alarm fire," Cavanaugh said. "We've got a hundred men here and twenty-two pieces of apparatus."

"People in the Museum were asking, 'Where's Allen?'" Allen Porter said. "And at one point one of the firemen was overcome by smoke, and they were putting him in an ambulance, and there was a bald head like mine, and they thought, 'Oh, dear . . . there goes Allen.'"

Barr and d'Harnoncourt had stayed to the bitter end of the day. While the crew had been removing the pictures Barr had gone around the galleries feeling the walls for heat in order to determine where there was the most danger, and, like d'Harnoncourt, he had helped to lug pictures as well as direct the others.

"René sent the staff home finally," Mrs. Shaw said. "I stayed, obviously, because the place was crawling with press. By the end of the day René was absolutely exhausted and he seemed terribly upset. Actually the newspaper stories got better and better. The AP reported that the extent of the damage was very small, that the fire was out in twenty minutes, but the afternoon papers had a headline that somebody had died, and that was true. René looked at that and said, 'Why do they have to pick the worst things?' René was never one to blame anyone for anything. He took the responsibility for all the bad things and not the good ones."

No one at the end of the day knew for certain how bad the bad things were or how many good ones there were to be thankful for. Everyone knew it could most certainly have been a very great deal worse.

"The dollar loss," said the NFPA report, "has been reported as high as $300,000 for the building and $400,000 for the contents." It was a rough guess.

"The night of the fire," Mrs. Barr told me, "Sarah Rubenstein, the Comptroller, had a dream of what it would cost to put the Museum in working order again—$850,000. It turned out to be just that."

It had cost less than that to build the main building of the Museum in 1939. Such was the nature of inflation even in 1958.

There had been more than 2,000 paintings in the Museum when the fire happened. Of these some 530 were exposed to smoke, and by March 1959 eighty-four of them had been cleaned and four of these had received "major treatment." (Cézanne's "Pine and Rocks" and Gris's "Still Life" had been lined; Kuniyoshi's "Self-Portrait" had been "infused and restretched," and Orozco's "Zapatistas" had been "re-infused and restretched.") By comparison, these troubles were minor indeed.

The big Monet "Water Lilies" was burned to a crisp, stretcher and all, a total loss. Nothing was left but "small charred fragments." A large canvas, "Festival of St. John's Eve," by the Brazilian Cândido Portinari, to whom the Museum had given a one-man show in 1940 (he was a discovery of Lincoln Kirstein) "was burned through the upper half and torn beyond repair." Seven other canvases had been severely damaged, and Barr gave a brief report of what had happened to them to the Committee on Museum Collections when it met just a week after the fire.

The Portinari got thrown out by mistake. The charred frame with remnants of the canvas had been too large to remove during the fire, and the next day a clean-up crew that the Museum had hired to help the regular staff had swept it out with other refuse. "The City Rises," by Boccioni, a large, brilliant oil that the Museum had bought with Mrs. Guggenheim's funds in 1951, was badly burned, one third of it beyond repair, but Barr felt that the rest of it might be salvaged. In his regard, it was the most serious loss of all, since it was unique, like no other painting by Boccioni, and therefore irreplaceable. (It was, however, very expertly restored and repainted, and with a legend explaining what part of it is the original, it hangs today with the Museum's permanent collection.) The smaller Monet "Water Lilies," which was hanging in the stair hall, was charred over its entire surface and was considered "probably a 'total loss.' " It turned out to be. Its surface was a mass of bubbles, like a sheet of boiling tar. (The Museum gave it to the Institute of Fine Arts at New York University so that students in its conservation laboratory might study it.) "The Jungle" by the Cuban painter Wifredo Lam suffered "some damage in the upper left corner." It was painted in gouache on paper, and it had been covered with Plexiglas. If it had not been, it would have vanished. Instead, it was cleaned of smoke and soot, and it is back in the collection. "Faust I" by Jan Muller was charred along one edge, but was otherwise intact. Larry Rivers' "Washington Crossing the Delaware" fared less well. While only one small area in the lower right corner was burned, the whole surface had been discolored by the heat and smoke. The picture was painted in a mixture of oil and washes, pencil and charcoal, and it was unvarnished, which made it almost impossible to clean. Rivers, however, was satisfied with what was done to it, and it, too, is back in the collection.

There were two other casualties, both of which after a period of prolonged and careful recuperation regained their places on the Museum's walls. One was Tchelitchew's "Hide and Seek" ("*Cache-Cache*"). Its entire surface, painted in oil on canvas with intricate and subtle glazes, was discolored, and while Barr hoped that much of its brilliance could be restored, he thought it unlikely that it could be brought back to its original state. The oil medium proved to be tougher than Barr thought, for when the smoke and soot were cleaned off the colors looked unharmed. The other was Jackson Pollock's "Number 1," which the Museum had bought in 1950, two years after it was painted. It had been hanging on the third-floor landing during the fire (it was approximately 6½ by 9 feet) and its entire surface had been covered with a heavy smoke deposit. It presented a very special problem. Pollock used house paint and radiator paint and almost anything he could lay his hands on, and he had put them on an unprimed cotton canvas. When Barr made his report, he was in grave doubt that it could be restored. He was overpessimistic. It was, but it is in such fragile condition that the Museum will not let it out of the building except under rare conditions.

Just two pieces of sculpture were in the least damaged by the fire—Brancusi's "Bird in Space" and Calder's "Lobster Trap and Fish-tail." The Calder had hung (it is a mobile) from the ceiling above the main staircase. (One evening at the end of the opening of an exhibition Barr and a friend were coming down the stairs of the nearly deserted Museum, and as they got to the landing they saw a stocky figure leaning back and blowing up at the mobile to make it move. "Hello, Sandy," Barr said. It was Calder.) Neither the Brancusi nor the Calder offered any substantial problems to the conservators.

The Museum's conservator was a young woman named Jean Volkmer, who had been trained by Sheldon and Caroline Keck. Keck was at the time the conservator for the Brooklyn Museum and is one of the great experts on the care and restoration of works of art in our time. Miss Volkmer had come to the Museum to work in the Circulating Exhibitions Department, helping to mount shows, but had insisted that she wanted to learn restoration and told Dorothy Miller, who was impressed by her eagerness, that unless the Museum would help her to get such training she would leave. The Kecks took her on as an apprentice, and Mrs. Keck said, according to Miss Miller, that "she has the best hands for this work we've ever seen." However, when there are severe restoration problems, they are rarely undertaken without consultation. A confidential (but unsigned) report dated March 6,

1959, concerned primarily with Boccioni's "The City Rises," says: "The fire-damaged pictures have been examined by many experts, to get a widespread opinion as to possible treatment. One of these experts was Paul Coremans." Coremans was the director of the conservation laboratory in Brussels, the center for such work for all of the Low Countries. It was he who had supervised the restoration of the Van Eyck altarpiece in Ghent and was regarded (he has since died) as the grand master of his demanding profession. The intricacy and subtlety of the work, as described in the report on the Boccioni, chemical test of pigments, the use of X-ray, of varnishes, solvents, a plaster mold of the impasto surface, and so on, is beyond the capacity of a layman to understand—at least of this layman. John McAndrew (who is presently devoting himself to raising money to save the art and architecture of Venice) said, "What they did with the damaged pictures afterwards was extremely ingenious. You know, they spend more on conservation than any comparable museum in the world— partly because they're so fussy, but largely because artists today use store paints and tubed paints and unsized canvas. The paper in collages turns brown, and pictures on unsized canvas I don't think will last more than a generation unless they're coated with plastic back and front."

In his report to the Acquisitions Committee, Barr mentioned the problem of the large number of pictures that had suffered, though none seriously, from smoke. Cleaning them, he said, was going to be a long, slow process, possibly involving inflammable solvents, and this created a security problem. It was not, however, one which offered as many hazards as transferring the entire collection to a warehouse.

Obviously the first order of business was to get the Museum back into business. Before the day of the fire was over, crews were already sweeping up; by the next day carpenters were wielding their hammers, and the materials for rebuilding were piling up on the sidewalk of 53rd Street. Where windows had been smashed there were panels of Masonite. *The New Yorker* reported that it had heard that 300 men were at work, scrubbing, plastering, painting. It looked that way. "Hard as it is to believe," the magazine reported, "the building has already come to life—has even begun to sparkle a little in its old, bold fashion." According to a Museum press release issued ten days after the fire, there were actually about 150 men at work. The release also announced the reopening of the Seurat exhibition, the exact date to depend "on how fast the plaster on the new cinderblock gallery walls dries." It opened on May 1 and Seurat was followed on March 24 by the reopening of the Juan Gris exhibition. On April 29 the Museum posted a sign on its front entrance which thanked "everyone for the many kind messages and generous offers of help" and said that the first-floor galleries had been redesigned and rebuilt (with fireproof materials, you may be sure) for the Seurat show and that the sculpture garden and the garden restaurant were open. Furthermore, to make up for lost time, the hours that the Museum was open had been extended—eleven a.m. to ten p.m. on weekdays and from one to seven on Sundays. After the Gris show closed and the Museum was shut for more extensive repairs, a different sign was put up at the suggestion of Elizabeth Shaw, who had sent a memorandum to d'Harnoncourt; he jumped at it. It read:

> It seems to me that every day there is a small group of disappointed art lovers disembarking from taxi cabs in front of the Museum or arriving on foot from Fifth Avenue. As the summer continues I suspect that we will have a few out-of-towners show up every day. Do you think it would be a friendly gesture to add a line to our sign saying we are sorry we are closed and pointing out that other museums in this area can be visited and giving their hours and addresses? The Crafts Museum, Whitney, and Primitive Museum might be listed.

The "kind messages and generous offers of help" came from everywhere. "Every museum in the world you've ever heard of and some you haven't wrote or wired," Elizabeth Shaw said. They came from officials, from artists, from friends of the staff, and from many strangers. They came from Europe and South America and Australia, Hawaii and Japan (in June 1954 a Japanese house had been opened for exhibition in the Museum's garden). They came from dealers offering trained hands to transport pictures, from museums offering the services of restorers, from collectors offering the loan of pictures. "The whole of New York wept for you last night," Rosalind Constable of *Time* wrote to Mrs. Shaw. "There was in fact an extraordinary atmosphere of grief abroad. The lovers of the Museum gathered at dusk along the street outside, and gazed up in silence." Monroe Wheeler had a cable from his old friend Jean Cocteau: "*Sommes auprès de toi cher Monroe avec toute notre tendresse.*" One woman wrote: "As I emerged from Elizabeth Arden's at noon yesterday my heart fell into my boots." She enclosed a check. "The Museum is lucky to have saved so much," she said. "After all, there might have been civil war with Chicago!" Toni Hughes, an artist, wrote to Barr:

"When I read about the Museum in the paper this morning I felt as though a friend had been hurt. From the first time I saw a Matisse when the Museum was in the Heckscher Bldg up until this morning's headlines, the museum has been a part of my life—to love and to criticize." The Norwegian Consul and his wife were having lunch in the Museum's penthouse when the fire broke out. He wrote: "We were trapped with some fifty other members for two hours. The staff did a wonderful job in saving 99.99 percent of your paintings. We left the next morning for Paris." There were quite literally dozens and dozens of such missives.

"It was very touching to get the expressions of support from all over the world," Mrs. Shaw said, "but it was a double reminder to René of the responsibility he was carrying. If it was this important . . . But he knew it was important."

D'Harnoncourt spent the night at Allen Porter's apartment on 54th Street just down the block from the Museum's garden. Barr went back to his apartment on the corner of 96th Street and Madison Avenue. "You should have smelled Alfred when he got home," Mrs. Barr said.

Both men were exhausted (Barr, who is slight of build, had lost seven pounds that day). Indeed, almost everyone who worked for the Museum was wrung out with effort, strain, and shock. The kind of euphoria that is engendered by a crisis, however, kept them going through the next few weeks until the Museum's doors were again open. Not only were saws humming and hammers pounding in the Museum, but typewriters were snapping out letters to members and to potential donors, press releases, acknowledgments of telegrams and cables and letters, and the minutes of emergency trustee meetings. Everyone who had lent a painting to the Gris or Seurat show got a letter asking if the Museum might continue to hold his treasure for the reopening and remove any traces of smoke that might have touched them. No one refused.

A number of men and women, some of whom lived at a great distance, had asked if there was any way in which they might get hold of a few square inches of the damaged Monet "Water Lilies." A sculptor wrote from England asking if he could "beg, borrow, or buy" the "ruined Monets." He wrote, "It is only under ruined conditions that I can come near to the masters. I have saved up some money for works of Art. . . ." These requests were, of course, politely declined. One elderly man naïvely, but kindly, offered to lend the Museum a color reproduction of a painting of water lilies that hung in his recreation room, in case it would be any help in restoring the damaged pictures.

Two days after the fire, at an emergency meeting of the Board of Trustees, Henry Allen Moe moved that "the President and the Chairman of the Board be authorized to appoint a committee for all purposes connected with the fire, including all questions concerned with the opening of the Museum and rearranging of exhibitions. . . ." Philip Johnson was appointed consulting architect to the committee. "There should be a news release," the motion said, "to the effect that the Museum will not be opened until steps have been taken to assure the safety of the public and works of art according to the highest possible standards of safety."

It was also decided at this meeting that there should be an Emergency Committee to raise funds, as it was believed that the insurance would fall far short of what was needed to put the house in order. Mrs. Donald B. ("Beth") Straus and August Heckscher were asked to be co-chairmen and accepted. Mrs. Straus was then chairman of the Museum's Junior Council (she has played an extremely important role in the Museum since that time, as we shall see). Heckscher was a member of the Junior Council. They did what is customary in such circumstances: they asked a long list of people prominent in the arts, letters, theater, and other "media" and a certain number of known patrons of the arts (known, that is, for the amplitude of their purses) to be a committee of patrons. On a letterhead which listed eighty-seven names (including husbands and wives) and ended with the conventional "list incomplete," a letter went out to the members of the Museum, saying that the goal was $250,000 and that "It seems fitting that it [MOMA] should turn now to the friends who have been both enthusiastic and faithful." Two weeks after the fire (and before the letter went to members) seven trustees had given or pledged $28,000 and, in contributions ranging from $1 to $2,500, "friends" had given an additional $16,000. By the end of May Mrs. Shaw could report to the press that the total had reached $120,000. On June 12 a form letter over William A. M. Burden's signature, as President of the Museum, went to members saying that the building would be closed until late September or early October; when it reopened it would be completely air-conditioned, have more library space, "fireproof, flexible partitions in the galleries," and "on the northeast corner of the building" there would be "a separate six-story major circulation staircase." It would also have "a well-equipped conservation laboratory." Not surprising. To make it up to the members for excluding them for four months, their memberships would be extended by that many months; to each student member was sent a copy of *What Is Modern Painting?* by Barr.

There were other knotty problems. Insurance on the damaged paintings was one of them. A Washington *Star* columnist, Betty Beal, reported that the Washington insurance-brokerage firm that handled the Museum's insurance estimated that it would have to settle for "the paintings only" for "over $400,000." A clipping of the column arrived on Mrs. Shaw's desk and she sent it on to Barr asking if this indeed was so. Barr was disconcerted. "I had estimated our maximum loss at around $300,000," he replied. "In a conversation with the insurance people, this was raised to $400,000 just to be on the safe side. The actual settlement will probably be considerably less." He added, "I consider it extremely indiscreet [of the insurance broker] to give it to a columnist." There was, however, an immediate payment to the Museum of $135,000 "advanced against the total," a figure based on the estimated market value of the two lost Monets. The Museum had an interesting, possibly unique, insurance policy on its collections. The values on individual works of art did not need to be set until there was occasion to make a claim. The total collection at that time was insured for $3,000,000 "for any single occurrence." Obviously the fire loss came nowhere near that figure, but it meant that the insurance was paid on what the picture would bring in the current market. The value on the big Monet was set at $100,000 and on the small one at $35,000.

Another problem, more delicate in its way and more disturbing, was the matter of Rubin Geller, the electrician found dead on the second floor. A telegram of condolence was sent to Geller's widow almost the minute the tragedy was discovered. It was sent by Mrs. Shaw and signed with Burden's and the Museum's names. A little over a month later, on May 21, a letter went from Burden to Mrs. Geller enclosing a check for $3,000 "as an expression to you and your family of our sincere sympathy." It also noted: "We understand that this is an amount equal to that paid to you by your husband's trade union."

Geller was not a Museum employee. He worked for a sub-contractor who was in turn working for a firm that was installing the air-conditioning system, and legally the Museum seems to have had no obligation. What they sent was, they said, "over and above whatever was due her [Mrs. Geller] in accordance with the Workmen's Compensation Law." They were fearful, however, that the Geller family might sue, and of what the press might make of it, especially if such a suit ever came to court. Even the serving of papers would make a story.

Mrs. Shaw consulted Richard Koch, a lawyer with the firm that represented the Museum, about how the Museum should act and what, if anything, it should say if the press called for a statement. Koch (who learned so much about the workings of the Museum as the result of the fire and other matters about which he was consulted that he became the Chief of Administration for the Museum in 1959) said, in essence: accept the papers, whether they are properly served or not, and say nothing to the press except that the matter is being referred to the Museum's lawyers. If there is a wrangle, it would, in any case, be between the insurance companies representing Geller, the contractors, and the Museum. It was publicity that the Museum was concerned about—not money. Nelson Rockefeller, by this time Governor of New York, received a few anonymous letters telling of Mrs. Geller's plight ("To my knowledge the only income Mrs. Geller has coming in is from compensation," one letter said. "She only gets $98.00 a month. No one can live on that") and asking him to provide for her. ("The family and friends are quite surprised that you, Mr. Rockefeller, did not take care of the widow in some way.") There was a suit, but it never got to court. It was settled for $35,000 and the matter was dropped. Its residue was a sense of horror in the minds of those who accepted the Museum's responsibility primarily as their own, and in this case, it would seem, it was d'Harnoncourt more than anyone else.

According to Mrs. Parkinson, it was not until several months after the fire that d'Harnoncourt's doctor told him that he was not only physically but nervously exhausted and that he must rest. "He collapsed much later than the others," she said. "About a year later he was a very sick man. We sent him to Europe for two or three months," and she added, "René was never really the same again. He had always been so vigorous, but from then on he had to take care of himself."

When the Museum reopened to the public on October 8 it did so with a lavish gesture. We are not only open for business, it seemed to say, but we are as safe as a church, as permanent as the Faith, and have the unqualified confidence of everyone in the security of our custodianship. In the west galleries on the first floor was the modest collection which Philip Goodwin had assembled and which his family had given to the Museum. It was modest only in scale; in quality it was excellent. It was "shown in a special gallery to honor the donor and the things he loved." In the third-floor gallery were collages, drawings, tapestries, prints, and sculptures by the Alsatian Jean Arp. In the Auditorium Gallery, a couple of flights below street level, was a show of photographs called *Architecture Worth Saving*. (The Museum was early engaged in what has since become a major crusade for the preservation of architectural landmarks.) But the big splash was on the second and third floors.

Here was an exhibition of *Works of Art: Given or Promised* to the Museum. "Their extraordinary quality is obvious," Barr wrote in a special issue of the *Bulletin*. "Their enormous value makes them, practically speaking, irreplaceable." Here were two new-old Cézannes, one a "promised gift" of William S. Paley (who later became the Museum's President) and one a gift of Mrs. David M. Levy, "the donor retaining a life interest." [3] Mrs. Levy also gave a splendid Degas, "At the Milliner's," on the same conditions. There were a Gauguin, a Klee, a Delaunay, two Légers, a Matisse, a Miró, a Mondrian, and so on down the alphabet to Vuillard (three of them) by way of nine Picassos, two Renoirs, two Seurats, and two smashing Toulouse-Lautrecs. This was not all, but it gives the flavor. Surely American artists must have noticed that there was not a single piece by any of them in the lot, unless Lipchitz, who had come to America as a refugee during the war, was one of them. The same was by no means true of the Goodwin collection, with its Nadelman and Dove, its Noguchi and Marin and Demuth.

Two nights before the Museum reopened to the public there was a large dinner in the penthouse for trustees and committee members, critics and donors and lenders of pictures or sculptures to the exhibitions, and a few artists. At "table #1" gubernatorial candidate Rockefeller, as Chairman of the Museum's Board, was host to Mrs. Parkinson, the president of the International Council; James Soby, in his role as chairman of the Department of Painting and Sculpture; Aline (Mrs. Eero) Saarinen, at that time associate art critic of the *New York Times*; Mrs. Edward Root, a member of the International Council and the wife of an avid collector; [4] Dr. Charles R. Hulbeck, a lender; Mrs. Samuel A. Marx, a trustee; and M. Jean Arp, the artist whose work was downstairs, as guest of honor. (He had changed his name from Hans to Jean after his Dada period.)

After thanking those present and "thousands of individuals throughout the country" for contributing to the Emergency Fund, Rockefeller managed to mention Conger Goodyear (he was not going to get caught in that trap again) and told how the building, now about

---

3 The Internal Revenue Service no longer permits gifts made in such a manner to qualify for tax-deductibility. Museums regard this with dismay.

4 Edward Root left his collection to the Munson-Williams-Proctor Museum in Utica, New York.

twenty years old, was being rapidly outgrown. "Our attendance has more than doubled, our membership has grown sevenfold," he said, and though a lot has been accomplished in the last few months to improve the Museum's facilities, "We still lack a great deal of space to show the Museum's collection in all its diversity . . . and we lack the resources to execute fully the program for which we are qualified by our knowledge and experience." He also said that his dinner guests would "be glad to know" that Burden and d'Harnoncourt and other insiders were "studying plans for additional building and exploring ways and means to raise the necessary funds."

Glad to know? It was going to cost them $25,000,000 and a stupendous amount of arm-twisting. The phoenix was on the wing.

*Blanchette Hooker Rockefeller
(Mrs. John D. III) . . . Hookie wishes to be
as useful as possible to the Museum of Modern
Art and she maintains a very keen interest in the
varied programs at both Asia House and Japan
House. "It seems there are always things to be
worked on," she writes, "and, besides, I have a very
busy husband who likes to travel, four grown
children and five grandchildren. This just about
fills my days to the limit of my capacity."
Chapin School Alumnae Bulletin, 1972*

Chapter XIX *The Ladies Move In*

Shortly after the Museum reopened following the fire, William Burden, by his own account, found himself pricked by the horns of a fearful dilemma. Should he accept President Eisenhower's invitation to serve as His Excellency the Ambassador Extraordinary and Plenipotentiary of the United States of America to Belgium, or should he continue as President of the Board of Trustees of the Museum of Modern Art? How best could he serve his country? In somewhat such terms, in any case, he presented his decision to his fellow trustees in person and by letter. No one seemed to think the dilemma was a very real one or took it very seriously, and, of course, he became Ambassador Burden early in 1959. There was, after all, a good precedent for his decision. Another President of the Museum, Jock Whitney, had gone off to be Ambassador to the Court of St. James's in London just a few years before, and he had performed with distinction.

In the opinion of many of the staff, Burden was a somewhat remote President of the Museum, parsimonious of his time as of his wealth. He came regularly to the meetings of the board and frequently to meetings of the Committee on the Museum's Collections, of which he had been chairman from 1947 to 1950. Himself a collector, he enjoyed the position of public as well as private acquisitor and the discussions that took place between the curators (and especially Barr) and the committee members. But he was a businessman, "a man of affairs," an "aviation expert" who at the time he became the Museum's President was a Special Assistant for Aviation to the Secretary of Commerce. He did not regard the presidency of the Museum as Goodyear and Clark and Nelson Rockefeller had, as a major preoccupation—as a patient on whose pulse he needed to keep a frequent finger. That is not to say he was not conscientious or friendly. "He called the staff by their first names," I was told, and when he was first elected in 1953 he suggested that a tea be held "for the entire staff" in the Museum penthouse so that he might meet them. "The men in the shops," it is recorded, "preferred that he visit them downstairs while they were on the job, which he did. Tea was served in Mrs. Rockfeller's guest house for department heads to have an opportunity to meet him."

Obviously he had not been the kind of trustee who haunted the Museum, and he was not that sort of President. He did not drop in to see d'Harnoncourt; d'Harnoncourt was expected to visit him at his office at 630 Fifth Avenue, a few blocks from the Museum, if he had policy matters to discuss. In general, however, their consultations took place by telephone, "pretty much on a rubber-stamp basis," as a member of the administration staff recalls. Policy was made by d'Harnoncourt so far as the operations of the Museum were concerned, and generally concurred in, it appears, by Burden, a not unreasonable situation considering the regard in which d'Harnoncourt's sense of fitness, timing, and flair were held by the trustees.

When Burden left to occupy the embassy in Brussels, a very different atmosphere enveloped the Museum. At the urging of her brothers-in-law, Nelson and David, and somewhat to the dismay of her husband, who was up to his eyes in the affairs of the new Lincoln Center, and wished her at his side, Mrs. John D. Rockefeller 3rd let herself be elected President of the Museum. She could scarcely decline. The Museum had since the beginning been a Rockefeller responsibility, a protectorate, one might almost say, and it behooved Abby Rockefeller's progeny to keep her beloved wild oat green. They were not remiss in so doing, and, in a sense, they had groomed John's wife to assume a somewhat matriarchal position in the Museum much like that once occupied by her mother-in-law. Not, to be sure, that she was the sort of woman who could be manipulated against her will, but when she became a Rockefeller she was quite aware that she was assuming a role with very stringent demands, a public aspect that was inescapable, a private aspect that was clannish, and she had shared "the boys'" admiration and affection for their mother.

She was not unaccustomed to considerable wealth when, as Blanchette Hooker, she had married into vast wealth. Her mother was Blanche Ferry of Detroit, whose family fortune was made in the seed business, and her father was Elon Huntington Hooker, a distinguished civil engineer who became president of the Hooker Electrochemical Company. Like the well-trained and intellectually adept young woman she was, she went from Miss Chapin's School (as it was then called) in New York to Vassar College, where her consuming interest was in music, not in art. She is a tall woman whom Aline Saarinen described accurately as a "cool, pale beauty with a regally poised head that gives her the look of a Despiau sculpture." ("I have never seen Blanchette with a hair out of place," a friend of hers who lives in the same apartment building on Beekman Place said to me. Her apartment has a sweeping view of the East River, lighted at night by a huge Pepsi-Cola sign in red neon which happily, if surprisingly, keeps it from being the dullest river view in New York.) She has a quiet voice which has assurance without insistence and an easy but not a casual manner. When you have her attention, you have her full attention, and she speaks with what for her is frankness, though she is used to being careful of what she says. One of the present curators of the Museum said of her, "If there is ever a natural aristocracy—I don't mean an aristocracy of money but of pure quality—she would be my candidate for the queen." When those who have worked with her and for her speak of her, it is almost always with extravagance—a combination of respect and admiration, far more tinged with affection than with awe. When Henry Allen Moe was asked if she was a good President, he answered simply, "You're damn right she was." It is said that of all the family she is the only one for whom, when she telephones her brother-in-law Nelson, he runs to the phone.

Moe was Chairman of the Board at the time when Mrs. Rockefeller (whom I shall call Blanchette to distinguish her from her mother-in-law, Abby) became President. John 3rd "didn't have a damn bit of interest in the Museum," Moe said. It was a perpetuation of his father's lack of interest in Abby's enthusiasm for modern art. And, he added, "Blanchette was following in the footsteps of her mother-in-law and doing it awfully well."

She did not come to it unprepared.

In 1948, when she was in her very early forties, she somewhat reluctantly accepted a challenge offered her by Nelson to form a Junior Council for the Museum. His reason for wanting such a group seemed —indeed, turned out to be—plausible. Many of the trustees were getting on in years, and if new blood could be found in a group of young, well-heeled enthusiasts who might be groomed for the board, there was less danger that the board's arteries might harden. The Junior Council was not, however, to be a new version of the Junior Advisory Committee that had made such an infernal nuisance of itself by meddling in the Museum's policies, its programs for exhibitions, its self-esteem, and even in its decisions about hiring and firing members of the staff, and which, being unheeded, quit in a body in 1944. Heaven forbid! This was to be a sort of peaceable cutting garden out of which ornamental blossoms might be plucked to replenish the bouquet. It was to have its own programs (under the eye of the trustees and the curatorial staff, of course), but it would not—could not, by its nature —put sand in the Museum's transmission.

Blanchette went at the organization of the Junior Council with her customary calm and clear-headed energy, and she enlisted as her lieutenant Mrs. Donald B. Straus, called "Beth," the wife of a distinguished labor mediator who is a scion of the "one-'s' Strauses" of R. H. Macy & Co. proprietorship. Mrs. Straus is a pretty, feminine, and outgoing woman behind whose ready smile and easy manner lie a perceptive and lively intelligence and very considerable executive skill. Had Nelson's suggestion achieved no other end than to get these two women involved in and devoted to the Museum, it would have more than proved its validity. In actuality, it did what he hoped it would do. It not only gathered a small but useful harvest of interest and support among a group of young-middle-aged men and women who could afford to be useful to the Museum with money or work, but it also provided a testing ground for possible trustees out of which the board in subsequent years plucked half a dozen members, and, presumably, will continue to pluck.

By the time Blanchette Rockefeller chaired the first meeting of the Junior Council in February 1949, she and Beth Straus had persuaded thirty men and women (men were harder to persuade than women) to be members. Five years later it had sixty-three members and in 1971 it had shrunk a bit to fifty-two. In that year William Rubin, Curator of Collections, said, "Outside the regular things we do, some of the most important things that happen at the Museum are initiated

by the Junior Council. It's an organization that creates a flexibility that
the Museum wouldn't have otherwise." It initiated in its first years a
lecture series, a symposium, and an "art-lending service" for members
of the Museum the purpose of which was to promote the sale of paintings and prints and small sculptures by young artists chosen by a
Junior Council committee. For $3 to $35 members could rent the
works for a period of two months to see if they liked them enough to
buy them. The price range then was limited from $25 to $750 (it is
recently from $35 to $2,500). Its rationale was "to encourage the
wider purchase of original contemporary art . . . to help younger
and lesser known artists . . . and to stimulate the potential collector.
. . ." In its first three years it sold 106 pieces and distributed $15,862.50
"among fifty galleries and the fifty-six artists they represent." The
scheme was the brainchild of Walter Bareiss, one of the council members who subsequently became a trustee and, for a brief period in the
Museum's recent turbulent history, the Acting Director. There are
now dozens of lending services modeled on this one in dozens of
American museums, though San Francisco claims that it got there first
and disputes the Modern's right to claim that it initiated the idea.

Since its inception the council has organized and financed a variety
of what might be called nourishing side-dishes to the Museum's menu
of meat and tossed salads and occasionally frothy deserts. The council
has put its weight heavily behind talk. It has organized lecture series,
initially called *The Related Arts of Today*. It has sponsored sympo-
siums on everything from automobile design (with Philip Johnson as
moderator) to *The Writer Looks at Painting*. It has sponsored poetry
evenings at which Marianne Moore and W. H. Auden and William
Carlos Williams were the stars in the early days. It has arranged for
film series—one in 1965, for example, called *The Independent Film:
Selections from the Film-Makers Cooperative* and another of four
films and a symposium with the mole-like title *Whither Underground?*
It has organized exhibitions of young printmakers, of "recent" drawings and sculptures and paintings by Amercians, and you may be sure
the final selection had to be approved by the Museum's curators lest
the exhibitions which went traveling not fit the "standards" of the
Museum's taste. In 1964, at the instigation of James Thrall Soby, the
Junior Council set out to collect television documentaries on artists,
interviews with them, tapes of them at work, and comments on them.
With the help of the three major networks, New York's Channel 13
(WNDT), and what was then called National Educational Television,
they established a Television Archive of the Arts. By January 1967

they had about seventy programs stored away for future art historians. The council has also been in charge of selecting the Museum's offering of Christmas cards, which, together with some commissioned editions of prints, and books such as a *Guide to Modern Art in Europe* (in cooperation with Pan American Airways), have helped to pay the expenses of its programs.

From the time when Blanchette Rockefeller was appointed the council's first chairman, that office has been designated by the trustees and not by vote of the council, which, however, selects its own executive committee. There has always been a scramble to get onto the selection committees of the council—the committees that pick the pieces for the lending service, for the exhibitions, for the Christmas cards. The council's appeal to the curatorial instincts and urges of its members has unquestionably been a factor in keeping it not only alive but lively.

The Junior Council was by no means Blanchette Rockefeller's only preparation for high office on the Museum's board. She felt it incumbent upon her to know something about the art the Museum so treasured, and with Barr's guidance she started to buy sculpture and painting. Her first acquisition was a bronze horse and rider by Marini of which Barr had showed her photographs. When it turned up at Beekman Place, it was a great deal larger than she had had any notion it would be. It looked as out of place among the Chinese porcelains and sculptures, the Impressionist paintings, and the English furniture as if it had wandered out of its stall into the front hall of the apartment. As Aline Saarinen said, "She needed a stable," and so she commissioned Philip Johnson to remodel a brownstone house on East 52nd Street into a "guest house" which was also to become her private gallery. It was as impeccably modern on the inside in Johnson's spare manner as it was impeccably unostentatious on the outside. Accompanied by Barr and Johnson, she went to art galleries, hopefully not letting it be known who she was, and bought Rothko and Motherwell, Tomlin and Pollock and de Kooning. She also bought more sculpture to supplement a Lipchitz that Nelson and Tod Rockefeller gave her as encouragement, including Giacometti's six-foot "Pointing Man," an almost string-like figure which Blanchette's children called "No Dessert."

The guest house was to Blanchette almost precisely the equivalent of Abby's gallery on the sixth floor of the house on 54th Street, and Blanchette's "Johnny" (as she calls her husband) was as little at home with modern art as Abby's John had been. She shared with her hus-

band, however, an admiration for the arts of Asia (he was at one time
president of the Japan Society, had been responsible for erecting a
Japanese house for temporary exhibition in the Museum's garden, and
was a founder of Asia House), and they collected with discrimination
and enthusiasm. In the gallery of their house at Pocantico the arts of
ancient and modern Asia deploy themselves with ease among the
modern arts of America and Europe.[1] The guest house became an
informal arm of the Museum. It was there that small parties were held
and committees of trustees and staff frequently met. It was presided
over by a butler named Charles, who could and frequently did run
up luncheons for a small number of trustees and donors to the Museum,
for Important Persons and those who were being wooed. There, too,
were cocktail parties and small dinners and the ever present hazard of
someone accidentally backing into the shallow pool which separated
the main room on the first floor from the rooms in the back. Stepping-
stones crossed the pool, a concession, perhaps, by Johnson to the
Rockefellers' taste for things Japanese.

The Junior Council had been in existence for a little over seven
years when Blanchette Rockefeller found herself chairman of a far
more ambitious, far-reaching, and influential program than the Junior
Council ever intended to be. This was the International Council; she
was already on the Executive Committee, the Collections Committee,
the Exhibitions Committee, and by that time was honorary chairman
of the Junior Council, of which Beth Straus was the chairman. (It is
said that when she was appointed to the Committee on the Museum's
Collections—or Acquisitions Committee, as it was usually called—she
took a weekend to fix in her memory the catalogue of the collections
with the names of the pictures, their artists, and how they had been
acquired by the Museum.) The International Council did not spring
fully armed from the brow of the Museum's Jove-like Nelson, but it
was the offspring of a brainchild of his.

You will recall that not long after the end of World War II the
Department of Circulating Exhibitions had gone into the doldrums. It
was expensive to run, and the need and demand for its exhibitions was
by no means as great as it had been in the Museum's early days. Elodie
Courter had married and left the Museum, and Porter McCray, who
had replaced her (and who was a member of the Coordination Com-

---

1 In recent years they have turned their attention to collecting American
painting of the nineteenth century with the discriminating advice of E. P. Richardson, for many years the director of the Detroit Art Institute and still the foremost authority on American art.

mittee which ran the Museum after Barr was fired as Director), had found it advisable to shift the emphasis of the department away from shows to send to other museums and concentrate primarily on shows for educational institutions and especially colleges. Museums which in the 1930s were virgin territory ripe for the missionary shows of modern art from the Museum became after the war collectors and borrowers of such works on their own. There is no question that the Museum's circulating shows had, as William M. Milliken, the director of the Cleveland Museum, said, made an "extraordinary impression" and in doing so had changed the attitudes of institutions everywhere in the country toward what the Museum defined as "modern" and Boston boorishly (from the Modern's point of view) called "contemporary." Surely it had affected a change in the teaching of art history in colleges and the programs of college museums. In 1939 the Rockefeller Foundation had given the Museum a grant to "expand its programs of exhibitions especially prepared for smaller institutions with limited funds," and shows that could be installed in school classrooms, corridors, or even gymnasiums were being shipped out for fees as little as $10 to $30. During the war the Museum, as we have noted, worked as much for Nelson Rockefeller as for anyone else, and under contract to the office of the Coordinator of Inter-American Affairs it helped to prepare all sorts of materials of and about the arts for export to Latin America.

The end of the war in Europe did not conclude Rockefeller's official concern with Latin America or with the export of American art. In 1944 he became an Assistant Secretary of State for Latin American Affairs, a position he occupied for only a year. He was back in New York in 1946 and once again President of the Museum, a job he retained until 1953. During part of this time he also served as Chairman of the International Development and Advisory Board of the Truman program known as "Point Four" for economic assistance to "underdeveloped areas" throughout the world. In 1953 he became Under Secretary of the Department of Health, Education and Welfare, but before he left New York for this rather temporary job (he resigned in 1954) he had persuaded (if that is the word) the Rockefeller Brothers Fund to make a five-year grant to the Museum for what was formally called the International Circulating Exhibitions Program. The idea behind such a program was to let it be known especially in Europe that America was not the cultural backwater that the Russians during that tense period called "the cold war" were trying to demonstrate that it was. The American State Department's attempts to export our arts for exhibition had been largely aborted by dissident Congressmen, as we have noted, who could not abide any art more sophisticated than *Saturday Evening Post* covers.

It was with this ukase from the trustees and financial encouragement from the Fund that McCray, who had taken a year's leave from the Museum in 1951 to work in Paris for the exhibition section of the Marshall Plan, shifted the emphasis in traveling exhibitions from domestic to primarily foreign circulation. The Museum now had, and was delighted to have, the whole world (or at least the world outside the Iron Curtain) in which to proselytize—though this time the exportable religion was home-grown rather than what had been in the past its primary message, the importable faith from Europe. In the first year of the International Program, McCray shipped out twenty-five exhibitions, twenty-two of which represented "various aspects of modern American art." The other three were "devoted to the arts of other countries," and were circulated in the United States. Off to Europe, to Canada, to Latin America, and, indeed, to Japan went shows of *Modern American Painters and Sculptors*, of *The Skyscraper*, of post-war architecture, prints, photographs, and in came *The Modern Movement in Italy: Architecture and Design* and *The Architecture of Japan*. It was only a beginning. The Museum also bought the United States pavilion at the Venice Biennale from the Grand Central Art Galleries, which had been built in 1929 for its own shows when they were an artist's cooperative gallery. After the war the pavilion was made available to the Museum, and the shows sent there were selected by Barr and Sweeney and Dorothy Miller. The federal government (which meant the State Department) was not interested in taking it over, and was unmoved by the fact that it was the only pavilion at the Biennale that was not owned by its nation's government. The internationally minded staff and trustees of the Museum were shocked that America should not be represented at this most prestigious, if intensely political, international art show where all the European countries and Russia were blowing their cultural horns while America, in a manner of speaking, stayed home and sucked its thumb. At the moment it seemed essential that the United States be represented at the Biennale by its most sophisticated art institution, and there was no doubt in anyone's mind at the Museum what that was. From 1954 to 1962, without government help, the Museum made itself responsible for exhibitions by distinguished American artists at Venice.

The pavilion was, the Museum has long since discovered, no bargain. It became an expense that the Museum was unable or unwilling to bear, and though it still owns it, the exhibitions put on there in recent years have been the doing of the National Collection of Fine Arts, one of the many arms of the Smithsonian Institution.

In 1956 the International Program adopted a new face, a new financial structure, a new entity, and a new name. Eliza Parkinson, by that time a trustee for many years, had the idea that the Museum ought to be able to get support for the International Program in much the same way that the Metropolitan Opera got patronage through its National Council. Rockefeller and René d'Harnoncourt worked out a plan with two prongs to it, and asked Blanchette to run it. The first was that the International Program of the Museum should be supported not just by the Museum, not just by New Yorkers, not just by foundations, but that it should be supported by men and women interested in the arts all over America—not many of them, mind you, but a relative few who could afford to put up $1,000 a year to be members of the council. They were to be carefully chosen and individually solicited. This was to be no mass charity; into it was built (though it was not called that) a basic snob appeal which combined exclusivity with cultural beneficence, one of the aspects of art patronage that is characteristic of our age—but no more of ours than of any other age. Added to this, however, was the ingredient of patriotism: if the federal government won't support a program to tell the world about our arts, it is our duty as concerned citizens to do so. Those who were approached were collectors, men and women known to be concerned with their local art institutions, men and women who fall under that somewhat loose but useful appellation "prominent citizens," who like to be identified with causes, and who get a certain titillating sense of *noblesse oblige* from "lending" their names and appearing at meetings and parties given for their benefit.

Blanchette Rockefeller was the first president of the International Council, and she and Eliza Parkinson, who succeeded her after the first couple of years, spent an inordinate amount of time writing letters to likely candidates for membership, talking with those who came to New York, and convincing museum directors in other cities that the council was not trying to steal their patrons. It merely wanted to involve them in a program to make the American arts known to the capitals (and who knew? perhaps the provinces) of the world. In time the museum directors enthusiastically, it seems, came around. In the first year there were seven members. Now there are approximately 145 members in seventeen countries, producing an income for the International Council of nearly $200,000.

The council is a separate corporation from the Museum, but no one

would suggest that it is an independent corporation. When the Rockefeller Brothers Fund grant for the International Program for five years
was about to run out, a new agreement was reached between the fund,
the Museum, and a new corporation called the International Council
at the Museum of Modern Art (there was subsequently a day-long
hassle of the members about whether "at" should be changed to "of,"
and "of" prevailed). This agreement stipulated that the council should
be set up as a membership corporation under the laws of New York
State. (There are many such non-profit corporations in New York.)
This corporation was to aim at a goal "utimately" of $160,000 in mem-
bership dues. The Museum was to provide the programs under supervision of the director of its International Program (namely, Porter
McCray) and these were to be "reviewed and amended" by the council
"as it sees fit," but "in keeping with existing MOMA standards." The
Museum, moreover, would "undertake all necessary negotiations and
arrangements to carry out the Council's plan." In other words, "of"
more nearly defined the council's relations to the Museum than "at."
The role assumed by the Rockefeller Brothers Fund was to be a di-
minishing one, starting with a contribution of $125,000 the first year
and decreasing each year so that by the fifth year (1961–62) it would
contribute a final $50,000, and from then on the council would be on
its own, presumably with enough members to carry it.

The International Council was less than three years old when Burden
left for Brussels and Blanchette Rockefeller took his place as President
of the Museum. However, not only had marked successes been achieved
by the council's exhibitions, most notably a show of *The New American Painting* which was shown in eight European countries in 1958–59,
but there had been ructions in the palace.

The New American Painting, which might have been a rehearsal for
the vast show of the New York School that the Metropolitan Museum
put on twelve years later for its centennial, was assembled by Dorothy
Miller, according to d'Harnoncourt, "at the request of European institutions for a show devoted specifically to Abstract Expressionism in
America." [2] Something was known of these painters, mostly New
Yorkers, in Europe, as they had been included in earlier exports of the
International Program of the Museum and the appetite had been whet-
ted for more. They were received with the full range of critical en-

---

[2] The artists included in the exhibition were William Baziotes, James Brooks,
Sam Francis, Arshile Gorky, Adolph Gottlieb, Philip Guston, Grace Hartigan,
Franz Kline, Willem de Kooning, Robert Motherwell, Barnett Newman, Jackson
Pollock, Mark Rothko, Theodoros Stamos, Clyfford Still, Bradley Walker
Tomlin, Jack Tworkov.

thusiasm and disgust, but with almost no indifference. A Milan critic said, "It is not now. It is not painting. It is not American." A critic in Rotterdam said, "No matter how subjective their work may be, it has a communicative power because they live under the spell of their time, which is also our time. . . ." The critic for *Le Figaro Littéraire* in Paris asked, "Why do they think they are painters? We would end up by being, I won't say convinced—for the only greatness here is in the size of the canvases—but disarmed if we did not deplore the terrible danger which the publicity given to such examples offers, as well as the imprudence of the combined national museums in offering official support all too generously to such contagious heresies." A reporter from the *Manchester Guardian* who saw the show at the Tate Gallery in London said, "I have never seen so many young gallery-goers sitting down in a silent daze." John Russell, the critic for the London *Sunday Times*, wrote in part, "However often we may have heard of the size, the assurance, the headlong heedless momentum which characterize them all, we are still bowled over by these qualities when we are, as it were, physically involved in them. For involved we are, as if by some vast upheaval, not of Nature, but of our notion of human potentialities."

The result was more than merely appraisal, favorable or unfavorable. It was, in some respects, like the reaction to the Armory Show of 1913. Whereas one London headline read, "This is not art—it's a joke in bad taste" (an almost unmistakable echo of Royal Cortissoz' outburst of forty-six years before: "This is not a movement and a principle. It is unadulterated cheek."), you will find today vast canvases by many of these artists hanging sedately on the walls of the Tate, part of its permanent collection. You will also find them in European private collections and in the stock of dealers in Paris and Milan and Rome. There is no question that early in its career the International Council had achieved its primary purpose—to make Europe, especially, aware of the vitality of American art. D'Harnoncourt was moved to say in a reprinting of the catalogue which originally accompanied the exhibition, "For us, our reward is the pleasure of knowing that this exhibition and those before it have won for American art widespread recognition and acclaim abroad."

There was, however, trouble at home—unrest among the staff, and a feeling of uneasiness about the way in which the International Council was getting too big for its boots. The council was not the principal cause of discord. The Museum, although d'Harnoncourt was the Director, was still being run by the Coordination Committee, or, if not run, at least subjected to policies made by that group, which was, as it had long been, d'Harnoncourt, Wheeler, Barr, and McCray. Discontent bubbled up into what was then called (and still is by those who remember it) "the revolt of the Young Turks." In 1959 Burden decided that to keep peace in the Museum family he should let the staff have a chance to blow off steam, to discuss their grievances against the Coordination Committee, and try to restore the kind of *esprit de corps* which, in spite of routine in-fighting, had sustained the Museum since it first opened. One should bear in mind that this was a considerably underpaid staff of very able young and youngish people and that the trustees were quite aware that "the help" was working for far less than it was worth. To put it in franker terms than the trustees would have put it, the staff was being bilked; instead of being rewarded for their loyalty, their long hours, their expertise, and their dedication with proper salaries, staff members were being patted on the head and given occasional *bonnes bouches*. Burden invited all of the Young Turks, Blanchette and David Rockefeller, and the members of the Coordination Committee to spend a long weekend at his summer place in Maine.

The Young Turks were led by Arthur Drexler, who was, as Eliza Parkinson put it, "terrifically a Young Turk then; by comparison he's almost square now." Standing behind him were Elizabeth Shaw, head of Public Information, Richard Griffith of the Film Library, Emily Woodruff Stone, in charge of Membership and "special events," and Steichen of Photography in spirit if not in fact. None of these departments was represented on the Coordination Committee, they felt strongly that they should have some say in Museum policy, and they had made petitions to the board to let their voices be heard. Mrs. Parkinson put it somewhat differently: "They felt they had to be in on all the decisions. They have to tell us [the trustees] everything. René always talked to everybody, but he always talked to them alone. There had been a lot of discontent. René dominated the Maine meeting, and he let them scream and yell." There were echoes here of the attitude of the trustees toward the Junior Advisory Committee which had resigned some years before in a body because the trustees wouldn't listen to it.

The focus of the principal attack was Porter McCray and the International Council. "I think they were awfully jealous," Mrs. Parkinson said, "because the International Council had become very important and it entailed a lot of travel and they all wanted to travel. He represented the Museum and there were all those parties that they'd hear about. But the fact was that he was setting up a little museum within

the Museum. He ran the international program as a little empire."
Whether the staff was jealous or not, it was concerned, and the term
"empire building" recurs frequently in discussions of the attack on
the International Council over what is referred to as "the Maine meeting." "There was a good deal of feeling," Elizabeth Shaw said, "on the
part of the curatorial staff and me and Emily that a parallel structure
was being set up. They were hiring their own curators. They had their
own public-information service. They were making exhibitions. Its
own membership at $1,000 was taking money away from other mem-
bership. It was a separate thing and people thought it should be reinte-
grated into the Museum. There was a great deal of discussion about it
that weekend, with more people listening, including Bill Burden and
other trustees. Before that it had been just staff muttering. We also
wanted more say in policy."

The upshot took the staff somewhat by surprise. D'Harnoncourt dissolved the Coordination Committee and said he would set up another
committee that embodied the heads of all the departments. Porter
McCray was, according to Mrs. Parkinson, greatly shaken by the attacks on him, but Arthur Drexler was equally shaken when Porter
McCray ultimately resigned. The conditions on which McCray was
instructed by d'Harnoncourt to run his department, Mrs. Parkinson
(who was then president of the council) said, were not possible for
him to accept. "Arthur came to me," she recalled, "and said, 'I never
really thought he would go.' The Young Turks always wanted to
shake up the four at the top, but it never occurred to them that they
could do it."

D'Harnoncourt did indeed dissolve the Coordination Committee,
but, Mrs. Shaw said, "We never did get the committee we wanted and
which he promised us. René really hated committees. It was partly his
deafness."

It was not until 1961, two years after the Maine meeting, that Mc-
Cray resigned. "The ladies were moving in," he said. But he also said,
"Alfred was the real fly in the ointment. He controlled the loan of
materials from the collection, and we weren't allowed to show any
artists who weren't represented in the Museum's collection. In the
Documenta in Germany, the second show, Alfred wouldn't let us
show Rauschenberg or Jasper Johns just because the Museum didn't
have any." (Actually, the Museum bought several works by Johns in
1958.)

The ladies had indeed moved in. Blanchette Rockefeller by this time
had been President of the Museum for two years and Eliza Parkinson

was the president of the International Council, which, let it be recorded, grew in influence as it was integrated into the functions of the
Museum. Its long arm under the directorship of Waldo Rasmussen,
who succeeded McCray, has reached not just into Europe and South
America (where there have long been members of the council, who
have eased its path) but also into India and Australia and Japan. Rasmussen, whose admiration for McCray as an administrator and as a
man of "impeccable taste" is undiminished by the passage of time,
came to the Museum in 1954 to work for McCray as a secretary and
clerk in the shipping department of the council. He had worked his
way through college as an expert stenographer, and he had been employed for two years in the Portland (Oregon) Museum. His ambition
was to find a job that would make it possible for him to study at the
Institute of Fine Arts in New York in the evenings and eventually to
get a job at the Museum of Modern Art. "Instead," he said, "I was
working there two weeks after I got to New York." (He had a wife
and two small children to support, and for four years he went to the
institute for evening courses.) His first encounter with modern art,
he says, was an exhibition called *Three Spanish Masters: Picasso, Miró
and Juan Gris.* It was one of the Museum's traveling shows, and he
had seen it in the Portland Museum. "So," he said, "I really started to
learn about modern art from the Museum before I ever came here."
It was, he says, d'Harnoncourt and Mrs. Parkinson who heeled him
in gradually to run the council after McCray's resignation. "I was
pretty young," he says. He was thirty-three.

At the dinner which reopened the Museum after the fire, Nelson
Rockefeller did not say that the goal which he and Burden had set in
their exploration of ways to raise funds was $25,000,000. There is
buried not so deep in Rockefeller's character an ambition to make
things bigger, more highly visible, more monumental. One need only
consider the mall that he has perpetrated on the city of Albany to see
that this is so. Possibly this giantism may stem from his having participated as a very young man in the building of Rockefeller Center, by
all odds the greatest urban complex of its day and one of the hand-
somest ever erected anywhere. But, whatever its source, bigness and
mortar are part and parcel of Rockefeller's image of himself, an image
which he apparently hopes to impress on everyone within eyeshot and
on the eyes of generations yet unborn.

Some years before the fire Rockefeller had proposed that the Museum should have a drive for funds—a mere $3,650,000. This was in the late 1940s, and Stephen Clark and Henry Allen Moe had thought it was an ill-advised move. They believed that the Museum should explore ways to live within its means—by which they did not mean the fees from admissions, memberships, sales of books, and the income from its small endowment; they meant that plus what one could expect from the generosity of trustees and friends. Moe wrote a memorandum to this effect, with Clark's concurrence, and the memorandum was sent to Rockefeller.

"Nelson would have none of it," Moe says. "We all had lunch at the Century Club one day, and he said in effect, 'Henry, what you're proposing may make fiscal sense, but I'm not used to this down operation. I'm used to expanding operations, and if this report is adopted by the board I would have to resign from the presidency.' It was as flat as that. I said, 'Well, Nelson, of course I won't present it.'"

The campaign to raise the money was started. "We met one evening," Moe recalls, "Clark, Jock Whitney, Nelson, and myself, and the consensus of this meeting was that they should go out and raise X million, I don't remember how much. I was asked to speak first, and I said, 'You'll never make it.' Stephen said it more forcefully, and, being more a man of money than myself, he carried more weight, but they went ahead. We walked out of the meeting, Stephen and I. We said, 'You're the younger generation, and if you want to do it this way, it's up to you. We won't impede you, we won't criticize you, we won't hinder you in any way, but it's up to you to do it. And so we bade them good evening—all very pleasantly, of course. But it was a flub completely. They abandoned it entirely."

The Thirtieth Anniversary Drive, as it was called, for $25,000,000 was by no means a flub. The ashes of the fire were still in everyone's mind at 53rd Street. D'Harnoncourt was persuaded that the Museum needed space, and space meant money. Nelson Rockefeller had other ideas. He wanted to build a special building for the International Council, and it took a good deal of persuading to talk him out of that and into agreeing that he would back the drive. The arguments were convincing. The Museum's budget for the fiscal year that ended in June 1959 called for operating expenses of just over $2,000,000 a year, an increase of $500,000 from five years before. In the twenty years since the "new building" had been built and Nelson Rockefeller had become President for the first time, attendance at the Museum had more than doubled, and the Museum had more than four times as many members. The number had reached 31,000. The objects in the collections had increased from 2,685 items to 18,510, and there was no place to put a great many of them in the Museum. Consequently, the Museum had rented more than 4,000 square feet in warehouses for what it called "the invisible collections." The total sum of the goal for the drive was divided into $12,000,000 for "building," (which included "operation and maintenance,") $8,850,000 for "program," and $4,150,-000 for "current operation."

The drive officially started with a dinner at the Four Seasons Restaurant (designed by Philip Johnson in the Seagram Building, of which he was associate architect with Mies van der Rohe), and Nelson (now Governor) Rockefeller introduced James Hopkins Smith, Jr., as chairman of the drive and made a speech. It was nice to be able to say that $9,250,000 was already in the kitty, "subscribed by the trustees and their families." The groundwork had been done by a "Steering Committee" whose chairman was Gardner Cowles, the publisher of, among many other things, *Look* Magazine. Mrs. Albert D. Lasker, who had once been an art dealer and by this time was the widow of an extremely successful advertising tycoon, a collector of paintings, a neighbor of Blanchette Rockefeller on Beekman Place, and the confidante of any number of political figures including Adlai Stevenson, was co-chairman. There were fifteen on the Steering Committee (including, of course, Blanchette Rockefeller, Eliza Parkinson, and Beth Straus) plus five members of the staff—Barr, Sarah Rubenstein, Elizabeth Shaw, Emily Stone, and Wheeler. Emily Stone (then Emily Woodruff), who had joined the staff to promote membership in 1947, was the staff member who, more than any other, was responsible for coordinating the efforts of the various committees and, in general, seeing that no sand got into the gears of the machinery. It was she who wrote the final report. It was d'Harnoncourt, according to Eliza Parkinson, who "very much dominated" the drive.

Successful drives almost inevitably have to rely on gimmicks, and the Museum tried several. Alfred Barr put up an exhibition on the second floor of the Museum which he called *A Bid for Space*. To dramatize the cramped quarters of the Museum and the desperate lack of wall space for exhibiting its collections, he hung pictures cheek by jowl and one above the other to the ceiling in a manner not unlike the common practice of nineteenth-century galleries both private, as in Mrs. Potter Palmer's castle in Chicago and Mrs. Carnegie's house at 91st Street in New York, and public, as in the Metropolitan Museum or the Louvre. Many people who came to the Museum were struck by the nostalgia of Barr's hanging and thought it "charming." He made his point, nonetheless.

For the second time in its career the Museum held an auction. This time, however, it sold none of its own treasures. On April 27, 1960, at the Parke-Bernet Galleries in New York, fifty works of art "donated by private collectors, artists and American and European dealers" were put on the block. There were six watercolors and drawings, six sculptures, and thirty-eight paintings. Four sculptors gave pieces (Marini, Arp, Moore, and Giacometti), all of them rather small in scale, and two painters gave pictures, Miró an oil and Dubuffet a collage. Several galleries, including Wildenstein, Perls, and Janis, gave pieces, and so, of course, did a number of trustees. Nelson Rockefeller gave a Braque, Henry Luce a little Renoir landscape, Ambassador Burden a Cézanne, Walter Bareiss another Braque, Mrs. Lasker a Picasso, and so on. Admission to the auction was by invitation, but it was not by any means a local affair. The sale was piped into Dallas, Chicago, and Los Angeles by closed-circuit television, and after all expenses had been paid the Museum was able to add $504,000 to its growing hoard. Burden's Cézanne, a still-life called *"Les Pommes,"* brought the highest price in the sale—$200,000.

By the last day of 1960 more than $3,600,000 had been added to the original sum announced at the Four Seasons, and the total stood at $12,900,000, or somewhat better than half the goal. In the following month the Rockefeller Foundation gave a grant of $1,500,000, "of which $1,000,000 was earmarked for an International Study Center." And then, as Mrs. Stone says in her report, "Everyone felt that the enthusiasm for the Drive had slackened."

There is no shot of adrenalin to stiffen a flagging drive like what is called in the foundation business a "challenge grant." A benefit exhibition of Soby's collection had picked up a mere $15,500 (not bad for a benefit exhibition, to be sure) and Beth Straus's "committee of forty-two ladies" was hard at work getting new members. (They got more than 1,000 before they were through.) Eliza Parkinson was plugging away as chairman of the Special Gifts Committee. (She went over her goal of $2,000,000 by more than $700,000.) But what made light appear at the end of the tunnel was an offer by the Rockefeller Brothers Fund "to match all new gifts and pledges from November 1961 through December 31, 1962, up to a total of $4,000,000." As Mrs. Stone says in her report: "This wonderful pledge gave a fresh incentive to everyone concerned. The Avalon and Old Dominion Foundations gave $500,000 toward the Publications Program and many Trustees and close friends contributed again to the campaign." On December 28, three days before the deadline for matching the grant, the Ford Foundation came charging in like a knight in a gold Model T with $1,000,000, a grant "in memory of Edsel Ford." So the Rockefeller Brothers' $4,000,000 was now $8,000,000 and the total in the kitty was $23,000,000. By a piece of magic bookkeeping which I do not begin to understand, $3,000,000 of IBEC notes, "a gift from John D. Rockefeller, Jr., made at the beginning of the campaign which had never been added to the funds received" (why?), were valued by the trustees at 85 percent of par, and they added $2,550,000 to the "total receipts of the Drive." And so they were over the top and announced that they had a net of $25,262,000.

I had been told by the president of another New York museum that "85 percent of the money came from the Rockefellers." This is an exaggeration, but not a flagrant one. Nelson and David and John D. Jr., each gave "more than a million," according to the report. John D. 3rd was in the $100,000-to-$999,000 category. Mrs. Prentice gave her houses next door to the Museum in 1960, "retaining life-time possession" of them. She died in June 1962 at the age of ninety-one. Add to these the $6,000,000 from the Brothers Fund and $1,500,000 from the Rockefeller Foundation and the IBEC notes and one approaches 50 percent of the total. Actually $20,000,000 of the $25,000,000 raised came either from Rockefeller sources (foundations or private) or donations of other trustees. The only non-Rockefeller trustees who gave over $1,000,000 were Mrs. Edsel Ford and John Hay Whitney.

If you have managed to stay awake through this recital of figures, you have done better than some members of the Museum staff who against their will and their temperaments were corralled into the fund-raising process. Instead of tending the store, they were individually making calls on prospective donors, each accompanied by a trustee— "the trustee to make the appeal, the staff member to amplify the needs." There were those who considered this kind of promotional work an imposition, much as faculty members in a college look on fund-raising as an administrative headache of which they want no part. What to do with all that nice money, however, was something else again.

The Photography Department, for example, was to get space it had never had before, as special funds were solicited for the Edward Steichen Photography Center. The Department of Architecture and Design was to have its own display space called The Philip Goodwin Galleries, and there was to be a new Paul J. Sachs Gallery of Drawings and Prints. It is, to be sure, a classic condition in very nearly all institutions that when they are bursting at the seams and the seams are let out, there is fat to fill them almost immediately, so that the relief from the pinch is never more than a temporary surcease. It did not take long for the Museum to demonstrate this truism.

In November 1962 ground-breaking ceremonies at the Museum were on television "live," and in the following June an announcement was made that was of great moment to the New York art world. The Museum's next-door neighbor on 54th Street, the Whitney Museum of American Art, had outgrown its home and was going to move uptown to 75th Street and Madison Avenue into a brand-new building designed by Marcel Breuer, who had once built a house with a "butterfly" roof in the Modern's backyard. The Whitney's "old" building (only nine years old, to be sure) was to become part of the Museum of Modern Art. The land on which the Whitney's first uptown home had been built (it had moved from the Village) had been donated by the Modern in 1949 with the agreement that if the Whitney ever decided to move, the Modern would have first refusal of the building. The land was returned (6,800 square feet of it) as a "gift" and the building was sold to the Modern for "an undisclosed price," or, at a rough but not uneducated guess, $1,500,000. Study centers which had been planned for the new construction were now put in the ex-Whitney and unhoped-for elbow room was achieved.

Just about a year later, on May 27, 1964, the Museum reopened with what might be called a twenty-one-gun salute to itself. There was a formal dinner in the new garden wing, an enormous empty gallery. Lady Bird Johnson was the Guest of Honor; Adlai Stevenson was there, so were a great many of the people who had contributed to the drive, the men and women prominent on the committees, and the loftier members of the staff. D'Harnoncourt was on Mrs. Johnson's left; Barr on Mrs. Douglas Dillon's. (Mr. Dillon was at that time Secretary of the Treasury.) There were artists in profusion this time (invited at the insistent suggestion of William S. Paley) and diplomats and politicians. There were, of course, speeches, preserved for posterity in the Museum's next *Annual Report*. Burden concentrated on the artists. ("While the Museum of Modern Art exists for the public, it exists because of the artists. And as we are dedicated here to the art of our time, it is the artists of our time whom we honor above all.") Mrs. Johnson, speaking from the new terrace at the east end of the garden to a crowd of about 5,000 presumably invited guests, got off a few clichés ("Art is the window to man's soul" and "Culture is an international language" and "Ideas . . . have a universality that transcends language barriers") entirely appropriate to the "re-dedication," as it was called, of the Museum. There was some muttering among provincial New Yorkers about her "Texas twang," but they were charmed by her all the same. The main address was by the eminent theologian Dr. Paul Tillich, but as he was ill and unable to be there, it was delivered by Dr. William Pauck of the Union Theological Seminary of New York. There were no clichés in this speech. "There is a rule," he said, "in the life of the spirit, unfortunate but inescapable, 'the rule of the forgotten breakthrough.'" And after elaborating on this he said, "The past history of the Museum happened in a period of continuous artistic rebellions and many breakthroughs in a short time. . . ."

It was a cool evening and a breeze rustled the leaves in the beeches and birches of the garden and sent the water from the fountains slightly flying; the muttering of 5,000 guests made the speeches difficult to follow. It was a party, not a solemn occasion, for most of the people there.

"Nothing," John Canaday, the *New York Times* art critic, wrote the following Sunday, "could have more spectacularly demonstrated the awesome reputation that the Museum of Modern Art has built for itself than the attention it received last week simply by reopening in enlarged format. You could hardly pick up a newspaper or a magazine without finding a forecast or a report of the museum's Second Advent." He was completely accurate. Not only did the press coverage reach into every corner of the country, but so did radio and television. NBC devoted its *Sunday* show to a tribute to the Museum, and for an hour Aline Saarinen walked about the Museum interspersing her comments on the works of art with interviews that she had pre-recorded with the artists—Chagall, Giacometti, Miró, Calder, Henry Moore, and Stuart Davis. *Newsday* found it "fascinating . . . if there is any criticism of the interviews it's that they were too brief. One could have listened for hours. . . ." On CBS-TV Mike Wallace interviewed Alfred Barr and a group of artists, some at the Museum and some in their studios—Rauschenberg, Indiana, Oldenburg, Marisol, and Segal. It was a half-hour show and had mixed reviews.

The expanded building itself, however, had universally favorable notices, and so, for the most part, did the institution itself. Ada Louise Huxtable, once a young member of the Museum's staff, but by 1964 the nation's best-known newspaper critic of architecture, found "The new museum . . . just about as perfect for its purpose and as expressive of its standards as any structure could be. . . . One of New York's most subtly effective structures, its refined simplicity quietly understating the care of its detailing and the sensitivity of its relationships to older buildings. . . ." John Canaday found the Museum "transformed." "It has a quality," he wrote, "of solidity and permanence and, above all, of balance that is brand new. There is now adequate space for extensive exhibition of a really magnificent permanent collection . . . bringing the museum's historical function into better balance with its other function as jury and proselytizer for contemporary experiments."

There had been no major exhibitions during the time the Museum was having its wings added (I refrain from mentioning its halo), but except for six months from the beginning of December 1963 until it re-dedicated itself in the following May, business went on pretty much as usual with the sounds of saws and hammers in the background. During those six months it lent works from its collections to the National Gallery in Washington, the Cleveland Museum, the Chicago Art Institute, the Carnegie in Pittsburgh, and the Museums of Fine Arts in Boston and Houston. It also sent a large group of Picassos to Montreal and Toronto, which had jointly organized a "major Picasso retrospective." The International Council, with Eliza Parkinson as its president and Rasmussen as it director, was busily sending shows to Asia, Africa, Australia, Latin America, and Europe, and providing American ambassadors with American paintings to hang on the walls of their residences. It had also given a Children's Art Carnival—whose prototype had been devised by Victor d'Amico for the Museum in the 1940s and had been part of the American Pavilion at the Brussels World's Fair of 1958—to the National Children's Museum in New Delhi. Children and adults had crowded into the Art Center of the Museum's affiliate, the Institute of Modern Art, which held classes in the annex at 21 West 53rd Street, and when the Museum reopened, the Art Center moved lock, stock and barrel to new quarters at 4 West 54th Street. Publications continued to pour out of the office over which Monroe Wheeler presided; there were twenty-five of them in the years 1963–65. They ranged from slim issues of the Museum *Bulletin* to full-dress catalogues such as *Bonnard and His Environment* by James Elliott, J. T. Soby, and Monroe Wheeler, *Architecture Without Architects* by Bernard Rudofsky, and *Alberto Giacometti* by Peter Selz.

No one had foreseen quite what the effect of the expanded facilities, the new galleries and gardens, the new study centers, the new library facilities, the new rooms for entertainment and meetings would have on the budget and, equally surprising, on the morale of the staff.

"Before we had the drive and the new building," a senior member of the staff said, "the Museum was run more like a club. Everybody loved René, and René had a personal relationship with all of his top staff. The thing that happened that I feel was inevitable was that after the drive the Museum became so big and dispersed that even René could not keep this personal dialogue with everybody . . . and . . . when they planned the drive, they didn't take into consideration how expensive it would be to run a much bigger shop."

In the five years from 1960–61 to 1964–65 the operating expenses of the Museum increased by just about a million dollars. $900,000 of this happened between 1964 and 1965. The cost of everything went up as the size of the building increased—general administration, building maintenance (of course), and the cost of curatorial and educational activities. The Museum's total expenses in 1964–65 were $3,334,123. Five years later in 1969–70 they were more than twice that, $7,194,100. What had been a small surplus of $53,000 in 1964–65 was in 1969–70 a smashing deficit of $1,200,000 plus.

It fell to Eliza Parkinson, newly installed as President of the Board, to watch this spiral, which at first looked like a small twister raising a little dust on a far horizon, turn into a tornado of great force. She became President in 1965, after the drive was over and the building was reopened. David Rockefeller, as Chairman of the Board, was looking for someone to take Burden's place, and he proposed to the Nominating Committee that Mrs. Parkinson be asked to be "Acting President."

"I was on the Nominating Committee then," Henry Allen Moe said. "I guess I still am. I said, 'Nothing doing, David. She rates being President and she will be a very good President.' "

Dr. Moe's judgment, as it usually did in the Museum's deliberations, prevailed.

"She was a very good President," he said, "a great President. Everyone trusted her, and she knew them all and she was there day by day. She has a man's judgment about affairs . . . but this is not the women's-lib way of putting it."

Eliza Parkinson's qualifications for being President of the Museum have, in some degree, run in and out of this narrative, from the time as a very young woman she had sat on the floor at the meetings of the first Junior Advisory Committee and had to shout to make herself heard above the clamor of youthful argument. It was she who was first determined to get the Museum embedded in education, and to her "education" had the specific meaning of the New York City schools. It was she, you will recall, who got funds first from the Advisory

Committee. It was she also who had interviewed Victor d'Amico to run the department. ("I remember interviewing him," she says, "He is a very interesting man, but I don't remember why I interviewed him. I guess it was because Alfred wasn't much interested and therefore asked me to because it was an Advisory Committee project.") She was elected a trustee of the Museum in 1939, during the war, but it was not until René d'Harnoncourt took over as Director that she became really active in the affairs of the Museum. She had the most profound respect for him as the glue that held the Museum together, who could handle the staff and the trustees with equal felicity and interpret them to each other. She also found it a delight to work with and for him, and their minds complemented one another. They became very close friends. Whereas Blanchette Rockefeller was the kind of Museum President who accepted the problems that were presented to her with calm and dignity and a cool head, Eliza Parkinson was the kind to seek out problems and attempt to solve them before they became urgent. She spent a great deal of time writing notes to members of the board or talking with them on the phone, telling them of problems that would be discussed at the next meeting and making her position clear. On issues that might be troublesome if dropped unannounced into the board's laps, she had already forestalled opposition or at least laid out the ground rules for discussion. It was a technique she learned from d'Harnoncourt. She was at the Museum almost every working day, and she got to know a great many of the staff as close friends. She was open in her discussions with them, and they felt they had her backing of their best interests with the trustees. She also enjoyed them, and they her. Hers is a lively intelligence, singularly free from cant. Her concern with art is a great deal more than fashionable, and while she has been advised by members of the staff, and particularly by Dorothy Miller, about what she has bought, her taste is adventurous and personal. In her apartment on East 72nd Street, designed by Arthur Drexler, are not only a number of American pictures left her by her aunt Lizzie Bliss (a Prendergast, several Davieses, Hoppers, and so on) but works by her friend Loren MacIver, by Rothko, Albers, and Still. She says that she has never paid more than $3,000 for anything. She had the advantage of attending the best and most exclusive course anywhere in the purchase of modern painting, sculpture, and photography—the Acquisitions Committee of the Museum.

When Blanchette Rockefeller's "Johnny" had decided that she was spending too much time on the affairs of the International Council, Eliza Parkinson took over as its president, a job at which she plugged away on a very nearly full-time basis for seven years. There was scarcely a nook or cranny in the Museum that she did not know or a member of the staff whose personality and performance she had not become familiar with and about whom she had not made up her mind, for she is not one not to have firm opinions about people.

Her opinions, however, are subject to change. Nothing demonstrated this more emphatically than the curiously volcanic careeer of Bates Lowry, who became the third Director of the Museum of Modern Art on July 1, 1968.

*"How would you like to be the director of the
Modern Museum? I hear the salary's good."
"Who cares about the salary? What's the
severance pay?"
A "two-liner" current in New York
in the spring of 1972*

Chapter XX *"Good Old Modern"*

By 1968 a number of faces that had long been familiar at 11 West
53rd Street had disappeared, and their easily recognizable steps were
no longer heard in the corridors of the fourth and fifth floors. Allen
Porter ("Mr. Museum") had retired at the age of sixty-two in 1965,
and he was living in his bright red-and-white remodeled wooden
church "up the Hudson" in Barrytown, New York. Surrounded by
needlepoint, much of it of his own making, photographs of Greta
Garbo, Victorian furniture and bibelots, he cultivated his garden. He
also rode each day fifteen or twenty miles on a bicycle given to him by
his colleagues when he retired. As this is written, he still does.

Monroe Wheeler retired in 1967, but he kept an office in the gray-
stone mansion next to the Museum on the west, one of two buildings
owned by the Museum which it has not yet been able to afford to tear
down and replace, though a scheme for it was in the plans published
at the time of the drive. It was once the headquarters of the Theatre
Guild. Wheeler's old friend Glenway Wescott said jokingly, "There
was joy at the Museum among the young at getting rid of him because
of his tyrannousness. . . . The best of the Museum was a triumvirate.
Alfred, of course, was the soul. René was the wit, the mind, the spirit,
the person who could get the trustees to do anything, and Monroe was
the technician." It was Wheeler who sweated over the budgets for exhibitions and struggled, not always successfully, to make the curators

or guest directors give him accurate estimates. "He'd fuss at them, and when he knew what they had to have, he would go to René, who would then go to the trustees, and if necessary, he would find financing from outside sources." Wheeler seems never to have missed an excuse or an opportunity to travel, and while he was on the staff he was as likely to be in Europe or India or South America as at the Museum. He was a sort of official ambassador not just to foreign museums and collectors but to artists as well, an arranger of loans and exhibitions, of borrowings and lendings, and since his retirement he has still on occasion acted the same role. He has, a staff member said, "a fantastic gift for getting people to lend things to the Museum. He convinces them that it's a privilege."

James Thrall Soby retired as chairman of the Collections Committee in 1967. He had been Barr's most loyal friend and supporter on the board for more than two decades, and it is frequently said that his taste was a mirror of Barr's, though this does him less than justice. Like anyone's taste, his was the reflection of his education (much of it at the hands of Chick Austin of the Wadsworth Atheneum in Hartford) and the time and the morality in which he grew up. The time was the Depression, which scarcely touched him, for he was the son of wealth, and the morality was the conventional liberalism of the New Deal, though it did not seem conventional at the time, especially to prosperous Hartford society. In that milieu Soby was, or seemed to be, a renegade, with outlandish appetites for the perverse in art. It was he who so frequently responded to the attacks of critics and groups of artists against the Museum's policies, which meant against its taste or the emphasis it placed on this or that artist or group of artists. He enjoyed a good scrap in defense of the palace in which he was a dedicated chamberlain (he was not above the internal politics), and he got on well with the help. He had both humor and a kind of humility (by no means humbleness) that endeared him to the staff, and though he worked for no recompense but gratification, he worked as hard as anyone in the Museum. He withdrew from active participation in the Museum's daily affairs because of his wife's recurring ill health, which had an unfortunate effect on his own.

Nelson Rockefeller, by the mid-'60s completely involved in politics and a furious and consuming ambition in the arena of public affairs, rarely turned up at the Museum, even for trustees' meetings. It has been reported that his brother David, Chairman of the Board, wrote him a note to the effect that he had missed forty-five consecutive meetings. "He came to the next meeting," a trustee said, "and stayed half an hour." It was suggested to me by a member of his family that he might "love to come back and take over the Museum again when he stops being Governor." (This was said in 1971.) Like nearly all of his family (his brothers Winthrop and Laurance are the exceptions; their concern is with "the environment"), he feels a filial duty to the Museum. When some of the trustees suggested in the late 1960s that it might make sense to sell the Museum building and land and re-establish it where there was more room for expansion much farther west and where, furthermore, it might help to upgrade a run-down section of the city by establishing a new "center of education and culture," Rockefeller said, in effect, "I want the Museum to stay on Rockefeller property, and if it doesn't, count me out."

Nelson's concern with the Museum—or, perhaps more accurately, the Museum's concern with him—was elaborately demonstrated in the summer of 1969 with a large exhibition directed by Dorothy Miller called *Twentieth Century Art from the Nelson Aldrich Rockefeller Collection.* A very rich dish it was, and beautifully served. According to Miss Miller, who has long advised him about buying pictures, he has become "extremely expert." He still keeps track of what is going on at the dealers' and at museums, and he likes to move the objects in his collection around lest they become so familiar in one place that they become part of the furniture, a practice of many devoted collectors but of few who buy just to possess and to display their possessions. The day he moved into the Governor's mansion in Albany, a splendid Victorian pile, he asked Miss Miller and Barr to come and help him hang the paintings. Barr had to decline, but Miss Miller said she would be delighted. There was to be a dinner that evening at seven, and, she said, "We couldn't find a hammer, so we used a child's tomahawk" to drive nails for the small pictures in the little reception room. The movers helped with the big pictures. "Nelson took off his jacket," Miss Miller says, "and said, 'Come on, let's get to work.' He spent the first three hours of his governorship pushing pictures around in the mansion." (Some years before, Sidney Janis had remarked that Rockefeller was not only "exceptionally receptive to advanced ideas" as a collector but so adept at hanging big canvases that "any gallery would be delighted to have him around as a handyman.") He has for a good many years employed a full-time curator to watch over his various collections. It is said that he has stopped buying primitive [1] and mod-

---

1 His great collection of Mexican, African, and Oceanic art, bought with the impeccable advice of d'Harnoncourt, was given in memory of his son, Michael, to the Metropolitan Museum in 1969. Michael lost his life on an anthropological expedition in the South Pacific.

ern art (indeed, is selling some at auction) and is buying Chinese porcelains, a throwback, one might say, beyond his mother's taste to the
taste of his father. He is also building a sumptuous Japanese house at
Pocantico Hills.

Steichen was gone. Iris Barry was long gone. Lincoln Kirstein was
disaffected—indeed, disgusted. Not long ago he called the Museum
"the greatest promulgator of trash in history." Dorothy Dudley,
who has not been part of this narrative but was for about thirty
years the Registrar of the Museum, an innovator in museum techniques, and the author of the authoritative book on her profession,
was gone. (After her retirement she married a man who had been a
friend for years, a sea captain, and they moved to Maine to live.)
Dorothy Miller retired in 1969 from the Museum, and busied herself
profitably in advising not only private collectors but business patrons
of the arts as well. She officially still lives in New York, but she has a
white clapboard house dating from about 1800 on the elm-lined Main
Street of Stockbridge, Massachusetts, which she keeps open much of
the year and where Alfred and Marga Barr spend a good deal of their
time.

In 1967 Barr retired. In 1968 d'Harnoncourt retired. Barr had been
there thirty-eight years, d'Harnoncourt had been Director for nineteen. The precocious kids of modern art had become the grand old
men. The young curate who had presided over the galleries in the
Heckscher Building retired as senior theologian of the college of aesthetic cardinals.

The press when Barr retired was, as you might suspect, filled with
encomiums of his career, his contribution to scholarship, and his
invention of the modern art museum, not just of the Museum of
Modern Art. "In the old days," *Newsweek* reported, "a museum was a
stately cenotaph for defunct genius, full of the hush and odor of sanctity. But Barr changed all that and literally seduced the public off the
street with showmanship and scholarship." In the *Saturday Review*,
Katherine Kuh, an old hand at such matters, wrote, "Every modern
gallery models itself to some extent on this pioneer New York prototype. Even the Metropolitan is beginning to borrow certain of Mr.
Barr's techniques . . ." and furthermore "the museum's most useful
innovations and services . . . are now standard practice throughout
America and Europe." Barr was praised for dedication to his cause,
though it had not been many years before that he was being charged
with a Barnum-like sensationalism and running a three-ring circus,
"the favorite target of sniping critics." He was commended for the

clarity and simplicity of his jargon-free writing about the arts, the adventurousness of his taste, and his personal modesty about the influence that he had had on the taste of a generation. "Although he is modest to the point of embarrassment," *Newsweek* said, "he is one of the rarest and most valuable men a culture can produce. He is sensibility become operational. . . ."

Barr disliked above all things being called a "tastemaker," and when John Canaday had called him in the *New York Times* in 1960 "the most powerful tastemaker in American art today and probably in the world," Barr had responded, "The artists lead; the Museum follows, exhibiting, collecting and publishing their work. In so doing it tries to act with both wisdom and courage, but also with awareness of its own fallibility." It was characteristic of him to disavow his influence, though he can have been in little doubt of it. In his reply to Canaday he recalled an Aesop fable about two flies perched on the axle tree of a chariot. "What a dust do we raise!" said one to the other. In a letter to *Newsweek,* which recalled this exchange at the time of Barr's retirement, he wrote, "Really I am not 'the most powerful tastemaker in American art today.' I am simply one of the Museum's 38 trustees and one of the 384 members of its staff." The implication of the Museum's influence is clear.

Two years before Barr's retirement Philip Johnson said to Richard Lemon, who was working on an article on the Museum for the *Saturday Evening Post*, "We have one great thing at the Museum, and that's Alfred Barr. He has energy, will, and evangelistic fervor and a sense of history and an eye so young and brilliant he makes sheep out of the rest of us." One of the Museum's long-time trustees referred to the "sheep" and "the Barr cult," and a disaffected laborer in the Museum's vineyard said, "Alfred never risked a qualitative analysis in his life, and he supported the dollar values of all those negotiable securities. . . ." There has always hung over the Museum, and therefore over Barr, the cloud of commercial manipulation, the accusation that it was in business to support the dollar values of its trustees' collections, that it exerted an exaggerated and unhealthy influence over the art market, that it was, as Andrew Ritchie said, "the Bourse." No one will deny the Museum's influence on the art market or the value to artists and dealers and collectors of its nod of approval, but no one suggests that Barr or any of his colleagues profited financially from the power they exerted. Indeed, when Barr and his generation retired, the trustees were embarrassed that they had made no adequate provision for pensions and had to scurry around and improvise a retirement program. Their salaries had been in the same range as professional salaries, and the board was ashamed to retire them on half-pay. The upshot was that it figured what it should have been paying them over the years and gave them half of *that*—as though they had been promoted at the last minute from colonel to brigadier general and retired at a brigadier's pension. "I don't think," one of Barr's colleagues said to me, "that Alfred ever made much more than $10,000 a year." He finally made twice that and more, and for years Mrs. Barr has continued to teach the history of art at the Spence School in New York.

Katherine Kuh asked Barr a series of questions about his career for her *Saturday Review* article because, as she said, since "Mr. Barr has been written about voluminously, both pro and con, we decided it would be interesting to hear what he has to say about himself and about the museum." In answer to her question about "the most important contributions" of the Museum, he mentioned seven things which I will summarize: First, the very fact of the establishment of the Museum in New York, which lacked a museum concerned with the recent past—"which, of course, includes the present." Second, the Museum's concern with *all* of the visual arts. Third, that its effect on universities had been the acceptance of modern art as a legitimate field of study and publication. Fourth, "the Museum's collections." Fifth, the Museum's exhibitions and its traveling shows. Sixth, its seven exhibitions of primitive and pre-Columbian art, and finally (seventh), "The most beautiful garden on Manhattan." He had, in other words, accomplished everything he had set out to do when he wrote the first prospectus for the Museum in 1929 and had a beautiful garden besides.

D'Harnoncourt was weary and he was eager to retire, perhaps over-eager. He had warned the Museum, but not prepared it for his withdrawal, for the absence of his comforting presence, his ability to absorb conflict and make it disappear, his kindliness, his paternal reassurance, his deft and almost invisible handling of his trustees, his subtle common sense. He had made no apparent effort to discover and train a successor, and there was no younger member of his staff who suited him or his trustees as his replacement. "René got more and more dreamy," an old friend of his said, "and more yielding to the headstrong young—the department heads and the directors of exhibitions." The realization of his ambition to see the Museum grow physically and in influence, to blossom with new galleries for the collections, new study centers, a new international center for research, all of which was to be accomplished by the Thirtieth Anniversary Drive, had created financial problems for the Museum which he had not anticipated. The deficit rose, as we have seen, at a frightening rate. He had had a phenomenal record of getting financial support for the Museum and for getting the trustees to make up deficits as they occurred with increasing rapidity but not with increasing cause for alarm. "He thought that as long as he had three mounts, Mount Rockefeller, Mount Whitney, and Mount Guggenheim," the friend said, "he didn't need to worry about what went on in the valleys. It was under René that the big deficit began, and this makes it very difficult to bring in new money, new millions. The new multimillionaires don't like to put their money in an organization that has a big deficit."

"Why is it that when we double the size of the Museum," Paley asked, "we triple our expenses?" The money men on the board, might, of course, have anticipated this and planned for it. They were as aware as anyone of the effect of inflation on their budget; they do not seem to have been aware of the almost inevitable inflation that took place in the Museum's staff. The expansion of the custodial and maintenance staff with the expansion of the plant was obvious. It was a great deal less obvious that a bigger museum was going to have to provide more curatorial staff. More places to show pictures meant more correspondence about borrowing them and more typists to write the letters dicated by more and more assistant curators. As unquestionably the biggest and most important museum of twentieth-century art anywhere in the world, it attracted a constant stream of inquiries from collectors, from scholars, from other museums, from dealers. The paperwork increased, and so did the turnover in the staff. Whereas it had not long ago been considered a privilege to say proudly that one was on the staff of the Museum of Modern Art ("You know, I work at MOMA"), now the young had discovered that it was useful to say that one *had* worked for the Museum when applying for a job elsewhere that paid more or was more interesting. So, many of them came with no intention of staying for more than a few months, to have "the Modern," so to speak, in their pasts. Those who did stay demanded not only more money, which was reasonable, but also more say in Museum policies of all sorts, which was met, after negotiations, with reassurances that sounded more real than they were.

These financial and personnel troubles d'Harnoncourt did not foresee, or if he foresaw them, their outlines were misty. In any event, they had not been prepared for when he retired in the summer of 1968. He also had not prepared his trustees for a challenge to the traditional concept of a museum, especially a museum called Modern, a museum with a contradiction written into its title, a contradiction which had served it well. As Beth Straus said, "The Museum is imitating itself." She said this in 1970; John Canaday had said it nearly a decade before in the *New York Times*. It had taken to collecting its own past; it was reviving its own revivals. It was rediscovering its discoveries—Art Nouveau, Dada and Surrealism; good old reliables in retrospect—Picasso, Matisse, Calder, even Walker Evans for the third time; good old movies and good old architects—Mies van der Rohe, Le Corbusier, Frank Lloyd Wright. It was repreaching old sermons in the best, or at least the oldest, homiletic tradition. Somehow it was "business as usual" even more than was usual. The Museum had not, however, quite made its peace with the idea that it was no longer leading the pack by a full lap but was running to keep up with dealers and other museums which it once had considered provincial and which had learned at MOMA's knee. It had, in essence, done its job too well. The time was past when it could say, "This is modern," and an eager and somewhat awed, if special, public nodded its head and said, "If you say so, then it must be." The time had also passed when it could say, "This is *good* design," and have its word taken as gospel, though it went right on saying it and displaying it. The odor of the Bauhaus which seemed to hang on so much of what it said was *good* seemed awfully stale thirty-five years after the Bauhaus was disbanded. The Museum still had the power to set secondhand dealers rummaging around for discarded bentwood chairs designed and manufactured by Thonet or his imitators, or bent plywood ones by Aalto. It could even inspire manufacturers to invent their own impure versions of such works. The Museum had not lost the capacity to be doctrinaire, but it had, to a very considerable degree, lost its capacity for being the first to discover art to be doctrinaire about. It was no longer the ultimate ambition of every young artist to have his work displayed at the Modern. Indeed, "modern" in the context of the Museum has become dated. Some years ago my daughter, when she was a teenager, was asked if she liked an elaborate Victorian pin-tray; she answered without hesitation, "Not for me. Give me good old modern!"

The Museum was good and old and modern when d'Harnoncourt decided to retire, and when he retired, Eliza Parkinson retired as President at the same time. "She had the timing just right," Henry Allen Moe said. "She came to me and said the time has come, and I said you've got to stay, and she said I will not, and she told me the reason, and I had to agree with her. She said we were getting into a period of financial stringency, and it will be a man's job to raise money, and said that she was incapable of this sort of thing."

Before either the President or the Director retired, however, the search for d'Harnoncourt's successor had been under way, and the committee assigned to this task had emerged with the name of Bates Lowry, professor of the history of art and chairman of the department at Brown University in Providence, Rhode Island. Lowry, who was then forty-three and is a very tall man, nearly as tall as d'Harnoncourt, came to the notice of the larger art community as a result of the floods in Florence in November 1966 which had wrought such havoc in the museums and libraries of that ancient Mecca of art-lovers, connoisseurs, scholars, and trippers. He and Professors Sidney J. Freedberg of Harvard and Millard Meiss of Princeton went into action at once and organized CRIA (Committee to Rescue Italian Art). Within a matter of a few days they had, with the help of other scholars and a host of energetic and knowing philanthropoids, organized a drive which raised $2,500,000. According to Mrs. Arthur A. Houghton, Jr., who with Edward M. M. Warburg was co-chairman of the New York committee, "Bates worked around the clock. He almost lost his senses from fatigue. Of course, he also had his department at Brown to run—but he never lost his equilibrium." Philip Johnson had done a building for Brown and had declared Lowry to be "an ideal client," and Johnson's word carried a great deal of weight with his fellow Museum trustees. Everything in his background seemed to indicate that Lowry was just what the Museum needed. He was respected as a scholar (he had taught the history of architecture at the Institute of Fine Arts, whose standards of scholarship are exceedingly rigorous); he had been "in on trying to set up a small liberal-arts college in Riverdale, California," as he said, and he had been chairman of the art department at Pomona College, where he had taught the history of painting and sculpture "and modern" and run the art gallery. So he combined administrative experience with gallery experience with scholarship with the ability to deal with architects. He was, moreover, personable, and his very size seemed to echo in the minds of the trustees the father image that d'Harnoncourt had for so long been to many of them. His manner was pleasantly direct, his smile ready, and, as one of those who worked with him at CRIA said, he was "something of a personality kid."

He joined the staff of the Museum several months before d'Harnoncourt moved out, and, rather to d'Harnoncourt's dismay, he insisted that he wanted to be the head of the Painting and Sculpture Departments as well as Director of the Museum. He had decided that this was the way to resolve a power struggle which Barr had left behind when he retired—a contest primarily between William Rubin and William Lieberman for control of the painting and sculpture collections and exhibitions. D'Harnoncourt, who knew better than anyone (except perhaps Barr) the burdens of being Director, thought that Lowry was taking too much on his plate, but he had, after all, been party to Lowry's appointment and he meant to support him. It is now said that he was deeply worried about Lowry's attitude.

Lowry's plans and ambitions for the Museum were basically scholarly. He was eager to forward d'Harnoncourt's plans for a new International Study Center, which was also one of Eliza Parkinson's primary concerns. He wanted to be sure that the entire collection was available to scholars, even though not all of it could possibly be on display at one time. "Pictures will be on racks that pull out," he said. "The Film Library will be in the study center so that scholars can consult individual films. There has never been any real study, for example, of the influence of films on modern painting and sculpture. . . . We plan to have archives of all kinds of materials dealing with the modern artist—letters, taped conversations, photographs." He wanted the Museum to publish a Journal of Modern Art. "There is no single place now," he said, "for the serious scholar of modern art to publish scholarly papers." He regretted the "split between the academic institutions and the museums," for "both worlds suffer from the spilt. The principal reason why it is difficult for museums to compete with the universities for good men is that we can't offer tenure or sabbaticals." He wanted to continue to enlarge and refine the collections, to have more gallery space. "Space is our major problem," he said and talked about plans to build farther west on 53rd Street. He also wanted the Museum's exhibitions to reflect what was going on now, this instant. "Our great problem," he said, "is not being able to bring exhibitions to the Museum that deal with current work quickly enough. We're scheduled up to 1971 [this was said in the spring of 1968]. The time lag shouldn't be that long. Artists want to know what is new; so do students. There is a sharp distinction between art-gallery shows and museum shows." [1]

Lowry's appointment was announced in May 1967, but he had a commitment to fulfill to Brown University; he became Director of Painting and Sculpture on January 1, 1968, but he did not actually take

[1] The foregoing quotations from Lowry are taken from an article entitled "Conversation with Bates Lowry," written by the author between the time of the announcement of his apppointment and his taking over. It appeared in *Art in America*, September–October 1968.

over the directorship of the Museum until July 1968. It was assumed
by everybody at the Museum, both staff and trustees, that d'Harnoncourt, though he planned to spend a great deal of his time at his summer cottage on Long Island or in Key West, where he also had a
house, would lend the same kind of calm, reasonable guiding hand to
the new Director that had characterized his nineteen years as Director.

It was not to be so. Fewer than six weeks after Lowry took over,
d'Harnoncourt was run down by a car and killed. Just before noon on
an August morning he was walking along a country lane on his way
back from the post office in Cutchogue to his cottage in New Suffolk,
Long Island. The car which struck him was driven by a forty-eight-
year-old widow, the mother of two, and she was arrested at the scene
for drunken driving and charged with criminally negligent homicide.
His funeral was held in a village graveyard on Long Island, and one of
his staff said, "It was dreadful," by which she meant that it was em-
barrassingly emotional. One of the senior executives of the Museum
was "crying at the top of his lungs like a little boy."

"Nelson Rockefeller spoke for the entire art world in mourning
d'Harnoncourt's death," *Newsweek* reported, " 'the tragic loss of a
uniquely creative human being who combined the best qualities of the
old and new worlds. . . . His influence on art in America will be felt
for many years.' " In the same obituary Barr was quoted as saying,
"He brought harmony to the Museum of Modern Art with his connoisseurship, understanding and self-effacement," and "he developed the art of installation to a point that isn't equaled anywhere in
the world."

On October 8th two thousand people gathered in the Museum garden for a memorial tribute to d'Harnoncourt. The staff member who
remembers the funeral as "dreadful" remembers the memorial service,
if it can be called a service, as "marvelous." While the Governor and
his wife and the Mayor of New York and Mrs. Lindsay sat with their
hands folded in their laps under the yellowed leaves, they listened to
the Concentus Musicus of Vienna, conducted by d'Harnoncourt's
nephew, Nikolaus Harnoncourt, play Bach's Brandenburg Concerto
No. 4. They heard William Paley preside and David Rockefeller and
the painter Robert Motherwell and Arthur Drexler speak of their
dead friend and colleague. "The Museum's existence as an essential
part of contemporary artists' lives," Motherwell said, "contributed in a
basic way to the transplantation of modern art to America and to its
extraordinary growth and flowering here." There was no question in
anyone's mind of the part that d'Harnoncourt played in making this

so. Indeed they had in their hands a handsomely designed and printed
red-brown booklet with d'Harnoncourt's name and dates on its cover
and a title page which read "A Tribute/ October 8, 1968, Sculpture
Garden, The Museum of Modern Art;" in it ten statements attested to
his prowess, the richness of his personality, his devotion to the arts. "I
worked so closely with René for twenty-eight years," Monroe
Wheeler, who contributed a short biography to the "Tribute," said,
"that for me his passing marks the decline of one life as well as the
close of another." Barr concluded his statement with, "I think he was
a great man. I know he was a noble man." The balance of speculation
and knowledge in Barr was perfectly in character. There were statements from Abe Fortas, who praised d'Harnoncourt for his contribution to the welfare of American Indians, Henry Allen Moe, Richard
Lippold, the sculptor, William S. Lieberman ("René d'Harnoncourt
was not a scholar; he was a humanist. He was a champion and he had
style."), Eliza Parkinson (who noted that the Museum "under his leadership and guidance" had grown to "approximately five times the size
it was in 1949 when he became Director."), Robert Goldwater, the
director of the Museum of Primitive Art, and finally Bates Lowry
about whom, of course, there was a great deal of curiosity and speculation among the two thousand who sat on the hard little folding chairs.
"No one," he wrote

> could work as closely, daily, with René d'Harnoncourt as I have
> done from the day my appointment as his successor was an-
> nounced a year ago without having the substance of his being
> touched. We worked with an exhilaration and a zest for explora-
> tion that would bring the Museum ever closer to the ideals to
> which he had devoted his life. He was a large man who was large
> in spirit, a gallant man who was generous with his love and praise,
> a wise man who solved problems with humor and kindness. We
> thought he was indestructible. We still do.

Lowry was quite right. D'Harnoncourt's presence is still very much
felt at the Museum, and every time there seems to be a misjudgment
about policy or about personnel or about the hanging of an exhibition,
someone wishes he were there with his finger cocked in his eye and
his seemingly tangential parables to straighten it out. His mourners
were not easily turned away from his memory, and there were many
who were eager to retain their claims to his affection. "He gave himself
unsparingly to his colleagues," Eliza Parkinson wrote. And Bill Lieber-

man said, "To anyone with whom he ever worked he was a friend, to many their best."

His successor scarcely had time to catch his breath before he found himself, in a manner of speaking, on the street. Lowry's tenure as Director of the Museum was brief and stormy, and it had the effect of causing a rift in the Board of Trustees and a polarization of the staff from which the Museum still has not, two Directors later, entirely recovered.

When Eliza Parkinson retired as President, William S. Paley took her place. He was the inventor and chairman of the Columbia Broadcasting System, and he had been a trustee of the Museum since the mid-'30s. David Rockefeller, who continued as Chairman of the Museum's Board, persuaded Paley that it was his turn to take over. Paley had not been a particularly active trustee and was therefore something of a stranger to the Museum's staff. He had, however, been a generous member of the board, a donor of paintings to the Museum's collections, and a regular contributor to the Museum's purse. He had come through handsomely at the time of the drive, as also had the CBS Foundation. His office on the northeast corner of the top floor of "Black Rock," as the CBS building, designed by Eero Saarinen, is called, looks down on the roof of the Museum, a reminder to Paley of his responsibilities and often, it must seem to him, of a cross he bears. Paley is a collector, and his office, conventionally furnished, is also expensively, albeit conventionally, hung with proper modern paintings that reflect a taste for Impressionists and Post-Impressionists and would strike only the most conservative taste as daring. Paley is part of the Whitney rather than the Rockefeller axis of the Museum. His wife is Mrs. Jock Whitney's sister.

Lowry's plans for the future of the Museum, as he spoke of them before he occupied d'Harnoncourt's office, seemed sound. The direction in which he wanted the Museum to grow was rooted in the scholarly traditions established by Barr, and his concepts of service to other institutions, to artists, and to the Museum's public bore the marks of d'Harnoncourt's inspiration and practice. Precisely what went wrong that caused him to be summarily dismissed is differently explained by each person one asks. There are those on the staff who say, "He was a good man, a nice man, we liked him. He just was in the wrong job." There are others who say that when he took the job over he suffered from *folie de grandeur*, that he was "too big for his boots," and that "he lost his head" when he was faced with the intensity and variety of the Museum's problems. "He was too much of an academic and too little of a humanist," one staff member said in explaining that Lowry, in pursuing his intense interest in the development of the International Study Center, made the mistake of setting up "a parallel power structure" within the Museum. He saw it as an organization with its own director and staff which would be separate from the functions and scholarship of the curators and the Librarian. "Instead of carefully integrating the Study Center into other functions of the Museum," I was told, "he thought it could be established by fiat." This led to a feeling that he did not make any attempt to take the staff into his confidence and try to bring them along with him as participants. Instead they felt that he was pushing a program down the Museum's throat more or less to spite them. The result was that he alienated those whose confidence he most needed to win. Lowry was not the first administrator at the Museum to discover that to treat the curatorial staff in a high-handed manner is to cut one's own throat.

His troubles, however, by no means stopped with the staff, for he managed to alienate a good many of his trustees as well. He apparently lacked the tact necessary to deal with a board that was used to the firm but gentle and witty ways of d'Harnoncourt, the *savoir-faire* and poise of Wheeler, and the somewhat mystical quality of Barr's quiet firmness. He is said to have overplayed his joviality in an attempt to establish an intimacy with the board, and instead of warming to him, they thought it gauche and their initial enthusiasm cooled. He made the mistake of being casual with them when he should have been businesslike. He endeared himself neither to the trustees nor to the staff when he declared, "I am going to make this a great museum." They were stupefied; they knew quite well who had already made the Museum great.

The board found him extravagant and unwilling to face the realities of a budget, an attitude by which boards are universally put off, especially when so much of the financing comes out of their own pockets. (One is reminded of Stephen Clark's remark to Victor d'Amico many years before, to the effect that "to wealthy people money is not just money; it's a symbol. You waste a penny or a thousand dollars, it's the same thing." Lowry clearly did not understand this.) Lowry's attitude was implicit in a remark he made to me in 1968: "Don't ask me about statistics," he said, "I can never remember how many people work for the Museum or things like that." He expected the money to flood in from somewhere, and where it came from and how was the trustees' business. One of Lowry's colleagues said, "You really can't blame him for being extravagant," and went on to explain that the way in which the trustees talked about spending millions and millions on expansion of the Museum, on grandiose plans for buildings as though they only had to ask for money to get it, did not create an atmosphere in which watching the pennies seemed important.

Precisely what precipitated the crisis which caused Paley and David Rockefeller to fire Lowry after he had been Director of the Museum for less than ten months is not on the record, nor on people's lips. But in the best traditions of the communications business they invited him in no uncertain terms to get out ("Has MOMA gone network?" someone said), and they did it without consulting the Executive Committee of the Museum's board. This, too, caused trouble. Ralph F. Colin, long a member of the board and a vice-president of the Museum, a lawyer who has been successfully battling for the rights of artists for years, and not only Paley's personal lawyer but an attorney for CBS, questioned at a meeting of the trustees Paley's action taken without the knowledge or consent of the board. Paley was evidently infuriated by this challenge to his judgment and authority, especially from a man with whom he had been so closely associated for so long, and he asked for, and got, Colin's resignation. He also dismissed him as his personal attorney, and a few months later Colin's CBS account was given to Roswell Gilpatric, the senior partner of the firm of Cravath, Swain and Moore.

The official date of Lowry's "resignation" (according to Paley's "Report of the President" in the Museum's *Biennial Report 1967–69*) was May 15, 1969. The news was released before that, and on May 12 Grace Glueck of the *New York Times*, who knows a story when she sees one or can dig one out if she suspects one, found a trustee willing to make a public statement. He said, "With a good board and a good director, how can such a crisis arise? I believe there was connivance against him." The trustee was John de Menil of Houston and New York, the president of Schlumberger, Ltd., "an international company operating in oil engineering, electronics and space." He had been on the Museum's board for ten years, and, according to Miss Glueck, he "charged that 'clannish' staff members interested in 'retaining their influence' misrepresented Mr. Lowry to members of the board of trustees." "His views," she said, "are in disagreement with those of other trustees who expressed disappointment over what they characterized as Mr. Lowry's lack of administrative ability, his failure in staff and trustee relationships and his assumption of certain responsibilities that might have been delegated."

Two trustees had worked closely with Lowry when he was running the CRIA organization; they were Edward Warburg and Beth Straus. Neither of them was consulted by the "search committee" or by Paley or Rockefeller before Lowry was hired. I mentioned this to Monroe Wheeler, who said, "There were other trustees who weren't consulted who might have been." David Solinger, the president of the board of the Whitney Museum, ran into David Rockefeller not long after the Lowry incident and said to him, "When you've got friends like X [meaning de Menil] you don't need enemies." "David was not amused," he told me. "I think he was deeply hurt by the whole thing, that his and Paley's decision should be disputed or that their right to fire Lowry should be questioned. Some people think that the only function of a board is to give money and to hire and fire the director."

For the second time in its history the Museum found itself without a Director, and for the second time it was administered by an inter-regnum committee. This time it was called the Operating Committee. Its chairman was a trustee, Walter Bareiss, and with him were Wilder Green, the Director of the Exhibition Program, and Richard Koch, the Director of Administration.

Bareiss, as we have seen, was the man who introduced the Art Lend-ing Service to the Junior Council. He was (and is) a collector, and when it was decided that there should be an exhibition of works of art from the collections of members of the Junior Council, Barr and Dorothy Miller visited his, among others. They were greatly im-pressed. He had a very large and distinguished collection of prints, "boxes and boxes of them from Albrecht Dürer on down," Miss Miller said, "a very great span." He also had Bonnards and Cézannes, and, "as he was of German origin," some German Expressionists, "and not only that but Pollock and de Kooning—the current scene." As a result of this evidence of concern, he was invited to be on the Acquisitions Committee, and in 1964 he was elected to the board. In the spring of 1967 he was appointed by the board as chairman of the Collections Committee and also chairman of the Painting and Sculpture Exhibi-tions Committee. He replaced James Soby, and he took on a hornets' nest. All had not been well in the Painting and Sculpture Department since Andrew Ritchie had left to become director of the Yale Art Gallery in 1958, and all was by no means ideal from his point of view even then. The old problem of contention between whoever was head of the Painting and Sculpture Department and Barr was never re-solved. What got bought was Barr's prerogative, in fact if not in theory. For a while after Ritchie left, Soby, as he so often did, came in to pinch-hit and while serving as Acquisitions chairman also acted as department head. In 1958 Peter Selz, who had established a scholarly reputation in the modern field with a book called *German Expressionist Painting* and was chairman of the art department at Pomona College and director of its gallery, was hired as a curator at the Museum, and he subsequently hired William Seitz, who was working in the Princeton art department and its museum. Seitz, who is a painter and scholar, was the first graduate student in the fine arts at Princeton to take his doctorate in modern art, and it had been Barr who had persuaded the department to let him do it. He was also responsible for the first one-man exhibition of a modern painter at Princeton: he did a show of Arshile Gorky. Selz stayed for seven years, and was encouraged—indeed, urged—by d'Harnoncourt to accept a job at Berkeley. Seitz left because of a misunderstanding, according to Dorothy Miller. "Something was said by René at a meeting that he misunderstood," she says, "and the next day he accepted a job at Brandeis. It was a very sad thing that we lost him." [2]

It was into this vacuum that Bareiss stepped and into which he attempted to let some air. Selz and Seitz had left. Barr was about to retire, so was d'Harnoncourt. Bareiss had been asked to look into the advisability of combining the directorship of the Painting and Sculpture Department with the job that Barr had held as boss over the collections. All this was before Lowry had appeared on the horizon, much less on the doorstep. It was not until after he had departed and the interregnum committee had been set up that Bareiss undertook the job he had initially been asked to do. His colleagues on the Operating Committee, Koch and Green, were old hands in the Museum's affairs. Koch, as we have seen, is a lawyer who got deeply involved with the Museum's problems at the time of the fire in 1958 and stayed on as chief member of the administrative staff. Wilder Green was first introduced into the Museum by Arthur Drexler and worked in the Architecture and Design Department. During the reconstruction of the Museum in the early '60s he was, as a colleague put it, "the goat." All sorts of matters having to do with the building program landed in his lap and he evidently managed them "with extraordinary equanimity." He was later moved to the Programs Department under Wheeler, and when the Operating Committee was set in motion he was in charge of programming and relations with the curatorial staff.

2 Seitz replaced Sam Hunter at Brandeis. Hunter left Brandeis to become director of the Jewish Museum in New York. Hunter had been a curator at the Modern under Ritchie, and had left to become acting director of the Minneapolis Museum of Fine Arts. To complete the circle, Hunter is now teaching at Princeton.

Koch was head of administration, and Bareiss was engaged in trying to straighten out the mess in the upper echelons of the curatorial staff that Lowry had inherited and, as it happened, had greatly aggravated by insisting that he be Director and Chief Curator and in charge of the collections all at the same time.

Bareiss' solution to the problem was to put William Lieberman in charge of everything to do with painting and sculpture and prints and drawings as well. Under Lowry's regime the department had been expanded and three associate curators had been added. Offices had been shifted around at considerable expense of both money and, evidently, of efficiency as well. In 1968 William Rubin, who had done exhibitions for the Museum as a guest director in the past (a show of Matta's paintings in 1958, for example, and the big Surrealist and Dada show of 1968 which d'Harnoncourt had asked him to organize more than ten years before), was appointed Curator of the painting and sculpture collections. "I was strictly an art historian," he said, "though I was a collector and I knew a good deal about the art market, which Alfred thought was important. It's the only collection in the world that I'd have given up teaching to curate." Rubin's first appearance in the Museum was when he was a child and came to the Saturday art classes that d'Amico had instituted. (He was a pupil of d'Amico's at the Fieldston School, and, he said, "They let me invent a course; when I was a senior in high school I gave a course in the comparative aesthetics of music and art.") He had done his graduate work in history of art at Columbia under Meyer Schapiro and Millard Meiss, taught full-time at Sarah Lawrence College, and given a graduate seminar for the City University of New York. After he came to the Museum he took on a teaching assignment at the Institute of Fine Arts as an adjunct professor. ("It was a study of the decade 1905–1915," he said. "We got to 1910.") He came to the Museum with the title of Curator, and when Lieberman was appointed by Bareiss as Director of Painting and Sculpture in 1969, Rubin became Chief Curator.

What Bareiss created turned out to be a can of worms. As of October 1, 1969, the staff of the Painting and Sculpture Department in addition to Lieberman and Rubin included seven associate curators, six assistant curators, six curatorial assistants, a researcher, three secretaries, and a custodian, or almost exactly three times the number of bodies it took to open and run the Museum in 1929, just forty years before.[3] The department was unwieldy, "more than anyone but a

3   The total staff of the Museum on October 1, 1969, was 451.

wizard," as Dorothy Miller put it, "could handle." There was friction. One of the associate curators quit, unable to work for Bill Lieberman. Rubin made it quite clear that he was going to report not to Lieberman but to the Director (when there was a Director): "that was crucial because in the kind of thing I do, you can't clear everything every time you have to turn around." The situation boiled up into a crisis, and the trustees had to step in to re-establish peace. Lieberman was determined not to relinquish any of the prerogative Bareiss had given him; Rubin was damned if he was going to be a step below Lieberman on the ladder and report to him. A committee (what else?) was appointed by the trustees to resolve the matter, and the "solution" it came up with was to make Lieberman Curator of Drawings and other works on paper (prints and watercolors), Rubin to be in charge of the painting and sculpture collections, and Kynaston McShine, who had been an associate curator, in charge of painting and sculpture exhibitions. McShine declined the title of "Acting Director" as being more to his discredit in terms of his career than to his credit. So a truce was established, even if peace was not.

But this truce was not yet in the process of negotiation when Paley announced that a new Director of the Museum had been appointed. He was John Hightower and he had come into prominence in the art world as the executive director of the New York State Council on the Arts. A protégé of Nelson Rockefeller and of Henry Allen Moe, he was thirty-seven, and he had a name not only for his ability to convince the hard-nosed legislators in Albany of the virtues of supporting the *avant-garde* arts but also for running a highly complex operation with verve and flexibility. He was, in other words, regarded as a promising administrator as well as a man of a new era in the democratic purveyance of the arts. The members of the arts council, whose bidding he guided and did, were a sophisticated group of patrons, promoters, dilettantes, and scholars of the arts with whom he found it, if not easy to deal, at least a great deal more than just possible. They liked him, his style, and his concept of the breadth of the council's responsibilities to all of the arts and to all of the people who might be touched by them. Moreover, he had humor and an easy manner and tact. He was running by far the most ambitious arts council in the nation (except for the National Council on the Arts of the federal government) and was generously praised by Nelson Rockefeller for his performance. He looked to the second search committee at the Museum in two years like the answer to prayer, and they offered him a salary about double what they had ever paid Alfred Barr.

What Hightower looked like at a distance was not precisely what he looked like to the trustees, or at least the influential old guard of the trustees, once he was on the premises. They knew that they had not hired a scholar, but though Hightower had called himself a "tactful generalist and humanist," they had not let this sink in. It is, indeed, difficult to know what they thought they were getting other than a bright young man who would see things their way if they just said what their way was, and run the Museum the way it had been run by d'Harnoncourt. They were not in the least prepared to discover that they had a political humanist on their hands who did not think of the Museum as an inviolable treasure chest. They were shocked when he suggested that the masterpieces might be spread around so that they might be seen in communities where art was regarded as something that was to be found only in palaces built by and for the rich. They were even more shocked when he said that "Art is the process of living. There must be a correlation between the concerns of museums and the qualities of living," and that "pollution is as much an aesthetic concern as it is an industrial or economic problem." They were stunned when he remarked to a reporter that taking a Thanksgiving turkey out of the oven "could be a great artistic experience," and they scowled when he referred to the Museum as a "club." He obviously touched a jumpy nerve when he said that art "doesn't have to be thought of as a connoisseurship. It's fun. It doesn't always have to be savored like the bouquet of a fine wine." This was heresy!

After he had been Director for a little over ten months, Edward Warburg said, "John is only interested in society, not in art. His first question is, 'What's its social impact?' He believes that a modern museum must be related to political action. He's on a suicide course." At just about that same time another trustee, one who was invited to be on the board at Hightower's suggestion, Eric Larrabee,[4] called him up and asked how he was getting along. Hightower replied, "Well, I've been on the job eight days longer than Bates Lowry."

At nine thirty on the morning that Hightower turned up for his first day as Director of the Museum and was understandably in somewhat of a daze, William Lieberman came into his office. "You've simply got to fire Bill Rubin," he said. A little later the same day a friend of Hightower, the artist Ralph Ortiz, whose work is represented in the Museum, appeared in his office. They had worked together on a project

4 **Eric Larrabee**, who had been a member of the state arts council while he was provost for arts and letters at the State University in Buffalo, became Hightower's successor as Director of the New York State Council on the Arts.

for Harlem when Hightower was director of the state arts council. "I have three demands to make," he said. "I demand that the Museum show the work of more blacks, more Puerto Ricans, and more heterosexuals!" He wished Hightower luck, and went on his cheerful way.

It was not only with his trustees, obviously, that Hightower got into early trouble. One of the jobs he was told to do by the trustees was to cut the projected deficit, which, when he took over, was estimated at $1,800,000. Eighteen months later the staff had shrunk from 539 to 440—"mostly by attrition," but there had been a number of difficult confrontations. A few old heads (including Sarah Rubenstein's and Mildred Constantine's, Assistant Treasurer and Curator of the Design Collection respectively) had rolled, very much to the dismay of their colleagues. He had fired Inez Garson, who had replaced d'Amico as the head of Education, because, it was said, he wanted closer control himself over the educational programs of the Museum. He had also run head-on into Arthur Drexler, who had had hopes of being appointed Director of the Museum and who made no secret of the fact that he disapproved of Hightower's attitude, policies, and lack of background in the scholarship of the arts and judgment of them. Hightower invited Drexler to have a drink at the Century Club and tried to fire him. As Eric Larrabee said, "It didn't take." Drexler was in a stronger position with many of the trustees and the old-guard staff than Hightower was, and he made it quite clear that he was prepared to raise hell both within the Museum and, if it came to that, with the press. The matter was dropped.

What was not dropped was the problem of reducing the number of clerical personnel and the lower levels of the professional staff, and on Christmas Eve of 1970 Hightower found himself faced with a threatened strike. It was set off by the dismissal of eleven clerical and professional employees. Nothing came of that strike, but it forecast another which happened in the following August and which Grace Glueck in the *Times* characterized as "a remarkably low-key affair." This one too was precipitated by the dismissal of members of the staff, but there was now a newly formed union called the Professional and Administrative Staff Association with 200 members and an affiliation with the Distributive Workers of America, described as "an independent, liberally oriented union affiliated with the Alliance for Labor Action." The pickets, mostly young women with a very high quotient of good looks and pleasant manners, carried posters that were more notable for their humor than their bite. "MOMA was built on a ROCKY foundation," one proclaimed. Another was a reproduction of Wyeth's

"Christina's World" with a balloon coming from her mouth with "STRIKE" printed in it. Another read, "MOMA IS HAVING LABOR PAINS." The throw-aways that the pickets handed out to passers-by undertook to explain what the cut-backs in staff would mean to the public. It painted a dark picture of fewer loan exhibitions, sharply reduced library and study-center hours and services, fewer museum publications, cut-off of the growth of archives, fewer traveling exhibitions, and "fewer exhibitions of work by younger, less well-known, or controversial artists." Nobody on the board or on the senior staff denied that all of these things were true, but neither did they know where the money was to come from. "This is not a private club for the rich," said Virginia Allen, one of the young members of the professional staff (she was in the Painting and Sculpture Department), "it's an international institution that belongs to the people."

The strikers, who by no means represented all of the administrative and professional staff (there were many hold-outs and much resentment among some of the young members and between union and anti-union factions), thought that the future problems of the Museum's finances could be solved by government support. Other unions represented in the Museum—the guards, for example, belonged to the Building Service International Union—wanted no part of the professional and clerical revolt, and paid no attention to the picket lines. Some of the upper-echelon staff, though not involved themselves, were uneasy about crossing the lines and did not. A good deal of hard feeling was engendered by the stealing of personnel records, telephoned threats at night by striking employees to those who were not striking, the issuance of statements which, according to the Museum, had no basis in fact, the prevention of films, intended for showing at the Museum, from being delivered, and so on.

A long article in the *Village Voice*, a lively local tabloid, gave the union's reasons for the strike and strongly supported it. The piece was much the fullest and most articulate statement of the strikers' "grievances" against the Museum, Hightower, Paley, the trustees, the senior curators, administrators, corporations, and, indeed, the ruling classes. It was filled with quotes from the dissidents. "Machiavelli's 'The Prince' has been the operating manual for the Museum," one striking employee said, and another is quoted as saying that it is "ruled by the people who rule this world" (i.e., Paley and David Rockefeller). Another staffer in defense of Bates Lowry and his regime said, "I don't think he understood that anyplace in the world such evil existed as existed in the Museum of Modern Art." The strikers, the reporter noted, weren't complaining about the trustees but about "the fact that they didn't have access to them, that only department heads and a few others represented issues to the trustees, and that they were seeing the museum they loved deteriorate, but risked losing their jobs if they spoke out." One of the things they spoke out about to the *Village Voice* reporter, Robin Reisig, was that they were "trained in art history far more than their supervisors," that "many of the younger staff members started taking seriously what they had been taught in school. . . . They weren't interested in palling around with the rich and looking down on 'workers.'. . . This glorified self-image of being an aristocrat doesn't work any more." They took issue with "another major Picasso show" and were quoted as saying, "We all *know* he is a great artist. The museum is a mausoleum, proving again and again how great Picasso is." And, furthermore, the report said, "many of its staff members feel MOMA could do more 'to serve the public rather than serve the ruling classes.' "

The article mentioned parenthetically that "(The Museum has had a very large deficit in recent years)," a detail that was not further explored except to say several columns later, "MOMA pleads poverty, predicting a deficit of $1.3 million for this fiscal year. Hightower wrote employees that if the trend toward growing deficits was not reversed, by 1978 the museum would 'have no alternative to closing our doors.' " The intention of the article, however, was not to mediate the dispute or to give both sides of the argument, but to state and support the strikers' position in the standard and frequently useful tradition of factional journalism. It did not point out, as Hightower often had, that the reason for the deficit which necessitated cutting the staff was that the Museum was trying to supply more services for more people, not for fewer, than it could afford to pay for, and that one of its greatest problems was that the public (not "the ruling classes") came in such great numbers that the size of the buildings could not effectively accommodate them. It did not say that it was almost impossible for anyone who wanted to look at the exhibits not to find himself staring between the necks of people in front of the work of art he came to look at, or that the crowds necessitated an increased number of guards for practical security purposes in the face of increasing vandalism and theft of works of art. It was surely the Museum's fault for making modern art of such interest to so many people that it could not keep up with the demand it had created, but it was not the kind of error that it wished it had not committed. Quite the contrary. It had been largely responsible for the fact that the young staffers were "trained in art history far more than their supervisors," because of its influence on the teaching of art history in colleges which, until it came along, ignored anything in the least unacademic or revolutionary that happened after 1875. There had been nobody to teach the older members of the Museum staff; to all intents and purposes, they had invented the history of modern art and made it into a discipline. The Museum's problem, as the director of another museum wrote to me, was that it had become "the victim of its own success."

The strike, which had started on August 20, was over by September 5, and the union announced a "tremendous breakthrough" in Museum-employee relations and a contract that was "a historic one, whose adoption at other museums would constitute an extraordinary development." Hightower said that "many of the provisions, particularly those relating to educational benefits and matters of policy, may well become benchmarks for the entire museum profession." Actually, though there was a wage adjustment (the annual minimum salary was raised from $4,700 to $5,750 with an across-the-board increase of 7½ percent for all association members), most of what the striking union got was lip service. The trustees' decision to cut the staff in order to reduce the deficit remained, but, as the *Times* reported, "a little time was gained in the contract for those marked for dismissal." The Museum promised to try harder to get government support for its programs. The residue of the strike was one of bitterness within the staff, dismay within the board, and an apparent weakening of Hightower's position with both.

On July 30, 1971, less than a month before the strike, Hightower was quoted in the *Times* as saying, "The Museum of Modern Art will be around for a while, and hopefully, I will be too." Though there was already considerable speculation about how long he would last in the job, Paley publicly said, "I think he's doing just fine. As things stand, he's Director of the Museum and he'll continue to be Director." The fact was that Hightower had become the focal point, the magnet to attract all the ills the Museum world was heir to, all of the conflicts between those who believed that the sole functions of a museum are historic and aesthetic and those who believed that it must become a social and political mirror of the dissatisfactions of artists and an active force in resolving community problems which are essentially political. In a *Members Newsletter* in November 1970 Hightower had declared his position: "Many of the nation's problems are aesthetic," he wrote,

> as evidenced by the glut of neon down every main street in America. The solution of America's main street blight, however,

will not be made aesthetically. It will be made politically. Despite this literally glaring fact, no museum in the country is willing to take a stand on an issue which in any way involves a political commitment.

Artists have traditionally been the most conscientious and, at times, the most provocative critics of society, and our obligation, as a museum, is to reflect the concern and work of the artist. As a modern museum, our responsibility is more complicated, for we must reflect most importantly the work and concerns of the artists of the present day, who feel that their work cannot be divorced from the humanism that provokes it.

Later in the same letter he said, "Were we, as The Museum of Modern Art, to wait fifty years from now to reflect on what was artistically valid in terms of this work, we would cease to be a museum of modern art."

Hightower attracted fire not just by such statements as this. The exhibition called *Information,* in which there was a "Dial-a-Poem" section, included a few tapes by "radicals" and "revolutionaries" in a wide selection that "ranged from work by poets such as Frank O'Hara and Barbara Guest to radical 'concrete' poetry composed almost as collage from newspaper headlines." Hightower wrote:

> Congressman Shirley of Iowa was one person who took exception. His aide called to find out the reasoning behind including statements by Eldridge Cleaver and Bobby Seale on a taped anthology of important contemporary poetry and statements of the last decade. The curious question that lingered after the telephone conversation was whether or not the Museum enjoyed a federal tax exemption. On another occasion, several FBI agents spent the day at the Museum on the Dial-a-Poem phones.

Here were echoes of the voices of Congressmen Dondero and Busbey and their attacks on radicalism in the arts in the 1940s and of still earlier days during the Depression when the government stepped in and prevented the WPA Federal Theatre from producing one of its shows called *The Living Newspaper* because it criticized Mussolini's Italy.

This was a diversion compared with other problems that Hightower had inherited and some he created for himself. He was in charge of a financial sieve from which the money was pouring out faster than it was being poured in, and he was aware that plugging up some of the holes in a sieve was still not going to make it into a container. He found himself subjected to pressures from minority groups who demanded representation in the Museum not on the grounds of the quality of their art but on the mere fact of its existence. He found himself caught in a crossfire between curators and between factions of employees. His early statements about his being opposed to museums as "elegant warehouses for beautiful things" had not gone down well with those who collected and nurtured such things, though in the course of his first year he had greatly altered his attitude toward the Museum's collections and said so.

In the fall of 1970 Hightower tried to turn the minds of the trustees to a consideration of his policies, which he hoped to make theirs, and the result was an *ad hoc* committee with Walter Bareiss as its chairman. For a time it looked as though Hightower might be getting somewhere in changing the Museum's philosophy to encompass the social and political problems of the arts as well as sticking to what had so long been its collecting, research, caretaking, and proselytizing concerns. Instead, the committee (or, more precisely, its chairman, Bareiss) came up with an "*aide-mémoire*" which set a list of priorities for the Museum that spelled out quite precisely what can only be called "business as usual." The only unusual thing about the memorandum was that its author found it necessary to draw a distinction between "modern" and "contemporary," a matter over which tempers had flared many years before. "For purposes of this Report," the *aide-mémoire* said, "the term 'modern' applies generally to the art dating from 1870 and the term 'contemporary' applies to the art created today." Barr, if he saw the memorandum (which he unquestionably did as a trustee), must have shaken his head in disbelief at such a solecism. But to Hightower the *aide-mémoire* and a more formal memorandum that followed it was something more than a gaffe; it was a straightjacket. And not only he but important members of the staff, most particularly Drexler and Rubin, saw the memorandum as an invasion of their prerogatives and took it upon themselves to tell the trustees that "policy of this kind was none of their damn business." The trustees approved the memorandum "unanimously."

An even more serious problem for Hightower, however, was that he found himself *persona non grata* with a number of the older and most powerful trustees for the simple reason that he was not René d'Harnoncourt, nor a reasonable facsimile thereof. He had none of d'Harnoncourt's soothing style, none of his aristocratic social self-possession, none of his deliberate, quiet elder-statesmanship which they had found so comforting and protective. He could not by any stretch of the imagination be a father figure to them; he was young, his humor and his language and laughter were unabashed. One of the senior trustees who had been on the committee which chose him said, "He doesn't come from a cultured background, and he doesn't know anything about art." He could neither provide them with d'Harnoncourt's reassurance and his genius for display, nor with Barr's aesthetic conviction and guidance. His statements about art and social imperatives made them not just uneasy; they thought he had betrayed them. His response to this in the press was, "Sure, some of the things I said put them off—though they weren't any different from what I said when they considered me for the job."

It seems quite clear in retrospect that the trustees did not know what they wanted from him as Director because they had not considered seriously what they wanted the future of their Museum to be. The *status-quo-ante*-Lowry appears to have been what they thought reasonable enough for the time being. What the Museum had been for the last fifteen years, from the time of its twenty-fifth birthday when its wave had crested and begun to decline into generalized, sparkling, rather bodiless foam, seemed satisfactory. It was a pleasant, popular, often piquant but not outrageous curatorial showcase and guessing game. Its best days were a tough act to follow, but the trustees did not want a tough man to follow them.

Hightower was not tough enough. He arrived filled with a crusading spirit and a considered, albeit, skeptical attitude toward the Museum's traditions. He learned, perhaps too quickly, to accept them; if he wanted to keep his job, he had no choice. It might have been better to have flouted them and retired bloody rather than just blue, to have departed with an obscenity rather than with a friendly handshake. But that was not his nature any more than it was his nature to be a father image on the one hand or a toady on the other. He tried to do his best on his own terms. In the trustees' terms, he failed. He was the wrong man in the wrong place at the wrong time.

The emphasis should be on *place*. His ideas about what a museum should be in 1970 were surely no more radical than, probably not as radical as, Alfred Barr's had been in 1929, nearly a generation and a half earlier. Barr had a philosophy and a plan about the functions of a museum which were shocking. What an outrageous thing it was to consider that movies and photographs, cooking utensils and typewriters and motorboat propellers had any conceivable place in an art museum! What did a museum have to do with billboards and book bindings, with housing developments, shoeshine stands and office buildings? They were all right in their place, but until Barr put them there, their place was not in an art museum. Barr had created a new kind of museum with an encompassing philosophy that gave dignity to all of the visual arts of living, not just the arts that had been regarded as "fine." He had with his museum created a new kind of *place*.

Hightower's attitude to the arts had sprung from an entirely different environment and time. His convictions about the relation of the arts to society (which is to say how people live) was not a contradiction of the ideas Barr fought for but an extension of them. Unlike Barr, Hightower wanted to improve people's enjoyment and understanding of the arts not by precept and example, as the Museum had done, but by participation, by making the arts a part of their lives, not something about which to be reverent but something to take to heart, enjoy, and learn from. To put his theories into practice Hightower did not need an old place, a place that had established its philosophy, its credentials, and its satellites and was happy with them, however admirable that place might be. He needed a brand-new place with brand-new backing by men and women as enthusiastic about his concept of a museum as Barr's early backers either were or were soon persuaded to be when he set out on his missionary errand. If Hightower was the wrong man at the wrong time at the wrong place at the Museum of Modern Art, he had been the right man, at the right time, in the right place as director of the New York State Council on the Arts. There, with the strong backing of Nelson Rockefeller and Seymour Knox, chairman of the council, both staunch conservatives in many matters but not in art, he had successfully waged a campaign for the new radicalism in the propagation and distribution of the arts.

These facts and qualifications could not have made less difference to Paley and David Rockefeller when they decided that they had given Hightower plenty of time to prove himself as Director of the Museum, and that he was not their man. Hightower was summoned to Paley's office on a morning early in January 1972 and was handed a letter of resignation which he was told to sign. Hightower, however, said that he would like to write his own letter of resignation: he was told that he might "if you get it back here by three this afternoon." On January 5 Rockefeller and Paley jointly sent a memorandum to the trustees which began, "We regret to inform you that Mr. John Hightower has resigned as Director of the Museum of Modern Art." It enclosed a copy of the press release and a copy of Hightower's letter of resignation. As the *Times* noted, "it was understood that the resignation had been requested." In his letter directed to "Dear David and Bill" Hightower noted that he had reduced the Museum's budget by "just under $800,000," that a professional union which "will, I am sure, be of benefit to the entire museum profession" had been formed, and that he had fostered programs which gave the Museum "a chance to expose the work of younger and more experimental artists." He then said what he planned to do. "I feel," he wrote, "that my commitment to all the arts and their inherent capacities as a humanizing influence for society can better be pursued elsewhere."

The Paley-Rockefeller letter advised the trustees that "Mr. Richard Oldenburg, Director of Publications at the Museum since 1969, has agreed to assume responsibility as Acting Director, supported by an administrative committee consisting of our top level curatorial and administrative personnel. A search committee will be appointed immediately to recommend a successor to Mr. Hightower."

There was surely no reason for the letter to mention, though it must have occurred to some of those who received it, that the Board of Trustees of the Museum of Modern Art had achieved the dubious distinction, unmatched by any other museum one can summon to mind, of having fired three out of the four Directors it had ever hired.

*By creating museums for modern art, we have
abandoned the traditional approach of art museums
to art. A museum of this sort is more like a trade
fair, exhibiting works made for the moment, but not
given any collective value, except in so far as
fashion decrees that they are "in."*
DILLON RIPLEY *in* The Sacred Grove, *1969*

Chapter **XXI** *Living Dangerously in
the Seventies*

When Professor Mather at a gathering in honor of the young Museum in 1934 said, "The business of every modern museum is to live
as dangerously as possible," he could not have had an inkling of the
kinds of dangers that would beset the Museum nearly four decades
later. If it was born and grew up in a cultural desert, it was now
teetering on a conspicuous pinnacle. He could not have known, for
example, that the greatest dangers to threaten the Museum were the
direct result of its remarkable success. He would have been surprised
to find it the victim of an over-popularity which created many of its
financial problems. Not even an admission fee of $1.75 (it had climbed
gradually from 25 cents in the late 1930s) could keep down the crowds.
It was the victim of its scholarly resources, both alive and on paper,
which caused dealers and collectors and students, the press and the
broadcasters to be constantly at it for information. Most of all, it was
the victim of its own missionary zeal. It had sold its doctrine so well
that the very institutions that had looked to it for inspiration and
interpretation of the dogma had grown weary of its authority and
turned against it. "It had worked itself out of a job," a painter who has

431

also run a university art department wrote. "The very effectiveness of its programs alienated those it had instructed." And a museum director of the same generation said, "It became the prisoner of its own success and the taste of its founding generation. Although a succession of younger people came in, none stayed long. Finding themselves out of step, they left." Still another historian and caretaker of culture, who said that "in one sense the success of MOMA has also been its undoing," added quite reasonably, "But then most institutions, particularly in this rapidly changing world, have a life span of only so long, and the fact that it was vital and vigorous for almost a quarter or a third of a century is a remarkable record indeed."

No one denies the depth or breadth of the Museum's influence, not only in America but in Europe. In the 1930s, as an English critic observed, modern art "had very little support from the great established museums in Europe or England. . . . Germany and Italy outlawed it, France left it to private collectors and dealers, England actively disliked it. The great German collections were dismantled by Hitler, the main figures were refugees, and so on. The MOMA really was the only sanctuary of learning and good sense. Barr especially had a quite extraordinary breadth of sympathy. . . . The Museum is still thought of as *the* modern museum in the U.S.A. and even in the world." Glenway Wescott said, "It is its mystique that has impressed me about the Museum more than anything else in modern life. The Museum has had an influence in this country greater than I've known any cultural agency to have anywhere in the world." In January 1972, J. Carter Brown, the director of the National Gallery in Washington, a man a full generation younger than Barr and d'Harnoncourt, called the Museum "the most significant tastemaking factor in twentieth-century America." He added, "I was there on Saturday and was reminded all over again what a fabulous achievement it was."

It is interesting and pertinent that Brown said "was," not "is." For by many the Museum is looked upon as rather old-fashioned, a dear relic of a great age of experimentation and ferment in the fine and applied arts and in their ways of being presented to a skeptical public. It is a comforting reminder of the youth and vigor and brashness of a radical generation that fought its way out of the Depression, through a world war, and wound up rather smugly wondering about the insolence and bad manners of a new generation of radicals.

But the feelings of nostalgia, coupled with those of a kind of frustration, are deeper and more thoughtful than that. There is a belief on the part of some of the Museum's old friends and admirers (I have no idea how many and can judge only from the sample with whom I have talked or corresponded) that the Museum should become the treasure house and showcase of the era known as "Modern." "I think if I were the Chairman of the Board," one said to me, "I would really make the Museum on 53rd Street an historical document of its time, and if members of the board wanted to play the museum game of the moment with contemporary art, I would get loft space in SoHo and begin a completely new chapter in what might turn out to be questionable but lively museology for the future." Another said, "I have come to the conclusion that 'modern art' is a thing of an era and that the Museum of Modern Art is, or should be, like the Baroque Museum in Vienna or the Ca' Rezzonico [of eighteenth-century arts] in Venice." Someone else frivolously (or at least not seriously) suggested that the Museum should be called The Barr Museum of Modern Art, as its great collection was in fact the creation of his personal taste.

The present staff of the Museum, of course, wants no part of packaging the Museum's past in a dignified time capsule, but neither does it want its treasures dispersed to other more traditional museums. "All of our gallery space," Arthur Drexler said, "including the 1964 additions, would fit into the main hall of the Metropolitan Museum, and yet everyone acknowledges that this is the greatest collection of all the arts of the twentieth century. One third of our space is devoted to temporary exhibitions. All of this activity takes place in this container, which was originally set up as a sort of private club. The collection is in warehouses; it's in basements and attics. It's piled on top of itself, inaccessible mostly. The trustees are just not able to grasp what the problem is, in fact, at this moment. This thing ought to be not just twice its size but six times its size. . . . I think we have a moral responsibility to this collection, and it is idle to talk about giving it to the Met. Where would they put it?" He also thinks it is idle talk to attach the Museum to an era. "People make the mistake," he said, "of thinking that the Museum makes the art. These things come in waves." It is up to the Museum, he believes, to identify the first ripples which someday become waves, then study them, chronicle them, and exhibit them. "Take for example the current Italian show [*Italy, the New Domestic Landscape*]—we've been working on it for years. We know more about the new Italian design than anybody in Italy." He suggested that there may be something developing now in Japan that in ten years will be as revolutionary. It would then be the Museum's responsibility to do for Japan what it has done for Italy.

Not long after Hightower's departure and the appointment of

Oldenburg as Acting Director, one of the trustees said to me, "This time we're not going to be rushed into a decision." The board was evidently satisfied (or, in any case, the Executive Committee was) that Oldenburg, who had come into the Museum to run the Publications Department two years after Wheeler's retirement, was an administrator with an unflappable calm and good sense who could, with the support of the "top-level curatorial and administrative staff," keep the Museum running smoothly. They were impressed by the skill with which he had straightened out what they regarded as a mess in the Publications Department; it had been saddled with an unconscionable inventory. They were also impressed by his easy presence and social assurance, by his poise which was coupled with humor, and by the evident fact that he was not over-awed either by the trustees or by the job they asked him to do. He was not the sort to jump into grandiose schemes as Lowry had, nor to try to alter the direction of the Museum's path as Hightower seemed to. He would feel his way. He would not ruffle the feathers of his colleagues or of his board, and he would make them feel themselves a part of any steps he might take.

Before coming to the Museum he had been managing editor of the trade department of the Macmillan Company, an old and solid publishing firm in New York, and before that he had worked for Doubleday and Company as head of the design department of that vast publishing empire. He had graduated from Harvard, spent a year in the Harvard Law School, and was for a time assistant to the director of financial aid in Harvard College. His relation to the arts was tangential: Claes Oldenburg, the Pop artist, is his brother. He was not an art historian (a lack for which Hightower was attacked and of which Lowry was suspected of having an overdose). When I suggested to one of them that the trustees might be wise to decide what they wanted their Museum to become before they settled on a Director, my comment was brushed aside as irrelevant, and not surprisingly so. What I had suggested was not in the tradition of the relationship that had existed between trustees and Directors of the Museum since the start.

The trustees of the Museum have prided themselves (not always with reason, as we have seen) on not interfering with the Director or with the curators in matters of artistic policy. They have, moreover, regarded themselves as almost unique among museum boards in letting the Director have his head. On the other hand, there has probably never been a museum board that got more fun, from the very first, out of the institution it controlled. In the earliest days, as in the latest, the Museum has been a place for members of the board to display their taste and their acumen—from the opening exhibition of Cézanne, van Gogh, Gauguin, and Seurat and the second show of *Nineteen Living Americans,* which the trustees helped to choose, to the exhibition of Picasso to celebrate Barr's seventieth birthday in 1972. There were quite a number of paintings in the show that were promised to the Museum but were still in trustee collections.

Part of the fun they have had has been the Museum's parties, the dinners in honor of the opening of exhibitions, at which they foregather in "black tie" and long dresses to celebrate the artist (if he is alive and willing), their "distinguished guests," and each other. (It has been said with some accuracy that "control of the guest list is control of the institution.") When it was suggested by the officers that expenses for social occasions be reduced along with other economies that were being made, one of the trustees asked Hightower if he thought they meant it. "Good God," he replied, "of course not!" A more subtle and essentially more gratifying part of the fun that the trustees have long enjoyed has been the deference with which they have been treated by the Directors (until Lowry) and by staff members who have added a note of culture and Upper Bohemianism to their dinner parties. They are greeted at the Museum as though they were nobility, and curators drop what they are doing, no matter how urgent it might be, to show them new acquisitions, let them into exhibitions in the process of preparation, and make them privy to what is new and exciting—tips, in a manner of speaking, on the culture and conversation market. Their collections are not infrequently formed but also hung with curatorial advice, not just in the case of Nelson Rockefeller, but of anyone on the board who asks for it. Eyebrows are now and then raised at preferential treatment that is given to members of the board and by no means least to Philip Johnson, who is not only a trustee and a generous donor of works of art but the Museum's architect. "I've told them again and again," he said to me, "that they're crazy to have a member of the board as their architect. That makes me my own client." The fact is that there never has been an architect for the Museum who was not a trustee, since Philip Goodwin, with Stone as his associate, designed the "new building" which is still the nucleus of the Museum. When a reporter for *New York* magazine asked Johnson, "What do you look for in a trustee?" he replied, "Money." And when she asked, "Is that all?" he said, "That's three things. Money money money."[1]

[1] "The Manhattan Arrangement of Art and Money" by Sophy Burnham, *New York,* December 8, 1969.

There is no question that the Museum's trustees have paid richly for the preferential treatment they have received. The Museum would not have come into being without their personal benefaction, and it could not have continued to exist, much less grown to such proportions or influence, without it. Now, however, it is apparent that the era of such support for the Museum is drawing to a close. Mount Rockefeller, Mount Whitney, and Mount Guggenheim no longer represent the kind of support on which the Museum once could count. Mount Guggenheim, of course, disappeared years ago when Mrs. Guggenheim died. There seems to be no evidence that the next generation of Rockefellers, the children of Nelson and David and John, have any particular interest in the Museum or that they will carry on the family tradition of its support. The same is true of Jock Whitney, who has been a pillar of the Museum in more respects than just financial. Possibly the Rockefeller Foundation can be counted on in the future unless the status of foundations in general is sharply altered, as some influential legislators would like to see. There are evidently many Westerners and Midwesterners who are not in the least sanguine about the vast amounts of money made available to institutions that they suspect politically by Eastern foundations. But even the Rockefeller and the Ford foundations examine largely without family prejudices and predilections the funds they give, and they demand, in most cases, that institutions which are the recipients of their beneficence demonstrate their public urgency by finding other funds to match in whole or in part the grants the foundations give.

When the striking employees protested that the Museum did not try hard enough to get government funds to meet its deficit, they had a grandiose notion of the extent to which federal and state governments can or are willing to support any single institution. They were aware of what has become a trend in the partial financing of cultural institutions, but the competition for the public "cultural dollar" is as fierce as for the private cultural dollar. No one knew this better than John Hightower, who, when he was running the New York State arts council, had been on the receiving end of thousands of pleas for help. Dollars from the business community which in recent years have been directed toward the arts have gone largely to such seemingly bottomless pits as symphony orchestras and to shoring up the limp finances of over-extended cultural centers. The Business Committee for the Arts, of which David Rockefeller is a moving spirit, advises corporations on how they can effectively steer a portion of their charitable gifts to art institutions. It is a relatively new organization, and so far the contributions it has steered to museums have been scarcely more than a helpful drop in the bucket. Such funds as the Museum has received from industry have been for specific exhibitions such as the Italian design show or programs such as the Film Library's "Cinéprobe," or the salary that was provided for Edward Steichen by the photography industry.

So the money problems which the trustees of the Museum and Richard Oldenburg, who was officially appointed Director on June 28, 1972, face is a far cry from those of the Museum in its early days. Private philanthropy has by no means run out, but the numbers and kinds of cultural institutions in these days of what Jacques Barzun has called "America's love affair with culture" have proliferated at a fearsome rate. New museums, ambitious new cultural centers, new orchestras, dance groups, repertory theaters, art schools, graphic workshops, architectural preservation groups, community galleries . . . each has a legitimate claim on the private cultural dollar, and each has its angels, some of whom are archangels like the big foundations and some of whom are mere *putti* like the lowest category of members of the Museum of Modern Art. Obviously in a great many cases the hopes of the cultural upstarts and their ambitions have far outrun their means of support. A modern museum, very fancy, very grand, in Pasadena had to close down. It made the Museum of Modern Art look frightfully old-fashioned, but it almost immediately ran into both personnel and financial problems. As this is written, there is good reason to hope it may find the means to open again. In Atlanta a $13,000,000 cultural center which incorporates a museum and an art school had to evict for lack of funds a theater group, a ballet troupe, and an opera company, and cut back its symphony programs because it could not afford to do otherwise. And the costs of culture keep going up. Not only have unions pushed wages up in symphonies, for example, but they have insisted on less rehearsal time and extra pay for playing "difficult" music. "Culture" is the least of their concerns, and community pride demands that the funds to keep the orchestra going be found somewhere. Not enough is found and so the number of programs and the amount of new music to be played are sharply cut.

The analogy of the symphony with the problems of not only the Modern Museum but all art museums is not difficult to draw. Like the orchestras, the museums first have to cut back their programs—the number of special exhibitions, the hours the library is open, the funds expended on improving their archives and their educational programs. At the very moment when more and more services are demanded of them by the community there is less and less likelihood that the museums can afford the services. At the very moment of the Museum's financial anguish, a number of other museums in New York that are not partially supported by the city were threatened with having to pay a whopping real-estate tax on the extremely valuable property they occupy. As everyone knows, the cities are as frantic to find money as the museums, and, like the museums, they turn to the federal government after they feel they have squeezed the local community to the politically possible limit.

The Museum has long been subjected to pressures from the community of artists, to attacks on its exhibition policies, on the choice of the artists it showed and purchased, on playing favorites (too much abstract art, too little abstract art, too many Europeans and too few Americans). As William Rubin said, "Every time we buy a work by one artist we insult 10,000 others whose work we don't buy." But in 1969 a new kind of attack filled the street outside the Museum garden with demonstrators, the air with speeches, and the columns of the *New York Times* with quoted invective and demands. There were about 300 demonstrators, and some of them carried signs which read "BURY THE MAUSOLEUM OF MODERN ART," and "DUMP DADA AND MOMA." At Lowry's instructions, the 54th Street gates to the garden were opened and the demonstrators came in. Whoever could get his hands on the portable loudspeaker could have his say. They said some measured and some unmeasured things. There were demands to rename the Museum "The Malcolm X Institute of Black Nationalism," and the *Times* reported that "one man wanted the Museum's research department dedicated to the work of South Vietnam's National Liberation Front." But the demands of the group, which represented the "Black Bloc" of the Art Workers Coalition, basically consisted of a wing of the Museum to be devoted to work by black artists, "extension into the black, Spanish and minority communities," and a public hearing to examine "the Museum's relationship to artists and to society." The demonstration was peaceful. There was no chanting, and no one either did any damage or was damaged.

The Museum had been warned earlier by the Art Workers Coalition that there might be a sit-in at the Museum unless it agreed to a public hearing. Lowry had averted this by promising that a special Committee on Artists' Relations was being formed by the Museum in which artists would participate. Its purpose, he said, was "to explore problems concerning the relationships of artists and museums." The Museum was feeling the fringes of a storm that had broken out the year before in Europe when students had moved against the Venice

Biennale and the Documenta at Kassel in West Germany. Hightower inherited the storm even before he officially became Director. He was asked by the Art Workers Coalition—of which the sculptor Takis Vassilakis, an artist in residence at the Center for Advanced Visual Studies at the Massachusetts Institute of Technology, was the principal spokesman—to meet with them at an artists' cooperative called "Museum" on Broadway. What they wanted, primarily, was a strong voice for artists in the running of the Museum; they wanted one third of the board to be made up of artists, and they demanded that the Museum sell everything it owned that was over thirty years old. Furthermore, they objected that "nothing meaningful could happen for artists at the Museum until the rich, dictatorial trustees go." They invited Hightower to become a member of the Coalition.

Hightower's responses to their demands on that evening in March 1970 did him no good with "the rich dictatorial trustees." He was quietly sympathetic, coolly politic, and by and large non-committal. He could scarcely have been otherwise, short of telling the Coalition to go jump in the lake. "Most of them [the powerful trustees] recognize the need to change," he said. "The most important are in sympathy with my point of view as they understand it." It was an optimistic statement, but he believed it. "There's not enough discussion with artists on the part of the Museum," he said. He could have added that, except for several architects, no artist had ever served on the Museum's board. The ostensible reason for the board's reluctance to include artists in its numbers was that it could not do so without seeming to favor some factions of the arts over others, though obviously this was what the Museum did every day in the selection of the artists it exhibited and those whose work it purchased. By and large, however, there has always been a basic mistrust and suspicion between artists and patrons, and the Museum offered no exception.

The Modern was by no means the only New York museum that was subjected to scrutiny, criticism, and, in a minor sense, invasion by the organized (if that is not too precise a word) artists. The Guggenheim Museum was the unwilling host to a visitation of eighteen members of the Art Workers Coalition on Flag Day 1970, who scattered leaflets about and hung a large flag on which was painted "PEACE OR DEATH" from Mr. Wright's spiral ramp and painted in washable color the word "UNIVERSALITY" on a wall. A meeting of the American Association of Museums at the Waldorf-Astoria Hotel in New York was, to all intents and purposes, broken up by a group that called itself the New York Artists Strike Against Racism, Sexism, Repression and War.

After the keynote speech by Nancy Hanks, chairman of the National Endowment for the Arts, Ralph Ortiz got the floor rather more by demanding it than by being given it, and shouted that museums must change radically "to meet the needs of all the people." "Must we wait for protesters to be murdered on the lawns of our museums?" he asked. His group had several days before staged a sit-in on the steps of the Metropolitan Museum "to condemn its open-door policy on a day that artists had declared a protest strike." Instead of letting itself be shut down for a day by the strikers (as the Whitney and Jewish museums had), it expressed its sympathies with the strikers by staying open five hours longer than it usually did.

The attacks by the Artists Strike on the assembled museum directors provoked some interesting response which said more about how the winds blow than about where they might ultimately drive the fleet of museums into a safe harbor. "I do not have any solution," August Heckscher, the New York City Administrator for Parks, Recreation and Cultural Affairs, said in a speech which he called "Museums in Crisis." "I admit that as a cultural bureaucrat I shall continue to press the institutions with which I have something to do to serve the public in ever widening numbers, to stress participation and involvement over the recondite and exclusive museum functions. I take some comfort from believing that in adopting this approach I am also serving the spirit of the age and the nature of modernity." Nelson Rockefeller got a "standing ovation" at the conference. He said, among other things, "Our nation is coming of age. For the first time politicians can get a plus instead of a minus for supporting this field. Young people today are less concerned about material things than spiritual values. If we do not provide opportunities for spiritual self-realization as well as material advances, our society will find itself shriveling." On his way out of the conference an artist said to him, "Stop praising yourself. We want to know what more you're going to do." When Rockefeller asked, "What's sexism, and what does it have to do with art?" one of the crowd said, "Ask Mrs. Rockefeller. She should be governor and not you."

The Museum of Modern Art continued to be the primary target of protest, not necessarily for what it had done but because of its high visibility and the ease with which it could be made a sitting duck. In April 1972 it was treated to what might be called "Ladies Day," when a group called Women in the Arts staged a demonstration, all dressed up to kill, on 53rd Street. There were about 300 of them and they played the placard game which the Museum seems to inspire. Some wore signs reading "MOMA PREFERS PAPA," and "SIGMUND, THIS IS WHAT WE WANT, AN END TO DISCRIMINATION." The ladies handed out leaflets in which they said that of the 1,000 one-man shows that the Museum had held only 5 had been the work of women. The truth of the matter (not that it mattered to the demonstrators) was that the Museum had held 293 one-artist shows since it opened and that 27 of them had been the work of women. "That's a rebuttal?" one demonstrator wanted to know.

Nearly three years before this demonstration a member of the Art Workers Coalition who is also a critic, Lucy Lippard, had quite succinctly said not only what was rather vaguely in the minds of many of her fellow members of the Coalition, if I guess correctly, but also in the minds of a good many professional museum people who had long followed the fortunes of the Museum. "There seems little hope for broad reform of the Museum of Modern Art," she said. "It has done a great deal in the past and now seems to have become so large and unwieldy that it has outgrown its usefulness. What is really needed is not just an updated Monolith of Modern Art, but a new and more flexible system."

"Broad reform" of the Museum, in the sense that Miss Lippard evidently meant it, would mean removing the Museum radically further from its original purposes than over the last forty years it has removed itself. It would not mean reformation in the sense of getting rid of heresies and getting back to fundamental principles; it would mean deserting its initial purposes, which were to present to a serious public a kind of art to which it was not accustomed and to open its eyes to a new belief in a new aesthetic doctrine. The early Museum was intended as a place of contemplation in which the faithful, and those who might be converted, could measure, evaluate, accept, or discard a developing art called "modern." The Museum knew its own mind, which is to say that Alfred Barr knew his own mind, and what was important to him determined the nature of the Museum and more particularly what the Museum presented to the public as worthy of contemplation and respect. Little by little in the first decade it added articles to the faith. To the arts called Fine—that is, to painting and sculpture—it added the arts called Minor—graphic art, photographic art, cinematic art, and the arts of the environment, architecture, design, landscape architecture. It also added to the nature of the faithful—that is to say, to its clientele or constituency or congregation. It very early did an exhibition of African sculpture, in the spring of 1935, and by promoting it in Harlem made a special and evidently successful effort to "interest the

Negroes of New York," as the *Bulletin* said. The show attracted an average of 1,000 visitors a day, "an increase of almost 6 percent" over average attendance. Moreover, the Museum got a grant from the General Education Board to make fifteen sets of photographs of the 500 objects in the show so that the Museum might distribute sets to Negro colleges and one set to the 135th Street (i.e., Harlem) branch of the New York Public Library, and keep one for itself. The photographs were made by Walker Evans, and he and the novelist John Cheever made all 1,500 prints. It was, one might say, merely a drop in the black bucket, but it evidenced an interest in the black community (or the Negro Community as it was then called) that was very nearly unique among New York museums in the early '30s.

Its constituency broadened as it introduced art classes in the Museum and initiated a new era in art teaching through d'Amico's program, the Committee on Art Education, and later through the Children's Carnival, now permanently installed in Harlem. Still farther afield went the traveling exhibitions, carrying the news, the objects (or photographs of them), and the doctrine to colleges in every corner of the country, to schools and to museums both large and small, many of which felt called upon to establish their own museums of modern art within their museums. Modern-art societies sprang up, as in Cincinnati, whose modern-art society was loosely affiliated with the Cincinnati Art Museum and sponsored its own exhibitions in the museum's galleries. All through the early years Barr kept a tight rein on what was permitted to issue from the Museum with its approval. Its traveling shows were models of display and of orthodoxy, as its publications were models of early scholarship in the modern arts and of bookmaking. Life in the Museum was arduous, devout, unsparing of itself or of the energies of its staff, whose devotion was matched only by its zeal and often by its fatigue.

But something else was happening to its constituency. The Museum was becoming chic. If it was considered "moderately amusing" and rather naughty by old New York society, it was becoming very nearly *de rigueur* for the Upper Bohemian society to be present at its evening openings of exhibitions where only those who were invited were supposed to appear. Here was where the editors of the fashion world came to see but more particularly to be seen by the theatrical world, the literary world, and the world of collectors, dealers, miscellaneous intellectuals, and debutantes. There was an aura of safe but heady adventurousness about the Museum, a sense of being identified with *le dernier cri* that appealed to the "bright young people" and to those who either

wished they were still young, who wouldn't be caught dead not knowing the name of the most obscure Surrealist, or who had the young in
tow. Identification with the Museum was considered not only sophisticated but urbane. Not only were the openings chic; being able to speak
the language of modern art, with its quite special vocabulary, was chic.
Owning it was still more chic, and to have something that the Museum
wanted to borrow for an exhibition was chicest of all. Some unknown
(to me) wag called the Museum a "finishing school for male and female dilettantes."

A danger the Museum faced when it moved into the glass-and-marble
palace on 53rd Street in 1939 was that the art would get lost in the
miasma of the fashionable. The threat to its initial integrity grew
greater as the surroundings grew gaudier. Parkinson's law, long before
Professor Parkinson invented it, went to work at once. Office space
abhors a vacuum, so does gallery space. More space meant more people
and more paperwork, the creation of more jobs, more miscellaneous
exhibitions, more sideshows, more jealousies and intramural skirmishes.
The first era of firings began. Frances Collins, Tom Mabry, John Mc-
Andrew, Sarah Newmeyer, and Alfred Barr were all thrown out in
fairly rapid succession. The excuse was that there was no way to run
this new big business except by being businesslike. How it happened
to be big business instead of the intellectual center it had set out to be
seemed irrelevant at that moment. A great deal of money was tied up
in the Museum or committed to it, a lot of very expensive and high-
powered backing by the board stood behind it, a lot of reputations
were involved, and so was the value of a great deal of art owned by
the Museum's best friends and most loyal supporters.

It would be not only unjust but inaccurate, in my judgment, to say,
as has often been said, that the primary concern of the Museum's
trustees was to protect their investments in art. As we have noted,
being a trustee of the Museum was a great deal of fun for most of
them, for many were museum directors *manqués*. It was also the source
of a good deal of social prestige for others who liked to find themselves
associated with the Rockefellers and Whitneys and Blisses and Cranes,
with the Clarks and Warburgs and Lewisohns. There is nothing uncommon about this attitude. Scarcely anyone who sits on a charitable
or educational board anywhere is above liking to be identified with a
group of people who "matter" in their community, whether it be the
vestry of a country church or the board of a hospital or the committee
of a dog show. Boards collectively are usually very different from
board members individually, and as a rule they are often far more

conservative as a group than as separate members. Like all such rules, this one is liberally peppered with exceptions.

One of the inescapable truths about the Museum and the dangers of the 1970s is that on its board and in very influential positions are some of the very same persons who were there twenty, thirty, and nearly forty years ago when they were young and the Museum was in its childhood and youth: William S. Paley, the President, Eliza Parkinson and Jim Soby, Vice-Presidents, Jock Whitney and Henry Allen Moe, Vice-Chairmen, are still there. So, of course, are David (Chairman), Nelson, and Blanchette Rockefeller. They are what the Art Workers Coalition calls "the rich dictatorial trustees," and, from the coalition's point of view, not without reason. They are indeed rich, and they control the rudder of the Museum. Such men and women will move slowly, cautiously, and quite probably, though with some reluctance, in the direction that the Art Workers Coalition wants them to—that is, toward a new concept of the Museum's role in the community, a role that bears out the Museum's initial charter as an educational institution but at the same time tries to maintain its early determination to be a great museum in the traditional sense of a great collection. It faces the question of whether it should become more and more of what one of its friends calls "a settlement house of the arts" or more and more like the Frick Museum in New York or the Phillips Gallery in Washington, a remarkable community-owned treasure, unaggressive but available to those who want to find richness and gratification, challenge and revelation in its treasures. The Museum of Modern Art is now neither a settlement nor a treasure house, neither leader nor follower, neither a Museum nor Modern.

What Modern meant when the Museum was founded is not what it means today. Modern was an attitude, a frame of mind, a conception of art characteristic of an era, and it was what it was because the Museum of Modern Art said that it was. That is why Modern today means Yesterday. But if the word Modern has had its meaning changed by the Museum of Modern Art, so has the word Museum had its meaning changed. It used to mean a place for what history had decided was worth putting in the deep-freeze. Whatever the effect the Museum of Modern Art may have had on the tastes of a generation, whatever it may have done to make the arts available to a vast number of people whom they might otherwise have escaped, however much it has done to improve the lot of the living artist by creating an atmosphere in which he is both more free and more respected than he has ever been before on this continent, however ephemeral these accomplishments may turn out to be in the long run, there is one effect of the existence of the Museum of which we can be sure. There is no question that because of Alfred Barr and René d'Harnoncourt museums will never be the same again anywhere in the world.

So be it.

But that is not to say that an eager, imaginative, disrespectful, and determined young cabal, now sitting hands-in-lap on the Museum's board, could not (indeed, might not) strike out on its own, as Abby Rockefeller and Lizzie Bliss and Mary Sullivan did. With the kind of initiative that opened the museum called Modern in 1929 and turned it into a cultural tidal wave by doggedness and brilliance, such a cabal might (indeed, could) start something just as unthinkable—a museum that is not a Museum, neither modern nor old nor good but, like its once youthful foster parent, prophetic and fresh and outrageous.

A Brief Chronology of the Museum of Modern Art, Including a List of Exhibitions, 1929–1972

In a very real sense the history of the Museum of Modern Art, so far as most persons are concerned, is the exhibitions it has displayed. It therefore seems appropriate to list the hundreds of exhibitions shown at the Museum. Between the time the Museum opened in 1929 and the end of 1972 there were more than a thousand, but the reader will not find all of them in the list that follows. Some exhibitions have been omitted for what seem to me good reasons. There have been, for instance, frequent shows of "Recent Aquisitions," sometimes a piece or two of sculpture or a few paintings or a group of prints. To list the items in these shows would fill another volume, and merely to list them, as they were billed, as "Recent Aquisitions" means nothing. Omitted from this list are also "Summer Exhibitions." Sometimes they were private collections lent anonymously; sometimes they were selected works from the Museum's collections, but in any case they have been recorded in the Museum's listings merely as "Summer Exhibitions." There have also been a great many shows of children's work from New York City schools and from the children's and young people's classes at the Museum. I have omitted these along with the annual Children's Holiday Carnival. There were constantly changing print and drawing shows, up for short periods of time lest they be damaged by overexposure to light; they often were given fanciful titles, which are meaningless in retrospect.

The first exhibition entitled "The Museum Collection: Painting and Sculpture" was held in 1933. Since then there have been a great many exhibitions drawn from the Museum's various collections, miscellanies for which there are no published catalogues. Unless they were given specific titles they have been omitted from the following list. Indeed, since the Museum moved into its "new" building in 1939, some portions of the permanent and study collections have always been on exhibition. On a few occasions, such as the celebration of the Museum's twenty-fifth anniversary, very grand exhibitions have been drawn from the collections and perpetuated by distinguished publications. Such a volume was *Masters of Modern Art,* now long out of print.

Those exhibitions whose titles in the list are followed by an asterisk (*) were accompanied (or sometimes followed) by published catalogues or related books bearing the Museum's imprint. This by no means represents a complete list of all of the Museum's publications which would have to include bulletins, how-to-do-it books, calendars, teaching portfolios, and, as mentioned in Chapter XII, studies that were not attached to any specific exhibition and a number of independent scholarly works of enduring value.

1929

MAY—*Mrs. Rockefeller, Miss Bliss, and Mrs. Sullivan invited A. Conger Goodyear to be chairman of a committee to organize a new museum for modern art.*
JULY—*Preliminary charter granted by the State of New York to the Museum of Modern Art (MOMA).*
AUGUST—*Alfred H. Barr, Jr., appointed Director of MOMA, Jere Abbott Associate Director.*
OCTOBER—*A. Conger Goodyear elected President of the Board of Trustees.*
NOVEMBER—*MOMA opened with its first loan exhibition* (Cézanne, Gauguin, Seurat, and van Gogh *) *in the Heckscher Building, Fifth Avenue and 57th Street, New York.*
Paintings by Nineteen Living Americans *

1930

Establishment of Junior Advisory Committee.
    Painting in Paris from American Collections *
    Weber, Klee, Lehmbruck, Maillol *
    Forty-six Painters and Sculptors Under Thirty-five Years of Age
    Charles Burchfield: Early Watercolors, 1916–1918 *
    Homer, Ryder, and Eakins *
    Corot, Daumier *
    Painting and Sculpture by Living Americans *

1931

Death of Lizzie P. Bliss and conditional bequest of her collection to MOMA.
    Toulouse-Lautrec, Redon *

German Painting and Sculpture *
Memorial Exhibition: The Collection of Miss Lizzie P. Bliss *
Henri Matisse *
Diego Rivera *

1932

MOMA moved to town house at 11 West 53rd Street; Library established; Department of Architecture established; first showing of work by photographers.
Modern Architecture: International Exhibition *
Murals by American Painters and Photographers *
A Brief Survey of Modern Painting *
Persian Fresco Painting—Facsimiles of Seventeenth Century Frescoes in Isfahan
American Painting and Sculpture, 1862–1932 *

1933

Department of Circulating Exhibitions established; the Bulletin of the Museum of Modern Art *started publication; first exhibition of furniture and decorative arts; first one-man photography show.*
American Folk Art: The Art of the Common Man in America, 1750–1900 *
Early Modern Architecture: Chicago, 1870–1910 *
Maurice Sterne, 1902–1932 *
Color Reproductions of Mexican Frescoes by Diego Rivera *
Toulouse-Lautrec Prints and Posters
Fruit and Flower Paintings
Sculptors' Drawings
The Museum Collection: Painting and Sculpture
Objects: 1900 and Today *
The Work of Young Architects in the Middle West *
American Sources of Modern Art (Aztec, Mayan, Incan) *
Project for a House in North Carolina by William T. Priestly
Gauguin Woodcuts and Watercolors
Modern European Art
A House by Richard C. Wood
Walker Evans: Photographs of Nineteenth Century Houses
Gifts and Loans from the Collection of Mrs. Saidie A. May
Edward Hopper: Retrospective Exhibition *
Painting and Sculpture from Sixteen American Cities *

1934

Accession of the Lizzie P. Bliss Collection; permanent charter granted by New York State Board of Regents; Machine Art exhibition initiated the design collection.
Philadelphia Savings Fund Society Building by Howe and Lescaze
International Exhibition of Theatre Art *

Machine Art *
Early Museum Architecture
The Lillie P. Bliss Collection *
Whistler: Portrait of the Artist's Mother
Housing Exhibition of the City of New York *
The War: Etchings by Otto Dix
The Making of a Museum Publication
Color Reproductions: Modern Watercolors and Pastels
National Exhibition of Art by the Public Works of Art Project
Modern Works of Art: Fifth Anniversary Exhibition *

1935

*The Film Library (now Department of Film) established in quarters in
CBS Building on Madison Avenue; first exhibition of black art.*
Gaston Lachaise: Retrospective Exhibition *
George Caleb Bingham, the Missouri Artist, 1811–1879 *
African Negro Art *
European Commercial Printing of Today
Fernand Léger: Painting and Drawings
Ignatz Wiemeler, Modern Bookbinder *
Modern Architecture in California
Le Corbusier *
Vincent van Gogh *

1936

*Plans to construct a new museum building announced; acquisition of four
houses on West 53rd Street; gift of 36 oils and 105 watercolors to MOMA
from Mrs. John D. Rockefeller, Jr.; Boston Museum of Modern Art in-
corporated; first showing of films at MOMA.*
Posters by Cassandre *
The Architecture of Henry Hobson Richardson *
New Acquisitions: The Collection of Mrs. John D. Rockefeller, Jr.
Cubism and Abstract Art *
Modern Painters and Sculptors as Illustrators *
Architecture in Government Housing *
Modern Exposition Architecture
Edward Steichen's Delphiniums
New Horizons in American Art *
American Art Portfolio
John Marin: Watercolors, Oil Paintings, Etchings *
Fantastic Art, Dada, and Surrealism *

1937

*MOMA moved to temporary quarters in the concourse of the Time-Life
Building in Rockefeller Center; educational project initiated as two-year
experiment with New York City high schools; first comprehensive photog-*

raphy exhibition; gift of site of present sculpture garden by John D. Rocke-feller, Jr.
> Vincent van Gogh (second showing) *
> Rugs Designed by American Artists
> Modern Architecture in England *
> Posters by E. McKnight Kauffer *
> Photography, 1839–1937 *
> Prehistoric Rock Pictures in Europe and Africa *
> Paintings by Paul Cézanne from the Museum
> Twelve Modern Paintings
> Project for a Community Center by Architects, Painters, and Sculptors Collaborative
> A Brief Survey of the American Film
> The War: Etchings by Otto Dix and "Armoured Train," a painting by Gino Severini
> Sculpture by William Edmondson
> The Town of Tomorrow
> Paintings for Paris by Thirty-six Living Americans
> Spanish and U.S. Government Posters
> The Making of a Contemporary Film
> The Museum Collection and Extended Loans

1938

Construction of new building at 11 West 53rd Street underway; first exhi-bition sent by MOMA to Europe; first Useful Objects exhibition.
> A New House by Frank Lloyd Wright ("Fallingwater") *
> American Folk Art *
> Subway Art (Murals and Sculpture for Subway Stations)
> Luis Quintanilla: An Exhibition of Drawings of the War in Spain *
> Alvar Aalto: Architecture and Furniture *
> Masters of Popular Painting: Modern Primitives of Europe and Amer-ica *
> Three Centuries of American Art (*Trois Siècles d'Art aux Etats Unis,* exhibited at the Jeu de Paume, Paris) *
> Competition for a Wheaton College Campus Art Center
> Walker Evans: American Photographs *
> The Prints of Georges Rouault *
> Useful Household Objects Under $5.
> Bauhaus, 1919–1928 *

1939

Tenth Anniversary year; opening of the new building at 11 West 53rd Street; resignation of A. Conger Goodyear as President of MOMA; election of Nelson A. Rockefeller as President and Stephen C. Clark as Chairman; initiation of regularly scheduled film showings in MOMA auditorium; in-auguration of Young People's Gallery; opening of the Library.
> Three Centuries of American Architecture
> Williamsburg Competition
> Art in Our Time: Tenth Anniversary Exhibition *

Charles Sheeler *
Picasso: Forty Years of His Art *
Useful Objects of American Design Under $10.*

1940

*Photography Department established with a basic collection and library;
Dance Archives established; Mrs. John D. Rockefeller, Jr., gave her collec-
tion of 1,600 prints to MOMA.*
  Smithsonian Competition for a Gallery of Art
  Modern Masters from European and American Collections *
  Italian Masters *
  Preview: Dance Archives
  Visual and Non-Visual Expression in Art
  The Work of Sharaku: Drawings and Prints
  American Designs for Abstract Film
  PM Competition: The Artist as Reporter
  Twenty Centuries of Mexican Art *
  Portinari of Brazil *
  Forty Years of the American Dance
  Two Great Americans:
      Frank Lloyd Wright, American Architect
      D. W. Griffith, American Film Master *
  The Ballet Today
  Useful Objects of American Design Under $10.
  American Color Prints Under $10.
  War Comes to the People, A Story Written with the Lens
  Sixty Photographs: A Survey of Camera Esthetics

1941

*Nelson A. Rockefeller replaced by John Hay Whitney as MOMA Presi-
dent for brief period; Presidency as well as Chairmanship of the Board
assumed by Stephen C. Clark; contracts signed with various government
agencies engaged in the war effort; various war programs initiated at
MOMA.*
  Pavlova Memorial Exhibition
  Indian Art of the United States *
  Tennessee Valley Authority: Architecture and Design
  Still Photographs from Hollywood Studios
  Britain at War *
  Sculpture and Sculptors' Drawings
  A History of American Movies * (*Film Index*, Vol. I.)
  A History of the Modern Poster
  Paul Klee *
  Masterpieces of Picasso
  National Defense Poster Competition
  Techniques of Painting (Advisory Committee Exhibition)
  Stockholm Builds
  Photographs by David Octavius Hill and Robert Adamson
  The Wooden House in America

Organic Design in Home Furnishings *
George Grosz
Buckminster Fuller's Dymaxion Deployment Unit
Isadora Duncan: Drawings, Photographs, Memorabilia
Image of Freedom (Photographs)
Joan Miró *
Salvador Dali *
Architecture of Eric Mendelsohn, 1914–1940
Useful Objects Under $10.
Silk Screen Prints Under $10.
American Photographs at $10.
Sculpture by Maillol, to Celebrate His Eightieth Birthday

1942

National Committee on Art Education initiated; first Children's Carnival of Art presented in MOMA garden.
Dancers in Movement: Photographs by Gjon Mili
Americans 1942: Eighteen Artists from Nine States *
U.S. Army Illustrators of Fort Custer, Michigan
Photographs of the Civil War and the American Frontier
Art in War: OEM Purchases from a National Competition
Henri Rousseau *
Two Years of War in England: Photographs by William Vandivert
Wartime Housing
Road to Victory (Photographs) *
Josephine Joy: Romantic Painter
New Rugs by American Artists
Camouflage for Civilian Defense
New Posters from England
Modern Architecture for the Modern School
How to Make a Photogram
The Americas Cooperate (Five Small Exhibitions)
Twentieth Century Sculpture and Constructions
United Hemisphere Poster Competition
The Museum and the War
Tchelitchew: Paintings and Drawings *
The Sculpture of John B. Flannagan *
Art from Fighting China
National War Poster Competition
Useful Objects in Wartime Under $10.
Twentieth Century Portraits *
Joe Milone's Shoe Shine Stand

1943

Five Serenade Concerts presided over by Virgil Thomson; publication of What Is Modern Painting? by A. H. Barr, Jr.; Photography Center opened on West 54th Street.
Brazil Builds *
Faces and Places in Brazil: Photographs by Genevieve Naylor

The Arts in Therapy
Americans 1943: Realists and Magic-Realists *
Birds in Color: Photographs by Eliot Porter
Helen Levitt: Photographs of Children
Yank Illustrates the War
Five California Houses
The Latin-American Collection of the Museum of Modern Art *
Religious Folk Art of the Southwest
War Caricatures by Hoffmeister and Peel
Five Paintings by Stanley Spencer
Tunisian Triumph: War Photographs by Eliot Elisofon
The Paintings of Morris Hirshfield
Airways to Peace (Photographs)
Bali, Background for War: The Human Problem of Reoccupation
Action Photography
Magazine Cover Competition: Women in Necessary Civilian Employ-
    ment
Alexander Calder *
Portraits (100 Years of Portrait Photography)
Marines Under Fire
Romantic Painting in America *

1944

Fifteenth Anniversary Exhibition, Art in Progress, surveys all aspects of
MOMA's program; Alfred H. Barr, Jr., dismissed as Director but does not
leave the Museum; René d'Harnoncourt joins the staff as Vice-President in
Charge of Foreign Affairs and Director of the Department of Manual Industries; Veterans' Art Center established; auction of "certain nineteenth-
century works," including many from the Bliss Collection, owned by the
Museum; Junior Advisory Committee dissolved.*
    Norman Bel Geddes' War Maneuver Models
    Modern Drawings *
    The American Snapshot *
    Modern Cuban Painters
    Look at Your Neighborhood
    Art in Progress—Fifteenth Anniversary Exhibition: *
        a. Painting, Sculpture, Prints
        b. Design for Use
        c. Built in U.S.A. 1932–1944 *
        d. Dance and Theatre Design
        e. Posters
        f. Photography
        g. Circulating Exhibitions
        h. Educational Services
        i. Film Library
    Picasso Exhibition for Mexico City
    Hayter and Studio 17: New Directions in Gravure
    American Battle Painting, 1776–1918 *
    Paintings by Jacob Lawrence
    Marsden Hartley *
    Lyonel Feininger *

Manzaanar: Photographs by Ansel Adams of Loyal Japanese-American
  Relocation Center
Building with Wood
The War Years: Color Reproductions of Works by Picasso, Matisse,
  Bonnard, 1939–1943
Are Clothes Modern? *

1945

Advisory Committee reconstituted.
  The Lesson of War Housing
  Power in the Pacific: Battle Photographs of Our Navy in Action on
    the Sea and in the Sky
  French Photographs: Daguerre to Atget
  Integrated Building: Kitchen, Bathroom, and Storage
  What Is Modern Painting? *
  Creative Photography
  Piet Mondrian
  Modern American Dance
  Georges Rouault *
  Stage Design by Robert Edmund Jones
  Paul Strand: Photographs, 1915–1945 *
  Works from the Museum Collection of Dance and Theatre Design:
    Ballet Drawings
  Tomorrow's Small House: Models and Plans *
  Stage Designs by Joan Junyer
  Fourteen Paintings by Vincent van Gogh
  Modern Textile Design
  Stuart Davis *
  Useful Objects, 1945
  Portrait of Ondine: Dance and Theatre Design

1946

*Nelson A. Rockefeller reelected President of the Board of Trustees with
John Hay Whitney as Chairman; James Johnson Sweeney appointed Direc-
tor of the Department of Painting and Sculpture; Film Library showed
"The History of the Motion Picture, 1895–1946"; Advisory Committee
dissolved.*
  If You Want to Build a House *
  Art of the South Seas *
  New Dormitories for Smith College
  Architecture in Steel: An Experiment in Standardization by Konrad
    Wachsmann
  A Home for U.N.O.: Must We Repeat the Geneva Fiasco?
  The Photographs of Edward Weston *
  New Furniture Designed by Charles Eames
  Marc Chagall *
  Original Illustrations for Children's Books
  Modern China (Tableware by Castleton)

Georgia O'Keeffe
A New Country House by Frank Lloyd Wright: Scale Model
New Photographers
Ballet Drawings by Franklin C. Watkins for "Transcendence"; Model
   by Eugene Berman for "The Island God"
Paintings from New York Private Collections
Photographs from the Museum Collection
Scenic Design by Arch Lauterer
Design Trends in Unit Furniture, Fabrics and Tableware
Fourteen Americans *
Modern Jewelry
Florine Stettheimer *
On Being a Cartoonist
Sixty-one Lithographs by Toulouse-Lautrec and Thirty-one Aquatints
   by Picasso for Buffon's *"Histoire Naturelle"*
"Le Tricorne" by Picasso
Useful Objects, 1946
Modern Rooms of the Last Fifty Years
Henry Moore *

1947

*Museum Collections established as a separate department with A. H. Barr,
Jr., as Director; James Thrall Soby appointed Director, Department of
Painting and Sculpture replacing James Johnson Sweeney; agreement with
Metropolitan Museum signed whereby MOMA would sell to the Metro-
politan certain paintings and sculptures that they agreed "have passed from
the category of modern to that of 'classic' "; Edward Steichen appointed
Director, Department of Photography.*
   The Theatre of Eugene Berman *
   Forty-six Recent Lithographs by Picasso from the Collection of Mrs.
      Meric Callery
   The Photographs of Henri Cartier-Bresson *
   Henry Hobson Richardson, 1838–1886: Architectural Masterpieces
   Printed Textiles for the Home
   Large-Scale Modern Paintings
   Taliesin and Taliesin West (Frank Lloyd Wright)
   Alfred Stieglitz Exhibition: His Photographs
   Alfred Stieglitz Exhibition: His Collection
   Two Cities: Planning in North & South America (Rio de Janeiro and
      Chicago's South Side)
   Robert Maillart: Engineer
   Boris Aronson: Stage Designs and Models
   Mies van der Rohe *
   One Hundred Useful Objects of Fine Design
   Ben Shahn *
   Three Young Photographers: Leonard McComb, Wayne Miller,
      Homer Page
   World of Illusion: Elements of Stage Design
   Highlights from the Film Library: Art and the Experimental Film
   Music and Musicians: Work by Six Photographers

1948

Veterans' Art Center became People's Art Center; Abby Aldrich Rocke-
feller (Mrs. John D., Jr.) died April 5th; d'Harnoncourt named Director
of Curatorial Departments.
   Portrait of Gertrude Stein by Picasso
   Stage Designs for the Ballet Society
   Gabo-Pevsner *
   Miró Mural (Commissioned for a Cincinnati Hotel)
   Lamb Wedge Lock Handle
   In and Out of Focus: A Survey of Today's Photography
   Pierre Bonnard *
   Louis Sullivan, 1856–1924
   Portraits in Prints
   Loren MacIver Mural Paintings
   New York Private Collections
   Fifty Photographs by Fifty Photographers
   Work from War Veterans' Art Center
   Recent Acquisitions: Bequest of Mrs. John D. Rockefeller, Jr.
   Bonnard-Picasso (Lithographs)
   Collage
   Photo-Secession Group: American Photography, 1902–1910
   Victor S. Riesenfeld Collection: Modern European Prints
   The Sculpture of Elie Nadelman *
   Christmas Exhibition: Useful Objects Under $10.
   Timeless Aspects of Modern Art *
   Photographs by Bill Brandt, Harry Callahan, Ted Croner, Lisette
      Model
   American Paintings from the Museum Collection

1949

Twentieth Anniversary year; Junior Council formed; d'Harnoncourt ap-
pointed Director of MOMA; Abby Aldrich Rockefeller Print Room estab-
lished; house by Marcel Breuer constructed in outdoor exhibition area.
   Hidden Talent Competition—Architecture
   The Exact Instant, One Hundred Years of News Photography
   From Le Corbusier to Niemeyer, 1929–1949
   Georges Braque *
   Frank Lloyd Wright: A New Theatre
   The House in the Museum Garden (Breuer) *
   Roots of Photography: Hill, Adamson, Cameron
   Lobmeyr Glass
   Master Prints from the Museum Collection
   Twentieth Century Italian Art *
   Art Nouveau from the Museum Collection
   Oskar Kokoschka *
   Realism in Photography: Steiner, Miller, Matsumoto, Sommer
   Prints by Gauguin, Vuillard, and Bonnard
   Sculpture by Painters

Painting and Sculpture in Architecture
Postage Stamp Design
Anni Albers Textiles
Modern Art in Your Life *
New Posters from Sixteen Countries
Six Women Photographers: Bourke-White, Levitt, Lange, Hoban,
   Babley, Larsen
Polio Poster Competition
Design Show: Christmas 1949
Roots of French Photography (Photography before 1870)
Paul Klee *

1950

*"Five Evenings with Modern Poets" (W. H. Auden, Marianne Moore,
e. e. cummings, William Carlos Williams, Robert Frost); cooperation with
Chicago Merchandise Mart in creation of "Good Design" shows initiated;
international competition for furniture design.*
   Percival Goodman War Memorial Model
   Photographs of Picasso by Gjon Mili and by Robert Capa
   Etchings by Picasso: The Sculptor's Studio *
   Mies van der Rohe: A Glass and Steel Apartment House for Chicago
   Charles Demuth *
   Franklin C. Watkins *
   Stieglitz and Atget Photographs
   New Talent: Drumlevitch, King, Parker
   Color Photography
   Prize Designs for Modern Furniture *
   Exhibition House by Gregory Ain *
   Posters from the Davis Collection
   Edvard Munch *
   Three Modern Styles
   Fifty-one American Photographers
   Carvers—Modelers—Welders
   Photographs by Lewis Carroll
   Skidmore, Owings and Merrill: Architects, U.S.A.
   Matthew Nowicki, Architect, 1910–1950 (Memorial)
   Chaim Soutine *
   Good Design
   New Talent (II): Bunce, Johnson, and Mundt

1951

*Grace Rainey Rogers Annex opened at 21 West 53rd St.; Art Lending
Service established by Junior Council; first exhibition of automobiles "as
art;" People's Art Center move to new annex.*
   Abstract Painting and Sculpture in America *
   Swiss Posters
   Korea—The Impact of War in Photographs
   Lebrun: Crucifixion

New Lamps (Design Competition)
Modigliani *
Japanese Household Objects
Abstraction in Photography
New Talent (III): Di Spirito, Kriesberg, Mintz
From the Alfred Stieglitz Collection
Modern Relief
Selections from Five New York Private Collections *
Le Corbusier: Architecture, Painting, Design
Some American Prints, 1945–50, from the Museum Collection
Twelve Photographers
Modern Bible Illustration
Lipchitz' "Birth of the Muses"
Forgotten Photographers
Eight Automobiles *
Prints by Max Beckmann
James Ensor *
Henri Matisse *
Memorable *Life* Photographs
Good Design
Five French Photographers: Brassaï, Cartier-Bresson, Doisneau, Ronis,
    Isiz

1952

*International program of circulating exhibitions initiated with Rockefeller
Brothers Fund grant;* Through the Enchanted Gate *television series spon-
sored by MOMA and National Broadcasting Company.*
Frank Lloyd Wright: Buildings for Johnson's Wax
Masterworks Acquired through the Mrs. Simon Guggenheim Fund
Picasso: His Graphic Art *
Odilon Redon: Drawings and Lithographs *
Posters by Painters and Sculptors
Sam A. Lewisohn Bequest
New Design Trends
Fifteen Americans *
New Talent (IV): Elliott, Power, Rogalski, Summers
Diogenes with a Camera I: E. Weston, Sommer, Callahan, Bubley,
    Porter, W. E. Smith
New York Times Posters
Architecture in the New York Area
French Paintings from the Molyneux Collection *
Understanding African Negro Sculpture
Then (1839) and Now (1952) (Photographs)
Two Houses—New Ways to Build: F. Kiesler and R. Buckminster
    Fuller
Recent American Woodcuts and Prints, by Marin, Hopper, and
    Weber
Good Design
Les Fauves *
Olivetti: Design in Industry *
New Talent (V): Goto, Hultberg, Kruger

Diogenes with a Camera II: A. Adams, Lange, Matsumoto, Man Ray, Siskind, Webb
De Stijl *

1953

Abby Aldrich Rockefeller Sculpture Garden opened; International Council of MOMA founded; privately owned U.S. Pavilion at Venice Biennale purchased by MOMA; property at 27 West 53rd St. acquired; 1947 agreement with Metropolitan Museum terminated; Katherine S. Dreier bequest to MOMA of 102 works of art announced; William A. M. Burden elected President of MOMA.

Built in U.S.A.: Post-War Architecture *
International Sculpture Competition: The Unknown Political Prisoner
Always the Young Strangers: Twenty-five Photographers
Edward G. Robinson Collection *
Four Poster Artists: Savignac, Games, Aicher, Bill
Georges Rouault *
Sculpture of the Twentieth Century *
Postwar European Photography
Recent American Prints, 1947–1953
Katherine S. Dreier Bequest
Kuniyoshi and Spencer
Expressionism in Germany
Varieties of Realism
Thonet Furniture
Jacques Villon: His Graphic Art *
Ten Automobiles *
Good Design
Architecture for the State Department
Premium Toys Designed for Industry
Léger *
New Talent (VI): Monroe, Schwartz, Sowers
Young American Printmakers

1954

Twenty-fifth Anniversary celebration; garden restaurant opened; Japanese house erected in outdoor area; publication of Masters of Modern Art.

Ancient Arts of the Andes *
Four American Graphic Designers: Lionni, Shahn, Matter, Martin
Signs in the Street
Edouard Vuillard *
Faces and Figures: Drawings from the Collection of the MOMA
Ceramics by Kitaoji Rosanjin
The Sculpture of Jacques Lipchitz *
Japanese Exhibition House
Niles Spencer
Japanese Calligraphy
Playground Sculpture: Winners of a Competition

Sculpture by Constantin Brancusi
Prints by Paul Klee
The Modern Movement in Italy: Architecture and Design
American Prints of the Twentieth Century
Twenty-fifth Anniversary Exhibitions: Paintings *
Modern Masterprints of Europe

1955

The Family of Man (Photographs) *
Good Design: Fifth Anniversary
Fifteen Paintings by French Masters of the Nineteenth Century *
Picasso: Twelve Masterworks
Textiles and Ornamental Arts of India *
New Talent (VII): Benrimo, Townley, Tyler
Prints from Europe and Japan
Etchings by Matisse *
The New Decade: Twenty-two European Painters and Sculptors *
Paintings from Private Collections * (Twenty-fifth Anniversary Ex-
   hibition)
U.P.A. "Form in the Animated Cartoon"
Léger Memorial
Giorgio de Chirico *
Yves Tanguy *
Two Graphic Designers: Bruno Munari and Alvin Lustig
Glass from the Museum of Modern Art Design Collection
Prints by Nolde and Kirchner
Latin American Architecture since 1945 *
New Talent (VIII): Craig, Fornas, Speyer
Vestments by Matisse

1956

*Property at 23 West 53rd St. acquired by MOMA from the Theatre Guild
for offices and storage (bookstore installed 1972).*
Diogenes with a Camera III: Bravo, Evans, Sander, Strand
Julio Gonzalez Retrospective *
Toulouse-Lautrec *
Diogenes with a Camera IV: Schenk, Garnett, Beraud-Villars, Burden
Family Service Association Posters
Recent Drawings U.S.A. *
New Talent (IX): Clerk, Hadji, Kabak
Kandinsky Murals
Twelve Americans *
Prints of Henri Matisse
Textiles U.S.A. *
Masters of British Painting, 1800–1950 *
Language of the Wall (Graffiti), photographs by Brassaï
Balthus *
Jackson Pollock *

1957

Children's Art Carnival sent to international trade fairs in Milan and Barcelona; International Council assumed sponsorship of MOMA's program of exhibitions abroad; exhibition of "Twentieth Century Design in Europe and America" sent to Japan.
The Graphic Work of Edvard Munch *
Buildings for Business and Government *
Travel Posters
New Talent (X): Cohen, Kohn, Schapiro
Picasso Seventy-fifth Anniversary *
Matta *
David Smith *
German Art of the Twentieth Century *
Seventy Photographers Look at New York *
Chagall
Gaudi *

1958

Fire in the Museum; Children's Carnival shown at Brussels World's Fair; "Design Today in America and Europe" prepared at request of Indian Government and established in New Delhi as core of India's first design collection; "New American Painting" exhibition shown in eight European cities.
Three Painters as Printmakers: Braque, Miró, Morandi
Seurat Paintings and Drawings
Juan Gris *
Fifty Selections from the Bareiss Collection
Jean Arp: A Retrospective *
Philip L. Goodwin Collection
Works of Art: Given or Promised
Architecture Worth Saving
Twentieth Century Design from the Museum Collection *
Ten European Artists (Prints)

1959

Thirtieth Anniversary Drive for $25,000,000 initiated to provide endowment, building, and program development. William A. M. Burden succeeded by Blanchette (Mrs. John D., 3rd) Rockefeller as President of MOMA.
Architecture and Imagery—Four New Buildings
Joan Miró *
New Talent (XI): David V. Hayes
Recent Sculpture U.S.A.
The New American Painting *
The Package *
New Talent (XII): Ronni Solbert

Three Structures by Buckminster Fuller *
New Images of Man *
The Artist in His Studio—Photographs by Alexander Liberman
Thirtieth Anniversary Special Installation—Towards the "New" Museum
Sixteen Americans *

1960

Announcement of gift by Mrs. E. Parmelee Prentiss of two brownstone houses at 5 and 7 West 53rd St., adjoining MOMA; "Jazz in the Garden" summer concerts initiated; Institute of Modern Art formed for People's Art Center and educational activities; auction of "Fifty Works Donated by Private Collectors" for benefit of Thirtieth Anniversary Drive.

New Talent (XIII): Peter Voulkos
The Sense of Abstraction in Contemporary Photography
Claude Monet: Seasons and Moments *
Homage to New York: A Self-Constructing and Self-Destroying Work of Art Conceived and Built by Jean Tinguely
Fifty Modern Paintings & Sculptures Especially Donated for the Benefit of the Thirtieth Anniversary Fund of the MOMA, New York
Portraits from the Museum Collection
Art Nouveau *
Jazz by Henri Matisse
New Spanish Painting and Sculpture *
New Talent (XIV): Baden, Gaudnek, and Rabkin
Visionary Architecture
Retrospective Exhibition: Museum of Modern Art Publications
The Drawings of Joseph Stella
Fernand Léger in the Museum Collection
Film Posters

1961

Henry Allen Moe elected Chairman of the Board of Trustees.

Mark Rothko *
James Thrall Soby Collection (Special Exhibition for the Benefit of the Museum's Thirtieth Anniversary Drive, M. Knoedler and Co., Inc., New York City) *
Max Ernst *
Steichen the Photographer *
Tangible Motion Sculpture by Len Lye
America Seen—Between the Wars
Futurism *
Boccioni Drawings and Etchings from the Collection of Mr. and Mrs. Harry L. Winston *
Japanese Vernacular Graphics
Richards Medical Research Building—Louis I. Kahn, Architect *
The Mrs. Adele R. Levy Collection—A Memorial Exhibition *
Fifteen Polish Painters *
Roads

Eero Saarinen, 1910–1961 (Memorial)
Diogenes with a Camera V: Clergue, Ishimoto, Brandt
The Art of Assemblage *
Max Weber—18 April 1881–4 October 1961, In Memoriam
The Last Works of Matisse: Large Cut Gouaches *
Chagall—The Jerusalem Windows
Orozco: Studies for the Dartmouth Murals
Redon, Moreau, Bresdin *

1962

*Ground broken for new "Garden Wing"; David Rockefeller elected
Chairman of the Board of Trustees; John Szarkowski appointed Director,
Department of Photography.*
Photographs by Harry Callahan and Robert Frank
Jean Dubuffet *
Frank Lloyd Wright Drawings *
Picasso—Eightieth Birthday Exhibition
Design for Sport *
Recent Painting U.S.A.: The Figure *
Walker Evans: American Photographs *
Ernst Haas: Color Photography
Mark Tobey *
The Museum of Modern Art Builds: Models and Photographs of Pro-
    posed Building Plans of Museum
The Bitter Years: 1935–41 (Farm Security Administration Photo-
    graphs)
Lettering by Hand *
Arshile Gorky, 1904–1948 *

1963

*Trustees announced successful completion of Thirtieth Anniversary Drive
and acquisition of Whitney Museum building adjoining MOMA garden at
20 West 54th St.; MOMA closed for five months starting December 2nd
for construction and remodeling; 125 paintings from MOMA collection
lent to National Gallery of Art, Washington, D.C., during closing.*
The Intimate World of Lyonel Feininger
Le Corbusier: Buildings in Europe and India
Emil Nolde, 1867–1956 *
Rodin *
Americans 1963 *
Five Unrelated Photographers: Heyman, Kraus, Liebling, White,
    Winogrand
André Derain in the Museum Collection
The Photographs of Jacques Henri Lartigue *
Hans Hofmann *
The Photographer and the American Landscape *
Medardo Rosso, 1858–1928 *
Stairs
"Fallingwater": A Frank Lloyd Wright House Revisited

1964

Museum opened May 27th with a series of exhibitions under the general title Art in a Changing World: 1884–1964; dedication of two new wings and enlarged sculpture garden by Mrs. Lyndon B. Johnson; opening of Philip L. Goodwin Galleries of Architecture and Design, Paul Sachs Galleries of Drawings and Prints, and Edward Steichen Photography Center.

Painting and Sculpture from the Museum Collections
Wilfred: Lumia Suite, Op 158
Family Portraits from the Museum Collections
A Selection of Drawings and Prints by Seventeen Artists from the Museum Collections
Edward Steichen Photography Center: Work from the Museum's Collection
Philip L. Goodwin Galleries of Architecture and Design: Work from the Museum's Collection
American Painters as New Lithographers
Stills from the Film Library Collection
The Photographer's Eye *
Two Design Programs: The Braun Co. The Chemex Corp.
Twentieth Century Engineering *
Pennsylvania Avenue, Washington, D.C.
The Photographic Poster
Contemporary Painters and Sculptors as Printmakers
Eduardo Paolozzi
Bonnard and His Environment *
Gunter Haese
Architecture Without Architects *
André Kertész (Photographs) *
Max Beckmann *

1965

Enlarged Abby Aldrich Rockefeller Print Room opened; Mrs. Bliss Parkinson elected President of MOMA Board of Trustees.

The Responsive Eye *
The Horror Film (Stills)
The Photo Essay
John S. Newberry: A Memorial Exhibition
D. W. Griffith: American Film Master *
Siskind Recently (Photographs)
American Collages
Modern Architecture, U.S.A.*
Giacometti *
Elliott Erwitt: Improbable Photographs
Glamour Portraits: Photographs
The Prints of Masuo Ikeda
Le Corbusier, 1887–1965 (Memorial)
Kay Sage Tanguy Bequest
Robert Motherwell *

Structures for Sound—Musical Instruments by François and Bernard Baschet *
The School of Paris: Paintings from the Florene May Schoenborn and Samuel A. Marx Collection *
Sculpture in Glass
Around the Automobile
René Magritte *
Chasubles Designed by Henri Matisse
Rauschenberg: Thirty-four Drawings for Dante's *Inferno*
Frederick J. Kiesler (Memorial)

1966

The Hampton Album (Photographs) *
Dorothea Lange (Photographs)
Mies van der Rohe Drawings *
"Greetings!" *
Turner: Imagination and Reality *
Marie Cosindas: Polaroid Color Photographs
Louis I. Kahn (Architecture)
The Career of an Actress: Sophia Loren (Film Stills)
Reuben Nakian *
The Object Transformed *
Bruce Davidson (Photographs)
Henri Matisse: Sixty-four Paintings *
Twenty Drawings: New Acquisitions
London/New York/Hollywood: A New Look in Prints
Toward a Rational Automobile
Walker Evans' Subway (Photographs) *
The Action Film (Stills)
The New Japanese Painting and Sculpture *
Contemporary Painters and Sculptors as Printmakers
Art in the Mirror
Chagall's "Aleko"
Photographs from the McAlpin Collection
Gaudi: The Sagrada Familia
The Taste of a Connoisseur: Paul J. Sachs Collection

1967

Alfred H. Barr, Jr., retired after thirty-seven years with MOMA, first as Director and subsequently as Director of Collections; appointment of Bates Lowry as successor to René d'Harnoncourt as Director of MOMA announced.
The New City: Architecture and Urban Renewal *
Calder: Nineteen Gifts from the Artist
Jerry N. Uelsmann (Photographs)
New Documents: Photographs by Arbus, Friedlander, and Winogrand
Posters for the Department of Film
Latin-American Art, 1931–1966
Jackson Pollock *

The Star Garden (A Place)
A European Experiment: Unique and Limited Edition Photographs by
    Brihat, Sudre and Cordier
Canada '67
Habitat '67 (Architecture)
Picasso: "Guernica," Studies and Postscripts
The Artist as His Subject
Stills from the Czechoslovakian Film Festival
Once Invisible (Photographs)
The 1960s: Painting and Sculpture from MOMA Collection
Architectural Fantasies: Drawings from the MOMA Collection
Lyonel Feininger: "The Ruin by the Sea"
Mutoscopes (Department of Film)
Jim Dine Designs for *A Midsummer Night's Dream* *
Jewelry by Contemporary Painters and Sculptors
The Sculpture of Picasso *
Prints by Picasso: A Selection from Sixty Years
The Star Vehicle: The Making of a Movie
Ray K. Metzker: Photographs
Frank O'Hara, In Memory of My Feelings *

1968

D'Harnoncourt retired as Director and replaced by Lowry in July; d'Harnoncourt killed by an automobile while taking a walk on Long Island; Mrs. Parkinson retired as President of Trustees and was succeeded by William S. Paley.
The Sidney and Harriet Janis Collection *
The Art of the Animator: The Storyboard
Word and Image: Posters and Typography from the Graphic Design
    Collection of the Museum of Modern Art, 1879–1967 *
Stills from the Jean-Luc Godard Film Series
Ben Schultz Memorial Exhibition (Photographs)
York House (Architecture)
Photography as Printmaking
Manhattan Observed *
Dada, Surrealism and Their Heritage *
Photographs before Surrealism
Christo Wraps the Museum
Recent Czech and Polish Posters
James Stirling: Three University Buildings
Cartier-Bresson: Recent Photographs
Art of the Real *
Garbo Film Stills
My European Trip: Photographs from the Car by Joel Meyerowitz
John Graham
Five Major Loans: Paintings Lent by Mrs. Bertram Smith and Norton
    Simon
Architecture of Museums *
Jean Dubuffet at the Museum of Modern Art *
Paul Caponigro: Recent Photographs
Monument to Six Million Jewish Martyrs by Louis Kahn

Tribute to Marcel Duchamp
Rauschenberg: Soundings
Brassaï Photographs *
Career of an Actor: Anthony Quinn (Film Stills)
Paris: May 1968. Posters of the Student Revolt
The Machine As Seen at the End of the Mechanical Age *
Eastern Kentucky and San Francisco: Photographs by William Gedney

1969

Lowry "resigned" in May; administration of MOMA assumed by a committee of three headed by Walter Bareiss, a trustee.
Julio Gonzalez
Stills from Lost Films *
Wall Hangings *
Function Without Form: Two Models for an Undesignable City
Willem de Kooning *
August Sander, 1876–1964: Photographs
Giacomo Manzu: Studies for "Portal of Death"
Kandinsky Watercolors
Ben Shahn, 1898–1969 (Memorial)
Painting for City Walls
Tamarind: Homage to Lithography *
Twentieth Century Art from the Nelson Aldrich Rockefeller Collection *
The New American Painting and Sculpture: The First Generation
The Career of an Actress: Katharine Hepburn (Film Stills)
Portrait Photographs
Urban Anticipations: Eugène Hénard, 1849–1923
Lucas Samaras: "Book"
Ludwig Mies van der Rohe "Memorial"
Robert Motherwell: "Lyric Suite"
Bill Brandt: Photographs
Claes Oldenburg *
Yugoslavia: A Report
George Grosz Drawings and Watercolors
Gary Winogrand: The Animals (Photographs) *
Ocean Projects: Hutchinson and Oppenheim
Drawings by Eric Mendelsohn, Architect
The Atget Collection (Selected Photographs)
The Graphic Constructions of Joseph Albers
A Salute to Alexander Calder *
Spaces *

1970

John Hightower appointed Director of MOMA in May.
Sherman's Campaign: Photographs by George N. Barnard
Mrs. Simon Guggenheim Memorial, 1877–1970
Joan Miró: Fifty Recent Prints

Hector Guimard *
Frank Stella *
Mark Rothko, 1903–1970 (Memorial)
The Japanese Film (Stills)
Photography into Sculpture
Theo van Doesburg: The Development of an Architect
Three Exhibitions
    a. Pop Art, Prints, Drawings & Multiples
    b. Popular Mechanics in Printmaking
    c. Preliminary Drawings
Protest Photographs
Photo-Eye of the Twenties *
Graphics I: New Dimensions
Information *
Archipenko: The Parisian Years
Barnett Newman, 1905–1970 (Memorial)
One-Eyed Dicks: Automatic Photographs of Bank Robberies
East 100th Street: Photographs by Bruce Davidson
Work in Progress: Architecture by Johnson, Roche, Rudolph
Stories by Duane Michals (Photographs)
Picasso: Master Printmaker
Robert Irwin
Painters for the Theatre
E. J. Bellocq: Storyville Portraits (Photographs)
The Nude: Thirty Twentieth Century Drawings
Paul Burlin, 1886–1969
Berenice Abbott: Photographs
Four Americans in Paris: The Collections of Gertrude Stein and Her
    Family *
Jasper Johns: Lithographs

1971

Strike of professional and clerical union members at MOMA.
Walker Evans (Photographs) *
Alexander Rodchenko
Surrealist Illusion from Museum Collection
Romare Bearden: The Prevalence of Ritual *
The Sculpture of Richard Hunt *
Will Insley: Ceremonial Space
Younger Abstract Expressionists of the Fifties
Technics & Creativity: Selections from Gemini G.E.L.
Manuel Alvarez Bravo (Photographs)
The Work of Frei Otto *
Clarence H. White (Photographs)
Matisse: Six Acquisitions
Posters by A. M. Cassandre
Projects: Keith Sonnier
A Selection of Drawings and Watercolors from Museum Collection
Architecture for the Arts: The State University of New York College
    at Purchase
Projects: Pier 18

Artist as Adversary *
Thomas Wilfred: Lumia
Photographs of Women
Projects: Mel Bochner
Barnett Newman *
Anton Heyboer; Etchings by Sol LeWitt; Henry Moore's "Elephant Skull"
American Prints from the International Program
Projects: Sam Gilliam
Education of an Architect: Point of View
Tony Smith/81 More
Projects: Nancy Graves
Photographs: Robert Adams and Emmett Gowin
Le Centre Beaubourg: A Museum of Modern Art for Paris
Seven Prints by de Kooning

1972

Hightower "resigned" as Director of MOMA; Richard Oldenberg named Acting Director and after six months appointed Director; David Rockefeller replaced as Chairman of the Board of Trustees by William S. Paley; Mrs. John D. Rockefeller 3rd elected President of the Board for the second time.

Naive Painting: A Selection from Museum Collection
Projects: Gatherings (Photographs by Lee Friedlander)
Picasso in the Collection of The Museum of Modern Art
Matisse: Jazz
Sculpture of Matisse
Graphics by Tadanori Yokoo
California Prints
Drawn in America
Barbara Morgan Photographs
Tchelitchew: Early Works on Paper
Projects: Richard Long
Projects: Emmanuel Pereire
Italy: The New Domestic Landscape *
Atget Trees (Photographs)
Projects: Richard Tuttle and David Novros
Symbolism, Synthetism, and the Fin-de-Siècle
European Drawings from the Collection
Kurt Schwitters
Photographs by Henry Wessel Jr.
African Textiles and Decorative Arts *
Philadelphia in New York: Ninety Modern Works from the Philadelphia Museum of Art
Etchings Etc.
Diane Arbus (Photographs)
Dubuffet: Persons and Places
Gaston Novelli
Classic Car: Cistalia Gt. 1946

Index

Aalto, Alvar, 317, 409
Abbott, Berenice, 329–30
Abbott, Jere, 21–22 and *n*., 27–30, 37, 47, 50, 51, 52, 59, 61, 66, 68, 70, 74, 84, 93, 94–5, 106, 109, 116, 149, 150, 178, 215, 244, 249, 323, 352; collection of, 22, 71
Abbott, John E., 111–13, 184, 201, 215, 223, 224–6, 235, 242, 247, 258–9, 271, 273, 276, 352
Abbott, Mrs. John E., *see* Barry, Iris
Abstract Expressionists, 35, 299, 310, 387
Abstractionists, 137–41
Ackerman, Frederick, 182
Adams, Ansel, 158–60, 213, 259
Addison Gallery, 293*n*.
African Negro Art show, 139
African Negro Sculpture show, 271, 441–2
Airways to Peace show, 345
Akermark, Margareta, 331–8 *passim*, 355
Albers, Joseph, 400
Albert, Prince: Crystal Palace Exposition, 91

Albright-Knox Gallery, Buffalo, 9, 10, 72, 134*n*., 209, 298, 301, 312
Aldrich, Larry: collection of, 311–12
Aldrich, Nelson W., 4, 292
Aldrich, Winthrop, 4
Allen, Frederick Lewis, 256
Allen, Virginia, 423
Amberg, George, 219–20, 225, 249, 262, 280, 332, 333–4, 335–6
America, 274
America Can't Have Housing show, 90
American Abstract Artists, 299
American Art News, 42–3
American Art Today show, 196–7, 203
American Association of Museums, 439
American Biograph and Muscotope Co., 114, 331, 333
American Federation of Art, 196
American Folk Art: The Art of the Common Man in America, 1750–1900 show, 107
American Institute for Persian Art and Archaeology, 107
American Institute of Architects *Journal*, 182
American Institute of Graphic Arts, 218

Russell Lynes

Russell Lynes was born in Great Barrington, Massachusetts, in 1910. He went to school in the Berkshires and in New York, graduated from Yale in 1932, and then went to work as a clerk at Harper & Brothers, publishers. He was subsequently Director of Publications at Vassar College and a school principal. He joined the editorial staff of *Harper's Magazine* in 1944 and was its managing editor from 1949 to 1968. He is now a contributing editor. He has written essays and articles for many magazines and lectured in many universities and museums. He is the author of nine books (including this one) of which *The Tastemakers, The Domesticated Americans, Confessions of a Dilettante,* and *The Art-Makers of Nineteenth Century America* have been largely concerned with the social history of the arts in America. For a number of years he wrote a column for *Harper's* called "After Hours" and another column for *Art in America* on "The State of Taste." For six years he was the president of The Archives of American Art. He was one of the founding members of the Landmarks Preservation Commission of New York, is currently president of the MacDowell Colony and a member of the New York City Art Commission.